The Palestine Yearbook of International Law, Volume 19 (2016)

The Palestine Yearbook of International Law

Editor-in-Chief

Ardi Imseis

Consulting Editor

Anis F. Kassim

Assistant Editors

Reem Al-Botmeh
Ata R. Hindi

Editorial Board

Anis F. Kassim   Ardi Imseis
Camille Mansour   Ghassan Faramand
Jamil Salem   Reem Al-Botmeh
Ata R. Hindi

Advisory Board

Georges M. Abi-Saab   Awn Al-Khasawneh
Ahmed Abouelwafa   Mahmoud Mubarak
Abdallah Alashaal   Mohammad K. Al-Musa
Badriya Al-Awadhi   Anis M. Al-Qasem
Mohammed Bedjaoui   Muhammad M. Al-Saleh
Salah Dabbagh   Moufid M. Shehab
Riad Daoudi   Muhammad Y. Olwan
Nabil Elaraby   Muhammad Aziz Shukri

VOLUME 19

The titles published in this series are listed at *brill.com/pyil*

The Palestine Yearbook of International Law, Volume 19 (2016)

Edited by

Ardi Imseis

BRILL
NIJHOFF

LEIDEN | BOSTON

The *Palestine Yearbook of International Law* is published in cooperation with the Birzeit University Institute of Law, under whose auspices it is edited. Established in 1993, the Institute of Law is research based and aims to contribute to the modernization of Palestinian legal structures both at the academic and professional levels.

All e-mail correspondence concerning the Yearbook should be sent to the Editor-in-Chief at: iol.pyil@birzeit.edu. Posted correspondence may be sent to: Attn: *Palestine Yearbook of International Law*, BZU Institute of Law. P.O. Box 14, Birzeit. Palestine. Telecommunication may be directed to the Institute of Law, at: Tel: (972) (2) 298-2009; Fax: (972) (2) 298-2137.

Typeface for the Latin, Greek, and Cyrillic scripts: "Brill". See and download: brill.com/brill-typeface.

ISSN 1386-1972
E-ISSN 2211-6141 (e-book)
ISBN 978-90-04-35680-1 (hardback)

Copyright 2018 by Koninklijke Brill NV, Leiden, The Netherlands.
Koninklijke Brill NV incorporates the imprints Brill, Brill Hes & De Graaf, Brill Nijhoff, Brill Rodopi, Brill Sense and Hotei Publishing.
All rights reserved. No part of this publication may be reproduced, translated, stored in a retrieval system, or transmitted in any form or by any means, electronic, mechanical, photocopying, recording or otherwise, without prior written permission from the publisher.
Authorization to photocopy items for internal or personal use is granted by Koninklijke Brill NV provided that the appropriate fees are paid directly to The Copyright Clearance Center, 222 Rosewood Drive, Suite 910, Danvers, MA 01923, USA. Fees are subject to change.

This book is printed on acid-free paper and produced in a sustainable manner.

Contents

PART 1
Articles

All Roads Lead to Rome: Why Palestine Remains the Issue   3
  Ardi Imseis

The Right to Rebel against Violations of Human Rights: A New Role for the Responsibility to Protect?   8
  Chiara Redaelli

Atrocities, Accountability and the Politics of Palestinian Statehood   42
  Jasmine Moussa

Prosecuting Israeli Perpetrators of International Crimes under Universal Jurisdiction Laws: Prospects for Success?   96
  Salma Karmi-Ayyoub

Occupants, Beware of BITs: Applicability of Investment Treaties to Occupied Territories   136
  Ofilio J. Mayorga

The Fragmentation of International Law: Contemporary Debates and Responses   177
  Musa Njabulo Shongwe

PART 2
Review Essay

Review Essay: Neo-colonial Transformations of Occupied Territory – and of the International Law of Occupation?   223
  Valentina Azarova

VI CONTENTS

PART 3
Materials

SECTION A
United Nations Documents

Report of the Special Rapporteur on the Situation of Human Rights in the Palestinian Territories Occupied Since 1967, U.N. Doc. A/HRC/31/73   241

Human Rights Situation in the Occupied Palestinian Territory, Including East Jerusalem, Report of the Secretary-General, U.N. Doc. A/HRC/31/44   269

Report of the UN Secretary General on Israeli Practices Affecting the Human Rights of the Palestinian People in the Occupied Palestinian Territory, Including East Jerusalem, U.N. Doc. A/71/364   294

Report of the Special Rapporteur on the Situation of Human Rights in the Palestinian Territories Occupied Since 1967, U.N. Doc. A/71/554   319

SECTION B
United Nations Resolutions

U.N. Human Rights Council Resolution 31/33 (2016) – Right of the Palestinian People to Self-determination   355

U.N. Human Rights Council Resolution 31/34 (2016) – Human Rights Situation in the Occupied Palestinian Territory, Including East Jerusalem   358

U.N. Human Rights Council Resolution 31/35 (2016) – Ensuring Accountability and Justice for All Violations of International Law in the Occupied Palestinian Territory, Including East Jerusalem   369

U.N. Human Rights Council Resolution 31/36 (2016) – Israeli Settlements in the Occupied Palestinian Territory, Including East Jerusalem, and in the Occupied Syrian Golan   374

U.N. Security Council Resolution 2334 (2016)   385

CONTENTS VII

SECTION C
European Court of Justice

Opinion of Advocate General Sharpston, Case C-79/15 P, Council of the European Union v Hamas 391

SECTION D
International Criminal Court

Report on Preliminary Examination Actions 2016 (Excerpts) 421

SECTION E
Cases

Sokolow v. Palestine Liberation Organization [U.S.], August 31, 2016 433

Index 473

PART 1

Articles

All Roads Lead to Rome: Why Palestine Remains the Issue

Ardi Imseis

This volume year was notable for a number of reasons, not least the ongoing conflicts engulfing the Arab world. Whether in Syria, Yemen, Iraq, Libya, Egypt or elsewhere, the impact of these events, in both human and political terms, has been unprecedented. From the promise of the Arab Spring to the subsequent devolution of a number of Arab societies into all-out war within or between one another, hundreds of thousands have been killed, maimed and tortured, and millions have been forced to seek refuge in exile or within internally displaced camps.

As one would expect, there is no shortage of explanations as to why and how this situation has transpired and what needs to be done about it. Some have assigned principal blame to the compounded failures and excesses of generations of Arab dictatorial rule. Others have charged failures in Western foreign policy in the Middle East, in particular the invasion of Iraq by the United States (US) in 2003 and its aftermath. In truth, it is difficult to exclude either of these factors, as the strength of Arab autocracy has long found its primary basis of support in the convergence of its own interests with those of hegemonic external powers, rather than the will of those governed. It should come as no surprise, therefore, that proponents of both positions have voiced separate calls for "intervention" in some form or another, citing all manner of international legal norms along the way – some well-established, others less so.

An important element of these narratives has been the drawing of connections between the human toll exacted by these ongoing present-day wars with other grim episodes in history, usually as a way of underscoring the need to do more to alleviate the plight of innocents under the rubric "never again". This, of course, isn't new. Just as international legal historians draw important connections between the Holocaust and the object and purpose of the Genocide Convention, the International Bill of Rights or the Fourth Geneva Convention, these claims justifiably seek to rouse sufficient political will to do something to save humanity, lest we be condemned to re-live history. Moreover, the connections drawn have rightly gone beyond the Holocaust, with other episodes – Cambodia, Srebrenica, Rwanda (and the list is long) – highlighted by those who want to ensure that justice is somehow done.

Throughout all of this, one has been hard pressed to find any sustained mainstream mention of Palestine or the Palestinian people's own historical and ongoing experience in coping with the ravages of war and conflict, and how what is now going on elsewhere in the region relates to it.[1] Politically, this is odd, as Palestine's plight is directly linked to Western hegemonic meddling in the region and prolonged disenfranchisement under autocratic and unrepresentative rule. It is just as odd from an international law standpoint, given that many of the lessons drawn from WWII, subsequently translated into conventional international law in the post-war period, have direct relevance to Palestine. This is not least the case, because Palestine's plight as a prolonged and festering wound upon the conscience of the international community underscores the long-term negative consequences of sustained and widespread violations of international refugee, human rights and humanitarian law. Whether forced exile, wholesale dispossession, collective punishment, military occupation, or racial and religious discrimination, there is no shortage of compelling parallels to be made through and with Palestine when addressing the dire situation now prevailing elsewhere in the region.

In many respects then, one might say that all roads do lead to Rome in the Middle East. To overlook what is happening in Palestine has become easy, given the scope and scale of the suffering elsewhere in the region. But it is precisely because of the cankerous and protracted nature of the Palestine question, with

---

1   From an international institutional perspective, one example of this is found in UNHCR's reporting on global trends in forced displacement in 2015, where it is erroneously reported that "[m]ore than half (54%) of all refugees worldwide came from just three countries: the Syrian Arab Republic (4.9 million), Afghanistan (2.7 million), and Somalia (1.1 million)". It is further erroneously reported that Jordan is a "top host" country, with some 664,100 refugees within its borders. *See* UNHCR, *Global Trends: Forced Displacement in 2015*, at 3, http://reliefweb.int/sites/reliefweb.int/files/resources/576408cd7.pdf. None of these statements appears to take into account the fact that as of 2015, over 5 million Palestine refugees were registered with the United Nations Relief and Works Agency, over approximately 2 million of whom reside in Jordan. *See generally*, UNRWA website *at*: https://www.unrwa.org/palestine-refugees. Of course, UNHCR does not have a mandate to provide protection and assistance to Palestine refugees who reside within UNRWA's areas of operation by virtue of art. 1D of the 1951 Convention Relating to the Status of Refugees. Nevertheless, this would not seem to be sufficient reason to exclude Palestine refugees from being appropriately recognized as refugees in the public record. Indeed, elsewhere, the same UNHCR report includes "5.2 million Palestine refugees registered by UNRWA" in the total of 65.3 million forcibly displaced persons in 2015 (at 2).

its multitudinous spin-off effects, that policy-makers and scholars, including of international law, should keep it at the fore as we consider how to manage and ultimately emerge from the present quagmire. From the perspective of the "progressive development" of international law alone, what major area of public international law now in issue elsewhere in the region has not been influenced by Palestine's experience? Virtually the whole cannon of international humanitarian and human rights law has been tested on Palestinian civilians, as has the most fundamental principles of the United Nations (UN) Charter system on the State of Palestine. The self-serving responses of a hegemonic Israel have followed, with results that have had a lasting impact far beyond it. Long before 9/11 and the evolution of the present day conflagrations in the Middle East, Israel's engagement with the Palestinians raised issues that have now become commonplace in the consideration of mainstream international law and order: preemptive self-defense; preventative war; the "war on terror"; anti-Jihadi counterinsurgency; mass-arrest and incarceration; "targeted" assassination; militarization of civil policing; aerial drone warfare; and usurpation of natural resources of an occupied territory. One could go on. The variety of material and legal techniques used by Israel and its military-industrial-security complex to subjugate the Palestinian people have been exported far and wide,[2] with effects that today manifest themselves elsewhere in the Arab world.

One of the other reasons it has been easy to overlook Palestine has been the sheer routine nature of it. As with previous years, this was demonstrated by events in 2016. The State of Palestine's resort to multilateral fora to highlight its plight and affirm its international legal personality continued. In this connection, and as part of its on-going preliminary examination into the situation in Palestine, a delegation from the Office of the Prosecutor of the International Criminal Court visited the West Bank and Israel, and the UN Security Council passed resolution 2334. While the content of the former event remains secret, the content of resolution 2334 offered the most fulsome denouncement of Israel's settlement enterprise by the Council in history. This includes the Council's important and novel call "upon all States ... to distinguish, in their relevant dealings, between the territory of the State of Israel and the territories occupied since 1967," a potential source of hope for advocates of the Boycott, Divestment and Sanctions movement.[3] Notwithstanding these developments, Palestinian multilateralism continued to have little recognizable positive material impact on the day-to-day reality of Palestinians on the ground, a situation

---

2 *See, e.g.*, Jeff Halper, War Against the People: Israel, the Palestinians and Global Pacification (2015).

3 S.C. Res. 2334, U.N. Doc. S/RES/2334 (Dec. 23, 2016), para. 5.

made worse by the ongoing political divisions between Fatah and Hamas. For its part, Israel maintained its policy course of open and increased civilian settlement in Palestine with the accompanying forced transfer of Palestinians looming large, particularly in the central West Bank and East Jerusalem. It also maintained its stifling system of movement restrictions on Palestinian people and goods in the West Bank, its draconian blockade of the Gaza Strip, its mass incarceration of political prisoners including hundreds without charge or trial, and its persecution of human rights defenders. Despite efforts taken by Israeli Prime Minister Benjamin Netanyahu to publically undermine the Obama administration, most notably following US-led negotiations on Iran's nuclear program in 2015, the US government approved an unprecedented USD 38 billion aid package to Israel in the twilight of president Obama's term. In short, Israel continued to deploy its matrix of control over Palestine and its resources with usual US support, while the Palestinians continued to rely on non-violent international legal and multilateral mechanisms to resist.

As with previous volumes of the Yearbook, the papers presented here cover a variety of topics, some relevant to how international law can be employed to press for just outcomes for the oppressed both in Palestine and beyond, others of more general interest. This is in addition to the usual array of legal materials, documents, judicial decisions and an extended review essay.

Chiara Redaelli leads the way with an article that examines the right to rebel under international law. In challenging the State-centric nature of conventional understandings of international law and order, this paper argues that the responsibility to protect (R2P) doctrine could provide a legal basis for the right to rebel against gross and systematic violations of human rights committed within the confines of the territorial State. It posits that if international law now contemplates the existence of a norm that allows forcible interventions by States into the internal affairs of other States in order to guard against gross human rights violations, there is no reason why the law should not allow the right of the victims of such violations to mount a resistance of their own.

From there, Jasmine Moussa offers an examination of UN General Assembly resolution 67/19 of 29 November 2012 with reference to the law on statehood. Her paper argues that while the resolution did not constitute the definitive act that constituted Palestine as a State under international law, it represented a watershed event that crystalized its ability to act as a State on the international plane. This has been important for a number of reasons, not least owing to the desire for accountability for past and on-going war crimes and crimes against humanity and the complete collapse of any notion of peace talks.

Salma Karmi-Ayoub then provides an analysis of criminal cases brought under universal jurisdiction laws against Israeli officials accused of committing war crimes. It demonstrates that political interference has been the principal reason such cases have yet to result in any high-profile convictions. It nevertheless proposes that universal jurisdiction remains a viable option for pursuing accountability and its success is more likely so long as litigation strategies focus on lower-level actors, where the perpetrators or victims are nationals or residents of forum jurisdictions and cases can be better integrated into broader advocacy strategies.

From there Ofilio Mayorga examines the unique interplay between bilateral investment treaties (BITs) and the law of belligerent occupation. His paper notes that with the proliferation of BITs since the 1990s, protected persons in occupied territories subject to them can turn to investment-treaty arbitration to challenge the acts of the occupant in real time and seek compensation for their losses. The continuity of BITs in times of belligerent occupation implies that they must coexist with international humanitarian law, subject to the operation of the latter under the *lex specialis* rule. Although the co-application of these two bodies of international law may result in the dilution of investment-treaty guarantees, case studies demonstrate that BITs offer the prospect of an effective enforcement mechanism of international humanitarian law that would otherwise not exist during occupation.

Finally, Musa Njabulo Shongwe looks at the matter of the fragmentation of international law through an assessment of contemporary debates in the literature. His contribution describes why and how fragmentation is a problem in international law through examination of substantive and procedural aspects of case law. The paper argues that although fragmentation is inevitable, it is a manageable feature of international law that must constantly be grappled with in dealing with normative conflicts and structural coherence in the system.

The Right to Rebel against Violations of Human Rights: A New Role for the Responsibility to Protect?

Chiara Redaelli*

I   Introduction   9
II Rebellions in International Law between Neutrality and Codification   10
   A   *The Principle of Neutrality*   10
   B   *Early Recognitions of the Right to Rebel against Heinous Atrocities: Historical Overview*   13
   C   *Codifications of the Right to Rebel in Domestic Law*   17
   D   *Codifications of the Right to Rebel at the International and Regional Levels*   18
   E   *National Liberation Movements and the Right to Struggle in the Name of Self-determination*   22
III Grounding the Right to Rebel: A New Role for the Responsibility to Protect?   25
   A   *Is there a Right to Collective Self-defense against Human Rights Violations?*   25
   B   *The Central Role of States in the R2P Doctrine*   27
   C   *The Right to Protect Oneself: Reconstructing the R2P Doctrine*   30
IV Practical Implications of Recognizing a Right to Rebel   33
   A   *Governments Committing Gross and Systematic Violations of Human Rights*   33
   B   *Opposition Groups Rebelling against Gross and Systematic Violations of Human Rights*   37
V   Concluding Remarks   40

---

*   Chiara Redaelli is a PhD Candidate and Teaching Assistant at the Graduate Institute of International and Development Studies (International Law Department). Before starting her PhD, she worked with UNHCR in Bangladesh and China. She also consulted for the Geneva Academy of International Humanitarian Law and Human Rights. Her research interests focus on international humanitarian law, human rights and *jus ad bellum*.

I   Introduction

The right to rebel is a neglected topic in international law. The reasons for this lack of interest are to be found in the centrality of States as subjects of international law and their understandable reluctance to address non-State violence in terms of right. This approach is reflected in the tendency to look at opposition groups as illegitimate, frequently labelling them as terrorists. However, non-State armed groups are highly heterogeneous and their aims and motivations to use violence should matter at the international law level.

This paper argues that the responsibility to protect (R2P) could provide the theoretical basis for the right to rebel against gross and systematic violations of human rights. The R2P doctrine maintains that each State bears the primary responsibility to protect the population within its borders; when it fails to do so, this responsibility is shared with the international community. In extreme circumstances, and where authorized by the United Nations Security Council (UNSC), foreign States may use force in order to stop gross and systematic violations of human rights. If international law accepts forcible interventions by States into the internal affairs of other States in order to guard against gross human rights violations, why should it negate the right of the victims of such violations to mount a resistance of its own?

International law has increasingly addressed the use of force by States within their borders. International humanitarian law (IHL) regulating non-international armed conflicts (NIACs) is now a fully developed field of studies. On the other hand, State violence in peaceful times has been taken away from the *domaine reservée*: the respect of international human rights law (IHRL) does matter at the international level, as confirmed by the R2P doctrine.

Both R2P and the increasing attention for the respect of human rights by governments are in line with a top-down approach that pervades nearly all fields of international law. States are the central subjects at the international level; what happens within their borders might affect their legitimacy in the eyes of their peers, *inter alia*, but in no way does it grant a right to rebel to non-State actors within those borders.

This paper challenges this traditional top-down approach. Several scholars have demonstrated that non-State actors can become subjects of specific branches of international law, such as IHL and IHRL. Now may be the time to take a step further and recognize a more active role for non-State actors. Victims of heinous human rights violations should not be passive subjects, waiting for foreign States to react to violations of their human rights. Granting them rights would be pointless without a related right to defend and protect them. International law would thus regulate both State and non-State violence, and the latter would be legitimate at least when directed to stop massive and systematic human rights violations.

This article is organized as follows. First, it focuses on the attempts of international law to address the right to rebel. Generally speaking, international law does not prohibit, nor expressly allow rebellions. Nevertheless, the right to rebel has been at the center of an animated debate through the centuries; furthermore, it has been object of codification at the domestic, regional, and international level. This paper then examines the ways in which the R2P doctrine could operate as legal basis for the right to rebel against human rights violations. Finally, it investigates what it could mean, in practice, to recognize a right to rebel, especially with regard to foreign interventions.

II   Rebellions in International Law between Neutrality and Codification

A   *The Principle of Neutrality*

Nowadays, the overwhelming majority of armed conflicts are internal in character.[1] Nonetheless, rebellion as an independent subject of study has received scant attention in international law. Primary sources as well as scholars extensively focus on IHL governing non-international armed conflicts, but seldom engage with rebellion in itself. This approach is reflected in the tendency to look at opposition groups as illegitimate, frequently labelling them as terrorists.[2]

Rebellions are intrinsically and ontologically against the authority or "sovereign". They are not simply a form of dissent; they threaten the very existence of State power. Consequently, domestic law tends to consider rebels as criminals or terrorists. This should come as no surprise: the rebel is a person who refuses to recognize the incumbent government, who opposes its power and considers it legitimate to use force to dislodge it. Hence, it is understandable that domes-

---

1   The War Report: Armed Conflict in 2014 7 (Annyssa Bellal ed., 2015).

2   Olivier Corten, La Rébellion et Le Droit International: Le Principe de Neutralité En Tension 70 (2014) [*hereinafter* Corten]; "Comme on le sait, le « rebelle » de l'un est souvent le « terroriste » de l'autre". *See also* Frédéric Mégret, *Beyond the 'Salvation' Paradigm: Responsibility To Protect (Others) vs the Power of Protecting Oneself*, 40 Security Dialogue 575, 578 (2009) [*hereinafter* Mégret (2009)].

THE RIGHT TO REBEL AGAINST VIOLATIONS OF HUMAN RIGHTS

tic law criminalizes such acts: "comment le droit peut-il en même temps poser la règle et énoncer les circonstances légitimes de sa violation?"[3]

The criminalization of rebellion at the domestic level does not necessarily imply that violent oppositions to government are prohibited at the international level.[4] This was confirmed in the *Tinoco* case, where the arbiter had to establish whether a government that assumed power in violation of a previous Constitution could be considered a *de facto* government:

> It is ably and earnestly argued on behalf of Costa Rica that the Tinoco government cannot be considered a *de facto* government, because it was not established and maintained in accord with the constitution of Costa Rica of 1871. To hold that a government which establishes itself and maintains a peaceful administration, with the acquiescence of the people for a substantial period of time, does not become a *de facto* government unless it conforms to a previous constitution would be to hold that within the rules of international law a revolution contrary to the fundamental law of the existing government cannot establish a new government. This cannot be, and is not, true. The change by revolution upsets the rule of the authorities in power under the then existing fundamental law, and sets aside the fundamental law in so far as the change of rule makes it necessary. To speak of a revolution creating a *de facto* government, which conforms to the limitations of the old constitution, is to use a contradiction in terms.[5]

Insurrection is a fact. International law simply acknowledges its existence and determines the applicable legal framework internal to the insurrection itself.

---

3 Frédéric Mégret, *Le droit international peut-il être un droit de résistance? Dix conditions pour un renouveau de l'ambition normative internationale*, 39 Études Internationales 39, 40 (2008) [*hereinafter* Mégret (2008)]. *See also* Corten, 242.

4 Annyssa Bellal and Louise Doswald-Beck, *Evaluating the Use of Force During the Arab Spring*, 14 Y.B. Int'l Humanitarian L. 3, 13 (2011) [*hereinafter* Bellal and Doswald-Beck]. *See also* Corten, 77.

5 Tinoco (Gr. Brit. v. Costa Rica), 1 R.I.A.A. 369 (1923). In Costa Rica in 1917, Federico Tinoco overthrew the Government of President Alfredo González. The new President retained power until 1919, when he went in exile in Europe. During its government, Tinoco promulgated a new Constitution and concluded some agreements with foreign companies. When Tinoco left the country, the new government declared all the acts of the former president null and void. This decision affected also the agreements concluded with the British companies. *See* Aleksandar Marsavelski, *The Crime of Terrorism and the Right of Revolution in International Law*, 28 Conn. J. Int'l L. 243, 276 (2012–2013) [*hereinafter* Marsavelski].

The evaluation of the facts does not clarify whether rebels actually possess a *right* to use force to overthrow a previous government. Instead, it aims at ascertaining whether the situation amounts to a non-international armed conflict, which triggers the application of IHL, or is a mere case of "internal disturbances and tensions",[6] regulated by domestic law.[7] This distinction is exclusively based on the intensity and the modalities in which the insurrection is conducted, not on the causes and aims of the parties.

The neutrality of international law towards rebellions is the result of a tension between two contrasting factors.[8] On the one hand, international law is first and foremost "un ordre normative de validation d'une certaine forme de pouvoir, la souveraineté, détenu par un certaine type d'acteur, en l'occurrence, l'État".[9] International law is primarily made by States for States and it is thus understandable that it fails to address rebellions in terms of legitimacy. On the other hand, sovereignty needs justification and should be grounded in something more than mere power.[10] This implies that sovereignty needs to be legitimate in the eyes of those subordinated to its power. Consequently, international law does not allow rebellions in order to preserve State sovereignty; nonetheless, it does not prohibit them either, allowing peoples to react in case a government loses its legitimacy.

---

6   Protocol Additional to the Geneva Conventions of 12 August 1949, and relating to the Protection of Victims of Non-International Armed Conflicts art. 1(2), June 8, 1977, 1125 U.N.T.S. 609.

7   Corten, 76. International human rights law applies during both armed conflicts and in peaceful times. However, certain human rights instruments contain clauses which grant the possibility to derogate from some provisions in case of emergency or similar circumstances. *See, e.g.*, International Covenant on Civil and Political Rights art. 4, Dec. 16, 1966, 999 U.N.T.S. 171; European Convention for the Protection of Human Rights and Fundamental Freedoms art 15, as amended by Protocols Nos. 11 and 14, Nov. 4, 1950, ETS 5, 213 U.N.T.S. 222 [*hereinafter* European HR Convention]; American Convention on Human Rights art. 27, Nov. 22, 1969, O.A.S. Treaty Series No. 36, 1144 U.N.T.S. 123. *See also* Lindsay Moir, The Law of Internal Armed Conflicts 195–197 (2004).

8   *See* Accordance with international law of the unilateral declaration of independence in respect of Kosovo, Advisory Opinion, 2010 I.C.J. Rep. 403 (July 22), Declaration of Judge Simma, para. 9; "The neutrality of international law on a certain point simply suggests that there are areas where international law has not yet come to regulate, or indeed, will never come to regulate".

9   Mégret (2008), 40.

10   Anne Peters, *Humanity as the Alfa and Omega of Sovereignty*, 20 Eur. J. Int'l L. 513, 518 (2009) [*hereinafter* Peters].

THE RIGHT TO REBEL AGAINST VIOLATIONS OF HUMAN RIGHTS

B   *Early Recognitions of the Right to Rebel against Heinous Atrocities:*
         Historical Overview

The debate on the right to rebel has received strikingly little attention in recent years. However, this has not always been the case. The idea of an armed intervention aimed at protecting foreign populations from the abuses of the sovereign and of a related right of the population to rebel against the oppressor was already present in European philosophical traditions of the Middle Ages.

At the time, the debate focused on the instances when a war could be considered to be just. Thomas Aquinas (1225–1274) identified three criteria for the *bellum justum*: 1) legitimate authority (*auctoritas principis*); 2) just cause (*justa causa*); and 3) right intention (*recta intentio*), namely pursuing good and avoiding evil.[11] Successive canonists embraced this approach and largely developed the *bellum justum* doctrine. The authority to use force was deemed to descend from God: the prince was granted its legitimacy inasmuch as he was *minister dei*. On the other hand, war was seen as punishment. During the 16th and 17th centuries, when religious wars were common, this meant that the use of force was just when directed against heathens. Similarly, the idea of war as punishment was invoked by Europeans to justify their claims over the New World.[12]

During the early Middle Ages, another cause of just war emerged among scholastic writers, namely armed intervention on behalf of the oppressed. The idea was first suggested by Ambrose (339–397) in the *De Officiis Ministrorum*[13] and then further elaborated by Francisco de Victoria (1480–1546), who advanced the progressive idea of the *jus defendi innocentes a morte iniusta*, "the right to defend innocents from unjust death".[14] The recognition of what we could call a responsibility to protect *ante litteram* gave rise to an animated discussion as to whether the right to defend oppressed people would also imply a right of the victims to defend themselves against the sovereign.

Protestants believed that sovereign authority comes from God. Due to its divine function as God's "lieutenant to command the rest of mankind", the sovereign was inviolable and *legibus soluto*.[15] Nonetheless, his absolute authority was not arbitrary; albeit not bound by his own rules, the sovereign had to follow

---

11   Yoram Dinstein, War, Aggression and Self-Defence 66 (2011).

12   Simon Chesterman, Just war or Just peace? Humanitarian Intervention and International Law 10 (2001) [*hereinafter* Chesterman].

13   *Id.*, 14.

14   Davide Rodogno, Against Massacre: Humanitarian Interventions in the Ottoman Empire, 1815–1914 24 (2012).

15   Luke Glanville, Sovereignty and the Responsibility to Protect: A New History 35 (2014) [*hereinafter* Glanville].

the laws of God. The sovereign and its people were bound by a unique relationship: the ruler had to govern and protect its population according to the laws of God; in return, the subjects to its power would be obedient and faithful.[16] Therefore, Protestants accepted the right of foreign forces to intervene in order to defend oppressed people from the abuses of the tyrant:

> Unless we wish to make sovereigns exempt from the law and bound by no statutes and no precedents, there must also of necessity be someone to remind them of their duty and hold them in restraint.[17]

Catholics, Presbyterians and Calvinists had a substantially different approach. For them, sovereign authority comes from the people, thus the people have a right to rebel against oppression as well as a right to seek foreign intervention. Therefore, a right to intervene in favor of oppressed people would exist only if a correspondent, internal right to react is recognized in the victim population. As explained by Tuck:

> The reason for this limitation is that a wrong done to another does not give me the right to avenge him, unless he would be justified in avenging himself and actually proposes to do so. Assuming, however, that these conditions exist, my aid to him is an act of cooperation in a good and just deed; but if [the injured party] does not entertain such a wish, no one else may intervene, since he who committed the wrong has made himself subject not to every one indiscriminately, but only to the person who has been wronged. Wherefore, the assertion made by some writers, that sovereign kings have the power of avenging injuries done in any part of the world, is entirely false, and throws into confusion all the orderly distinctions of jurisdiction; for such power was not [expressly] granted by God and its existence is not to be inferred by any process of reasoning.[18]

The debate between canonists contributed to set the basis of an intense dispute on intervention in favor of oppressed people that gained momentum during the 17th century. This is probably the period when humanitarian in-

---

16   *Id.*, 36–37.

17   Richard Tuck, *Grotius, Hobbes and Pufendorf on Humanitarian Intervention, in* Just and Unjust Military Intervention: European Thinkers from Vitoria to Mill 103 (Stefano Recchia and Jennifer M. Welsh eds., 2013) [*hereinafter* Tuck].

18   *Id.*, 101.

tervention received the most extensive attention before the 20th century.[19] The two authors that most influenced the debate were Hugo Grotius and Emer de Vattel.

Hugo Grotius's (1583–1654) *De jure belli ac pacis* is the first comprehensive systematization of the use of force.[20] Its merit lies in a secularization of the just war doctrine, both with regard to the just causes of war and the legitimate authority to begin a conflict. Systematizing the ideas expressed by de Victoria and Gentili, he argued for the existence of a legal right to wage war against a sovereign who oppresses his subjects.[21]

Grotius recognizes that "it is a rule established by the laws of nature and of social order, and a rule confirmed by all the records of history, that every sovereign is supreme judge in his own kingdom and over his own subjects, in whose disputes no foreign power can justly interfere".[22] Nonetheless, when a sovereign "abandon[s] all the laws of nations"[23] and causes grievances to the people under its jurisdiction, then it loses "the rights of independent sovereign."[24] As a consequence, foreign countries could intervene in order to protect the oppressed population. Nonetheless, the same right is not granted to the victims themselves. According to Grotius, "it would be fraught with the greatest dangers if subjects were allowed to redress grievances by force of arms".[25] The reason, he continues, is that individuals "cannot transfer their natural allegiance from their own sovereign to another".[26] However, the same limitation does not apply to foreign powers, which are not tied by the same bond with the sovereign and can thus intervene on behalf of the oppressed.

Emer de Vattel (1714–1767) is the author who more extensively focused on the inviolability of internal affairs of the sovereign. In his view, the international community is a "society of independent states"[27] governed by the law of nations, which he defined as "the law of sovereigns; free and independent states are moral persons, whose right and obligations we are to establish in this treatise".[28] The merit of Vattel is that he grounded the law of nations on the will of States. Taking distance from previous discourses on the natural law, present

---

19 *Id.*, 96.

20 Chesterman, 9.

21 *Id.*

22 Hugo Grotius, *De jure belli ac pacis*, II, XXV, §8 (1625).

23 *Id.*

24 *Id.*

25 *Id.*

26 *Id.*

27 Glanville, 56.

28 *Id.*

for instance in Grotius, he adopted a positivist approach, whereby States consent to the law which binds them.[29]

According to vattel, sovereignty implies that states have the right to be free from external interference:

> Enfin, toutes ces choses [i.e. the internal affairs of the state] n'interessant que la Nation, aucune Puissance Etrangere n'est en droit de s'en mêler ni ne doit y intervenir.[30]

Thus Vattel clearly articulated the right of non-intervention as a corollary of State sovereignty. Nonetheless, he also admitted the right to wage war in two circumstances.[31] First, drawing on Pufendorf and Wolff, he recognized the right of nations to use force to punish a State that committed an injury.[32] Second, he acknowledged the right to intervene in favor of oppressed populations. In contrast with the ideas of Bodin and Grotius, he claimed that people subject to tyranny under a sovereign have the right to forcibly resist that sovereign: "those monsters who, under the title of sovereigns, render themselves the scourges and horror of the human race ... are savage beasts, whom every brave man justly exterminate from the face of the earth".[33]

The discourse on intervention to protect oppressed people and their right to rebel against the tyrant lost its appeal during the 19th century.[34] The central role of State sovereignty and the emergence of its corollary, the principle of non-intervention, obfuscated any references to the legitimacy of revolts.[35] International law adopted a neutral attitude towards the right to rebel, neither legitimizing or banning it. Nonetheless, attempts to recognize the right to stage armed rebellions eventually emerged in international law, albeit in a timid and sporadic fashion.

---

29   *Id.*, 57.

30   Rosario Sapienza, Il principio di non intervento negli affair interni 43 (1990).

31   According to Vattel, waging war was one of the main prerogative of State sovereignty: "as long as the ruler is capable of defending the self-interest of his State in this way, his authority cannot be challenged on any legal grounds". *See* Jens Bartelson, *Double binds: sovereignty and the just war tradition, in* Sovereignty in Fragments: The Past, Present and Future of a Contested Concept 94 (Hent Kalmo and Quentin Skinner, 2010).

32   Chesterman, 18.

33   Glanville, 58; Corten, 233.

34   Tuck, 112.

35   Mégret (2008), 53.

THE RIGHT TO REBEL AGAINST VIOLATIONS OF HUMAN RIGHTS

C   *Codifications of the Right to Rebel in Domestic Law*

From the Middle Ages, the debate on when, if ever, people can rise up and take arms against the sovereign was extensively fueled by philosophers and theologians. During the 18th century, the question gained momentum with the American and French revolutions.[36]

The American Declaration of Independence (1776) recognizes that "all men are created equal, that they are endowed by their Creator with certain unalienable Rights, that among these are Life, Liberty and the pursuit of Happiness".[37] Government's legitimacy is grounded on the respect of these rights as well as on the consent of the governed. Consequently, "whenever any Form of Government becomes destructive of these ends, it is the Right of the People to alter or to abolish it, and to institute new Government, laying its foundation on such principles and organizing its powers in such form, as to them shall seem most likely to effect their Safety and Happiness".[38] Rebellion is thus lawful when directed at overthrowing a government that violates the inalienable rights of all men. However, the American Declaration does not contemplate allowing the people to abuse this right: "Governments long established should not be changed for light and transient causes".[39] In any case, "when a long train of abuses and usurpations, pursuing invariably the same Object evinces a design to reduce them under absolute Despotism, it is their right, it is their duty, to throw off such Government, and to provide new Guards for their future security".[40]

The French Declaration of the Rights of Man and Citizen – (1789) was greatly influenced by the American Declaration, but it was also able to innovate it adopting a more direct approach.[41] Notably, it mentions resistance to oppression among the natural and imprescriptible rights of man.[42] During the 18th and 19th Centuries, French history saw several overthrows and changes of power[43] and each of the new French governments recognized the right

---

36   Syméon Karagiannis, *Qu'est-il, en droit international, le droit à la résistance devenu?* 76 Revue trimestrielle de droits de l'homme 949 (2008) [*hereinafter* Karagiannis].

37   United States Declaration of Independence (July 4, 1776).

38   *Id.*

39   *Id.*

40   *Id.*

41   French Declaration of the Rights of Man and Citizens (Aug. 1979) [*hereinafter* French Declaration].

42   *Id.*, art. 2: "The aim of all political association is the preservation of the natural and imprescriptible rights of man. These rights are liberty, property, security, and resistance to oppression".

43   Karagiannis, 950–951.

to rebel. Notably, the Declaration of the Rights of Man and Citizen – (1793) affirms that: "the law ought to protect public and personal liberty against the oppression of those who govern"[44] and that "Resistance to oppression is the consequence of the other rights of man".[45] Therefore, "when the government violates the rights of the people, insurrection is for the people and for each portion of the people the most sacred of rights and the most indispensable of duties".[46]

Recognitions of the right to rebel can also be found in contemporary Constitutions. One example is the German Basic Law (1968). After the Second World War, the memory of the Nazi period was still vivid in German people's minds; therefore, the drafters of the constitution wanted to make sure to introduce a mechanism to react to abuse of power by the government. Article 20(4) thus establishes that: "All Germans shall have the right to resist any person seeking to abolish this constitutional order, if no other remedy is available".[47] Similarly, the Portuguese Constitution (1976) recognizes that: "Everyone shall possess the right to resist any order that infringes their rights, freedoms or guarantees and, when it is not possible to resort to the public authorities, to use force to repel any aggression".[48] Other Constitutions recognize the right to rebel,[49] notably in East European countries,[50] in almost all Latin-American States,[51] and in a number of African[52] and Asian ones.[53]

D *Codifications of the Right to Rebel at the International and Regional Levels*

International law is generally indifferent towards the right to rebel. Nonetheless, this does not mean that it is completely silent on the matter. Contrasting sources address directly or indirectly the right to rebel, leaving to the interpreter a great margin of appreciation as to whether such right exists under international law. Some scholars argue that the recognition of a right to rebel would be impossible, lacking a clear acknowledgement in international law. Other

---

44   French Declaration, art. 9.

45   *Id.*, art. 33.

46   *Id.*, art. 35.

47   German Basic Law art. 20(4) (1968). *See also* Marsavelski, 272.

48   Constitution of the Portuguese Republic art. 21 (1976).

49   Tony Honoré, *The Right to Rebel*, 8 Oxford J. Legal Stud. 34, 42 (1988) [*hereinafter* Honoré]; Mégret (2008), 54.

50   *See e.g.* Ukranian Constitution art. 55 (1996); Constitution of Estonia art. 54 (1992).

51   *See e.g.* Constitution of Peru art. 82 (1979).

52   *See e.g.* Constitution of Uganda art. 3 (1995).

53   *See e.g.* Constitution of Timor Leste art. 11 (2002).

THE RIGHT TO REBEL AGAINST VIOLATIONS OF HUMAN RIGHTS 19

authors affirm that recognizing human rights without a right to rebel against their violations would be pointless:

> The right to rebel ... must be a secondary rather than a primary right. It exists only when a wrong has been committed. Its point is to provide remedy in the event of the violation on a large scale of primary rights like the right to freedom from arbitrary arrest. The sustained denial of those rights may arguably amount to such oppression or exploitation as justifies rebellion.[54]

IHRL offers contradictory support for the existence of a right to rebel. The preamble of the Universal Declaration of Human Rights recognizes that: "whereas it is essential, if man is not to be compelled to have recourse, as a last resource, to rebellion against tyranny and oppression, that human rights should be protected by the rule of law". Despite discussions among the drafters of the Declaration, rebellion was only mentioned in the preamble for fear that it could destabilize governments.[55]

Successive human rights treaties failed to explicitly recognize a right to rebel. Notably, Article 5(1) of the International Covenant on Civil and Political Rights (ICCPR) establishes that:

> Nothing in the present Covenant may be interpreted as implying for any State, group or person any right to engage in any activity or perform any act aimed at the destruction of any of the rights and freedoms recognized herein or at their limitation to a greater extent than is provided for in the present Covenant.[56]

This provision would seem to exclude the right to rebel, as it is arguable that internal conflicts could lead to "destruction of any of the rights and freedoms recognized herein". On the other hand, an armed protest against a government which grossly and systematically violates human rights could be interpreted as excluding an abuse of rights.[57]

Some scholars claim that the existence of a right to peaceful protest under international law would rule out *a contrario*, a right to armed rebellion. The

---

54 Honoré, 38.

55 Johannes Morsink, The Universal Declaration of Human Rights: Origins, Drafting, and Intent 312 (2009).

56 Bellal and Doswald-Beck, 12.

57 *Id.*

right to protest is not expressly acknowledged in human rights treaties. However, its existence is protected by the right to peaceful assembly and the freedom of expression. Article 21 of the ICCPR establishes that:

> The right of peaceful assembly shall be recognized. No restrictions may be placed on the exercise of this right other than those imposed in conformity with the law and which are necessary in a democratic society in the interests of national security or public safety, public order (*ordre public*), the protection of public health or morals or the protection of the rights and freedoms of others.

This article clarifies under what terms the right of assembly is protected. First, the assembly has to be peaceful.[58] Second, it should not constitute a threat to "the interests of national security or public safety, public order (*ordre public*), the protection of public health or morals or the protection of the rights and freedoms of others". Therefore, an armed demonstration would be prohibited and State law enforcement personnel could intervene to disperse it. But could an armed demonstration be compared to a rebellion? What are the limits and differences between the two situations? Most importantly, what if the government forcefully represses a peaceful assembly and the population reacts by having resort to the use of force?[59]

At the regional level, human rights treaties adopt an even more conflicting approach. The European Convention of Human Rights[60] expressly allows States Parties to use lethal force when it is absolutely necessary "in action lawfully taken for the purpose of quelling a riot or insurrection". Furthermore, in the case *Yazar and others v. Turkey*, the European Court of Human Rights condemned Turkey for the dissolution of a political party on the basis that it did not threaten the Turkish democratic regime:

---

58 Stankov and the United Macedonian Organisation Ilinden v. Bulgaria, Apps. No. 29225/95 and 29221/95, 2001 Eur. Ct. H.R.

59 For instance, this is what happened in Libya and Syria. In February 2011, a wave of peaceful protests took place in Libya. The Qaddafi regime brutally reacted, repressing the protests recurring to the use of force. On month later, Al-Assad repressed peaceful protests in Syria and State forces killed more than 4,000 people as a result. Consequently, protesters started to take the streets – this time armed – leading to an internal armed conflict. *See Syria Profile: Timeline*, BBC News (Apr. 11, 2017), http://www.bbc.com/news/world-middle-east-14703995; *Libya Profile: Timeline*, BBC News (Mar. 1, 2017), http://www.bbc.com/news/world-africa-13755445.

60 European HR Convention art. 2(2)(c).

As the HEP did not advocate any policy that could have undermined the democratic regime in Turkey and did not urge or seek to justify the use of force for political ends, its dissolution cannot reasonably be said to have met a "pressing social need".[61]

The *ratio* underpinning the decision is that a plurality of views, guaranteed by the freedom of expression and of assembly, is one of the cornerstones of democracy and it should therefore not be limited, save in circumstances where the very existence of the democratic order is under threat. *A contrario*, it would be possible to argue that States could lawfully react against revolutionary movements that aim at the overthrow of government through the use of force.[62] Nonetheless, it seems fair to affirm that this reasoning would not apply if the opposition group is fighting against a non-democratic government, such as in Libya and Syria, where the regimes negate the pluralism of views befitting of democracies and were the first to initiate the use of force against their own people.

Other regional human rights instruments seem more open towards rebellions. In the Arab world, the Universal Islamic Declaration on Human Rights (1981) recognizes that "Every individual and every people has the inalienable right to freedom ... and shall be entitled to struggle by all available means against any infringement or abrogation of this right".[63] Similarly, the Arab Charter on Human Rights (2004) recognizes that "all peoples have the right to resist foreign occupation".[64]

More innovative is Article 20(2) of the African Charter of Human and Peoples' Rights (1981), which states that: "colonized or oppressed peoples shall have the right to free themselves from the bonds of domination by resorting to any means recognized by the international community". Some authors consider it as a simple restatement of the right to self-determination, acknowledged in Article 20(1) of the Charter, granting peoples a right to resist against colonial and racist domination.[65] Other scholars highlight the unique character of this provision and consider it to be a much broader recognition of the right to

---

61   Yazar and others v. Turkey, Apps. No. 22723/93, 22724/93 and 22725/93, 2002 Eur. Ct. H.R., §60.

62   Corten, 285; Bellal and Doswald-Beck, 12.

63   Universal Islamic Declaration on Human Rights art. II Right to Freedom (1981). *See also* Marsavelski, 274–275.

64   Arab Charter on Human Rights art. 2(4) (2004).

65   Corten, 240.

rebel.[66] In favor of the latter approach is the wording of the Article, which extends the right to resist to all oppressed people, and not only to those under colonial domination, alien occupation, and racist regimes. Furthermore, oppressed peoples can have recourse to "any means", and not only to peaceful means as established in the European Convention of Human Rights. [67]

E   *National Liberation Movements and the Right to Struggle in the Name of Self-determination*

It is well established that international law prevents States from denying the right to self-determination to peoples subject to colonial domination, foreign occupation or racist regimes[68] In line with this approach, the United Nations General Assembly (UNGA) has condemned any forms of foreign intervention directed to help the subjugating and/or aggressor state in these situations.[69]

---

66   Shannonbrooke Murphy, *Unique in International Human Rights Law: Article 20 (2) and the Right to Resist in the African Charter of Human and Peoples' Rights*, 2 Afr. Human Rts. J. 465, 465 (2011).

67   *Id.*, 473.

68   *See, e.g., Declaration on the Granting of Independence to Colonial Countries and Peoples*, U.N. Doc. A/RES/1514 (XV), para. 4 (Dec. 14, 1960); where the Assembly asks for the cessation of "all armed action and repressive measures of all kind directed against dependent peoples ... in order to enable them to exercise peacefully and freely their right to complete independence". *Strict observance of the prohibition of the threat or use of force in international relations, and of the right of peoples to self-determination*, U.N. Doc. A/RES/2160 (XXI), para. 1(b) (Nov 30, 1966): "Any forcible action, direct or indirect, which deprives peoples under foreign domination of their right to self-determination and freedom or independence and of their right to determine freely their political status and pursue their economic, social and cultural development constitutes a violation of the Charter of the United Nations". *Definition of Aggression*, U.N. Doc. A/RES/3314, preamble (Dec. 14, 1974); "the duty of States not to use armed force to deprive peoples of their right to self- determination, freedom and independence, or to disrupt territorial integrity". *See also* Antonio Cassese, Self-Determination of Peoples: A Legal Reappraisal 194 (1999) [*hereinafter* Cassese].

69   *See, e.g.,* resolutions on: *Question of southern Rhodesia*: U.N. Doc. A/RES/2262 (XXII), (Nov. 3, 1967); U.N. A/RES/2383 (XXIII), (Nov. 7, 1969); U.N. Doc. A/RES/2508 (XXIV), (Nov. 2, 1969); U.N. Doc. A/RES/2796 (XXVI), (Dec. 10, 1971); U.N. Doc A/RES/2945 (XXVII), (Dec. 1, 1972); U.N. Doc. A/RES/34/192, (Dec. 18, 1972). *See also* the resolutions on: *The importance of the universal realization of the right of peoples to self-determination and of the speedy granting of independence to colonial countries and peoples for the effective guarantee and observance of human rights*: U.N. Doc. A/RES/2649 (XXV), (Nov. 30, 1970); U.N. Doc. A/RES/2787 (XXVI), (Dec. 6, 1971); U.N. Doc. A/RES/2955 (XXVII), (Dec. 12, 1972); U.N. Doc. A/RES/3070 (XXVIII), (Nov. 30, 1973); U.N. Doc. A/RES/3246 (XXIX), (Nov. 29, 1974); U.N. Doc. A/RES/3382 (XXX), (Nov. 10, 1975); U.N. Doc. A/RES/31/34,

During the decolonization period, the UNGA recognized that when a State deprives its people of the right to self-determination, the population can struggle against the State and "seek and receive" external support to this end. The questions widely debated by the international community and the scholarship regarded the means by which peoples could struggle in defense of their right to self-determination, and the way in which foreign help could be granted. Would it include the use of force, or would it be limited to a peaceful resistance?

The *Declaration on Principles of International Law concerning Friendly Relations and Cooperation among States in Accordance with the Charter of the United Nations* (1970) states that:

> Every State has the duty to refrain from any forcible action which deprives peoples ... of their right to self-determination and freedom and independence. In their actions against, and resistance to, such forcible action in pursuit of the exercise of their right to self-determination, such peoples are entitled to seek and receive support in accordance with the purpose and principles of the Charter.[70]

This is further confirmed by Article 7 of the *Definition of Aggression*, which states that:

> Nothing in this Definition, and in particular article 3, could in any way prejudice the right to self-determination, freedom and independence ... particularly peoples under colonial and racist régimes or other forms of alien domination; nor the right of these peoples to struggle to that end and to seek and receive support, in accordance with the principles of the Charter and in conformity with the above-mentioned Declaration.[71]

Both resolutions recognize a right to struggle and to seek foreign help, but do not specify whether it would include also the use of force, or would be limited

---

(Nov. 30, 1976); U.N. Doc. A/RES/32/14, (Nov. 7, 1977); U.N. Doc. A/RES/33/24, (Nov. 29, 1977); U.N. Doc. A/RES/33/24, (Nov. 29, 1978); U.N. Doc. A/RES/34/44, (Nov. 29, 1979); U.N. Doc. A/RES/35/35 [A-B], (Nov. 14, 1980); where the general Assembly condemned "the establishment and the use of armed groups with the view to putting them against the national liberation movements".

70   *Declaration on Principles of International Law concerning Friendly Relations and Cooperation among States in Accordance with the Charter of the United Nations*, U.N. Doc. A/RES/25/2625, (Oct. 24, 1970).

71   *Definition of Aggression*, U.N. Doc. A/RES/3314, (Dec. 14, 1974).

to peaceful means.[72] The issue is further complicated by Article 1(4) of the Additional Protocol I to the Geneva Conventions, which expressly extends to national liberation movements prisoner of war (POW) status and the norms of IHL governing international armed conflicts.[73] This circumstance could be read as an indirect way to recognize their legitimacy at the international level,[74] but it is unclear whether it would also imply a right to receive forcible support.[75] These uncertainties could lead to the conclusion that "liberation movements have no legal right to use force to secure self-determination, but they do not breach international law by using force (defensively) against its forcible denial".[76]

The practice of States during the decolonization era shows that, on the one hand, the Western block believed that external intervention could entail only peaceful means. On the other hand, the Communist block pushed for a right to forcible intervention in favor of people fighting against colonial domination and apartheid. From the analysis of resolutions adopted by the UNGA and the UNSC, it is possible to discern a general consensus towards interventions in favor of peoples struggling for their right to self-determination: although a right to direct armed intervention was never recognized, nonetheless less

---

72 A forcible intervention in favor of national liberation movements would be a clear violation of the general ban on the use of force, enshrined in Article 2(4) of the Charter of the United Nations (UN). Nevertheless, in the 1960s, several socialist countries advanced the idea that "a derogation from the Charter system" would be possible "to the effect that third States can use force in collective self-defence against a State forcibly denying self-determination"; *see* Cassese, 199.

73 Protocol Additional to the Geneva Conventions of 12 August 1949, and relating to the Protection of Victims of International Armed Conflicts art. 1(4), June 8 1977, 1125 U.N.T.S. 3; "The situations referred to in the preceding paragraph include armed conflicts in which peoples are fighting against colonial domination and alien occupation and against racist régimes in the exercise of their right of self-determination, as enshrined in the Charter of the United Nations and the Declaration on Principles of International Law concerning Friendly Relations and Co-operation among States in accordance with the Charter of the United Nations". *See also* Ben Saul, *Defending "Terrorism": Justifications and Excuses for Terrorism in International Criminal Law*, University of Sidney Law School, Legal Studies Research Paper No. 08/122, at 11 (2006) [*hereinafter* Saul], http://ssrn.com/abstract=1291584.

74 Cassese, 196. Natalino Ronzitti, Le guerre di liberazione nazionale e il diritto internazionale 73 (1984) [*hereinafter* Ronzitti]. Mégret (2008), 50.

75 Eliav Lieblich, International Law and Civil Wars: Intervention and Consent 222 (2013).

76 Saul, 10; Cassese, 151–153.

THE RIGHT TO REBEL AGAINST VIOLATIONS OF HUMAN RIGHTS

grave forms of use of force, such as the provision of weapons and other military assistance, were generally endorsed by the UNGA and UNSC.[77]

As it is clear from the above, although international law addresses the right to rebel, it does so in a limited fashion, regulating specific situations, instead of adopting a more coherent and comprehensive approach. International law governing support for national liberation movements and struggles against colonial domination and apartheid is perhaps the clearest validation of any right to use of force to rebel.[78] Nonetheless, it is striking how such recognition is granted to cases of self-determination and negated to victims of genocide, war crimes, ethnic cleansing and crimes against humanity that may be subject to such crimes by their own national governing authorities. While there is an emerging norm that contemplates that these heinous human rights violations may trigger the exercise of the responsibility to protect by the international community, including forcible interventions from without, the possibility that any similar right to use force from within vests in the very population subject to these violations remains unrecognized.[79]

III Grounding the Right to Rebel: A New Role for the Responsibility to Protect?

A *Is there a Right to Collective Self-defense against Human Rights Violations?*

The right to self-defense is recognized both in domestic and international law, and operates as a circumstance precluding the wrongfulness of an otherwise

---

77   *See, e.g., Question of Namibia*, U.N. Doc. A/RES/35/227 [A-J], (Mar. 3, 1981): "The General Assembly ... calls upon Member States, specialized agencies and other organizations to render increased and sustained support and material, financial, *military* and other assistance to the South West Africa's people's Organization to enable it to intensify its struggle for the liberation of Namibia" (emphasis added). *See also*, among others: *South Africa-Zambia*, U.N. Doc. S/RES/393 (July 30, 1976); *Angola-South Africa*, U.N. Doc. S/RES/428, (May 6, 1978); *Angola-South Africa*, U.N. Doc. S/RES/447, (Mar. 28, 1979); *South Africa-Zambia*, U.N. Doc. S/RES/466, (Apr. 11, 1980); *Angola-South Africa*, U.N. Doc. S/RES/577, (Dec. 30, 1985); *Lesotho-South Africa;* U.N. Doc. S/RES/580, (Dec. 30, 1985); *South Africa*, U.N. Doc. S/RES/581, (Feb. 13, 1986); *Mozambique-Southern Rhodesia*, U.N. Doc. S/RES/411, (June 30, 1977); *Southern Rhodesia-Zambia*, U.N. Doc. S/RES/424, (Mar. 17, 1978); *Southern Rhodesia-Zambia*, U.N. Doc. S/RES/455, (Nov. 23, 1979). Ronzitti, 99; Cassese, 152 & 199–200.
78   Mégret (2008), 49–51.
79   *Id.*, 52.

unlawful act. At the State level, Article 51 of the Charter of the United Nations (UN) acknowledges a "right to individual or collective self-defense if an armed attack occurs against a Member of the United Nations".[80] Similarly, at the individual level, Article 31 of the Rome Statute excludes individual criminal responsibility when "the person acts reasonably to defend himself or herself or another person ... against an imminent and unlawful use of force in a manner proportionate to the degree of danger to the person or the other person or property protected".[81]

International law does not provide for a right to self-defense of non-State actors, with the only exception of subjugated peoples struggling to exercise their right to self-determination.[82] The gap is understandable: States are clearly not willing to confer non-State actors a right to use violence against them. States are granted a monopoly on the use of force and this circumstance is usually welcomed: when correctly exercised, internal sovereignty can protect people from human rights abuses.[83] Nonetheless, States' exclusivity over the use of force can be equally dangerous: "[b]y concentrating the authority to use force in States, the destructive potential of violence is vastly magnified, since States often command greater resources and organizational capacities than other communities".[84]

What if a State uses force to violate the human rights of the people under its jurisdiction? Would the population have a right to self-defense? Ben Saul affirms that: "a State policy of genocide, or violent persecution, against an ethnic group ... is clearly serious enough to trigger group self-defence". However, he adds that: "[s]elf-defence does not confer a license to use violence in a strategic way in protest at a generalized policy of State oppression".[85]

Other authors point out that denying the right of non-State actors to collective self-defense would be unreasonable, given the asymmetry between State and opposition groups in NIACs.[86] Despite the principle of equality, parties to a non-international armed conflict are *de facto* in a worse position than governmental forces, as they do not enjoy immunity from national prosecution. This would seem preposterous when the conflict originated from heinous violations of human rights committed by the government, such as in Libya and Syria – in

---

80   Christine Gray, International Law and the Use of Force 114 (2008).

81   Antonio Cassese, The Oxford Companion to International Criminal Justice 57–58 (2009).

82   Saul, 52.

83   Karima Bennoune, *Sovereignty vs. Suffering? Re-Examining Sovereignty and Human Rights through the Lens of Iraq*, 13 Eur. J. Int'l L. 243 (2002).

84   Saul, 54.

85   *Id.*, p. 37.

86   Bellal and Doswald-Beck, 22.

THE RIGHT TO REBEL AGAINST VIOLATIONS OF HUMAN RIGHTS 27

this case, "the State would benefit from a right on the basis of its own wrong".[87] Annyssa Bellal and Louise Doswald-Beck thus wonder whether "the international community should call for an exception in cases of violence in the form of individual or even collective self-defence. The present situation in non-international conflicts is the equivalent of punishing a State for exercising its right to self-defence against the unlawful aggression of another State".[88]

In sum, recognizing the right to collective self-defense of non-State actors that engage in armed activities against a government which violates human rights is both desirable as well as logical, from a strictly rights-based perspective. Nonetheless, the centrality of States in international law and their understandable reluctance to grant non-State actors this right leaves little hope in this regard. This does not mean that the international community does not allow for the rectification of gross violations of human rights committed by governments. Rather, dealing with such violations falls to States, and not individuals, to protect. State practice in recent years has shown that States have exercised this function through recourse to the notion of R2P. Yet, despite the importance of this emerging norm, the fact of it remaining subject to the will of States, rather than the victimized population itself, is a problematic factor that needs to be addressed.

B   *The Central Role of States in the R2P Doctrine*

The R2P doctrine maintains that each State bears the primary responsibility to protect the population within its borders from the most heinous violations of its human rights; when it fails to do so, this responsibility is shared with the international community. In extreme circumstances, States may use force in order to stop gross and systematic violations of human rights in other States – at least with the authorization of the UNSC. States are thus the central actors of R2P, either as single entities or as members of the international community. Individuals are simply seen as victims and they are not considered to be active players, capable of contributing to their own protection from heinous crimes.[89]

A close examination of the international documents that address R2P confirms this approach. Nearly none of them mentions civil society. Instead, the focus is exclusively on the role of States and the international community, as well as on the means by which to exercise peaceful or forcible interventions.[90] Perhaps the only exception is the International Commission on Intervention

---

87   *Id.*

88   *Id.*

89   Mégret (2009), 577–8.

90   *Id.*, 578.

and State Sovereignty (ICISS) Report on the Responsibility to Protect,[91] whereby it recognizes the communities' role in preventing gross violations of human rights:[92]

> When solutions are needed, it is the citizens of a particular state who have *the greatest interest and the largest stake* in the success of those solutions, in ensuring that the domestic authorities are fully accountable for their actions or inactions in addressing these problems, and in helping to ensure that past problems are not allowed to recur.[93]

Furthermore, the role of civil society is seen as instrumental in granting legitimacy to foreign intervention:

> By showing a commitment to helping local efforts to address both the root causes of problems and their more immediate triggers, broader international efforts gain added credibility – domestically, regionally, and globally. This credibility is especially important when international action must go beyond prevention to reaction, and especially when that reaction necessarily involves coercive measures, and ultimately the use of armed force.[94]

Again, the focus is on the international community. Helping local efforts does not seem to have a value *per se*. Instead, the ICISS Report highlights its instrumental role in enhancing the credibility of international efforts.

A similar approach is adopted with regard to the post-conflict phase. Local communities are recognized as the ones who will have to take over the responsibility of their own State. To this end, the international community should help civil society "set up a political process between the conflicting parties".[95] However, the importance of avoiding a situation where the international community monopolizes the post-conflict process is presented by the ICISS

---

91   International Commission on Intervention and State Sovereignty, *The Responsibility to Protect* (International Development Research Centre 2001), at 17, para. 2.30 [*hereinafter* ICISS Report] (emphasis added). The ICISS was the first to address systematically and comprehensively the concept of R2P. Its report shows the effort of the commission to set the basis for the development of this new idea, distinguishing it from previous controversial concepts such as humanitarian intervention.

92   *Id.*

93   *Id.*, 17, para. 2.30 (emphasis added).

94   *Id.*, 19, para. 3.4.

95   *Id.*, 45, para. 5.30.

THE RIGHT TO REBEL AGAINST VIOLATIONS OF HUMAN RIGHTS

Report as justified only because of its ultimate impact on the legitimacy of the international intervention, not on any impact it may have in empowering those in need of protection:

> This process of devolving responsibility back to the local community is essential to maintaining the legitimacy of intervention itself. Intervening to protect human beings must not be tainted by any suspicion that is a form of neo-colonial imperialism.[96]

Two considerations emerge from the above. First, in the ICISS Report, the local community's involvement is often seen as instrumental to legitimize the actions of the international community and not as a goal with intrinsic value *per se*. Second, ICISS fails to mention the role of civil society *during* the commission of atrocities. This could be read as a reflection of the principle of neutrality and of the reticence of the international community when it comes to non-State actors involved in internal conflicts.[97]

The centrality of the international community of States in saving oppressed populations is not a unique feature of emerging R2P doctrine. As aforementioned, the idea that victims are objects of salvation and not active subjects of emancipation can be traced back to the Middle Ages. As noted by Anne Orford, this approach draws upon "paternalistic descriptions of the need for international intervention" and on "images of the Security Council as a benevolent patriarch".[98] The international community is thus seen as the "guarantor of the values of human rights and democracy",[99] the sole actor capable to save victims of heinous atrocities.

This narrative is not limited to military intervention. The same approach can be found for instance in interventions undertaken by humanitarian agencies during refugee crises. Studies have been conducted on the stereotype of the refugee as a vulnerable and helpless victim in need of aid, incapable of playing a role in her own protection. Often, this vision leads to negative consequences, such as the development of dependency syndrome and the inability to reintegrate into society outside of refugee camps.[100]

---

96 *Id.*, 45, para. 5.31.

97 Mégret (2009), 580.

98 Anne Orford, *Muscular humanitarianism: reading the narratives of the new interventionism*, 10 Eur. J. Int'l L. 679, 693 (1999) [*hereinafter* Orford].

99 *Id.*, 694.

100 Barbara Harrell-Bond, *The experience of refugees as recipients of aid*, *in* Refugees: Perspectives on the Experience of Forced Migration 151–153 (1999).

Thus, in the case of interventions based on R2P, the local community is surely a victim and requires help. However, it is often the case that the very beneficiaries of such help are not recognized as active players that could have a more active role in addressing their own plight. In such circumstances,

> missing is any sense of the agency of the peoples of the states where intervention is to be conducted. There is no sense in which these peoples are understood to be themselves actively working to shape their communities and their world, except to the extent of seeking the protection of the international community. Only the hero of the story, the international community, has any capacity to animate or shape the people of target states.[101]

C *The Right to Protect Oneself: Reconstructing the R2P Doctrine*

The R2P doctrine embodies a top-down approach that pervades nearly all fields of international law: States are the central subjects at the international level; what happens within their borders would not grant any particular right to rebel. However, if international law accepts forcible interventions against human rights violations, why should it negate the right of victims to react to such violations? Victims should not be passive subjects, waiting for foreign States to react to violations of their human rights: granting them such rights would be pointless without a related right to defend and protect them.[102]

Frédéric Mégret has highlighted several reasons why we should welcome a right to resist in populations subject to heinous human rights violations.[103] First, historically peoples have proved able to entirely stop or at least minimize atrocities. The success of the Rwanda Patriotic Front in halting the genocide of the Tutsi, while the international community was unable to provide effective help, is a clear example of the potential of a well-organized resistance.[104] On the other hand, if we think of the forcible intervention in Libya, it is not hard to wonder whether the same could be said for foreign interventions conducted under the rubric of R2P.

Second, the victims of human rights violations are the ones who have the strongest interest in taking action. Therefore, unlike foreign interventions, victims' resistance is likely to occur. People would not have to negotiate a consen-

---

101   Orford, 695.

102   Honoré, 34; "Unless in certain conditions we have the right to rebel, much talk on human rights can be dismissed as empty rhetoric".

103   *See* Mégret (2009) and Mégret (2008).

104   Mégret (2009), 583.

THE RIGHT TO REBEL AGAINST VIOLATIONS OF HUMAN RIGHTS 31

sus between a litany of contrasting foreign and outside interests: their primary concern would be to protect themselves and to survive.[105]

Furthermore, the population could react in a timely and efficient manner. As Mégret explains, "[t]he great strength of local civil society is that it is in a sense always already there, and that its efforts at resistance will often have begun in direct response to patterns of violence".[106] Even when an international intervention does happen and helps to protect the population it is highly unlikely that it will be prompt. This is understandable, as the international community needs to find an agreement on the intervention. As highlighted by Mégret:

> All in all, the resistance paradigm offers a view of fighting atrocities that is more decentralized, bottom-up, empowering, people-based and spontaneous, where international intervention runs the risk of being centralized, top-down, paternalistic, state-based and institutional.[107]

Some might point out that there is a major difference between international interventions under the R2P framework and rebellions against heinous crimes. In the first case, there is the need of an authorization of the UNSC whereas no such authorization would be required for the second case.[108] However, this requirement is a highly-debated issue in the literature.

The first controversial question regards the discretionary power of the UNSC in qualifying situations as "threat to peace".[109] UNSC practice shows an "inconsistent record in terms of fulfilling its Charter mandate to maintain international peace and security".[110] Clearly an excessive interventionism would not be a welcome outcome. However, this issue would not rise in case of peoples' resistance against heinous crimes.

The considerable discretion of the UNSC raises in turn a second problem, namely whether there is a *duty* of the Council to intervene.[111] Previous practice

---

105   *Id.*, 584.

106   *Id.*

107   *Id. See also* Mégret (2008), 51–52.

108   *A More Secure World: Our Shared Responsibility. Report of the High-Level Panel on Threats, Challenges and Change*, U.N. Doc. A/59/565 (2004), at paras. 207–209 [*hereinafter* A More Secure World]; *2005 World Summit Outcome*, U.N. Doc. A/RES/60/1, (Oct. 24, 2005), at para. 139. *See also* Peters, 537.

109   Antonio Cassese, International Law 347 (2nd ed., 2005); Peters, 538.

110   Emma McClean, *The Responsibility to Protect: The Role of International Human Rights Law*, 13 J. Conflict & Security L. 123, 137 (2008).

111   Peters, 538; Cristina G. Badescu, Humanitarian Intervention and the Responsibility to Protect: Security and Human Rights 50–52 (2011).

demonstrates that the risk is not an excessive interventionism, but instead a reluctance to authorize military action. The exercise of the veto power by the permanent five members (P5) has proved to be the principal obstacle to interventions for humanitarian reasons, as demonstrated by the debates on the necessity to intervene in Syria.[112] This has led some authors to consider interventions to stop genocide, crimes against humanity and the like without the authorization of the UNSC. The discussion was fueled by the North Atlantic Treaty Organization (NATO) intervention in Kosovo, which was regarded *ex post facto* as "illegal, yet legitimate".[113]

While this article is not the place to engage with these debates, these considerations highlight the controversial nature of the responsibility to protect doctrine and of UNSC authorization to intervene through its invocation. Recognizing a right to rebel against violations of human rights as lawful, even in the absence of previous authorization of foreign intervention of the UNSC, would not raise the specter of these debatable issues and would allow for a timely and efficient response by the victims of these violations.

Some authors point out that – authorization by the UNSC notwithstanding – certain issues would remain unresolved. First, at what point would the violation of human rights be so serious as to trigger a right to rebel?[114] This question is not new: the same question rose with regard to interventions in the name of R2P. Despite the ICISS Report not having answered the question, in 2004 the United Nations High Level Panel on Threats, Challenges and Change specified that "there is a collective international responsibility to protect ... in the event of genocide and other large-scale killing, ethnic cleansing or serious violations of international humanitarian law".[115] This approach was embraced during the high-level meeting of the UNGA and included in the 2005 World Summit Outcome, where the R2P was linked to the protection of victims of genocide, war crimes, ethnic cleaning and crimes against humanity.[116] In line with these documents, the same threshold could apply to the right to rebel.

---

112   Carsten Stahn, *Between Law-breaking and Law-making: Syria, Humanitarian Intervention and 'What the Law Ought to Be*, 19 J. Conflict & Security L. 1, 13 (2013).

113   The Independent International Commission on Kosovo, *The Kosovo Report. Conflict, International Response, Lessons Learned* (2000), at 53; Olivier Corten, Le droit contre la guerre: L'interdiction du recours à la force en droit international contemporain 819–836 (2008).

114   Corten, 251; Mégret (2008), 56.

115   *A More Secure*, para. 203.

116   *2005 World Summit Outcome*, U.N. Doc. A/RES/60/1, §§ 138–140 (Oct. 24, 2005). *See also* Secretary General, *In Larger Freedom: Towards Development, Security and Human Rights for All*, U.N. Doc. A/59/2005, para. 135 (Mar. 21, 2005).

THE RIGHT TO REBEL AGAINST VIOLATIONS OF HUMAN RIGHTS   33

Second, would the opposition group retain a right to resist in case it commits human rights violations?[117] *Jus ad bellum* and *jus in bello* are fundamentally distinct branches of law. The reasons why a conflict started do not affect the equal application of IHL to all the parties to the conflict: "from the humanitarian point of view, the victims of the conflict on both sides need and deserve the same protection, and they are not necessarily responsible for the violation of *jus ad bellum* committed by "their" party".[118] The indifference of IHL to the *jus ad bellum* operates also in the other direction. The fact that a party to the conflict violates IHL does not affect its right to use force, if it is in conformity with international law. The same reasoning would apply to the right to rebel: the way in which the rebellion is conducted would not undermine the original right to react to heinous human rights violations.

IV   Practical Implications of Recognizing a Right to Rebel

A   *Governments Committing Gross and Systematic Violations of Human Rights*

From a theoretical point of view, recognizing a right to rebel against heinous crimes does not seem preposterous. The importance of empowering the people most directly affected and the lack of prompt action, if any, by the international community are just a few of the reasons why resistance should be welcomed and legitimized at the international level. The discourse becomes more problematic when the focus turns on the practical implications of recognizing a right to rebel. Why should the international community move in this direction, and how might such a move fit within the current international law system?

From a close analysis of recent State practice emerges the conclusion that the international community is increasingly concerned by gross violations of human rights. Notably, two trends have emerged from State practice. On the one hand, the international community tends to consider governments that commit heinous crimes against their people as illegitimate. On the other hand, opposition groups that fight against human rights violations are recognized as legitimate representatives of the population and receive moral and material

---

117   Corten, 251.

118   Marco Sassoli et al., *How Does Law Protect in War?*, https://www.icrc.org/casebook/doc/book-chapter/fundamentals-ihl-book-chapter.htm#b_ii;   https://www.icrc.org/en/document/how-does-law-protect-war-o; François Bugnion, *Jus ad Bellum, Jus in Bello and Non-international Armed Conflicts*, 6 Y.B. Int'l Humanitarian L. 167, 172 (2009).

help from foreign countries. The way power is exercised by the government towards the people under its jurisdiction is not part of the *domaine reservée* anymore: sovereignty implies responsibility for the protection of human rights towards the population and the international community.[119] State practice reflects this perception of sovereignty as responsibility and is reshaping the traditional approach towards governments that violate human rights in a gross, systematic and widespread manner. This is well illustrated by the recent events that unfolded in Libya and Syria.

In 2011, following the onset of the Arab Spring, tensions arose in Libya. On 15 February 2011, demonstrations started in the country. The government harshly reacted, killing several protesters. Within a few days, clashes increased and triggered an internal conflict.[120] The international community reacted immediately, condemning the actions undertaken by the government of Libya against the opposition and affirming that Libya's leader, Colonel Muammar Gaddafi, had lost his legitimacy. President Obama maintained that: "when a leader's only means of staying in power is to use mass violence against its own people, he has lost the legitimacy to rule".[121] Furthermore, the United Kingdom (UK) claimed that: "it is clear that this is an illegitimate regime that has lost the consent of its people".[122] By June 2011, several countries defined Gaddafi's government as illegitimate and recognized the National Transitional Council (NTC), the leading authority of the opposition group, as the representative of Libyan people.[123]

119　Peters, 524.

120　BBC, *Libya Profile: Timeline* (Mar. 1, 2017), http://www.bbc.com/news/world-africa -13755445.

121　Stefan Talmon, *The Difference between Rhetoric and Reality: Why an Illegitimate Regime May Still be a Government in the Eyes of International Law*, EJIL: Talk! (Mar. 3, 2011) [*hereinafter* Talmon (2011)], http://www.ejiltalk.org/the-difference-between-rhetoric-and-reality-why-an-illegitimate-regime-may-still-be-a-government-in-the-eyes-of-international-law/; Jonte van Hessen, *De Facto Regimes in International Law*, 23 Utrecht J. Int'l & Eur. Law 31, 37 (2012).

122　Talmon (2011).

123　The statement by the Chair of the Libya Contact Group clearly expresses this view: "Qadhafi and his regime had lost all legitimacy and he must leave power allowing the Libyan people to determine their own future ... In contrast with the current regime, the INC is a legitimate interlocutor, representing the aspirations of Libyan people". *See* Statement by Foreign Secretary William Hague following the Libya Contact Group meeting in Doha, Apr. 13, 2011, paras. 2 & 7. The Libya Contact Group was created during the London Conference on Libya on 29 March 2011. It included European powers, the United States, some Middle East countries and international organizations. The objective of the group is to: "provide leadership and overall political direction to the international effort in close coordination with the UN, AU, Arab League, OIC, and EU to support Libya; provide

The Ministry of Foreign Affairs of the Republic of the Maldives, for example, stated that: "through its actions including gross and systematic human rights violations, which appear to amount to war crimes and crimes against humanity, the government of Muammar Gaddafi has lost its legitimacy and its right to govern".[124] Similarly, Russia affirmed that: "Colonel Gaddafi has forfeited his legitimacy due to his actions ... indeed we need to help him go".[125] The League of Arab States[126] and the European Union[127] shared the same position.[128]

The international community adopted a similar reaction in the Syrian case. In March 2011, pro-democratic demonstrations erupted in Deraa; the government responded with fire, killing several people who took part in the demonstration. The episode triggered protests in the whole country, which were forcibly quelled by governmental forces. On 3 October 2011, the Syrian opposition forces formed the Syrian National Council (SNC) with the aim of overthrowing President Assad.[129] Following widespread human rights and humanitarian law violations

---

a forum for coordinating the international response on Libya; and provide a focal point in the international community for contact with the Libyan parties". *See* U.K. Foreign & Commonwealth Office, *London Conference on Libya: Chair's statement* (Mar. 29, 2011), https://www.gov.uk/government/news/london-conference-on-libya-chairs-statement. *See also* Christian Handerson, *International Measures for the Protection of Civilians in Libya and Côte D'Ivoire*, 60 Int'l & Comp. L. Q. 767, 776–777 (2011); Stefan Talmon, *Recognition of the Libyan National Transitional Council*, 15 ASIL: Insights (2011) https://www.asil.org/insights/volume/15/issue/16/recognition-libyan-national-transitional-council.

124 Presidency of the Republic of Maldives, *Maldives Recognises Libyan National Council as sole representative of the Libyan people* (Apr. 3, 2011), Ref: 2011–256, http://www.presidency maldives.gov.mv/Index.aspx?lid=11&dcid=5071.

125 *Gaddafi has lost all legitimacy – G8*, News24 (May 27, 2011), http://www.news24.com/ Africa/News/Gaddafi-has-lost-all-legitimacy-G8-20110527; *G8 summit: Gaddafi isolated as Russia joins demand for Libyan leader to go*, The Guardian (May 27, 2011), https://www .theguardian.com/world/2011/may/27/g8-gaddafi-libya-russia.

126 League of Arab States, *The Implications of the Current Events in Libya and the Arab Position*, Council Resolution 7360 (Cairo, Mar. 12, 2011), U.N. Doc. S/2011/137 (Mar. 15, 2011), Annex; whereby the Council decided: "*To cooperate and communicate* with the Transitional National Council of Libya and to provide the Libyan people with urgent and continuing support as well as the necessary protection from the serious violations and grave crimes committed by the Libyan authorities, which have consequently lost their legitimacy".

127 European Council, *Declaration on developments in Libya and the Southern Neighbourhood region*, EUCO 7/1/11, REV 1 (Apr. 20, 2011).

128 Stefan Talmon, *Recognition of Opposition Groups as the Legitimate Representative of a People*, 12 Chinese J. Int'l L. 219, 238–239 (2013) [*hereinafter* Talmon (2013)].

129 *Syria: The story of the conflict*, BBC News (Mar. 1, 2016) http://www.bbc.com/news/ world-middle-east-26116868.

committed by the government, several countries declared that Assad could not be considered as legitimate representative of its people, while the SNC was seen as a credible alternative to the regime.[130] On 20 November 2012, the UK recognized the National Coalition of the Syrian Revolutionary and Opposition Forces (NCS) as the "sole legitimate representative" of the Syrian people[131] and specified that: "a credible alternative to the Assad regime is emerging that has the growing support of the Arab League, the European Union, the United States and an increasing number of other countries".[132] The European Union, the United States, France, Turkey and six Gulf States made a similar declaration, recognizing the opposition group as the legitimate government.[133] The same view was shared by the UN Secretary General Ban Ki-moon, who affirmed that: "For many months, it has been evident that President Assad has lost his legitimacy",[134] and further affirmed by Kofi Annan, special envoy of the UN in Syria: "the current [Syrian] government has lost all legitimacy".[135]

The Libyan and Syrian cases clearly show that the international community recognizes undemocratic regimes as *de jure* governments. Nevertheless, this attitude changes substantially when the incumbent government "turns against its own people,... uses heavy weapons, fighter aircraft and tanks to fire on its people".[136] In these cases, it can be noticed an emerging consensus in recognizing that governments that commit heinous crimes against their own people lose their legitimacy and should go.[137] What does it mean in practice? The lost of legitimacy of the incumbent government leaves room for the recognition of another entity as the legitimate representative of the people.[138] This is confirmed by the declarations of States and international and regional organizations with regard to the situation in Libya and Syria, whereby it emerges that declarations on the illegitimacy of the Libyan and Syrian governments were coupled with the recognition of the Libyan National

---

130   *Syria conflict: UK recognizes opposition, says William Hague*, BBC News (Nov. 20, 2012), http://www.bbc.com/news/uk-politics-20406562.

131   *Id.*

132   *Id.*

133   *Id.*

134   *Secretary-General's remarks to the General Assembly on the situation in Syria*, UNRIC (June 7, 2012), http://www.unric.org/it/siria/28132-the-secretary-generals-remarks-to-the-general-assembly-on-the-situation-in-syria-new-york-7-june-2012.

135   Kofi Annan, *My departing advice on how to save Syria*, Financial Times (Aug. 2, 2012), http://www.ft.com/cms/s/2/b00b6ed4-dbc9-11e1-8d78-00144feab49a.html#axzz4Linkl4DB.

136   Talmon (2013), 238.

137   *Id.*

138   Talmon (2013), 239.

THE RIGHT TO REBEL AGAINST VIOLATIONS OF HUMAN RIGHTS

Transitional Council and of the National Coalition of the Syrian Revolutionary and Opposition Forces.

B *Opposition Groups Rebelling against Gross and Systematic Violations of Human Rights*

During the first months of the Libyan conflict, several States recognized the NTC as the legitimate representative of Libyan people, but were always very careful in underlying that Gaddafi was still the *de jure* head of government. The only exception was France, whose Foreign Minister affirmed that: "the National Transitional Council is the only holder of governmental authority in the contacts between France and Libya and its related entities".[139] The situation dramatically changed in subsequent months. On July 15, 2011, during the Libyan Contact Group meeting, 32 States declared that:

> The Contact Group reaffirmed that the Qaddafi regime no longer has any legitimate authority in Libya and that Qaddafi and certain members of his family must go. Henceforth and until an interim authority is in place, participants agreed to deal with the National Transitional Council (NTC) as the legitimate governing authority in Libya …The Group urged all relevant parties to explore ways and means of paving the way for the formation of an interim government to ensure a smooth and peaceful transition of power with the widest popular support possible. In line with the NTC's "Road Map", the formation of an interim government should be quickly followed by the convening of a National Congress with representatives from all parts of Libya.[140]

This position was widely endorsed by the overwhelming majority of the international community. The League of Arab States decided "to cooperate and liaise with the Interim Transitional National Council of Libya" and added that the Libyan authorities "have forfeited all legitimacy" due to the grave violations of human rights committed against the Libyan population. The role of the NTC as representative of Libyan people also emerged in UNSC Resolution 2009 (2011), where the Council encouraged

---

139 Dapo Akande, *Recognition of Libyan National Transitional Council*, EJIL: Talk! (2011), http://www.ejiltalk.org/recognition-of-libyan-national-transitional-council-as-government-of-libya/; Talmon (2013), 238.

140 *Fourth Meeting of the Libya Contact Group Chair's Statement*, 15 July 2011, Istanbul, para. 4.

the National Transitional Council to implement its plans to: (a) protect Libya's population, restore government services, and allocate Libya's funds openly and transparently; (b) prevent further abuses and violations of human rights and international humanitarian law and to put an end to impunity; (c) ensure a consultative, inclusive political process with a view to agreement on a constitution and the holding of free and fair elections.[141]

By attributing to the opposition group tasks that typically fall to governments, the UNSC *de facto* recognized its authority. The UNSC resolution was adopted in September, when it was clear that Gaddafi was about to lose the conflict and the rebels had the control of the majority of the country.[142] On September 21, the African Union recognized the National Transitional Council as the *de facto* Libyan government.[143]

Similarly, considerations of the illegitimacy of the Syrian government were coupled with declarations of recognition of the National Coalition of the Syrian Revolutionary and Opposition Forces (the so-called Syrian Opposition Coalition, or SOC).[144] On 20 November 2012, the UK recognized it as the "sole legitimate representative" of the Syrian people[145] and specified that: "a credible alternative to the Assad regime is emerging that has the growing support of the Arab League, the European Union, the United States and an increasing number of other countries".[146] The United States (US),[147] the European Union, several European Countries, Turkey and the League of Arab States made a similar declaration, recognizing the opposition group as the legitimate representative of the Syrian people.[148] What do these recognitions mean in practice? Despite the fact that they may be just political declarations, in both cases they led to some forms of intervention in favor of the rebels.

On 13 March 2011, the UNSC authorized member States to take "all the necessary measures ... to protect civilians and civilian populated areas under

---

141 U.N. Doc. S/RES/2009, §5 (Sept 16, 2011).

142 *Libya Profile: Timeline*, BBC News (Mar. 1, 2017), http://www.bbc.com/news/world-africa-13755445.

143 *Id.*

144 The SOC replaced the Syrian National Council (SNC). *See* Talmon (2013), 220.

145 *Syria conflict: UK recognizes opposition, says William Hague*, BBC News (Nov. 20, 2012), http://www.bbc.com/news/uk-politics-20406562.

146 *Id.*

147 *Id.*; President Obama defined the coalition as the "sole legitimate representation of the aspirations of the Syrian people".

148 Talmon (2013), 221–223.

THE RIGHT TO REBEL AGAINST VIOLATIONS OF HUMAN RIGHTS

threat of attack in the Libyan Arab Jamahiriya, including Bengazi".[149] The intervention was aimed at protecting civilians. Nonetheless, this meant in practice attacking governmental forces and hence helping the opposition groups. Furthermore, mentioning Bengazi, the stronghold of the rebels, in the resolution is a sign of support towards the rebels.[150]

Following the alarming expansion of Daesh, which gained control over key areas in Syria and declared a caliphate in the territory from Aleppo to Diyala (an eastern Iraqi province), in February 2015 the US and Turkey signed an agreement to arm and train a selected pool of members of the Syrian opposition forces.[151] Saudi Arabia and Qatar armed the rebels as well, while some European countries supplied weapons to the Kurds fighting against the Islamic State of Iraq and Syria (ISIS), also known as Daesh.[152] Although weapons and other material support were specifically provided to fight Daesh, there was no guarantee that the rebels would have used the arms only against Daesh and not also against governmental forces.[153]

State practice in Libya and Syria demonstrates that gross and systematic violations of human rights can jeopardize the legitimacy of the government, leaving "room for another legitimate representative of the State's people", namely the opposition group.[154] The recognition of a right to rebel would fit well in this scenario. The responsibility to protect doctrine provides that States have the responsibility to protect their citizens from widespread, systematic and grave breaches of human rights. State practice demonstrates that, when they fail to do so, their legitimacy might be undermined. At the same time, the

---

149 U.N. Doc. S/RES/1973, (Mar. 17, 2011).

150 Dapo Akande, *What does UN Security Council Resolution 1973 permit?* EJIL: Talk! (Mar. 23, 2011) http://www.ejiltalk.org/what-does-un-security-council-resolution-1973-permit/.

151 Turkey and US agree to train and arm Syrian rebels in fight against ISIS, The Guardian (Feb. 19, 2015), http://www.theguardian.com/world/2015/feb/19/turkey-us-train-syrian -rebels-fight-isis.

152 *Germany to supply arms to Kurds fighting IS in Iraq*, BBC News (Sep. 1, 2014), http://www .bbc.com/news/world-europe-29012159.

153 This is not the place to analyze whether providing arms to and training opposition groups in Syria was lawful under international law. Nonetheless, it is worth mentioning that the prohibition to intervene in favor of rebels is well established in international law. First and foremost, the UN Charter establishes the ban on the use of force (UN Charter art. 2(4)) and the principle of non-intervention (UN Charter art. 2(7)). Furthermore, the International Court of Justice excluded such possibility in the *Nicaragua* case (para. 228), where the ICJ explained that the arming and training of opposition groups "can certainly be said to involve the threat or use of force" against a foreign country.

154 Talmon (2013), 239.

recognition of a right to rebel would legalize the armed resistance of the population against gross violations of human rights committed by the regime. In these cases, States have provided military support to the rebels without meeting the condemnation of the international community. The right to resistance would determine the bases and the limits of such support, which should be exercised as subsidiary measure.

V   Concluding Remarks

Arguing for a right to rebel might seem like an abstract, if wishful, exercise. Surely international law, as it currently stands, is not going to recognize the existence of this right any time soon and some may welcome this fact as a positive outcome. Speaking about a right to rebel will raise the concern of even the most open-minded and liberal scholars. One issue regards the entity to which the right to rebel would be granted. Non-State armed forces are heterogeneous groups that change and evolve rapidly. Who could guard against a legitimate armed opposition from producing a system of government worse than that which it overthrows through the invocation of the right to resist? Likewise, there are other risks connected with the recognition of a right to rebel. Using violence to stop human rights violations could potentially increase these violations, jeopardizing the protection of civilians further. Moreover, even when the rebellion *per se* does not contribute to human rights violations, it does not guarantee that it will be able to stop State's violence. Nevertheless, the intervention in Libya demonstrates that the same critiques can be directed to foreign interventions aimed at protecting the population. Recurring to armed force, be it by States or non-State groups, is always risky and should be looked at as the last resort, guided by the principles of necessity and proportionality.[155]

Marco Sassoli correctly noted that

> ... a world without armed groups would be a better world, as would a world without war. However, armed groups are simply a reality, just as armed conflicts are a reality. Those who developed IHL did not like armed conflicts, but they did not simply state that armed conflicts should not exist. They also accepted that armed conflicts exist and tried to design rules

---

155   Frédéric Mégret, *Beyond 'Freedom Fighters' and 'Terrorists': When, if Ever, is Non-State Violence Legitimate in International Law?* (Apr. 6, 2009), http://papers.ssrn.com/sol3/papers.cfm?abstract_id=1373590.

applicable to these situations, accepted by those involved in this sad reality.[156]

Similarly, armed resistance against gross and systematic human rights violations will not cease to exist simply because we ignore it. Recognizing a right to rebel against heinous violations of human rights does not necessarily mean that the victims will recur to armed resistance lightly. As Mégret notes, "[v]ictims of atrocities might ... go through agonizing dilemmas about whether to resist, and if so when and how".[157] None would thoughtlessly start a war. Nonetheless, the recognition by the international community of a right to rebel would grant the victims some recognition and legitimization at the international level.

Granting rights without conceding means to react against their violations would be pointless. International law should not serve as a shield for States to commit atrocities. Instead, it should learn from history, acknowledging that too often the international community has not been able to prevent or stop human rights violations, while the local resistance has proved successful. The right to rebel would thus lead to a re-construction and re-consideration of the responsibility to protect doctrine. If sovereignty does entail responsibility, then first and foremost it should be a responsibility of the State towards its people, which would have a right to resistance in case the government does not respect its responsibility. The international community would have a subsidiary role, sustaining and supporting the legitimate efforts of the people fighting against heinous violations of human rights.

---

156   Marco Sassòli, *Taking Armed Groups Seriously: Ways to Improve Their Compliance with International Humanitarian Law*, 1 J. Int'l Humanitarian Legal Stud. 5, 50 (2010).

157   Mégret (2009), 584.

Atrocities, Accountability and the Politics of Palestinian Statehood

*Jasmine Moussa**

I   Introduction   42
II Impunity and the Quest for Palestinian Statehood   47
III Does Palestine Qualify as a State Under International Law? Recent Developments in an Old Debate   50
IV "Statehood", Recognition and UN Membership   58
   A   *The Law and Politics of UN Admission*   60
   B   *"Statehood" Without UN Membership: Circumventing the Security Council*   64
V   Challenges to General Assembly Resolution 67/19: (In)Consistency with Security Council Resolutions?   66
VI Implications of Palestine's New Status   70
   A   *Institutional Implications*   71
   B   *Multi-lateral Treaty Participation*   72
   C   *Standing before International Courts*   76
   D   *Immunity from Jurisdiction and Standing before Domestic Courts*   79
   E   *State Succession and the Validity of Treaties Concluded by the PLO and Palestinian Authority*   86
VII Conclusion   94

I   Introduction

Events over the past five years have reignited debate on the status of Palestine. Is Palestine a State or a semi-sovereign entity? Is it an occupied State whose

---

* PhD in Law (University of Cambridge), LLM in Public International Law, with Distinction (LSE). The views expressed in this article are the author's own and do not represent the views of any of the institutions to which she is affiliated. The author would like to thank Ardi Imseis, Editor-in-Chief of the Palestine Yearbook of International Law for his valuable editorial input. Any mistakes or omissions remain the author's own.

ATROCITIES, ACCOUNTABILITY AND THE POLITICS 43

sovereignty is in abeyance, or does it enjoy some other *sui generis* international status? Is Palestine entitled to the trappings of sovereignty? Can it conclude agreements and participate in multilateral treaties that are open only to States? Does it have standing before international courts such as the International Criminal Court (ICC)? These questions have resurfaced after Palestine's bid, in 2009, to accept the ICC's jurisdiction for crimes committed in its territory during Israel's "Operation Cast Lead" – a massive air and ground offensive against the Gaza Strip under the pretext of stopping weapons smuggling into Gaza and rocket fire into Israel. The attacks, which targeted the densely-populated cities of Gaza, Rafah and Khan Younis over twenty-two days, killed approximately 1,400 Palestinians. Palestine's recent bid to accede to the Rome Statute of the ICC and seek accountability for alleged Israeli crimes has its origins in the international community's response to this conflict. The desire for accountability, the failure of peace talks and the persistence of Israeli settlement activity have all motivated Palestine's strategy of seeking recognition through membership of international institutions.[1] Interestingly, this strategy re-conceptualizes international law and international organizations as tools for asserting sovereignty, rather than restricting it.[2]

Under this strategy, Palestine applied for membership of the United Nations (UN) Educational, Scientific and Cultural Organization (UNESCO), which voted overwhelmingly in favor of Palestinian membership.[3] Failing to acquire UN membership, Palestine then pursued a diplomatic campaign to change its status within the UN from "observer" to "non-member observer *State*". On 29 November 2012 (exactly 65 years after the adoption of UN General Assembly

---

1   Yoffie has termed this Palestine's "Plan B", which he argues replaced attempts to seek bilateral recognition by individual States. While the momentum and success of Palestine's current endeavor to join international organizations, and participate in international treaties is unprecedented, as identified by Yoffie, this strategy is not new. Neither has Palestine abandoned the parallel process of seeking recognition by States that have not yet recognized it. *See* Adam G. Yoffie, *The Palestine Problem: The Search for Statehood and the Benefits of International Law*, 36 Yale J. Int'l L. 497, 499, 501 (2011).

2   *Id.* Ethan Bronner, *In Israel, Time for Peace Offer May Run Out*, N.Y. Times (Apr. 2, 2011), http://www.nytimes.com/2011/04/03/world/middleeast/03mideast.html?pagewanted=all.

3   UNESCO Res. 36 C/76, *Records of the General Conference*, 36th Session, 11th Plenary Meeting, Vol. 1 (Oct. 31, 2011); *Palestinian Flag Raised at UNESCO*, UNESCO Media Services (Dec. 13, 2012), http://www.unesco.org/new/en/media-services/single-view/news/palestinian_flag_raised_at_unesco/.

Resolution 181 which partitioned Palestine), the UN General Assembly (UNGA) adopted Resolution 67/19 (2012) upgrading Palestine's status.[4]

Resolution 67/19 (2012) elicited mixed responses from UN member States, with some regarding it as an implicit recognition of Palestinian statehood[5] and others consigning it to the realm of pure symbolism.[6] Israel's representative denied that the resolution could confer statehood on the Palestinian Authority (PA) – Palestine's interim self-government body – as the latter arguably failed to meet the relevant criteria. Neither would it enable the PA to participate in international treaties, organizations, or conferences as a State. He also claimed that the resolution violated the PA's fundamental binding commitments.[7] Although he did not clarify what these commitments were, it is likely he was referring to the Oslo Accords, in which the Palestine Liberation Organization (PLO) – recognized by the UNGA since 1974 as the legitimate representative of the Palestinian people – committed not to unilaterally alter arrangements

---

4 After laying the groundwork for the "creation" of Israel through partitioning Palestine on 29 November 1947, ironically the UNGA – whose membership changed drastically following the decolonization movement – played a key role in "re-creating" Palestine throughout the following sixty-five years. *See* G.A. Res. 181, *Future government of Palestine*, U.N. Doc. A/Res/181 (II) (Nov. 29, 1947). It has been argued that the GA acted ultra vires in partitioning Palestine. *See* Hans Koechler, *The Palestine Problem in the Framework of International Law: Sovereignty as the Crucial Issue of a Peaceful Settlement of the Palestinian-Israeli Conflict*, presented at *1991–2000: The Palestinian-Israeli Peace Process – A critical evaluation of ten years of negotiations between the Palestinian Authority and Israel* (Madrid, Sep. 30–Oct. 1, 2000), http://i-p-o.org/palestine-sovereignty.htm#_ftnref20; Hans Kelsen, The Law of the United Nations, A Critical Analysis of Its Fundamental Problems 193, 195–197 (1950); Clyde Eagleton *Palestine and the Constitutional Law of the United Nations*, 42 Am. J. Int'l L. 397–399 (1948).

5 The Palestinian President called the resolution a "birth certificate of the reality of the State of Palestine". Turkey's Foreign Minister stated that granting Palestine non-Member Observer State status was a "first step" and a "booster" that created momentum towards a negotiated, comprehensive solution to the conflict. The UN Committee on the Inalienable Rights of the Palestinian People shared this view, stating that since Palestinian membership in the UN was still pending before the UNSC, progress on Palestine's status in the United Nations would help safeguard the two-State solution. *See General Assembly Votes Overwhelmingly to Accord Palestine 'Non-Member Observer State' Status in United Nations*, U.N. Doc. GA/11317 (Nov. 29, 2012), https://www.un.org/press/en/2012/ga11317.doc.htm.

6 The US representative also criticized the resolution, stating that "today's vote should not be misconstrued by any as constituting eligibility for UN membership. It does not. This resolution does not establish that Palestine is a state." *See Explanation of Vote by Ambassador Susan E. Rice, U.S. Permanent Representative to the United Nations, Following UN General Assembly Vote on Palestinian Observer State Status Resolution*, United States Mission to the United Nations (Nov. 29, 2012), http://usun.state.gov/briefing/statements/201226.htm.

7 *See* U.N. Doc. GA/11317.

reached with Israel. This understanding was later endorsed in the Road Map and UN Security Council (UNSC) Resolution 1515. In fact, Israel had declared in its decision on the Wye River Memorandum that "a unilateral decision by the [PA] on the establishment of a Palestinian State, prior to the achievement of a *Final Status Agreement* would constitute a substantive and fundamental violation of the *Interim Agreement*".[8]

The view denying any legal effect to UNGA Resolution 67/19 and disputing Palestine's standing as a State was also expressed in academic literature. According to one commentator, "the practice of admitting contested entities and even undoubtedly non-States to this club [of non-member States] proves that nominally calling an entity a non-member *State* does not automatically accord it with statehood".[9]

Far from being ineffective or symbolic, however, Palestine's new status within the UN has had important political and legal implications. In terms of its political consequences, the new status gives much-needed momentum to Palestine's push for greater recognition as a State by other States. In October 2014, Sweden became the first Western European State to officially recognize Palestine,[10] a move that spurred a number of European parliaments (the United Kingdom (UK),[11] Spain,[12] Portugal,[13] Ireland,[14] Italy,[15] France[16] and

---

8   Israel Ministry of Foreign Affairs, *Government Decision on the Wye River Memorandum* (Nov. 11, 1998), http://www.mfa.gov.il/MFA/ForeignPolicy/Peace/Guide/Pages/Government %20Decision%20on%20the%20Wye%20River%20Memorandum%20-N.aspx.

9   Jure Vidmar, *Palestine and the Conceptual Problem of Implicit Statehood*, 12 Chinese J. Int'l L. 1, 9 (2013) [*hereinafter* Vidmar].

10   *See* Steven Erlanger, *Sweden to Recognize Palestinian State*, N.Y. Times (Oct. 3, 2014), https://www.nytimes.com/2014/10/04/world/europe/sweden-to-recognize-palestinian-state.html.

11   Hansard, Division 54, Column 44–128 (Oct. 13, 2014) (U.K.).

12   *Boletín oficial de las cortes generales congreso de los diputados x legislature*, Serie D: General (Nov. 26, 2014), at 38.

13   *Portuguese parliament passes motion in support of 'Palestine' recognition*, Jerusalem Post (Dec. 12, 2014) http://www.jpost.com/Arab-Israeli-Conflict/Portuguese-parliament -passes-motion-in-support-of-Palestine-recognition-384494.

14   Dáil Éireann, Private Members Business (Sinn Féin) (Dec. 9, 2014), http://www.oireachtas .ie/viewdoc.asp?fn=/documents/ThisWeek/PMB-DAIL-2014/document36.htm.

15   *Italian parliament approves symbolic recognition of Palestine*, Jerusalem Post (Feb. 27, 2015), http://www.jpost.com/Israel-News/Politics-And-Diplomacy/Italian-parliament-approves -symbolic-recognition-of-Palestine-392425.

16   *Résolution portant sur la reconnaissance de l'État de Palestine*, Texte adopté n° 439, Petite loi (Dec. 2, 2014), http://www.dekamer.be/FLWB/PDF/54/0721/54K0721007.pdf.

Belgium[17]) to adopt resolutions recognizing Palestinian statehood and urging their executive authorities to follow suit.[18] This culminated in the European Parliament's symbolic motion, in December 2014, to overwhelmingly express its support "in principle" for the recognition of Palestine.[19] Most recently, on 13 May 2015, the Holy See officially recognized Palestinian statehood in a bilateral treaty.[20] In terms of its legal implications, the UNGA vote has also had important institutional implications. In addition, it has allowed Palestine to accede to multilateral treaties open only to States, including the Rome Statute of the ICC.

In a dramatic turn of events, on 16 January 2015 the ICC Prosecutor opened a preliminary investigation into alleged crimes committed during the July-August 2014 war in the occupied Palestinian territory (oPt) after Palestine acceded to the Rome Statute.[21] Less than three years earlier, the Prosecutor had rejected a similar bid by Palestine in respect of crimes allegedly committed during Israel's 2009 military operation in Gaza. In explaining this significant reversal of policy, the Prosecutor's office referred to UNGA Resolution 67/19 (2012), which had upgraded Palestine's status to a "non-member observer State". Curiously, the Office of the Prosecutor of the ICC (OTP) found that it could not exercise jurisdiction over the events of 2009, as Palestine's new status "did not retroactively validate the previously invalid 2009 declaration lodged without the necessary standing".[22] How is it that Palestine, which had no standing (*i.e.* was not a State) in 2009, could suddenly have standing in 2012? The OTP's conclusion seems to suggest that UNGA Resolution 67/19 "created" or "constituted" a State of Palestine in a "big bang" kind of moment.[23]

This article examines the question of whether UNGA Resolution 67/19 has "constitutive" effects, and if not, then what are the resolution's legal im-

---

17 *Résolution Visant à la reconnaissance de l'état palestinien par la belgique*, Chambre des représentants de belgique Doc 54 0721/ (2014/2015) (Feb. 5, 2015).

18 Unlike Sweden's decision, such resolutions are unbinding in respect of the executive branches of their respective States.

19 *European Parliament resolution on recognition of Palestine statehood*, European Parliament (Dec. 17, 2014), www.euparl.europa.eu.

20 *Vatican causes stir with treaty recognizing Palestine as a state*, The Washington Post (May 13, 2015), http://www.washingtonpost.com/world/middle_east/vatican-officially -recognizes-the-state-of-palestine/2015/05/13/265624f2-f97d-11e4-9ef4-1bb7ce3b3fb7 _story.html.

21 ICC-CPI, *The Prosecutor of the International Criminal Court, Fatou Bensouda, Opens a Preliminary Examination of the Situation in Palestine,* ICC-OTP-20150116-PR1083 (Jan. 16, 2015), https://www.icc-cpi.int/Pages/item.aspx?name=pr1083.

22 *Id.*

23 *See* Vidmar, 14.

plications? It responds to critics who argue that the resolution is of no legal value through the following structure: Section (II) contextualizes the debate on Palestinian statehood within the broader narrative of accountability for Israeli crimes in the oPt. Section (III) analyses the doctrinal debate on whether Palestine does, in fact, meet the criteria for statehood. Section (IV) discusses Palestine's circumvention of the UNSC in favor of the legitimating authority of the UNGA. Section (V) investigates one of the most important challenges to UNGA Resolution 67/19, namely its purported inconsistency with existing commitments of the PLO and PA[24] and relevant UNSC resolutions. Section (VI) explores the legal consequences of Palestine's new international status, focusing on five areas: institutional aspects; multi-lateral treaty participation; standing before international courts; sovereign immunity and standing before domestic courts; and State succession to international treaties. These five areas indicate that Resolution 67/19 is not necessarily "constitutive" of Palestinian statehood; however, upgrading Palestine's status in the UNGA may be considered the watershed event that crystallized Palestine's ability to act as a State. This role is essential for the purely practical consideration that determining the exact date when Palestine crossed the threshold of statehood is objectively impossible.

II   Impunity and the Quest for Palestinian Statehood

The recent bid for Palestinian statehood was triggered by the UN Human Rights Council's (HRC) response to Israel's "Operation Cast Lead". In January 2009, the HRC set up the *United Nations Fact Finding Mission on the Conflict*

---

24   For the purposes of this paper, the PLO and the PA are often referred to collectively as they are in effect both responsible for the Palestinian entity's foreign relations, or have been over certain periods of history. The PLO was established in 1964 and was recognized by the UNGA as the "representative of the Palestinian people" in 1974 (UNGA Res. 3236 (XXIX), 22 November 1974). In that capacity, the PLO was responsible for negotiations with Israel, which in turn recognized the PLO as the official representative of the Palestinian people in 1993. Simultaneously, the 1993 Declaration of Principles (DOP) between Israel and the PLO, led to establishment of the PA as an interim self-governing body. Over time, the PA has assumed *suo motu* some responsibilities in the sphere of foreign relations (e.g. the Palestinian Ministry of Foreign Affairs is officially part of the Palestinian Authority). It did not, however, replace the PLO's representative or foreign relations functions. In 1994, the PLO established a "Negotiation Affairs Department" to oversee the implementation of the Interim Agreement and the Permanent Status talks. Although the PLO and the PA are legally distinct, in practice their authorities in the areas of representation and foreign relations overlap.

in Gaza, which produced a report (also known as the "Goldstone report") in September 2009.[25]

The 452-page report described the attack against Gaza as "a deliberately disproportionate attack designed to punish, humiliate and terrorize a civilian population"[26] and documented numerous atrocities by Israeli forces in the Gaza Strip, amounting to war crimes and crimes against humanity.[27] It also reported violations of the human rights of Palestinian protestors and detainees in Israeli prisons,[28] and of Israeli protesters demonstrating against the attacks in Gaza.[29] The report found that Palestinian armed groups had also committed war crimes by launching indiscriminate attacks against southern Israel from June 2008 to July 2009, which resulted in four fatalities (three of which were civilians) as well as physical and psychological injury and damage to civilian property. It also found that the Palestinian security forces had committed violations of international human rights law (IHRL) in the oPt.[30]

Among its numerous recommendations, the Goldstone report requested that the UNSC establish an independent Committee of Experts to monitor and report on domestic proceedings undertaken by the Israeli Government and the authorities in the Gaza Strip to investigate and prosecute serious violations of international humanitarian law (IHL) and IHRL throughout the duration of the conflict. In the absence of good-faith investigations, the UNSC was requested to consider referring the situation in Gaza to the ICC Prosecutor.[31] The issue of domestic proceedings is essential to determining admissibility before the ICC; a case is only admissible if the State concerned is itself unwilling or unable genuinely to carry out a prosecution.[32]

---

25   *See* H.R.C., *Report of the Human Rights Council on its Ninth Special Session*, U.N. Doc. A/HRC/S-9/2 (Jan. 9 & 12, 2009), at 5, para. 14.

26   H.R.C., *Report of the United Nations Fact-Finding Mission on the Gaza Conflict*, U.N. Doc. A/HRC/12/48 (Sep. 25, 2009), para. 1893. Although international pressure on the Palestinian UN delegation in Geneva initially delayed adoption of the report, the ensuing domestic (and international civil society) outcry led the Palestinian Authority, in coordination with their allies in the HRC, to call for a Special Session in October 2009, during which the report was endorsed.

27   *Id.*, paras. 1885- 1895, 1921–1934, 1935–36.

28   *Id.*, paras. 1938–43.

29   *Id.*, paras. 1762–74, 1903, 1948–49.

30   *Id.*, paras. 1648, 1652, 1653, 1659, 1688–1691, 1900–01, 1911, 1950–53, 1954–56.

31   *Id.*, paras. 1969.

32   Rome Statute of the International Criminal Court arts. 17(1)(a), 2187 U.N.T.S. 90 (July 17, 1998). A series of measures ensued over the next two years to implement the Goldstone report's recommendations. At the international level, the UNGA adopted resolution

ATROCITIES, ACCOUNTABILITY AND THE POLITICS

In the aftermath of the report, the Palestinian government began a series of unilateral steps to trigger the ICC's jurisdiction. In January 2009, the PA made a declaration under Article 12(3) of the ICC Statute, which provides that a "State may, by declaration lodged with the Registrar, accept the exercise of jurisdiction by the Court with respect to the crime in question".[33] The OTP initiated a preliminary examination of whether there was a reasonable basis to proceed with an investigation. This included considering whether the preconditions for the Court's exercise of its jurisdiction had been met.[34] The OTP made the exercise of the Court's jurisdiction contingent upon a finding that Palestine qualified as a State for the purposes of Article 12(3). In order to make such a

---

64/10, on 5 November 2009, which endorsed the Human Rights Council's report of its twelfth special session and called on Israel and the Palestinian authorities to undertake credible and independent inquiries into the alleged violations. The UNGA called on the parties once again to conduct impartial investigations in its resolution 64/254 in February 2010. Two months later, the HRC established a Committee of Independent Experts to monitor the progress of domestic proceedings in Israel and the OPTs, in compliance with the relevant UNGA resolutions. In its report, submitted to the HRC on 18 March 2011, the Committee concluded that although Israel has domestic mechanisms in place to investigate alleged war crimes, it had not opened any investigations related to Operation Cast Lead. It also noted a number of impediments to the independence and effectiveness of these mechanisms, concluding that Israel's failure to cooperate precluded a comprehensive assessment. The Committee was also unable to conclude that the *de facto* authorities in Gaza had carried out independent and credible investigations, while the PA had discharged its responsibility to impartially investigate allegations of serious violations in the West Bank. *See* G.A. Res. 64/10, *Follow-up to the report of the United Nations Fact-Finding Mission on the Gaza Conflict*, U.N. Doc. A/RES/64/10 (Nov. 5, 2009). G.A. Res. 64/254, *Second follow-up report of the United Nations Fact-Finding Mission on the Gaza Conflict*, U.N. Doc. A/RES/64/254 (Feb. 26, 2010), para. 3; U.N. H.R.C. Res. 13/9, *Follow-up to the report of the United Nations Independent International Fact-Finding Mission on the Gaza Conflict*, U.N. Doc. A/HRC/RES/13/9 (Apr. 14, 2010), para. 9; *Report of the Committee of independent experts in international humanitarian and human rights laws to monitor and assess any domestic, legal or other proceedings undertaken by both the Government of Israel and the Palestinian side, in the light of General Assembly resolution 64/254, including the independence, effectiveness, genuineness of these investigations and their conformity with international standards*, U.N. Doc. A/HRC/15/50 (Sep 23, 2010).

33 The text of the declaration is available at: http://www.icc-cpi.int/NR/rdonlyres/74EEE201-0FED-4481-95D4-C8071087102C/279777/20090122PalestinianDeclaration2.pdf.

34 *See* ICC-CPI, *Update on Situation in Palestine* (Apr. 3, 2012), paras. 2–3 [*hereinafter* ICC Palestine Update], http://www.icc-cpi.int/NR/rdonlyres/C6162BBF-FEB9-4FAF-AFA9-836106D2694A/284387/SituationinPalestine030412ENG.pdf; ICC-CPI, *Letter to the UN High Commissioner on Human Rights* (Jan. 12, 2010), http://www.icc-cpi.int/NR/rdonlyres/FF55CC8D-3E63-4D3F-B502-1DB2BC4D45FF/281439/LettertoUNHC1.pdf.

determination, the OTP convened a "roundtable discussion", and accepted numerous submissions by academics, experts, regional organizations and NGOs on whether Palestine's Article 12(3) declaration met statutory requirements.[35]

In April 2012, more than three years after the PA lodged its declaration, the OTP declined to initiate a preliminary investigation, stating that the preconditions for the exercise of jurisdiction were not met. It gave the following reasons: (1) the competence for determining whether an entity qualified as a "State" lay with the competent bodies of the UN or the ICC Assembly of State Parties; (2) although Palestine's application for admission to the UN had no direct link with Palestine's Article 12(3) declaration, the process "informs the current legal status of Palestine";[36] and (3) the status of Palestine in the UNGA was one of "observer" and not "non-member State".[37] The OTP therefore decided not to proceed with the investigation. Two years later, the UNSC's Committee on the Admission of New *Members* adopted a similarly formalistic conception of statehood to deny Palestine admission to the organization.[38]

III   Does Palestine Qualify as a State under International Law? Recent Developments in an Old Debate

The question of Palestinian statehood remains highly contested[39] and partly rests on the well-tried debate of whether recognition is constitutive or declara-

---

35   In favor, *see*: John Quigley, *The Palestine Declaration to the International Criminal Court, in* Is there a Court for Gaza? A test bench for International Justice 429–440 (Chantal Meloni & Gianni Tognoni eds., 2012) [*hereinafter* Quigley (2012)]; John Quigley, *The Palestine Declaration to the International Criminal Court: The Statehood Issue*, 35 Rutgers L. Rec. 257–263 (Spring 2009); Allain Pellet, *The Palestinian Declaration and the Jurisdiction of the International Criminal Court*, 8 J. Int'l Crim. Justice 981, 997 (2010). Against *see*: Daniel Benoliel and Ronen Perry, *Israel, Palestine, and the ICC*, 32 Mich. J. Int'l L. 73, 126 (2010) [*hereinafter* Benoliel and Perry].

36   ICC Palestine Update, para. 7.

37   *Id.*, paras. 5–7.

38   *Report of the Committee on the Admission of New Members*, U.N. Doc. S/2011/705 (Nov. 11, 2011), http://palestineun.org/report-of-the-committee-on-the-admission-of-new -members-s2011705/#more-523.

39   *See* James Crawford, *Creation of the State of Palestine: Too Much Too Soon?* 1 Eur. J. Int'l L. 307 (1990) [*hereinafter* Crawford (1990)]; Francis Boyle, Palestine, Palestinians and International Law (2003); Katherin W. Meighan, *Note, The Israel-PLO Declaration of Principles: Prelude to a Peace?* 34 Va. J. Int'l L. 435 (1994); Frederic L. Kirgis, *Admission of "Palestine" as a Member of a Specialized Agency and Withholding the Payment of Assessments in Response*, 84 Am. J. Int'l L. 218, 219 (1990); James L. Prince, Note, *The*

ATROCITIES, ACCOUNTABILITY AND THE POLITICS 51

tory. According to the declaratory theory of recognition, an entity is considered a State if it meets certain criteria. These, as set forth in Article 1 of the 1933 Montevideo Convention, are defined territory, permanent population, effective government, and capacity to enter into foreign relations.[40] The first two criteria are rarely controversial.

In Crawford's view, State practice and judicial precedents indicate that the four criteria of statehood should be read together to imply "independence" or effectiveness, which is the central criterion for statehood. Actual rather than formal independence is "perhaps the most difficult of all the criteria of statehood to assess correctly; in some cases it may well be impossible of objective ascertainment".[41] Crawford defines independence as: (1) the existence of an organized community on a particular territory, exclusively exercising governing power; and (2) the absence of exercise by another State of self-governing powers over that territory.[42] Substantial external control of the State is regarded as a fact precluding actual independence. In other words, formal independence is not achieved if the foreign power has a special claim of right to exercise governmental authority over the putative State, as in the case of Taiwan or if it maintains discretionary authority to intervene in the internal affairs of the putative State. There are exceptions to this, however, such as in the case of Monaco which was recognized as an independent State and admitted to the UN although France asserted "undefined powers of intervention".[43]

According to the constitutive theory, statehood derives from recognition, which is itself discretionary. In other words, an entity cannot be considered a State unless it is so recognized by other States, the determination of statehood thus constituting a political act. The act of recognition is therefore a precondition for acquiring international personality. Conversely, the declaratory

---

    International Legal Implications of the November 1988 Palestinian Declaration of Statehood, 25 Stanford J. Int'l L. 681 (1989); Anis Kassim, *The Palestinian Liberation Organization's Claim to Status: A Juridical Analysis Under International Law*, 9 Denver J. Int'l L. & Pol. 1, 18–25 (1980).

40   Montevideo Convention on the Rights and Duties of States, Dec. 26, 1933, 165 L.N.T.S. 19 [*hereinafter* Montevideo Convention].

41   Rosalyn Cohen, *Concept of Statehood in United Nations Practice*, 109 U. Penn. L. R. 1127, 1169 (1961) [*hereinafter* Cohen].

42   James Crawford, The Creation of States in International Law 62, 76 (2nd ed., 2006) [*hereinafter* Crawford (2006)]. To prove lack of real independence, one must show "foreign control overbearing the decision-making of the entity concerned on a wide range of matters and doing so systematically and on a regular basis". James Crawford, Brownlie's Principles of Public International Law 76 (8th ed., 2012) [*hereinafter* Brownlie].

43   Crawford (2006), 71–75.

theory posits statehood as a matter of law, not fact. Statehood is a legal status, independent of recognition and the criterion of whether a State exists is effectiveness. Recognition therefore does not determine personality under international law.[44]

Crawford rejects the constitutive theory, arguing that it is counter-logical and untenable in light of contrary State practice.[45] He argues that the implications of the constitutive theory are that a non-recognizing State would be entitled to deny the rights of statehood to any State it did not recognize by intervening in its affairs or ignoring its nationality.[46] Nonetheless, he acknowledges that recognition has an important legal and political function. In particular, it may act as evidence of an entity's status. Another critique of the constitutive theory is that it does not clarify the "degree" of recognition necessary to "constitute" a State. Is it enough that a majority of States recognize a particular entity as a State? Or must there be unanimity in the international community?[47]

Shaw agrees with the view that the declaratory approach better reflects State practice; however, he also suggests that actual practice leads to a middle ground between the two approaches.[48] He implies that the constitutive approach becomes relevant in those cases where the factual situation is unclear or when the criteria of statehood are not fully realized; in such a case, recognition by other States can be constitutive. For example, in the case of the European Community's and the United States' (US) premature recognition of Bosnia-Herzegovina in April 1992, international recognition compensated for lack of effectiveness.[49]

The question of whether recognition is similarly necessary to "constitute" Palestine because of lack of effectiveness admits no easy answer. The indeterminacy and inherent inconsistency of the doctrine of "effectiveness" lend credence to both sides of the argument.[50] The main proponents of Palestinian statehood, namely Boyle, Quigley, and Falk each approach the role of recogni-

---

44 *Id.*, 4–5; Martin Dixon, Textbook on International Law 133 (7th ed., 2013) [*hereinafter* Dixon]. *See also* Malcolm Shaw, International Law 445 (6th ed., 2008) [*hereinafter* Shaw (2008)].

45 Crawford (2006), 21, 24–25. In further support of the declaratory theory, *see* Conference on Yugoslavia, Arbitration Commission, Opinion No. 8, July 4, 1992, 92 I.L.R. 162, at 199, para. 2; Montevideo Convention art. 3. *See also* William T. Worster, *Law, Politics and the Conception of the State in Recognition Theory*, 27 Boston U. Int'l L. J. 115, 118–19 (2009) [*hereinafter* Worster].

46 Crawford (2006), 27.

47 Dixon, 134.

48 Crawford (2006), 447–448.

49 *Id.*, 448–51, 461–2.

50 Worster, 116–17.

ATROCITIES, ACCOUNTABILITY AND THE POLITICS

tion differently.[51] Boyle constructs a historical legal argument for Palestinian statehood, arguing that Palestine exists as a State because it has been widely recognized as one throughout various stages of its history.[52] He argues that under the League of Nations system, Palestine was a Class 'A' Mandate, and hence was accorded provisional recognition (in Class 'A' Mandates latent sovereignty was vested in the populations of the territories themselves).[53] Termination of the 'A' Mandates resulted in either "automatic" independence or transfer to the UN Trusteeship system. Since Palestine did not become a UN Trust Territory, the termination of the mandate must have led to independence.[54] In addition, Israel's acceptance of UNGA Resolution 181 (1947), which partitioned Palestine into a Jewish and an Arab State, effectively meant that it had recognized the Arab State or Palestine.

In response to Boyle, Crawford[55] has argued that State practice, with the exception of the case of Iraq, does not generally support the contention that class 'A' Mandates were granted automatic independence upon termination of the Mandate. He also argues that although the relevant Jewish organization accepted GA Resolution 181, the Arab League and the Arab High Committee for Palestine did not. The competent UN organs therefore did not insist on the resolution's implementation.[56] Instead, war erupted between the parties in 1948 leading to a completely different territorial configuration.

---

51   *See also* John Dugard, *International (In)justice and Palestine, in* Is there a Court for Gaza? A test bench for International Justice 581–594 (Chantal Meloni & Gianni Tognoni eds., 2012) [sovereign independence in the juridical sense]. Dugard argues that "the declared purpose of the ICC is 'to put an end to impunity', which means that a purposive interpretation of the ICC Statute would support acceptance of the Palestinian declaration, it would not be unreasonable for the ICC Prosecutor to accept the Palestinian declaration". *See also* Vera Gowlland-Debass, Note on *Legal Effects Palestine's Declaration Under Article 12(3), in* Is there a Court for Gaza? A test bench for International Justice 513–524 (Chantal Meloni & Gianni Tognoni eds., 2012) [*hereinafter* Gowlland-Debass].

52   Francis Boyle, *The Creation of the State of Palestine*, 1 Eur. J. Int'l L. 301, 302 (1990) [*hereinafter* Boyle (1990)].

53   *See also* Winston P. Nagan and Alitza M. Haddad, *Recognition of Palestinian Statehood: A Clarification of the Interests of the Concerned Parties*, 18 U.C. Davis J. Int'l L. & Pol. 343, 349–350, 373–74 (2012) [*hereinafter* Nagan and Haddad].

54   It has even been argued that the Permanent Court of International Justice (PCIJ) regarded Palestine as a State for the Mavrommatis Palestine Concessions Case; *see* Mavrommatis Palestine Concessions Case (Greece v. UK), 1924 P.C.I.J. Ser. A No. 2. John Quigley, The Statehood of Palestine: International Law and the Middle East Conflict 59–60 (2010) [*hereinafter* Quigley (2010)].

55   Crawford (1990), 307.

56   Note however that the PLO recognized UNGA resolution 181 in the 1988 Proclamation of Statehood, as well as later in the DOP. It also recognized UNSC Resolutions 242 and 338.

Alternatively, Quigley argues that Palestinian statehood has been effective ever since the Palestine National Council (PNC) declared independence in 1988.[57] In his view, this declaration, which was recognized by UNGA Resolution 43/177 (1988), was "definitive, determinative and irreversible". More than 83 States immediately recognized Palestine as an independent State, meaning that many States believed Palestine fulfilled the criterion of "capacity to enter into foreign relations".[58] Quigley also refers to the practice of according UN observer status to national liberation movements, including the PLO, as a precursor to the emergence of a State. He adds that Palestine was represented at the UNSC during discussions that directly affected it, a privilege exclusively reserved for States.[59] Finally, he argues that Israel itself had itself implicitly recognized Palestinian statehood through insisting in 1993 that the PLO recognize Israel – a sovereign act of foreign relations and the archetypal conduct reserved for States.[60]

Crawford, on the other hand, contends that Palestine could not have fulfilled the criterion of "effectiveness" at the time of the PNC's declaration of independence in 1988, since Israel continued to function as a government in Palestine. This seems to be confirmed by international treaty practice. For example, in 1989, Palestine attempted to accede to the 1949 *Geneva Conventions and Additional Protocols*. In its capacity as depository of the Conventions, however, the Swiss government was apprehensive due to the "uncertainty within the international community as to the existence or non-existence of a State of Palestine".[61]

According to Crawford, the establishment of the "Palestinian Interim Self-Governing Authority" (PA) did nothing to change that reality since the PA – as its name implies – is no more than an interim, local-government body with restricted powers. Israel carefully reserved for itself certain rights and privileges, including in the field of foreign relations and external security[62], depriv-

---

57 Palestine National Council, Declaration of Independence, Nov. 15, 1988, in *Letter dated 18 November 1988 from the Permanent Representative of Jordan to the United Nations addressed to the Secretary-General*, U.N. Doc. A/43/827, S/20278, 27 I.L.M. 1668 (1988).

58 *See* Boyle (1990), 303; John Quigley, *The Israel-PLO Interim Agreements: Are they Treaties?*, 30 Cornell Int'l L. J. 717, 724 (1997) [*hereinafter* Quigley (1997)].

59 Quigley (1997), 723.

60 *Id.*, 725.

61 Crawford (2006), 440; Quigley (2012), 432.

62 *See* DOP, Article VIII: "In order to guarantee public order and internal security for the Palestinians of the West Bank and the Gaza Strip, the Council will establish a strong police force, while Israel will continue to carry the responsibility for defending against external threats, as well as the responsibility for overall security of Israelis for the purpose

ing the PA of jurisdiction over essential issues that were to be settled in the permanent status negotiations, such as the status of Jerusalem, settlements, and military locations. The PLO there cannot be considered any more than a national liberation movement recognized as representing a non-State legal entity (Palestine), which explains its capacity to perform various acts, such as entering into treaties.[63]

Shaw supports this view, adding that by accepting the Oslo Accords, the PLO itself tacitly accepted that Palestine did not already exist as a sovereign State. Even if the PLO had indeed claimed statehood before the Oslo Accords, Shaw argues that their acceptance of the Oslo Accords effectively led to the relinquishment of any such claim.[64] This argument can be easily rebutted, however, since the Interim Accords contain the proviso that "neither Party shall be deemed, by virtue of having entered into this Agreement, to have renounced or waived any of its existing rights, claims or positions".[65]

Quigley, on the other hand, argues that since 1995, Palestine has fulfilled the Montevideo criteria, including the criterion of "effectiveness". In his view, even if Palestine did not meet the criteria for statehood in 1988, then the facts on the ground certainly changed since the conclusion of the 1995 Interim Agreement. According to this view, transfer of territorial control by Israel to the PA through the Interim Agreement is sufficient basis for the existence of a Palestinian state, as Palestine now satisfied the criterion of control of a population over a certain territory.[66] Similarly, Gowlland-Debass argues that the Oslo Accords represent no more "than the transfer of belligerent administrative powers and responsibilities from the occupying Israeli military administration to the Palestinian National Authority in preparation for full Israeli withdrawal from the [occupied Palestinian territory (oPt)]".[67]

In 2005–2006, two parallel developments resulted in huge implications for the Palestinian government's exercise of "effective control". First, Israel unilaterally evacuated its military forces and settlers from the Gaza Strip (while

---

of safeguarding their internal security and public order"; Agreement on the Gaza Strip and the Jericho Area, (Cairo, May 4, 1994), U.N. Doc. S/1994/727 (June 20, 1994), Art. V (1) (b): "This jurisdiction does not include foreign relations, internal security and public order of Settlements and the Military Installation Area and Israelis, and external security".

63 Crawford (2006), 437–38.

64 Malcolm Shaw, *The Article 12(3) Declaration of the Palestinian Authority*, 9 J. Int'l Crim. Justice 301, 307 (2011).

65 Israeli-Palestinian Interim Agreement on the West Bank and the Gaza Strip art. 31(6), Washington, D.C., Sep. 28, 1995.

66 Quigley (1997), 724.

67 Gowlland-Debass, 523.

remaining in control of Gaza's airspace, sea space and border entry points). Second, Palestine suffered from an internal political split after Hamas won the Palestinian legislative elections in January 2006. Although initially Hamas established a national unity government with Fatah, violence broke out between the two factions, resulting in Hamas' takeover of Gaza and the PA's appointment of a Fatah-led government in the West Bank.[68]

Two important legal questions emerged from this: namely, which entity is in "effective control" of the Gaza Strip (Israel, Hamas or the PA?); and, can Gaza and the West Bank still be considered one "State"? The answer to the first question is complicated by a dictum of the International Court of Justice (ICJ) in its *Wall* advisory opinion. The Court dismissed the argument that Israel's construction of the wall was consistent with its inherent right of self-defense under Article 51 of the UN Charter on the grounds that Israel exercised control in the oPt's from where the attacks originated and that "Israel [did] not claim that the attacks against it [were] imputable to a foreign state".[69] Although this does not necessarily mean that Palestine is not a State (Israel did not try to impute Hamas' attacks to Palestine or any other State), it is clear that the Court considered the oPt to be under the authority and control of Israel as an Occupying Power.[70] Admittedly, this decision preceded the Israeli "disengagement" from Gaza; however, those arguing that the Gaza Strip remains occupied refer to the extensive control still maintained by Israel over Gaza.[71]

Even if the PA was not in full control of the Palestinian territories, Quigley argues that the "control requirement has been relaxed in international practice when the putative State was seen to have a right to statehood and where there was no competing entity seeking statehood in the same territory".[72] This is based on the idea that statehood and sovereignty can exist in the "juridical sense", regardless of effectiveness, and that this exists as a matter of right in previous colonies and entities with a right to self-determination.[73] The influence of the perceived legitimacy of Palestine's cause on Palestine's right to statehood is confirmed by a number of UNGA resolutions, including the text of

---

68   *See* Michael Karayanni, Conflicts in a Conflict: A Conflict of Laws Case Study on Israel and the Palestinian Territories 50 (2014) [*hereinafter* Karayanni].

69   *Legal Consequences of the Construction of a Wall in the Occupied Palestinian Territory,* Advisory Opinion, 2004 I.C.J. Rep. 136, 194, para. 139 (July 9) [*hereinafter* ICJ Wall Advisory Opinion].

70   *Id.,* 167, para. 78.

71   Karayanni, 51.

72   Quigley (1997), 724.

73   Gerard Kreijen, State Failure, Sovereignty And Effectiveness: Legal Lessons from the Decolonization of Sub-Saharan Africa 148–149 (2004).

ATROCITIES, ACCOUNTABILITY AND THE POLITICS 57

UNGA Resolution 67/19 itself, which repeatedly refers to the Palestinian people's right to self-determination, freedom and sovereignty over their territory.[74]

Quigley further argues that, since Israel is only a belligerent occupant "there is no doubt" that Israeli occupation neither displaces nor transfers sovereignty.[75] He adds that since Israel cannot claim sovereignty over Palestine, Palestine is the only sovereign in Gaza and the West Bank even though it does not have complete control.[76] This is not affected by the fact that Israel continued to handle some aspects of Palestine's foreign relations, particularly since "the PLO did not cede all foreign relations to Israel"[77] but remained a party to several bilateral and multilateral treaties indicating its treatment as a State.[78] The view that Palestine could meet the test of independence without complete foreign relations autonomy is supported by State practice. For example, when the UK formally ended its "Protection" over Egypt, the 1922 Declaration of Independence maintained "Four Reserved Points", including the conduct of foreign relations.[79] However, Egypt was considered a sovereign State and had the capacity to participate in multilateral treaties, such as the 1929 Convention Relative to the Treatment of Prisoners of War.[80] Egypt was later admitted to the League of Nations in 1937 then became an original member of the UN in 1945, although it still had British troops stationed on its territory under the 1936 Anglo-Egyptian Treaty of Independence.[81] As indicated below, numerous States have been admitted to the UN although they did not strictly meet the juridical criteria of statehood.

---

74 G.A. Res. 67/19 preamble, arts. 1, 6, *Status of Palestine in the United Nations,* U.N. Doc. A/RES/67/19 (Nov. 29, 2012). The GA has consistently recognized the illegality of the Israeli occupation and Israeli settlement activities. *See* G.A. Res 49/149, U.N. Doc. A/RES/49/149 (Feb. 7, 1995); G.A. Res. 52/66, U.N. Doc. A/RES/52/66 (Dec. 10, 1997).

75 Cohen, 1152; Lord McNair and Arnold D. Watts, The Legal Effects of War 368 (1966); Hague Regulations annexed to the Hague Convention No IV – Laws and Customs of War on Land arts. 42–56, Oct. 18, 1907, 205 Cons. T.S. 277 [*hereinafter* Hague Regulations]. Consequently, treaties between the occupied State and third States survive the occupation.

76 Quigley (1997), 729.

77 *Id.*

78 *See also* John Quigley (2010); John Quigley, The Case for Palestine: An International Law Perspective (2005).

79 *See* Elena Vezzadini, *Nationalism by Telegrams: Political Writing and Anti-Colonial Resistance in Sudan, 1920–1924,* 46 Int'l J. African Hist. Stud. 27 (2013).

80 Convention relative to the Treatment of Prisoners of War, July 27, 1929, 118 L.N.T.S. 343.

81 Treaty of Alliance Between the United Kingdom of Great Britain and Northern Ireland and Egypt, Aug. 26, 1936, 173 L.N.T.S. 402. *See* Majd Khadduri, *The Anglo-Egyptian Controversy,* Proceedings of the American Academy of Political Science, 24 no. 24 (Jan. 1952), at 82, 88.

Finally, the issue of Hamas' control over the Gaza Strip has cast doubts over the Palestinian government's exercise of effective control. The question of the extent of territorial control required in order for a government to be considered "effective" has not been settled under international law.[82] In spite of Hamas' de facto authority over the Gaza Strip, the PA still claims that its legal authority extends to all the oPt.[83] Israeli withdrawal from Gaza is therefore a partial withdrawal from the single self-determination unit that constitutes Palestine. This has been confirmed by resolutions of the UN, such as UNSC Resolution 1860 (2009), which stipulated that "the Gaza Strip constitutes an integral part of the territory occupied in 1967 and will be a part of the Palestinian state". In 2011, negotiations on a national reconciliation between Fatah and Hamas, brokered by Egypt, led to the conclusion of an accord followed by the Hamas-Fatah Doha Agreement of 2012. In June 2014, the two factions finally formed a national unity government.

Even if this agreement were not in place, however, the claim that Hamas' position in Gaza undermines the PA's "effectiveness" confuses recognition of States and recognition of governments under international law.[84] It is not uncommon for a State to lack control over a particular part of its territory. This does not mean that its statehood can be denied. The PA is the internationally recognized government of Palestine; whether or not it is in complete control of the territory of Palestine. This is highly determinative of "effectiveness" since it is widely considered that "the existence of stable and effective government has inevitably become linked to some extent to the question of recognition of governments".[85]

IV   "Statehood", Recognition and UN Membership

The mainstream view in doctrine is that recognition is a bilateral act exercised by States. It is not a competence of any international organization, including the UN or any of its organs. According to this view, statehood and UN membership should not be conflated. UN membership does not guarantee universal recognition and is not binding on member States, which may still

---

82   Cohen, 1138.

83   *Id.*, 51.

84   *See* Michael Kearney, "Comment" on Eugene Kontorovich, *Guest Post: Effective Control and Accepting ICC Jurisdiction*, Opinio Juris (Aug. 4, 2015) http://opiniojuris.org/2014/08/04/guest-post-effective-control-accepting-icc-jurisdiction/.

85   Cohen, 1135.

ATROCITIES, ACCOUNTABILITY AND THE POLITICS   59

refuse to recognize any other member State.[86] In fact, several States have been recognized as such without being members of the UN. For example, Japan, Liechtenstein and San Marino were parties to the ICJ Statute before becoming members of the UN, while Nauru instituted proceedings in the ICJ against Australia under Article 93(2) of the Statute before becoming a UN member.[87] Similarly, Switzerland was almost universally recognized as being a State although it only became a UN member in 2002. The Holy See (Vatican City) is recognized as a State by 177 other States,[88] without ever being a member of the UN (however, it has been a non-member observer State since 1964).[89] Non-admission to the UN therefore does not negate the possibility that an entity is a State under international law. In other words, the legal effect of admission to the UN should not be overstated.

It has been suggested that UN admission (and possibly UNGA non-member observer State status) constitutes a form of "collective recognition". While UN membership is not necessary to establish an entity as a State, however, admission to the UN undeniably constitutes important evidence of statehood. One view takes this even further to assert that "when an entity joins the UN, this ends any doubt pertaining to its legal status – it definitely is a State", although the reverse is not necessarily true.[90] So although, in the examples mentioned above, Liechtenstein, San Marino, Nauru and Switzerland were States before joining the UN, it would be very difficult to argue that an entity that is already a UN member is not a State. For example, Israel remains unrecognized by a large number of States, although it has been a member of the UN since 1949.[91] Few would be able to argue that Israel is not a State, however, in spite of this lack of recognition. UN membership, at the very least implies that an entity is a State, since membership is exclusively open to States. The presumption that a UN member meets the criteria of statehood is a difficult one to rebut.

---

86   Shaw (2008), 466.

87   Crawford (2006), 191–192.

88   *See* The Permanent Mission of the Holy See to the United Nations, Our History, https://holyseemission.org/contents//statements/58ba0b742bc1b.php.

89   *See* G.A. Res. 58/314, *Participation of the Holy See in the work of the United Nations*, U.N. Doc. A/RES/58/314 (July 16, 2004).

90   Vidmar, 20.

91   Martin Wählisch, *Beyond a Seat in the United Nations*, 53 Harvard J. Int'l L. 226, 232, 241 (2012) [*hereinafter* Wählisch].

A   *The Law and Politics of UN Admission*

In regulating membership of the UN, the organization's political organs are required to interpret and apply the ill-defined juridical criteria of statehood. Article 4 of the UN Charter, which encapsulates the conditions and mechanism for admission to the UN, stipulates the following:

(1)   Membership in the United Nations is open to all other peace-loving *states* which accept the obligations contained in the present Charter and, in the judgment of the Organization, are able and willing to carry out these obligations.

(2)   The admission of any such *state* to membership in the United Nations will be effected by a decision of the General Assembly upon the recommendation of the Security Council (emphasis added).

Admission involves two distinct issues: the procedural mechanisms by which the application for admission is considered (paragraph 2) and the applicable legal criteria (paragraph 1).[92] The legal criteria for UN admission have always attracted a certain degree of controversy as they involve an element of political discretion.[93] In her review of State practice in 1962, Higgins stated that the traditional legal criteria of statehood are not always adhered to when admitting new States to the UN.[94] Both the procedural and legal aspects were subjects of separate advisory proceedings before the ICJ.

Because Article 4 of the UN Charter was drafted very broadly, it remained up to States and the relevant organs of the UN to develop its precise meaning through practice. The admission procedure is a competence shared by the UNSC and the UNGA. The UNSC first recommends the admission of a State,

then the UNGA makes a decision regarding admission. It is the practice within the UN that a State requesting membership submits a request to the UNSG who refers the request to the UNSC. The UNSC may then refer the request to the Committee on Admission of New Members, which must make a unanimous decision and return to the UNSC with a recommendation. The UNSC may then make a positive recommendation to the UNGA.[95] During the first

---

92   Thomas D. Grant, Admission to the United Nations: Charter Article 4 and the Rise of Universal Organization 12 (2009) [*hereinafter* Grant].

93   Crawford (2006), 180.

94   Rosalyn Higgins, the Development of International Law through the Political Organs of the United Nations 11–57, 54 (1963).

95   Yuen-Li Liang, *Conditions of Admission of a State to Membership in the United Nations*, 43 Am. J. Int'l L. 288–303 (1949) [*hereinafter* Yuen-Li Liang]. The Charter does not specify

ATROCITIES, ACCOUNTABILITY AND THE POLITICS 61

two decades of the UN's existence, a large number of States were denied admission through the casting of vetoes in the UNSC. Since then, membership in most cases has been automatic: of the 85 cases since 1963 only five faced objections.[96]

Since the organization's inception, the substantive (legal) criteria of article 4(1) have, proved controversial, particularly the question of statehood. This was subject to an ICJ Advisory Opinion in 1948.[97] According to the ICJ, article 4(1) could be interpreted to mean that an applicant should be admitted to the UN if it fulfilled five criteria. It had to "(1) be a State; (2) be peace-loving; (3) accept the obligations of the Charter; (4) be able to carry out these obligations; (5) be willing to do so".[98] The word "State" is not defined but is generally understood to reflect the definition of the term under general international law.

Practice within the Committee on Admission of New Members indicates a chief concern with the applicant's "effectiveness" as a State and its independence. This was the case with the admission of Mongolia, which was delayed for ten years under the pretext of lack of independence. The same objection arose in the case of Transjordan. UNSC members have used the criterion of "independence" to justify objecting to the admission of a number of States, including Kuwait, whose initial application was vetoed by the Soviet Union

---

whether UNSC recommendation occurs through an ordinary vote – which requires the affirmative vote of the five permanent members (article 27(3)) – or through a procedural vote (permanent members have no veto (Article 27(2)). This issue was settled by cross-reference to UN Charter Article 18(2), according to which the issue of membership was considered an 'important question' to be settled by a two-thirds majority of the UNGA. By analogy, admission would also be considered an "important question" in the UNSC, to be decided through an ordinary rather than a procedural vote. Practice in the UN has reaffirmed this interpretation. *See* Grant, 14.

96   *Id.*, 23.

97   Another Advisory Opinion of the International Court of Justice addressed the following questions that were left unanswered by the ambiguous text of Article 4: (1) must the UNGA follow the UNSC's recommendation, or can it admit a new State in spite of a negative recommendation? (2) is the UNGA authorized to take action where the veto has resulted in a deadlock in the Council? The Court rejected the view that a "recommendation" by the UNSC could include a negative recommendation. Article 4(2) therefore only envisaged a favorable recommendation by the UNSC. This ended any possible claim that the UNSC's determination was a mere "recommendation" with no binding legal effect. *See* Competence of the General Assembly regarding Admission of a State to the United Nations, Advisory Opinion, 1950 I.C.J. Rep. 4, 9 (Mar. 3).

98   Admission of a State to the United Nations (Article 4 of the Charter), Advisory Opinion, 1948 I.C.J. Rep. 57, 62 (May 28).

partly on grounds of lack of independence from the UK. It was later admitted without opposition.[99]

More recently, the admission of the European microstates and the Pacific small-island States indicates a move towards a standard of "formal" independence rather than actual effectiveness. "Formal" independence, such as when "the powers of government in a territory are vested in the separate authorities" of that territory, or when there is a formal grant of full power from the previous sovereign, may justify admitting a State to the UN.[100] According to this view, the delegation of government competence such as foreign affairs and defense to another State does not derogate from independence.

The international community has recognized various States and admitted them to the UN notwithstanding the absence of one or another of the criteria of statehood. For example, Vietnam was admitted to the UN in 1950, although it had not gained formal independence from France, neither did it have a stable and effective government. India was one of the original members of the UN in 1945, although it only formally gained independence from the UK two years later. The Democratic Republic of Congo (DRC) did not have effective government when it was admitted to the UN in 1960, and Belgian and foreign troops had not yet withdrawn from DRC territory. Similarly, Guinea-Bissau was recognized and admitted to the UN as soon as Portugal agreed to recognize it and withdraw its forces, but before Portuguese withdrawal actually took place.[101] Transjordan and Cyprus were both admitted to the UN although they had agreements with the UN allowing for the stationing of British troops and granting the UK extensive military rights in their territories. In none of these cases did lack of independence preclude the eventual admission of the applicant.[102] In fact one view argues that, since statehood is a matter of both fact and law, the definition of "State" should not be read narrowly when considering admission to the UN.[103] Because the criteria of UN membership are sufficiently malleable and indeterminate, the exception to actual effectiveness seems to be the rule. In fact, upon the admission of Israel to the UN, the USA made the following remarks:

---

99 Yuen-Li Liang, 294.

100 Crawford (2006), 67.

101 Quigley (1997), 725.

102 Cohen, 1144–45.

103 The USA made an argument to that effect to support Israel's admission to the UN in 1949. *See* Yuen-Li Lang, 300–301.

… neither at San Francisco nor subsequently had the United Nations considered that complete freedom to frame and manage one's own foreign policy was an essential requisite of United Nations membership … The term 'state,' as used and applied in Article 4 of the Charter of the United Nations, may not be wholly identical with the term 'state' as it is used and defined in classic textbooks of international law…. [and thus Israel exercised] complete independence of judgment and of will in forming and in executing its foreign policy.[104]

Ironically, 65 years later, an overly formalistic definition of statehood and effectiveness was used to obstruct Palestine's admission to the UN. The Committee on the Admission of New Members examined Palestine's membership application through five informal meetings between September and November 2011. In its final report, the Committee stated that it "was unable to make a unanimous recommendation to the Security Council".[105] In the UNSC, member-States were in sharp disagreement over the same issues.

In particular, views differed as to whether Palestine had "effective control" over its territory in view of both Hamas' *de facto* control over the Gaza Strip and Israel's control – in its capacity as Occupying Power – over most of the Palestinian territory. Some members of the Committee also stated that Hamas' position in the Gaza Strip meant that the PA could not be considered an effective government and questioned whether Palestine was indeed a "peace-loving" State, since Hamas had not renounced violence.[106]

In response, a number of other States maintained that occupation could not act as a bar to statehood and that Israel's continued presence in the West Bank is what has obstructed full exercise by the PA of its authorities. These states referred to the reports of the World Bank, the International Monetary Fund (IMF), and the Ad Hoc Liaison Committee for Coordination of the International Assistance to Palestinians, which all concluded that Palestine was ready for statehood. They also argued that in spite of the Oslo Accords' restrictions on the PA's competence in the area of foreign relations, over 130 States had already recognized Palestine and exchanged relations with it.[107]

---

104   *Id.*, 300.

105   *Report of the Committee on the Admission of New Members*, U.N. Doc. S/2011/705 (Nov. 11, 2011), para. 21, http://palestineun.org/report-of-the-committee-on-the-admission-of-new-members-s2011705/#more-523.

106   *Id.*, paras. 11, 12, 16.

107   *Id.*, paras. 11–15.

Because of these divisions within the Council, it has not yet decided on the issue of Palestinian membership.[108]

B "Statehood" without UN Membership: Circumventing the Security Council

Although the UNGA does not formally have the power to admit members to the UN without the UNSC's recommendation, it has competence (by virtue of institutional practice rather than any provision within the UN Charter) to grant observer status.[109] Most observers in the UNGA are international and regional organizations and other entities such as National Liberation Movements; however, a small number of States have enjoyed observer status, such as Austria, Bangladesh and the Holy See.[110]

In 1974, the UNGA invited the PLO to "participate in the sessions and the work of the General Assembly in the capacity of observer".[111] In 1988, after the PNC proclaimed Palestinian statehood in the West Bank and Gaza Strip, the UNGA voted to replace the designation "Palestine Liberation Organization" with "Palestine" in the UN system.[112] In January 1989, for the first time, the PLO itself directly submitted a request to the UNSC to participate in its debate. The UNSC extended the invitation in spite of the objection of the US.[113]

---

108 Wählisch, 226.

109 Daniel Costelloe, *The Status of Palestine at the General Assembly*, Cambridge J. of Int'l and Comp. L. (Blog) (Nov. 29, 2012) [*hereinafter* Costelloe], http://cilj.co.uk/2012/11/29/the-status-of-palestine-at-the-general-assembly-2/.

110 Vidmar, 6–8.

111 G.A. Res. 3237 (XXIX), *Observer status for the Palestine Liberation Organization*, U.N. Doc. A/RES/3237 (XXIX) (Nov. 22, 1974). In 1975, the UNSC made a similar request at the instigation of the delegate of Egypt. The Council conferred upon the PLO the "same rights of participation as are conferred when a Member State is invited to participate under rule 37". This practice was repeated several times from 1975 to 1988. *See* SCOR, Session, 1859th meeting, U.N. Doc. S/PV 1859 (1975). The PLO was invited neither under rule 39 (members of the secretariat, experts, representatives of international and regional organizations) nor rule 37 (States not members of the UNSC). But it enjoyed *the same rights of participation* as States under rule 37.

112 The UNGA also transferred its session to Geneva in order to host PLO Chairman Yasser Arafat (who had been refused a visa by the US). G.A. Res 43/177, *Question of Palestine*, U.N. Doc. A/RES/43/177 (Dec. 15, 1988). G.A. Res. 43/49, *Report of the Committee on Relations with the Host Country*, U.N. Doc. A/RES/43/49 (Dec. 2, 1988).

113 *See* SCOR, 44th Session, 2841st mtg., UN Doc S/PV 2841 (1989); Repertoire of the Practice of the Security Council, at 58, http://www.un.org/en/sc/repertoire/89-92/89-92_03.pdf. *See also* Quigley (1977), 722.

No attempt was made by the Palestinian leadership to apply for membership of the UN until 2011. Failing to achieve membership, Palestine launched a diplomatic campaign to change its status within the UN from "observer entity" to "non-member observer State". This was achieved through UNGA Resolution 67/19, which also reaffirms the Palestinian people's "right to self-determination and to their independent State of Palestine on the Palestinian territory occupied since 1967"[114] and expresses hope that the UNSC would consider favorably Palestine's application to full membership of the UN.[115] It also specifies the boundaries of the putative Palestinian State as the territories occupied since 1967. Although UNGA resolutions are generally non-binding, the UNGA can make binding decisions on issues within its areas of competence.[116] Because the GA has some measure of discretion in granting non-member observer State status, it would appear that resolution 67/19 falls squarely within the UNGA's competence.[117]

Notably, the UNGA's assessment of the facts on the ground in Palestine was decisively in favor of Palestinian statehood, unlike the UNSC's Committee on Admission of New Members. UNGA Resolution 67/19 (2012) commended "the Palestinian National Authority's 2009 plan for constructing the institutions of an independent Palestinian State within a two-year period". It also welcomed the positive assessment reached by the Ad Hoc Liaison Committee composed of the UN, World Bank and International Monetary Fund (IMF) to assess Palestine's readiness for statehood from an institutional perspective, which had determined in April 2011 that the PNA was above the threshold of a functioning State. The resolution also recalled in its preamble that Palestine is a full member of UNESCO, the Economic and Social Commission for Western Asia, the League of Arab States, the Non-Aligned Movement and the Organization of Islamic Conference and that it has been recognized by 132 States. It further reaffirmed the Palestinian people's right to "sovereignty over their territory" and "to independence in their State of Palestine on the Palestinian territory occupied since 1967".[118] The UNGA therefore acknowledged that Palestine

---

114   U.N. Doc. A/RES/67/19 (Nov. 29, 2012), para. 1.

115   *Id.*, para. 3.

116   Legal Consequences for States of the Continued Presence of South Africa in Namibia (South West Africa) notwithstanding Security Council Resolution 276 (1970), Advisory Opinion, 1971 I.C.J. Rep. 16, 50 (June 21); "it would not be correct to assume that because the General Assembly is in principle vested with recommendatory powers, it is debarred from adopting, in specific cases within the framework of its competence, resolutions which make determinations or have operative design".

117   Wählisch, 253–4.

118   U.N. Doc. A/RES/67/19 (Nov. 29, 2012), preamble & para. 1.

generally fulfilled the formal criteria of statehood under the 1933 Montevideo Convention.

Just as UN admission is not synonymous with "recognition", UNGA Resolution 67/19 does not "recognize" Palestine in the formal sense of the word. States that have voted against Resolution 67/19 or that refuse to recognize Palestine in their bilateral relations cannot be compelled to do so. The resolution may therefore be considered a form of "collective" or widespread recognition among those consenting States, to the same extent that UN membership is. Palestine has therefore been able to use the concept of an upgraded "non-member observer *State* status" to circumvent the selective formalism and "pedantic literalism"[119] of the UN Committee on Admission of New Members and the UNSC.

V Challenges to General Assembly Resolution 67/19: (In)Consistency with Security Council Resolutions?

Immediately following the adoption of UNGA resolution 67/19 (2012), the delegate of Israel implied that the resolution contradicted the undertakings of the Palestinian government throughout the peace process as well as resolutions of the UNSC. Canada's Foreign Minister similarly claimed that the resolution undermined the two-State solution and violated UNSC Resolutions 1515 (2003) and 1850 (2008).[120] He referred to UNGA Resolution 67/19 as an "utterly regrettable decision to abandon policy and principle," and threatened to consider "all available next steps" as a result.[121] Canada then proceeded to recall its Heads of Mission to the UN in New York and Geneva in protest against the vote.[122]

The argument that UNGA Resolution 67/19 violates resolutions 1515 (2003) and 1850 (2008) of the UNSC is untenable for three principal reasons. First, these two resolutions do not provide any binding solution or outcome to the final status negotiations. Resolution 1515 (2003), adopted under Chapter 7 of the UN Charter, endorsed the Road Map and its vision of a two-State solu-

---

119   Stephen Schwebel, Justice in International Law 573–574 (1994).

120   Canada, Global Affairs Canada, *Address by Minister Baird to United Nations General Assembly in Opposition to Palestinian Bid for Non-Member Observer State Status* (Nov. 29, 2012), http://www.international.gc.ca/media/aff/speeches-discours/2012/11/29a .aspx?view=d.

121   *Id.*

122   Campbell Clark, *Canada temporarily recalls Palestinian, UN envoys, but says it isn't breaking off relations*, The Globe and Mail (Nov 30, 2012), http://www.theglobeandmail .com/news/politics/canada-temporarily-recalls-palestinian-un-envoys-but-says-it-isnt -breaking-off-relations/article5832220/.

tion to the Palestinian-Israeli conflict. The resolution, which consists of three short operative paragraphs, makes no reference to the outcome of the final status arrangements other than "to achieve the vision of two States living side by side in peace and security".[123] UNSC Resolution 1850 (2009) similarly adopted under Chapter 7, calls on both parties to fulfil their obligations under the Road Map and refrain from any steps that would prejudice the outcome of the negotiations. It also declares it support for the parties agreed principles for bilateral negotiations and their efforts to "reach their goal of concluding a peace treaty resolving all outstanding issues".[124] The resolutions provide no time frame within which to reach a final settlement, nor any details pertaining to the terms of such a settlement.

This view is confirmed by the ICJ's decision in the accordance with international law of the unilateral declaration of independence in respect of Kosovo (hereinafter Kosovo Advisory Opinion). The ICJ was faced with a similar claim by Serbia that Kosovo's Interim Institutions of Self-Government had acted in violation of UNSC Resolution 1244 (1999) by issuing the unilateral declaration of independence.[125] The ICJ rejected this claim on the grounds that UNSC Resolution 1244 (1999) did not intend to prejudice the outcome of the negotiating process or to make conditions regarding the final status of Kosovo. This is although Resolution 1244 (1999) was adopted under Chapter 7 of the UN Charter, provided for an interim administration of Kosovo, and also explicitly reaffirmed Serbia's territorial integrity.[126] If this analysis is applied to the situation in Palestine, it cannot be claimed that a unilateral decision by the PA to achieve the status of a non-member observer State in the UNGA prior to reaching a Final Status Agreement constitutes a violation of relevant UNSC resolutions.

Secondly, the ICJ also held in the Kosovo Advisory Opinion that the legality of the declaration must be assessed in light of its broader context.[127] It referred to the failure, in 2007, of negotiations between the parties and to the UN Special Envoy's statement that after one year of direct talks, it seemed to him that the parties would be incapable of reaching an agreement on Kosovo's status.[128] It is against this backdrop that the declaration was adopted on 17 February 2008.

---

123   S.C. Res. 1515, U.N. Doc. S/RES/1515 (Nov. 19, 2003), para. 2.

124   S.C. Res. 1850, U.N. Doc. S/RES/1850 (Dec. 16, 2008), paras. 2–3.

125   Accordance with international law of the unilateral declaration of independence in respect of Kosovo, Advisory Opinion, 2010 I.C.J. Rep. 403 (July 22).

126   *Id.*, paras. 96–118.

127   *Id.*, para. 104.

128   *Id.*, para. 64–73.

Similarly, in the case of Palestine, the latter's bid to unilaterally pursue international recognition and accept the ICC's jurisdiction must be assessed within the context of the stalled peace process and Israel's prolonged military occupation. Ever since the beginning of the Israeli-Palestinian peace process with the conclusion of the Declaration of Principles and the Oslo I Accords,[129] the process has been fraught with major setbacks.[130]

More recently, and in response to repeated stalemates, in 2003 the Quartet[131] produced a Road Map to a Permanent Two-State Solution to the Israeli-Palestinian Conflict.[132] The Road Map foresaw the completion of the final status negotiations and the establishment of an independent Palestinian State by 2005. It was endorsed by the UNSC in Resolution 1515. However, throughout the negotiation process, Israel persisted in its policy of expanding settlement activity in violation of international law and relevant UN resolutions. This motivated the Palestinians to press forward with their agenda for a unilateral dec-

---

129 Although a detailed discussion of the peace process is outside the scope of this paper, a brief overview reveals the futility of the decades-long negotiations process. In 1993, Israel and the PLO concluded the Declaration of Principles (DOP), setting the stage for a series of other interim agreements (See Declaration of Principles on Interim Self-Government Arrangements (Oslo I), Sept. 13, 1993, Israel-PLO, 32 I.L.M. 1525 (1993), hereinafter the Oslo I Accords). The DOP provided for Israeli recognition of the PLO as the representative of the Palestinian people, and the PLO's recognition of Israel's right to exist. It also established the PA and provided for Israeli withdrawal from the Gaza Strip and parts of the West Bank over a five year period, as well as partial transfer of Israeli authority from the civil administration of Palestine. It expressly excluded the conduct of Palestine's foreign affairs from its ambit, while providing for the establishment of a "temporary international or foreign presence". The final status issues (borders, settlements, refugees and the status of Jerusalem) were postponed and were to be resolved through separate negotiations by 1999. In 1995, the two parties concluded the Interim Agreement on the West Bank and Gaza Strip, which provided for Israeli withdrawal from the major West Bank towns except for Hebron, where it would keep troops to protect settlers. In 1997, Israel agreed to withdraw from Hebron and in 1998 the Wye River Agreement was concluded, providing for more Israeli redeployments. These agreements gradually increased the scope of territorial and jurisdictional authority exercised by the PA. Both parties continually argued that the other was in violation of the agreements, with the result that the peace process remained stalled.

130 For an overview of the Oslo Process, see Peter Malanczuk, *Some Basic Aspects of the Agreements Between Israel and the PLO from the Perspective of International Law*, 7 Eur. J. Int'l L. 485 (1996) [*hereinafter* Malanczuk]; Quigley (1997), 720- 725; Shaw (2008), 246–7; Karayanni, 41. The full text of these agreements can be found in: 7 Palestine Y.B. Int'l L. (1992–94).

131 The US, Russia, EU and the UN.

132 Quigley (2011), 190.

ATROCITIES, ACCOUNTABILITY AND THE POLITICS

laration of independence, as the territory of the putative Palestinian State kept diminishing through new facts created by Israel on the ground.[133] A number of other developments further complicated the situation, leading to additional obstacles to the peace process. First, in 2002, Israel embarked on the construction of the so-called separation wall/barrier, which was the subject of an ICJ Advisory Opinion in 2004. This was largely perceived as a vindication of the Palestinian cause and the right to self-determination for the Palestinian people.[134] Notwithstanding this, Israel proposed in bilateral talks in 2012 that the boundary line between the two States follow the controversial wall and thus leave all of occupied Jerusalem inside of Israel.[135] Israel also demanded that the PLO recognize it as an ethnically Jewish state.[136]

Secondly, in 2005 Israel implemented its unilateral "disengagement plan", evacuating its military forces and settlers from the Gaza Strip, while maintaining control over Gaza's airspace, territorial waters, border crossings and some aspects of its civil administration.[137] Subsequently, in 2007, Hamas seized control in Gaza, leading to a rift between Hamas and the PA. Since then, Israel has maintained a blockade over the Gaza Strip compounding exponentially an already grave humanitarian crisis. In December 2008, Israel launched "Operation Cast Lead", in which 1,400 Palestinians were killed. This was followed in 2014 by a fifty-day military campaign against Gaza dubbed "Operation Protective Edge", which killed more than 2,140 people, more than 1,400 of whom were civilians.[138] In light of this, it is evident that the peace process and bilateral talks have not succeeded in achieving a final settlement. Bilateral talks – even

---

133   Particularly significant is the massive growth of Israeli settlements. In 1989, just after the Palestine's first declaration of independence, it was estimated that 190,800 Israeli settlers lived in the oPt. Twenty years later, this number had grown to half a million, covering almost 45% of the occupied West Bank. See PLO Negotiations Affairs Department, *The Historic Compromise: The Palestinian Declaration of Independence and the Twenty-Year Struggle for a Two-State Solution* (2008), available at: http://carim-south.eu/carim/public/polsoctexts/PS2PAL005_EN.pdf. *See also* Winston P. Nagan and Aitza M. Haddad, *Recognition of Palestinian Statehood: A Clarification of the Interests of the Concerned Parties*, 18 U.C. Davis J. Int'l L. & Pol'y 343, 349–350, 373–74 (2012) [*hereinafter* Nagan and Haddad].

134   *See, generally*, ICJ Wall Advisory Opinion.

135   Nagan and Haddad, 413.

136   *Id.*, 420.

137   Benoliel and Perry, 104.

138   UN Office for the Coordination of Humanitarian Affairs, *Occupied Palestinian Territory: Gaza Emergency Situation Report* (Sep. 4, 2014), http://www.ochaopt.org/documents/ocha_opt_sitrep_04_09_2014.pdf.

with the mediation of the Quartet and the US administration – have failed in achieving agreement on the final status of Palestine and are unlikely to succeed in the near future. This is supported by the conclusions of the 2012 Report of the UN Secretary General on the Peaceful Settlement of the Question of Palestine, which states that there had been little progress towards peaceful settlement throughout the previous year, and that confidence between the parties continued to erode in spite of efforts by the UN and the Quartet.[139] As with the case of Kosovo's declaration, therefore, it would seem unreasonable to expect Palestine not to unilaterally pursue international recognition when all attempts at a negotiated settlement indicate a clear dead end.

VI   Implications of Palestine's New Status

UNGA resolution 67/19 neither creates Palestine as a State nor recognizes the already existing State of Palestine (as recognition is a purely bilateral act). However, contrary to Vidmar's contention, by acknowledging Palestine's statehood the resolution could carry an implicit confirmation of this statehood, at least within the UN system.[140] By stating that Palestine fulfils the criteria of statehood (in the resolution's preamble) and designating it as a non-member "observer State", it has allowed Palestine to crystallize its status and therefore *act* as a State. Since 29 November 2012 Palestine has been able, for example, to accede to multilateral conventions open only to States, irrespective of recognition. Similarly, the ICC Prosecutor's statement that the ICC may only exercise its jurisdiction in Palestine as of 29 November 2012 indicates that Palestine's capacity to *act* as a State arises only after that date. Although Palestine arguably already possessed treaty-making capacity before 29 November 2012,[141] in practice it was unable to exercise this capacity in the multi-lateral sphere. As a result of the adoption of Resolution 67/19, Palestine may now participate in the development and creation of international law (through membership of

---

139   *Peaceful Settlement of the Question of Palestine, Report of the Secretary General*, U.N. Doc. A/67/364-S/2012/701 (Sep. 12, 2012).

140   Vidmar, 13.

141   *See* Dapo Akande, *Palestine as a UN Observer State: Does This make Palestine a State?* EJIL Talk! (Dec. 3, 2012), http://www.ejiltalk.org/palestine-as-a-unobserver-state-does -this-make-palestine-a-state/.

multilateral treaties) and bring claims at the international level (under both the ICJ and ICC statute).[142] It is therefore a full subject of international law.

Resolution 67/19, however, has no implications for the exercise of bilateral relations (which is exclusively governed by bilateral recognition). In this sphere, recognition remains, by and large, constitutive. For example, Palestine may not be able to conclude a bilateral treaty with the US or the UK (*exercise of relations*) although it has the *capacity* to do so.[143]

A *Institutional Implications*

The most obvious implications of Palestine's new status are its institutional implications within the UN system. Some of these institutional implications are reflected in the UN Charter itself.[144] According to Article 35(2), Palestine may now place items on the agenda of the UNSC and UNGA. Others can arguably be deduced through an analogy with the Holy See (Vatican City), the only other entity currently recognized as a non-Member observer State in the UN.[145]

The Holy See has had observer status at the UN since 1964. According to UNGA resolution 58/314 (2004) and its annex, the Vatican City (Holy See) may participate in UNGA discussions and in the UN specialized agencies, as well as the regional commissions. It contributes financially to the UN budget. It has the right of inscription on the speakers' list after the last member-State and before all other observers and the right to co-sponsor resolutions making reference to the Holy See. It has the right to intervene and to reply, and to have its communications circulated as official documents.[146] Some of these rights had already been enjoyed by Palestine before 2012 as a result of its "enhanced" observer status.[147]

---

142   A subject of international law is one that "has direct rights and responsibilities under the system, can bring international claims and can participate in the creation, development and enforcement of international law"; *see* Robert McCorquordale, *The Individual in the International Legal System, in* International Law 285 (Malcolm Evans ed., 3rd ed., 2010).

143   *See* Dixon, 136.

144   U.N. Office of Legal Affairs, *Issues related to General Assembly Resolution 67/19 on the status of Palestine in the United Nations* (Dec. 21, 2012), para. 10 [*hereinafter* UN Memo Palestine], http://palestineun.org/wp-content/uploads/2013/08/012-UN-Memo-regarding-67-19.pdf.

145   For a detailed discussion, *see* Crawford (2006), 221–233; Shaw, 243–44; Cedric Ryngaert, *The Legal Status of the Holy See*, 3 Goettingen J. Int'l L. 829 (2011).

146   G.A. Res. 58/314, *Participation of the Holy See in the work of the United Nations*, U.N. Doc. A/RES/58/314 (July 16, 2004); *Participation of the Holy See in the work of the United Nations: Note by the Security-General*, U.N. Doc. A/58/871.

147   UN Memo Palestine, para. 11.

On the other hand, the Holy See does not have the right to vote in the UN system, to put forward candidates in the UNGA, or to sponsor resolutions. In conferences convened under UN auspices for "all States" the Holy See has the same rights as any other participating state.[148] Although it has been argued that the Holy See's non-member observer State status is the product of very specific historical circumstances and therefore cannot form the basis of an analogy with Palestine,[149] it is quite clear that this is not the view adopted within the UN system. The UN Secretariat has indicated that Palestine's new status is in itself sufficient to confer upon Palestine all the rights enjoyed by States that are not members of the organization, whether in respect of participation in meetings, conferences[150] and multilateral treaties,[151] or in terms of referring to Palestine as a "State" or "country", to its authorities as the "government" and to the Chairman of the PA as the "President" or "Head of State".[152]

B   *Multilateral Treaty Participation*

Each multilateral treaty has its own specific provisions regulating which entities may become parties. As a State, it is clear that Palestine may now participate in treaties that are generally open to States as a manifestation of its exercise of statehood. For example, the Vatican is a party to several multilateral treaties (under the designation of either the Vatican City or the Holy See), including the 1949 Geneva Conventions (since 1951) and their Additional Protocols of 1977 (since 1985).[153]

The Summary of Practice of the Secretary General indicates how the Secretary-General deals with accession by States to multilateral treaties, including in cases where the status of the entity in question is unclear. The Summary of Practice distinguishes between three different cases. The first case is that of treaties that are open only to UN member States and States Parties to the ICJ Statute. The second case is that of treaties open to "all States" under

---

148   U.N. Doc. A/RES/58/314; U.N. Doc. A/58/871.

149   *See* Nimrod Karin, *Letter to the Editor from former Deputy Legal Adviser to Israel's Permanent Mission to the United Nations,* Just Security (Apr. 8, 2014), http://justsecurity .org/9165/letter-editor-deputy-legal-adviser-israels-permanent-mission-united-nations/. Karin argues that no analogy may be drawn between Palestine and the Holy See, which was recognized as a State before joining the UN as a observer non-member State.

150   UN Memo Palestine, paras. 17–18.

151   *Id.,* paras. 13–16.

152   *Id.,* paras. 3–7.

153   Fionnuala Ní Aoláin, *States, Almost States, Non-State Actors and the Geneva Conventions: Palestinian President Abbas's attempt to join the Club,* Just Security (Apr. 2, 2014), http:// justsecurity.org/8777/states-states-non-state-actors-geneva-conventions/.

the so-called "Vienna formula". This formula was devised to allow State-like entities to join multilateral treaties where they had been denied accession to the UN or to the ICJ Statute for political reasons, given that they had succeeded in joining a UN specialized agency (where there was no "veto").[154] For example, the Vienna Convention on the Law of Treaties (VCLT) was opened for signature "by all States Members of the United Nations or of any of the specialized agencies or of the International Atomic Energy Agency or Parties to the Statute of the International Court of Justice, and by any other State invited by the General Assembly of the United Nations to become a party to the Convention".[155] The Cook Islands therefore became a party to various multilateral conventions based on its membership in the World Health Organization (WHO), UNESCO, and the Food and Agricultural Organization (FAO).[156] Third, there are treaties open to "all States" or "any State" without further specification, such as the Convention on the Suppression and Punishment of the Crime of Apartheid (the Apartheid Convention). For the purposes of becoming parties to such treaties, it is not within the Secretary General's competence to determine whether an entity constitutes a State. According to the Secretary General, if he were to receive an instrument of accession from an entity with unclear status, he would defer to the UNGA.[157] This would take the form of a direct request for the UNGA's opinion or a determination based on prior practice if there are "unequivocal indications from the Assembly that it considers a particular entity to be a State".[158] As an example, the Summary of Practice mentions the cases of Guinea-Bissau and Vietnam. These were both invited, in 1973, to attend the Third UN Conference on the Law of the Sea as States. They were therefore considered from then on to fall under the "all States" formula although they were not yet members of the UN or any of its specialized

---

154 U.N. Office of Legal Affairs, Treaty Section, Summary of Practice of the Secretary-General as Depositary of Multilateral Treaties, U.N. Doc. ST/LEG/7/Rev.1 (1999), para. 79 [*hereinafter* UN Summary of Practice].

155 *Id.*, para. 81.

156 *Id.*, para. 85–86. There are very few cases in which the UN Secretary-General declined to accept the accession of a State-like entity to a multilateral convention. In 1969, Poland forwarded to the Secretary-General a communication from the German Democratic Republic, in which it expressed its desire to accede to the 1968 Convention on the Non-Applicability of Statutory Limitations to War Crimes and Crimes against Humanity (754 U.N.T.S. 73). No depositary action was taken, however, since the German Democratic Republic did not meet the requirements of the "Vienna formula" provided for in the Convention (*see Id.*, para. 88; U.N. Y.B. Int'l L. 1969, at 549).

157 UN Summary of practice, para. 81.

158 *Id.*, paras. 82–83.

agencies, or parties to the ICJ Statute (in fact, Guinea-Bissau remained under Portuguese occupation until 1974). Similarly, a number of newly independent States were included in the "all States" formula based on UNGA resolutions that welcomed their accession to independence, such as Brunei.[159]

As neither a member of the UN or a party to the ICJ Statute, Palestine could not become a party to treaties under the first category. However, its accession to membership of UNESCO has allowed it to accede to multilateral treaties within the second category, which use the "Vienna formula". Palestine therefore deposited with the Secretary General on 2 April 2014 instruments of ratification of fifteen international treaties, including the VCLT, the Vienna Conventions on Diplomatic and Consular Relations, the International Covenant on Civil and Political Rights (ICCPR), the International Covenant on Economic, Social and Cultural Rights (ICESCR), the Convention on the Elimination of All Forms of Discrimination against Women (CEDAW), the Convention on the Rights of Persons with Disabilities (CRPD), the International Convention on the Elimination of All Forms of Racial Discrimination (CERD), the Convention against Torture and Other Cruel, Inhuman and Degrading Treatment or Punishment, the Convention on the Rights of the Child (CRC) and its Optional Protocol on the Involvement of Children in Armed Conflict (CRC-OPAC).[160] The UN Secretary General accepted this immediately and Palestine has since become a full party to all these treaties.

Palestine can also accede to multilateral conventions using the "all States" or "any States" formula. UNGA Resolution 67/19 is conclusive evidence that Palestine constitutes a State for the purposes of UNGA practice. The Secretary General would therefore have to defer to the decision of the UNGA and allow Palestine to accede to any such conventions. Palestine therefore acceded to a number of additional treaties, including the Apartheid Convention, the four Geneva Conventions and their Additional Protocols[161] and The Hague Convention (IV) respecting the Laws and Customs of War.[162] In January 2015, Palestine acceded to four other multilateral conventions prohibiting certain

---

159   *Id.*, paras. 83–84.

160   ICRC, *Treaties and State Parties to Such Treaties: Palestine*, https://www.icrc.org/applic/ ihl/ihl.nsf/vwTreatiesByCountrySelected.xsp?xp_countrySelected=PS.

161   *Id.*

162   ICRC, *Treaties, State Parties and Commentaries, Convention (IV) respecting the Laws and Customs of War on Land and its annex: Regulations concerning the Laws and Customs of War on Land. The Hague, 18 October 1907*, https://www.icrc.org/applic/ihl/ihl.nsf/States .xsp?xp_viewStates=XPages_NORMStatesParties&xp_treatySelected=195.

ATROCITIES, ACCOUNTABILITY AND THE POLITICS

means and methods of warfare, which use the "all States" formula.[163] It also acceded in December 2012 to the three conventions on the protection of cultural property during armed conflict, deposited with the Director General of UNESCO.[164]

One argument holds that multilateral treaty accession simply acknowledges that an entity is a State only for the purposes of each particular treaty and not under general international law. It therefore cannot "imply" statehood. Otherwise, one would be faced with the bizarre outcome that States may be created or constituted by the UNESCO Governing Council (through admission to membership of this specialized agency) or through the UN Secretary-General, in his capacity as depository.[165] This argument, however, is untenable. The UN Secretary-General's determination does not create or constitute a State; it simply confirms the status of a pre-existing State, whose status was in doubt, therefore allowing it to exercise the attributes of statehood. This is not contingent on recognition by other States, since the State – under the declaratory theory – already exists as a matter of objective fact. In other words, treaty-making capacity does not "constitute" Palestine as a State (particularly since Palestine already had treaty-making powers), but its ability to participate in multilateral treaties that are only open to states confirms its statehood.[166]

---

163   Convention on Prohibitions or Restrictions on the Use of Certain Conventional Weapons Which May be Deemed to be Excessively Injurious or to Have Indiscriminate Effects (and Protocols), Oct. 10, 1980, 1342 U.N.T.S. 137; Protocol I (Non-Detectable Fragments); Protocol III (Incendiary Weapons); Convention on Cluster Munitions, May 30, 2008, 2688 U.N.T.S. 39.

164   Hague Convention for the Protection of Cultural Property, 1954, Hague Protocol for the Protection of Cultural Property, 1954, Second Hague Protocol for the Protection of Cultural Property, 1999.

165   Vidmar, 19.

166   At another level, Palestine has come under intense criticism from the US and Israel for acceding to multilateral conventions, including international human rights and humanitarian treaties. In fact, Israel retaliated by freezing $200 million in tax revenues and cutting electricity to parts of the West Bank, as a form of collective punishment as well as reneging on an agreed prisoner release. *See* International Federation for Human Rights, *Palestine Accedes to International Human Rights Conventions* (Apr. 10 2014), https:// www.fidh.org/International-Federation-for-Human-Rights/north-africa-middle-east/ israel-occupied-palestinian-territories/15112-palestine-accedes-to-international-human -rights-conventions. This is ironic as new States are typically encouraged to accede to multilateral conventions, particularly in the area of human rights. For example, practice in the European Community (now European Union) has made recognition conditional upon respect for international human rights obligations.; Photini Pazartzis, *Secession*

C *Standing before International Courts*

The statutes of international courts are essentially international treaties that contain specific provisions on accession like any other international treaty. However, the ICJ is a special case since its statute forms an integral part of the UN Charter (Article 92). The Court is therefore open to all members of the UN, which automatically become parties to the Statute (Charter Article 93(1)) by virtue of that membership. States that are not members of the UN may also access the Court in accordance with Article 93(2) of the Charter, which provides that "[a] state which is not a Member of the United Nations may become a party to the Statute of the International Court of Justice on conditions to be determined in each case by the General Assembly upon the recommendation of the Security Council".

Article 34(1) of the ICJ Statute provides that "[o]nly states may be parties in cases before the Court". In other words, entities that are not States do not have standing to appear in contentious proceedings. In the case of Switzerland, the UNGA and UNSC required Switzerland to undertake to accept all the Statute's provisions, including all obligations of UN member States such as compliance with the ICJ's decisions, and to contribute towards the ICJ's expenses.[167] Similar conditions were imposed on Japan, Liechtenstein, and San Marino which – as mentioned earlier – also became parties to the ICJ Statute before becoming UN member States.[168] Since the UNSC's positive recommendation is required, it is questionable whether Palestine would be able to accede to the ICJ Statute, notwithstanding UNGA Resolution 67/19.

However, it would still be possible for Palestine to access the ICJ without becoming a party to the Statute. Statute Article 35(2) stipulates that "the conditions under which the Court shall be open to other states shall, subject to the special provisions contained in treaties in force, be laid down by the Security Council ...". UNSC Resolution 9 (1946), which operationalizes Article 35(2), provides that the ICJ shall be open to a State not party to the Statute provided that it has previously deposited with the registrar "a declaration by which it accepts the jurisdiction of the Court, in accordance with the Charter of the United Nations ... and undertakes to comply in good faith with the decision of

---

    and International Law: The European Dimension, in Marcelo G. Kohen (Ed.), Secession: International Law Perspectives 365 (2006); European Community: Declaration on Yugoslavia and on the Guidelines on the Recognition of new States in Eastern Europe and the Soviet Union, International Legal Materials, Vol. 31, No. 6 (Nov. 1992),1485–1487.

167   G.A. Res. 91(I), *Conditions on which Switzerland may become a Party to the International Court of Justice* (Dec. 11, 1946). *See* Shaw (2008), 1072.

168   Grant, 260.

ATROCITIES, ACCOUNTABILITY AND THE POLITICS 77

the Court".[169] Such a declaration may be particular (in respect of a particular dispute) or general (in respect of all disputes or a particular class of disputes). The Federal Republic of Germany filed such a general declaration in 1961, on the basis of which it became a party to proceedings in the ICJ in the *North Sea Continental Shelf* case.[170] Albania and Italy filed particular declarations to access the court before they became UN members.[171] Even though this course of action is potentially available to Palestine, the ICJ would not be able to exercise jurisdiction in any dispute concerning Israel without the latter's consent. However, the Palestinian government has already announced plans to bring cases against other States that have accepted the ICJ's compulsory jurisdiction for various international law violations against Palestine.[172]

As for the ICC, Palestine acceded to the Rome Statute after submitting a second Article 12(3) declaration accepting the ICC's jurisdiction "over crimes committed within the Occupied Palestinian Territory, including East Jerusalem, since June 13 2014". As with other treaties using the "all States" formula, Article 125(3) of the Statute simply provides that "[t]his Statute shall be open to accession by all States". Similarly, a "State" may validly lodge an Article 12(3) declaration. The Rome Statute does not limit this to UN member States and is therefore subject to the UNGA's determination and the practice of the UNSG.

Some scholars have drawn attention to the fact that during the vote on UNGA Resolution 67/19, a number of States sought to obtain assurances from the PA that it would not seek to join either the ICC or the ICJ Statute. It is unclear whether such assurances were ultimately given.[173] However, it is now evident that even if they were, such assurances have no legal effect.

Unlike its first Article 12(3) declaration, Palestine's second declaration is not required to establish standing. Rather, it is necessary to establish retroactive jurisdiction over the events of June–July 2014 (since the Statute entered into force for Palestine on 2 April 2015). The ambiguous wording of Articles 11(2) and 12(3) of the Statute do not indicate clearly whether a State that is already a party to the Statute may make a declaration accepting retroactive jurisdiction.

---

169   S.C. Res. 9, U.N. Doc. S/RES/9 (1946). *See also* Grant, 261.

170   North Sea Continental Shelf (Fed. Rep. of Germ. v. Den., Fed. Rep. Germ. v. Neth.), 1968 I.C.J. Rep., Pleadings, Vol. 1, at 6, 8, 151.

171   Corfu Channel (U.K. v. Alb.), 1949 I.C.J. Rep. 4 (Apr. 9); Monetary Gold Removed from Rome in 1943 (It. v. Fr., U.K. and U.S.), 1954 I.C.J. Rep. 19 (June 15).

172   *Palestinians plan to sue Britain over 1917 Balfour act*, BBC News (July 27, 2016), http://www.bbc.com/news/world-middle-east-36893974.

173   *See* Costelloe.

On the other hand, the Court's Rules of Procedure arguably allow States party to make declarations under Article 12(3) establishing retroactive jurisdiction.[174]

The ICC Prosecutor has already initiated a preliminary investigation into the situation in Palestine. In her press release on the matter, the Prosecutor stated that:

> while the change in status did not retroactively validate the previously invalid 2009 declaration lodged without the necessary standing, Palestine would be able to accept the jurisdiction of the Court from 29 November 2012 onward, pursuant to articles 12 and 125 of the Rome Statute.[175]

This indicates that the ICC may exercise its jurisdiction retroactively, but only as of 29 November 2012 (the date of adoption of UNGA Resolution 67/19). For the purposes of the ICC Statute, Palestine is only considered a State as of that date. Does this mean that, for the purposes of ICC jurisdiction, UNGA Resolution 67/19 is, in effect, constitutive?

It is possible to explain the Prosecutor's practice without abandoning the declaratory theory of recognition. Under this theory, the question must surely arise as to when precisely Palestine first became a State and began to accrue international rights and responsibilities. Given the indeterminacy of the concept of "effectiveness", this question is not one that can be answered precisely. The need thus arises to designate an approximate date for the "beginning" of Palestinian statehood. The date of adoption of GA Resolution 67/19 is a reasonable candidate. Since it is the date that the majority of the international community collectively decided to officially call Palestine a "State" within the UN, for the first time.

---

174   ICC-CPI, Article 44(1), Rules of Procedure and Evidence, http://www.icc-cpi.int/en_menus/icc/legal%20texts%20and%20tools/official%20journal/Documents/RulesProcedureEvidenceEng.pdf. This is arguably confirmed by the decision of the Pre-Trial Chamber to exercise jurisdiction in the Kony case and by the travaux préparatoires of Article 12(3). *See* Alexander Wills, *The ICC's Retroactive Jurisdiction, Revisited*, Opinio Juris (Jan. 29, 2013), http://opiniojuris.org/2013/01/29/the-iccs-retroactive-jurisdiction-revisited/; ICC-CPI, *Warrant of Arrest For Joseph Kony Issued On 8 July 2005 as Amended on 27 September 2005*, ICC-02/04-01/05 (Oct. 13, 2005), http://www.icc-cpi.int/iccdocs/doc/doc97185.PDF.

175   ICC-CPI, *The Prosecutor of the International Criminal Court, Fatou Bensouda, opens a preliminary examination of the situation in Palestine* (Jan. 16, 2015), https://www.icc-cpi.int/Pages/item.aspx?name=pr1083.

D *Immunity from Jurisdiction and Standing before Domestic Courts*

Although the mainstream view is that recognition is not constitutive of statehood,[176] in some cases, recognition is "constitutive of the rights and duties associated with full statehood".[177] This is particularly evident in the domestic sphere. In some jurisdictions, the act of recognition itself is what creates legal effects in the domestic jurisdiction, such as endowing a State with sovereign immunity. Sovereign immunity – which involves both immunity from process and immunity from execution of domestic court judgments – therefore becomes a domestic consequence of international recognition.[178] State immunity only arises if the entity claiming immunity can be sued as a State.[179] Whether an entity enjoys immunity from the jurisdiction of the courts of another State will depend, first and foremost, on the domestic law of that State. Though conceptually distinct, questions of standing before foreign courts are closely related to questions of sovereign immunity.

In most common-law jurisdictions, the judiciary defers to the executive on matters of recognition,[180] while in most civil law jurisdictions courts may independently assess whether an entity is a State according to objective criteria. Recognition in common law jurisdictions may therefore be constitutive with respect to its internal consequences, since the act of recognition is what creates legal effects in the domestic jurisdiction.[181] In civil law jurisdictions, recognition is merely declaratory even with respect to its internal consequences, as an entity may enjoy standing and immunity as a state irrespective of recognition.

---

176 *See* Vidmar, 11.

177 J.A. Wade, *Executive and Judiciary in Foreign Affairs: Recognition of Foreign Lawmaking Entities, in* Essays on International and Comparative Law: In Honour of Judge Erades 238 (1993).

178 International crimes do not affect the operation of sovereign immunities, which are simply a bar to jurisdiction. Jurisdictional Immunities of the State (Germ. v. It., Greece Intervening), Judgment, 2012 I.C.J. Rep. 99, para. 93–97 (Feb. 3).

179 *See* Katherine Reece Thomas, *Non-Recognition, Personality and Capacity: The Palestine Liberation Organization and The Palestinian Authority in English Law*, 29 Anglo-Am. L. Rev. 228, 245 (2000) [*hereinafter* Thomas].

180 According to Benvenisti, "in common law countries the rule is that courts do not form their views on [matters of recognition of foreign states and governments]. Instead they must refer to the ministry of foreign affairs. A certificate issued by the latter shall be conclusive evidence to the truth of its contents". *See* Eyal Bienvenisti, *Judicial Misgivings Regarding the Application of International Law: An Analysis of Attitudes of National Courts*, 4 Eur. J. Int'l L. 159, 172 (1993 I).

181 Shaw, 471.

Paradoxically, where an entity's status is in question, recognition and non-recognition will have the same consequences. A non-recognized entity has no standing to sue or to be sued before the domestic courts of another State. In other words, if an entity cannot be sued because it does not constitute a State then the courts are unable to exercise jurisdiction (as the case is inadmissible). Effectively, the result would be the same were the entity in question to enjoy procedural immunity (which is a bar to jurisdiction).[182]

In most common-law States that do not recognize Palestine, theoretically, the latter cannot sue or be sued before the domestic courts. For example, in the UK, domestic courts consider that entities unrecognized by the British Foreign Office do not exist as States, and hence do not enjoy immunity from proceedings.[183] Neither can they be sued, as they have no standing. An "executive certificate" presented by the Foreign Office is regarded as conclusive evidence of whether or not a State is sovereign.[184] The same practice is followed in other common law jurisdictions, such as Singapore.[185]

Although this also applies in theory in the US, courts have frequently departed from this strict division of powers, giving rise to much controversy. One example is the 1991 *Klinghoffer* case, which arose after the killing of Leon Klinghoffer aboard the Achille Lauro in 1985. In this case, a US Appellate Court upheld a New York Court's decision, in which the latter arrogated to itself the authority to determine whether the PLO constituted a State and was therefore entitled to sovereign immunity. After examining the relevant facts, the court held that the PLO did not constitute a "State" as it did not fulfil the relevant criteria under US law (defined territory, fixed population, capacity to exercise

---

182 *See* Thomas 245.

183 State Immunity Act 1978, s. 6 (U.K.). *See* Shaw, 472–75. This is also known as the "one-voice" policy. While British courts have consistently deferred to the executive and declined to make any independent pronouncements on the status of an entity, these courts have also devised the legal fiction of "delegated authority", based on a wide interpretation of relevant executive certificates, to pronounce on the sovereign acts of unrecognized governments of unrecognized States. *See* Republic of Somalia v. Woodhouse Drake and Carey (Suisse), SA [1993] QB 54, 65–6 [U.K.]; Sierra Leone Telecommunications Co Ltd v Barclay's Bank plc, 114 ILR 466, 475–78 [U.K.]; Kuwait Airways v Iraqi Airways et al., HL [2002] (Nos 4 and 5) (CA) [U.K.], paras. 351–60. *See also* Thomas, 242–43, 251.

184 Section 21 of the UK State Immunity Act states that an executive certificate by the Secretary of State "shall be conclusive evidence on any question- (a) whether any country is a State for the purposes of Part 1 of this Act ..." *See* Carl Zeiss Stiftung v Rayner and Keeler Ltd (No. 2) [1967] 1 AC 853 House of Lords [U.K.].

185 Woo Anthony v Singapore Airlines Ltd and Other Actions [2003] SGHC 190, [2004] 3 LRC 342 [Sing.].

effective government, and capacity to enter into genuine relations with other States). It therefore was not entitled to sovereign immunity or to immunity under the US-UN Headquarters Agreement (as its mission was an "observer" mission). However, the Court found that the PLO had standing as an unincorporated association "doing business" in New York. It also stated that although the PLO had no standing to sue in US Courts, "there is no bar to suit when an unrecognized regime is brought into suit as a defendant".[186]

The *Klinghoffer* decision was widely criticized. In terms of substance, the Court's conclusions regarding the PLO's lack of defined territory, fixed population and capacity to enter into foreign relations have been described as a selective interpretation of the relevant facts. In addition, the Court ignored precedents establishing judicial deference to the executive on matters of recognition. By bypassing the executive and making a determination as to whether the PLO constituted a State, the Court of Appeals arguably ignored the principle of separation of powers and relied on subjective criteria to assess Palestinian statehood.[187] It then devised the legal fiction of considering the PLO an unincorporated association in order to find a way to attach legal personality to it. The courts again denied that Palestine met the criteria of statehood in subsequent cases, similarly relying on the argument that as the executive branch had not recognized the PLO/PA as a State, it was not entitled to sovereign immunity.[188]

In February–March 2015 two contradictory decisions were issued in US Federal Courts, with important implications for Palestine's standing in the US. In the first *Sokolow* decision (*Sokolow I*), a New York Federal Court found the PLO and PA liable for acts of terrorism that occurred during the second *Intifada* against US nationals, ordering the payment of $218.5 million in damages (tripled to $ 655.5 million under the 1992 *US Anti-Terrorism Act*).[189] The

---

186 Klinghoffer v. SNC Achille Lauro, United States (Court of Appeals) 96 ILR 74.

187 *See* Is there a Court for Gaza? A test bench for International Justice 429–440 (Chantal Meloni & Gianni Tognoni eds., 2012); Smith (1992), 185–87. Eric T. Smith, "State Recognition Under the Foreign Sovereign Immunity Act: Who Decides, the Judiciary or the Executive? Klinghoffer v. Palestine Liberation Organization, 937 F.2d 44 (2d Cir. 1991)" 6 *Temp. Int'l & Comp. L.J.* 169 (1992), 185–87.

188 Knox v. Palestine Liberation Organization, 306 F. Supp.2d 424 (SDNY 2004), at 443, 446 and Ungar v. Palestinian Authority 315 F. Supp.2d 164 (DRI 2004) [U.S].

189 Sokolow v. Palestine Liberation Organization et al, U.S. District Court, Southern District of New York (SDNY 2008), 9/30/2008, No. 04-00397 [U.S.].

decision was overturned on appeal on 31 August 2016, on the grounds of lack of jurisdiction (*Sokolow II*).[190]

Under the 1992 Act, US Federal Courts are granted jurisdiction over "acts of terrorism" and a right of action for US citizens injured by such acts. In *Sokolow I*, the Court rejected the defendants' motion for dismissal for lack of subject matter jurisdiction, based on a claim of sovereign immunity. The Court stated that

> ... in previous similar lawsuits, the PLO and PA raised, and the courts rejected, the same sovereign immunity arguments now asserted in this litigation. Defendants have failed to demonstrate any change of circumstances, be it legal or factual in nature, that would affect the applicability and/or preclusive effect of the prior holdings of those courts (emphasis added).[191]

The defendant was therefore estopped from raising sovereign immunity arguments. Notwithstanding this procedural bar, the court proceeded to refute the immunity claim on its substance. It stated that:

> While the PLO and PA argue their sovereignty, they do not claim individual statehood status. Their assertion of immunity derives from the claimed sovereignty of the State of Palestine. Defendants contend that they are essential agencies of Palestine, performing core governmental functions and, as such, are entitled to immunity. Palestine, whose statehood is not recognized by the United States, does not meet the definition of a "state," under United States and international law, and hence does not constitute a foreign state ...[192]

The Court based its jurisdiction on the grounds that the PLO's activities and continuous and systematic presence in the United States meant that it was "at home" in the US (a doctrine enunciated by the US Supreme Court to exclude jurisdiction over foreign corporations that are neither incorporated in the US nor have their principal place of business there). This entailed that the

---

190   *Sokolow v. Palestine Liberation Organization et al*, 2nd U.S. Circuit Court of Appeals, (2nd Cir 2016), 31/08/2016, No. 15-3135 [U.S.].

191   *Sokolow v. Palestine Liberation Organization et al.*, 583 F. Supp. 2d 451 at 458, (SDNY 2008), 9/30/2008 Memorandum Decision and Order [U.S.].

192   *Id.*

Court could exercise general personal jurisdiction.[193] Less than a month later, a Washington federal court found in the *Kleiman* case, that the PA was not "at home" in the US as its principal place of business was the West Bank and Gaza Strip.[194]

As in the *Klinghoffer* case, in both *Sokolow I* and *Kleiman*, the Court considered the PLO/PA as a foreign corporation, although in *Sokolow I* the Court acknowledged that by their own admission, the defendants did not consider themselves a foreign corporation. In addition to the "at home" test, *Sokolow I* relied on the principle of comity to establish jurisdiction since, the court held, there was no conflict with any other sovereign interest or foreign country legislation.[195]

The Court's confused logic is revealed in its discussion of the PLO/PA's responsibility for attacks carried out by Hamas, a non-State actor operating out of the oPt. It found the PLO/PA responsible, through what seems to rest on principles of attribution of conduct to States, implying that the New York Court effectively treated the PLO/PA as a State that (a) has effective control over the whole territory of Palestine; and (b) may be held responsible for the actions of non-State actors operating from within that territory.[196]

In its appeal against the *Sokolow I* decision, the appellant challenged the Court's jurisdiction, but not on the ground of sovereign immunity. In fact, the appellate brief accepted that the PLO/PA was a foreign, unincorporated association, arguing that it was not "at home" in the US, but in Palestine. It stated that "the United States does not recognize the PA as a sovereign government. JA-359 ("Palestine, whose statehood is not recognized by the United

---

193 "Petition for a writ of mandamus, in Re the Palestinian Authority and Palestine Liberation Organization in the United States Court of Appeals for the Second Circuit (3 Dec 2014); "Complaint", *Sokolow v. Palestine Liberation Organization et al.*, U.S. District Court, Southern District of New York, No. 04-00397, (filed 16 January 2014), para. 3 [U.S.].

194 Adam Klasfeld, *Palestinian Groups Skate DC Civil Terror Suit*, Courthouse News Service, http://www.courthousenews.com/palestinian-groups-skate-dc-civil-terror-suit/.

195 *See Second Circuit Ends "Doing Business" Test in New York for General Jurisdiction*, Holland & Knight, http://www.hklaw.com/publications/Second-Circuit-Ends-Doing-Business-Test -in-New-York-for-General-Jurisdiction-02-12-2015/?utm_source=Mondaq&utm _medium=syndication&utm_campaign=View-Original.

196 Solon Solomon, *The Palestinian Authority Jury Award: Implications on Liability of Non-States and Damages for Psychological Harm*, EJIL! Talk (Feb. 26, 2015), http://www.ejiltalk .org/the-palestinian-authority-jury-award-implications-on-liability-of-non-states-and -damages-for-psychological-harm/.

States, does not meet the definition of a "state")".[197] This is a curious admission, particularly given the changed circumstances created by UNGA resolution 67/19. It is only slightly mitigated by the appellant's implied distinction between the PLO/PA (the "non-sovereign government" or "governing authority" in Palestine) and the State of Palestine itself. Just as in the *Kleiman* decision, the Court of Appeals in *Sokolow II* found that jurisdiction could not be based on the "at home" test for lack of a sufficient connection to the US. It did not, however, consider the appellants' other arguments.[198]

In some jurisdictions (particularly civil law jurisdictions), courts are not legally required to defer to the executive on matters of State recognition (although courts often seek guidance from the government on such matters).[199] In *Democratic Republic of East Timor, Fretilin v. The Netherlands*,[200] the District Court of The Hague examined whether East Timor qualified as a State and therefore enjoyed *persona standi in judicio*. The case related to an export license granted by the Netherlands for the delivery to Indonesia of three corvettes, which were alleged by the plaintiffs to be intended for use in the war in East Timor. The Court was of the opinion that lack of recognition by the Netherlands and the majority of the international community was not decisive and that, "according to current legal opinion, this question must be decided independently by a court of law, irrespective of the question of recognition".[201] It then proceeded to decide the case "on the basis of the factual criteria for statehood laid down by international law."[202] The court decided against the appellant, on the basis that, at the time of proceedings, Indonesia was in effective control of East Timor, and the latter therefore did not fulfil the factual criteria for statehood. The court also declared that the Fretilin Liberation Front, which claimed to act as the authority in East Timor, lacked legal personality under Dutch law. The court therefore found the case inadmissible.[203]

---

197 Sokolow v. Palestine Liberation Organization et al, United States Court of Appeals for the Second Circuit, Case 15-3151, Document 119, 01/29/2016, p. 8 [U.S.].

198 Sokolow v. Palestine Liberation Organization et al, Justia U.S. 2nd Circuit Court of Appeals Opinion Summaries (1 September 2016) [U.S.], available at: http://us2ndcircuitcourtof appealsopinions.justia.com/2016/09/01/sokolow-v-palestine-liberation-org/.

199 Benvenisti (1993 I), 173.

200 Democratic Republic of East Timor, Fretilin, and Others v. The Netherlands, District Court of The Hague, [1980] 87 ILR 73.

201 *Id.*, 74.

202 *Id.*

203 *Id.*, 76.

In the case of *Parent v. Singapore Airlines Limited (SAL)*,[204] the Quebec Superior Court examined whether Taiwan constituted a State, notwithstanding Canada's non-recognition.[205] The Canadian Department of Foreign Affairs and International Trade refused to issue a certificate under the State Immunity Act, stating in a letter to SAL that "Canada has a one-China policy which recognises the People's Republic of China, with its government located in Beijing, and it has full diplomatic relations with that government. Canada does not have diplomatic relations with 'Taiwan' or the 'Republic of China'".[206] By interpreting the Sovereign Immunity Act widely, the Court found that in the absence of an executive certificate, it was up to the Court to determine whether immunity applied, based on the evidence adduced.[207] The Court proceeded to examine whether Taiwan had the attributes of statehood as defined in public international law, and held that it did (Taiwan had a defined territory, permanent population, effective government and could conduct relations with foreign States, since at the time Taiwan maintained diplomatic relations with 27 States).[208] As a consequence, Taiwan was also entitled to sovereign immunity.[209]

Allowing domestic courts to assess whether an entity qualifies as a State is in keeping with the declaratory theory of recognition. Although domestic courts carry out this assessment with reference to the "factual" or legal criteria of statehood, as the above cases indicate, courts may differ widely in this assessment and in their definition of "effectiveness". In many cases, domestic courts, even in civil law jurisdictions, will be influenced by the executive's position with respect to a certain entity. In States where courts defer to the executive in matters of recognition, recognition is only constitutive with respect to an unrecognized States' ability to exercise bilateral relations with that State and the internal consequences of statehood. It has no bearings on the unrecognized State's capacity to act as a State at the international level, such as through acceding to multilateral treaties open only to States or entering into relations with other States that recognize it.

---

204   Parent and Others v. Singapore Airlines Limited and the Civil Aeronautics Administration, Canada, Superior Court of Quebec (22 October 2003) [2003] 133 ILR 264.

205   The facts related to the crash of a passenger airline operated by Singapore Airlines Limited (SAL) in an airport in Taiwan, which was under the authority of the Civil Aeronautics Association (CAA). The SAL argued that the CAA was responsible for the accident. The CAA claimed on its part that, as part of the Government of Taiwan, it was entitled to immunity from jurisdiction.

206   *Id.*, 272, para. 25.

207   *Id.*, 277, paras. 39–43.

208   *Id.*, 271, 280–81, paras. 55–57.

209   *Id.*, 281, para. 58.

Upgrading Palestine's status in the UNGA has no effect in States that have already recognized Palestine as a State. In such cases, Palestine may have standing; however, sovereign immunity applies without controversy (as a matter of customary international law to the extent incorporated into the domestic laws of the States concerned).[210] The main controversy arises, however, with respect to states that have not recognized Palestine, such as the US, UK, Canada, Australia and most European Union member states. In common law jurisdictions where the judiciary defers to the executive on matters of recognition, Palestine's new status in the UN is unlikely to have any significant impact. This is not the case, however, in civil law jurisdictions such as the Netherlands and Quebec, where courts do not formally defer to the executive on matters of recognition. In such jurisdictions, it is conceivable that domestic courts could find that Palestine fulfills the factual criteria of statehood and therefore enjoys standing in domestic courts and also enjoys sovereign immunity. The recent decision by the UNGA to upgrade Palestine's status to a non-member observer State may prove to be of persuasive value in such cases.

E   *State Succession and the Validity of Treaties Concluded by the PLO and Palestinian Authority*

In the immediate aftermath of the Oslo Process, much academic literature addressed the legal nature of agreements concluded between Israel and the PLO, and their binding force in light of Palestine's disputed status.[211] Benvenisti argued that the Declaration of Principles should be considered a binding treaty concluded between two full-fledged subjects of international law.[212] Weiss, on the other hand, maintained that as an entity lacking the attributes of statehood in 1993, the PLO was not endowed with the authority to create binding international obligations through treaties.[213] According to his argument, the DOP is "nonbinding or, at most, an agreement to agree", and "imposes no substantive legal obligations on Israel".[214] The debate centers on whether non-State actors may be parties to binding international treaties. Indeed, Article 3 of the Vienna Convention on the Law of Treaties (VCLT) envisages this pos-

---

210   Palestine is not a party to the UN Convention on Jurisdictional Immunities of States and Their Property, G.A. Res. 59/38, annex, GAOR, Fifty-Ninth Session, Supplement No. 49 U.N. Doc. A/59/49 (Dec. 2, 2004).

211   *See* Malanczuk, 488–89; Quigley (1997).

212   Eyal Benvenisti, *The Israeli-Palestinian Declaration of Principles: A Framework for Future Settlement*, 4 Eur. J. Int'l L. 542, 545 (1993) [*hereainfter* Benvenisti (1993 II)].

213   Jeffrey Weiss, *Terminating the Israel-PLO Declaration of Principles: Is it Legal under International Law?* 18 Loy. L.A. Int'l & Comp. L.J. 109, 126–128 (1995).

214   *Id.*, 141.

sibility, while State practice also confirms that non-State actors may become parties to treaties.[215]

Assuming that the agreements entered into by Israel on the one hand, and the PLO and PA on the other, are binding international agreements, would they continue in force for the new State of Palestine? This question has arisen in the literature on the subject, mainly in the following terms: does Palestine succeed to the rights and obligations of the pre-statehood "Palestinian non-State entity", or as a "newly independent State", is it entitled to a "clean slate" according to which it may repudiate all prior treaty commitments?[216] The question thus framed, however, does not accurately present how the law of State succession, identity and continuity applies in the context of the case of Palestine. Can Palestine be considered a "newly independent State" at all if it was never an Israeli "colony" (its territory merely fell under Israeli belligerent occupation)? Considering Palestine a "newly independent State" presupposes that the predecessor (presumably Israel) concluded treaties on Palestine's behalf, or was responsible for its foreign relations, which is clearly not the case. It is therefore unclear whether the case of Palestine can be considered one of succession at all, or rather of the continuity of the international legal personality of the PLO and the PA. Another question is whether today's Palestine can be said to continue the legal personality of the Palestine that existed as an Ottoman Territory and then as a British mandate. Finally, how does the issue of recognition influence this legal analysis?

There is a fundamental difference between State continuity, where the State continues to exist in spite of changes in government, territory or population, and State succession (which occurs when there is a transformation in sovereignty). A State is said to continue if its legal personality remains intact. In the case of State succession, a question arises as to the fate of international treaties concluded by the predecessor State. This question is addressed by the law of State succession, which is both ambiguous and insufficiently developed.[217] Generally, the guiding principles are the "clean-slate" theory,[218] which advocates a rupture of treaty relations after a succession of States, and its

---

215 *See* Benvenisti (1993 II), 544–45; Valentin Jeutner, *Water Claims of an Independent Palestine in Practice, in* Palestine Membership in the United Nations: Legal and Practical Implications 308 (Mutaz Qafisheh ed., 2013).

216 Jeutner, 340–341.

217 Matthew Craven, The Decolonisation of International Law: State Succession and the Law of Treaties 11 (2007).

218 Advocates of these theory include: Lord McNair, The Law of Treaties (1986), 592; Erik Castrén, *On State Succession in Practice and Theory*, 24 Nordisk Tidsskrift Int'l Ret 55, 66–67 (1954).

opposite, the "universal succession" theory, which is based on the continuity of treaty relations.[219] Doctrine has remained sharply divided between these two theories. Under the 1978 Vienna Convention on State Succession in Respect of Treaties (VCSST) (which is not yet in force), the "clean slate" is applicable to all newly independent States (NISs) (or former colonial dependencies), whereas "universal succession" is applicable in cases of secession and dissolution. Categorizing instances of changes in sovereignty into either of these categories has proven controversial. Certain types of treaties are subject to a rule of *ipso jure* continuity, such as treaties establishing boundaries and other territorial regimes.[220]

Although the relationship between recognition and State identity and continuity is underexplored, recognition theory could have important implications for questions of State continuity and succession. First, recognition is an important, if not decisive, factor in State identity and extinction.[221] In other words, whether a State is considered a "new State" or a continuator to a predecessor state depends both on the claim of the State concerned and recognition by the international community.

Secondly, in a case such as that of Palestine, where the predecessor is most likely a non-State actor or semi-sovereign entity (the PA) rather than another State, it would seem recognition would have to be merely declaratory. Since the constitutive theory of recognition proposes that the State is "constituted" or created by the act of recognition, it implies a rupture of legal relations with

---

219   Daniel P. O'Connell, State Succession in Municipal and International Law, Vol. 1, 9 (1967) [*hereinafter* O'Connell (1967)]; Arthur B. Keith, Theory of State Succession 6, 17–26 (1907), 6, 17–26; Arrigo Cavaglieri, *Effets juridiques des changements de souverainete territoriales*, 15 Revue de Droit International et de legislation Compare 219–248, 224 (1934) [*hereinafter* Cavaglieri]; Andrew Clapham, Brierly's Law of Nations (6th ed., 1963), 151–154; Oppenheim's International Law 158 (Sir Robert Jennings, Sir Arthur Watts eds., 8th ed., 1955); Anthony Aust, Modern Treaty Law and Practice 372–73 (2nd ed., 2007).

220   *Official Records of the UN Conference on Succession of States to Treaties*, Vol. III, U.N. Doc. A/CONF.80/16/ Add.2, 34); Vienna Convention on Succession of States in Respect of Treaties arts. 11, 12, 1946 U.N.T.S. 3, Aug. 23, 1978 [*hereinafter* VCSST]; Gabčíkovo-Nagymaros (Hung. v. Slovakia), Judgment, 1997 I.C.J. Rep. 7 (Sep. 25), para 123; Henry Wheaton, Elements of International Law §29–30 (8th ed., 1866); John Westlake, International Law 66–67 (1904); William E. Hall, A Treatise on International Law 114–115 (1924); Charles C. Hyde, International Law, Chiefly as Interpreted and Applied by the United States 1538 (2nd ed., 1945); Oppenheim's International Law 159, 166 (Sir Robert Jennings, Sir Arthur Watts eds., 8th ed., 1955). *See also* Cavaglieri, 226.

221   Crawford (2006), 669–671; Kevin Bühler, *State Succession, Identity/Continuity and Membership in the UN, in* State Succession: Codification Tested Against the Facts 195 (Eisemann and Koskenniemi eds., 2000) [*hereinafter* Bühler].

the predecessor and a transformation of legal personality and of sovereignty. The declaratory theory of recognition, however, presupposes that the "new State" already existed prior to recognition, which is easier to reconcile with the notion of continuity of legal personality. Legal relations are thus preserved and the question of succession does not arise.[222]

Thirdly, continuity of legal personality can arise in the form of reversion, provided third State recognition exists. According to this doctrine, a State may "revert" to or restore its prior sovereignty, lost or suspended due to colonization or dismemberment. In this case, all rights and obligations of the restored sovereign, prior to the invasion, remain unaffected. Restored sovereignty in such cases operates retroactively when it is restored.[223] The most poignant example of reversion is the Baltic States' reversion to their pre-Soviet independence in 1990 under the claim their independence was "restored" after having been lost during the illegal Soviet invasion in 1940.[224] A critical factor in this case was "their self-perception as having emerged from an illegal regime of occupation to restore their pre-1940 independence".[225] The Baltic States therefore did not consider themselves successors to the USSR.

The doctrine of reversion is the antithesis of the doctrine of *debellatio*, which holds that sovereignty can be lost once the occupier imposed its "effective control" over the occupied territory. Reversion is based on the notion that the underlying illegality of the occupation can prevent "effective control" from displacing the presumption of the continuity of statehood.[226] This was the approach taken by legal scholars in relation to Poland, Czechoslovakia, Austria, Albania and Ethiopia after World War II and the previously mentioned case of the Baltic States after the collapse of the Soviet Union. The notion that "illegal effectiveness does not affect the sovereignty of States victims of an illegal occupation"[227] is an application of the maxim *ex injuria jus non oritur*. In these cases, treaties ratified by the illegal occupant do not continue in force for the occupied territory. States that had fallen under such occupation, therefore,

---

222   Crawford (2006), 667–668.

223   *Id.*, 698–99; Brownlie, Ch. 19.

224   Rein Müllerson, *The Arms Control Obligations of the Former Soveit Union,* 33 Va. J. Int'l L. 299, 310–12(1992–93). However, it is unclear that the doctrine of reversion could applied in the case of Palestine, which was arguably never fully sovereign, but went from being a Mandate to being an occupied territory.

225   *See* Yael Ronen, *Status of Settlers Implanted by Illegal Territorial Regimes,* 79 Brit. Y.B. Int'l L. 194 (2009).

226   Crawford (2006), 703.

227   Gowlland-Debass, 522.

chose to accede rather than succeed to international treaties extended by the occupant, a practice that underscored the inherent illegality of the occupation.

Because the concept of change in sovereignty is ambiguous, the 1978 Vienna Convention on the Succession of States in Respect of Treaties (VCSST) stipulates that a succession of States means the "replacement of *one state by another* in the *responsibility for the international relations of a territory*" (emphasis added). Article 16 VCSST establishes the right of a NIS to repudiate treaties concluded by its predecessors (defining a NIS as a "successor State the territory of which immediately before the date of the succession of States was a *dependent territory for the international relations of which the predecessor State was responsible*").[228] This provision was devised to address the question of the fate of treaties concluded in the case of typical colonies and dependent territories. Article 34 VCSST stipulates that States emerging out of separation of parts of the territory of a State (secession and dissolution) are subject to a rule of universal succession. Where there is no transformation in the sovereignty of the State, no question of succession arises and a continuity of legal relations is presumed.[229]

The VCSST presupposes that State succession only occurs when one State replaces another in the "responsibility for international relations" over a particular territory. Treaty succession therefore centers on whether treaties concluded by the predecessor State continue to bind the newly independent successor State. This leads to two important questions in the context of the present case. First, can succession occur between a non-State actor (or a semi-sovereign entity) and a State? Secondly, who was responsible for the international relations of pre-statehood Palestine, Israel or the PLO (followed by the PA), keeping in mind that as a belligerent occupant, Israel never exercised sovereignty over Palestine?

---

228 VCSST art. 2(f). In clarifying this definition, Waldock stated that the term "covers a State formed either through the secession of part of the metropolitan territory of an existing State or through the secession or emergence to independence of a colony; but it excludes a State formed by a union of States, by a federation of a State with an existing State, by the termination of the protection of a protected State or by the emergence of a trusteeship or mandated territory to independence." Humphrey Waldock, *Third Report on Succession in Respect of Treaties*, Y.B. Int'l L. Comm. (1970) vol. II, 27, para. 9. However, in his Fifth Report, Waldock's examination of State practice led him to the conclusion that the practice of different categories of dependent territories did not differ materially. See Waldock, *Fifth Report on Succession in Respect of Treaties*, Y.B. Int'l L. Comm. (1972) vol. II, 3–17.

229 Crawford (2006), 667–668.

As a belligerent occupant, Israel exercises its authority in the oPt through a military government[230] and only has some temporary, limited rights of administration. Contemporary international legal scholars are almost unanimous in considering that sovereignty is vested in the people under occupation, and not the Occupying Power.[231] Although the UN treaty monitoring bodies and the ICJ have found that Israel's obligations under international human rights treaties apply in the oPt, this stems from Israel's obligations as a belligerent occupant, within the territories under its jurisdiction and control. It in no way implies that Israel exercises sovereignty in the oPt.[232]

The notion of "responsibility for international relations" of a territory is no less ambiguous than the notion of "change in sovereignty". According to Article IX of the *Interim Agreement*, the Palestinian Council (*viz.* the PA) had no authority in the sphere of foreign relations (with some exceptions such as foreign trade, economic assistance and educational, scientific and cultural relations). This was intended to ensure that the PA would not have the full attributes of sovereignty. In spite of this, in practice Palestine (and before it the PA and PLO) conducts its own foreign relations, including its foreign relations with Israel, with which it has a number of bilateral treaties.

Palestine could also conceivably claim that it has "reverted" to its prior legal personality, under the British Mandate or as an Ottoman territory. This possibility is foreseen by UNGA Resolution 181, which provided in Part I(C) that the projected Arab and Jewish States were to make Declarations to the UN as a prerequisite for their independence. The proposed Declarations stipulated in Chapter 3(1) that:

> The [Jewish and Arab] State[s] shall be bound by all the international agreements and conventions, both general and special to which Palestine has become a party. Subject to any right of denunciation provided for therein, such agreements and conventions shall be respected by the State throughout the period for which they were concluded.

---

230   Joel Singer, *Aspects of Foreign Relations under the Israeli-Palestinian Agreements on Interim Self-Government Arrangements for the West Bank and Gaza*, 28 Isr. L. Rev. 268, 274 (1994).

231   Orna Ben-Naftali, Aeyal Gross and Keren Michaeli, *Illegal Occupation: Framing the Occupied Palestinian Territory*, 23 Berkley J. Int'l L. 551, 554 (2005).

232   Although Israel contests the applicability of its human rights obligations within the oPt, it has extended a number of multilateral treaties to occupied East Jerusalem. *See* Theodor Meron, *Applicability of Multilateral Conventions to Occupied Territory*, 72 Am. J. Int'l L. 542 (1978).

The Declaration also provided for both the Arab and Jewish States' succession to the debts and assets of Mandate Palestine. This followed from the provisions of the Palestine Mandate, which had considered Mandate Palestine the successor to the Ottoman Empire in the territory of Palestine.[233]

Reversion to a State of Palestine that existed under the Ottoman Empire, the British Mandate over Palestine, or the Arab State created under UNGA Resolution 181 (leaving aside the question of whether this State ever came into being) is complicated by the question of whether Palestine ever enjoyed sovereignty under these regimes and therefore whether reversion to a non-sovereign entity is possible. Equally problematic is the assertion that Palestine's sovereignty was never displaced by Israeli occupation, but only held in abeyance. Finally, the limits of the territorial claims of a Palestine based on some historic configuration of that State are unclear.

Palestine's practice so far indicates that despite rooting its historical legal claims in UNGA Resolution 181, the State of Palestine regards itself as continuing the legal personality of the PLO/PA. It maintains the same seat in the UN in New York albeit under a different name, and has maintained its seat in regional organizations such as the Arab League. Issues of State continuity are subjective and depend to a large extent on the State's claim and recognition by other States. If Palestine were to consider itself a new State, then it is possible that it would seek to apply the "clean slate" principle to repudiate its prior treaty obligations. However, doctrine recognises that where a dependent territory had some measure of international legal personality, the presumption of continuity of treaty relations is stronger.

Prior to the conclusion of the VCSST, doctrine supported the proposition that dependent territories that had already achieved a degree of international legal personality before independence would be presumed to continue their prior legal personality (and hence could not be regarded as "new" States).[234] O'Connell, for example, espoused a rule of universal succession "in the case of independence of territories that possessed international personality or were semi-sovereign States".[235] Colonies and dependent territories that had, in the process of gaining independence, been recognized as possessing some treaty-making powers were therefore subject to a rule of universal

---

233 Quigley (2010), 59–60, 93.

234 Buhler, 195–96.

235 Daniel P. O'Connell, *Independence and Succession to Treaties*, 38 Brit. Y.B. Int'l L. 84, 141, 165 (1962) [*hereinafter* O'Connell (1962)].

succession.[236] This position was also reflected in the International Law Association's work on State succession, which concluded that most dependent territories attained independence within a constitutional framework, and thus the "maximum possible degree of legal continuity was achieved".[237] Although the International Law Commission in its codification of the law of State succession did not differentiate between so-called "semi-sovereign" entities and colonial dependencies (all were subject to the "clean-slate" principle),[238] this has been criticized.[239]

There are very few precedents of treaty succession where the predecessor was not a State, but a non-State entity. One example is the case of East Timor, whose immediate predecessor was the UN Transitional Arrangement in East Timor (UNTAET). UNTAET concluded the *Timor Gap Treaty* with Australia on behalf of East Timor,[240] which the Government of East Timor accepted upon independence.[241] Although this may indicate that the practice here was one of treaty succession, it may equally indicate that the treaty only continued in force after confirmation by the new sovereign. Although State practice in this area is inconclusive, the presumption of Palestine's universal succession to the treaties of the PLO/PA would seem to be stronger. In fact, Palestinian President Mahmoud Abbas already implicitly accepted this in September 2015, when he stated the following:

> we declare that as long as Israel refuses to commit to the agreements signed with *us* which render *us* an authority without real powers, as long as Israel refuses to cease settlement activity and to release the fourth group of Palestinian prisoners in accordance with *our* agreements, Israel leaves us no choice but to insist that we will not remain the only ones

---

236 JES Fawcett, The British Commonwealth in International Law 144 (1963); D. J. Harris, *Cases and Materials on International Law*, 640 (7th ed., 2010).

237 International Law Association, *The Effect of Independence on Treaties, A Handbook* xiii (1965) [*hereinafter* ILA Handbook].

238 Francis Vallat, *First Report on Succession in Respect of Treaties*, Y.B. Int'l L. Comm. (1974) Vol II, part 1, 70, para 401.

239 *See* O'Connell, (1962), 86, 103, 178–179; O'Connell (1967), 88; Daniel P. O'Connell, *Independence and Problems of State Succession, in* The New Nations in International Law and Diplomacy 7, 21, 25 (William O'Brien ed., 1965) [*hereinafter* O'Connell (1965)]; ILA Handbook, xiii

240 *See* Gillian Triggs, *Legal and Commercial Risks from Investment in the Timor Gap*, 1 Melbourne J. Int'l L. 1, 9–10 (2000).

241 Timor Sea Treaty Between the Government of East Timor and the Government of Australia 2002, 2003 Austl. T.S. 13.

committed to the implementation of these agreements while Israel continuously violates them. We therefore declare that we cannot continue to be bound by these agreements and that Israel must assume fully all of its responsibilities as an Occupying Power because the *status quo* cannot continue. The decisions of the Palestine Central Council last March are specific and binding.[242]

Although this does not amount to a clear repudiation of the *Oslo Accords* as widely reported,[243] it implies that Palestine is building a case against Israel based on the latter's material breach of mutually binding agreements. At no point did Palestine purport to repudiate the Oslo Accords on the grounds of the "clean slate" doctrine under the law of State succession. In fact, the President of Palestine referred to the agreements as "agreements signed by us", which indicates the substitution of the PLO for the State of Palestine as a party to these treaties.

VII   Conclusion

Palestine's recent bid to gain international recognition as a State originated in its desire to end impunity for violations of IHL on its territory by acceding to the Rome Statute of the ICC. The process of achieving membership of UNESCO, and then non-member observer State status in the UNGA has had important implications for Palestine's capacity to act in the international sphere, and to a lesser extent, in the domestic sphere.

Although Palestine arguably existed as a State prior to the adoption of UNGA Resolution 67/19, it is this resolution that allowed Palestine to join multilateral treaties reserved only for States. As a result, Palestine may now participate in the development and creation of international law and bring claims at the international level. As of November 2012, Palestine has had standing before international courts, such as the ICC. In other words, it is a full subject of international law with the full attributes of statehood.

---

242   *See* Statement by H.E. Mr. Mahmoud Abbas, President of the State of Palestine at the General Debate of the United Nations General Assembly at its 70th Session (Sept. 30, 2015), https://gadebate.un.org/sites/default/files/gastatements/70/70_PS_en.pdf.

243   See excerpt of Abbas' speech, translated into English: Louis Charbonneau and Hugh Bronstein, *Israel Undermines U.S. Peace Effort, Palestinian Abbas Tells U.N*, Reuters (Sep. 30, 2015), http://www.reuters.com/article/us-un-assembly-palestinians-idUSKCN0 RU2D420150930.

Resolution 67/19 does not create or constitute the State of Palestine; however, it does acknowledge, confirm and therefore crystallize Palestine's right to *act* as a State, allowing it to exercise the attributes of statehood. It serves a pragmatic purpose by allowing the international community (and precisely UN bodies and treaty depositories) to take 29 November 2012 as the date after which Palestine could be considered a State. By acknowledging the pre-existing reality that Palestine has fulfilled the conditions of statehood, the resolution helped crystallize Palestine's already-existing statehood. In other words, the resolution gave it the capacity to act under international law.

While Palestine's new status has no formal consequences in the field of bilateral relations and the domestic jurisdictions of States (which are governed by bilateral recognition), this status may affect Palestine's *persona standi in judicio* in jurisdictions that do not require courts to defer to the executive on matters of recognition (such as various civil law jurisdictions). Similarly, if domestic courts consider that UNGA Resolution 67/19 has persuasive value, it may affect Palestine's sovereign immunities.

Adhering to the declaratory theory of recognition also implies that Palestine's legal personality (before 29 November 2012) has remained intact. Although the way in which the law of State succession applies to the case of Palestine remains unclear, Palestine's practice so far indicates that it considers itself the continuator to the PLO and the PA, and that it will not seek to repudiate treaties concluded by either on the grounds of a purported "clean slate". Palestine could also conceivably make the claim that it continues the legal personality of Ottoman Palestine or the Palestine Mandate, although this would likely rest on political rather than legal considerations and would serve to underscore the illegality of Israel's presence in the OPT over the past five decades.

Prosecuting Israeli Perpetrators of International Crimes under Universal Jurisdiction Laws: Prospects for Success?

*Salma Karmi-Ayyoub**

I   Introduction   98
II The Principle and Practice of Universal Jurisdiction   101
   A   *Definition of (Criminal) Universal Jurisdiction*   101
   B   *Scope and Application of UJ at the National Level*   102
   C   *Israeli and Western Opposition to Universal Jurisdiction Cases against Israeli Officials*   104
III Obstacles to Universal Jurisdiction Cases against Israeli Officials   107
   A   *Technical Obstacles to Universal Jurisdiction Cases*   108
      1   Subsidiarity   108
         i   History of the Al Daraj Case   108
         ii The Spanish Proceedings   109
         iii Conclusions on the Al-Daraj Case   111
      2   Presence of the Suspect within the Jurisdiction   111
   B   *Political Obstacles to Universal Jurisdiction Cases*   114
      1   Changes in Legislation in Response to Israeli Lobbying   114
         i   Spain   115
         ii The United Kingdom   115
         iii Belgium   117

---

* Salma Karmi-Ayyoub is a criminal barrister and external consultant for Palestinian human rights organization Al-Haq. She holds a post-graduate degree in law and was called to the Bar of England and Wales in 2007, after which she practiced criminal law at Tooks Chambers, where she was awarded tenancy. From 2009 until 2012, she headed an international litigation project at Al-Haq and worked on cases in various jurisdictions concerning persons and companies involved in human rights abuses. Ms. Karmi-Ayyoub continues to work with human rights organizations and solicitors' firms on legal projects concerning Palestine and has a particular interest in the question of Palestine and the International Criminal Court.

PROSPECTS FOR SUCCESS? 97

2 Political Interference in Cases 118
  i Decisions of Attorneys-general: The United Kingdom &
    New Zealand 118
  ii Immunity from Prosecution 119
  iii Political Interference in Judicial Processes 121
3 Israeli Non-cooperation with Investigations 123
IV Ways Forward 125
  A *Reasons to Continue Pursuing UJ* 125
  B *Recommendations for Future Cases* 129
    i Focusing on Lower-level Perpetrators 130
    ii Cases in Which Perpetrators or Victims have Strong
      Links to Foreign Jurisdictions 131
    iii Advocacy Initiatives that Strengthen UJ 133
V Conclusion 134

Abstract

This article will review criminal cases brought under universal jurisdiction (hereinafter "UJ") laws against Israeli officials[1] accused of committing human rights violations against Palestinians. It will describe the challenges to bringing such cases and suggest that political opposition is the main reason there has yet to be such a prosecution. It will propose that UJ remains a viable option for pursuing accountability for Palestinian human rights violations but will suggest ways in which the chance of success for future cases can be improved arguing, in particular, that cases more likely to succeed are those which focus on lower-level perpetrators, in which perpetrators or victims are nationals of forum jurisdictions and that are better integrated into broader advocacy strategies.

---

1 This article is limited to an analysis of criminal UJ cases and therefore does not include civil cases that have been brought under laws providing for the exercise of universal or extra-territorial civil jurisdiction, such as in the US under the Alien Tort Statute and the Torture Victim Protection Act. For more information about such cases, see the Centre for Constitutional Rights which has brought civil cases on behalf of Palestinians under these laws: http://ccrjustice.org/. For information about a civil case brought in Quebec by the Palestinian village of Bil'in against two Canadian companies that were involved in building an Israeli settlement on village land, *see* Al Haq, *Update on the case of Bil'in v. Green Park in Canada – Hearings schedules 22–25 June* (Oct. 13, 2010), http://www.alhaq.org/advocacy/topics/settlements-and-settler-violence/238-update-on-the-case-of-bilin-v-green-park-in-canada-hearings-scheduled-22-25-june.

I   Introduction

In 2001, victims of the Sabra and Shatila massacres in Lebanon lodged a complaint with a Belgian court against then-Israeli prime minister Ariel Sharon and other officials for their alleged complicity in those events which the court agreed to investigate. This marked the first ever UJ case brought by Palestinians against Israeli officials and provoked a diplomatic incident when the Belgian Consulate in Tel Aviv was attacked. Supporters of Ariel Sharon, including the Mayor of Jerusalem, insulted the Belgian Prime Minister when he visited Israel in 2002, and Israel vigorously lobbied Belgium to drop the case.[2]

At the same time, Belgium was under intense pressure from the United States (US) to change its UJ laws in order stop cases filed by victim groups against, amongst others, former US president George H. W. Bush and General Tommy Franks for crimes allegedly committed in Iraq. After several court battles and mounting political pressure, Belgium eventually introduced legislative changes in 2003 that significantly curtailed the scope of its UJ laws.[3] The *Sharon* case, meanwhile, was closed on the basis that, as a serving prime minister, Sharon had immunity from prosecution.[4]

Despite the failure of the *Sharon* case in Belgium, there have been at least ten more attempts to bring UJ cases against Israeli officials in Western European countries as well as one case in New Zealand since 2001. Most cases have been based on evidence implicating suspected perpetrators in the commission of torture or of grave breaches of the Fourth Geneva Convention as a result of military operations in the Gaza Strip.[5] These attempts include a successful arrest

---

2   Chibli Mallat, *Introduction: New Lights on the Sharon case*, 12 Palestine Y.B. Int'l L. 183–190 (2002–2003).

3   Wolfang Kaleck, *From Pinochet to Rumsfeld: Universal Jurisdiction in Europe 1998–2008*, 30 Mich. J. Int'l L. 933–936 (2009) [*hereinafter* Kaleck].

4   Chibli Mallat, Michael Verhaeghe, Luc Walleyn & Laurie King-Irani, *Sharon Trial: 12 February 2003 decision of Belgian Supreme Court*, Electronic Intifada (Feb. 19, 2003), https://electronic intifada.net/content/sharon-trial-12-february-2003-decision-belgian-supreme-court-explained/4413.

5   This refers strictly to UJ cases – *i.e.* those in which neither perpetrator nor victim are nationals of forum States and in which the crime did not take place on the territory of the forum State. Later, I refer to more recent cases in which either the perpetrator or victims are nationals of the forum jurisdiction, therefore not included in this list. Nine of the criminal UJ cases referred to here are in the public domain and the tenth is a confidential case brought by the Palestinian human rights organization Al-Haq. It is possible that there have been other cases that are not in the public domain and of which the author does not have knowledge. For a synopsis of the majority of UJ cases against Israeli officials to date, *see* Palestinian Centre for

warrant application against former Israeli Foreign Minister, Tzipi Livni, in the United Kingdom (UK) in 2009[6] and against Doron Almog, former Chief of the Southern Command of the Israeli army, also in the UK in 2005. An arrest warrant was also issued against Moshe Yaalon, former Chief of Staff of the Israeli army, in New Zealand in 2006, and in Spain, in 2008, a criminal investigation was opened into former Israeli Defense Minister, Binyamin Ben-Eliezer, and other high-ranking Israeli officials for their alleged involvement in war crimes.[7]

The Palestinian Centre for Human Rights, which has been at the forefront of bringing most of these cases, views UJ as "an essential tool in the fight against impunity".[8] Similarly, the Palestinian human rights organization, Al-Haq, sees UJ as "a significant step forward in the international struggle against impunity".[9] Indeed, the use of UJ by Palestinian human rights organizations has largely been a response to a situation of pervasive Israeli impunity for crimes committed in the occupied Palestinian territory (oPt) in which Palestinians are unable to achieve legal redress at either the local or international levels. In particular, the Palestinian legal system is unable to exercise jurisdiction over Israeli nationals who have committed crimes,[10] the Israeli legal system is unwilling to do so,[11] and the international community has repeatedly failed to take meaningful

---

Human Rights, *The Principle and Practice of Universal Jurisdiction: PCHR's work in the occupied Palestinian territory* (2010) [*hereinafter* PCHR UJ], http://pchrgaza.org/files/Reports/English/pdf_spec/PCHR-UJ-BOOK.pdf.

6 Ian Black, *Tzipi Livni arrest warrant prompts Israeli government travel 'ban'*, The Guardian (Dec. 15, 2009), http://www.theguardian.com/world/2009/dec/15/tzipi-livni-arrest-warrant-israeli.

7 PCHR UJ, 121–122 & 129–131.

8 *Id.*, 10.

9 Al-Haq, *Al-Haq position paper on the threat to universal jurisdiction in the wake of the UK arrest warrant against Tzipi Livni* (2010), at 2, http://www.alhaq.org/attachments/article/276/28-1-Position%20Paper%20on%20Universal%20Jurisdiction%2028%20Jan%202010.pdf.

10 Nasser Rayyes, *The rule of law and human rights within Palestinian National Authority territories*, 10 Palestine-Isr. J. (2003).

11 The general pattern of institutional and functional deficiencies of Israel's judicial systems to investigate and prosecute alleged war crimes committed by Israeli officials against Palestinians in the oPt, evidencing a lack of willingness on the part of the Israeli authorities to ensure accountability for Israeli perpetrators of international crimes, has been well documented by human rights organizations and the UN. *See, e.g.*, FIDH, *Shielded from accountability: Israel's unwillingness to investigation and prosecute international crimes* (Sep. 2011), https://www.fidh.org/IMG/pdf/report_justice_israel-final-3-2.pdf; H.R.C, *Report of the Independent Commission of Inquiry on the 2014 Gaza Conflict*, U.N. Doc. A/HRC/29/52 (June 24, 2015), para. 76.

action to prevent Israeli violations of international law.[12] Cases against Israeli officials under UJ laws in foreign domestic jurisdictions have, therefore, provided a mechanism for seeking much-needed accountability.

However, in spite of the strenuous efforts of human rights organizations to use UJ, no case brought against an Israeli official has ever resulted in a prosecution. The many obstacles to exercising UJ suggest it might be difficult to ever achieve a trial of an Israeli official under UJ. This raises a question as to whether UJ is a viable mechanism for pursuing accountability for Israeli crimes that should continue to be pursued by whatever means available.

In this paper, I will briefly survey the last fifteen years of UJ litigation against Israeli officials and describe the main challenges and obstacles to such cases that have emerged. I will suggest that the main reason there is yet to be a prosecution of an Israeli official has been political opposition to prosecutions from Israel and forum State governments, rather than any legally meritorious reason, such as an insufficiency of evidence implicating alleged perpetrators in crimes. I will propose that UJ cases should continue to be pursued despite the difficulties of securing a successful outcome because there are currently so few alternative avenues available to Palestinians for achieving accountability. However, I will make certain recommendations designed to improve the potential for success in future cases. In particular, I will suggest that cases more likely to succeed are those which focus on lower-level perpetrators, in which perpetrators or victims are nationals or residents of forum jurisdictions, and that are better integrated into broader advocacy strategies.

The paper is structured in three parts. Part I defines the concept, scope and applicability of criminal UJ and outlines the political context in which UJ cases against Israeli officials are brought. Part II describes the main challenges and obstacles faced by UJ cases with reference to specific examples. First it outlines the technical obstacles to the exercise of UJ, namely: (i) subsidiarity; and (ii) the requirement for the physical presence of a suspect within the jurisdiction. It then turns to the obstacles that have arisen, directly or indirectly, as a

---

12   For instance, Israel repeatedly failed to implement recommendations of several UN Security Council resolutions. For a list of the UN Security Council resolutions that Israel has ignored (as of 2002), *see* Stephen Zunes, *United Nations Security Council resolutions currently being violated by countries other than Iraq*, Foreign Policy In Focus (Oct. 1, 2002), http://fpif.org/united_nations_security_council_resolutions_currently_being_violated _by_countries_other_than_iraq/. For a discussion of how the UN has failed to enforce its resolutions regarding Israeli actions in Jerusalem, *see* Michael Dumper, *Jerusalem, in* Routledge Handbook on the Israeli-Palestinian Conflict 121, 130 (J. Peters & D. Newman eds., 2013).

result of political opposition to cases, namely: (i) countries limiting the scope of their UJ laws; (ii) political interference in cases; and (iii) Israeli non-cooperation with investigations. Part III draws conclusions and makes recommendations as to how to increase the chances of success in future UJ cases.

II The Principle and Practice of Universal Jurisdiction

To appreciate the complexities of UJ litigation, we shall need a precise definition of what UJ actually is, as well as an understanding of the application of UJ at the national level – in particular, the existence of differences in the jurisdictional laws and practices of forum States. A further difficulty arises from issues connected with political opposition to UJ cases against Israeli officials. These matters are discussed below.

A *Definition of (Criminal) Universal Jurisdiction*

UJ refers to the assertion by one State of its jurisdiction over crimes committed in the territory of another State, by and against nationals of another State where the crime poses no direct threat to the vital interests of the State asserting jurisdiction. In other words, UJ amounts to the claim by a State to prosecute crimes in circumstances where none of the traditional links of territoriality, nationality, passive personality or the protective principle exists at the time of the commission of the alleged offence.[13]

Under customary international law, States are entitled to exercise UJ over the international crimes of genocide, torture, war crimes and crimes against humanity because the heinous nature of the crimes means that their suppression and punishment is a matter of concern to the international community as a whole.[14] Numerous international treaties oblige States Parties to exercise forms of UJ over crimes, as defined in those treaties, when a suspect is present on their territory.[15] For example the 1949 Geneva Conventions oblige High Contracting Parties to exercise jurisdiction over grave breaches of the Conventions even when the alleged perpetrator is the national of, and

---

13 Council of the European Union, *AU-EU Expert Report on the Principle of Universal Jurisdiction,* 8672/1/09 REV 1, 7 (Apr. 16, 2009) [*hereinafter* AU-EU Expert Report].

14 Luc Reydams, Universal Jurisdiction: International and Municipal Legal Perspectives 3 (2004). *See also*, Antonio Cassese, *Is the bell tolling for universality? A plea for a sensible notion of universal jurisdiction,* 1 J. Int'l Crim. Justice 589, 591–592 (2003) [*hereinafter* Cassese].

15 AU-EU Expert Report, 7–8.

the crime took place on the territory of another State,[16] and the Convention against Torture provides for UJ over the crime of torture.[17]

B *Scope and Application of UJ at the National Level*

The principle that UJ may be exercised over the commission of serious international crimes is well established in international law. Indeed, Israel was the first country to use universal jurisdiction laws to prosecute Adolf Eichmann, a former Nazi lieutenant colonel, for the commission of serious international crimes in a trial that was held in Jerusalem in 1961.[18] Moreover, many States have laws providing for the exercise of UJ.[19] In spite of the broad recognition of the principle of UJ, however, there is a lack of uniformity in its application and over the requirements for its exercise at the national level. The reason is that the application of UJ at the national level depends on the rules of the domestic legal system that is exercising jurisdiction and, in addition, it may be derived from both treaty and customary law, the exact parameters of which lack clarity.[20]

For example there is a lack of agreement over whether customary law permits the exercise of so-called "UJ *in absentia* in which a State exercises UJ over persons even when they are not present in the State's territory.[21] Until recently,

---

16   Geneva Convention (I) on Wounded and Sick in Armed Forces in the Field art. 49, Aug. 12, 1949, 75 U.N.T.S. 31; Geneva Convention (II) on Wounded, Sick and Shipwrecked of Armed Forces at Sea art. 50, Aug. 12, 1949, 75 U.N.T.S 85; Geneva Convention (III) on Prisoners of War art. 129, Aug. 12, 1949, 75 U.N.T.S. 135; Geneva Convention (IV) relative to the Protection of Civilian Persons in Time of War art. 146, Aug. 12, 1949, 75 U.N.T.S. 287 [*hereinafter* Fourth Geneva Convention).

17   Convention against Torture and Other Cruel, Inhuman or Degrading Treatment or Punishment arts. 5(2) & 6(1), Dec. 10, 1984, 1465 U.N.T.S. 85.

18   Dominik Lasok, *The Eichmann Trial*, 11 Int'l Comp. L. Q. 355–374 (1962).

19   Amnesty International, *Universal jurisdiction: a preliminary survey of legislation around the world–2012 update*, AI-Index IOR 53/019/2012, (Oct. 2012) at 2 [*hereinafter* Amnesty UJ]; G.A. Res. 69/174, *The scope and the application of the principle of universal jurisdiction: Report of the Secretary-General*, U.N. Doc. A/69/174 (July 23, 2014), para. 63 [*hereinafter* UNSG UJ Report).

20   *See, generally*, AU-EU Expert Report; Cassese.

21   Alexander Poels, *Universal Jurisdiction in Absentia*, 23 Neth. Q. Hum. Rts. 65–84 (2005). In Congo v. Belgium, International Court of Justice judges were divided on whether this type of UJ is permitted under customary international law; *see* Arrest Warrant of 11 April 2000 (Dem. Rep. Congo v. Belg.), 2002 I.C.J. Rep. 3 (Feb. 14) [*hereinafter* ICJ Arrest Warrant]. *See also* Roger O-Keefe, *Universal Jurisdiction: Clarifying the Basic Concept*, 2 J. Int'l Crim. Justice 735–760 (2004); which argues that the ICJ judges' conclusions on the legality of UJ *in absentia* wrongly conflate two issues that are independent of one another: prescrip-

Belgium and Spain allowed for this type of UJ but, under political pressure from certain countries (particularly the US, Israel and China), they were both forced to change their laws.[22] Some States have also argued that such an exercise of jurisdiction represents an infringement of their sovereignty.[23] Currently, the matter is left for interpretation by States, some of which require the presence of the perpetrator in the forum State in order for UJ proceedings to be initiated whilst others allow for UJ trials *in absentia* if the alleged perpetrator has been present within the country at least once during the investigation or trial phase, and in some cases the presence of the suspect is not a requirement for proceedings to be initiated.[24]

Similarly, it is widely accepted that UJ should operate subsidiarily. In other words, it should be exercised when the territorial or nationality State is unwilling or unable to prosecute the crime.[25] However, in reality, subsidiarity is not a condition for the exercise of UJ in all countries and it is questionable whether it is in fact a requirement for the exercise of UJ under international law.[26] Furthermore, countries that do have the subsidiarity requirement interpret the concept differently. Thus, for instance, in Spain the test for subsidiarity is legal inactivity by the territorial State caused by an inability or unwillingness to investigate the case. By contrast, in Germany, a much broader test is applied – if the territorial State has investigated the "complex" of crimes in which the alleged perpetrator in the UJ case is implicated, even if it has not

---

tive jurisdiction (a State's jurisdiction to prescribe their criminal law) and enforcement jurisdiction (the manner of that law's enforcement) – the latter being dependent on the municipal law of each State.

22 Kaleck, 932–936. *See also* Human Rights Watch, *The world needs Spain's universal jurisdiction law* (May 27, 2009), http://www.hrw.org/news/2009/05/27/world-needs-spain-s-universal-jurisdiction-law.

23 *See, e.g.*, the arguments put forward in *Arrest Warrant* by the Democratic Republic of the Congo in their application to institute proceedings against Belgium in response to a Belgian court's issuance of an arrest warrant *in absentia* against the then-Foreign Minister.

24 UNSG UJ Report, para. 66.

25 *The rule of law and transitional justice in conflict and post-conflict societies: Report of the Secretary-General*, U.N. Doc. S/2004/616 (Aug. 23, 2004), para. 48.

26 Harmen Van de Wilt, *Universal Jurisdiction under Attack: An Assessment of African Misgivings towards International Criminal Justice as Administered by Western States*, 9 J. Int'l Crim. Justice 1043, 1050 (2011). *See also*: Cassese; AU-EU Expert Report, para. 14; for differing opinions on whether subsidiarity is a requirement of UJ under customary law. To complicate matters further, the provisions of Geneva Conventions that oblige High Contracting Parties to exercise UJ, and which may form the basis for the exercise of UJ by States in certain cases, do not contain the subsidiarity principle but, on the contrary, make prosecution by the forum jurisdiction the primary obligation.

carried out investigations into the involvement of the alleged perpetrator himself, that is sufficient to block UJ proceedings.[27]

UJ therefore represents a principle that is well-defined in international law, but interpreted and applied differently by national jurisdictions, creating practical difficulties for practitioners of UJ. It makes it difficult, for example, to prepare a case in UJ for submission to several judicial fora, as some Palestinian human rights organizations have considered doing. In general, UJ litigation has to be tailored to the national legal system of the country in which the case is to be brought.[28]

C   *Israeli and Western Opposition to Universal Jurisdiction Cases against Israeli Officials*

Before turning to the specific obstacles that have arisen in UJ cases involving alleged Israeli suspects, it is also important to understand that cases are brought within a context of vehement and sustained Israeli opposition to the Palestinian use of the law as a means of peaceful redress for their predicament.[29] This means that all attempts to seek UJ prosecutions of Israeli officials face, in addition to the legal and practical complexity of such litiga-

---

27   This issue arose in a case filed against Donald Rumsfeld in Germany on allegations of war crimes and torture committed against Iraqi detainees over which Rumsfeld was accused of having command responsibility. The German Federal Prosecutor declined to investigate on the basis that the "complex" of crimes was under investigation in the United States and that it did not matter whether the Rumsfeld himself had been investigated or whether the exact same crimes were being investigated. It should be noted that in Germany, the lack of subsidiarity operates as a factor entitling the prosecutor to exercise his or her discretion to decline to investigate or prosecute a universal jurisdiction case rather than as a legal requirement for the exercise of jurisdiction; *see* Human Rights Watch, *Universal Jurisdiction in Europe: The State of the Art*, HRW Index vol. 18, No. 5(D) (June 2006), at 32–33 [*hereinafter* HRW UJ in Europe]. *See also* Human Rights Watch, *The legal framework for universal jurisdiction in Germany* (2014), at 5–6, https://www.hrw.org/sites/default/files/related_material/IJ0914German_0.pdf.

28   The author has personal knowledge of discussions between Palestinian human rights organizations about increasing the efficiency of UJ cases by compiling one evidence file against one or several perpetrators that can be submitted to several jurisdictions depending on where the alleged perpetrators happen to be travelling.

29   For example, in 2009, Prime Minister Netanyahu stated that he would not allow any prosecutions of Israelis in association with "Operation Cast Lead"; *see Netanyahu vows never to let Israelis be tried for war crimes*, Ha'aretz (Oct. 12, 2012), http://www.haaretz.com/news/netanyahu-vows-never-to-let-israelis-be-tried-for-war-crimes-1.6248.

tion, the very significant obstacle of political pressure aimed at preventing cases from going ahead.[30]

Israeli opposition to UJ cases began with the *Sharon* case in Belgium in 2001, when Israel lobbied Belgium to restrict its UJ laws to ensure that the case could not proceed. Israel has subsequently lobbied the governments of all countries in which UJ cases against its officials have been brought to intervene to prevent them from going ahead.[31] The response from States has largely been one of acquiescence to such lobbying, apparently because forum governments believe that considerations of international diplomacy and perceived national interest should trump the pursuit of justice in individual cases. As a result, three countries – Spain, the United Kingdom (UK) and Belgium – have changed their laws to restrict the application of UJ. In addition, the governments of at least three countries – the UK, The Netherlands and New Zealand – have intervened in judicial processes to prevent cases against Israeli officials from proceeding (see below).

Moreover, since the publication of the report of the United Nations (UN) Fact-Finding Mission on the Gaza Conflict in 2009 (or the so-called "Goldstone Report"), Israel seems to have formulated a foreign policy aimed specifically at preventing Palestinian legal cases from being successful. For instance, when speaking in a lecture entitled "Challenges to Israeli Foreign Policy" at the Israel Council on Foreign Relations in 2010, Israel's then Deputy Foreign Minister, Dani Ayalon, defined the use of the law by Palestinians as a "main challenge" for Israel in the "coming decade" stating that "[t]oday the trenches are in Geneva in the Council of Human Rights, or in New York in the General Assembly,

---

30   This predicament is not unique to cases against Israel officials. In fact, political opposition to cases is a problem faced by all UJ litigation directed against officials of powerful nations. It has meant that up until now the only successful prosecutions have been of perpetrators of developing countries and generally only of middle and low-ranking perpetrators. For an overview of UJ prosecutions (*i.e.* cases in which charges have been brought as opposed to merely investigations opened) which demonstrates that perpetrators have been from Rwanda, the former Yugoslavia, the Democratic Republic of the Congo, Sudan, Liberia, Afghanistan, Iraq, Myanmar, Mauritania, Argentina, Guatemala, Algeria and Chad; *see* Joseph Rikhof, *Fewer places to hide? The impact of domestic war crimes prosecutions on international impunity* (Conference Paper) (2008), at 20–28 [*hereinafter* Rikhof], http://www.ccij.ca/content/uploads/2015/07/Rikhof.pdf. In addition to the cases mentioned in Rikhof's piece, there is currently an on-going UJ trial of a Nepalese army general in the UK; *see Nepalese office Kumar Lama trial adjourned*, BBC News (Mar. 18, 2015), http://www.bbc.co.uk/news/uk-england-sussex-31932371.

31   Kaleck, 932–936.

or in the Security Council, or in the Hague ... [or in] the ICJ".[32] As part of its policy, Israel has claimed that Palestinian legal initiatives amount to a form of "lawfare" aimed merely at the "de-legitimization" of Israel – a claim which is made in order to discredit the Palestinian use of the law without having to engage in the substance of the arguments made, and to suggest that democratic countries fighting terrorism have a common interest to ensure that such cases are unsuccessful.[33] Thus, the Israeli Ministry of Foreign Affairs website has a webpage dedicated to the topic of "lawfare"[34] and the Israeli government has recently established a special Knesset subcommittee on "lawfare" to discuss how to combat Palestinian legal initiatives.[35]

Israel has also mounted several diplomatic campaigns to thwart legal initiatives aimed at holding Israeli officials accountable for their actions. For instance, Israel, assisted by the US, led a long (and ultimately unsuccessful) campaign to pressure the Palestinian Authority (PA) not to join the International Criminal Court (ICC).[36] Israel also applied pressure on the PA, reportedly including threats to inflict damage on the Palestinian economy, in order to delay a vote on the Goldstone Report at the UN Human Rights Council in October 2010.[37] Israel subsequently lobbied Western States and the UN

---

32   Israeli Ministry of Foreign Affairs, *Deputy FM Ayalon: Challenges for Israeli Foreign Policy* (Jan. 6, 2010), http://mfa.gov.il/MFA/PressRoom/2010/Pages/DepFM_Ayalon_Challenges_ Israeli_Foreign_Policy_6-Jan-2010.aspx.

33   "Lawfare" is a term that has been defined to mean "the strategy of using – or misusing – law as a substitute for a traditional military means to achieve an operational objective". Although the term originated in the 1970s, it has been used more recently by the US administration in support of the "war on terror" to accuse adversaries of fabricating or capitalizing on allegations that US soldiers have committed war crimes in order to undermine population support for US military interventions; *see* Charles J. Dunlap, Jr., *Lawfare: A Decisive Element of 21st-Century Conflicts?* 54 Joint Force Q. 35–39 (2009).

34   Israeli Ministry of Foreign Affairs, FAQ: the campaign to defame Israel, http://mfa.gov.il/ MFA/ForeignPolicy/FAQ/Pages/FAQ_Attack_Israeli_Values.aspx#delegit.

35   Lahav Harkov, *Livni to head new Knesset subcommittee on Lawfare*, Jerusalem Post (Aug. 17, 2015), http://www.jpost.com/Israel-News/Livni-to-head-new-Knesset-subcommit tee-on-lawfare-412382.

36   *See, e.g.,* Barak Ravid, *Palestinians refuse clause in UN draft barring criminal charges against Israel*, Ha'aretz (Nov. 27, 2012), http://www.haaretz.com/israel-news/palestinians -refuse-clause-in-un-draft-barring-criminal-charges-against-israel.premium-1.480931. *Kerry's offer: You Release Terrorists, They'll Renew Talks*, Arutz Sheva (Mar. 24, 2013), http:// www.israelnationalnews.com/News/News.aspx/166504#.VwKvKEeming.

37   Jonathan Cook, *How Israel bought off UN war crimes probe*, Electronic Intifada (Oct. 6, 2009), https://electronicintifada.net/content/how-israel-bought-uns-war-crimes -probe/8477.

Secretary-General to ensure that the Goldstone Report's recommendations would not be implemented by the UN Security Council.[38] More recently, Israel also mounted a smear campaign against William Schabas, head of the UN commission of inquiry into the 2014 Gaza conflict, who was viewed as being too sympathetic to the Palestinians, forcing him to resign before completing his mandate.[39] Similarly, Israel has refused to cooperate with the last three UN special rapporteurs on human rights in the oPt, namely: Richard Falk, who was rapporteur between 2008 and 2014;[40] Marakim Wibisono, who was appointed after Richard Falk and resigned his position due to Israeli non-cooperation in January 2016;[41] and current Special Rapporteur, Michael Lynk.[42]

III   Obstacles to Universal Jurisdiction Cases against Israeli Officials

Apart from the issue of political opposition by Israel to UJ and the unwillingness of many forum governments to pursue such cases, there are also technical obstacles to a successful prosecution of UJ cases which are discussed below.

---

38   Al Haq, *Is the Goldstone Report Dead, High Commissioner?* (Feb. 4, 2010), http://www
.alhaq.org/advocacy/targets/united-nations/391-qis-the-goldstone-report-dead-high
-commissioner; Marian Houk, *UNSG Ban Ki-Moon target of Israeli lobbying against
Goldstone report*, UN-Truth (Oct. 24, 2009), http://un-truth.com/ban-ki-moon/unsg-ban
-ki-moon-target-of-israeli-lobbying-against-goldstone-report; Roni Sofer, *Minister Shalom
to UN Chief: Bury Goldstone Report*, Ynet News (Oct. 23, 2009), http://www.ynetnews.com/
articles/0,7340, L-3794423,00.html; Canaan Liphshiz, *Jewish lobbying sways EU against
support of Gaza Goldstone report*, Ha'aretz (Mar. 10, 2010), http://www.haaretz.com/
jewish-lobbying-sways-eu-against-support-of-goldstone-gaza-report-1.266404; US dodges
UN debate on Goldstone Gaza report, Ha'aretz (Nov. 4, 2009), http://www.haaretz.com/
news/u-s-dodges-un-debate-on-goldstone-gaza-report-1.4761.
39   *Head of UN war crimes inquiry resigns after Israel accused him of pro-Gaza bias*, The
Guardian (Feb. 3, 2015), http://www.theguardian.com/world/2015/feb/02/un-war-crimes
-inquiry-resigns-israel-gaza-palestine.
40   UN OHCHR, *ICJ should assess legal status of prolonged Israeli occupation of Palestine,
says UN rights expert* (Mar. 21, 2014), http://www.ohchr.org/EN/NewsEvents/Pages/
DisplayNews.aspx?NewsID=14421&.
41   UN OHCHR, *Special Rapporteur on the Occupied Palestinian Territory resigns due to continued lack of access to OPT* (Jan. 4, 2016), http://www.ohchr.org/en/NewsEvents/Pages/
DisplayNews.aspx?NewsID=16922&LangID=E.
42   UN OHCHR, *Human Rights: New UN Special Rapporteur on Palestine launches first official mission* (July 8, 2016), http://www.ohchr.org/EN/NewsEvents/Pages/DisplayNews
.aspx?NewsID=20247&LangID=E.

A   Technical Obstacles to Universal Jurisdiction Cases

The primary technical obstacles are the principle of subsidiarity and, in some jurisdictions, the requirement that the suspect should be physically present within the forum State in order for UJ proceedings to be initiated.

1   Subsidiarity

In accordance with the principle of subsidiarity, some domestic legal systems will only exercise UJ if it can be demonstrated that the territorial or nationality State or an international jurisdiction is unable or unwilling to hear the case.[43] This prevented a case from proceeding in Spain against former Israeli Defense Minister, Binyamin Ben-Eliezer, and six other senior Israeli officials for their involvement in the Al-Daraj attack. The case demonstrates the difficulty in persuading foreign national courts of the fact that Palestinians lack an effective remedy within the Israeli justice system.[44]

i   History of the Al Daraj Case

The Al-Daraj bombing concerned the 2002 assassination of a Hamas leader Saleh Shehadeh, in Gaza in which the Israeli army dropped a one-ton bomb on an apartment block in Gaza City causing extensive property damage and killing and injuring scores of civilians. Victims in the case had originally requested the Israeli Military Advocate General (MAG) to investigate the case. He decided, on the basis of an internal army review, that the death of civilians was unintentional and therefore not to open a criminal investigation. In 2003, the Israeli Supreme Court was petitioned to declare the decision of the MAG not to investigate the case null and void and in June 2007 a hearing was held on the matter. Without ruling on the question of whether the operation might constitute a war crime, the court recommended that "an objective and independent" body should be established to investigate the case in order to establish the responsibility of the State (rather than the criminal responsibility of the persons involved in the operation) and to pay compensation to victims in appropriate cases. Subsequently, in 2008, the court denied the claimants' petition stating, *inter alia*, that there were no demonstrated defects in the MAG's reasoning.

---

43   HRW UJ in Europe, at 32.

44   Palestinian Centre for Human Rights, *PCHR take Al Daraj Case to Constitutional Court* (Apr. 16, 2010), http://www.pchrgaza.org/portal/en/index.php?option=com_content& view=article&id=6441:pchr-take-al-daraj-case-to-constitutional-court-challenge -restrictions-on-universal-jurisdiction-law-in-spain-&catid=58:universal -jurisdiction&Itemid=214.

PROSPECTS FOR SUCCESS? 109

Meanwhile in January 2008, acting on the Israeli Supreme Court's recommendation, then-Israeli Prime Minister Ehud Olmert established a commission of enquiry into the case composed of two former Israeli army generals and an ex-official of the Israeli General Security Services. The commission had the status of a military enquiry and therefore the procedure, witness testimonies and final report were to remain confidential. Furthermore, the commission would only be able to provide non-binding recommendations to the army. In 2011, the commission produced a report concluding in similar terms as the earlier internal army review that the consequences of the Al-Daraj attack were unintended and unforeseen, and recommended that there should be no criminal investigation. Victims in the case had also lodged civil claims against the military for compensation which were eventually dismissed.[45]

ii   *The Spanish Proceedings*

In June 2008, Palestinian victims of the Al-Daraj attack, represented by the Palestinian Centre for Human Rights (PCHR) and Spanish lawyers, petitioned a Spanish court to investigate the Israeli officials for their involvement in the bombing. In January 2009, the court formally opened a criminal investigation into the case in response to which Israel sent a large dossier to the court detailing the existence of ongoing judicial proceedings regarding the incident in Israel and arguing that the Spanish investigation should be closed. The Spanish State Prosecutor filed a motion with the court requesting the closure of the investigation on the basis of the arguments put forward in the Israeli dossier; but in May 2009, the court upheld its decision to investigate the case, concluding that the Israeli commission of enquiry did not constitute a criminal investigation and that "... the judicial authorities of Israel have not initiated any criminal proceedings with the objective of determining if the events

---

45   PCHR UJ, at 129–130. Palestinian Centre for Human Rights, *Israel's Al-Daraj Commission Illustrates Long-Standing Institutionalisation of Impunity and Unwillingness to Genuinely Investigate Alleged War Crimes* (Mar. 1, 2011), http://www.pchrgaza.org/portal/en/index.php?option=com_content&view=article&id=7261:israels-al-daraj-commission-illustrates-long-standing-institutionalisation-of-impunity-and-unwillingness-to-genuinely-investigate-alleged-war-crimes&catid=58:universal-jurisdiction&Itemid=214. Palestinian Centre for Human Rights, *PCHR take Al Daraj Case to Constitutional Court* (Apr. 16, 2010), http://www.pchrgaza.org/portal/en/index.php?option=com_content&view=article&id=6441:pchr-take-al-daraj-case-to-constitutional-court-challenge-restrictions-on-universal-jurisdiction-law-in-spain-&catid=58:universal-jurisdiction&Itemid=214. Sharon Weill and Valentina Azarov, *Universal jurisdiction once again under threat*, Electronic Intifada (June 10, 2009) [*hereinafter* Weill and Azarov], https://electronicintifada.net/content/universal-jurisdiction-once-again-under-threat/8284.

denounced could entail some criminal liability". The court also expressed serious doubts about the independence and impartiality of the Israeli MAG, the Israeli Attorney General and the commission of enquiry, as well as about their functional separation from the executive branch of the State.[46]

The State Prosecutor appealed this decision to a Spanish appeals court (the National High Court) which, in June 2009, reversed the lower court's decision, ruling that the investigation should be closed. The appeals court stated that the case was being adequately investigated in Israel, observing that the MAG had taken into account an army review when declining to open an investigation, that civil complaints had been lodged by the victims, and that criminal proceedings were pending in the form of the petition that had been brought to the Israeli Supreme Court and the subsequent commission of enquiry. The court also noted that the latter constituted an adequate investigation since, amongst other things, its decisions were subject to judicial review. In addition, the court stated that any conclusion that the MAG, Attorney General and commission of enquiry lacked independence and impartiality, ignored "the evidence of the existence of a social and democratic rule of law [in Israel] under which the members of the executive and judicial branches are subject to the law".[47]

PCHR appealed this decision to the Spanish Supreme Court, on the grounds that there had been a breach of the right to due legal process (it was argued that the original Prosecutor's appeal to the National High Court was procedurally improper) and a violation of the right to effective judicial protection because, *inter alia*, the Spanish appeals court had erred in finding that criminal proceedings into the Al-Daraj attack were pending in Israel.

In 2010, the Spanish Supreme Court upheld the appeal court's decision to close the investigation. It rejected the first ground of appeal, ruling that there had been due process in the case consistent with procedural guarantees. As regards the second ground of appeal, the Supreme Court relied on a decision of the Spanish Constitutional Court that the right to judicial protection would only be violated if a lower court judgment were unreasonable or manifestly arbitrary. The Supreme Court went on to rule that the appeals court decision had been detailed, well-reasoned and its conclusions regarding the status of

---

46   PCHR UJ, at 130. *See also* Weill and Azarov.

47   Unofficial translation of the judgement of the Spanish National High Court provided by the Centre for Constitutional Rights, https://ccrjustice.org/sites/default/files/assets/ National%20High%20Court%20-%20Appeals%20Majority%20Decision%20of%20 07.09.2009_ENG.pdf.

PROSPECTS FOR SUCCESS? 111

investigations in Israel reasonable, and therefore that there had been no violation of the right to judicial protection in the case.[48]

iii   *Conclusions on the Al-Daraj Case*

The *Al-Daraj* case illustrated the difficulty in persuading foreign domestic courts that it is not possible for Palestinians to obtain an effective remedy in Israel. It also highlights the perception that exists in many countries, as articulated in the Spanish appeals court decision, that Israel is a Western-style democracy, operating under the rule-of-law with a fair and robust judicial system. They therefore consider it inappropriate under the subsidiarity principle to pursue UJ cases against Israeli perpetrators. In order to overcome the subsidiarity requirement, special effort will need to be made to persuasively present to domestic courts the deficiencies of the Israeli judicial system and to demonstrate that the quasi-investigative steps that Israel sometimes carries out into military operations, such as those it took after the Al-Daraj attack, do not constitute independent, effective, and impartial investigations.

The case also raises questions over the integrity of national judicial processes in the face of political pressure which, although it cannot be proven, is likely to have influenced the appeal court's decision in the case; for at the time the ruling was handed down, Spain was being lobbied heavily by Israel to prevent the case from going ahead and restricted its UJ laws later that same year, partly in order to appease Israel. In addition, Spain's Foreign Minister condemned the investigation, and reportedly sought to reassure his Israeli counterparts that the case would not go ahead. Indeed, the case only reached the Spanish appeals court because the State Prosecutor adopted Israel's arguments and decided to oppose the investigation.[49]

2   Presence of the Suspect within the Jurisdiction

In many countries, there is a requirement that the suspect be present within the jurisdiction before a UJ investigation or prosecution can proceed.[50] Unlike the majority of successful UJ cases to date, in which perpetrators have been

---

48   Tribunal Supremo, Sala de lo Penal, Sección 1 (Supreme Court, Criminal Chamber, Section 1), Appeal No. 1979/2009, Judgment, Mar. 4, 2010 (in Spanish), http://estaticos .elmundo.es/documentos/2010/04/13/auto_gaza.pdf. Palestinian Centre for Human Rights, *PCHR to take Al Daraj case to Constitutional Court in Spain; Challenge Restrictions on Universal Jurisdiction law in Spain* (Apr. 16, 2010), http://pchrgaza.org/en/?p=6516.

49   *See* Palestinian Centre for Human Rights, *PCHR will Appeal to Supreme Court against Spanish Appeal Court's Decision* (June 30, 2009), http://pchrgaza.org/en/?p=2342.

50   HRW UJ in Europe, at 28–30.

resident in forum States as part of immigrant or asylum communities, Israeli perpetrators tend to live in Israel and to travel to foreign jurisdictions only for short periods of time.[51]

This poses an obstacle to UJ cases in countries in which presence is a requirement because it means that suspects are able to enter and leave the jurisdiction before national authorities have had time to carry out investigations and execute arrests. It can also pose an obstacle in countries in which presence is not a strict requirement because State prosecutors who have discretion over which cases to investigate are often reluctant to invest resources in pursuing investigations in which a suspect is not resident in the country.[52] To add to the difficulty, as a result of the relative success of UJ cases that have been brought against Israeli officials in the past, many Israeli officials avoid travelling to certain jurisdictions or take precautions to hide their travel plans so that their appearance in a foreign country where a case could be filed is unknown.[53]

An example of a UJ case in which the presence requirement was an obstacle was that involving Ami Ayalon in Holland in 2008. Lawyers acting on behalf of the Palestinian Center for Human Rights submitted a criminal complaint to the Dutch Prosecutor concerning Ayalon's involvement in torture. Ayalon was the former head of the Israeli General Security Services and then-Israeli Minister-without-Portfolio. Ayalon was visiting The Netherlands for five days and a request for urgency was included in the complaint. However, the prosecutor's investigation was delayed in order for a decision to be reached by the College of Procurators-General on whether Ayalon had diplomatic immunity.

---

51 In Europe, where most of the successful UJ prosecutions have taken place, almost all the defendants were already living in forum countries as part of an immigrant or asylum community. This includes, for instance, trials of Rwandan nationals in Belgium; see Luc Reydams, *Belgium's First Application of Universal Jurisdiction: The Butare Four Case*, 1 J. Int'l Crim. Justice 428–438 (2003) [*hereinafter* Reydams]; trials of Congolese and Afghan nationals in Holland: HRW UJ in Europe, at 71–80; and the trial of an Afghan national in the UK: *Afghan Zardad jailed for 20 years*, BBC News (July 19, 2005), http://news.bbc .co.uk/1/hi/uk/4695353.stm.

52 HRW UJ in Europe, at 28–32.

53 It is reported that some Israeli officials have stopped travelling to Spain and the UK on account of fear of arrest; see PCHR UJ, at 122, 131; Ian Black, *Tzipi arrest warrant prompts Israeli government travel 'ban'*, The Guardian (Dec. 15, 2009), http://www.theguardian .com/world/2009/dec/15/tzipi-livni-arrest-warrant-israeli. In some cases, it also appears that Israeli officials have kept their travel plans secret or changed their travel plans at the last minute, causing confusion over whether or not they have travelled to the forum jurisdiction (there are examples of cases in which this happened of which the author has personal knowledge).

Although the College reached a decision on the sixth day that Ayalon lacked immunity, the prosecutor decided that an investigation could not be initiated because Ayalon had by that time left the jurisdiction.[54]

Lawyers in the case appealed the prosecutor's decision to an appeals court on the basis that Ayalon's presence in the country, however brief, met the jurisdictional requirements for opening an investigation. The Dutch appeals court ruled, however, that whilst presence for short periods of time is a sufficient ground for establishing jurisdiction, the case was based on the Convention against Torture which obliges States Parties to exercise UJ against "suspects". Therefore, in order for jurisdiction to be established, the Public Prosecutor would have had to make a determination that Ayalon was indeed a suspect (*i.e.* someone reasonably suspected of committing the offence of torture) whilst he was visiting the country.

The court noted that the Prosecutor had undertaken no investigations into Ayalon (except to request advice as to whether he had immunity from prosecution) and had therefore not made the determination that Ayalon was a suspect. Furthermore, the court viewed the information contained in the complaint filed against Ayalon as too general in nature to disclose reasonable grounds to suspect that he had committed an offence. The court concluded that: "[t]he Netherlands does not now have jurisdiction over the complainee [Ayalon] since the Public Prosecution Service carried out no investigation whatever into the complainee's alleged role or share in the torture of the complainant ... and also since the complainee was not arrested at that time and is no longer in the Netherlands".[55]

The main lawyer in the case, Liesbeth Zegveld, has argued that the court's decision regarding jurisdiction is confusing because, on the one hand, it states that in torture cases presence of the suspect is a sufficient precondition for the exercise of jurisdiction and, on the other hand, rules that presence does not actually establish jurisdiction but that action on the part of the prosecutor – namely carrying out an investigation in order to categorize as a person as a suspect – is needed to activate jurisdiction. She argues that this reasoning wrongly conflates the question of jurisdiction, which should be independent of prosecutorial action, with that of the sufficiency of evidence against a

---

54   PCHR UJ, at 126–128.

55   Al Shami v Ayalon, Appeal judgment, No K08/0386 Rechtspraak.nl: BK7374, para. 15 (English translation) contained in Oxford Reports on International Law – ILDC 673 (NL 2009), at 9–10 [Neth.].

particular suspect.[56] Indeed there is reportedly still a considerable degree of confusion in The Netherlands regarding the meaning of the presence requirement. In any event, the Ayalon case demonstrates how the presence requirement poses an obstacle to UJ cases although, as discussed below, delay in the case may also have been caused by political pressure.

By contrast a case in which prosecutorial discretion posed an obstacle to a UJ prosecution concerns a request Al-Haq made to the British police in 2010 to investigate a high-ranking Israeli official on the basis of evidence implicating him in a *prima facie* case involving the commission of grave breaches of the Fourth Geneva Convention. The police refused to investigate the case, claiming that resource limitations meant they had to prioritize the investigation of domestic cases and, in view of the wide discretion given to State prosecutors under English law over whether to investigate cases, it was decided not to appeal the decision.[57]

The presence requirement and prosecutorial discretion over whether to investigate cases in which perpetrators are not resident in the forum jurisdiction therefore pose significant obstacles to UJ cases.

B *Political Obstacles to Universal Jurisdiction Cases*

Perhaps more difficult to overcome, however, than the technical obstacles to the exercise of jurisdiction are the political obstacles to UJ cases that can consist of the imposition of restrictions to UJ legislation as the result of lobbying by Israel, direct political interference by forum governments in cases, and Israeli refusal to cooperate with the investigation process.

1 Changes in Legislation in Response to Israeli Lobbying

Lobbying by Israel of foreign governments in response to specific cases has caused certain countries, namely Spain, the UK and Belgium, to restrict their UJ laws by narrowing the basis upon which jurisdiction may be asserted or by limiting the right of private parties to initiate prosecutions. This has meant that it will be more difficult to bring cases in those countries in the future.

---

56 Liesbeth Zegveld and Jeff Handmaker, *Universal jurisdiction: state of affairs and ways ahead*, International Institute of Social Studies, Working Paper No. 532 (Jan. 2012), at 7–8, http://www.iss.nl/news_events/iss_news/detail/article/34133-wp-532-universal-jurisdiction-state-of-affairs-and-ways-ahead-a-policy-paper-by-l-zegveld/.

57 Confidential case of which the author has personal knowledge.

PROSPECTS FOR SUCCESS?

i   *Spain*

Until 2009, Spain's laws provided for UJ over international crimes. There was no requirement that the suspect had to be present within the jurisdiction before a criminal investigation could be opened or charges brought.[58] However, the *Al-Daraj* case brought under these laws provoked intense lobbying by Israel of Spain to change its laws. Israel's Defense Minister, Ehud Barak, reportedly stated that, "I intend to appeal to the Spanish foreign minister, the Spanish minister of defense and, if need be, the Spanish prime minister, who is a colleague of mine, in the Socialist International, to override the decision".[59] As noted above, the Spanish Foreign Minister also reportedly told his Israeli counterpart that he would seek to have the law changed.[60]

As a result of political pressure from Israel – in addition to pressure reportedly exerted by China and the US over UJ cases brought in Spain concerning crimes committed in Tibet and Guantanamo Bay respectively – Spain changed its laws in 2009 to limit jurisdiction over international crimes to offences committed against Spanish nationals or where the perpetrator was present in Spain or if Spanish interests were affected. In 2014, the law was further restricted to prevent the investigation of cases in which the perpetrator was not present on Spanish soil. Interestingly enough, the new law was passed the day after a Spanish judge issued an arrest warrant against the former Chinese president, Jiang Zemin, over alleged human rights abuses in Tibet – the legislative changes having reportedly been made in order to appease China. As a result, it is no longer possible to bring UJ cases in Spain unless there is a Spanish connection.[61]

ii   *The United Kingdom*

Until 2011, it was possible for private citizens to apply directly to the UK magistrates' court for an arrest warrant in UJ cases as effectively the first step in

---

58   HRW UJ in Europe, at 86–90. Kaleck, 954–958.

59   *Israel urges Spain to halt 'cynical' Gaza war crimes probe*, Ha'aretz (May 4, 2009), http://www.haaretz.com/israel-urges-spain-to-halt-cynical-gaza-war-crimes-probe-1.275337.

60   Human Rights Watch, *The world needs Spain's universal jurisdiction laws* (May 27, 2009) http://www.hrw.org/news/2009/05/27/world-needs-spain-s-universal-jurisdiction-law.

61   Rosa Fernandez, *The 2014 Reform of Universal Jurisdiction in Spain: From All to Nothing*, Zeitschrift für Internationale Strafrechtsdogmatik (2014) [*hereinafter* Fernandez], http://zis-online.com/dat/artikel/2014_13_883.pdf; Ashifa Kassam, *Spain moves to curb legal convention allowing for trials of foreign rights abuses*, The Guardian (Feb. 11, 2014), http://www.theguardian.com/world/2014/feb/11/spain-end-judges-trials-foreign-human-rights-abuses.

initiating a private prosecution.[62] In September 2011, however, after sustained Israeli lobbying of the British government, and in the aftermath of a successful arrest warrant application against the former Israeli Foreign Minister, Tzipi Livni, the law was changed. Private applications for arrest warrants now require the consent of the Director of Public Prosecutions.[63] This has effectively removed the right of private parties to apply for arrest warrants by placing applications under the control of the prosecutor who, furthermore, is entitled to consider the government's view on the "public interest" of pursuing the case when deciding whether or not to grant permission for the arrest warrant application.[64]

The pressure exerted by Israel on Britain to change its UJ laws was intense and sustained. It included Israel summoning Britain's ambassador to warn him that Britain's ability to play a role in the Middle East peace process had been damaged by the Livni affair. Israel also stated that its officials would not visit the UK until the issue had been addressed and the Israeli ambassador openly called on the UK to change its laws.[65] In addition, when Britain's Foreign Minister visited Israel in 2010, Israel reportedly postponed a high-level meeting because the government had not yet taken action to change English law.[66]

Yet the British government had clearly been willing to change the law to prevent further applications from being made against Israeli officials. For instance, both the British Prime Minister and Foreign Minister reportedly expressed their opposition to the arrest warrant in the Livni case when speaking to their Israeli counterparts and promised to change the law.[67] Britain's Prime Minister even reportedly broke off climate-change talks in Copenhagen, after

---

62   HRW UJ in Europe, at 94–98.

63   Police Reform and Social Responsibility Act, 2011, c. 13, s153 (U.K.).

64   Crown Prosecution Service, *War Crimes/Crimes Against Humanity Referral Guidelines* (Aug. 2015), http://www.cps.gov.uk/publications/agencies/war_crimes.html#e.

65   Ian Black, *Tzipi Livni arrest warrant prompts Israeli government travel 'ban'*, The Guardian (Dec. 15, 2009), http://www.theguardian.com/world/2009/dec/15/tzipi-livni -arrest-warrant-israeli.

66   Harriet Sherwood, *Israel sparks legal row during William Hague visit*, The Guardian (Nov. 3, 2010), http://www.theguardian.com/world/2010/nov/03/israel-war-crimes-row -william-hague.

67   Ian Black, *Gordon Brown reassures Israel over Tzipi Livni arrest warrant*, The Guardian (Dec. 16, 2009), http://www.theguardian.com/world/2009/dec/16/tzipi-livni-israel-arrest -warrant.

PROSPECTS FOR SUCCESS?

the Livni warrant had been issued, to call Tzipi Livni and reassure her that she was "most welcome in Britain any time".[68]

iii   *Belgium*

Until 2001, Belgium had UJ over crimes against humanity, genocide and war crimes as a result of a law passed in 1993, and amended in 1999, which provided for UJ over international crimes.[69] In 2001, victims lodged a complaint against Ariel Sharon for his alleged involvement in the Sabra and Shatila massacres in Lebanon and other victim groups also filed complaints against high-profile figures, including George H. W. Bush and Dick Cheney for war crimes allegedly committed in the 1991 Gulf War. The cases provoked intense lobbying of Belgium by Israel and the US to change its laws. As a result, in April 2003, Belgium amended its UJ laws to restrict the rights of private parties to bring cases by stipulating that only the State Prosecutor could initiate UJ prosecutions, unless the alleged crime had occurred on Belgian soil, the alleged defendant was a Belgian citizen or present in Belgium, or the victim was a Belgian citizen or resident in Belgium for at least three years.[70]

However, when the changes to the law did not prevent a case from being filed in May 2003 against US General Tommy Franks for war crimes in Iraq, the US applied further pressure on Belgium to change its laws, including threatening to withhold funding for NATO operations in Belgium.[71] As a result, in August 2003, Belgium overhauled its UJ law by introducing a new legislative scheme that repealed the original law, incorporated its provisions into Belgium's ordinary penal code and, in doing so, relinquished the universal elements of the original law.[72] As a result, Belgium's ability to exercise jurisdiction over international crimes (that it is not obliged by treaty to prosecute under

---

68   Adrian Blomfield, *Brown calls Livni to express regret at arrest warrant*, The Telegraph (Dec. 16, 2009), http://www.telegraph.co.uk/news/worldnews/middleeast/israel/6827382/Brown-calls-Livni-to-express-regret-at-arrest-warrant.html.

69   The Act Concerning the Punishment of Grave Breaches of the Geneva Conventions and their Additional Protocols passed in 1993 provided Belgian courts with UJ over 20 specific war crimes. Amendments to the law passed in 1999 broadened the scope of the Act to provide for UJ over a larger number of international crimes, including crimes against humanity and genocide. *See* Eric Leonard, *Global Governance and the State: Domestic Enforcement of Universal Jurisdiction*, 16 Hum. Rts. Rev. 143, 151 (2015) [*hereinafter* Leonard].

70   Kaleck, 932–936; Leonard, 153.

71   Ian Black, *US threatens NATO boycott over Belgian war crimes law*, The Guardian (June 13, 2003), http://www.theguardian.com/world/2003/jun/13/nato.warcrimes.

72   Damien Vandemeersch, *Prosecuting International Crimes in Belgium*, 3 J. Int'l Crim. Justice 400, 402 (2005); Reydams, 428–438.

the *aut dedere aut iudicare* principle) is now restricted to cases in which the perpetrators are Belgian nationals or residents, or the victims are Belgian nationals or were living in Belgium for at least three years at the time when the crime was committed. Additionally, if the accused is not present on Belgian soil, the State Prosecutor is entitled to dismiss the case if it is considered not to be in the interests of justice to pursue it.[73]

Lobbying of the governments of Belgium, the UK and Spain by Israel and other countries has therefore resulted in changes to UJ laws that have significantly restricted the ability of complainants to initiate UJ cases in those countries.

2   Political Interference in Cases
Forum governments have also apparently interfered in the progress of cases in order to stop them from proceeding after commencement. In particular, attorneys-general have made decisions to close cases, thereby allowing Israeli officials immunity from prosecution. Moreover, it is possible that governments have also interfered directly in judicial processes in order to prevent cases from succeeding.

i   *Decisions of Attorneys-general: The United Kingdom & New Zealand*
In certain common law countries, including the UK and New Zealand, UJ prosecutions require the authorization of the Attorney-General. Constitutionally, the Attorney-General, as Chief Legal Advisor of the Crown, is independent of government. However, he or she is simultaneously a government minister and therefore a political appointee.[74] The role of the Attorney-General in authorizing prosecutions, therefore, creates great scope for political considerations to affect decisions about whether to prosecute cases. Indeed, in the UK, the Attorney-General is even allowed to consult government ministers in order to

---

73   HRW UJ in Europe, at 37–38; Kaleck, 932–936; Human Rights Watch, *Belgium: Universal jurisdiction law repealed* (Aug. 1, 2003), https://www.hrw.org/news/2003/08/01/belgium-universal-jurisdiction-law-repealed.

74   For a description of the role of the United Kingdom Attorney-General, *see* Attorney General's Office, *Protocol between the Attorney-General and the Prosecuting Departments* (July 2009) [*hereinafter* UK Attorney General Protocol], https://www.gov.uk/government/uploads/system/uploads/attachment_data/file/15197/Protocol_between_the_Attorney_General_and_the_Prosecuting_Departments.pdf. For a description of the role of the New Zealand Attorney-General, *see* Cabinet Office (Government of New Zealand), *Cabinet Manual: Attorney-General* (2008), http://www.cabinetmanual.cabinetoffice.govt.nz/4.2.

decide whether a prosecution is in the public interest and to stop prosecutions that are considered to harm "national security".[75]

In 2006, the New Zealand Attorney-General stopped the prosecution of Moshe Yaalon, former Israeli Defense Forces Chief-of-Staff. A district court issued an arrest warrant against Yaalon, who was visiting the country. Evidence was presented to the court that demonstrated Yaalon's involvement in the Al-Daraj attack which the judge concluded as "good and sufficient reasons to justify arrest".[76] After the warrant was issued, however, the Attorney-General directed the court to stay the prosecution claiming that "... the materials supplied to support the allegations could not be relied upon to show a *prima facie* case against the defendant".[77] It is difficult to understand how the Attorney-General could have come to such a different conclusion than an independent judge based on the evidence. It has been suggested that the case was thus blocked for political reasons.[78]

Although there is yet to be a UJ case in the UK against an Israeli perpetrator which has reached the stage of requiring the authorization of the Attorney-General, strong political ties between Israel and the UK mean it is quite likely that the Attorney-General would refuse authorization for the prosecution to proceed if a case were to reach that stage.[79]

ii   *Immunity from Prosecution*

Immunity from prosecution is also an obstacle. Certain high-ranking State officials such as heads-of-State and foreign ministers are entitled to immunity from criminal prosecution by foreign States for the period that they are in

---

75   UK Attorney-General Protocol, paras. 4(b) & 4(e).

76   PCHR UJ, at 125.

77   *Id.*, at 125–126.

78   *Id.*

79   For example, a United Kingdom case in which a prosecutor was entitled to take into account international relations concerns when deciding whether a prosecution was in the public interest is that of: R (on the Application of Corner House Research) v. Director of The Serious Fraud Office, [2009] [2008] UKHL 60 (Judgment) [U.K.]. The Director of the Serious Fraud Office had discontinued an international bribery investigation as a result of receiving threats from a Saudi Arabian official that Saudi Arabia would withdraw from counter-terrorism co-operation arrangements with the UK if the investigaiton continued – threats that if acted on it was considered would endanger national security. The court decided that the Director of the Serious Fraud Office had behaved properly in taking into account such threats when deciding whether the investigation was in the public interest.

office.[80] This prevented the case in Belgium in 2001 against then-Israeli Prime Minister, Ariel Sharon, from going ahead[81] and the same thing occurred in a case in the UK in 2004 against Shaul Mofaz who was then-Israeli Defense Minister.[82] However, the obstacle posed by this form of immunity is not very significant because the immunity applies only to a relatively small number of positions and only for the period of time that the person is in office.

By contrast another type of immunity, "special mission" immunity, might pose a more significant obstacle to cases, at least in the UK. Special mission immunity applies to persons who are on a special mission, which is a temporary diplomatic mission sent by one State to another, with the consent of the latter, as a means by which to conduct ad hoc diplomacy outside the framework of permanent diplomatic relations.[83]

This form of immunity was applied by the UK government to Tzipi Livni, apparently to protect her from prosecution when she was not entitled to personal immunity. In October 2011, Tzipi Livni, then head of the Israeli opposition travelled to the UK and an application to apply for a private arrest warrant against her was refused after a certificate issued by the UK Foreign and Commonwealth Office declaring that she was on a special mission and therefore entitled to immunity from prosecution.[84]

It is highly questionable whether Tzipi Livni's visit really amounted to a "special mission". In particular, Livni had claimed to be visiting the UK in order to "celebrate" the UK's change in the law in September 2011 (restricting the

80   ICJ Arrest Warrant, paras. 51–61.

81   Kaleck, 933.

82   Application for Arrest Warrant Against General Shaul Mofaz, Bow Street Magistrates' Court (Feb. 12, 2004) (unreported) paras. 11–14, http://www.geneva-academy.ch/RULAC/ pdf_state/Application-for-Arrest-Warrant-Against-General-Shaul-Mofaz.pdf. According to the decision of the District Judge in the case, the categories of high-ranking State officials entitled to personal immunity from criminal prosecution, which were mentioned in the ICJ Arrest Warrant (Dem. Rep. Congo v Belg.) are non-exhaustive. The judge decided that defense ministers had similar duties to foreign ministers and were therefore also entitled to immunity from prosecution. The author is unaware of any challenge or appeal against this decision, which appears to extend the category of state officials entitled to personal immunity beyond those decided in ICJ Arrest Warrant.

83   Convention on Special Missions arts. 1(a) & 2, Dec. 8, 1969, 1400 U.N.T.S. 231; *Khurts Bat v The Investigating Judge of the German Federal Court v The Government of Mongolia, The Secretary of State for Foreign and Commonwealth Affairs*, [2011] EWHC 2029 (Admin), para. 24 [U.K.].

84   Crown Prosecution Service, *CPS statement in relation to Ms Tzipi Livni's visit to the UK* (Oct. 6, 2011), http://blog.cps.gov.uk/2011/10/cps-statement-in-relation-to-ms-tzipi-livinis -visit-to-the-uk.html.

PROSPECTS FOR SUCCESS? 121

rights of private parties to initiate cases)[85] rather than to conduct State diplomacy, and the pro-Israel lobbying group, Bicom, claimed to have "facilitated" her visit.[86] Furthermore, the certificate declaring that Livni's trip was a Special Mission was provided and dated two days after the arrest warrant application against her had been made, and when Livni was already in the country, raising questions as to when the UK government had consented to her trip as a special mission.[87] The case is viewed by many as one in which the UK government provided Livni with diplomatic "cover" to ensure that she was not prosecuted.[88]

Whilst it is possible for lawyers to challenge government decisions to apply special mission immunity to visiting officials by way of judicial review, it is difficult to succeed in such cases because decisions concerning immunity are traditionally considered to be within the remit of government and the courts are therefore reluctant to look behind government declarations in order to examine the real situation.[89] Special Mission immunity might therefore continue to pose an obstacle to UJ cases brought against Israeli officials in the UK.

iii   *Political Interference in Judicial Processes*

It seems that the governments of forum States have also interfered directly in judicial processes in order to prevent prosecutions of Israeli officials from going ahead. An example is the Doron Almog case in the UK in 2005. A magistrates' court issued a warrant for Almog's arrest on the basis of evidence implicating him in the Al-Daraj bombing. Almog was on an El Al airlines flight to the UK to attend an event at the time. However, unidentified persons leaked the information that a warrant for Almog's arrest had been issued and the Israeli embassy warned him not to disembark from his plane when it arrived at the airport. The British police subsequently made no attempt to board the plane in order to arrest Almog, claiming they were unable to obtain confirmation of their

---

85   Daniel Machover and Raji Sourani, Changes to UK law didn't protect Tzipi Livni, Al Jazeera English (Oct. 10, 2011), http://www.aljazeera.com/indepth/opinion/2011/10/20110912402659549.html.

86   Bicom, *Livni meeting Hague in UK today following law change* (Oct. 6, 2011), http://www.bicom.org.uk/news-article/livni-meeting-hague-in-uk-today-following-law-change/.

87   Crown Prosecution Service, *CPS statement in relation to Ms Tzipi Livni's visit to the UK* (Oct. 6, 2011), http://blog.cps.gov.uk/2011/10/cps-statement-in-relation-to-ms-tzipi-livinis-visit-to-the-uk.html.

88   Ben White, *A very special mission*, The New Statesman (Oct. 8, 2011), http://www.newstatesman.com/blogs/the-staggers/2011/10/special-mission-livni-visit.

89   Khurts Bat v The Investigating Judge of the German Federal Court v The Government of Mongolia, The Secretary of State for Foreign and Commonwealth Affairs, [2011] EWHC 2029 (Admin), paras. 33–34 [U.K].

legal right to board it (even though the legal position was not complicated) and that they feared a clash with Israeli air marshals if they did. As a result, Almog was allowed to leave the jurisdiction without being arrested.[90] The case raised serious questions about whether the UK authorities deliberately thwarted Doron Almog's arrest.

Similarly, in Holland in 2008 a criminal complaint concerning the involvement of Ami Ayalon, former head of the Israeli General Security Services, in torture was submitted to the Dutch prosecutor. Ayalon was visiting The Netherlands for five days and because of the brevity of his stay, a request for urgency was included in the complaint. However, the prosecutor failed to initiate an investigation because a decision as to whether Ayalon had diplomatic immunity was delayed. The decision took six days to be made, by which time Ayalon had already left the jurisdiction.[91] It is difficult to imagine how it could have taken so long to arrive at a relatively straightforward decision on immunity and, indeed, the Israeli media reported that "discreet talks between Israel and Holland prevented the arrest of ... Ami Ayalon".[92]

In addition, a case brought against Israeli officials under Spain's newly restricted UJ laws might also have been prevented from going ahead through government interference. In 2010, Spanish victims of the Israeli attack on the Gaza Freedom Flotilla petitioned a Spanish court to open an investigation into the alleged commission of crimes by Israeli Prime Minister Binyamin Netanyahu and six other Israeli officials, because of their involvement in the Flotilla attack. The Court opened a case finding "strong evidence" of "crimes against humanity, illegal detention, deportation and torture".[93] In June 2015, however, the case had to be closed because of a 2014 change in the law that required alleged perpetrators in UJ cases to be present in Spain in order for investigations to proceed.[94] Nonetheless, in November 2015, the court issued

---

90   PCHR UJ, at 122; Andy McSmith *Keeping the Peace? The El Al flight and the Israeli army officer*, The Independent (Feb. 20 2008), http://www.independent.co.uk/news/uk/home-news/keeping-the-peace-the-el-al-flight-and-the-israeli-army-officer-784407.html; Dominic Casciani, *Police feared 'airport stand-off'*, BBC News (Feb. 19, 2008), http://news.bbc.co.uk/1/hi/uk/7251954.stm.

91   PCHR UJ, at 126–128.

92   Itamar Eichner, *Minister Ayalon evaded arrest in Holland*, Ynet News (Oct. 7, 2008), http://www.ynetnews.com/articles/0,7340, L-3606332,00.html.

93   Inigo Sanez de Ugarte, *La Fiscalia de la Audencia Nacional reclama que el TPI investigue el asalto israeli a la flotilla de Gaza, Eldiario.es* (Jan. 14, 2013) [*hereinafter* Ugarte], http://www.eldiario.es/politica/Fiscalia-Audiencia-TPI-investigue-Gaza_0_90291294.html.

94   Charlotte Silver, *Did Israeli interference block justice in Spain?* Electronic Intifada (Feb. 19, 2016), https://electronicintifada.net/content/did-israeli-interference-block-justice

PROSPECTS FOR SUCCESS?

an order instructing the Spanish police to place the names of the suspects on the police database and to notify the Court if they visited the country in order that the case could be re-instated and arrests executed.[95]

The day after the Court's order, an Israeli Foreign Ministry spokesperson told the Times of Israel: "We consider [the case] to be a provocation. The Israeli embassy in Madrid is in touch with Spanish General Prosecutor in order to close the file as promptly as possible. We hope that this will be over soon".[96] A month later, on 22 December 2015, Spain's National Court annulled the lower court's order, removing the names of the Israeli officials from the police database in a ruling that, according to the claimants' lawyer, was unprecedented and likely to have been the result of political pressure from Israel.[97]

3   Israeli Non-cooperation with Investigations

Finally, a potential obstacle to UJ cases is Israel's refusal to cooperate with foreign prosecuting authorities that wish to conduct international crimes investigations within Israel and the oPt. Israel's stance for several years has been to refuse to cooperate with UN-mandated international investigations such as the UN Fact-Finding mission into "Operation Cast Lead" in 2009[98] and the UN commission of inquiry on the 2014 Gaza conflict.[99] It will almost certainly therefore also refuse to cooperate with UJ investigations of foreign national authorities. Whilst it is theoretically possible to prosecute UJ cases without the cooperation of the territorial State, such cases are rare and the great majority

-spain/15741. Judah Ari Gross, *Spanish court shelves probe into Gaza flotilla raid*, Times of Israel (June 12, 2015), – http://www.timesofisrael.com/spanish-court-shelves-probe -into-gaza-flotilla-raid/.

95   Charlotte Silver, *Did Israeli interference block justice in Spain?* Electronic Intifada (Feb. 19, 2016) https://electronicintifada.net/content/did-israeli-interference-block -justice-spain/15741.

96   *Spanish judge seeks to prosecute PM over 2010 flotilla raid*, Times of Israel (Nov. 17, 2015), http://www.timesofisrael.com/spanish-judge-seeks-to-prosecute-pm-over-2010-flotilla -raid/.

97   Charlotte Silver, *Did Israeli interference block justice in Spain?* Electronic Intifada (Feb. 19, 2016), https://electronicintifada.net/content/did-israeli-interference-block- justice-spain/15741.

98   UN General Assembly, *Report of the United Nations Fact-Finding Mission on the Gaza Conflict*, U.N. Doc. A/HRC/12/48 (Sep. 25, 2009), para 20.

99   Itamar Eichner, *UN report calls for international investigation into alleged Israel, Hamas war crimes*, Ynet News (June 22, 2015), http://www.ynetnews.com/articles/0,7340, L-4671512,00.html.

of successful UJ prosecutions to date have involved the cooperation of the territorial State authorities.[100]

Indeed, the expectation that Israel would not cooperate with national investigations has been an obstacle in at least one case concerning complicity in Israeli crimes – that of the Dutch crane company, Riwal, in The Netherlands. In 2009, Al-Haq lodged a criminal complaint against Riwal (both the company and its directors) under The Netherlands' International Crimes Act which provides for jurisdiction over international crimes committed extra-territorially by Dutch nationals. The Dutch prosecutor investigated the company for its involvement in constructing the wall and settlements in the West Bank but needed to carry out a search of the Tel Aviv branch office in order to know the full extent of the company's activities.[101] The prosecutor eventually decided not to pursue the case citing the predicted lack of cooperation by the Israeli authorities in the investigation as one of the reasons for the decision.[102]

Although Israeli non-cooperation has generally not posed an obstacle to the UJ cases targeting Israeli perpetrators that have reached the stage of investigation, the reason is that most of these cases have focused on high-level officials whose involvement in crimes is based on their command responsibility (their position of effective command or authority over subordinates who have physically perpetrated crimes). Therefore, the information required to implicate them has been obtainable from open sources.[103]

---

100   For example, the Mauritanian general Ely Ould Dah was convicted under UJ laws by a French court for the crime of torture, even though the prosecuting authorities were unable to carry out any territorial investigations; *see* Ould Dah v France, App. No. 13113/03, 2009 Eur. Ct. H.R. For a review of cases demonstrating that prosecutions have generally involved cooperation between prosecuting and territorial State authorities in the gathering of evidence, *see* HRW UJ in Europe.

101   Al Haq, *Prosecutor dismisses war crimes case against Riwal* (May 14, 2013), http://www .alhaq.org/advocacy/targets/accountability/71-riwal/704-prosecutor-dismisses-war -crimes-case-against-riwal. Statement of investigators in the case (personal communication) (Mar. 2011).

102   National Public Prosecutor's Office (Rotterdam), Letter of dismissal (May 13, 2013) [*hereinafter* Riwal Letter of Dismissal], http://www.alhaq.org/images/stories/Brief_Landelijk _Parket_13-05-2013_ENG__a_Sj_crona_Van_Stigt_Advocaten.pdf.

103   *See* PCHR UJ. An exception is the case of Doron Almog in the United Kingdom. Almog had discussed on Israeli army radio how he had ordered the destruction of 59 homes in Rafah and this statement was relied upon to demonstrate his direct responsibility for the crime; Statement of Daniel Machover, solicitor in the case (private communication) (Mar. 2016).

However, there are problems with the strategy of pursuing only high-ranking officials, for such perpetrators are generally shielded from prosecution. In future, therefore, it may be advisable (for the reasons reviewed below), to shift to a strategy of pursuing middle- and lower-ranking officials or private persons. However, the difficulty which is then likely to arise is that the evidence needed to implicate perpetrators will tend not to be in the public domain and therefore not easily obtainable without the cooperation of the Israeli government, which will likely not be forthcoming. Furthermore, when any case approaches the stage of prosecution – even cases that have relied on open source evidence to reach the investigation stage – the national authorities of the forum State will be likely to want to carry out their own investigations in Israel or the oPt, in order to pursue the case further. Israeli non-cooperation with investigations is therefore likely to create practical difficulties in gathering evidence in future cases, thus posing an obstacle that will need to be overcome.

IV   Ways Forward

This review of the UJ cases brought against Israeli perpetrators shows that no case has reached the stage of prosecution despite the fact that evidence of crimes has generally been compelling enough to persuade courts or national prosecutors to open investigations into the alleged perpetrators. In the majority of cases, forum State governments have, in response to Israeli lobbying, taken some form of legislative or political action that has either prevented the case from going ahead or has made it more difficult to bring future cases. Furthermore, in two of the three cases reviewed here that were ostensibly thwarted by technical obstacles to the exercise of jurisdiction – the *Al-Daraj* case in Spain and the *Ayalon* case in The Netherlands – it is probable that political opposition played a role in preventing the cases from succeeding. In particular, in Spain, political pressure may have affected the progress of the case and the decision of the Appeals Court not to investigate, and in The Netherlands, it seems that political pressure was behind the delay in reaching a decision on immunity that ultimately prevented the case from going ahead. In other words, politics has been the main obstacle to UJ cases brought against Israeli officials.

A   *Reasons to Continue Pursuing UJ*
This begs the question of whether Palestinian victims and the human rights organizations and lawyers representing them should continue pursuing UJ litigation given that the odds appear to be stacked so heavily against achieving

a prosecution and conviction of alleged perpetrators. Whilst it is reasonable to suggest that Palestinians should, as a result, stop engaging in UJ litigation there are several factors that militate in favor of a decision to continue pursuing UJ cases, at least for the time being.

Firstly, it is clear that achieving legal accountability for Israeli crimes is a paramount need for Palestinians, given their subjugation to an on-going regime of widespread and systematic human rights abuse in the form of Israel's occupation of the oPt, in which Israel enjoys almost complete impunity.[104] Apart from the jurisdiction of the ICC, which has recently become available as result of Palestine's membership of the ICC – and the potential of which remains uncertain – UJ litigation represents one of the only mechanisms currently available for achieving legal accountability for Palestinian victims of Israeli crimes; for that reason, arguably even if only as a matter of principle, UJ litigation should continue to be pursued.[105]

Secondly, despite the setbacks that have occurred, most countries are moving towards a greater acceptance and application of the principle of UJ. This suggests that the likelihood of there being a successful case against an Israeli perpetrator will increase with time. For a start, most countries have incorporated some form of UJ legislation into their domestic law. According to a survey carried out by Amnesty International in 2012 for example, 147 States have laws providing for UJ over one or more international crimes.[106] Similarly, the International Committee of the Red Cross (ICRC) reported in 2014 that around 100 States had established UJ over serious violations of international humanitarian law.[107]

Furthermore, on the international level, States have signaled a commitment to developing and implementing UJ. In particular, since 2009 the Sixth Committee of the UN General Assembly has annually discussed "the scope and application of UJ" and passed an annual resolution reiterating its commit-

---

104   As to the subjugation of the Palestinians to a long-standing regime of human rights violations and the existence of a prolonged situation of impunity, *see* U.N. General Assembly, *Report of the United Nations Fact-Finding Mission on the Gaza Conflict*, U.N. Doc. A/HRC/28 (Sep. 25, 2009), 1958, paras. 198–209.

105   Palestine acceded to the Rome Statute of the ICC in January 2015 and shortly afterwards the prosecutor of the ICC opened a preliminary examination into the situation in Palestine. For the prospects that ICC membership will lead to a trial of Israeli officials for war crimes, *see* Salma Karmi-Ayyoub, *Palestinian membership of the International Criminal Court*, Al Jazeera Centre for Studies (July 9, 2015), http://studies.aljazeera.net/en/reports/2015/07/20157972711804703.html.

106   Amnesty UJ, at 2.

107   UNSG UJ Report, para. 63.

ment "to fighting impunity" through UJ.[108] In 2014, it also established a working group to develop the concept of UJ.[109] Moreover, States' ratifications of the Rome Statute and of its complementarity principle – which puts the onus for prosecuting international crimes in the first instance on States – has brought into being a greater commitment to investigating and prosecuting international crimes at the national level.[110]

For instance, the European Union has made a policy commitment to ending impunity for perpetrators of international crimes within its borders and has created an infrastructure for transnational cooperation in the investigation of crimes, demonstrating a recognition of an emerging practice of formal UJ litigation and the need for it to be systematic and coordinated.[111] Several European countries, as well as the US and Canada, have also established specialized units dedicated to the prosecution of international crimes and to the detection of international crime suspects when they enter the country.[112]

---

108   *See, e.g.*, G.A. Res. 68/117, *The scope and application of the principle of universal jurisdiction*, U.N. Doc. A/RES/68/117 (Dec. 18, 2013).

109   For a description of the UJ agenda item, *see* Sixth Committee, U.N. General Assembly, Sixty-sixth session: The scope and application of the principle of universal jurisdiction (Agenda item 84), http://www.un.org/en/ga/sixth/66/ccopeAppUniJuri.shtml. For the establishment of the universal jurisdiction working group, *see* G.A. Res. 69/124, *The scope and application of the principle of universal jurisdiction*, U.N. Doc. A/RES/69/124 (Dec. 18, 2014).

110   Rome Statute of the International Criminal Court arts. 1 & 17, 2187 U.N.T.S. 90 (July 17, 1998) [*hereinafter* Rome Statute].

111   In 2002, the EU established a network of national contact points to ensure cooperation between national authorities in the investigation of international crimes. The network includes European countries, as well as the US and Canada, all of which have specialized units for the prosecution of international crimes and/or procedures for detecting international crimes suspects when they enter the country. In 2011, a secretariat for the network was established; *see* Council Decision 494/JHA of 13 June 2002, *setting up a European network of contact points in respect of persons responsible for genocide, crimes against humanity and war crimes*, 2002 O.J. (L 167), 1–2; Council Decision 335/JHA of 8 May 2003, on the investigation and prosecution of genocide, crimes against humanity and war crimes, 2003 O.J. (L 118), 12–14. *See also* Eurojust, Members of the Genocide Network, http://www.eurojust.europa.eu/Practitioners/Genocide-Network/Pages/members.aspx; Network Secretariats, http://www.eurojust.europa.eu/about/structure/Pages/network-secretariats.aspx.

112   Redress and FIDH, *Strategies for the effective investigation and prosecution of serious international crimes: the practice of specialized war crimes units* (Dec. 2010) [*hereinafter* Redress and FIDH Report], http://www.redress.org/downloads/publications/The_Practice_of_Specialised_War_Crimes_Units_Dec_2010.pdf.

In addition, the trend of increased commitment to UJ is not confined to Western countries and there seems to be a greater willingness (which did not previously exist) amongst some non-Western countries to pursuing UJ. This is demonstrated in recent cases, such as the trial in 2015 of Hissene Habre, former president of Chad, in Senegal[113] and the opening of a criminal investigation in 2014 by the Argentinean Federal Court into complaints filed by members of a Paraguayan indigenous group over crimes committed by the Paraguayan government in the late 1960s and 1970s.[114]

In short there is a global UJ movement which is growing in strength. As the ICRC has put it, "... the exercise of the principle of universal jurisdiction is gaining more acceptance and ... states are willing to prevent and tackle impunity for war crimes perpetrated beyond their borders".[115] This would seem, therefore, to be the wrong time to abandon bringing UJ cases against Israeli perpetrators.

Finally, there are positive by-products of even unsuccessful UJ litigation. For example, the process of bringing litigation provides a platform on which to showcase and raise awareness of Israeli crimes. In particular, litigation may attract publicity to a case, helping to ensure that issues which would not otherwise be adequately reported in the media – such as the crimes that form the basis of the litigation, or Israel's culture of impunity that has caused victims to seek accountability in a foreign jurisdiction – receive media coverage. Litigation that does not result in a prosecution or conviction can also provide preliminary rulings in the form of decisions by prosecutors and courts of first instance to open investigations that confirm the existence of strong evidence of the commission of international crimes by Israeli officials, and can impose a *de facto* ban on Israeli travel to certain countries. Such actions contribute to Israel's isolation and therefore help to apply pressure on it to desist from its unlawful actions.

In addition, indirect benefits can be derived from the investigation of cases that do not reach the stage of prosecution. For instance, the investigation by the

---

113 Human Rights Watch, *Q&A: The case of Hissene Habre before the Extraordinary African Chambers in Senegal* (Aug. 31, 2015), https://www.hrw.org/news/2015/08/31/ qa-case-hissene-habre-extraordinary-african-chambers-senegal.

114 International Working Group for Indigenous Affairs, *Ache people of Paraguay: Madrid conference on a forgotten genocide* (June 12, 2014), http://www.iwgia .org/news/search-news?news_id=1014. Rick Learns, *Genocide of the Ache people of Paraguay will be tried in Argentina*, Indian Country Today Media Network (Aug. 18, 2014), http://indiancountrytodaymedianetwork.com/2014/08/18/genocide-ache-people -paraguay-will-be-tried-argentina-156444.

115 UNSG UJ Report, para. 64.

PROSPECTS FOR SUCCESS?

Dutch prosecutor of the company Riwal in The Netherlands, for involvement in constructing the wall and settlements in the West Bank, caused Riwal to voluntarily divest itself from its Israeli operations.[116] The prosecutor's decision to investigate the case, which would have involved his making the determination that Riwal's activities were capable of amounting to an aiding and abetting or war crimes in order to allow him to invoke his powers of investigation, also constitutes evidence that certain types of corporate involvement in the Israeli occupation amount to (and will be viewed by prosecutors as amounting to) crimes, which is useful in advocacy initiatives that try to dissuade companies from involvement in the occupation. Therefore, UJ litigation, even if ultimately unsuccessful, can make an important contribution to efforts to isolate and apply pressure on Israel for its human rights violations.

B   *Recommendations for Future Cases*

There are several reasons for continuing to resort to UJ cases as part of the struggle to achieve Palestinian rights. The fact remains, however, that prosecutions of Israeli officials face obstacles not encountered in prosecuting perpetrators from other less powerful countries. In order for there to be a successful case against an Israeli perpetrator in the future these obstacles will therefore need to be overcome.

As a starting point, lawyers and human rights organizations engaged in litigation should be less opportunistic and more strategic in their case selection.[117] This means that the merits of a case should be assessed in terms not only of the strength of the evidence but also in terms of the ability of the case to overcome the various obstacles it will encounter in any given jurisdiction. In order to reduce the likelihood of political interference in cases, for example, it is worth considering bringing litigation in suitable UJ countries outside the Western world and which are more sympathetic to the prosecution of Israeli perpetrators.[118]

---

116   Riwal Letter of Dismissal.

117   This is not to suggest that lawyers have not carefully considered the merits of UJ cases before bringing them, but the author's impression is that there has sometimes been a tendency, especially during the early years of bringing litigation, to select cases based mainly on whether the perpetrator is known to have plans to travel to a foreign jurisdiction with little consideration of the obstacles to the case.

118   For instance South Africa might provide a promising jurisdiction in light of the fact that South African police have reportedly agreed to execute arrest warrants against Israeli officials for their role in the attack on the Gaza Freedom Flotilla should they enter the country; *see* Charlotte Silver, *Top Israeli officials face arrest in Spain, South Africa*, Electronic Intifada (Nov. 17, 2015), https://electronicintifada.net/blogs/charlotte-silver/

Moreover, the review of the obstacles encountered by UJ cases suggests that focusing specifically on lower-level perpetrators, on cases in which perpetrators or victims are nationals or residents of forum States, and in ensuring that litigation is better integrated into broader advocacy strategies will also increase the chance of success. Each of these ideas is explored in turn below.

i   *Focusing on Lower-level Perpetrators*

Focusing UJ litigation on lower-lever perpetrators has several potential advantages. Firstly, such perpetrators will not have diplomatic immunity and cases against them might provoke less of a political backlash from Israel and from forum State governments. Secondly, such perpetrators, if they are not expecting cases to be filed against them, will not take the same precautions, as many high-level Israeli officials do, of refraining from traveling to UJ jurisdictions or of concealing their travel plans so that it is not known when they are visiting a jurisdiction until it is too late to file a case.

Thirdly, focusing UJ cases on lower-level officials makes the most efficient use of the jurisdictions currently available for prosecuting Israeli perpetrators in the light of Palestine's recent accession to the Rome Statute of the ICC. The reason is that, under the Rome Statute's complementarity principle, the ICC is barred from investigating any case that a "State which has jurisdiction over it" is investigating or prosecuting. The State with jurisdiction usually refers to the territorial or nationality State but could conceivably include a State that is investigating a case under UJ laws.[119] Thus, a national UJ investigation might bar the ICC from proceeding with the same case whilst, paradoxically, a national jurisdiction in which UJ litigation is brought could, under the subsidiarity principle, decide that the ICC is the correct forum for the investigation.[120]

---

top-israeli-officials-face-arrest-spain-south-africa. Although for the suggestion that the ANC government is "selling out the Palestinian struggle in favour of an elitist agenda of the leadership's business interests and wealth accumulation" and that efforts to secure prosecutions of South African nationals that serve in the Israeli army have therefore been unsuccessful, *see* Eddie Cottle, *South Africa: Will the ANC government ever prosecute South Africans serving in the Israeli Defence Force?* All Africa (Apr. 21, 2015), http://allafrica.com/stories/201504211399.html.

119   Rome Statute art. 17(1).

120   For example, under Spanish law, a UJ case cannot proceed under the subsidiarity principle if an investigation into the same case has been initiated by the territorial or nationality state or by an international court; *see* Fernandez, 724. Indeed, in the Gaza Freedom Flotilla case that was opened in Spain in 2010, the concurrence of several jurisdictions – Israel, Turkey and the ICC's preliminary examination – caused the investigating judge to refer the case to the Spanish Supreme Court so that it could decide on Spain's jurisdiction

PROSPECTS FOR SUCCESS? 131

In order to avoid such a situation, UJ litigation should focus on cases that the ICC cannot or is unlikely to want to prosecute, namely against lower-level perpetrators (the ICC tends to focus on high-ranking officials in accordance with its purpose of prosecuting only the most serious crimes) and on cases that otherwise fall outside of the ICC's jurisdiction.

Lower-level perpetrators that might be suitable targets for UJ cases and that, until now, have not been the subject of litigation, are the many officials involved in authorizing or executing crimes that Israel commits in a non-military context as part of its occupation of the West Bank (such as home demolitions, land confiscations and settlement construction). Unlike lower-ranking soldiers involved in military operations whose identity is difficult to discover without Israeli government cooperation, and where the evidence required to prosecute them is often not in the public domain, the officials involved in "governance crimes" tend to have formal positions within the State bureaucracy so that their identities are easy to obtain, and much of the evidence of their crimes is a matter of public record.[121]

ii   *Cases in Which Perpetrators or Victims have Strong Links to Foreign Jurisdictions*

There are indications that a move away from bringing pure UJ cases to those involving the exercise of extra-territorial jurisdiction more broadly could also be a useful strategy. For a start, it is now only possible in certain jurisdictions, as a result of the imposition of legislative restrictions on the application of UJ, to bring cases in which either the perpetrators or victims are nationals or residents of the forum State. Indeed, there have been several recent, relatively successful cases in which victims have been nationals of forum States. In 2010, a Spanish court opened an investigation into Israeli Prime Minister Binyamin Netanyahu and other officials for their role in the attack on the Gaza Freedom

---

and both the investigating judge and the Spanish prosecutor expressed the view that the referral of the case to the ICC should be preferred; *see* JCI No. 5, Decision of 17.6.2014 – Auto, Diligencias Pre-vias 197/10 (cited in Fernandez, n70). For a discussion of Spanish laws that prevent the investigation of extra-territorial crimes over which the ICC could have jurisdiction and how this inverts the ICC's complimentary principle, *see* Fernandez, 725 & n71.

121   For example, a B'tselem report on settlements describes in detail the bureaucratic process of establishing Israeli settlements and the governmental and quasi-governmental agencies involved making it easy to discover which officials are involved in the process of establishing settlements. *See* B'tselem, *Land Grab: Israel's settlement policy in the West Bank* (May 2002), at 20–22, https://www.btselem.org/download/200205_land_grab_eng .pdf.

Flotilla following applications by Spanish victims which lead to a finding of strong evidence of the commission of international crimes and for a short period of time (before likely political interference in the case) to suspects' names being listed on the police database for arrest should they enter the jurisdiction. In 2014, a Turkish court also issued arrest warrants against several serious Israeli military commanders following the start of a trials *in absentia* for their role in authorizing the Gaza Freedom Flotilla attack[122] and it is reported that following an application by a South African victim of the attack, the South African police have agreed to enforce the Turkish arrest warrants if wanted persons to step onto South African soil.[123]

Moreover, in order to help overcome the presence requirement that exists in many jurisdictions and to increase the willingness of national prosecutors to investigate cases, it is important to focus on perpetrators who are nationals or residents of forum countries. The fact that, for example, around one-third of ICC member States have Rome Statute implementing legislation allowing for the exercise of extra-territorial jurisdiction over nationals (and sometimes also residents) who have committed international crimes provides an avenue for bringing such cases.[124]

The types of perpetrators that could be targeted under an extra-territorial application of jurisdiction include persons who have dual Israeli and forum State nationality and persons who reside permanently or for significant periods of time in forum jurisdictions. Consideration should also be given to pursuing litigation against the many foreign-domiciled companies and cor-

---

122 Nora Barrows-Freidman, *Turkish court issues "historic" arrest warrants for Israeli army commanders*, Electronic Intifada (June 2, 2014), https://electronicintifada.net/blogs/nora-barrows-friedman/turkish-court-issues-historic-arrest-warrants-israeli-army-commanders; IHH Humanitarian Relief Foundation Commission on Human Rights and Law, *The Mavi Marmara Case* (Dec. 10, 2012), at 6, http://www.ihh.org.tr/fotograf/yayinlar/dokumanlar/134-Mavi%20Marmara%20Hukuk%20Raporu%20-%2010%20Aral%C4%B1k%202012%20-mavi-marmara-legal-report.pdf. The case in Turkey was reportedly brought on more than one jurisdictional basis, including a purported territorial basis as the *Mavi Marmara* ship on which the Israeli raid was carried out is a Turkish ship (although flagged by the Comoros islands), as well as on a UJ basis as a result of the nature of the crimes.

123 Charlotte Silver, *Top Israeli officials face arrest in Spain, South Africa*, Electronic Intifada (Nov. 17, 2015), https://electronicintifada.net/blogs/charlotte-silver/top-israeli-officials-face-arrest-spain-south-africa.

124 Amnesty International, *Rome Statute Implementation Report Card: Part One*, AI-Index IOR 53/011/2010 (2010), at 7, https://www.amnesty.org/en/documents/IOR53/011/2010/en/.

PROSPECTS FOR SUCCESS? 133

porate officers involved in Israeli human rights violations in the oPt.[125] The existence of campaigns that have raised public awareness about the issue of corporate complicity in Israel's occupation, and into which such litigation could be integrated, suggests that bringing cases against companies domiciled in forum States for involvement in Israeli crimes could well be a worthwhile endeavor.[126]

iii   *Advocacy Initiatives that Strengthen UJ*

Finally, Palestinians and their supporters must understand the extent of the political opposition that exists to UJ cases against Israeli perpetrators. They should therefore ensure that, in addition to preparing cases for submission to courts and prosecutors, time and effort are spent on activities that are ancillary to legal work: on advocacy initiatives that create a less hostile and more con-ducive political environment for bringing cases, for instance. Indeed it is no coincidence that all successful UJ prosecutions to date have either concerned crimes that are subject to virtually universal condemnation, such as those committed under Nazi Germany, in Rwanda and in the former Yugoslavia – where international tribunals have been established to prosecute offenders – or in countries that have a reputation for being conflict-ridden places where atrocities have taken place, and in which, consequently, the "politics" of bring-ing cases is relatively low.

This suggests that, in order for there to be a successful UJ case against an Israeli perpetrator, the notion of prosecuting Israeli officials needs also to become uncontroversial. Of course, this is a difficult position to achieve in the light of the extent of Western support for Israel but there are, nonetheless, cer-tain measures that could be taken to help foster a sense amongst publics of forum States that Israel's occupation is unacceptable and that UJ is therefore a necessary measure for addressing Israeli impunity for the commission of seri-ous international crimes.

Firstly, there should be more effective advocacy generally aimed at raising awareness of Israel's egregious human rights record. Secondly, and as was evi-dent from the ruling in the *Al-Daraj* case in Spain, the fact that Palestinians are unable to obtain an effective remedy for serious human rights violations

---

125   See the website of the Israeli NGO "Who Profits" for a list of wholly or partly foreign-owned companies that are active in the OPT: http://www.whoprofits.org.

126   For public campaigns that have raised awareness of the issue of corporate complicity in the Israeli occupation, *see, e.g.*, Boycott Divestment and Sanctions movement, Stop G4S, https://bdsmovement.net/activecamps/g4s; Stolen Beauty, Boycott Ahava products and expose the ugly secrets from the Dead Sea, http://www.stolenbeauty.org/.

in Israel itself needs to be more effectively demonstrated. In particular, foreign courts and prosecutors need to be persuaded of the fact that, despite Israel's image as a law-abiding, Western-style democracy, the Israeli judicial system allows Israeli officials, particularly high-ranking officials and those implementing State policy, to enjoy impunity for crimes committed against Palestinians.

Finally, UJ cases should be better integrated into broader advocacy strategies that build popular support for the objective of achieving accountability for Israeli crimes. Ideally UJ litigation would be in the vanguard of a series of initiatives to raise awareness of and create change in those aspects of Israeli policy that are reflected in the case under litigation. For example, in the UK in recent years, there have been many advocacy initiatives aimed at raising awareness of the treatment of Palestinian children in Israeli military detention. For example, there was a government-funded lawyers' delegation to the oPt in 2011,[127] and campaigning groups have written numerous letters to the government on the issue.[128] In addition, a debate on the topic of Palestinian child detainees was held in parliament in 2016, in which the member of parliament leading the discussion recommended that a watch list should be compiled of persons responsible for the ill-treatment of Palestinian children in order that they can be arrested and prosecuted under UJ laws if they enter the UK.[129] These advocacy initiatives are likely to have created a greater chance of success for future UJ in the UK concerning the ill-treatment of Palestinian children, or at least they have ensured that there is popular support for the prosecution of such cases.

V   Conclusion

This analysis of the challenges and obstacles to prosecuting Israeli officials under UJ laws has sought to demonstrate that the main reason there has not yet been a successful prosecution of an Israeli perpetrator is Israeli political opposition to such cases, combined with a lack of political will on the part of

---

127   Children in Military Custody/Foreign and Commonwealth Office, *Children in Military Custody* (June 2012), at 2, http://www.childreninmilitarycustody.org.uk/wp-content/uploads/2012/03/Children_in_Military_Custody_Full_Report.pdf.

128   *See, e.g.*, Lawyers for Palestinian Human Rights, *Concerning the forcible transfer of Palestinian children in violation of the Fourth Geneva Convention*, Letter to Foreign and Commonwealth Office (June 1, 2012), http://lphr.org.uk/wp-content/uploads/2014/04/LPHR-DCI-Urgent-Action-Forcible-Transfer-1.pdf.

129   Hansard HC, Vol. 604 (no.92), col 81WH (Jan. 6, 2016) [U.K.].

foreign governments to support prosecutions. Although it will be difficult to overcome these obstacles, UJ should continue to be pursued since it offers one of the only mechanisms currently available for challenging Israeli impunity for human rights violations committed against Palestinians. Furthermore, the indications are that the UJ movement globally is growing in strength, meaning that the likelihood of a successful case against an Israeli perpetrator will increase with time. In addition, there are positive by-products of the process of bringing litigation for the struggle to achieve of Palestinian human rights: even unsuccessful litigation helps to raise awareness of Israeli crimes and to imposes a cost on complicity in the Israeli occupation.

In order to increase the likelihood of success in future cases, however, the cases that are brought must be more strategically chosen. In particular, there should be an increased focus on lower-level perpetrators and on cases in which either the perpetrator or the victim have links to the forum jurisdiction. There should also be a greater emphasis on advocacy efforts that help to create a more conducive political environment for successfully bringing such cases to court.

THE PALESTINE YEARBOOK OF
INTERNATIONAL LAW XIX (2016) 136–176

Occupants, Beware of BITs: Applicability of Investment Treaties to Occupied Territories

*Ofilio J. Mayorga**

I   Introduction   137
II The Status of Treaties in Occupied Territories   144
    A   The Traditional View: Prior Treaties do not Bind the Occupant   145
    B   The Contemporary View: Treaties as "Laws in Force" in Occupied Territories   152
III Are Occupants Immune to the Arbitral Jurisdiction of BITs in Force in Occupied Territories?   161
    A   The Limits of the Occupant's Immunity from Local Law   163
IV The Co-Application of the Law of Belligerent Occupation and BITs   168
    A   The Jurisdiction ratione personae of Investment Tribunals and the Concept of "Protected Persons" under the Fourth Geneva Convention   170
    B   Substantive Investment Protections during Belligerent Occupation   172
V   Conclusion   176

---

*   International Associate, Foley Hoag LLP; LL.M. '10 (University of Michigan Law School, Ann Arbor); M.A.L.D. '09 (The Fletcher School of Law and Diplomacy, Tufts University); *Licenciado en Derecho*' 06 (Universidad Americana, Nicaragua); Member of the Bars of Nicaragua and New York. Email: omayorga@foleyhoag.com. The author would like to thank Pierre D'Argent, Sarah Cartmell, Professor Dino Kritsiotis, Andrew Loewenstein and participants at the 24th Annual Conference of the Australian and New Zealand Society of International Law (ANZSIL) for their generous comments on previous drafts. Liz Glusman and Carol Kim also provided outstanding support in completing this article. All opinions and errors remain the author's own, and should not be attributed to Foley Hoag LLP or to any other person.

I Introduction

Foreign investors may suffer losses when the territory in which they had invested falls under military occupation. The occupation authorities could either seize[1] or destroy foreign-owned assets in the course of military operations or as part of an annexation plan. They may also enact regulations affecting the value of foreign investments.[2]

In assessing the legality of the occupant's acts, civilians would normally turn to international humanitarian law (IHL).[3] Indeed, one of the goals of IHL is to minimize the risk of economic loss to civilians, including nationals of neutral States, in times of armed conflict.[4] To that end, IHL prohibits the confiscation,[5] pillaging[6] and wanton destruction[7] of private property in occupied territories.

---

1   Germany's spoliation of occupied territories during World War II included the confiscation of property and the "[s]eizure of foreign holdings in the banks and private safety deposit vaults"; *see* Jacob Robinson, *Transfer of Property in Enemy Occupied territory*, 39 Am. J. Int'l L. 216, 219–220 (1945). Another instance where an Occupying Power interfered with foreign economic interests in occupied territory was after the Six-Day War of 1967, when Israel seized several oil fields in the Sinai Peninsula. These oil fields were partially owned by the Italian state oil corporation; *see* Edward R Cummings, *Oil Resources in Occupied Arab Territories under the Law of Belligerent Occupation*, 9 J. Int'l L. & Econ. 533 (1974).

2   *See* Ernst H. Feilchenfeld, *The International Economic Law of Belligerent Occupation*, Carnegie Endowment for International Peace (1942), at 86–87 [describing Germany's extensive use of its regulatory powers in occupied Belgium during World War I: "During the War of 1914–1918 Belgium was subjected to a regulated economy through occupation decrees governing production and consumption, prices, labor, banking, etc."].

3   The terms "international humanitarian law (IHL)", "the laws of armed conflict (LOAC)", and "laws of war" are used interchangeably in this article to describe the rules that govern the conduct of belligerents during active armed hostilities and occupation.

4   *See* Gerhard Von Glahn, The Occupation of Enemy Territory: A Commentary on the Law and Practice of Belligerent Occupation 197 (1957) [*hereinafter* Glahn]; discussing the status of private neutral property in occupied territories: "Little needs to be said about the position of private property owned by neutrals of and located in territory under military occupation. Just as private neutral citizens are subject to the same treatment as is meted out to the indigenous population, so private neutral property shares in every respect the treatment accorded to private property owned by citizens of the occupied area".

5   Hague Regulations annexed to the Hague Convention No IV – Laws and Customs of War on Land art. 46, Oct. 18, 1907, 205 Cons. T.S. 277 [*hereinafter* Hague Regulations]; "Family honor and rights, the lives of persons, and private property, as well as religious convictions and practice, must be respected. Private property cannot be confiscated".

6   Hague Regulations art. 47; "Pillage is formally forbidden".

7   Geneva Convention Relative to the Protection of Civilian Persons in Time of War art. 53, Aug. 12, 1949, 75 U.N.T.S. 287 [*hereinafter* Fourth Geneva Convention]; "Any destruction by the Occupying Power of real or personal property belonging individually or collectively to

IHL also limits the occupant's regulatory powers to what is necessary to restore and maintain public order and civil life.[8]

Despite the inviolability of private property in wartime, IHL treaties do not allow victims of IHL violations to seek redress for their economic losses.[9] Historically, civilians had to wait for the conclusion of a peace treaty to asses the feasibility of a claim against the occupant.[10] Today, however, civilians may file complaints before regional human rights courts or even the International Court of Justice (ICJ) through the mechanism of diplomatic protection.[11] But

---

private persons, or to the State, or to other public authorities, or to social or co-operative organizations, is prohibited, except where such destruction is rendered absolutely necessary by military operations".

8   Hague Regulations art. 43. This provision lays out the occupant's legislative powers: "The authority of the legitimate power having in fact passed into the hands of the occupant, the latter shall take all the measures to restore, and ensure, as far as possible, public order and safety, while respecting, unless absolutely prevented, the laws in force in the country". Article 43 was amplified, rather than superseded, by the Fourth Geneva Convention art. 64. *See, e.g.*, R. T. Yingling & R. W. Ginnane, *The Geneva Conventions of 1949*, 46 Am. J. Int'l L. 393, 422 (1952); "Under [Article 64], the criminal law and courts of the occupied territory must be continued in effect for ordinary criminal offenses committed by the local inhabitants and which do not involve the occupation forces. This principle is an amplification of Article 43 of the Hague Regulations and is consistent with American practice in Germany and Japan during World War II". Accordingly, both provisions must be read together in assessing the legality of the occupant's acts.

9   *See, generally*, Harvard Program on Humanitarian Policy and Conflict Research, *Policy Brief Reparation for Civilians Living in the Occupied Palestinian Territory (OPT): Opportunities and Constraints under International Law* (May 2010), at 9, http://www.hpcrresearch.org/publications/applied-research/hpcr-policy-briefs; "Thus, the truth of the matter is that IHL, while arguably affirming that victims of IHL violations have a conceptual right to compensation, does not take that one step further to actually allow victims to enforce that right".

10   *See* Von Glahn, 189; explaining that compensation for losses in occupied territory may have only been possible after a peace treaty was signed. In short, compensation depended on the will of the occupant or the victim's own government: "To whom can the owner turn for compensation for his losses when an occupant violates the immunity of private property? It is unfortunate but true that international law does not provide an answer to this question. In some instances the treaty of peace following the military occupation provided for compensation; normally, however, unless the occupant voluntarily pays for the loss sustained, the owner can turn only to his own government for payment, after the end of occupation".

11   *See* Robert Kolb, Advanced Introduction to International Humanitarian Law 195 (2014) [*hereinafter* Kolb]; "Civil complaints by individuals for reparation of losses flowing from war crimes or other breaches of IHL are possible at international human rights courts,

OCCUPANTS, BEWARE OF BITS   139

these options have their own limitations and may not always be available to
the victims of IHL violations.

With the proliferation of Bilateral Investment Treaties (BITs) since the
1990s, civilians may now turn to investment-treaty arbitration to challenge the
acts of the occupant in real time and seek compensation for their losses.[12] In
fact, several Ukrainian companies are invoking the Russia-Ukraine BIT of 1998
to bring investment claims against Russia for the alleged seizure of their assets
in occupied Crimea.[13] Russia has refused to participate in these proceedings
because it considers that the claimants' investments fall outside the scope of
protection of the Russia-Ukraine BIT.[14]

---

like the [European Court of Human Rights], or in front of international tribunals such as
the ICJ by the device of diplomatic protection (in other words, a State has to spouse the
claim of the individual possessing its nationality and bring it in its name to the international court)".

12   Investment treaties are international legal instruments entered into by two or more
States to protect the economic interests of their nationals in foreign territories. Each
contracting party undertakes to provide investors from other countries with legal protection against egregious governmental interference, such as failure to accord fair and
equitable treatment, expropriation without just compensation, discrimination based
on national origin, and gross negligence in preventing physical harm. In case of breach,
investment treaties usually entitle foreign investors to submit their claims against the
host State to international arbitration. These agreements include Bilateral Investment
Treaties (BITs), regional economic agreements such as NAFTA and DR-CAFTA, and
Free Trade Agreements (FTAs). The first BIT was concluded in 1959 between Germany
and Pakistan. Today more than 3,000 investment treaties are in force. *See, e.g.*, Latham &
Watkins Client Alert, *Investment Treaty Arbitration: A Primer* (July 29, 2013), https://www
.lw.com/thoughtLeadership/LW-investment-treaty-arbitration-primer.

13   The majority of States do not recognize Russia's annexation of Crimea; *see* G.A. Res
68/262, *Territorial Integrity of Ukraine*, U.N. Doc. A/RES/68.282 (Mar. 27, 2014). Professor
Michael Bothe has correctly pointed out that non-recognition in this case means that
Crimea is currently under Russia's occupation and, therefore, the Hague Regulations and
the Fourth Geneva Convention apply; *see* Michael Bothe, *The Current Status of Crimea:
Russian Territory, Occupied Territory or What?* 53 Military L. & L. War Rev. 99, 101 (2014).
In support of the proposition that Russia's annexation of Crimea in 2014 was unlawful,
see, generally, Thomas D Grant, Aggression Against Ukraine: Territory, Responsibility, and
International Law (2015) [*hereinafter* Grant].

14   *See* Luke Eric Peterson, *First UNCITRAL arbitral tribunal is finalized to hear claim
that Russia is liable for harm befalling investments in annexed Crimean Peninsula*, Int'l
Arbitration Reporter (July 14, 2015), https://www.iareporter.com/articles/first-uncitral
-arbitral-tribunal-is-finalized-to-hear-claim-that-russia-is-liable-for-harm-befalling
-investments-in-annexed-crimean-peninsula.

Russia's non-appearence, however, does not remove the obvious jurisdictional hurdles the claimants must overcome to succeed in these claims. Like virtually all investment treaties, the Russia-Ukraine BIT protects investments made by investors of either Contracting Party in the territory of the other Contracting Party.[15] Because the disputed investments in these cases were not made by Ukrainian investors in Russian territory – in fact, they remain Ukrainian investments in Ukrainian territory despite Russia's purported annexation of Crimea – the chances of investment tribunals deciding these claims on the merits are thin.[16] But if they do, and if Russia is held liable, they may find, either explicitly or implicitly, that Crimea is now Russian territory.[17]

---

15 *See, e.g.*, arts. 1(1–2) & 2(2) of the Russian Federation–Ukraine BIT (1998) http://invest mentpolicyhub.unctad.org/IIA/country/219/treaty/2859; "Article 1. Definitions: For the purposes of this Agreement: 1. "Investments" shall denote all kinds of property and intellectual values, which are put in by the investor of one Contracting Party on the territory of the other Contracting Party in conformity with the latter's legislation ... 4. "Territory" shall denote the territory of the Russian Federation or the territory of the Ukraine and also their respective exclusive economic zone and the continental shelf as defined in conformity with the international law. Article 2. Encouragement and Protection of Investments. 2. Each Contracting Party shall guarantee, in conformity with its legislation, the complete and unconditional legal protection of investments of investors of the other Contracting Party."

16 *See, e.g.*, Yarik Kryvoi, *Protecting Foreign Investors in Crimea: Is Investment Arbitration an Option?* CIS Arbitration Forum (July 29, 2014), http://www.cisarbitration.com/2014/07/29/ protecting-foreign-investors-in-crimea-is-investment-arbitration-an-option (suggesting that investment treaty claims are likely to be dismissed for lack of jurisdiction because Crimea is not part of Russian territory).

17 To avoid validating Russia's unlawful annexation, arbitral tribunals could decide that the Russia-Ukraine BIT applies extraterritorially. This would allow the tribunals to hold Russia liable under the Russia-Ukraine BIT while acknowledging that Russia's alleged wrongful conduct took place in what is still Ukrainian territory. However, the extraterritorial application of BITs as a result of the *de facto* control of one of the contracting parties over the territory of another State is extremely doubtful. In its Wall advisory opinion, the International Court of Justice (ICJ) found that the International Covenant on Civil and Political Rights (ICCPR) and the Convention on the Rights of the Child (CRC) applied to acts carried out by a State in the exercise of its jurisdiction outside its own territory. To support this finding, the Court relied on the fact that the scope of application clause in both treaties expressly covered "all individuals within [the State's] territory *and subject to its jurisdiction*" (emphasis added); *see* Legal Consequences of the Construction of a Wall in the Occupied Palestinian Territory, Advisory Opinion, 2004 I.C.J. Rep. 136, 102–113 (9 July). Likewise, the ICCPR's Human Rights Committee (HRC) has interpreted the phrase "within its territory *and subject to its jurisdiction*" in Article 2(1) of the ICCPR as a disjunctive conjunction (emphasis added); *see* Symeon Karagiannis, *The Territorial*

The latter scenario shows that the misapplication of investment treaties in situation of occupation could result in the judicial validation of unlawful territorial annexations. To avert this outcome, foreign investors should bring their claims in situations of occupation with the law of belligerent occupation. This is the only way investors could successfully invoke the legal protections of BITs without undermining the sovereignty of the occupied State.[18]

The thesis of this article is that occupants are bound by BITs in force in the occupied state.[19] Under Article 43 of the Hague Regulations of 1907, occupants

---

Application of Treaties, in The Oxford Guide to Treaties 320 (Duncan B. Hollis ed., 2012). This means that the ICCPR binds a State not just for acts within its territory but also in areas where the State exercises effective control, *i.e.*, in occupied territories. But unlike these and other human rights treaties which have been found to apply extraterritorially, BITs do not have "jurisdiction" clauses. Therefore, the scope of application of most BITs is restricted to the territory of the contracting parties and does not seem to extend to investments subject to the jurisdiction or control of a contracting party outside its own borders; *see, e.g.*, Russian Federation–Ukraine BIT, arts. 1(1), 1(4).

18   It has been suggested elsewhere that the law of occupation is "deficient" and does not adequately protect foreign investors in illegally annexed territories like Crimea. As a result, the argument goes, policy considerations would support extending the treaties of the annexing State, including its BITs, to the annexed territory by virtue of the "moving treaty-frontiers rule". *See, generally*, Richard Happe and Sebastian Wuschka, *Horror Vacui: Or Why Investment Treaties Should Apply to Illegally Annexed Territories*, 33 J. Int'l Arbitration 245 (2016). But the "moving treaty-frontiers" rule cannot be applied to instances of illegal annexation, even where the occupation endures across time. This is a rule of State succession; *see, e.g.*, Hubert Beemelmans, *State Succession in International Law: Remarks on Recent Theory and State praxis*, 15 B.U. Int'l L. J. 71, 99 (1997). As such, it presupposes the legal transfer of part of the territory of one State to the territory of another State; *see* Vienna Convention on Succession of States in Respect of Treaties art. 15, Aug. 23, 1978, 1946 U.N.T.S. 3. The application of the moving treaty-frontier rule to an illegally annexed territory – *i.e.* occupied territory – would result in the protection of foreign investments at the expense of the sovereignty of the ousted government. There is merit in searching for a pragmatic solution to the apparent legal vacuum foreign investors may confront in occupied territories. But as this article will show, the law of occupation is perfectly capable of safeguarding the economic interests of foreign investors under pre-occupation BITs while protecting the territorial integrity of the occupied State at the same time.

19   In a recent interview, Mark McNeill, a partner at a major international law firm, expressed a similar view while briefly commenting on the rights of non-Ukrainian investors against Russia for violations of BITs in force in Ukraine: "The general rule is that an occupying power must respect the existing laws in force in the occupied territory, which may include commitments made under investment treaties. As such, a non-Ukrainian investor could potentially hold the Russian Federation responsible for violations of

"shall take all the measures in [their] power to restore and ensure, as far as possible, public order and [civil life], while respecting, unless absolutely prevented, the laws in force in the country."[20] Where the constitution of the occupied State grants valid pre-occupation treaties the status of domestic law, Article 43 of the Hague Regulations requires the occupant to respect the BITs of the occupied State.[21] If so, foreign investors could bring investment-treaty claims against an occupant for the breach of their rights – as modified by the law of occupation – under the BITs of the *de jure* sovereign.

Thus, foreign investors who suffer losses in occupied territories should not bring their claims under BITs between the occupant and the investor's home country. Rather, foreign investors should invoke BITs between the occupied State and their home country.[22] To illustrate, if Russia unlawfully seizes the assets of a German investor in Crimea, the investor should file her claim under the Germany-Ukraine BIT instead of the Germany-Russia BIT.[23]

It could be argued that the occupant is not bound by the BITs of the displaced sovereign because it is not a party to any of them. To be sure, States are not bound by obligations to which they have not consented.[24] But in times of occupation, the occupants' consent to comply with BITs in force in occupied territories is expressed "indirectly" or "derivatively" in Article 43 of the Hague

---

investment protections contained in Ukraine's investment treaties."; *see* Alison Ross, *Crimea claims threatened against Russia*, Global Arbitration Review (July 10, 2015), http://globalarbitrationreview.com/news/article/33957/crimea-claims-threatened-against-russia.

20   Hague Regulations art. 43.

21   For an overview of how different States incorporate international treaty obligations into their domestic law, *see, generally,* Anthony Aust, Modern Treaty Law and Practice 159–177 (2013) [*hereinafter* Aust].

22   When an award of damages based on a BIT between the occupying power and the home State of the investor implies a change of sovereignty in the occupied territory, the courts of a State that does not recognize the annexation may refuse to enforce it.

23   Nationals of the occupied State are not foreign investors. Therefore, they could never invoke BITs to claim damages for unlawful acts that took place in the territory of the State of which they are nationals, even if the territory is under the effective control of a foreign power.

24   This is the principle *res inter alios acta* according to which "an agreement only has force and effect as between the parties. It cannot give rights to or require action of one who is not party to the agreement"; *see* James R Fox, Dictionary of International and Comparative Law 281 (3rd ed., 2003). The principle *res inter alios acta* was codified in Article 34 of the Vienna Convention on the Law of Treaties. This provision states: "A treaty does not create either obligations or rights for a third State without its consent"; *see* Vienna Convention on the Law of Treaties art. 34, May 23, 1969, 1155 U.N.T.S. 331 [*hereinafter* VCLT].

Regulations.[25] This form of consent not only includes the occupant's submission to the substantive guarantees of the applicable BIT, but also to its dispute resolution provisions.[26]

This article proceeds as follows. Part II discusses the status of treaties in occupied territories. Until the beginning of the second half of the 20th century, it was assumed that the treaties of the displaced sovereign did not bind military occupants. But this view is incompatible with the temporary and precarious nature of belligerent occupation. After discussing primary and subsidiary sources of international law – including recent State practice, ICJ jurisprudence, the work of the International Law Commission (ILC) and contemporary scholarship – Part II concludes that the treaties in force in the occupied State bind the Occupying Power as a result of the latter's obligation to respect the laws in force in occupied territories.

Even so, most legal scholars claim that occupants are immune to the laws of the occupied State despite Article 43 of the Hague Regulations.[27] In practice, this means that the inhabitants of occupied territories may not use the laws in force in the occupied State to sue the occupant and its agents. From this perspective, foreign investors could not assert their rights under pre-occupation BITs against the occupant. In response, Part III demonstrates that the occupants do not have absolute immunity from the laws of the occupied State under the LOAC. Although the immunity of the occupant's armed forces and civilian personnel is justified in wartime,[28] this immunity does not apply to the

---

25 *See, generally*, Chittharanjan F. Amerasinghe, Jurisdiction of International Tribunals 89 (2003) [*hereinafter* Amerasinghe]; explaining that the consent to the creation of the ICTY and the ICTR by Yugoslavia and Rwanda was indirect or derivative: "Consent may be given to the establishment of a tribunal and to its jurisdiction indirectly or derivatively. *This is a new concept in the identification of consent.* The consent given by the two states concerned, namely Yugoslavia and Rwanda, to the creation of the ICTY and the ICTR respectively illustrates this kind of consent" (emphasis added).

26 Domestic investment laws could also be an independent source of jurisdiction for the settlement of investment disputes by an arbitral tribunal during occupation. In cases where the investor brings a claim against the occupant under a domestic investment law, the question of the applicability of BITs to occupied territories does not arise; *see, e.g.*, Makane Moise Mbengue, *Consent to Arbitration Through National Investment Legislation*, Investment Treaty News (July 19, 2012), https://www.iisd.org/itn/2012/07/19/consent-to-arbitration-through-national-investment-legislation.

27 *See* n 104.

28 *See, e.g.*, Office of General Counsel, Department of Defense, United States, *Law of War Manual* (June 2015, updated May 2016) [*hereinafter* US Law of War Manual]; "Section 11.8.5: "Immunity of Occupation Personnel From Local Law. Military and civilian personnel of the occupying forces and occupation administration and persons accompanying

144   MAYORGA

damages claims submitted to an arbitral tribunal sitting outside the occupied State – and therefore, far removed from the influence of the occupant.

Part IV explains the impact of the concurrent application of the law of occupation and BITs in investor-State disputes. One of the effects of the interaction between these two bodies of law may be that the jurisdiction of an investment-treaty tribunal could be limited *ratione personae* to those considered "protected persons" under the Fourth Geneva Convention of 1949. More importantly, because IHL is *lex specialis*, the substantive protections generally accorded to investors in times of peace may be diluted during occupation.

Finally, Part V concludes with a discussion on how investment arbitration can contribute to the enforcement of IHL in occupied territories.

II   The Status of Treaties in Occupied Territories

The law of occupation has been codified primarily in two major treaties: 1) the Hague Regulations of 1907; and 2) the Fourth Geneva Convention of 1949.[29] Neither treaty expressly provides whether the treaties of the occupied State bind the occupant. Further complicating this inquiry is the fact that State practice is limited and that it has attracted little attention from legal scholars. But as will be demonstrated below, treaties incorporated into the domestic legal system of the occupied State before the occupation are "laws in force" under Article 43 of the Hague Regulations. Therefore, the occupant must respect the occupied State's treaties unless prevented by military necessity.

---

them are not subject to the local law or to the jurisdiction of the local civil or criminal courts of the occupied territory, unless expressly made subject thereto by a competent officer of the Occupying Power". *See also* Office of the Judge Advocate General, Canada, *The Law of Armed Conflict at the Operational and Tactical Levels* (2001); "Section 1210. Occupying Force Exempt From Local Laws. 1. Members of an occupying force are not subject to the jurisdiction of the local courts as their offices will be dealt with under the military law of their own armed forces. The occupant will generally ensure that some system of law is available to handle legal problems arising between inhabitants of the occupied territory and members of the occupation force."

29   The Hague Regulations of 1907 and the four Geneva Conventions of 1949 are widely considered part of customary international law. *See, generally,* Yutaka Arai-Takahashi, The Law of Occupation: Continuity and Change of International Humanitarian Law, and its Interaction with International Human Rights Law 55–64 (2009) [*hereinafter* Arai-Takahashi].

A   *The Traditional View: Prior Treaties do not Bind the Occupant*

Throughout the second half of the 19th century and until a few decades after the end of World War II, it was assumed that the treaties of the occupied State did not bind the occupant, especially in matters related to trade, commerce, and the treatment of aliens. The presumption against the continuity of treaties in occupied territories was a corollary of the widely-held view at the time that "treaties between warring states were *automatically abrogated* with the outbreak of war".[30]

For example, the United States (US) Judge Advocate General School's text on Belligerent Occupation of 1944 states that an occupant "may regulate, restrict or prohibit trade in the occupied territory unrestrained by treaty stipulations of the legitimate sovereign."[31] Likewise, the International Committee of the Red Cross's (ICRC) commentaries to the Fourth Geneva Convention claim that the Occupying Power "is not bound by the treaties concerning the legal status of aliens which may exist [in occupied territories]".[32] G.I.A.D. Draper echoed this proposition in his Hague Academy lectures of 1965. According to him, "[t]he Occupying Power, having established its position as such, does not thereby become bound by the treaties concluded between the Occupied State and neutral States relating to the treatment of aliens".[33] None of these sources explains why.

L. H. Woolsey delved into this problem in detail when discussing Japan's obligations toward alien residents in occupied Chinese territory before the outbreak of World War II. Woolsey was particularly concerned with the continuity of the rights and privileges that China had granted to Americans and American missionary societies through several treaties dating back to the 19th century.[34] These rights included the right to "reside and carry on trade, industry and manufactures in the Open Ports" as well as the right to "rent, purchase houses, places

---

30   Arnold Pronto, *The Effect of War on Law – What Happens to Their Treaties when States Go to War?* 2 Cambridge J. Int'l & Comp. L. 227, 230 (2013) (emphasis added) [*hereinafter* Pronto].

31   Morris Zimmerman, The Law of Belligerent Occupation 71 (JAGS Text No. 11, The Judge Advocate General's School 1944) [*hereinafter* JAGS Text No. 11].

32   Commentary on the Geneva Conventions of 12 August 1949: IV Geneva Convention Relative to the Protection of Civilian Persons in Time of War 49 (J. S. Pictet et al., eds., ICRC 1958) [*hereinafter* Fourth Geneva Convention commentary].

33   Draper, G.I.A.D, *The Geneva Conventions of 1949* (Volume 114) (Collected Courses of the Hague Academy of International Law, the Hague Academy of International Law 1965), at 127.

34   L.H. Woolsey, *Peaceful War in China*, 32 Am. J. Int'l L. 314, 314–315 (1938) [*hereinafter* Woolsey].

of business and other buildings and rent or lease land and build thereon".[35] China also allowed foreign steam vessels to navigate inland waters for the transportation of passengers and merchandise by virtue of a treaty concluded in 1895. Furthermore, under the system of extraterritoriality,[36] Americans and other alien residents were not subject to the jurisdiction of Chinese courts and Chinese law. Instead, they could only be "tried in civil and criminal cases by consular officers who [applied] the laws of the nationality of the defendant".[37]

For Woolsey, "territorial" or "localized" treaties creating rights *in rem*, such as navigational rights on Chinese inland waters, survived in times of occupation because they followed the territory. As a result, he concluded, they "become a limitation on the fee in the hands of the military occupant".[38] On the other hand, Woolsey believed that alien residents could not claim from the occupant the same rights and privileges that they had claimed from the legitimate government on matters involving residence, travel, trade and tariffs because the occupant is "supreme".[39]

Based on Woolsey's analysis, one could hardly claim that the BITs of the displaced sovereign bind the occupant. BITs do not confer rights *in rem*,[40] and, therefore, they do not follow the territory. If anything, BITs fall within the type of treaties the ICRC and G.I.A.D. Draper regarded as "relating to the treatment of aliens" because they require Contracting Parties to accord foreign in-

---

35   *Id.*

36   The system of extraterritoriality through consular courts has fallen into desuetude. *See, generally*, Paweł Czubik & Piotr Szwedo, *Consular Jurisdiction, in* Max Planck Encyclopedia of International Law 1–2 (2013); "Consular jurisdiction today is regarded as being of historical significance only. However, remnants of it may be found in contemporary international law. Consular jurisdiction excluded the judicial competence of the receiving State with regard to the nationals of the sending State. Foreigners were subordinated to consuls who exercised judicial authority. Such exclusion infringed the sovereignty of the receiving State in the contemporary meaning of this notion. Consular jurisdiction was a feature of those times when personalism, as opposed to territorialism, dominated as a rule of attribution of judicial authority. It remained a characteristic of relations between European and non-Christian States, which were regulated through capitulations."

37   Woolsey, 315.

38   *Id.*, 320. *See also* JAGS Text No 11, 24.

39   Woolsey, 319.

40   *See, e.g.*, Zachary Douglas, *The Plea of Illegality in Investment Treaty Arbitration*, 29 ICSID Rev. 174 (2014). "An investment treaty does not create property rights or regulate the means for their acquisition; an investment treaty instead provides an additional layer of protection once property rights defined under the laws of the host State have been acquired in the manner prescribed by those laws."

OCCUPANTS, BEWARE OF BITS

vestors certain standards of protection, such as, fair and equitable treatment, full protection and security, and most-favored-nation treatment.[41]

Woolsey also insinuated that treaties granting extraterritorial privileges could be binding on the occupant because they derived from a special grant of a portion of sovereignty.[42] But he ultimately rejected the idea after concluding that occupants were not bound by "prior contracts".[43] Citing the *Waller* incident of 1895 and the *Casablanca Arbitration* of 1907,[44] Woolsey also acknowledged that judicial and State practice did not support the continuity of extraterritorial privileges during occupation.

The *Waller* incident arose after a court-martial set up by French occupying forces in Madagascar prosecuted an American citizen.[45] The French court prosecuted John Waller despite a provision in the 1867 commercial treaty between the US and the Queen of Madagascar, which gave the American Consul in Madagascar exclusive jurisdiction over criminal or civil offenses committed by American citizens.[46]

For its part, *Deserters of Casablanca* arbitration involved a jurisdictional conflict between the German consular authorities and the French occupying forces over German nationals in Morocco.[47] This conflict arose when the German Consul in Casablanca tried to grant consular protection to German nationals who had deserted from the French foreign legion. France argued that the German consulate's actions encroached upon the exclusive right of jurisdiction that an occupying nation enjoys over its soldiers and acts likely to endanger its safety, even in a country granting extraterritorial jurisdiction. Germany, on the other hand, argued that France did not have the right to claim a right of jurisdiction over German nationals, even if they belonged to the French foreign legion. Although the Arbitral Tribunal refused to formulate an absolute rule giving preference to either of the "two concurrent jurisdictions",

---

41   *See, generally*, Jeswald W Salacuse, The Law Of Investment Treaties 131 (1st ed., 2010).

42   Woolsey, 319; "It is true that certain other treaty rights, such as extraterritoriality, may be claimed on the ground that they are derived from a special grant of a portion of the sovereignty of China and that therefore the military occupant takes subject to them."

43   Woolsey, 319.

44   *Id.*

45   *See* John B Moore, *Digest of International Law* (Vol. 2, Washington Government Printing Office 1906), at 204–212. *See also: Waller is in France*, The San Francisco Call (Apr. 21, 1895) [*hereinafter* Waller].

46   *See: Treaties and Conventions Concluded Between The United States of America and Other Powers Since July 4, 1776* (Washington Government Printing Office 1871), at 532.

47   *See: Deserters of Casablanca, Fra. v. Ger., Award*, 3 Am. J. Int'l L. 755 (1909).

it ultimately found that German consular officials did not have the right to protect German deserting from the French foreign legion.[48]

In any case, the assumption that the occupied State's treaties do not bind the occupying power – except for localized or territorial treaties – is misleading for at least three reasons.

First, the rule that only localized or territorial treaties bind the occupant appears to have been imported into the law of occupation from the now obsolete law of conquest. Indeed, the law of occupation as we know it today developed out of the law of conquest.[49] Until the first half of the 19th century, occupants considered themselves absolute owners of territories under occupation.[50] This is why, in the past occupation resulted in the transfer of sovereignty. But this view lost ground in 1907 with the adoption of the Hague Regulations.[51] Specifically, Article 43 of the Hague Regulations codified the key principle underlying the modern law of belligerent occupation: that occupation is a precarious and temporary condition which does not result in the transfer of sovereignty.[52]

---

48   For an illuminating analysis of this decision, *see* James Scott Brown, *The Casablanca Arbitration Award*, 3 Am. J. Int'l L. 698 (1909).

49   Von Glahn, 7; "The development of the existing rules governing military occupation was preceded by centuries during which no real distinction was drawn between military occupation on the one hand and conquest and subjugation on the other. Conquest of enemy territory was generally regarded as establishing annexation to the conqueror's real, and it was held that the successful sovereign was practically immune from nay limitations on his right to do as he liked in the occupied area."

50   *See* Doris A Graber, The Development of The Law of Belligerent Occupation 1863–1914 13 (1st ed., 1949).

51   *See* Romulus A. Picciotti, *Legal Problems of Occupied Nations after the Termination of Occupation*, 33 Mil. L. Rev. 25, 29 (1966); "As the nineteenth century drew to a close, the distinction between conquest and military occupation had been firmly established. Moreover, the illogical and oppressive fiction of substituted sovereignty as the basis for justification of the rights of the occupant was replaced by the broader and more natural foundation of military necessity and the duty owed by the occupant to the population. Simultaneously with these changing concepts, there developed a body of international law, much of it incorporated into the municipal law of many nations and almost universally recognized, delineating the scope of the rights of the occupant over the territory and limiting his freedom of action. The majority of these rules were incorporated in fourteen articles of the Hague Regulations annexed to the IV Hague Convention of 1907."

52   Arai-Takahashi, 42; "One of the general principles underlying Article 43 of the Hague Regulations is that belligerent occupation is a precarious and transitional authority with no conferral of sovereignty upon the occupying power."

OCCUPANTS, BEWARE OF BITS 149

Despite this development, certain occupation problems have continued to be examined through the lens of the law of conquest and State succession.[53] So the opinion that only localized treaties survive during occupation may well be the product of legal inertia in the law of occupation.

The localized-treaty rule is, in fact, a rule of State succession.[54] As such, it presupposes the lawful change of sovereign authority over a particular territory. Because the successor State acquires sovereignty over the territory of its predecessor, it is only logical that the former will continue to be bound automatically by the territorial treaties of the latter. But the status of non-localized treaties in cases of state succession is different. By virtue of the "moving treaty frontier" rule, the non-localized treaties of the predecessor State cease to have effect in the transferred territory; whereas the non-localized treaties of the successor State begin to apply to the incorporated territory.[55]

These principles, however, do not fully apply to occupied territories. Of course, if the successor State who acquires full sovereignty over the territory in question is bound by prior localized treaties, so is the occupant whose position is precarious and short of sovereignty. But the fate of non-localized treaties in

---

53 Professor Richard Baxter, for instance, attributed to legal inertia the prevalence of the concepts of war treason and war rebellion to explain the legal basis of the "duty of obedience" inhabitants of occupied territories owe the occupant: "The presence in international law of a theory which envisages a duty of obedience imposed by that law and characterizes certain acts hostile to the occupant as war treason or as war rebellion can only be explained in terms of history. It is particularly significant that these kindred concepts date from a period which was still one of transition from the rigorous law of conquest to the modern and more enlightened view of belligerent occupation. That they have persisted is a consequence of inertia in the law, which has failed to take account of later developments in warfare and in the law of occupation itself." *See* Richard Baxter, *The Duty of Obedience to the Occupant*, 27 British Y.B. Int'l L. 235, 257 (1950).

54 In the *Gabčíkovo-Nagymaros* case, the ICJ confirmed the customary status of Article 12 of the Vienna Convention on Succession of States in respect of Treaties, which provides that rights and obligations of a territorial character established by a treaty are unaffected by a succession of States. The Court held that the 1977 Treaty between Hungary and Czechoslovakia continued to be binding on Slovakia as a successor State because "it created rights and obligations "attaching to" the parts of the Danube to which it relates ..."; *see* Gabčíkovo-Nagymaros Project (Hung. v. Slovk.), Judgment, 1997 I.C.J. Rep. 7, 72 (Sept. 25).

55 *See, e.g.*, James Crawford, Brownlie's Principles of Public International Law 425 (8th ed., 2012); explaining the moving treaty boundaries principle as follows: "... the "moving treaty boundaries" principle holds that a transfer of territory from State A to State B is presumed not to affect existing treaties [of the annexing State]: State B's treaties cover the transferred territory whereas State A's cease to apply."

occupation is different. Although the non-localized treaties of the predecessor State cease to apply in cases of State succession, this does not mean that the non-localized treaties of the occupied State will cease to have effect in the occupied territory. Because occupation does not result in a change of sovereignty, the occupant takes the occupied territory as it finds it. Thus, the occupant must respect both localized and non-localized treaties unless prevented by military necessity.[56]

Second, the argument that the occupied State's treaties cease to apply during occupation because the occupant is "supreme" is unconvincing.[57] The only conceivable situation in which the occupant assumes supreme authority is in cases of subjugation or *debellatio, i.e.* when the government of the defeated State ceases to function and losses control of all its territory.[58] The governments of the Allied Powers, for example, assumed supreme authority over Germany's territory after the unconditional surrender of the German armed

---

56 The occupant's duty to respect the laws in force in the occupied territory is subject to the necessity exception contained in Article 43 of the Hague Regulations and Article 64 of Fourth Geneva Convention. Although Article 43 of the Hague Regulations states that the occupant may not repeal, modify or suspend the pre-existing legal system of the occupied territory unless "absolutely prevented", the phrase is not as restrictive as it appears. The consensus is that the phrase "absolutely prevented" is equivalent to necessity. Article 64 of the Fourth Geneva Convention clarified what amounts to "necessity" by spelling out "three specific dimensions" of the term. These three dimensions are: 1) the need of the Occupying Power to remove any direct threat to its security and the security of the members of its armed forces, administrative staff, and property; 2) the duty of the occupant to comply with its obligations under the Geneva Convention and customary international law; and 3) the need to ensure the "orderly government" of the occupied territory. *See, e.g.*, Yoram Dinstein, *Legislation Under Article 43 of the Hague Regulations: Belligerent Occupation and Peace Building*, Program on Humanitarian Policy and Conflict Research Occasional Paper Series 2, at 4–7 (Fall 2004) [*hereinafter* Dinstein].

57 Woolsey, 314, 319; "In this view, what becomes of the treaty rights of third Powers in the territory of occupation-for example, the rights of Americans, American institutions and American vessels in China? Can alien residents claim from the occupant the same rights and privileges that they claim from the legitimate government? Can consular courts of the United States continue to function? Do treaty tariffs and trade privileges continue? Do treaty rights of navigation subsist? *It would seem in principle, on the theory that the military occupant is supreme, that they do not, without his consent and approval, particularly the rights as to residence, travel, trade, tariffs, and the like.*" (emphasis added).

58 *Debellatio* occurs when the government of the defeated State ceases to function and losses control of all its territory. *See, generally*, Michael N Schmitt, *Debellatio, in* Max Planck Encyclopedia of International Law (2013), at para. 17 [*hereinafter* Schmitt].

OCCUPANTS, BEWARE OF BITS   151

forces in 1945.[59] In *Altstötter and others*, the US Military Tribunal at Nuremberg held that the German government's complete disintegration and unconditional surrender justified the Allies' assumption and exercise of supreme governmental power. Notably, the Tribunal concluded that as a result of the complete destruction of the German government, the Allied Powers were not subject to the limitations of the Hague Regulations.[60] Because of the governmental vacuum resulting from subjugation or *debellatio*, occupants were expected to assume supreme authority over occupied territories without the constraints of the Hague Regulations.[61]

Not only are instances of subjugation or *debellatio* rare today, but the concepts have lost their appeal since the adoption of the Fourth Geneva Convention and the First Additional Protocol in 1977.[62] The law of occupation as it stands today does not confer supreme authority to the occupant. In fact, no contemporary military manual refers to the occupant's authority as supreme.[63] The German military manual of 2013, for example, characterizes the occupant's authority simply as "occupational authority".[64] Therefore, an occupant may not rely on a purported supreme authority over occupied territories to ignore the ousted sovereign's international obligations.

Third, the *Waller* and the *Deserters of Casablanca* incidents do not stand against the continuity of the ousted sovereign's treaties. These cases simply confirm the exclusivity of the occupant's jurisdiction over persons who commit crimes or offenses affecting the security and stability of the occupation

---

59   *See* Declaration Regarding the Defeat of Germany and the Assumption of Supreme Authority by Allied Powers (signed 5 June 1945), http://avalon.law.yale.edu/wwii/ger01.asp.

60   In re Altstötter and Others (Justice Trial) United States Military Tribunal, Nuremberg, Germany, Dec. 4, 1947, I.L.R. 278, 280.

61   *See* R. Y. Jennings, *Government in Commission*, 23 British Y.B. Int'l L. 112, 136 (1946); asserting that as a result of Germany's extinction "... the whole *raison d'etre* of the law of belligerent occupation is absent in the circumstances of the Allied occupation of Germany, and to attempt to apply it would be a manifest anachronism."

62   Arai-Takahashi, 39. *See also* Schmitt.

63   *See, e.g.*, U.S. Department of the Army, FM 27–10, *Department of the Army Field Manual, The Law of Land Warfare, July 1956; Law of War Manual* (Office of General Counsel, Department of Defense, U.S.A. (June 2015, updated May 2016)); *Manual of the Law of Armed Conflict* (Ministry of Defense, U.K. 2004).

64   *Law of Armed Conflict Manual* (Federal Ministry of Defense, Berlin, Germany 1 May 2013), para. 527.

administration and its armed forces.[65] Waller was tried as a spy since he had allegedly warned the Hovas of an impending attack by the French.[66] And because desertion is also a crime over which the military courts of the occupant exercise exclusive jurisdiction,[67] the Casablanca tribunal dismissed Germany's claim that France violated the violated the extraterritorial jurisdiction of the German Consul. Accordingly, the *Waller* and *Casablanca* cases merely reflect the application of the principle of military necessity in occupied territories.[68] Neither case supports an absolute rule allowing the occupant to ignore the treaty obligations of the occupied State.

B *The Contemporary View: Treaties as "Laws in Force" in Occupied Territories*

By the middle of the 20th century, international law started to move away from the presumption that the outbreak of armed conflict *ipso facto* terminated or suspended existing treaties.[69] This development eventually reached the law of occupation.

The few authors who have addressed the issue recently agree that the treaty obligations of the displaced sovereign bind occupants. Eyal Benvenisti, for example, argues that the occupant should regard itself as bound by international

---

65   *See, e.g.,* Arai-Takahashi 157, 159; "Historically, the occupying power has always been vested with the power to set up military tribunals of its own to try offenses committed by native population against members of occupation forces or administration ... The jurisdiction of such tribunals ('occupation forces') is parallel to that entertained by existing indigenous courts. On one hand, native tribunals deal with offenses committed by inhabitants against other inhabitants or their property in occupied territory. On the other, occupation courts address all offenses against security of the occupation army or administration, and violations of laws and customs of war, including damage to communications and to the property of the occupying authorities. The local courts are not allowed to try offenses committed by nationals (members of army or of administrative personnel) of the occupying power, and those of its allies." Morris Greenspan, The Modern Law of Land Warfare 241 (1959) [*hereinafter* Greenspan]; " ... the local courts usually continue to exercise jurisdiction over the inhabitants except for crimes affecting the stability and security of the occupation regime itself, the occupation forces, or the war effort of the occupant."

66   *See* Waller.

67   *See, e.g.,* US Law of War Manual, Section 4.5.2.5; "<u>Deserters</u>. The deserter's relationship with his or her armed forces is a question of that State's domestic law and not international law States generally forbid members of their armed forces from desertion and generally regard members of the armed forces who desert as continuing to be members of their armed forces."

68   *See* Hague Regulations art. 43; Fourth Geneva Convention art. 64; Dinstein.

69   Pronto, 230.

agreements assumed by the ousted government prior to the occupation insofar as the agreements are relevant to the maintenance of public order and civil life in occupied territories.[70] Similarly, Professor Theodor Meron suggests that if the territorial sovereign ratifies a convention and adopts the necessary implementing legislation prior to the occupation, the occupant must respect the convention as part of the local legislation in force in occupied territories.[71]

Professor Meron advanced this idea after the discussions about Israel's international labor obligations in the occupied Palestinian territories at the 63rd International Labor Conference in 1977. In response to allegations of labor discrimination in violation of the International Labor Organization (ILO) Convention No. 111, Israel submitted a report to a special committee of the ILO concluding that "both the policy and the practice of the Government of Israel regarding the working population of the administered areas have been in full accord with the provisions of Convention No. 111".[72] However, Israel's right and duty to apply Convention No. 111 in occupied territories was contested at the conference.

Several delegates argued that an illegal regime which did not have sovereignty over the Palestinian territories could not apply Convention No. 111.[73] Israel objected to this stating that ILO Convention No. 111 applied to the administered territories because: 1) all the parties concerned, including Jordan and Israel, had ratified it; and 2) Convention No. 111 provided for the only yardstick

---

70   *See* Eyal Benvenisti, The International Law of Occupation 83 (2nd ed., 2012) [*hereinafter* Benvenisti (2012)].

71   *See* Theodor Meron, *Applicability of Multilateral Conventions to Occupied Territories*, 72 Am. J. Int'l L. 542, 550 (1978) [*hereinafter* Meron]. For the same view, *see also* Naomi Burke, *A Change In Perspective: Looking at Occupation Through the Lens of The Law Of Treaties*, 41 N.Y.U. J. Int'l L. & Pol. 103, 115 (2008–2009) [*hereinafter* Burke]. "A multilateral treaty that has been ratified by the occupied state is certainly a "law in force in the country." Therefore, in restoring and ensuring public order and civil life, an Occupying Power would be obligated to respect the international obligations of the occupied territory 'unless absolutely prevented' or unless its own security needs or its obligations under the Geneva Conventions towards the local population prevent it from doing so." Adam Roberts, *Transformative Military Occupation: Applying the Laws of War and Human Rights*, 100 Am. J. Int'l L. 580, 589 (2006); "Traditionally, the laws of war have been seen as the main-even the only-branch of international law applicable to occupations. However, there is no a priori reason why multilateral conventions on other matters should not be applicable to occupied territories."

72   Record of Proceedings, International Labour Conference, Sixty-Third Session, Geneva (1977), at 612.

73   Theodor Meron, 546.

to determine whether Israel had engaged in discrimination.[74] Professor Roberto Ago, Italy's delegate, supported Israel's position and stated that,

> *it is a very clear and unquestioned principle of general international law governing the duties of an occupying Power, irrespective of whether such occupation is legal or illegal, that the occupying Power, no matter what its position may be, is obliged to observe all the international conventions in force in the territory occupied.*[75]

More recently, during the occupation of Iraq in 2003, the Coalition Provisional Authority (CPA) modified the Iraqi labor code, citing Iraq's obligation to eradicate child labor under ILO Conventions No 138 and 182.[76]

Indeed, the phrase "laws in force in occupied territory" is not limited to "laws" in the strict sense; it should be read to include every component of a domestic legal system. The International Committee of the Red Cross (ICRC) has explained that "[t]he idea of the continuity of the legal system [under Article 64 of the Fourth Geneva Convention] applies to the whole of the law (civil law and penal law) in the occupied territory".[77] The ICRC further clarified that the reason Article 64 of the Fourth Geneva Convention refers only to the continuity of the penal laws of the occupied State, was that "[penal law] had not been sufficiently observed during past conflicts; [but] there is no rea-

---

74 Record of Proceedings, International Labour Conference, Sixty-Third Session, Geneva (1977), at 718; "Now that the question of the application of Convention No. 111 was to be handled by objective experts, we are being told that we may not apply that Convention – and yet Convention No. 111, which has been ratified by Israel, Egypt, the Syrian Arab Republic and Jordan, is the only – I repeat the only – agreed international standard for determining whether a member State of the ILO has practiced discrimination."

75 *Id.*, 716.

76 Benvenisti (2012), 83.

77 Fourth Geneva Convention commentary, at 335. Fourth Geneva Convention art. 64 reads as follows: "The penal laws of the occupied territory shall remain in force, with the exception that they may be repealed or suspended by the Occupying Power in cases where they constitute a threat to its security or an obstacle to the application of the present Convention. Subject to the latter consideration and to the necessity for ensuring the effective administration of justice, the tribunals of the occupied territory shall continue to function in respect of all offences covered by the said laws. The Occupying Power may, however, subject the population of the occupied territory to provisions which are essential to enable the Occupying Power to fulfil its obligations under the present Convention, to maintain the orderly government of the territory, and to ensure the security of the Occupying Power, of the members and property of the occupying forces or administration, and likewise of the establishments and lines of communication used by them."

son to infer *a contrario* that the occupation authorities are not also bound to respect the civil law of the country, or even its constitution".[78] Insofar they have been incorporated into the domestic law of a State, either through ratification or implementing legislation, treaties constitute another important piece of a legal system.[79] Therefore, there is no *a priori* reason for excluding treaties from the system of law the occupant is bound by in accordance with Article 43 of the Hague Regulations and Article 64 of the Fourth Geneva Convention.

The International Court of Justice (ICJ) appeared to ascribe to this view in its judgment in the *Armed Activities on the Territory of the Congo* [DRC] case in 2005. The Court stated that the occupant's obligations under Article 43 of the Hague Regulations comprised the duty to secure respect for the applicable rules of international human rights law. After concluded that Uganda was occupying the Ituri region, the ICJ held that Uganda,

> ... *was under an obligation, according to Article 43 of the Hague Regulations of 1907, to take all the measures in its power to restore, and ensure, as far as possible, public order and safety in the occupied area, while respecting, unless absolutely prevented, the laws in force in the DRC. This obligation comprised the duty to secure respect for the applicable rules of international human rights law and international humanitarian law, to protect the inhabitants of the occupied territory against acts of violence, and not to tolerate such violence by any third party.*[80]

This holding, however, does not explain how the Court incorporated the DRC's international human rights treaties into Article 43 of the Hague Regulations. Later, in another passage in its judgment, the Court relied on the extraterritorial application of human rights treaties to determine which rules of human rights law applied to Uganda's conduct as an Occupying Power.[81]

---

78   *Id.*

79   During a meeting of experts convened by the ICRC to discuss current challenges to the law of occupation, one participant indicated that the term "penal laws" in article 64 of Fourth Geneva Convention comprised laws in general, including decrees, ordinances, and court precedents, as well as administrative regulations and executive orders; *see* ICRC, *Expert Meeting: Occupation and other Forms of Administration of Foreign Territory* (Mar. 2012), at 58 [*hereinafter* ICRC Expert Meeting], https://www.icrc.org/eng/assets/files/publications/icrc-002–4094.pdf.

80   Armed Activities on the Territory of the Congo (Dem. Rep. Congo v. Uganda), Judgment, 2005 I.C.J. Rep. 168, 231 (Dec. 19) (emphasis added) [*hereinafter* Armed Activities].

81   *Id.*, 242–243; citing its Advisory Opinion of 9 July 2004, the *Legal Consequences of the Construction of a Wall in the Occupied Palestinian Territory*, the Court restated its position

The Court's reference to the extraterritorial application of international human rights treaties casts doubt as to whether it considered these treaties to be applicable because they were part of the law in force in the DRC.[82] Yet, the Court later indicated that the human rights treaties it had identified as applicable to Uganda's acts had been either acceded to or ratified not only by Uganda but also by the occupied State, the DRC.[83]

Because treaties ratified or acceded to by the occupied State are irrelevant to the analysis of the occupant's extraterritorial obligations, the Court seemed to have found these human rights treaties to be applicable also because they were part of the laws in force in DRC's occupied territory. To be sure, had the basis for the applicability of these treaties been their extraterritorial application alone, the analysis of Uganda's obligations under Article 43 of the Hague Regulations would have been unnecessary. In fact, the Court concluded that Uganda was responsible under several provisions of the Hague Regulations, including Article 43, for specific acts committed by its armed forces in violation of human rights treaties in the course of the occupation of the Ituri region.[84] This means that the Court did not rely on Article 43 of the Hague Regulations simply to find Uganda liable for its failure to prevent violations of human rights by third parties, but also for its own acts.

The International Law Commission's (ILC) Draft Articles on the "Effects of Armed Conflict on Treaties" could also be cited as a significant departure from the view that the ousted sovereign's treaties do not bind the occupant. Under

---

that "international human rights instruments are applicable "in respect of acts done by a State in the exercise of its jurisdiction outside its own territory", particularly in occupied territories".

82 The recent case law of the European Court on Human Rights (ECtHR) dealing with human rights in occupied territories is based on the extraterritoriality of the European Convention on Human Rights. Therefore, the ECtHR has not addressed the continuity of the occupied State's treaties under Article 43 of the Hague Regulations. In the landmark cases of *Loizidou v Turkey* and *Cyprus v Turkey*, the ECtHR confirmed that the concept of jurisdiction under Art. 1 of the European Convention was not confined to the territory of the Contracting States. Accordingly, the Court held Turkey liable for violations of the European Convention in Northern Cyprus without analyzing the obligations of an Occupying Power under article 43 of the Hague Regulations. *See, generally*, Loizidou v. Turkey, App. No. 15318/89, 1995 Eur. Ct. H.R.; Cyprus v. Turkey, App. No. 25781/94, 2001 Eur. Ct. H.R.

83 Armed Activities, 242–245. "The Court considers that the following instruments in the fields of international humanitarian law and international human rights law are applicable, as relevant, in the present case...".

84 *Id.*, 244.

draft Article 3, the existence of an armed conflict does not *ipso facto* terminate or suspend the operation of treaties as between States parties to the conflict, as well as between a State party to the conflict and a State that is not.[85] The definition of the term "armed conflict" includes "the occupation of territory which meets with no armed resistance."[86] Thus, a BIT between the occupied State and the State of origin of the investor would *a priori* continue to operate in occupied territories.

The ILC provided an indicative category of treaties the subject matter of which carries an implication that they continue in operation, in whole or in part, during armed conflict.[87] That list includes treaties of friendship, commerce and navigation and agreements concerning private rights.[88] According to the ILC commentaries to the Draft Articles, investment treaties not only qualify as agreements concerning private rights, but are also analogous to treaties of friendship, commerce and navigation.[89]

Additionally, some BITs contain so-called "war clauses". A "war clause" may require the host State to compensate a foreign investor for losses arising out of the destruction of property by government forces in cases of armed conflict, state of emergency, revolution, insurrection, civil disturbance, or similar events, unless said destruction was not required by the necessity of the situation.[90]

---

85 U.N. I.L.C., *Draft Articles on the Effects of Armed Conflict on Treaties, with Commentaries*, U.N. Doc. A/66/10, Y.B. Int'l L. Comm., Vol. 11 (2011); "Article 3. General principle. The existence of an armed conflict does not ipso facto terminate or suspend the operation of treaties: (a) as between States parties to the conflict; (b) as between a State party to the conflict and a State that is not".

86 *Id.*, commentary, art. 2.

87 *Id.*, commentary, art. 7; and art. 7, annex with indicative list of treaties.

88 *Id.*, art. 7 (e–f), annex with Indicative list of treaties.

89 *Id.*

90 Article 5 of the BIT between Libya and Austria provides an example of a war clause: "Compensation for losses: (1) An investor of a Contracting Party who has suffered a loss relating to its investment in the territory of the other Contracting Party due to war or to other armed conflict, state of emergency, revolution, insurrection, civil disturbance, or any other similar event, or acts of God or force majeure, in the territory of the latter Contracting Party, shall be accorded by the latter Contracting Party, as regards restitution, indemnification, compensation or any other settlement, treatment no less favourable than that which it accords to its own investors or to investors of any third state, whichever is most favourable to the investor. (2) An investor of a Contracting Party who in any of the events referred to in paragraph (1) suffers loss resulting from: (a) requisitioning of its investment or part thereof by the forces or authorities of the other Contracting Party, or (b) destruction of its investment or part thereof by the forces or authorities of the other Contracting Party, which was not required by the necessity of the situation, shall in any

The inclusion of a "war clause" in a BIT strongly suggests that the treaty continues to operate during armed conflict.[91]

But other than supporting a presumption of continuity of BITs during armed conflict in general, the utility of the Draft Articles on the Effects of Armed Conflict on Treaties is marginal in situations of occupation. By equating occupation to other situations of armed conflict, the ILC skirted the issue of the occupant's role in carrying out the international obligations of the occupied State.

The law of belligerent occupation presumes that the treaty obligations of the ousted sovereign are suspended because it has lost control of its own territory.[92] For this reason, the ousted sovereign is not internationally liable for violations of treaty rights in the occupied territory.[93] Yet, by failing to address situations of occupation in a separate article, the ILC overlooked the occupant's obligations under Article 43 of the Hague Regulations. As Burke aptly pointed out, "[i]f the termination and suspension of treaty obligations are considered to operate equally in times of armed conflict and occupation,

---

case be accorded by the latter Contracting Party restitution or compensation which in either case shall be prompt, adequate and effective and, with respect to compensation, shall be in accordance with Article 4 (2) and (3)." *See* http://investmentpolicyhub.unctad .org/Download/TreatyFile/199.

91 In fact, the very first investment treaty claim arose out of a situation of armed conflict. *See, generally*, Asian Agricultural Products Ltd v Sri Lanka, I.C.S.I.D. Case. No. ARB/87/3 (Final Award) (1991) 30 I.L.M. 580. The Tribunal did not even question whether the BIT in that case continued to apply despite the conflict.

92 Burke, 116.

93 The ousted sovereign could still be liable for investment treaty claims arising out of a "denial of justice" by local judges who remain at their post and continue to exercise jurisdiction over disputes between private parties during the occupation. Investment tribunals have used different tests to determine whether a denial of justice had occurred. *See, e.g.*, Rumeli Telekom A.S. and Telsim Mobil Telekomunikasyon Hizmetleri A.S. v. Republic of Kazakhstan, I.C.S.I.D. Case No. ARB/05/16, Award (July 9, 2008), at para. 619 (analyzing whether the decisions were "so egregiously wrong as to be inexplicable other than by a denial of justice."). Cf *Loewen Group, Inc. and Raymond L. Loewen v. United States of America*, ICSID Case No ARB(AF)/98/3, Award (26 June 2003), para. 132 (stating that a denial of justice occurs in cases of a "[m]anifest injustice in the sense of a lack of due process leading to an outcome which offends a sense of judicial propriety"). Though local judges are subject to the control and supervision of the occupant, they still owe allegiance to the legitimate sovereign. Their decisions, therefore, are pronounced in the name of the latter, not the occupant. *See* Fourth Geneva Convention commentary, 305. If, on the other hand, the local court's wrongful decision was influenced by the occupant, the displaced sovereign should not be held liable.

OCCUPANTS, BEWARE OF BITS

the additional positive duties of an occupying power [under Article 43 of the Hague Regulations] may be negated".[94] For this reason, Burke suggested a Draft Article providing for the occupant's duty to temporarily administer the obligations of the occupied State in accordance with Article 43 of the Hague Regulations.[95] Unfortunately, the ILC did not incorporate her suggestion.

In any case – despite the ILC's failure to specifically address situations of occupation – the opinion of contemporary scholars, recent State practice, and arguably the ICJ's decision in the *Armed Activities* case, suggest that the occupant is bound by treaty obligations assumed by the ousted sovereign before the occupation.

This is a corollary of the principle that the administration of occupied territory creates for the occupant "a situation which [is] essentially similar to that of the legitimate government of the country."[96] Only military necessity will excuse the occupant from complying with the obligations acquired by the *de jure* sovereign before the occupation.

In its Namibia advisory opinion, the ICJ held that: "[p]hysical control of a territory, and not sovereignty or legitimacy of title, is the basis of State liability

---

94 Burke, 104.

95 *Id.*, 116–117.

96 Societe eds Quais de Smyrna v. Greece, 5 I.L.R. 495 (1929). The occupant may also enjoy the privileges the occupied State had in its territory, unless prohibited by IHL. The Special Franco-Greek Arbitral Tribunal found that Greece, the occupant in Smyrna during the Greco-Turkish war following World War I, was entitled to the same exceptions that the Ottoman Government had under a concession agreement granted by the latter to a French company in 1867. The concession entitled the French company to levy dues on the loading and unloading of all merchandise coming into or leaving the docks of Smyrna. At the same time, in accordance with the concession and the Tariff Act of 1878, the Ottoman government was exempted from the payment of dues on "munitions of war" and the "luggage of soldiers". During the occupation of Smyrna, Greece used the docks for unloading all kinds of merchandise. It also refused to pay the French company any dues on merchandise intended for the use of the army claiming the same exemption enjoyed by the Ottoman authorities before the occupation. Finding in favor of Greece, the tribunal stated that: "During the occupation of Smyrna the Greek Government exercised there a political and military power and assumed the supreme administration of the town and its surroundings. In these circumstances it must be admitted that the occupation created for the Greek government a situation which was essentially similar to that of the legitimate government of the country." Thus, while Greece was under an obligation to respect the concession and the Ottoman tariff act, it also benefited from the exemption enjoyed previously by the Ottoman government.

for acts affecting other States."[97] It follows that the occupant assumes international responsibility for its acts despite not having acquired sovereignty over the occupied territory.[98] Given that the displaced sovereigns' obligations are suspended as a result of the occupation, the breach of a BIT in force in occupied territory would be attributable to the occupant and not to the *de jure* sovereign.

The assumption of international responsibility towards other States in relation to the occupied area and the continuity of the occupied State's treaties imply that the occupant must also honor the occupied State's offer to arbitrate any disputes arising from the breach of a BIT in force in the occupied State.[99]

---

97   Legal Consequences for States of the Continued Presence of South Africa in Namibia (South West Africa) notwithstanding Security Council Resolution 276 (1970), Advisory Opinion, 1971 I.C.J. Rep. 16, para. 118.

98   *See* Von Glahn, 32. "Although sovereignty does not pass from the legitimate ruler to the occupant, the latter assumes international responsibility for the occupied area, at least as far as his legal acts undertaken there are concerned, and those acts possess in relation to neutral states the same validity as if they had been acts of the legitimate sovereign of the occupied territory." *See also* Benvenisti (2012), 18.

99   Not all dispute resolution clauses in BITs and other international investment agreements are the same. Some investment treaties require foreign investors to submit their disputes to the "competent tribunal" of the host State before submitting them to an international arbitral forum. The United Kingdom–Argentina BIT, for example, allows foreign investors to resort to international arbitration only if, after 18 months, the domestic court to which the dispute was originally submitted has not rendered a final decision settling the matter between the parties. *See* article 8 of the Agreement between the Government of the United Kingdom of Great Britain and Northern Island and the Government of the Republic of Argentina for the Promotion and Protection of Investments (adopted 30 March 1994, entered into force 30 August 1995), http://investmentpolicyhub.unctad .org/Download/TreatyFile/126. The application of this type of dispute settlement clause in times of occupation raises several problems. Ideally, the courts of the occupied State will continue to function during the occupation as required by articles 54(1) and 64(1) of the Fourth Geneva Convention. But where the local judicial structure collapses as a result of the occupation, the occupant has the power to fill this vacuum by setting up courts to administer the laws of the occupied territory. In the former case, the aggrieved party should submit its claim to the competent municipal court before resorting to international arbitration. In the latter, the claimant should submit it to the competent court established by the occupant. However, none of these courts is likely to offer the claimant a reasonable possibility to obtain effective redress. Even if they continue to function, the judges of the municipal courts may be reluctant to review the acts of the Occupying Power. Furthermore, the judges of the courts set up by the occupant are likely to favor the occupation authorities. In either case, foreign investors could plead "futility" to be relieved from their obligation to resort to domestic proceedings. *See, e.g.,* Ambiente Ufficio

It is true that the occupant is not a party to the BITs of the occupied State. Accordingly, an investment-treaty tribunal could find that it lacks jurisdiction because the occupant did not expressly consent to international arbitration.[100]

In situations of occupation, however, the occupant's consent to international arbitration under the BITs of the occupied State is not direct. Instead, its consent is given through Article 43 of the Hague Regulations. In other words, consent in investor-occupant disputes is "indirect" or "derivative".

The concept of "indirect" or "derivative" consent in international law is not novel. Yugoslavia and Rwanda, for example, did not consent to the jurisdiction of the ICTY[101] and the ICTR[102] for international crimes committed in their territories the 1990s. These Tribunals were established by the United Nations (UN) Security Council (UNSC) under Chapter 7 of the UN Charter. But as a result of their UN membership, Yugoslavia and Rwanda had an obligation under Article 25 of the UN Charter to comply with the decisions of the UNSC. Their consent was thus "indirectly or derivatively given, because by signing the Charter ... they agreed to the UNSC taking decisions under Chapter VII that were binding on them."[103]

Similarly, the consent of the occupant to international arbitration under the BITs of the occupied State is indirectly or derivatively given, because by signing the Hague Regulations and Fourth Geneva Convention, the occupant has agreed to respect the laws in force in the occupied territory.

III Are Occupants Immune to the Arbitral Jurisdiction of BITs in Force in Occupied Territories?

The weight of scholarly opinion has for years maintained that the occupant's obligation to respect the laws of the occupied territory does not imply that the occupant and its agents are subject to those laws. Von Glahn, for example,

---

    S.p.A. v Argentine Republic, I.C.S.I.D. Case No. ARB/08/9, Decision on Jurisdiction and Admissibility (Feb 8, 2013) (Simma, Böckstiegel, Torres), para. 603 (recognizing the existence of the futility exception in international investment arbitration).

100 *See, e.g.*, ST-AD GmbH v The Republic of Bulgaria, P.C.A. Case No. 2011-06 (ST-BG), Award on Jurisdiction (July 18, 2013) 336 (Stern, Klein, Thomas); holding that: "for a claimant to benefit from the jurisdictional protection granted by an arbitration mechanism, there is a condition *ratione voluntatis*: the State must have given its consent to such procedure, which allows a foreign investor to sue the State directly at the international level."

101 *See* S.C. Res. 808, U.N. Doc. S/RES/808 (Feb. 22, 1993).

102 *See* S.C. Res. 955, U.N. Doc. S/RES/955 (Nov. 8, 1994).

103 *See, generally*, Amerasinghe.

noted that "[o]wing to his military supremacy and his alien character an occupant is not subject to the laws or to the courts of the occupied enemy state, nor have native courts jurisdiction over members of the occupying forces".[104] In practice, this means that the occupant is immune to the arbitral jurisdiction of the BITs in force in the occupied State.

Military necessity and security demands are, indeed, valid reasons why members of the occupying forces are not subject to the laws and the courts of the occupied State. The occupant's ability to maintain its war effort and public order would be impaired if its soldiers were required to appear before a domestic court anytime an inhabitant of the occupied territory filed a civil or criminal complaint. The necessity exception of Article 43 of the Hague Regulations and Article 64 of the Fourth Geneva Convention informs this logic.[105] Under this exception, the occupant is entitled to suspend any laws or political privileges that undermine the legitimate military purposes of the occupation and threaten the integrity of its military and civilian personnel.[106]

The *Waller* and *Casablanca* cases discussed in Part I above illustrate this point. The *Waller* incident dealt with espionage while the *Casablanca* arbitration involved desertion. These are exactly the type of offenses that threaten the stability of the occupation regime and the security of the occupant's forces.

---

104   Von Glahn, 108. *See also* Georg Schwarzenberger, International Law as Applied by International Courts and Tribunals 185 (Vol II., 1968) [*hereinafter* Schwarzenberger]; "Respect for local law by its temporary guardian is not necessarily identical with submission of the Occupying Power itself to the legal order of its enemy". APV Rogers, Law on the Battlefield 239 (3rd ed., 2012); "The law of the occupied territory continues in force except to the extent it is suspended or replaced by the occupier, but the occupier and its forces are not subject to that law". Yoram Dinstein, The International Law of Belligerent Occupation 136 (2009) [*hereinafter* Dinstein (2009)]; "It must be emphasized that local courts have no jurisdiction – either in criminal or in civil matters – *over the Occupying Power itself or over the members of the army of occupation.* This includes the "civilian component" of the military government in the occupied territory..." (emphasis added).

105   *See* n57.

106   *See, e.g.*, Greenspan, 223; "Naturally, the occupant will suspend or amend laws which are essentially political in nature, and political or constitutional privileges, as well as laws which adversely affect the welfare and safety of his command. Examples are laws relating to recruiting for the enemy forces, the right to bear arms, the right of assembly, the right to vote, freedom of the press, and the right to travel freely in the territory or leave it." Professor Alain Pellet suggests that the concept of military necessity in cases of prolonged occupations is exclusively tied to the security of the occupation forces. *See* Alain Pellet, *The Destruction of Troy Will Not Take Place, in* International Law and the Administration of the Occupied Territories 198 (Emma Playfair ed., 1992). Thus, military necessity can hardly help justify measures beyond that goal.

OCCUPANTS, BEWARE OF BITS

In both cases, France was allowed to ignore the extraterritorial privileges that the offenders would have otherwise enjoyed by virtue of the military necessity principle.

It is unclear whether the occupant enjoys immunity from local law in all circumstances, or whether this immunity applies only in cases of military necessity. Because an award of damages does not constitute a threat to the legitimate purposes of the occupant's war effort or the security of its forces, the occupant may not allege immunity from the jurisdiction of investment tribunals constituted under the BITs of the occupied State.

A   *The Occupant's Immunity from Local Law: Myth or Reality?*

The source of the occupant's immunity from the occupied State's laws is unclear. Professor Schwarzenberger correctly dismissed the claim that it derives from the equality of status of sovereign States.[107] In his view, it was more appropriate "to found this immunity on the freedom of belligerent States to exercise their discretion on the absence of limitations and prohibitions imposed on them by the standard of civilization or the laws of war".[108]

The question, then, is whether any provision in the applicable humanitarian treaties subjects the occupant to the laws of the occupied State. The only provision in the Hague Regulations that could do this is Article 43. But in Schwarzenberger's opinion, this provision was "hardly categoric".[109] According to him, the occupant's obligation to respect local law "is not necessarily identical with submission ... to the legal order of [the] enemy".[110] He claimed that Article 43 merely required the occupant " ... to apply the local public, criminal and civil law to all acts other than those of the Occupying Power or its agencies".[111] Ultimately, he considered the idea of the occupant being subject

---

107   Schwarzenberger, 184.

108   *Id.*, 185.

109   *Id.*

110   *Id.*

111   *Id.*, 183. This view was also voiced at the ICRC's expert meeting on current challenges to the law of occupation in 2012. During a discussion involving the legal regime applicable to the use of force in occupied territory, one of the participants challenged the argument put forward by other experts that "the duty incumbent upon the occupier to respect the laws in force in the occupied territory, contained in Article 43 of the Hague Regulations, would introduce another layer of norms that the occupying power would have to observe when resorting to force (particularly the rules of human rights law incorporated in the occupied territory's domestic legal order)". The expert challenging this idea asserted that "[Article 43] merely indicated that the people of the occupied territory should be able, as far as possible, to continue to live under their own legal order". *See* ICRC Expert Meeting

to the laws of the occupied State to be a far-reaching limitation of wartime sovereignty that was not codified in Article 43 of the Hague Regulations.[112]

Schwarzenberger tested the soundness of his interpretation of Article 43 against the principle of *effet utile*. This principle dictates that the provisions of a treaty must be construed so as to give them meaning rather than deprive them of it.[113] Schwarzenberger argued that because his reading of Article 43 still required the occupant to apply the local law to the acts of the local population *inter se*, Article 43's stipulated respect for the local law would still carry meaning.[114]

But Schwarzenberger's resort to *effet utile* to interpret Article 43 was unwarranted. The principle of *effet utile* applies only where the language in question is susceptible of two constructions, one of which will carry out and the other defeat its manifest object. But where neither of the two opposing constructions deprives it of meaning, the *effet utile* principle is unhelpful because it does not tell the interpreter which of the two possible meanings to adopt.[115] Here, the alternative construction of Article 43, *i.e.* that it subjects the acts of the occupant to the laws of the occupied State, does not deprive it of meaning. To the contrary, it gives it "maximum effect" by guaranteeing the inhabitants of occupied territories the rights and privileges they had *vis-à-vis* the legitimate sovereign under local law before the occupation.

Schwarzenberger's construction of Article 43 is also flawed because it goes against its plain meaning. In the *Free Zones of Upper Savoy* case, the Permanent Court of International Justice (PCIJ) suggested that the principle of *effet utile* may not be relied upon if it results in " ... doing violence to the [treaty's] terms".[116]

Report, 113; the debates at the ICRC expert meeting testify to a lack of consensus on the scope of the occupant's "local law" obligations under Article 43 of the Hague Regulations.

112   Schwarzenberger, 185.

113   *See* Cayuga Indians (Great Britain) v. United States, Award of the UK/USA Arbitral Tribunal (1926), UNRIAA, Vol. VI, 184.

114   Schwarzenberger, 183.

115   In its decision on jurisdiction, the *Cemex v. Venezuela* arbitral tribunal discussed the limits of the principle of *effet utile* thus: " ... one must recall that this principle does not require that a maximum effect be given to a text. It only excludes interpretations which would render the text meaningless, when a meaningful interpretation is possible". *See* Cemex Caracas Investments v Bolivarian Republic of Venezuela, I.C.S.I.D. Case No. ARB/08/15, Decision on Jurisdiction (Dec. 30, 2010) (Guillaume, Abi-Saab, von Mehren).

116   Free Zones of Upper Savoy and District of Gex (Fr v Switz), 1929 P.C.I.J. (Ser. A) no 22 (Order of Aug. 19), 13.

In interpreting a treaty provision, one must identify first the text's ordinary meaning.[117] Yet determining the ordinary meaning of a treaty term cannot be done in the abstract; it can only be done in the "context" of the treaty and in light of its "object and purpose."[118] Thus, the second step under the VCLT is to analyze the term in its "context," which assists in identifying that term's ordinary meaning and avoids an overly literal approach to interpretation.[119] A key reason for using the context in which a phrase occurs is to ensure that provisions of a treaty are mutually supportive. In particular, the context of a treaty term can include terms in other provisions of the same treaty. Finally, the third step under the VCLT is to identify the treaty's object and purpose, which "bring[s] the teleological element into the general rule [of treaty interpretation]".[120]

This three-step process reveals that Article 43 of the Hague Regulations does not grant the occupant immunity from the laws of the occupied territory. The plain meaning of Article 43 makes this clear. It provides that the occupant must ensure public order and civil life *while respecting*, unless absolutely prevented, the laws in force in the country". The term "respect" means to show deference, regard or consideration for someone or something.[121] Thus, on its face, Article 43 requires the occupant to show deference, regard, or consideration for the occupied territory's laws. If the laws of the occupied territory grant an individual a particular right or privilege, the occupant must respect it.

Contrary to Schwarzenberger's narrow interpretation of Article 43, this provision does not limit the occupant's obligation to simply ensuring that others comply with the laws of the occupied territory.[122] The use of the term "respect" in other provisions of the Hague Regulations confirms this point. The first clause of Article 46 of the Hague Regulations, for example, stipulates that "[f]amily honor and rights, the lives of persons, and private property, as well as religious convictions and practice, *must be respected*".[123] The phrase "must be respected" in Article 46 has the same connotation of the phrase "while respecting" used in Article 43. And no one questions that Article 46 imposes

---

117 Conditions of Admission of a State to Membership in the United Nations (Article 4 of the Charter), Advisory Opinion, 1948 I.C.J. Rep. 57 (May 28). Article 31(1) of the VCLT requires that a treaty be interpreted "in good faith in accordance with the ordinary meaning to be given to [its] terms ... in their context and in the light of [the treaty's] object and purpose"; VCLT art. 31(1).

118 *See, generally*, Aust, 209.

119 Richard K Gardiner, Treaty Interpretation 177 (2008).

120 *Id.*, 189.

121 *Respect, in* Random House Webster's Unabridged Dictionary 1640 (2nd ed., 1999).

122 Schwarzenberger, 183.

123 Hague Regulations art. 46.

upon the occupant and its organs the obligation to respect those rights. So, the context in which the term "respect" is used in the Hague Regulations negates Schwarzenberger's narrow interpretation of Article 43.

Finally, the occupant's blanket immunity would defeat the object and purpose of Article 43 of the Hague Regulations by putting the occupant in a privileged position compared to that of the *de jure* sovereign. Notably, in an arbitration from the inter-war period where Germany (the occupant) argued that it was not subject to the laws of Belgium (the occupied State), the arbitral tribunal held that "[t]he object of Article 43 of the Hague Regulations was not to put the occupant in a privileged position. Its object was to impose duties upon the occupant".[124]

Because the powers of the occupant are "incidental to war and for the purposes of war",[125] the occupant cannot claim privileges other than those that may be justified by military necessity. If the de jure sovereign was subject to the jurisdiction of an arbitral tribunal before the occupation, so is the occupant who is required to maintain the *status quo* in occupied territories.[126] Indeed, the occupant cannot claim absolute immunity to interfere with the rights of individuals in violation of the laws of war.[127]

The awards of mixed arbitral tribunals in the inter-war period also vindicate the idea that the occupant is subject to the laws of the occupied State. For

---

124 Milaire v German State, Germano-Belgian Mixed Arbitral Tribunal (Jan. 1, 1923), 2 I.L.R. 13; holding that: "The object of Article 43 of the Hague Regulations was not to put the occupant in a privileged position. Its object was to impose duties upon the occupant. Its meaning, properly interpreted, was that so long as the laws of the occupied territory, in particular its private law, were not abrogated they remained in force to their full extent."

125 Greenspan, 217; "The effect of military occupation, therefore, is to place the actual (de facto) ruling authority in the hands of the occupant. His rights are, however, only temporary not permanent. They are incidental to war and for the purposes of war". *See also* Julius Stone, Legal Controls of International Conflict 698 (1954); "The Occupant's authority is "military authority". Clearly this is not full sovereignty, but equally clearly it extends under the [Hague rules] to civil matters".

126 Hans-Peter Gasser and Knut Dorman, *Protection of the Civilian Population, in* The Handbook of International Humanitarian Law 275 (Dieter Fleck ed., 2013); "International law on belligerent occupation imposes on the occupying power the obligation, among others, not to change the status quo in the occupied territory...". The occupant, however, does not assume any rights or obligations related to the public debt of the legitimate sovereign; see Von Glahn, 156–159.

127 *Id.*, 276; suggesting that the scope of Article 43 goes beyond the prohibition to change the laws of the occupied territory: "Not only must the legal status of the territory remain unaltered, but also its political institutions and public life in general have to continue with as little disturbance as possible".

OCCUPANTS, BEWARE OF BITS

example, in finding Germany liable to pay compensation to a Belgian national who had been employed by the German Military Railway Administration in occupied Belgium during World War I, the Belgo-German Mixed Arbitral *Milaire v Germany* rejected Germany's argument that Article 43 of the Hague Regulations did not subject Germany's public institutions, in this case the German railway authority, to the laws of the occupied territory. According to the tribunal, "[the meaning of Article 43], properly interpreted was that so long as the laws of the occupied territory, in particular its private law, were not abrogated they remained in force to their full extent".[128] Because Germany did not abrogate the Belgian Statute on Industrial Accidents of 1903, the tribunal found the statute to be applicable to Germany, and thus, "treated the military railway administration of the Occupying Power as being subject to local law".[129]

Similarly, in *Cie. Des Chemins de fer du Nord v. German State*, the Franco-German Mixed Tribunal concluded that Germany's non-military exploitation of railway lines operated by a French company in Belgium at the outbreak of World War I was governed by the Belgian Civil Code rather than the Hague Regulations. Accordingly, the tribunal decided that Germany was required to pay the claimant the proceeds resulting from the commercial exploitation of the railway lines in accordance with Belgian civil law.[130] Had Germany operated the railway lines exclusively for military purposes, Germany's act would have fallen within its lawful powers under the Hague Regulations.

To be sure, the subjection of the occupant to the "laws in force" in the occupied territory does not mean that the occupant is subrogated for the territorial sovereign.[131] The occupant does not become a successor to the rights and duties of the occupied State in the strict sense because military necessity exempts it from the obligations of the ousted sovereign.

At any rate, the occupant's purported immunity from local law derives less from international law than from the sheer fact of its military might.[132] Indeed,

---

128 *See* Milaire v German State.

129 Schwarzenberger, 185. *See also* J. H. W. Verzijl, International Law in Historical Perspective 173–174 (1978).

130 Cie des Chemins de Fer du Nord v. German State, Franco-German Mixed Tribunal (Apr. 8, 1929), 5 I.L.R. 498.

131 *See, e.g.*, Schwarzenberger, 343; suggesting that the legal continuity of the occupied State's laws falls short of an endorsement of any principle of general succession of the Occupying Power to the rights and duties of the territorial sovereign in the law of belligerent occupation.

132 For example, Judge Christopher Greenwood notes that the occupant's power to command obedience over the local population in occupied territories derives from force, not law; *see* Christopher Greenwood, *The Administration of Occupied Territory in International Law*,

IHL requires that the courts of the occupied State shall continue to function during occupation.[133] But the fear of retaliation by the occupation authorities may explain why domestic courts have generally declined to exercise jurisdiction over the acts of the occupant.[134] Once that fear is removed, there is nothing in the law of occupation prohibiting a court from holding occupants liable for their IHL violations. Because an independent international tribunal sitting in Washington D.C., London, Paris, or The Hague, is unlikely to be intimidated by the occupant, there would be no reason for it to dismiss a case for lack of jurisdiction under a BIT.

IV   The Co-Application of the Law of Belligerent Occupation and BITs

The applicability of BITs to occupied territories entails that they must coexist with IHL, the *lex specialis* in occupied territories.[135] As a result, *prima facie* conflicts between investment guarantees and IHL norms are likely to emerge.

---

in International Law and the Administration of the Occupied Territories at 251 (Emma Playfair ed., 1992). Like any protected persons in occupied territories, local judges owe obedience to the occupant. See Fourth Geneva Convention Commentary, at 305; "[i]t may be mentioned in this connection that public officials and judges act under the superintendence and control of the occupant to whom legal power has passed in actual practice and to whom they, like any other protected person, owe obedience."

133   *See, e.g.*, Arai-Takahashi, 145; "The occupying power is generally required to maintain local courts and must not alter the status of judges".

134   *See* Tristan Ferraro, *Enforcement of Occupation Law in Domestic Courts: Issues and Opportunities*, 41 Isr. L. Rev. 331, 344, 347 (2008); indicating that local judges are constrained by the fear of retaliation from the occupant or the potential restriction of the domestic courts' jurisdiction by the occupant. *See also* McDougal and Feliciano, Law and Minimum World Public Order 772 (1961); discussing the case where the Norwegian Supreme court reviewed the international legality of a German occupation measure: " ... as could be expected, the justices were removed and replaced with less assertive ones".

135   Jenks indicated that instruments pertaining to the laws of war "must clearly be regarded as a *leges speciales* in relation to instruments laying down peace-time norms concerning the same subjects"; *see* C. Wilfried Jenks, *The Conflict of Law-Making Treaties*, 30 Brit. Y.B. Int'l L. 401, 446 (1953). Similarly, in its *Nuclear Weapons* advisory opinion, the ICJ regarded the law applicable in armed conflict as *lex specialis* in relation to human rights law; *see* Legality of the Threat or Use of Nuclear Weapons, Advisory Opinion, 1996 I.C.J. Rep. 226, para. 25 (July 8) [*hereinafter* Nuclear Weapons].

In a broad sense, normative conflicts occur where two rules that deal with the same subject-matter "suggest different ways of dealing with a problem".[136] Because BITs and IHL contain rules dealing with the protection of property, the separate application of BITs and IHL to the same dispute may produce conflicting results.

The Occupying State may claim, for example, that an investment tribunal lacks jurisdiction because neither the Hague Regulations nor Fourth Geneva Convention provides for the compulsory settlement of disputes through international arbitration. On the other hand, in order to prevent the dilution of investment protection standards, a foreign investor may resist the application of IHL on the basis that the arbitral tribunal cannot go beyond the "four corners" of a BIT.

Instead of applying one set of norms to the exclusion of the other, this type of conflict can be avoided through the method of "systemic integration". This method is sanctioned by Article 31(3)(c) of the VCLT, which requires treaties to be interpreted together with other "relevant rules of international law applicable in the relations between the parties".[137] It promotes complementarity between *prima facie* inconsistent regimes. The benefit of integrating BITs and IHL is twofold: first, it ensures that investment tribunals retain jurisdiction to hear investor-State disputes in wartime;[138] and second, it allows arbitrators to judge State conduct on the basis of the rules and expectations that inform the conduct of military professionals in occupied areas.[139]

For foreign investors, however, the systemic integration of BITs and IHL comes at a great price. As will be shown below, the jurisdiction *ratione personae*

---

136   I.L.C., *Fragmentation of International Law: Difficulties arising from the Diversification and Expansion of International Law, Report of the Study Group of the International Law Commission*, U.N. Doc. A/CN.4/L682 (Apr. 13, 2006), at para. ¶25 [*hereinafter* ILC Fragmentation].

137   *See* VCLT, art. 31(3)(c).

138   The International Law Commission (ILC) formulated and defended this principle of systemic integration in the 2006 report on the fragmentation of international law. According to the ILC, an international tribunal can rely upon this method to reach beyond the "four corners" of the particular instrument that confers it with jurisdiction to hear the dispute. In the case of investment arbitral tribunals, this means that they may apply and interpret investment treaties in relation to their normative environment, which include other regimes of international law, such as IHL. *See* ILC Fragmentation, paras. 410–423.

139   *See, e.g.*, David Kennedy, Of Law and War 102 (2006); "Military professionals the world over are emboldened by the confidence that what they do on the battlefield, in war, should be judged by different standards, tested by different rules, than what they do at home with their families, when their communities are at peace".

of an investment tribunal may be limited to "protected persons" under the Fourth Geneva Convention; and the substantive investment guarantees contained in BITs may be diluted during occupation.

A   *The Jurisdiction* ratione personae *of Investment Tribunals and the Concept of "Protected Persons" under the Fourth Geneva Convention*

Only "investors" are entitled to bring investment-treaty claims under a BIT. Most BITs define the term "investor" as: 1) natural persons who are considered nationals or citizens of one of the contracting Parties (the home State of the investor); or 2) companies and other legal entities which have a registered office or their seat in the territory of the home State.[140] Of course, the investor-claimant must also have an investment in the territory of the other contracting Party (the host State).[141]

But the personal scope of application of BITs does not necessarily overlap with the personal scope of application of the rules governing occupation. During occupation, not everyone enjoys "protected person" status under the Fourth Geneva Convention. Article 4 excludes from the protection of the Convention the following categories of persons: 1) nationals of the Occupying Power; 2) nationals of a co-belligerent, if their country and the Occupying Power maintain normal diplomatic relations; 3) persons who are protected by the First and Third Geneva Conventions (mainly members of the armed forces of a belligerent who are *hors de combat*); and 4) nationals of a State which is not bound by the Convention.[142]

---

140   *See, e.g.*, Article 1(2) of the Agreement between the Arab Republic of Egypt and the Federal Republic of Germany concerning the Encouragement and Reciprocal Protection of Investments.

141   Generally, the term "investment" in BITs is broadly defined as "any kind of asset" owned or controlled by an investor, including movable and immovable property, shares in companies, concessions and intellectual property rights. *See Id.*, art. 1(1).

142   Fourth Geneva Convention art. 4; "Persons protected by the Convention are those who, at a given moment and in any manner whatsoever, find themselves, in case of a conflict or occupation, in the hands of a Party to the conflict or Occupying Power of which they are not nationals. Nationals of a State which is not bound by the Convention are not protected by it. Nationals of a neutral State who find themselves in the territory of a belligerent State, and nationals of a co-belligerent State, shall not be regarded as protected persons while the State of which they are nationals has normal diplomatic representation in the State in whose hands they are." The provisions of Part II are, however, wider in application, as defined in Article 13; "Persons protected by the Geneva Convention for the Amelioration of the Condition of the Wounded and Sick in Armed Forces in the Field of August 12, 1949, or by the Geneva Convention for the Amelioration of the Condition

OCCUPANTS, BEWARE OF BITS 171

Thus, a foreigner may qualify as an "investor" under the applicable BIT, but he or she may not be a "protected person" under Article 4 of the Fourth Geneva Convention. Would an arbitral tribunal called upon to settle a dispute arising out of occupation measures have jurisdiction in cases involving a foreign investor who does not enjoy "protected person" status in occupied territory? Put differently, is the jurisdiction *ratione personae* of an arbitral tribunal limited to persons who qualify both as "investors" under the applicable BIT and as "protected" under the Fourth Geneva Convention?

Because Article 43 of the Hague Regulations is the "entry point" for BITs during occupation, the jurisdiction of an arbitral tribunal appears to be subordinated to the law of occupation. Thus, it could be argued that persons who are not "protected" under the Fourth Geneva Convention may not rely on Article 43 of the Hague Regulations as the basis for an arbitral tribunal's jurisdiction over the occupant. Although the personal scope of the Hague Regulations is broader than that of the Fourth Geneva Convention,[143] this is one area where the Fourth Geneva Convention appears to have replaced the Hague Regulations.[144] Accordingly, the concept of "protected persons" under the Fourth Geneva Convention must be read into the Hague Regulations as well. From this perspective, a claim may be made that an investment tribunal lacks personal jurisdiction over investors who do not fall within the definition of "protected persons" under the Fourth Geneva Convention.

Now, of the 4 categories of persons listed above who do not enjoy "protected person" status, categories 1) and 2) are the most significant to the application of BITs to occupied territories. The first category excludes the nationals of the occupant, even if they live in occupied territory. It follows that Russian investors in Crimea may not invoke the Russia-Ukraine BIT to challenge Russia's occupation measures. Under the second category, nationals of a co-belligerent State which maintains diplomatic relations with the occupying State would seem to be precluded from bringing investment treaty claims against the occupant. This means that, during the occupation of Iraq, for example, nationals of States

---

of Wounded, Sick and Shipwrecked Members of Armed Forces at Sea of August 12, 1949, or by the Geneva Convention relative to the Treatment of Prisoners of War of August 12, 1949, shall not be considered as protected persons within the meaning of the present Convention" (emphasis added). *See also* Fourth Geneva Convention commentary, 46.

143 The Hague Regulations apply to "inhabitants" in general, while in occupied territories the protections of the Fourth Geneva Convention only extend to "protected persons". This discrepancy has been noted by several scholars, including Dinstein; *see* Dinstein (2009), 61–62.

144 *See* Greenspan, 156.

which participated in the Coalition led by the US, such as the UK, Australia, Spain, and Poland,[145] would not have been able to bring claims against the US under Iraqi BITs.

B *Substantive Investment Protections during Belligerent Occupation*

Article 53 of the Fourth Geneva Convention prohibits the destruction of private property by the Occupying Power except where such destruction is rendered absolutely necessary by military operations.[146] Thus, the destruction of a civilian building, such as a restaurant, used regularly by members of a hostile armed group to plan attacks against the occupying forces may be lawful under IHL. Conversely, the destruction of the restaurant may be a breach of the full protection and security (FPS) standard of a BIT, if it is established that the military operation should have been preceded by an attempt to arrest the members of the armed group.[147]

To resolve this *prima facie* normative conflict, investment tribunals may resort to the method of "systemic integration" codified in Article 31(3)(c) of the VCLT. This provision requires treaties to be interpreted together with other "relevant rules of international law applicable in the relations between the parties". The ICJ followed a similar solution in *Nuclear Weapons* to determine the scope and content of the human right to life, as codified in the International Covenant on Civil and Political Rights (ICCPR), in times of armed conflict. The ICJ held:

> In principle, the right not arbitrarily to be deprived of one's life applies also in hostilities. The test of what is an arbitrary deprivation of life, however, then falls to be determined by the applicable lex specialis, namely, the law applicable in armed conflict which is designed to regulate the conduct of hostilities. Thus whether a particular loss of life, through the

---

145 *See* Jack L. Goldsmith, *Protected Persons Status in Occupied Iraq under the Fourth Geneva Convention*, Memorandum Opinion for the Counsel to the President (Mar. 18, 2004), at 9, http://nsarchive.gwu.edu/torturingdemocracy/documents/20040318.pdf.

146 Fourth Geneva Convention art. 53.

147 *See, generally,* Asian Agricultural Products Ltd. v. Republic of Sri Lanka, I.C.S.I.D. Case No. ARB/87/3,. The majority decision has been criticized elsewhere by the author for failing to take into account the fact that the State operation that resulted in the destruction of a shrimp farm owned by the claimant occurred in the context of an non-international armed conflict. *See* Ofilio Mayorga, *Arbitrating War: Military Necessity as a Defense to the Breach of Investment Treaty Obligations*, Harvard Program on Humanitarian Policy and Conflict Research, Policy Brief (Aug. 2013) [*hereinafter* Mayorga] (generally discussing the conflict between full protection and security guarantees under investment treaties and IHL's targeting norms).

OCCUPANTS, BEWARE OF BITS

use of a certain weapon in warfare, is to be considered an arbitrary deprivation of life contrary to Article 6 of the Covenant, can only be decided by reference to the law applicable in armed conflict and not deduced from the terms of the Covenant itself.[148]

In light of the ICJ's analysis in the *Nuclear Weapons*, the test of what constitutes a breach of investment treaty protections in occupied territories, such as the FPS standard or fair and equitable treatment, will be determined by reference to the applicable *lex specialis, i.e.,* IHL. This is also possible because investment treaties do not operate in isolation. As the majority opinion of the arbitral tribunal in the case *Asian Agricultural Products Ltd v Sri Lanka* stated:

> the Bilateral Investment Treaty is not a self-contained closed legal system limited to provide the substantive material rules of direct applicability, but it has to be envisaged within a wider juridical context in which rules from other sources are integrated through implied incorporation methods, or by direct reference to certain supplementary rules, whether of international law character or of domestic law nature.[149]

In case of destruction of foreign-owned property by occupation authorities in the course of military operations, the material scope of the FPS standard in the applicable BIT must be determined by reference to the concept of military necessity under Article 53 of the Fourth Geneva Convention. While the FPS standard generally limits the State's right to use force in times of peace, military necessity grants the parties to a conflict the ability to inflict a certain degree of injury, death, or destruction in order to defeat the enemy. Therefore, in situations of armed hostilities, the FPS standard will be substantially modified by IHL.[150]

Another investment protection guarantee that will likely be diluted with the application of a BIT to occupied territories is the right to receive compensation for the taking of private property that could be used as *materiel de guerre* or for the transport of things or persons. Most BITs provide that, in case of direct or indirect expropriations, the State must pay the foreign investor "prompt, adequate and effective compensation".[151] But according to Article 53, paragraph 2, of the Hague Regulations, the Occupying Power may seize "All appliances, whether on land, at sea, or in the air, adapted for the transmission of

---

148   Nuclear Weapons, para. 25.

149   *See* Asian Agricultural Products Ltd v Sri Lanka, 587.

150   *See* Mayorga.

151   *See, e.g.,* Russian Federation–Ukraine BIT art. 5.

news or for the transport of persons or things ... depots of arms, and, generally, all kinds of munitions of war ... even if they belong to private individuals, but must be restored and compensation fixed when peace is made".[152] Under this provision, the occupant may seize buses, aircraft, trucks, railway rolling stock owned by private individuals, and it is not required to pay compensation until the end of hostilities.[153] The termination of an armed conflict is, of course, difficult to predict. What is clear is that the meaning of "prompt" compensation for the taking of the type of items listed in Article 53 of the Fourth Geneva Convention will be assessed from the date peace is concluded.

There are instances of complementarity, though, where the enforcement of investment-treaty guarantees advances IHL norms. Article 52 of the Hague Regulations allows the occupant to demand requisitions in kind and services from the local inhabitants.[154] The concept "requisitions in kind" generally refers to the seizure of movable property, such as equipment and supplies for the proper functioning of the occupation authorities, or food for the members of the armed forces. Requisitions in services, on the other hand, include the temporary use of immovable property for the billeting or lodgment of troops. The requisition of private property must be done against payment of compensation, preferably in cash, and as soon as possible. Requisitioning for any other purpose other than the needs of the army of occupation, *i.e.* to satisfy the demand for food of the population of the Occupying Power at home, is unlawful under the Hague Regulations[155] and may result in an unlawful expropriation or even the breach of the fair and equitable standard of the applicable BIT.

The occupant's regulations may also come under the scrutiny of investment-treaty tribunals. It is true that occupants enjoy broad legislative powers under the Hague Regulations and the Fourth Geneva Convention, but any regulation passed without a legitimate desire to promote public order and civil life in the occupied territory may result in a compensable regulatory taking under a BIT.[156]

---

152   *See* Hague Regulations art. 52.

153   *See* Dinstein, 232–234.

154   *See* Hague Regulations art. 52.

155   *See* Dinstein, 227–229.

156   *See also* Edmund H Schwenk, *Legislative Power of the Military Occupant under Article 43, Hague Regulations*, 54 Yale L. J. 393, 398–399 (1944–1945); explaining the scope of the regulatory powers of the occupant under article 43 of the Hague Regulations: "While the occupant can restore public order and civil life only when they have been disrupted, he may legislate to ensure them in the absence of any disturbance ... Thus it follows that, when public order and civil life have remained undisturbed, the validity of legislation under Article 43 depends on whether or not the legislating occupant was motivated by a desire to ensure them".

In short, the law of belligerent occupation provides the substantive law in a dispute between an investor and an occupant. On the other hand, the arbitration clause of the applicable BIT operates as the enforcer of IHL in the dispute.

This type of interaction is more likely in cases of short-lived occupations which are exclusively motivated by the military objectives of one of the parties to an armed conflict. The best example of this would be the U.S. occupation of Iraq in 2003. But in cases like Crimea, where the occupant purports to annex the occupied territory in violation of international law, or in cases of prolonged occupations where the occupant no longer confronts an armed resistance, certain provisions in the Hague Regulations or the Fourth Geneva Convention which are specific to the realities of war may be irrelevant. In such situations, an investment tribunal could apply investment-treaty guarantees in isolation. But this does not mean that the law of occupation will cease to apply as a whole.[157] The legality of the acts of the occupants will still be subject to the general duty of maintaining and ensuring public order and civil life in the occupied territory.[158]

---

157 *See* Lauri Malsko, Illegal Annexation and State Continuity: The Case of the Incorporation of the Baltic States by the USSR 189, 193 (2003); concluding that the Hague Regulations applied to the Baltic States from the USSR's annexation in 1940 until their independence in 1991: " ... the Soviet military occupations of 1940, just as other occupations of that time, must be measured by the yardstick of the 1907 Hague Regulations ... Since the Soviet annexation of the Baltic States in 1940 lacked any ground in international law, and a significant segment of the international community refused to grant formal approval of Soviet conquest, the ultimate failure of the USSR to acquire a legal title over the Baltic States implies automatically that the regime of occupation as such was, as a matter of international law, not terminated until the independence of Estonia, Latvia and Lithuania was reestablished in 1991."

158 In the case of an illegal annexation that endures over time, international arbitral tribunals should resist the temptation of treating the entire period of occupation as a legal *nullum. See Id.*, 194; " ... the fact and reality of annexation practices cannot be completely ignored, as if they had never existed ... For instance, by imposing the Soviet economic system on the Baltic States, the USSR clearly violated the 1907 Hague rules of occupation. However, it is reasonable to argue that the principle *ex factis ius oritur* compels acceptance of certain aspects of the foreign-imposed Soviet economic system in the decades following the illegal annexation as facts of life. The whole Soviet occupation period cannot be regarded as a legal *nullum*. Thus, the foreign-imposed Soviet economic system in the whole Eastern Europe became a fact of life which was ultimately borne by the local population and as such was accepted by the international community. Since it was no longer legally questioned, neither internationally nor domestically, it would be artificial to maintain that the system continued to violate the 1907 Hague Regulations."

V   Conclusion

BITs incorporated into the domestic legal system of the occupied State are "laws in force" for the purposes of Article 43 of the Hague Regulations. Thus, the occupant must respect those BITs as a result of its obligation to ensure civil life and public order in the occupied territories.

This also means that the occupant has the right to suspend the application of BITs in force in occupied territories as any other domestic law or regulation. But the occupant may only exercise this power to guarantee the security of its forces and the legitimate military goals of the occupation. If the enforcement of investment guarantees does not affect either, the suspension of a BIT would be contrary to international law. In an investor-occupant dispute, for example, where it is clear that the Occupying Power has seized foreign-owned property as part of its overall effort to annex the occupied territory, the arbitral tribunal should resist any of the occupant's excuses to avoid the application of the BIT in question.

Moreover, the occupant cannot claim immunity from the arbitral jurisdiction of BITs in force in occupied territories. The reason for this is that arbitral proceedings will not undermine the security of the occupant's forces or the legitimate military goals of an occupation.

The continuity of BITs in times of belligerent occupation implies that they must coexist with IHL. Although the co-application of these two bodies of international law may result in the dilution of investment-treaty guarantees, BITs provide an effective enforcement mechanism of IHL that would otherwise not exist during occupation. Indeed, the lack of effective implementation and enforcement mechanisms is widely regarded as IHL's "Achilles heel".[159] This problem is particularly salient in the law of occupation. But the right of foreign investors to submit investment disputes against the occupant may certainly contribute to reducing the serious enforcement gap that undermines the law of occupation's role in preserving the territorial integrity of occupied States.

---

159   Kolb, 187–189.

The Fragmentation of International Law: Contemporary Debates and Responses

*Musa Njabulo Shongwe**

I   Introduction   178
II Manifestations of the Problems of Fragmentation   180
    A   *Conflicting Interpretations*   180
    B   *Special Law Claiming Exception or Priority*   182
        1   The *MOX Plant* Case   182
        2   The Southern Bluefin Tuna Case (*Australia and New Zealand v. Japan*)   185
        3   Belilos v. Switzerland   187
    C   *Other Examples*   189
III Addressing Treaty Conflicts by Applying Conflict Rules   192
    A   *Jus Cogens*   192
    B   *The Vienna Convention on the Law of Treaties and the* lex posterior *Principle*   194
    C   *Article 103 of the UN Charter*   196
    D   *Lex Specialis*   204
    E   *Hierarchical Considerations*   206
IV The Institutional Problem   207
V   The Big Debate   210
VI Concluding Remarks   218

Abstract

The fragmentation of international law is an undeniable issue in contemporary international law, which has received some considerable critical attention this past decade. Regardless of the fact that this is an age-old problem, its recent manifestations have sparked a debate in which two groups of international

---

*   Post-Doctoral Research Fellow at the South African National Research Chair in International Law, University of Johannesburg. Email: musanjabuloshongwe@yahoo.com.

scholars (positivists and realists) have expressed contesting views on whether fragmentation is a real problem to be solved, or simply a pure academic anxiety about the future of international law. This paper describes why and how fragmentation is a problem of international law, through case law examples of substantive and procedural aspects of fragmentation. The paper then analyses the value of international law mechanisms of dealing with normative conflicts, as well as the shortcomings of those tools. The paper reviews the ongoing debate as to whether fragmentation is a negative or a positive force in the international legal order. The paper contributes to the academic debate by arguing that because of the structural make-up of the international legal system, fragmentation is inevitable, but at the same time, it is a manageable phenomenon. It is argued that fragmentation is a permanent feature of the international legal system, and as such, its relevance to the future of international law must not be undermined. The paper also argues and recommends that the ever-important goal of ensuring unity and coherence of the international legal system should never be lost, and this argument is advanced in view of contemporary academic scholarship that seeks to put the matter of fragmentation to rest.

I   Introduction

Because of its many facets, the concept of fragmentation in international law does not carry a straight forward definition.[1] However, the fragmentation of international law denotes the fracture of the international legal order caused by the proliferation of specialized functional regimes of international law.[2] The proliferation of specialized regimes transforms international law into a network of legal orders that operate under their own primary principles and that may, at times, be at variance with general international law. The modern international legal system has indeed become an elaborate and fragmented

---

1   There is no universally accepted definition of "fragmentation" in international law. *See* Cheng Tai-Heng, *Making International Law without Knowing What It Is*, 10 Washington Univ. Glob. Stud. L. Rev. 1 (2011).

2   *See* Bruno Simma, *The Universality of International Law from the Perspective of a Practitioner*, 20 Eur. J. Int'l L. 265, 270 (2009). The International Law Commission has also described fragmentation as the disassociation of international law into "specialized and (relatively) autonomous rules or rule complexes"; *see* I.L.C., *Fragmentation of International Law: Difficulties Arising from the Diversification and Expansion of International Law*, in *Report of the International Law Commission, 58th Session*, U.N. Doc. A/61/10 (2006); U.N. Doc. A/CN.4/L.682 (Apr. 13, 2006), para. 8 [*hereinafter* ILC Report].

structure.[3] It is a legal system made up of many other sub-systems. That is why other scholars have defined fragmentation as "the increased proliferation of international regulatory institutions with overlapping jurisdictions and ambiguous boundaries".[4] Fragmentation, or the effects thereof, has also been described as the interaction between conflicting rules and institutional practices that culminate in the erosion of general international law.[5] Fragmentation therefore presents both normative and institutional problems for international law, and there is a correlation between the substantive and institutional aspects of fragmentation.[6]

The rapid development of modern international law has been characterized by increased levels of specialization. Matters once governed by general international law have become the field for specialist systems such as "trade law", "human rights law", "environmental law", "law of the sea", etc. – each possessing their own principles and institutions.[7] Specialized regimes have proliferated as a result of the practical needs of specialization in international law.[8] They have been designed to better regulate the particularities of a specific subject area more effectively than general international law.[9]

Normative conflicts have since occurred between general international law and its specialized branches and also between those branches *inter se*.[10] When the rules of a special regime are incompatible with either general international law or rules of another special regime, a conflict may occur which must be resolved by applying rules of international law[11] since the international legal

---

3   Bruno Simma and Dirk Pulkowski, *Of Planets and the Universe: Self-Contained Regimes in International Law*, 17 Eur. J. Int'l L. 485 (2006).

4   Eyal Benvenisti and George Downs, *The Empire's New Clothes: Political Economy and the Fragmentation of International Law*, 60 Stanford L. Rev. 595, 596 (2007).

5   Sahib Singh, *The Potential of International Law: Fragmentation and Ethics*, 24 Leiden J. Int'l L. 23, 24–25 (2011).

6   *See* Tomer Broude and Yuval Shany, The Shifting of Allocation of Authority in International Law 99 (2008).

7   ILC Report, para. 8.

8   Daniel Joyner and Marco Roscini, Non-Proliferation Law as a Special Regime: A Contribution to Fragmentation Theory in International Law 1 (2013).

9   Martii Koskenniemi and Paivio Leino, *Fragmentation of International Law: Postmodern Anxieties*, 15 Leiden J. Int'l L. 553–579 (2002).

10   *See* Andreas Fischer-Lescano and Gunther Teubner, *Regime Collisions: The Vain Search for Legal Unity in the Fragmentation of Global Law*, 25 Mich. J. Int'l L. 999, 1018 (2004).

11   These include the rules of interpretation under article 31 of the Vienna Convention on the Law of Treaties, rules of hierarchy and other legal techniques that are discussed further below.

system is decentralized and non-hierarchical. The conflicts and incompatibilities that may arise or have occurred between international norms of different regimes have brought about a considerable volume of legal scholarship and writings that reflect on the cohesiveness of international law.

This paper analyses legal theory on the fragmentation of international law with the view to understand whether conflicts within the international legal system present real problems that threaten the viability, credibility or reliability of the system, or, whether they present only manageable theoretical problems that may easily be overcome through legal reasoning and application of readily available legal mechanisms. For that purpose, the paper starts by highlighting some past and present problems of fragmentation of international law through case law examples. The effect of these problems is then highlighted through an identification of the shortcomings of tools provided by international law for the resolution of normative conflicts. From that analysis, the paper then presents an opinion based on academic debates on whether fragmentation is a positive or a negative phenomenon for the future of the international legal system. This paper provides a contribution in line with the past decade of scholarly work on fragmentation, most specifically, since the conclusion of the International Law Commission (ILC) study on fragmentation in 2006.

II   Manifestations of the Problems of Fragmentation

A   *Conflicting Interpretations*

Normative conflicts often give rise to legal issues, and these issues are based on the consideration of "specialty" or "generality" of the conflicting norms. The first clearest example of a conflict of interpretations of a rule of general international law became available in the comparison of the two cases: *Prosecutor v. Dusko Tadić* (1999)[12] and *Nicaragua v. United States of America* (1986).[13] In the *Tadić* case, the International Criminal Tribunal for the former Yugoslavia (ICTY) Appeals Chamber considered the responsibility of Serbia-Montenegro for the acts of Bosnian Serb militia in the conflict in the former Yugoslavia. For this purpose, it examined the jurisprudence of the International Court of Justice (ICJ) in the earlier *Nicaragua* case where the United States (US) had

---

12   Prosecutor v. Tadić, Case No.IT-94-1-A, A.Ch, Judgment (Int'l Crim. Trib. for the Former Yugoslavia July 15, 1999) [*hereinafter* Tadić Judgment].

13   Military and Paramilitary Activities in and against Nicaragua (Nicar. v. U.S.), Judgment, 1986 I.C.J. Rep. 14 (June 27), 64–65 [*hereinafter* ICJ Nicaragua].

THE FRAGMENTATION OF INTERNATIONAL LAW   181

not been held responsible for the acts of the Nicaraguan *contras* merely on account of organizing, financing, training and equipping them. Such involvement failed to meet the standard of "effective control".[14] The ICTY, for its part, concluded that "effective control" set too high a threshold for holding an outside power legally accountable for domestic unrest.[15] It was sufficient that the power has "a role in organizing, coordinating, or planning the military actions of the military group", that is to say that it exercised "overall control" over them for the conflict to be an "international armed conflict".[16] From this contrast it was observed that the *Tadić* decision did not suggest "overall control" to exist alongside "effective control" either as an exception to the general law or as a special (local) regime governing the Yugoslav conflict. It sought to replace the standard. Even though this may be a common occurrence in any legal system, its consequences for the international legal system (which lacks a proper institutional hierarchy) might be particularly problematic. The collision between the ICJ and the ICTY in this case brought about the initial anxiety over fragmentation. The fact that the ICTY had earlier referred to itself as a self-contained regime sparked more concerns over fragmentation.[17]

The *Nicaragua-Tadić* divide attracted considerable attention in the debate over the fragmentation of international law.[18] The ILC report stated that such conflicts create two types of problems: first, they diminish legal certainty because legal subjects are no longer able to predict the reaction of official institutions to their behavior and to plan their activity accordingly; and second, they put legal subjects in an unequal position *vis-à-vis* each other.[19] The *Nicaragua-Tadić* experience also draws attention to the issue of consistency within international courts[20] because the ICJ and the ICTY came to different conclusions on the legal effects of third-party involvement (particularly third party control

---

14   Tadić Judgment, para. 109.

15   *Id.,* paras. 115–116.

16   *Id.*

17   Prosecutor v. Tadić, Case No. IT-94-1-AR72, Decision on the Defense Motion for Interlocutory Appeal on Jurisdiction, para. 11. (Int'l Crim. Trib. For the Former Yugoslavia Oct. 2, 1995) [*hereinafter* Tadić Appeal].

18   *See* Mark Drumbl, *Looking Up, Down and Across: The ICTY's Place in the International Legal Order,* 37 New England L. Rev. 1037 (2003); Mohamed Shahabudde, *Consistency in Holdings of International Tribunals, in* Liber Amicorum Judge Shigeru Oda 633–650 (Nisuke Ando, Edward McWhinney and Rudiger Wolfrum eds., 2002).

19   *See, generally,* ILC Report.

20   Richard Goldstone & Rebecca Hamilton, *Bosnia v Serbia: Lessons from the Encounter of the International Court of Justice with the International Tribunal for the Former Yugoslavia,* 21 Leiden J. Int'l L. 95 (2008).

of rebel forces) on armed conflicts, and State responsibility for internationally wrongful acts.

B *Special Law Claiming Exception or Priority*

Special law occurs where an international court or institution makes a decision that deviates from how situations of a similar type have been decided in the past because the new case is held to be regulated, not under the general rule, but by an "exception" to it. The cases that follow below illustrate this point.

1 The *MOX Plant* Case

The *Mox Plant* case shows the marginalization of general international law by the European Court of Justice (ECJ).[21] It was observed how a special legal regime (the European regime) claimed priority over the general international legal system.[22] The matter was part of a series of cases brought by Ireland against the United Kingdom (UK) concerning the operation of a nuclear reprocessing plant at Sellafield, UK. In this case, the regime under the United Nations (UN) Convention on the Law of the Sea (UNCLOS) conflicted with the system under European Commission (EC) Law. A complaint had been raised by Ireland against the UK on account of the potential environmental effects of the plant under two international treaties.[23] One was the Convention on the Protection of the Marine Environment of the North-East Atlantic (OSPAR Convention) dealing with the protection of the environment of the North Sea, and the other was the UNCLOS. Having heard of these proceedings, the EC, for its part, raised a claim against Ireland on account of Ireland's having taken the conduct of the UK – another member State of the European Union (EU) – to international arbitration, that is to say, to be legally assessed under rules other than those of European law by bodies other than European ones. The Court condemned Ireland on all accounts. Ireland had failed to respect the exclusive

---

21 Case C-459/03, Comm'n v. Ireland, 2006 E.C.R. I-04635. There had been a series of cases brought by Ireland against the United Kingdom concerning the operation of the nuclear processing plant in Sellafield; *see* Dispute Concerning Access to Information Under Article 9 of the OSPAR Convention (Ir. v. U.K.), XXIII RIAA 59 (Perm. Ct. Arb. 2003), 42 I.L.M. 1118 [*hereinafter* Ireland v. UK]. The other cases are: MOX Plant (Ir. v. U.K.), Case No. 10, Order, Request for Provisional Measures of Dec. 3, 2001, ITLOS ICGJ 343, 41 I.L.M. 405 [*hereinafter* MOX Plant Provisional Measures]; MOX Plant (Ir. v. U.K.), 126 ILR 310 (Perm. Ct. Arb. 2003), 42 I.L.M. 1187.

22 *See* this discussion in: Martii Koskeniemmi, International Law: Between Fragmentation and Constitutionalism 1 (2006).

23 *See* Ireland v. UK.

THE FRAGMENTATION OF INTERNATIONAL LAW

jurisdiction of the ECJ, and its duty to cooperate under Article 10 of the EC Treaty which provides that:

> Member States shall take all appropriate measures, whether general or particular, to ensure fulfilment of the obligations arising out of this Treaty or resulting from action taken by the institutions of the Community. They shall facilitate the achievement of the Community's tasks. They shall abstain from any measure which could jeopardize the attainment of the objectives of this Treaty.

Upon considering the UK's objection to its jurisdiction on account that the same matter was pending before an OSPAR arbitral tribunal as well as the ECJ, the Arbitral Tribunal[24] observed that:

> ... even if the OSPAR Convention, the EC Treaty and the Euratom treaty contain rights or obligations similar to or identical with the rights set out in the [UNCLOS], the rights and obligations under these agreements have a separate existence from those under [the UNCLOS].[25]

Three different institutional procedures were raised in this case, namely: an Arbitral Tribunal set up under Annex VII of the UNCLOS; the compulsory dispute settlement procedure under the OSPAR Convention; as well as under the European Community and Euratom Treaties within the ECJ. The difficult questions arising were whether the problem was principally about the law of the sea, or about possible pollution of the North Sea, or about inter EC relationships.[26] All three rule-complexes appeared to address the same facts: the (universal) rules of the UNCLOS, the (regional) rules of the OSPAR Convention, and the (regional) rules of EC/EURATOM. It is not clear as to which of these should be determinative, how the rule-complexes link to each other, and most importantly, what principles or tools of public international law should be used in order to decide a potential conflict between them.[27]

This case therefore shows the ECJ treating the EU as a sovereign, whose laws override any other legal structure. In appealing to international law against the UK, Ireland was violating the sovereignty of European law. The Arbitral

---

24   Set up under Annex VII of the UNCLOS; *see* U.N. Convention on the Law of the Sea, Nov. 16, 1994, 1833 U.N.T.S. 397 [*hereinafter* UNCLOS].

25   MOX Plant Provisional Measures, para. 50.

26   ILC Report, para. 10.

27   *Id.*, para. 13.

Tribunal established under UNCLOS to consider the merits of the case displayed some comity or a degree of deference to the dispute's regional context by suspending the proceedings.[28] This was done on the basis that it was likely that aspects of the dispute fell within the exclusive jurisdiction of the ECJ,[29] which called into question the tribunal's jurisdiction over aspects of the claims before it.[30] Subsequently, in 2003, the tribunal suspended the proceedings, and stated that:

> ... bearing in mind considerations of mutual respect and comity which should prevail between judicial institutions both of which may be called upon to determine rights and obligations as between two States ... it would be inappropriate ... to proceed further with hearing the Parties on the merits of the dispute in the absence of a resolution of the problems referred to. Moreover, a procedure that might result in two conflicting decisions on the same issue would not be helpful to the resolution of the dispute between the Parties.[31]

The *MOX Plant* case was not the only case in which the ECJ viewed the EU as a special legal regime that claimed priority over the general international legal system. In *NV Algemene Transport-en Expeditie Ondememing Van Gend en Loos v Nederlandse Administratie der Belastingen* (*Netherlands Inland Revenue Administration*),[32] the ECJ stated that the European Community constitutes a

---

28 The Tribunal's order to suspend proceedings was made under its rules of procedure, which state that "subject to these rules, the Arbitral Tribunal may conduct the proceedings in such manner as it considers appropriate"; *see MOX Plant Provisional Measures. See also* Rules of Procedure, Arbitral Tribunal Constituted under Article 287 and Annex 1, UNCLOS art. 1.

29 It may also be noted that even if the content of the rights and obligations under these conventions was similar or identical, their application by one tribunal might result in a different outcome from their application by another tribunal on account of "differences in the respective context, object and purpose, subsequent practice of parties and *travaux préparatoires*"; Mox Plant Provisional Measures, para. 51.

30 *See* ILC Report, paras. 51–52.

31 *MOX Plant* (*Ir. v. U.K.*), Suspension of Proceedings on Jurisdiction and Merits and Request for Further Provisional Measures, Order No. 3, 2003 Perm. Ct. Arb. (June 24), paras. 21–28. Subsequently, the tribunal made a further order suspending the proceedings until a judgment of the ECJ; *see* Further Suspension of Proceedings on Jurisdiction and Merits, Order No. 4, 2003 Perm. Ct. Arb. (Nov. 13).

32 Case 26/62, NV Algemene Transport- en Expeditie Onderneming van Gend & Loos v. Netherlands Inland Revenue Administration, 1963 E.C.R. 1, para 3.

THE FRAGMENTATION OF INTERNATIONAL LAW

new legal order for international law for the benefit of which the States have limited their sovereign rights. The separate character of EU law was also confirmed in the subsequent cases of *Flamino Costa v ENEL*[33] and *Commission of the European Community v Grand Duchy of Luxembourg and Kingdom of Belgium*.[34]

2   The Southern Bluefin Tuna Case (*Australia and New Zealand v. Japan*)

This case, before the UN Law of the Sea Tribunal (ITLOS), demonstrates the problems incurred by the applicability of more than one regulation to a given case. This case was held at the World Bank headquarters in Washington as an Arbitral Tribunal.[35] The case[36] concerned the Southern Bluefin Tuna (SBT), a severely depleted species. The main areas to engage in fishing for SBT are Australia, Japan and New Zealand. The three States realized the dramatic reduction of SBT and in May 1993 they signed the Convention for the Conservation of Southern Bluefin Tuna (CCSBT). The main purpose of the CCSBT is to decide measures of management for the SBT and the total allowable catch. There was a total allowable catch of 11,750 tons. In 1998, Japan decided to start an Experimental Fishing Program (EFP) because of their uncertainty in the SBT stock assessment. New Zealand and Australia rejected the EFP because it is outside the framework of the Commission. The two states submitted the dispute to arbitration and filed a request for provisional measures with ITLOS against Japan. Japan challenged the jurisdiction of the ITLOS.[37] Japan claimed that even if the ITLOS claimed jurisdiction, provisional measures were not warranted. Under the CCBST, Japan felt that their actions presented no risk of irreparable injury to the SBT stock and that the two States would be fully compensated by future reductions in Japan's catch. Japan's final claim was that the two States resume negotiations with a new view on the total allowable catch, annual quotas and continuation of EFP. The defendants claimed that the Japanese EFP is a violation of its duty to cooperate in the conservation in the SBT treaty and UNCLOS.[38] Unilateralism was not part of the SBT Treaty

---

33   Case 6/64, Flaminio Costa v. E.N.E.L., 1964 E.C.R. 585, 593.

34   Case 90/63 & 91/63, Commission of the European Economic Community v Grand Duchy of Luxembourg and Kingdom of Belgium, 1964 E.C.R. 625.

35   *See* the case summary in Kerry Hancock, *Southern Bluefin Tuna Cases*, unpublished (2009), http://courses.kvasaheim.com/ps376/briefs/kehancockbrief4.pdf (visited 6 January 2016).

36   *Id.*

37   *Id.*

38   *Id.*

and would thoroughly hurt the framework of the defined regional fishery organization. One of the legal issues was whether the ITLOS under UNCLOS had jurisdiction to hear and decide this case.

In this case, Japan had argued, *inter alia,* that the 1993 Convention on the Conservation of the Southern Bluefin Tuna (CCSBT) applied to the case both as *lex specialis* and *lex posterior*, hence excluding the application of the 1982 UNCLOS.[39] It was, however, held that both the 1982 and the 1993 instruments were applicable. The Arbitration Tribunal stated that:

> It is a commonplace of international law and State practice for more than one treaty to bear upon a particular dispute. There is no reason why a given act of a State may not violate its obligations under more than one treaty. There is frequently a parallelism of treaties, both in their substantive content and in their provisions for settlement of disputes arising there under. The current range of international legal obligations benefits from a process of accretion and cumulation; in the practice of States, the conclusion of an implementing convention does not necessarily vacate the obligations imposed by the framework convention upon the parties to the implementing convention. The broad provision for the promotion of universal respect for and observance of human rights, and the international obligation to cooperate for the achievement of those purposes, found in the Articles 1, 55 and 56 of the Charter of the United Nations, have not been discharged for States Parties by their ratification of Human Rights Covenants and other human rights treaties [...] Nor is it clear that the particular provisions of the 1993 Convention exhaust the extent of the relevant obligations of UNCLOS. In some respects, UNCLOS may be viewed as extending beyond the reach of the CCSBT.[40]

The Tribunal spoke of "a process of accretion and cumulation" of international legal obligations,[41] which it regarded as beneficial to international law. In as much as this may be beneficial to international law, the question of course does arise whether this development might lead to a complete detachment of some areas of international law from others, without an overarching general international law remaining and holding the parts together. In arriving at this question, one would not have to go so far as to suspect that "powerful States

---

39   Southern Bluefin Tuna (Aust. v. Japan/N.Z. v. Japan), Award of 4 August 2000 (Jurisdiction and Admissibility), UNRIAA vol. XXIII (2004) 23, para. 38 (c).

40   *Id.*, paras 40–41.

41   *Id.*, para. 52.

THE FRAGMENTATION OF INTERNATIONAL LAW

labor to maintain and even actively promote fragmentation because it enables them to preserve their dominance in an era in which hierarchy is increasingly viewed as illegitimate, and to opportunistically break the rules without seriously jeopardizing the system they have created".[42]

In the author's view, to see such sinister motives at work behind the fragmentation phenomenon is not justified. A much more natural or realistic explanation may be submitted. The phenomenon of fragmentation of international law is nothing but the result of a transposition of functional differentiations of governance from the national to the international plane and from the regional to the universal plane; which means that international law today increasingly reflects the differentiation of branches of the law which are familiar to us from the domestic sphere. Consequently, international law has developed, and is still developing its own complete regulatory regimes which are increasingly competing with each other.

The doctrine of treaty parallelism addresses precisely the need to coordinate the reading of particular instruments or to see them in a mutually supportive light. At issue in the *Southern Bluefin Tuna* case was the relationship between the 1982 of the UNCLOS and a fisheries treaty concluded for the implementation of the former. It would have been awkward, and certainly not in accord with the intent of the parties, to read those instruments independently from each other. But as to how that relationship should be conceived (were they part of a "regime" or were they not?) may remain the subject of some other debate, particularly in view of the overlapping provisions on dispute-settlement. The Tribunal itself fully realized that it could not ignore the fact that the problem arose under both treaties.[43]

3   Belilos v. Switzerland[44]

The fragmentation of international law may also be illustrated by the treatment of reservations by human rights organs. In the 1988, the *Belilos* case at the

---

42   Eyal Benvenisti and George Downs, *The Empire's New Clothes: Political Economy and the Fragmentation of International Law*, 60 Stanford L. Rev. 595 (2007).

43   For the debate concerning the problems that emerge as a result of the Tribunal's preference of the dispute settlement provisions of the regional treaty (Convention for the Conservation of Southern Bluefin Tuna) to the (compulsory) provisions of Part XV UNCLOS, *see* Jacqueline Peel, *A Paper Umbrella Which Dissolves in the Rain? The Future for Resolving Fisheries Disputes under UNCLOS in the Aftermath of the Southern Bluefin Tuna Arbitration*, 3 Melbourne J. Int'l L. 53–78 (2002); Barbara Kwiatkowska, *The Ireland v. United Kingdom (Mox Plant) Case: Applying the Doctrine of Treaty Parallelism*, 18 Int'l J. Marine & Coastal L. 52 (2003).

44   Belilos v. Switzerland, App. No. 10328/83, 1988 Eur. Ct. H.R.

European Court of Human Rights (ECtHR) viewed an interpretative declaration made by Switzerland in its instrument of ratification as a reservation, and struck it down as incompatible with the object and purpose of the European Convention on Human Rights. The ECtHR discarded its legal validity as it was "couched in terms that are too vague and broad for it to be possible to determine their exact meaning or scope".[45] The invalidity affected only the reservation and not Switzerland's being party to the Convention. It was however held that Switzerland was bound by the Convention "irrespective of the validity of the declaration".[46] The *Belilos* decision was a much-debated departure from the law concerning the effect and severability of reservations.[47] In subsequent cases, the ECtHR has pointed out that the normal rules on reservations to treaties do not as such apply to human rights law. In fact, it was seven years after the *Belilos* judgment when the ECtHR, discussing the effect of certain territorial restrictions in Turkey's declarations, made it express that its role differed from that of the ICJ.[48] Article 36 of the ICJ Statute permitted "the attachment of substantive, territorial and temporal restrictions to the optional recognition of the Court's jurisdictional competence" and had served as a model for the corresponding provision in the European Convention. In the Court's view:

> ... a fundamental difference in the role and purpose of the respective tribunals [i.e. of the ICJ and the ECHR], coupled with the existence of a practice of unconditional acceptance ... provides a compelling basis for distinguishing Convention practice from that of the International Court.[49]

The Court thus dismissed Turkey's territorial delimitation, stating that the object and purpose of the Convention as an instrument for the protection of individual human beings require that its provisions be interpreted and applied so as to make its safeguards practical and effective.[50]

---

45   *Id.*, paras. 54–55.

46   *Id.*

47   Martii Koskenniemi and Paivi Leino, *Fragmentation of International Law? Postmodern Anxieties*, 15 Leiden J. Int'l L. 567 (2002) [*hereinafter* Koskenniemi & Leino].

48   Loizidou v. Turkey, App. No. 15318/89, 1995 Eur. Ct. H.R., para. 67.

49   *Id.*

50   *Id.*

THE FRAGMENTATION OF INTERNATIONAL LAW

C   *Other Examples*

Decisions of international tribunals and new patterns of State practice evincing a lack of coordination keep on emerging. This is because of the current framework of the system of international law. There have been some other notable institutional struggles most visible in the way the ICTY has taken positions that diverge from those taken by the ICJ.[51] The two tribunals have differed in their approach to their power to review UN Security Council acts. In the *Lockerbie* case,[52] the ICJ found that both Libya and the US were obliged to accept and carry out the decisions of the UN Security Council, and that by virtue of Article 103 of the Charter this obligation overrode whatever rights they may otherwise possess. An indication of provisional measures as requested by Libya would have been "likely to impair the rights which appear *prima facie* to be enjoyed by the United States by virtue of Security Council resolution 748 (1992)".[53] No review of the legality of that resolution was carried out. By contrast, after a disclaimer about not acting as a "constitutional tribunal", the ICTY Appeals Chamber expressly reviewed the legality of its own establishment.[54] While the Chamber accepted that the UN Charter left the UN Security Council much discretion as to its choice of measures, the power of the Tribunal did not disappear, especially "in cases where there might be a manifest contradiction with the Principles and Purposes of the Charter". Having concluded that it did have jurisdiction to examine the plea founded on the invalidity of its establishment, the conclusion followed almost as a matter of course that "the International Tribunal has been lawfully established as a measure under Chapter VII of the Charter".[55]

The ICTY has also taken a position diverging from that taken by the ICJ. In an Advisory Opinion delivered by the ICJ in 1996, the ICJ considered that armed reprisals in the course of an armed conflict should be "governed by the principle of proportionality".[56] In the *Martic* case,[57] the ICTY held that armed

---

51   Koskenniemi & Leino, 562–563.

52   Case Concerning Questions of Interpretation and Application of the 1971 Montreal Convention arising from the Aerial Incident at Lockerbie (Libya v. U.S.), Request for the Indication of Provisional Measures Order of 14 April 1992, 1992 ICJ Rep. 114 (Apr. 14), para. 39.

53   *Id.*, para. 41.

54   Tadić Appeal, para. 20.

55   *Id.*, paras. 21–22 & 40.

56   Legality of Threat or Use of Nuclear Weapons, Advisory Opinion, 1996 I.C.J. Rep. 226 (July 8), para. 46.

57   Prosecutor v. Milan Martić, Case No. IT-95-11-R61, T.Ch. I, (Int'l Crim. Trib. for the Former Yugoslavia Mar. 8, 1996), para. 17. The commentary appears in: Christopher Greenwood,

reprisals were altogether prohibited, prompting at least one commentator to reproach the Tribunal for a conclusion that was both unfounded and unnecessary. It is notable that these decisions were only a few months apart.

We may recall the earlier discussion of the ICTY Appeals Chamber where the *Nicaragua* decision was effectively overruled. That judgment was later challenged in the *Celebisi* case.[58] In that case the appellants argued that the ICTY was bound by the decisions of the ICJ because of the latter's position as the "principal judicial organ" of the UN.[59] The Appeals Chamber accepted that the Tribunal could not ignore the need for consistency with the general state of the law. But it stressed that the Tribunal was an "autonomous judicial body" and that there was no "hierarchical relationship" between it and the ICJ.[60]

The same questions were also discussed in yet another case when one of the accused (Žigić) made a motion appealing to suspend the procedure at the Trial Chamber while the Bosnian Genocide case was still pending before the ICJ. The argument was that the two tribunals "should not hold opposing views on the same factual or legal questions and that the Tribunal should follow the decisions of the ICJ because the ICJ is the principal judicial organ of the United Nations while the tribunal is a subsidiary organ".[61] The Trial Chamber dismissed the motion because in its view, the ICJ dealt with State responsibility while the ICTY dealt with individual responsibility. In addition, the ICTY had already pronounced on many issues involving considerations of the same kind. Moreover, the possibility of a contradiction was based purely on speculation.

Another example is found in the analysis of the case of *Prosecutor v. Delalić*.[62] In the interlude between the ICTY *Tadić* Appeal judgment and the ICJ *Bosnia Genocide* judgment, a defendant in the *Delalić* case argued that, in the first place, the ICTY was "bound" by the ICJ's Nicaragua test and, in the alternative,

---

Belligerent Reprisals in the Jurisprudence of the International Criminal Tribunal for the Former Yugoslavia, in International and National Prosecution of Crimes under International Law: Current Developments 539–558 (Horst Fischer, Klaus Kreß & Sasha Rolf Lüder eds., 2001).

58   Prosecutor v. Zejnil Delalić et al (Čelebići Camp), Case No. IT-96-21-A, Appeals Chamber, (Int'l Crim. Trib. for the Former Yugoslavia Feb. 20, 2001) [*hereinafter* ICTY Delalić et al. Appeals].

59   *Id.*

60   *Id.*

61   Prosecutor v. Miroslav Kvočka et al (Omarska, Keraterm and Trnopolje Camps), Case No. IT-98-30/1, T.Ch., Decision on the Defence Motion regarding Concurrent Procedures before International Criminal Tribunal for the Former Yugoslavia and International Court of Justice on the Same Questions (Int'l Crim. Trib. For the Former Yugoslavia Dec. 5, 2000).

62   ICTY Delalić et al Appeals, para 21.

THE FRAGMENTATION OF INTERNATIONAL LAW   191

that it was "undesirable" to have two courts with conflicting decisions on the same issue. The ICTY Appeals Chamber was not persuaded, noting that it was an "autonomous international judicial body that was not in any hierarchical relationship with the ICJ".[63] It added that it would necessarily "take into consideration other decisions of international courts" but may "come to a different conclusion".[64]

There is also a practice known as "judicial experimentalism" which is exercised by the diverse number of courts, and which is a potential contributing factor to fragmentation. Judicial experimentalism can easily convert to judicial activism and *ultra vires* missions. Judicial experimentalism is a technique familiar to judges of all kinds, whether common law, civil law, or international law. Each judge or arbitrator will approach the resolution of a dispute primarily from the perspective of an institutional actor looking at one specific issue, rather than as an arbiter with a global role in a broader scheme of public international law.[65] Consequently, the result of gap filling, as multiplied by numerous issue-specific international courts and tribunals, is a furthering of the fragmentation of international law. Issue specific tribunals perceive themselves as independent and, in the belief that their mandate is to address the "specific issues" before them. This practice prevails because treaties in general will stipulate that disputes must be resolved first in accordance with the terms of the treaty (often presumptively describing such agreements as "law") and subsequently in accordance with principles of international law.[66]

As noted above, in 1995 the Appeals Chamber of the ICTY reviewed the legality of its own establishment. While the Appeals Chamber acknowledged the UN Charter, and the powers of the UN Security Council, it held that the Appeals Chamber's powers did not disappear, and that "the International Tribunal has been lawfully established as a measure under Chapter VII of the Charter".[67] Notably, the same argument would apply to the ITLOS, the International Criminal Court, and the International Centre for the Settlement of Investment Disputes (ICSID) (under the auspices of the World Bank). However, undercutting this is the fact that none of these courts are structured to permit appeals to the ICJ. Arguably, if the UN had intended to ensure the

---

63   *Id.*, para. 24.

64   *Id.*

65   Marko Milanovic, *Norm Conflict in International Law: Whither Human Rights*, 20 Duke J. Comp. & Int'l L. 71 (2009) [*hereinafter* Milanovic].

66   *See, e.g.*, S D Myers Inc. v. Canada (U.S. v. Can.), Final Award on Costs, 48 NAFTA, 2002 Ch. 11 Arb. Trib.

67   Tadić Appeal, para. 95.

ICJ remains superior to these courts, an appeal or revision mechanism might have been introduced. It can therefore be argued that if such an incoherent international order exists, it implicitly requires a substantive alignment of international courts so that their decisions are focused on the common objective of providing certainty through a consistent jurisprudence.[68] The analysis of the cases above also shows that there is a great need to preserve both the unity and consistency of international law.

III   Addressing Treaty Conflicts by Applying Conflict Rules

International law provides a "tool set" designed to solve problems arising from incongruities and conflicts between existing legal norms and regimes, which consists of: *jus cogens* rules, Article 30 of the Vienna Convention on the Law of Treaties (VCLT), Article 103 of the UN Charter, the *lex specialis* principle, and hierarchical considerations. The application and efficacy of these tools is analyzed below.

A   *Jus Cogens*

In the survey of international law jurisprudence, *jus cogens* – that is the body of peremptory norms in international law – appears to have been rarely used to invalidate conflicting norms. This is because courts generally exhibit a tendency to do what they can to avoid norm conflicts.[69] It may seem that the ICJ has been reluctant to refer to *jus cogens* in its decisions because an explicit mention of the term can be found only in very few cases. An example that may be given is the decision of the ICJ which is most often referred to in relation to *jus cogens*: the *Nicaragua* case of 1986.[70] Hence, Ian Brownlie states that "*jus cogens* is like a car which has never left the garage".[71]

There are however a few cases where *jus cogens* were successfully invoked to resolve a norm conflict. One is the case of *Ferrini v. Federal Republic of Germany*.[72] In this case, the Italian Supreme Court held that while customary law prescribes immunity from jurisdiction of a foreign State for acts which

---

68   *See* Oil Platforms (Iran v. U.S.), 2003 I.C.J. Rep. 161 (Nov. 6).

69   Milanovic, 105.

70   ICJ Nicaragua, para. 190.

71   Antonio Cassese and Joseph Weiler, Change and Stability in International Law Making 175 (1988).

72   *See Judicial Decisions*, 14 Italian Y.B. Int'l L. 341 (2004) (providing relevant text of Ferrini v. Federal Republic of Germany).

THE FRAGMENTATION OF INTERNATIONAL LAW 193

are the expression of its sovereign authority, the immunity should be lifted when such acts amount to international crimes.[73] For the Court, violations of fundamental human rights encroach upon universal values protected by *jus cogens* norms, which lie at the top of the hierarchy of norms in the international legal order, and thus take precedence over conflicting law, including State immunity.[74] The most significant use of *jus cogens* as a tool for resolving norm conflicts was in the *Pinochet* case.[75] In this case, the issue arose whether immunity of a former head of State could be upheld against an accusation of his having committed torture while in office.[76] Referring to relevant passages in the *Furundžija* case,[77] the House of Lords held that "the *jus cogens* nature of the international crime of torture justifies states in taking universal jurisdiction over torture wherever committed". As the condition of "double criminality" was fulfilled, Pinochet could not plead immunity against a request for extradition to Spain. In the words of Lord Millett:

> International law cannot be supposed to have established a crime having the character of a *jus cogens* and at the same time to have provided an immunity which is co-extensive with the obligation it seeks to impose.[78]

In its analysis of this case, the ILC emphasized that "for the first time a local domestic court denied immunity to a former head of State on the grounds that there cannot be any immunity against prosecution for breach of *jus cogens*".[79] Indeed, this is the case that is most often cited as using *jus cogens* as a rule of norm in conflict resolution. However, the *Pinochet* case is criticized on the grounds that the reasoning of the *seriatim* opinions of their Lordships in *Pinochet* is notoriously difficult to decipher, because the holding of the House was emphatically *not* that *jus cogens* invalidated any conflicting rules on State

---

73 For analysis of the decision, *see* Pasquale De Sena & Francesca De Vittor, *State Immunity and Human Rights: the Italian Supreme Court Decision on the Ferrini Case,* 16 Eur. J. Int'l L. 89 (2005).

74 Andrea Gattini, *War Crimes and State Immunity in the Ferrini Decision,* 3 J. Int'l Crim. Just. 224 (2005).

75 Regina v. Bow Street Metropolitan Stipendiary Magistrate, Ex parte Pinochet Ugarte (No 3) [2000] 1 A.C. 147 (H.L. 1999) [U.K.] [*hereinafter* Pinochet].

76 *Id.*, at 213.

77 *Id.*, at 198. Prosecutor v. Anto Furundžija, Case No. IT-95-17/1, Judgment (Intl. Crim. Trib. for the Former Yugoslavia Dec. 10, 1998), paras. 153–154 [*hereinafter* Furundžija].

78 Pinochet, at 278.

79 ILC Report, para. 371.

immunity.[80] The majority of the Law Lords held that immunity *ratione materiae* did not cover the acts of torture imputable to Augusto Pinochet committed after 8 December 1988, the date the UK ratified the Convention against Torture (CAT). For most of the Law Lords, the ratification of the CAT by all the relevant State parties in the case and the expansive regime of jurisdiction established by this instrument seem to have been conclusive, rather than *jus cogens* proper.[81] This view is confirmed by the decision in *Jones v. Ministry of Interior of Saudi Arabia*,[82] where the House of Lords interpreted the *Pinochet* case as holding that the CAT waived or created an exception to immunities *ratione materiae* for the crime of torture. *Jus cogens* had precisely nothing to do with it.[83] The background, nature and effects of *jus cogens* were summarized by the ICTY:

> Because of the importance of the values it [the prohibition of torture] protects, this principle has evolved into a peremptory norm or *jus cogens*, that is, a norm that enjoys a higher rank in the international hierarchy than treaty law and even "ordinary" customary rules. The most conspicuous consequence of this higher rank is that the principle at issue cannot be derogated from by States through international treaties or local or special customs or even general customary rules not endowed with the same normative force.[84]

It is clear from the above discussion that courts rarely use *jus cogens* norms as a tool for resolution of normative conflicts.

B   ***The Vienna Convention on the Law of Treaties and the* lex posterior Principle***

Article 30 of the VCLT deals with priorities in the application of successive treaties relating to the same subject matter, and is an expression of the principle *lex posterior derogat lege priori* (later law overrules the earlier law). The

---

80   Milanovic, 76.

81   The State parties in the case were: Chile (State of nationality), Spain (State requesting Augusto Pinochet's extradition) and the United Kingdom (forum State).

82   Jones v. Ministry of Interior of Saudi Arabia [2006] UKHL 26, (2007) 1 AC 270, 298 (2006) 2 WLR 1424 [U.K.] (appeal taken from England].

83   *See also* Al-Adsani v. United Kingdom, App. No. 35763/97, 2001 Eur. Ct. H.R. (holding by 9 votes to 8 that the *jus cogens* prohibition of torture did not conflict with the law of state immunity). However, this case is distinguishable to the extent that is deals with immunity in civil matters.

84   Furundžija, para. 153.

THE FRAGMENTATION OF INTERNATIONAL LAW

lex posterior principle is well-embedded in domestic jurisprudence and often cited in an international law context as well. Nevertheless, there are few cases where it would have been applied as such. It may often be more useful to refer directly to the will of the parties than to the *lex posterior* principle to which it may simply give expression. In as much as it is a question of parties to the later treaty being different from parties to the earlier treaty, it is doubtful whether any meaningful role is left for the *lex posterior* principle.

In the case of *Slivenko v. Latvia*,[85] the ECtHR held that the European Convention on Human Rights controlled the content and/or application of an earlier bilateral treaty, or at least determined how the latter was to be interpreted and applied by the national authorities.[86] The issue in this case concerned the application of a 1994 Russian-Latvian Treaty as far as it concerned the deportation of certain former members of the Soviet army and their families from Latvian territory. The court examined the rights of the concerned individuals on the basis of the European Convention, to which Latvia had acceded at a later date, and concluded that:

> The (Russian-Latvian) treaty cannot serve as a valid basis for depriving the Court of its power to review whether there was interference with the applicant's rights and freedoms and, if so, whether such interference was justified.[87]

That view was based on an earlier admissibility decision in which the Court had specifically noted as follows:

> It follows from the text of Article 57 (1) of the [European Convention on Human Rights], read in conjunction with Article 1, that ratification of the Convention by a State presupposes that any law then in force in its territory should be in conformity with the Convention. In the Court's opinion, the same principles must apply as regards any provisions of international treaties which a Contracting State has concluded prior to the ratification of the Convention and which might be at variance with certain of its provisions.[88]

---

85   Slivenko v. Latvia, App. No. 48321/99, Judgment, 2003 Eur. Ct. H.R. 2003-X 265 [*hereinafter* Slivenko v. Latvia].

86   ILC Report, 126–127.

87   Slivenko v. Latvia, para 120.

88   Slivenko et al. v. Latvia, Decision as to the admissibility of 23 January 2002, 2002 Eur. Ct. H.R. (2002-II) 482–483 para. 60–61.

This is an important statement of principle. Under it, it seems difficult to deny that if the *lex posterior* should be read in favor of the European Convention on Human Rights, it should also favor any other later human rights treaties, if not any other later multilateral legislative treaties. Again, we are in the presence of a hierarchy that seems best dealt with by the notion of special "integral" obligations, such as obligations in human rights treaties that enjoy some kind of precedence over merely transactional bilateral instruments. However, it is difficult to determine if this is a case of *lex specialis* or *lex posterior*. The important point is that the bilateral treaty (the Russian-Latvian treaty) did not have a life that would be independent from its normative environment at the time of application. The construction of the bilateral treaty by reference to the later multilateral treaty was reasonable, and little else seems pertinent. It is difficult therefore to find a case in which the *lex posterior* principle as expressed by the VCLT has been applied exclusively to resolve a conflict case.

C   *Article 103 of the UN Charter*

Article 103 of the UN Charter is perhaps the most relevant stipulation regarding the primacy of State obligations under the Charter over other international obligations. Article 103 played a key role in the case of *Al-Jedda* before the House of Lords.[89] In this case, a grant of authority from the UN Security Council to certain member States was interpreted by the US as *inter alia* allowing them to engage in preventative detention without judicial review, in Iraq and Kosovo, respectively.

The background of the case is as follows:[90] in June 2004 the UN Security Council adopted Resolution 1546, which provided the legal framework for the continued presence of the coalition or multi-national forces (MNF) in Iraq after the occupation of the country came to an end. The resolution independently granted these forces some of the rights that they enjoyed as occupiers under the law of armed conflict. The specific right of concern here is the occupier's power to preventatively detain persons for security reasons, stipulated in Article 42(1) of the Fourth Geneva Convention[91] which states that: "The internment or placing in assigned residence of protected persons may be ordered only if the security of the Detaining Power makes it absolutely necessary", as well as in Article 78 thereof which provides that: "If the Occupying Power con-

---

89   R (In re Al-Jedda) v. Secretary of State for Defence [2007] UKHL 58; [2008] 1 A.C. 332 (appeal taken from England) [*hereinafter* Al-Jedda].

90   Case Summary in: Milanovic, 79–86.

91   Geneva Convention (IV) relative to the Protection of Civilian Persons in Time of War art. 42, Aug. 12, 1949, 75 U.N.T.S. 287.

THE FRAGMENTATION OF INTERNATIONAL LAW

197

siders it necessary, for imperative reasons of security, to take safety measures concerning protected persons, it may, at the most, subject them to assigned residence or to internment".[92] Acting under Chapter 7 of the UN Charter, the UN Security Council decided that:

> ... the multinational force shall have the authority to take all necessary measures to contribute to the maintenance of security and stability in Iraq in accordance with the letters annexed to this resolution expressing, *inter alia*, the Iraqi request for the continued presence of the multinational force and setting out its tasks, including by preventing and deterring terrorism".[93]

Letters were sent to the UN Security Council by US Secretary of State Colin Powell and then-interim Prime Minister of Iraq, Ayad Allawi, both emphasizing the ongoing security threats in Iraq and the need to put them to an end. In particular, Secretary Powell's letter outlined the duties of the MNF forces, stating that these "will include combat operations against members of (insurgent) groups, internment where this is necessary for imperative reasons of security", and "the continued search for and securing of weapons that threaten Iraq's security".[94] Under this authority, in October 2004 British troops of the MNF detained Mr. Al-Jedda as a security threat.[95] The detention was authorized and periodically reviewed by senior officers of the British army. Al-Jedda challenged his detention before English courts, relying on Article 5(1) of the European Convention on Human Rights.[96] The government opposed his challenge on two main grounds. First, it argued that in this particular situation the European Convention on Human Rights and the UK Human Rights Act did not apply extra-territorially. Second, even if they did, internment was

---

92   *Id.*, art. 43(1) further provides that: "Any protected person who has been interned or placed in assigned residence shall be entitled to have such action reconsidered as soon as possible by an appropriate court or administrative board designated by the Detaining Power for that purpose. If the internment or placing in assigned residence is maintained, the court or administrative board shall periodically, and at least twice yearly, give consideration to his or her case, with a view to the favourable amendment of the initial decision, if circumstances permit".

93   S.C. Res. 1546, U.N. Doc. S/RES/1546 (June 8, 2004), para. 10.

94   Al-Jedda, 332.

95   *Id.*

96   The European Convention on Human Rights being transformed into English law by virtue of the UK Human Rights Act, which enshrines the right to liberty of person and does not allow for internment on security grounds.

authorized by a binding resolution of the UN Security Council, which prevailed over Article 5(1) under the terms of Article 103 of the Charter. The government desisted from its first argument after the House of Lords decided the *Al-Skeini* case, in which it established that the UK Human Rights Act and European Convention on Human Rights do apply to persons detained by British forces in Iraq.[97] However, both the High Court and the Court of Appeal, and ultimately the House of Lords found against Al-Jedda on the basis of Article 103 of the UN Charter. Lord Bingham, who delivered the lead opinion, first dealt with Al-Jedda's argument that Article 103 was inapplicable, since Resolution 1546 merely authorized the UK to detain persons considered to be security threats, but did not oblige it to do so.[98] He did not find that argument persuasive. He considered that both state practice and academic opinion clearly favored the applicability of Article 103 to Council authorizations, as the importance of maintaining international peace and security could scarcely be exaggerated, and since authorizations have effectively replaced the system of collective security that was envisaged by the drafters. Lord Bingham then rejected the argument that Article 103 should not apply to the European Convention on Human Rights, due to the latter's special character as a human rights treaty, as Article 103 applies to all international agreements.[99] Lord Bingham concluded that there was a genuine norm conflict between a UN Charter obligation of the UK and Article 5(1) of the European Convention on Human Rights, and that the UN Charter obligation must prevail. He stated that:

> Thus there is a clash between on the one hand a power or duty to detain exercisable on the express authority of the UN Security Council and, on the other, a fundamental human right which the UK has undertaken to secure to those (like the appellant) within its jurisdiction. How are these to be reconciled? There is in my opinion only one way in which they can be reconciled: by ruling that the UK may lawfully, where it is necessary for imperative reasons of security, exercise the power to detain authorized

---

97   R (Al-Skeini and others) v. Secretary of State for Defence [2007] UKHL 26; [2007] 3 WLR 33 (appeal taken from Eng.). For the commentary on the decision, *see* Tobias Thienel, *The ECHR in Iraq: The Judgment of the House of Lords in R (Al-Skeini) v. Secretary of State for Defence*, 6 J. Int'l Crim. Justice 115 (2008). The case was also decided by: Al-Skeini et al v. U.K., App. No. 55721/07, 2011 Eur. Ct. H.R. *See also* Frederik Naert, *The European Court of Human Rights' Al-Jedda and Al-Skeini Judgments: an Introduction and Some Reflections*, 50 Mil. L. & L. War Rev. 315 (2011).

98   *Al-Jedda*, para. 33–34 (per Lord Bingham).

99   *Id.*

THE FRAGMENTATION OF INTERNATIONAL LAW 199

by UNSCR 1546 and successive resolutions, but must ensure that the detainee's rights under article 5 are not infringed to any greater extent than is inherent in such detention.[100]

Milanovic opines that in the *Al-Jedda* case, a presumption against norm conflict was applied.[101] Even though Resolution 1546 did prevail over Article 5(1) of the European Convention on Human Rights by virtue of Article 103 of the UN Charter, it did so only to the extent inherent in preventative detention. Even in cases of genuine norm conflict, especially those involving human rights, the scope of the conflict will be minimized through interpretation. Other methods of conflict resolution and avoidance could have been applied by the House in *Al-Jedda*, but they were either not relied on by the parties or were not to their Lordships' liking.[102] The fact that the primacy effect of Article 103 also extends to binding UN Security Council resolutions has been confirmed by both doctrine and practice,[103] as well as by the ICJ in the *Lockerbie* case.[104]

The application of Article 103 of the UN Charter in conflict resolution can also be observed in the cases of *Yusuf* and *Kadi*.[105] The background to these cases relates to the sanctions originally established by the UN Security Council in Resolution 1267 (1999) against the Taliban regime in Afghanistan. The sanctions regime was expanded by subsequent resolutions to the Al-Qaeda network and persons associated with it.[106] The UN Security Council set up a Sanctions Committee as its subsidiary body to monitor the implementation of sanctions, which maintained lists of suspected terrorists. UN member States were obliged to enforce sanctions against those listed individuals. Having this sanctions regime in view, the member states of the European Union (EU) decided that instead of implementing this regime individually in their respective domestic legal systems, they should do so through EU mechanisms. Thus the EU Council adopted several common positions, as well as Regulation No. 881/2002,

---

100 *Id.*, para. 39. *See* also Lord Roger concurring at para. 118; Lord Baroness Hale concurring at para. 125–26; and Lord Carswell concurring at para. 131.

101 Milanovic, at 83.

102 *Id.*

103 ILC Report, para. 331.

104 Questions of Interpretation and Application of the 1971 Montreal Convention arising from the Ariel incident at Lockerbie (Libya v. U.K.), Request for the indication of provisional measures, 1992 I.C.J. Rep. 114 (Apr. 14), para. 37 [*hereinafter* ICJ Lockerbie].

105 Joined Cases C-402/05 P & C-415/05 P, Kadi & Al Barakaat v. Council of the European Union, 2008 3 C.M.L.R. 41 (2008).

106 Chia Lehnardt, *European Court Rules on UN and EU Terrorist Suspect Blacklists*, 11 Am. Soc'y of Int'l L. Insights 1–2 (2007).

implementing the sanctions regime. As "Community Law", the Regulation had a direct effect in the legal orders of the member states and took precedence over any contrary domestic legislation. The assets of the applicant in the *Kadi* case were frozen on the strength of the sanctions regime. Kadi sought to annul the implementing regulation on the grounds that it violated his fundamental human rights protected by EU law, especially the rights enshrined in the European Convention on Human Rights, namely: the right to a fair hearing, the right to property and the right to judicial review.[107] One of his key arguments was that:

> [T]he Security Council resolutions relied on by the [EU] Council and the Commission do not confer on those institutions the power to abrogate those fundamental rights without justifying that stance before the Court by producing the necessary evidence. As a legal order independent of the United Nations, governed by its own rules of law, the European Union must justify its actions by reference to its own powers and duties *vis-à-vis* individuals within that order.[108]

The significance of this argument cannot be overemphasized, as it challenges the most fundamental operating assumption of Article 103 of the UN Charter. Like any rule of hierarchy, it can only prevail over a norm which is a part of the same legal order. As the US Constitution is the supreme law only in the US legal system, but not in the legal orders of France or China, so Article 103 of the Charter is superior law only in the international legal system. According to Kadi's argument, however, he was entitled to human rights protections under EU law, and that legal order "was independent of the United Nations". The UN Security Council resolution could not prevail over these rights, as it could not penetrate this independent legal order. This was one of the main themes of the Advocate-General's opinion in *Kadi*, as well as the decision on appeal of the European Court of Justice (ECJ). The EU Council submitted on the other hand that:

> First, that the Community, like the Member States of the United Nations, is bound by international law to give effect, within its spheres of competence, to resolutions of the Security Council, especially those adopted under Chapter VII of the Charter of the United Nations; Second, that the powers of the Community institutions in this area are limited and that

---

107   T-315/01, Kadi v Council and Commission, 2005 E.C.R. II-3649, para. 59.

108   *Id.*, para. 140.

THE FRAGMENTATION OF INTERNATIONAL LAW

they have no autonomous discretion in any form; Third, that they cannot therefore alter the content of those resolutions or set up mechanisms capable of giving rise to any alteration in their content and; Fourth, that any other international agreement or domestic rule of law liable to hinder such implementation must be disregarded".[109]

Hence, the parties submitted a much more fundamental question than the resolution of a single norm conflict – that of the relationship between general international law and EU law.[110] Only by finding that the two legal orders were one, if even autonomous to a great extent, would the Court be able to entertain the Article 103 argument. The Court went on to do just that. First, it held that:

> From the standpoint of international law, the obligations of the Member States of the United Nations under the Charter of the United Nations clearly prevail over every other obligation of domestic law or of international treaty law including, for those of them that are members of the Council of Europe, their obligations under the ECHR and, for those that are also members of the Community, their obligations under the EC Treaty ... With more particular regard to the relations between the obligations of the Member States of the Community by virtue of the Charter of the United Nations and their obligations under Community law, it may be added that, in accordance with the first paragraph of Article 307 EC, 'The rights and obligations arising from agreements concluded before 1 January 1958 or, for acceding States, before the date of their accession, between one or more Member States on the one hand, and one or more third countries on the other, shall not be affected by the provisions of this Treaty'.[111]

Furthermore,

> Article 224 of the Treaty establishing the European Economic Community (now Article 297 EC) was specifically introduced into the Treaty in order to observe the rule of primacy defined above. Under that provision, "Member States shall consult each other with a view to taking together the steps needed to prevent the functioning of the common market being affected by measures which a Member State may be called upon to take

---

109   *Id.*, para. 206.
110   *Id.*, para. 178.
111   *Id.*, para. 181 & 185.

[...] in order to carry out obligations it has accepted for the purpose of maintaining peace and international security".[112]

Thus, the Court held that:

Pursuant both to the rules of general international law and to the specific provisions of the Treaty, Member States may, and indeed must, leave unapplied any provision of Community law, whether a provision of primary law or a general principle of that law, that raises any impediment to the proper performance of their obligations under the Charter of the United Nations.[113]

Moreover,

Unlike its Member States, the Community as such is not directly bound by the Charter of the United Nations and that it is not therefore required, as an obligation of general public international law, to accept and carry out the decisions of the Security Council in accordance with Article 25 of that Charter. The reason is that the Community is not a member of the United Nations or an addressee of the resolutions of the Security Council, or the successor to the rights and obligations of the Member States for the purposes of public international law. Nevertheless, the Community must be considered to be bound by the obligations under the Charter of the United Nations in the same way as its Member States, by virtue of the Treaty establishing it. In that regard, it is not in dispute that at the time when they concluded the Treaty establishing the European Economic Community the Member States were bound by their obligations under the Charter of the United Nations. By concluding a treaty between them they could not transfer to the Community more powers than they possessed or withdraw from their obligations to third countries under that Charter.[114]

The Court thus rejected the applicant's argument that "the Community legal order is a legal order independent of the United Nations, governed by its own rules of law".[115]

---

112   *Id.*, para. 188.

113   *Id.*, para. 190.

114   *Id.*, paras. 192–95.

115   *Id.*, para. 208.

Article 103 of the UN Charter was given full attention in the *Lockerbie* case.[116] The governments of the UK and the US had requested Libya to surrender certain individuals in connection with the investigations into the bombing of an airplane over the village of Lockerbie in Scotland. The UN Security Council, acting under Chapter 7 of the Charter, supported the measures to be taken against Libya, which in turn considered the requests of the two above-mentioned governments incompatible with the Montreal Convention of 1971 for the Suppression of Unlawful Acts against the Safety of Civil Aviation, and submitted the dispute to the ICJ. At first, Libya asked the Court to indicate provisional measures, whereas the respondents argued that a binding decision of the UN Security Council did not permit such an indication. In its Orders of 14 April 1992 the ICJ stated that:

> Whereas both Libya and the United States, as Members of the United Nations, are obliged to accept and carry out the decisions of the Security Council in accordance with Article 25 of the Charter; whereas the Court, which is at the stage of proceedings on provisional measures, considers that *prima facie* this obligation extends to the decision contained in resolution 748 (1992); and whereas, in accordance with Article 103 of the Charter, the obligations of the Parties in that respect prevail over their obligations under any other international agreement, including the Montreal Convention;
>
> Whereas the Court, while thus not at this stage called upon to determine definitively the legal effect of Security Council resolution 748 (1992), considers that, whatever the situation previous to the adoption of that resolution, the rights claimed by Libya under the Montreal Convention cannot now be regarded as appropriate for protection by the indication of provisional measures.[117]

Judge Lauterpacht, in his separate opinion to the order of the ICJ in the *Application of the Genocide Convention* case, discussed the relationship between Article 103 of the UN Charter and *jus cogens*, and stated that:

> The concept of *jus cogens* operates as a concept superior to both customary international law and treaty. The relief which Article 103 of the Charter may give the Security Council in case of conflict between one of its

---

116   Libya v. U.S., Preliminary Objections, ICJ Reports (1998) 8. See case summary in: ILC Report (n 2) 180–181.

117   ICJ Lockerbie, para. 39–40.

decisions and an operative treaty obligation cannot – as a matter of simple hierarchy of norms – extend to a conflict between the Security Council resolution and *jus cogens*. Indeed, one only has to state the opposite proposition thus – that a Security Council resolution may even require participation in genocide – for its unacceptability to be apparent.[118]

This seems natural. If, as pointed out above, the UN Charter is not above *jus cogens*, then it also cannot transfer a power to contradict *jus cogens* to bodies that receive their jurisdiction from the Charter.[119]

D   Lex Specialis

Most of general international law is *jus dispositivum* so that parties are entitled to establish specific rights or obligations to govern their behavior. In the *North Sea Continental Shelf* cases, it was stated that "it is well understood that, in practice, rules of international law can, by agreement, be derogated from in particular cases or as between particular parties".[120] This was the situation in the *Right of Passage* case.[121] After having determined that the relevant practice accepted by both states (India and Britain/Portugal) established a limited right of transit passage, the ICJ concluded that it did not need to investigate what the content of general principles of law or custom on this matter was, and stated that "such a particular practice must prevail over any general rules".[122]

By virtue of international law being *jus dispositivum*, parties are entitled to derogate from it by establishing specific rights or obligations to govern their behaviour. The ICJ has pointed out that "it is well understood that, in practice, rules of (general) international law can, by agreement, be derogated from in particular cases or as between particular parties".[123] Therefore, international case-law appears to accept the *lex specialis* maxim, albeit without great elaboration.

---

118   Application of the Convention on the Prevention and Punishment of the Crime of Genocide (Bosn. Herz. v. Serb. & Montenegro), Further Requests for the Indiciation of Provisional Measures (separate opinion of Judge Lauterpacht), 1993 I.C.J. Rep. 407, 440, para. 10 (Sep. 13).

119   ILC Report, para. 181.

120   North Sea Continental Shelf (Fed. Rep. Ger. v. Neth./Fed. Rep. Ger. v. Den.), 1969 I.C.J. Rep. 42, para. 72 (Apr. 26) [*hereinafter* ICJ Continental Shelf].

121   Right of Passage over Indian Territory (Port. v. India), 1960 I.C.J. Rep. 6 (Apr. 12).

122   *Id.*, 44.

123   ICJ Continental Shelf, para. 72.

THE FRAGMENTATION OF INTERNATIONAL LAW

Four different situations may be distinguished. The maxim may operate: (a) within a single instrument; (b) between two different instruments; (c) between a treaty and a non-treaty standard; and (d) between two non-treaty standards. A relevant case example is where *lex specialis* regulates the relationship between *different* instruments. In the *Mavrommatis Palestine Concessions* case, the Permanent Court of International Justice was faced with two instruments that had a bearing on its jurisdiction: the 1922 Mandate for Palestine and the 1923 Protocol XII of the Treaty of Lausanne. The Court concluded that "in cases of doubt, the Protocol, being a special and more recent agreement, should prevail".[124] That view seemed to endorse both the *lex posterior* and the *lex specialis* maxims without entering into the question of their relationship.

A second case is the one where the *lex specialis* is resorted to in order to privilege a treaty standard over a non-treaty standard. In the *INA Corporation v. Government of the Islamic Republic of Iran*,[125] the corporation sought compensation for the expropriation of its 20 per cent share in an Iranian insurance company. The claimant argued that on the basis of international law and the Iran-United States Treaty of Amity (1955), compensation should be "prompt, adequate and effective".[126] The respondent held that the compensation was to be calculated on the basis of the net book value of the nationalized shares. The Tribunal considered that in cases of large-scale lawful nationalizations general international law no longer provided for full compensation. It did not, however, attempt to establish the exact content of the customary norm as it considered that for the purposes of the case: we are in the presence of a *lex specialis* in the form of the Treaty of Amity, which in principle prevails over general rules.[127] In the *Continental Shelf* case between Tunisia and Libya, the Court suggested that States might be able to opt out from the development of general law by these means.[128] It had been authorized by the Special Agreement to take into the "new accepted trends" in the Third UN Law of the Sea Conference. In this regard, the Court noted that:

> It would no doubt have been possible for the Parties to identify in the Special Agreement certain specific developments in the law of the sea

---

124 The Mavrommatis Palestine Concessions (Greece v. U.K.), Judgment, 1924 P.C.I.J. (ser. A) no. 2, at 2 (Aug. 30).

125 INA Corporation v. Iran, Iran-US C. Trib. Vol. 8, (1985-I), 378.

126 *Id.*

127 *Id.*

128 Continental Shelf (Tunis. v. Libya), 1982 I.C.J. Rep. 18, 38 (Feb. 24).

[...] and to have declared that in their bilateral relations in the particular case such rules should be binding as *lex specialis*.[129]

The *lex specialis* maxim seems like a "perfectly recognized and respectable judicial technique" of setting aside any examination of the content of the general law once the special rule had been found in a way that leaves open whether the special rule was an elaboration or an exception to that general law or whether there was any general law in the matter in the first place.[130] In the above cases, the Court accepted that general international law may be subject to derogation by agreement and that such an agreement may be rationalized as *lex specialis*. These cases illustrate the practice of international tribunals to give precedence to treaty law in matters where there is customary law as well – a practice that highlights the dispositive nature of custom and the tribunals' deference to agreements as the "hardest" and presumably most legitimate basis on which their decisions can be based. Thirlway summarizes the jurisprudence as follows:

> It is universally accepted that – consideration of *jus cogens* apart – a treaty as *lex specialis* is law between the parties to it in derogation of the general customary law which would otherwise have governed their relations.[131]

This argument is not to mean that customary international law would thereby become extinguished. It will continue to apply residually, and become fully applicable for instance when the special treaty is no longer in force or, as in the *Nicaragua* case, if the jurisdiction of the relevant law-applying organ fails to cover the treaty.[132]

E   *Hierarchical Considerations*

In as much as "general law" does not have the status of *jus cogens,* treaties generally enjoy priority over custom and particular treaties over general treaties.[133] Similarly, the ILC has held the view (as suggested by the ICJ *Right of Passage* case) that local customs, if proven, have primacy over general customary law

---

129   *Id.*, para. 24.

130   Hugh Thirlway, *The Law and Procedure of the International Court of Justice 1960–1989*, 61 Brit. Y.B. Int'l L. 104–106 (1990) [*hereinafter* Thirlway].

131   *Id.*, 147.

132   ICJ Nicaragua, para. 179.

133   Thirlway, at 143–144.

THE FRAGMENTATION OF INTERNATIONAL LAW
207

and, perhaps, the body of customary law has primacy over the general principles of law under Article 38(1)(c) of the ICJ Statute.[134] According to the ILC, this informal hierarchy follows from no legislative enactment, but emerges as a "forensic"[135] or a "natural"[136] aspect of legal reasoning. Any court or lawyer will first look at treaties, then custom and then the general principles of law for an answer to a normative problem. Much of the concern over the fragmentation of international law emerges from the awareness of the "horizontal" nature of the international legal system.[137] The rules and principles of international law are not in a hierarchical relationship to each other.[138] Nor are the different sources (treaty, custom, general principles of law) ranked in any general order of priority. Consequently, there is no general order of precedence between international legal rules. There is however an important practice that gives effect to the informal sense that some norms are more important than other norms and that in cases of conflict those important norms should be given effect to. In the absence of a general theory about where to derive this sense of importance, practice has developed a general consensus. Therefore, in the jurisprudence of international courts it is difficult to point to a single conflict case that has been found to have been decided purely on considerations of hierarchy. The tools as seen in the above cases form only part of the determination.

IV   The Institutional Problem

The growth and proliferation of international courts and tribunals[139] brings forth an institutional aspect of fragmentation. The proliferation of international

---

134   ILC Report, at 47.

135   Robert Jennings and Arthur Watts, Oppenheim's International Law Vol. I, Part I 26 (1992).

136   Mark Villiger, Customary International Law and Treaties: A Study of Their Interactions and Interrelations with Special Consideration of the 1969 Vienna Convention on the Law of Treaties 161 (1985).

137   ILC Report, at 166.

138   It must be noted however that there has developed a value system within the international community which accords a special status to the prohibition of aggression, promotion of human rights, and environmental protection. Therefore, it is now well settled that peremptory norms (*jus cogens*) and obligations *erga omnes* enjoy a higher status in the normative hierarchy. *See,* in this regard, John Dugard International Law: A South African Perspective 38 (2011).

139   Most international tribunals have been established in recent decades. *See* Roger Alford, *The Proliferation of International Courts and Tribunals: International Tribunals in Ascendance,* 94 Am. Soc'y Int'l L. Proc. 160 (2000).

courts has also stimulated the debate over fragmentation.[140] International courts and tribunals are growing numerically as well as qualitatively.[141] But what is the institutional impact of proliferation on the unity of international law? Simply put, there is a risk that a similar norm of international law may be interpreted differently by different international courts or tribunals. The proliferation of international courts and tribunals multiplies the possibility of diverging jurisprudence and forum shopping. The inherent danger in such a horizontal (or non-hierarchical) system is that the rights and obligations of subjects of international law may be determined according to the body that is seized of them.

With regard to international institutions, the problem of fragmentation has been viewed as arising in a number of ways. For instance, a conflict may arise when different tribunals assert jurisdiction on the same set of facts, or even when different tribunals diverge in their interpretations of the same treaty or customary norm.[142] The former is a problem of forum shopping, and the latter a problem of normative coherence or consistency. According to Leathley,[143] the growth of issue-specific tribunals has introduced new challenges for the international judiciary and has contributed to the fragmentation of international law. For example, courts and tribunals established by treaty face an immediate challenge to their legitimacy. Such courts have to justify the political will entrusted to them.

A prominent institutional problem is that of jurisdictional conflicts. Cases under conflict of jurisdiction concern instances of simultaneous seizing of more than one judicial body with the same matter; deviations in subsequent decisions rendered by different courts on cases with similar material facts; and legal questions, or cases in which conflict results from a different context than that in which the issue arose. The most commonly cited cases as examples

---

140   *See, generally,* Larissa van den Herik & Carsten Stahn, *Fragmentation, Diversification and 3D Legal Pluralism: International Criminal Law as the Jack-in-the-Box, in* The Diversification and Fragmentation of International Criminal Law 21–87 (Larissa van den Herik & Carsten Stahn, eds., 2012) [hereinafter Van den Herik & Stahn].

141   This means that their subject matter jurisdiction and specialization is also increasing. They are not only mandated to resolve inter-state disputes, but they also monitor and ensure respect for international law. *See* Karin Oellers-Frahm, *Multiplication of International Courts and Tribunals and Conflicting Jurisdiction – Problems and Possible Solutions,* 5 Max Planck Y.B. U.N. L. 68 (2001) [*hereinafter* Oellers-Frahm].

142   Gregory Fox, *International Organizations: Conflicts of International Law,* 95 American Soc'y Int'l L. Proc. 184 (2001).

143   Christian Leathley, *Fragmentation of International Law: Has the ILC Missed an Opportunity?* 40 NYU J. Int'l L. & Pol'y 259 (2007).

THE FRAGMENTATION OF INTERNATIONAL LAW 209

of conflicting jurisdiction[144] are the *Nicaragua* (1966)[145] and *Tadić* (1999)[146] cases which have been dealt with earlier. Another case of conflict is the case of *Loizidou v. Turkey* decided by the ECtHR.[147] There, the ECtHR was faced with questions concerning a reservation to declarations accepting the compulsory jurisdiction of the Court and the European Commission of Human Rights.[148] In particular, the reservation concerned the restriction of the territorial scope of the acceptance of jurisdiction made by Turkey to the then-valid Articles 25 and 46 of the European Convention on Human Rights, namely, the exclusion of acts having been committed in the Turkish Republic of Northern Cyprus. The Court found that a territorial restriction of the acceptance of its jurisdiction was not compatible with the Convention, thus giving a restrictive interpretation to Articles 25 and 46.[149] The novel issue to be decided by the Court was "what are the consequences for the declaration of acceptance if one of the reservations is found to be invalid?"[150] The Court found that the invalidity of the reservation did not affect the validity of the acceptance because the reservation was severable from the declaration.[151] This decision by the Court has been criticized for being in conflict with the jurisprudence of the ICJ,[152] regardless of the fact that the Court gave detailed reasons for the restrictive interpretation of the validity of reservations to the acceptance of jurisdiction, and reasons for its finding on the severability of reservations from the declaration. This is because the wording of the articles in question is similar to Article 36(3) of the ICJ Statute, which has always been broadly interpreted, and until now, has never been applied in a manner that would declare a reservation incompatible with the ICJ Statute.[153] The Court had never been confronted with

---

144 For the main points of the discussion on conflicting jurisdiction, *see* Oellers-Frahm, 78–91.

145 *See Tadić.*

146 *See ICJ.*

147 Loizidou v Turk., App No. 15318/89, 1995 Eur. Ct. H.R., Series A, Vol. 310 (Mar. 23) [*hereinafter* ECtHR Lozidou].

148 ECtHR Loizidou, para. 62.

149 *Id.*, para. 71.

150 *Id.*, para. 58.

151 *Id.*, para. 78.

152 Sir Robert Jennings, *The Proliferation of Adjudicatory Bodies: Dangers and Possible Answers,* 9 Am. Soc'y Int'l L. Bull. 5 (1995).

153 *See* Oellers-Frahm, 81; citing examples of the same question arising in the Certain Norwegian Loans (Fr. v. Nor.), 1957 I.C.J. Rep, 9 (July 6); Aerial Incident of 10 August 1999 (Pak. v. India), Judgment, 2000 I.C.J. Rep. 12 (June 21); Fisheries Jurisdiction (Spain v. Can.), 1998 I.C.J. Rep. 432 (Dec. 4).

the present question in particular; this question had only been discussed in separate opinions to judgments of the ICJ.[154] Other commentators argue that although the articles that the Court had to interpret were nearly identical, that does not mean that they have to be construed identically, for treaty interpretation has to give regard not only to the wording of the provisions but also to the purpose of the treaty itself, and the intent of the parties.[155] However, the existence of such a stance shows that the danger of conflicting jurisdiction due to the multiplication of international courts and tribunals is real.

The above examples demonstrate the pressing need for inter-court dialogue and respect for decisions of other judicial bodies as well as the importance of detailed reasoning in order to make comprehensible the result reached by each tribunal. It further demonstrates that if such an incoherent international order continues to evolve, it may require a hierarchical organization of international courts so that their decisions are focused on the common objective of providing certainty through a consistent jurisprudence.[156]

V   The Big Debate

Could it be possible that the concerns described above have been overly exaggerated? Is fragmentation a real cause for concern for the success/future of international law? Does fragmentation constitute a real threat to the international legal system? To be more specific, does the proliferation of specialized international norms and autonomous institutions threaten the unity, reliability and legal certainty of international law? These are the important questions that international lawyers have intensely debated over the past decade. The *big debate* started after the ILC published its conclusions on the study of fragmentation in 2006,[157] and it has been gaining momentum.

It must be noted that the body of recent academic works on the issue seems to have shifted the focus from analyzing and trying to resolve both the normative and institutional 'problems' of fragmentation. Moving away from the earlier concepts of 'normative conflicts', 'jurisdictional competition' etc, contributors to the fragmentation debate are now advancing transitional

---

154 *See*, in particular, the separate opinion of Sir Hersch Lauterpatch in Norwegian Loans, 9; and *Fisheries Jurisdiction*, par 36.

155 Oellers-Frahm, 82.

156 See *Oil Platforms (Islamic Republic of Iran v. United States of America)* 2003 ICJ Reports 161.

157 *See* ILC Report.

THE FRAGMENTATION OF INTERNATIONAL LAW   211

concepts such as "normative equivalence"[158] or parallelism between various
sources of international law, the "diversity"[159] of international norms, "normative constitutionalism",[160] "legal pluralism",[161] and convergence.[162] In my view,
these concepts, which are a departure from the original 'conflict-based analysis', give us an idea that there is a positive approach towards managing the
fragmentation of international law which seeks to exploit rather than change
the current fragmented state of the international legal order. In brief, fragmentation is now seen as less of a problem, and more of an opportunity.

The fragmentation of international law is an age-old issue that has trou-
bled jurists, philosophers and decision-makers in international relations.[163]
Although this problem is not new, it is today more magnified because of broader and deeper international relations that all require regulation, and which are
not fully coordinated, in part because international law remains fragmented.
The concept of 'fragmentation' as defined earlier, suggests a pre-existing unified legal order. However, some contemporary academics deny the fact that
international law was ever unified.[164] They argue that international law is by
its nature a fragmented legal system. Koskenniemi and Leino have pointed
out that:

---

158   They also use the term "normative parallelism" with reference to where similar or equiv-
      alent norms are developed within disparate legal regimes; *see* Ralph Michaels & Joost
      Pauwelyn, *Conflict of Norms of Conflict of Laws? Different Techniques in the Fragmentation
      of International Law, in* Multi-Sourced Equivalent Norms in International Law 19–42
      (Tomer Broude & Yuval Shany eds., 1st ed., 2011).

159   *See* van den Herik & Stahn; Nele Matz-Liick, *Structural Questions of Fragmenation*, 105
      Am. Soc'y Int'l L. Proc. 125 (2011)

160   *See* Jan Klabbers, Anne Peters & Geil Ulfstein, The Constitutionalisation of International
      Law 345 (2009); Karell Wellens, International Law in Silver Perspective: Challenges Ahead
      181 (2015).

161   *See* Paul Schiff Berman, Global Legal Pluralism: A Jurisprudence of Law Beyond Borders 11
      (2012).

162   Mads Andenas & Eirik Bjorge, A Farewell to Fragmentation: Reassertion and Convergence
      in International Law 1 (2015) [*hereinafter* Andenas & Bjorge].

163   *See* Wilfred Jenks, Conflict of Law-Making Treaties, 30 Brit. Y.B. Int'l L. 401 (1953); Jonathan
      Charney, *Is International Law Threatened by Multiple International Tribunals*, 271 Recueil
      des cours 101–382 (1998); Andeas Fischer-Lescano & Teubner Gunther, *Regime-Collisions:
      The Vain Search for Legal Unity in the Fragmentation of Global Law*, 22 Mich. J. Int'l L. 999–
      1046 (2004).

164   *See* Christian Tomuschat, *International Law as a Coherent System: Unity or Fragmentation,
      in* Looking to the Future: Essays on International Law in Honor of W. Michael Reisman
      324 (Mahnoush Arsanjani et al. eds., 2011); Nele Matz-Luck, *Structural Questions of
      Fragmentation*, 105 Am. Soc'y Int'l L. Proc. 125 (2011).

> International lawyers have always had to cope with the absence of a single source of normative validity; it may seem paradoxical that *they* should now feel anxiety about competing normative orders.[165]

According to Cogan, "there is no normal or absolute state of uniformity in law. There are always overlaps among rules and institutions, and there are always established mechanisms for their reconciliation".[166] The comprehensive study of fragmentation conducted by the ILC focused solely on the substantive problems of fragmentation, which they dubbed "the splitting up of the law into specialized boxes that claim relative autonomy from each other and from the general law".[167] While the ILC conceded that fragmentation creates conflict between rules and regimes, they curiously held the opinion that it did not create any practical legal difficulties. Additionally, the ILC Report did not address one of the most apparent manifestations of the fragmentation of international law, which is the establishment of numerous unrelated courts and tribunals, which has ultimately caused the rise of inconsistent development of international law and conflicting jurisprudence. In my view, there is a significant link between the fragmentation of "norms" and the fragmentation of "authority", which ought not to have been ignored. The ILC seems to have adopted the view that fragmentation is merely a technical problem that has emerged naturally with the increase of international activity, and may only be controlled by the use of technical streamlining and coordination. The ILC did however recognize that even though it is "not generally appropriate" to draw up a hierarchical structure of norms and rules in international law, it is true that "some rules of international law are more important than other rules and for this reason enjoy superior position or special status in the international legal system".[168]

The academic analysis of fragmentation after the ILC Report has seen the emergence of what I may classify as two schools of thought: the realists and the positivists. Realists maintain their anxieties over fragmentation. They generally worry about the problem of "choice of law" in international law. The earliest example of such anxiety advanced by Morgenstern[169] was the following: an organization may be called upon to deal with a legal situation in respect of which there exists a conflict of laws. A State may, for example, be party to

---

165   Martti Koskenniemi & Paivi Leino, *Fragmentation of International Law: Postmodern Anxieties*, 15 Leiden J. Int'l L. 558 (2002).

166   Jacob Cogan, *The Idea of Fragmentation*, 105 Am. Soc'y Int'l L. Proc. 123 (2011).

167   *See* ILC Report.

168   *See* ILC Report, para. 31.

169   Felice Morgenstern, Legal Problems of International Organizations 37 (1986).

THE FRAGMENTATION OF INTERNATIONAL LAW

two multilateral obligations that are arguably inconsistent. Such potential conflict obviously lies in the interaction or relationship between the general law and special (regional) laws. In this regard, Wouters, Hoffmeister and Tom Ruys (2006)[170] have also stated, by example, that:

> Institutional ambiguities created by the EC and EU Treaty on external representation of Europe are not conducive to achieving a generally satisfactory European status in the UN system. UN partners may well be ignorant of the European architecture, and they are not obliged to follow the legal details thereof. Therefore the question whether the EU or the EC or both should represent a European position in the UN is mostly left to the European institutions themselves.[171]

In this case, there is a clear need for the regulation of potential conflict. Fox[172] states that this problem is roughly analogous to situations confronted by domestic conflict of laws rules, in which a party has sufficient connection to two or more jurisdictions to subject that party to the laws of those jurisdictions simultaneously. When those laws are inconsistent or both jurisdictions have an interest in having their laws applied, modern choice of law theory describes the situation as a "true conflict" to be resolved by the forum's choice of law rules. The court seized then makes the choice and applies one law or the other as the rule of decision. However, if one jurisdiction is found not to have an interest in its law applied, a "false" conflict is said to exist, and the law of the sole "interested" state is applied.[173] The matter may end with application of the forum court's choice of law, but this is not the case with treaty law because under treaty law, if a state finds itself the subject of conflicting obligations, a decision by an international tribunal to apply one of those obligations does not relieve the State of complying with the other. Fox therefore views the problem of fragmentation as occurring due to free-standing treaty obligations and treaties having no formal institutional relationship with each other – relations which might be used to resolve conflicting obligations.[174]

---

170   Jan Wouters, Frank Hoffmeister & Tom Ruys, The United Nations and the European Union: An Ever Stronger Partnership 1 (2006).

171   *Id.*

172   Fox, 184.

173   *Id.*

174   *Id.*

On a similar note, Hafner[175] observes that generally each treaty enforcement mechanism considers itself committed first of all to applying only its own system or sub-system of standards. Hafner states that because most treaty bodies may only apply their own substantive law to disputes or situations brought before them (except for the ICJ), states may engage in forum shopping, resorting to the mechanism that corresponds best to their state interests.[176] Interestingly, Craven[177] has held a different view on the issue of fragmentation. According to him, fragmentation should not be viewed as being prominently associated with incoherence, disunity and uncertainty, but rather as "marks of successes".[178] According to Craven, the concern as to normative inconsistency and institutional weaknesses is therefore simply a manifestation of the maturity of the system and a demonstration of its normative breadth and depth. This sentiment forms the gist of the positivist school of thought in fragmentation theory. The same view was also held by Cassese and Koskenniemi. Cassese suggested that:

> The gradual interpenetration and cross-fertilization of previously somewhat compartmentalised areas of international law is a significant development: it shows that at least at the normative level the international community is becoming more integrated and – what is even more important – that such values as human rights and the need to promote development are increasingly permeating various sectors of international law that previously seemed impervious to them.[179]

Koskenniemi also suggested that:

---

175   Gerhard Hafner, *Pros and Cons ensuing from Fragmentation of International Law*, 25 Mich. J. Int'l L. 857 (2004).

176   *Id.*

177   Mathew Craven, *Unity, Diversity and the Fragmentation of International Law*, 14 Finnish Y.B. Int'l L. 5 (2003).

178   In this regard, Mathew Craven states also that the description by the use of the term "proliferation" is misleading since the multiplication of specialized tribunals is, by itself, a healthy phenomenon. In earlier academic evaluations, the successes of the diversification and expansion of international law are explicit. *See, e.g.,* Georges Aabi-Saab, *Fragmentation or Unification: Some Concluding Remarks*, 31 NYU J. Int'l L. & Politics 919, 992 (1999); Benedict Kingsbury, *Foreword: Is the Proliferation of International Courts and Tribunals a Systematic Problem*, 31 NYU J. Int'l Int'l L. & Politics 679, 686 (1999).

179   Antonio Cassese, International Law 45 (1st ed., 2001).

THE FRAGMENTATION OF INTERNATIONAL LAW   215

> Far from being a problem to resolve, the proliferation of autonomous or
> semi-autonomous normative regimes is an unavoidable reflection of a
> 'postmodern' social condition and a beneficial prologue to a pluralistic
> community in which the degrees of homogeneity and fragmentation re-
> flect shifts of political preference and the fluctuating success of hege-
> monic pursuits.[180]

The positivist school of thought correctly argues that normative fragmentation
is a natural and predictable consequence of the evolution of the international
legal system, rather than its disintegration. This is because fragmentation is
caused by the specialization of relations within the international community.[181]
According to Lapas, the proliferation of international sub-systems and its consequent fragmentation is determined by the requirements of the contemporary international community. Thus, substantive fragmentation seems to be a
perfect catalyst in the development or transformation of international law as
we know it, into the law of the future international community.[182] In my view,
this argument may be reasonable when one considers that international law
always seeks to transcend its prior limits; it is a constantly developing legal
system. I think that being conservative and seeking to maintain a perceived
state of 'uniformity' is an attitude that is adverse to international law's devel-
opmental interests. New legal regimes and institutions are required to solve
new problems. From that perspective, we can celebrate the proliferation of international law and institutions that brings about fragmentation.

Positivists also hold the view that international law is not fragmenting, but
is rather manifesting itself as a pluralist system.[183] It has been argued that international legal pluralism is a sign of the maturing of international law, and
should not be seen as posing a threat.[184] Indeed, the recognition and acceptance of the concept of legal pluralism can enrich international law, because
the proliferation of regional and specialized regimes will be acceptable provided that their inter-se relations and their coexistence with general international

---

180   Martti Koskenniemi, *What is International Law For?, in* International Law 89, 110 (Malcolm
      Evans, 1st ed., 2003).
181   Davorin Lapas, *Some Remarks on Fragmentation of International Law: Disintegration or
      Transformation?* 40 Comp. & Int'l L. J. S. Afr. 1, 28 (2007).
182   *Id.*, 29.
183   *See, eg,* William Burke-White, *International Legal Pluralism,* 25 Mich. J. Int'l L. 963, 978
      (2004).
184   Mario Prost & Paul Kingsley Clarke, *Unity, Diversity and the Fragmentation of International
      Law: How Much does the Fragmentation of International Organizations Really Matter?* 5
      Chinese J. Int'l L. 341 (2006) [*hereinafter* Prost & Clarke].

law does not threaten the whole structure of the international legal order. The world community swarms with myriad legal orders[185], as it will continue to be in the foreseeable future. It seems plausible therefore to argue that the international legal system can thrive in its fragmented state. It is from the very fragmentation and legal differentiation that international law can find its unity (unity in diversity).

Supporters of the positivist school of thought argue that the risks of fragmentation are rather more theoretical than real. According to Scott, fragmentation is not an inherently negative phenomenon. Scott argues in the context of environmental law that a conflation and overlap between mandates of international institutions provides an opportunity for improving synergy between policy and programs, and opportunity for the more effective implementation of environmental obligations.[186] Scott therefore suggests that rather than trying to reverse or minimize the phenomenon of fragmentation, it should be exploited for the purpose of advancing new norms of public interest.

With regard to the judicial aspects of fragmentation, positivists hold the opinion that the proliferation of international courts and tribunals strengthens the use of adjudicatory processes and strengthens the international rule of law.[187] They argue that it is through the decisions of regional and specialized tribunals that the development and application of international law is progressive.[188] I am of the view that the proliferation of international courts and tribunals can indeed be beneficial because more and more cases will in future be resolved through legal proceedings: having more courts is better than having few. The work of international courts strengthens the rule of law and "ensures more effective respect for international law".[189] According to Rao, the creation of multiple international judicial tribunals "is a sign of the growing maturity of international law".[190]

---

185 Antonio Cassesse, *Remarks on Scelle's Theory of 'Role Splitting' in International Law*, 2 Eur. J. Int'l L. 210, 231 (1990).

186 Karen Scott, *International Environmental Governance: Managing Fragmentation through Institutional Connection*, 12 Melbourne J. Int'l L. 178 (2011).

187 Ole Kristian Fauchland & Andre Nollkaemper, The Practice of International and National Courts and the (De-)Fragmentation of International Law 3 (1st ed., 2012) [*hereinafter* Fauchland & Nollkaemper].

188 *Id.*, 6.

189 Michal Balcerzak & Sebastian Sykuna, *Leksykonochronyprawczłowieka*, 100 podstawowychpojęć 457–458 (2010).

190 Pemmaraju Rao, *Multiple International Judicial Forums: A Reflection of the Growing Strength of International Law or Its Fragmentation?*, 25 Mich. J. INT' L. 925, 930 (2004).

THE FRAGMENTATION OF INTERNATIONAL LAW 217

Fauchland and Nollkaemper opine that the risk of conflicting judgments is largely a theoretical one.[191] In connection to that, Prost and Clarke have argued that "we cannot conclude, from the few cases of jurisdictional overlaps, that there is a general disagreement or disorder".[192] According to the positivist school of thought, international courts and tribunals conduct themselves, and should be viewed, more as instruments for the unity and integrity of international law, than as sources of its fragmentation.[193] From the judicial perspective therefore, I would argue that the dangers of fragmentation may have been overstated. This is indeed arguable because international judges are increasingly becoming aware of the responsibility they bear to construe international law in a coherent manner.[194] This means that some of the problems associated with fragmentation can be avoided through a coherent interpretation of international law by all courts and tribunals.

In the contemporary state of international legal literature, it would appear then that the anxieties over fragmentation have largely been exaggerated. According to the positivists, what is feared to be fragmentation today might simply be some unavoidable side-effects of integrative processes which, although undesirable, are not necessarily harmful to the international legal order as a whole. One might therefore become convinced that fragmentation should not be so feared. The final and perhaps more interesting point made by the positivists suggests that we should "keep calm and carry on".[195] According to Broude, the anxieties that existed before, such as "threats to the unity of international law and the loss of overall control", have since normalized.[196] The prevailing argument in contemporary scholarship therefore is that reasonable solutions do exist and can be drawn from international law principles whenever difficulties do arise. Broude's view is also supported by Andenas and Bjorge's most recent book which essentially attempts to close the debate.[197]

---

191   Fauchland & Nollkaemper, 6.

192   Prost & Kingsley, 370.

193   August Reinisch, *The Proliferation of International Dispute Settlement Mechanisms: The Threat of Fragmentation vs. the Promise of a More Effective System? Some Reflections from the Perspectives of Investment Arbitration, in* International Law between Universalism and Fragmentation: Festschrift in Honour of Gerhard Hafner 107 (Isabelle Buffard et al. eds., 2008).

194   Bruno Simma, *Universality of International Law from the Perspective of a Practitioner*, 20 Eur. J. Int'l L. 265 (2008).

195   Tomer Broude, *Keep Calm and Carry On: Martti Koskenniemi and the Fragmentation of International Law*, 27 Temple Int'l & Comp. L. J. 279 (2013).

196   *Id.*, 238.

197   Andenas & Bjorge.

VI   Concluding Remarks

Indeed, it is possible to keep calm and carry on, even though it is undeniable that that the international legal system is inherently flawed in terms of its internal coherence. In as much as we can accept the benefits of fragmentation, the following facts cannot simply be ignored: The international legal system has no centralized adjudicatory body, and the principle of free choice or consent laid down in Article 33(1) of the UN Charter: enables States to establish dispute settlement mechanisms according to their particular needs or requirements; States are free to settle their disputes by any peaceful means they so wish;[198] and States may adhere to different but parallel dispute settlement mechanisms for parallel or even similar obligations.[199] A rigid consideration of these factors tells us that the rights and obligations of legal subjects may still be determined according to the body that is seized of them. The result could be an uncertainty of the standards to be applied in any given case. In my view, coherence is not yet a given. It is a real concern therefore that the uncontrolled proliferation of international courts and tribunals still places the unity of international law in danger.

It may be observed additionally that most of the problems associated with fragmentation exist because of some *other defects* of the international legal system. Public international law has no centralized legislative organ and there are no future prospects of one. States have no obligation to become members of the UN, and the principle of state sovereignty is only curtailed by the growth of international organizations with decision-making powers,[200] which States have also joined through exercising their free will. State consent remains the key element for establishing jurisdiction under the ICJ Statute as well.[201] Therefore, States may continue to establish regimes and procedures for dispute settlement according to their own needs.[202] It is clear, then, that normative conflicts are still possible between general international law and special rules that claim to exist as an exception to or are at variance with gen-

---

198   Article 33 of the UN Charter provides that "states are free to settle their disputes by any peaceful means, be it judicial or non-judicial".

199   Gabrielle Marceau & Kyung Kwak, *Overlaps and Conflicts of Jurisdiction between the World Trade Organization and Regional Trade Agreements*, Canadian Yearbook of Int'l L. 83, 95–96 (2003).

200   Christian Tomuschat, *International Law as a Coherent System: Unity or Fragmentation, in* Looking to the Future: Essays on International Law in Honor of W. Michael Reisman 330 (Mahnoush Arsanjani et al eds., 2011) [*hereinafter* Tomuschat].

201   ICJ Statute, art. 36.

202   Tomuschat, 333.

eral international law. Most legal systems provide legal means and devices to solve possible conflicts of norms, and ensure their harmonious application. However, the international legal system is poorly equipped to avoid normative conflicts and the uneven application of international norms because it lacks clear legal guidance for the resolution of conflict of norms. This state of affairs poses a perpetual threat to the unity of the international legal system and I believe that it is still worthwhile to continually seek and employ more efficient methods of preventing disorder and ensuring unity.

PART 2

Review Essay

∵

Review Essay: Neo-colonial Transformations of Occupied Territory – and of the International Law of Occupation?

Andrea Carcano, the Transformation of Occupied Territory in International Law (The Hague: Brill, 2015)

Valentina Azarova*

I   Introduction   223
II Beyond Occupation Law   224
III Occupation and Transformation   226
IV Transformative Occupation Beyond Iraq   229
V   License to Transform?   232

I   Introduction

On 6 July 2016, the long-awaited Iraq Inquiry (or Chilcot Inquiry) report presented a scathing verdict of United Kingdom (UK) government ministers' justification for – planning and conducting of the 2003 invasion and occupation of Iraq. The planning was carried out before other options were exhausted, while the conduct "went badly wrong, with consequences to this day".[1] As a result, the UK's involvement amounted to violations of international law. The report's 2.6 million words are a reminder of the politics of belligerent occupation and the challenges they entail for international law, given what can be viewed as its checkered application and enforcement both historically and in ongoing situations of occupation. The question this begs is whether the international law of occupation is being remade, or at least unmade through the practice of

---

*   Valentina Azarova, Postdoctoral Fellow, Centre for Global Public Law, Koç University, Istanbul, Turkey.
1   Leon Watson & Michael Wilkinson, *Chilcot report: Tony Blair takes 'full responsibility' for Iraq war as Jeremy Corbyn 'apologises sincerely on behalf' of Labour party*, Telegraph (July 6, 2016), http://www.telegraph.co.uk/news/2016/07/06/chilcot-report-2003-iraq-war-was-unnecessary-and-invasion-was-no/.

States and international institutions – and, if so, how could international law be mobilized in response? As Chilcot notes, "[a]ll aspects of any intervention [and hence also occupation] need to be calculated, debated and challenged with the utmost rigour, and when decisions have been made, they need to be implemented fully". Certain manifestations of intervention, Carcano reminds us, also need to be rigorously ruled out from the beginning.

Carcano's work makes an important contribution to the work of others preoccupied with the law of occupation and its diverse contemporary applications.[2] Offering a detailed and thorough analysis of transformative measures undertaken in the context of belligerent occupation, his monograph addresses the phenomenon of "transformative" occupation administrations, with Iraq as a case-study. Carcano presents a searching analysis of the international project to "democratize" Iraq, and of the effectiveness, or rather ineffectiveness of international law in regulating occupiers by prohibiting transformative sprees and preventing them from being entrusted with an international mandate to administer foreign territory. Carcano reaffirms the bright-line rules of international law that limit the scope of authority of occupying States by drawing a balance between their interests, those of the people and government of the occupied territory and those of the international community. This essay argues that the broader lesson of Iraq and other historical transformative occupations that Carcano laboriously surveys concerns the nature and effects of the harm inflicted by ongoing contemporary situations of occupation that pursue territorial aggrandizement and political transformation – such as Israel's longest modern occupation of Palestinian territory which turned 50 in June 2017 – both on the rights of the population in the occupied territory and the integrity and effectiveness of international law.

II   Beyond Occupation Law

Notwithstanding its anachronisms, the law of occupation was always intended to be applied in conjunction with other international law norms.[3] Today, as Carcano describes, the law of occupation is co-applied not only with inter-

---

2   Yutaka Arai-Takahashi, *Preoccupied with occupation: critical examinations of the historical development of the law of occupation*, 94 Int'l Rev. Red Cross 885 (2012).

3   Matters pertaining to the acquisition of title to territory were deferred early on to the law of nations. Delegates at the Hague Peace Conference noted that "there are certain points which cannot be the subject of a convention and which it would be better to leave, as at present, under the governance of that tacit and common law which arises from the principles of the

REVIEW ESSAY

national human rights law, but the norms on territorial integrity, exclusive jurisdiction, self-determination, and the interstate use of force. Carcano "seeks to understand how this evolving framework responds to contemporary aspirations to use occupation as a means of improving the lives of people in an occupied territory by introducing pro-human rights reforms and enabling the pursuit of the right to (internal) self-determination".[4]

A number of historical occupations, such as those of Mesopotamia, Japan, and Germany, had transformative elements, that Carcano argues were unique in their constellation of the population's interests and the international community's imperatives. They are also outdated from a normative perspective given developments in the *lex specialis* of occupation and other international law, particularly the right to self-determination.

In contemporary international legal practice, the challenge to sovereignty flows from the political and legal activism of States. Carcano describes how States including invading powers already in control of territory have disingenuously mobilized legal arguments that blur the distinctions between occupation, international territorial administration (ITA) and post-conflict situations governed by the emerging framework of *jus post bellum*, in order to expand the scope of their permissive authority as occupying powers. The activities of States on foreign soil seldom benefit from genuine substantive multilateral endorsement, and often, the same powers that are on opposite sides of a given occupation are also members of the United Nations (UN) Security Council (UNSC), which issues such endorsements. In practice, where UNSC members do initiate or facilitate mandates for foreign territorial control, it is often for their own interests which means that such mandates can be instrumental for those States that initiate and facilitate their adoption.

Iraq is an illuminating case study of the application of the law of occupation, the political sensibilities of international law and the paradigmatic function of occupation law as an anti-colonial framework. Carcano's meticulous account of events in Iraq since 2003 exposes some of the blind spots in international legal practice in contemporary situations of occupation, and in particular an amnesia in relation to the ills that transpired during the international territorial administrations of the past. It is a warning against the potential emergence of a legal basis for transformative occupation. The Iraqi experience shows that such a move would backtrack on the political and normative achievements

---

law of nations"; *see* Proceedings of the Hague Peace Conference: Translation of the Official Texts 502 (1920).

4   Andrea Carcano, The Transformation of Occupied Territory in International Law 6 (2015) [*hereinafter* Carcano].

represented by the law of occupation and its reliance on conservation and military necessity as normative premises, making it less likely that occupying States and the international institutions that might bestow them with further authority will be held accountable for their potential wrongs.[5]

By authorizing transformative measures in occupied territory, we risk the erosion of the international law norms applicable to such situations, which are intended to safeguard against colonial practices by occupying States. Such realities not only distort the severity of the actions of the occupying State, but arguably also render into disrepute the effectiveness of restraints of occupation law. The colonial flavor and resonance of contemporary predatory practices that pursue the transformation of the status, demographic character and political order of occupied territory highlight the need to deter such practices particularly in foreign administrations and trusteeship-like regimes. In this respect, Carcano's work is an important and sobering reminder of the need to uphold an uncompromised rule-based approach in such precarious situations by keeping close tabs on the nature of the activities of occupying powers and their effects on the rights of the local population.

III   Occupation and Transformation

Carcano begins by tracing the genealogy of the law of occupation, its conceptual foundations, and its contemporary application in conjunction with other rules and regimes of international law. He posits that occupation law was intended as a safeguard against interference with or infringement on sovereign rights, which has been reified by the outlawing of colonial regimes, the crystallization of the law of self-determination, and the codification of the act and crime of aggression. In other words, the law of occupation has become, for better or worse, a centerpiece of the contemporary international law of anti-colonization.

In Chapter 1, Carcano observes that the law of occupation has always considered occupation as a factual state of affairs. Historically, as Carcano recounts, international law permitted States to pursue their political goals unhindered "within agreed spheres of influence".[6] Up until the turn of the 20th century, occupation permitted the pursuit of conquest and exploitation, and States were able to rely on the justness of their military objectives to single-handedly make changes to the occupied territory's legal, political and economic order.

---

5   *Id.*, 423.

6   *Id.*, 40.

REVIEW ESSAY

Yet transformative foreign administrations ended when the era of national sovereignty and self-determination began. Today, such changes are not only precluded by the law of military occupation, but also by UN Charter law on the use of force and on self-determination – hallmarks of the legal legacy of decolonization.

Contemporary situations of occupation are a form of temporary control and administration that protects the rights of the legitimate sovereign by limiting an occupier to the exercise of duty-bound authority over the population and property of the occupied territory. This hard-rule based body of rules aims to strike a balance between the interests of the occupier, the population and the ousted sovereign. Against this backdrop, Carcano maintains, "Transformative occupation is a form of occupation which is the antithesis of the model of occupation as administration and control of territory, as codified in the Hague Regulations".[7] If a foreign power's transformative measures were to be legitimate and lawful, Carcano remarks, they "could not turn on the mere caprices of the stronger nation".[8]

The decision-making powers of an occupier, as *de facto* administrator without international recognition, are restricted by the formal exceptions embedded in occupation law, which is authoritatively complemented by criteria of legality enshrined in human rights and humanitarian law, and subject to occupation law's normative underpinnings in the *jus ad bellum* on the use of force. Even though the "humanitarian" normative framework of the Geneva Conventions (1949) "demands action rather than inaction on the part of the occupying power to do its utmost to tackle issues which emerge during and as a result of the occupation", Carcano argues, the underlying occupier's "normative authority is limited functionally and temporally by the existence of the occupation".[9] With this in mind, the Postdam Declaration adopted during the occupation of Germany by the Allied Forces (1945–49) limited reforms to what was necessary to undertake the demilitarization and de-Nazification of the territory, as the groundworks for its future political and economic reconstruction and transformation.[10] Carcano observes that occupiers' activities are subject to close scrutiny since "as history teaches us, occupations can turn into annexation, exploitation, or a form of colonialism," adding that "the more closely

---

7   *Id.*, 37.

8   *Id.*, 57. *See also* Ralph Wilde, International Territorial Administration (2008).

9   *Id.*, 73.

10   *Id.*, 68.

current occupations resemble models of the colonial era, the more appropriate it becomes to speak of forms of neo-colonialism".[11]

In Chapter 2, Carcano implies astutely that the contemporary framework of international law applicable to situations of occupation, as an integrated framework of international laws that consists of norms and legal regimes beyond the specialized body of occupation law. These practices place the normative viability of the occupying power's mandate under pressure; further challenging the understanding of the mandate of occupation law as a trust. A crucial question Carcano raises is "whether this evolution has in some way affected the traditional tenets of the law of occupation in favour of transformative policies directed to advancing human rights and democracy and/or enabling the (internal) self-determination of a people under occupation".[12]

The co-application of complementary norms can reassert certain restraints on the occupier's authority through the imposition of simultaneous and composite obligations and responsibilities. It can also provide a lens for assessing the normative dimension of the administrative and legal "regime" established by the occupier in the occupied territory. The legality of the continuation of the occupation would be subject to a twofold test of lawfulness based the effects of its activities on the territory, people and its ousted sovereign; and the international status, rights and benefits the occupier might accrue from these revisions. Carcano submits that the occupier's "authority/duty to [implement such revisions should be limited to taking measures having effect solely during the occupation or also after it".[13] In other words, the occupier does not have unfettered, "autonomous normative authority"[14] to advance human rights and democratic principles,[15] and must ensure in good faith that any measures it undertakes in or vis-à-vis the occupied territory are limited in their temporal effect.

Could an occupier lawfully decide that the occupied State was not constituted in accordance with the right to self-determination, and take on the self-appointed role of enabling actual self-determination by removing the current political regime? Carcano submits that an occupying power's presence in foreign territory can become illegal by virtue of its violations of international norms on the use of force and self-determination,[16] without usurping the

---

11   *Id.*, 51.

12   *Id.*, 75.

13   *Id.*, 97.

14   *Id.*, 99.

15   *Id.*, 100.

16   *Id.*, 81–2.

real-time protection afforded by occupation law; in line with the distinction between *jus in bello* and *ad bellum*. Such unlawfully prolonged occupations undermine the core object and purpose of the law of occupation, as well as the protection afforded to the local population's future rights. Measures that exceed an occupier's limited authority could be considered tantamount to forcible or coercive action that deprives a people of the right to self-determination. This formulation is more appropriate and efficient in terms of normative pull to enforceability, in calling out the occupying state for engaging in illegal force to maintain the occupation.

Carcano rightly asserts that whether an occupation should give way to transformative measures is "an eminently political question that should be examined on a case by case basis".[17] Indeed, this resonates with an argument Carcano does not take up concerning the implications of the violations of the law on self-determination in Iraq, or the illegal force used in other ongoing occupations on the occupier's ability to lawfully exercise authority in the territory, and hence arguably also the relevance of the law of occupation in such situations. Be it as it may, if occupiers were to regularly aggregate this authority by turning occupations into 'transformative' regimes, the international law applicable to such situations would also likely be transformed to more willingly, and perhaps also unwittingly accommodate such revisions. Such practices risk marking the end of the contemporary regulatory era in which the international law applicable to non-consensual foreign administrations imposes constraining limits on the authority of occupiers even in relation to acts that are in theory intended to serve the interests of the local population.

IV   Transformative Occupation Beyond Iraq

In the second part of his work, which consists of Chapters 3 to 5, Carcano frames the occupation of Iraq as a case-in-point of "transformative pro-democratic occupation". Carcano unpacks and carefully analyses each layer of facts concerning the establishment and status of the Coalition Provisional Authority (CPA), *qua* occupying States, their activities, "normative production" and transformative measures to challenge traditional approaches to the regulation of structurally abusive situations of belligerent occupation, whereby the very purpose for maintaining the occupation is illegal in international law.

Chapter 3 observes the ambiguities surrounding the CPA's legal status and the mandate granted to it by the UNSC, particularly in Resolution 1483,

---

17   *Id.*, 107.

which became a basis for the CPA's self-proclaimed free-for-all mandate and authorities. It called States to "promote the welfare of the population", restore "stability" and, to this end, display "a pro-active role in the administration of Iraq so as to ensure the welfare of the Iraqi people".[18] In so doing, the UNSC came to validate the ensuing occupation and to provide a cover of legitimacy to an inherently unlawful situation that ensued from the continued use of illegal force to pursue regime change measures. Its resolutions essentially purported to turn the CPA into an administrator with an international mandate; in other words, turning a hostile occupier into a good-will ambassador charged with the people's interests. This construction of an international mandate was rendered a nefarious enabler with essentially no limit on the means that could justify such broadly formulated ends: "the CPA was implicitly authorised to do all that it thought was necessary to achieve them".[19]

The CPA, for its part, read the resolution to support contrarian interpretations of core international law norms. The CPA's *de facto* transformation into an international administrator, Carcano maintains, "essentially reflects a compromise intended to appease all of the UN Security Council's permanent members – members with opposing views concerning Operation Iraqi Freedom".[20] Carcano argues that UNSC Resolution 1483 was intended to be mired with constructive ambiguity so as to lend itself to broad and dynamic interpretation by the CPA noting that interested States who commissioned the resolution (*i.e.* UK and United States) simply wanted a green-light "to proceed as they had planned."[21]

Carcano substantiates this proposition in Chapter 4 by critically examining the "normative production" of the CPA based on UNSC Resolutions 1483 on security, judicial and legislative reforms. He also considers measures adopted in relation to the political and constitutional system under UNSC Resolution 1511, which effectively granted the CPA authority to organize elections and draft a constitution, which entailed irreversible changes. Carcano criticizes the UNSC for not having "openly stated that it was pursuing a process reputedly essential to the improvement of the situation in Iraq, rather than hiding behind an Iraqi presumed consent that was tenuous at best,"[22] and instead "abus[ing] its power by allocating sovereign tasks to a non-sovereign entity".[23] The UNSC took no measure to protect against CPA abuses, and left the "undermining"

---

18   *Id.*, 170.

19   *Id.*, 171.

20   *Id.*, 165–166.

21   *Id.*, 178.

22   *Id.*, 322.

23   *Id.*, 321.

REVIEW ESSAY

effects of the CPA's actions on "social cohesion, and hence the stability of Iraq" unexamined.[24] In a sense, the Chilcot Report, over a decade later, is the first concerned challenge to the validity of these measures.

Carcano suggests that minor amendments to the law of occupation appear on face value necessary; such as clarifications with regards to the limits of an occupier's authority to adopt measures in relation to the national economy and foreign investment. The law's silence on such matters is however not unjustified. The likelihood that such measures further the occupier's, as opposed to the local population's interests, and the effect they have on occupation law's central attachment to conservationism, arguably imply a prohibition on such likely intrusive measures that could disrupt the organic development of the occupied territory both under occupation and after its end. It is therefore perhaps also worth asking whether the UNSC can enable and authorize such measures without effectively looking to set aside the operation of occupation law, and whether this does not therefore distract, and perhaps also detract, from its principal institutional role as regulator and enforcer of UN Charter law, including the international norms on the use of interstate force and on the self-determination of peoples.

Hence, the present author supports others who have urged a cautionary approach to the revision or amendment of contemporary international law. Indeed, as Carcano observes, it ultimately became apparent that such measures were part of the illegitimate reforms carried out in Iraq, they "were illegal as they went beyond its normative competence both *ratione materiae* and *ratione temporis*, concerned as they were with regulating the future of Iraq rather than its present."[25] Giving way to the UNSC's legislative capacity in such situations is both ill-advised and incompatible to its principal mandate of conflict prevention and resolution, which given the power relations between occupier and occupied demand the immediate handover of power to the local authorities. Iraq is certainly no model for the Council's engagement with volatile realities of armed conflict.

Without guidance or a granular mandate, the UNSC permitted the CPA to set aside the law of occupation unabatedly and justify a broad gamut of reforms by claiming that they are intended to serve the needs and interests of the Iraqi people. This arrangement, Carcano notes, resembles "the sacred trust of civilisation under which European countries justified colonial rule".[26] Not unlike such policies, as Carcano observes in Chapter 5, the CPA's divisive legal argumentation and inherently coercive policies of democratization

24   *Id.*, 323.
25   *Id.*, 340.
26   *Id.*, 336.

(acquiesced by the UNSC) not only "breached the law of occupation and the right to self-determination",[27] but contributed to "the increase of already-existing conditions of insecurity and instability, paving the way for the beginning of the 'age of discord'.[28] Till this day, this state of affairs and a reality of political interference prevail. A similar reality has emerged from the actions of other occupying States that support – the secession of the occupied territory from that of the occupied State through the occupying State's support of secessionist entities, e.g. Armenia in Azerbaijan, Russia in South Ossetia and Abkhazaia, Transnistria and Crimea.

V   License to Transform?

In his concluding, Chapter 6, Carcano compares the two-phased occupation of Iraq with other transformative occupations in which the law of self-determination was applied to vet the legitimacy of measures based on the people's consent. Particularly, he notes, "fundamental decisions on why, whether, and when to adopt a new constitutional document or replace an existing one."[29] Carcano submits that the fact that the CPA was not "a substantially force-based enterprise throughout", and failed "to gain legitimacy through the policies it enacted," is "evidenced by the emergence of a gradual but steady insurgency."[30]

Carcano argues that given the legal and political flaws in the occupation of Iraq, the impact of this case of occupation on the law of occupation should be considered with caution. It risks alleviating the restraints on future occupiers, and perhaps also undermining the protections afforded to individual rights and protected persons in international humanitarian law. Carcano's erudite approach to the sensibilities of contemporary international law in relation to transformative foreign administrations, provides an authoritative assessment of the legality and legitimacy of the actions adopted during the occupation of Iraq. While regime change practices has been firmly outlawed by international law, he astutely assures those concerned with its grim, neo-colonial prospects, that nothing short of an activist, *lex ferenda* project to create new norms would provide a lawful exception to the conservationist principle. In other words, revisionist projects such as that of the CPA through the UNSC should be normatively pre-empted by the imperative of guaranteeing the effectiveness of

---

27   *Id.*, 410.

28   *Id.*, 343.

29   *Id.*, 422.

30   *Id.*, 414.

REVIEW ESSAY

occupation law. Such an approach would also be in line with the need to keep the UNSC in check to ensure it is not abusing the Article 103 supremacy clause, while refocusing its work on its conflict prevention duties through more diligent application of the *jus ad bellum*.

Despite having raised a host of danger-flags to this effect, Carcano appears to posit a curious suggestion that there may be a way to lawfully pursue democratization in a situation of occupation under existing international law and practice. If such reforms are carried out with extreme care and caution and under explicit UNSC authorization, Carcano argues, we can imagine a *detailed* mandate with explicit limitations on the authority of the international administrator in line both with the imperatives of international law and lessons learned from previous occupations.[31] Given the pitfalls of international territorial administration and the infancy of *jus post bellum*, the possibility for such change is hardly imaginable. Granting the UNSC as we know it a supervisory role over occupiers is likelier to invite practices reminiscent of the era of trusteeship and the "civilizing mission" of Western States, rather than offer real prospect of protection.[32] Carcano is not blind to these risks, and asserts that "the case of Iraq, for all the foregoing reasons, militates against the Security Council's support role in democratisation processes pursued through an occupying power".[33]

Authority over affairs in the occupied territory is a zero-sum game: in which the right to self-determination of people provides a near-absolute safeguard against an occupying power's abusive regime, only the most exceptional circumstances can the UNSC authorize an ex-occupier *qua* administrator, to exercise "an extraordinary level of supervision".[34] Such scrutiny should coincide with measures intended to bring the occupying States' presence and influence over the occupied territory to an end; instead of inductively approving any mandate for transformation, they should aim to relieve the population of the occupied territory from the adverse effects of an unlawfully prolonged occupation. Carcano denotes the growing demand for a pragmatic approach for such post-conflict situations, while skeptically questioning the capacity and good-will of occupying powers. It is expected that international law respond to the challenge posed by 'failed' States to international law and security, it must not undermine its basis in normative attachments that receive overwhelming support from States.

---

31   *Id.*, 435.

32   *See, generally*, Ralph Wilde, International Territorial Administration (2008).

33   *Id.*, 457.

34   *Id.*

All occupation administrations continue to benefit the political and economic interests of predatory actors (who often consider themselves above the law). Iraq is a case-in-point for the systemic economic exploitation that can ensue from the actions of powerful Western nations acting as self-proclaimed adjudicators of "democratic" standards and claiming supremacy over international law. To borrow from Elizabeth Wilmshurst's views on the invasion of Iraq, international law was "regarded simply as an impediment to be removed", stating: "we ignored the rule of law – the result was Iraq".[35] The displacement of the law of occupation essentially led to the upending of the rule of international law more broadly; including the law on the use of force and on sovereign equality. These are also the marks of a reality that establishes and perpetuates a situation of serious human rights violations.

They established an administration the effect of which was as taxing for its population as it was for the future of the country, with equally perilous effects for the integrity of international law, which the UNSC effectively bent to accommodate certain States' agendas.[36] Similar abuses and legal subversions characterize other ongoing occupations: the instrumentalization of self-determination law in Russia's annexation of Crimea;[37] the rejection of the application of the law of occupation by Israel in Palestine and Morocco in the Western Sahara inter alia; and the pursuit of different forms of foreign domination through secessionist movements in the context of Russia's continued occupation of Georgian territory, Armenia's occupation of Azerbaijani territory and Turkey's occupation of northern Cyprus.

Against the backdrop of ongoing expert and civil society struggles to reconcile with the challenges of the contemporary practice of the law of occupation and deconstruct its "ends and fictions",[38] Carcano's work provides an important contribution to the elucidation of this problematique, as well as a reminder of the deep-seated normative attachments of the international legal order. Attesting to the alarming threat posed by transformative occupation, apparent from the case of Iraq and the inadvertent long-term harms caused by the CPA,

---

35 Elizabeth Wilmshurst, *We ignored the rule of law – the result was Iraq*, The Guardian (July 7, 2016), https://www.theguardian.com/commentisfree/2016/jul/07/ignored-rule -law-war-result-was-iraq-un-charter-foreign-office-lawyer-2003.

36 International Committee of the Red Cross, *Occupation and Other Forms of Administration of Foreign Territory*, Expert Meeting (March 2012), https://www.icrc.org/eng/assets/files/ publications/icrc-002-4094.pdf.

37 Christopher Borgen, *Law, Rethoric, Strategy: Russia and Self-determination Before and After Crimea*, 91 Int'l Legal Stud. 216 (2015).

38 See e.g., Aeyal Gross, The Writing on the Wall: Rethinking the International Law of Occupation (2017).

REVIEW ESSAY

Carcano's scholarship both complements and revisits the working assumptions of works on the law of occupation by Benvenisti, Dinstein and Arai-Takahashi, while also straddling the works of Wilde on the lingering "civilizing mission" of international territorial administrations, Roth on antithetical nature of "democratic governance" in the context of governmental illegitimacy in international law, and Fox on "humanitarian" occupation. It frames a sub-category of transformative (pro-democratic) occupations that contributes to the analysis of the role of an occupying power, international institutions and international norms in such perilous situations, and shrewdly concludes that such actions and the divisive argumentation that states have used in furthering what can essentially be termed as an "assault"[39] on of international law. Carcano's work is a timely appeal to pre-empt and seek the reversal of the damage caused by divisive use to the "irreplaceable" bright-line rules of international law.

---

39   See, Jens Ohlin, The Assault On International Law (2015).

PART 3

Materials

SECTION A

United Nations Documents

∴

Report of the Special Rapporteur on the Situation of Human Rights in the Palestinian Territories Occupied Since 1967, U.N. Doc. A/HRC/31/73

United Nations
General Assembly
A/HRC/31/73

Human Rights Council
Thirty-first session
Agenda item 7
Human rights situation in Palestine and other occupied Arab territories

Report of the Special Rapporteur on the situation of human rights in the Palestinian territories occupied since 1967

Note by the Secretariat

The Secretariat has the honour to transmit to the Human Rights Council the report of the Special Rapporteur on the situation of human rights in the Palestinian territories occupied since 1967, submitted pursuant to Commission on Human Rights resolution 1993/2 A and Human Rights Council resolution 5/1. In it, the Special Rapporteur on the situation of human rights in the Palestinian territories occupied since 1967, Makarim Wibisono examines the overall lack of effective protection of the rights of Palestinians living under Israeli occupation since 1967 and addresses the non-cooperation of Israel with the mandate. He reviews allegations of violations of human rights related to the surge in violence in the Occupied Palestinian Territory in 2015. The report further illustrates continuing concerns regarding the protection of human rights and respect for international humanitarian law by reviewing selected recommendations related to the Occupied Palestinian Territory of the second universal periodic review of Israel. It also draws on communications addressed by the Special Rapporteur to the Government of Israel to illustrate continuing concerns.

UN DOCUMENTS

I Introduction

1. The present report examines the need for effective protection of the rights of Palestinians living under Israeli occupation since 1967. Since assuming his mandate in June 2014, the Special Rapporteur has been struck by the abundant amounts of information and reports on violations of international human rights law and international humanitarian law, on the one hand, and the seeming inability of the international community to match what is known of the situation with more effective protection of Palestinians in the Occupied Palestinian Territory.

2. The Special Rapporteur emphasizes the importance of Palestinian, Israeli and international civil society organizations, human rights defenders, United Nations actors and other international bodies working tirelessly to improve the situation of human rights and provide a protective presence for Palestinians against the effects of Israeli policies and practices related to the occupation. However, year after year, violations of international humanitarian law and of civil, political, economic, social and cultural rights continue to be reported. Key recommendations to the Government of Israel presented by the Secretary-General, the United Nations High Commissioner for Human Rights and independent mandate holders, such as the Special Rapporteur, to the General Assembly and the Human Rights Council remain largely unimplemented. In the present report, the Special Rapporteur examines the outcome of the second universal periodic review of Israel and discusses key recommendations made by States regarding areas of broad, ongoing concerns in the Occupied Palestinian Territory, on the issues of settlements, the blockade, Palestinian prisoners and detainees and accountability, and responses by the Government of Israel.

3. As an occupied people, under international humanitarian law, Palestinians in the Occupied Palestinian Territory are "protected persons". Yet there is a disconnect between the rights and protections afforded to them under international humanitarian law, and international human rights law in particular, and actual protection. Israel, as the occupying Power, holds the primary responsibility for addressing this disconnect. The Special Rapporteur wishes to illustrate some facets of the vulnerability of individual Palestinians resulting from Israeli policies and practices. He will do so by reference to letters of allegation and urgent appeals that he and other special procedure mandate holders addressed to the Government of Israel in 2014 and 2015, raising alleged violations of

international humanitarian law and international human rights law in specific cases.

4. While the mandate of the Special Rapporteur is focused on investigation of violations by Israel of the principles and bases of international law (see Commission on Human Rights resolution 1993/2 A), the Special Rapporteur has previously noted the fact that both Palestinians and Israelis have been victims of the protracted Israeli-Palestinian conflict. The scale of the impact, however, whether in terms of casualty figures or wider impacts, differs significantly in that the daily lives of Palestinians are affected by the Israeli occupation. The destructive impact of the Israeli-Palestinian conflict is particularly clear in times of active hostilities, such as in the summer of 2014 in Gaza, or as has been witnessed particularly in the fourth quarter of 2015, especially in the West Bank, during escalations in violence.

5. According to the Office for the Coordination of Humanitarian Affairs, in October and November 2015 the escalation of violence resulted in the deaths of more than 100 Palestinians and some 11,300 injured, and 17 Israeli fatalities and some 170 injured.[1] The Special Rapporteur wishes to reiterate two points, related to the current violence, which are interlinked. The first is that any wanton act of individual violence, whether committed by Palestinians or Israelis, is unacceptable and must be investigated and prosecuted in accordance with international standards. The second is that the upsurge of violence with serious concerns of excessive use of force by Israeli security forces in the context of attacks and alleged attacks by Palestinians and during clashes, and ongoing settler violence, is arising within a pre-existing context. Anyone seeking to quell the unrest would, notwithstanding the unequivocal position that individual perpetrators of crimes must be held responsible, need to look to the context and related root causes of the overall heightened tension. To simply condemn individual attacks does not offer any viable way out of the violence rolling over the Occupied Palestinian Territory.

6. It is part of the current context that there seems to be an atmosphere of despair, particularly among the Palestinian youth, at the prolonged interference by Israeli authorities in every aspect of Palestinian life, the general absence of accountability for violations and abuses committed against them and the absence of any immediate prospects of an improvement in the situation.

---

1 Office for the Coordination of Humanitarian Affairs, "Casualties in the Occupied Palestinian Territory and Israel, 1 October to 30 November 2015", 14 December 2015.

7. On 13 July 2014, in a letter addressed to the Secretary-General, the President of the State of Palestine, Mahmoud Abbas, formally requested that "the territory of the State of Palestine be placed under an international protection system by the United Nations". President Abbas highlighted the long-standing occupation and the prevention of the exercise of the right of Palestinians to self-determination. In the letter, three overarching objectives of the protection system for Palestine were detailed including ensuring respect for human rights, fundamental freedoms and international law and international humanitarian law and to providing protection for the Palestinian people and civilian population from the ongoing occupation and acts of aggression by Israel (see S/2014/514, annex).

8. On 21 July 2014, the Secretary-General transmitted the letter to the President of the Security Council (S/2014/514). On 21 October 2015, the Secretary-General, referencing his earlier letter, further transmitted a summary of historical precedents of international protection regimes for areas of territories and their inhabitants (see S/2015/809, annex). The Secretary-General requested the President of the Security Council to bring his letter dated 21 October 2015 and the accompanying annex to the attention of the members of the Security Council.

9. The Special Rapporteur will not comment on the specifics of the request for international protection, except to reiterate that long-standing Israeli policies and practices in the Occupied Palestinian Territory, such as continued settlement expansion, the construction of the wall, and the blockade of Gaza, are illegal under international law and well-known to entail ongoing and serious violations of the human rights of Palestinians.

II   Non-cooperation by Israel with the Mandate

10. The Special Rapporteur deeply regrets to report that he has been obstructed in his ability to fulfil his mandate by the lack of cooperation of Israel. The Special Rapporteur assumed the mandate as an impartial observer and has from the outset made great efforts to engage in dialogue with the Government of Palestine and the Government of Israel. He has repeatedly signaled that his only interest, as an independent expert, lies in the effective and even-handed implementation of the mandate.

11. The Government of Palestine has extended full cooperation with the mandate holder. The Special Rapporteur has met with several Palestinian officials, including during his two missions to the region, graciously facili-

tated by the Governments of Jordan and Egypt, in lieu of in situ missions, in September 2014 and June 2015.

12. In a letter dated 13 October 2015, the Special Rapporteur formally renewed his request to the Government of Israel to grant him access to the Occupied Palestinian Territory by the end of 2015. This followed similar letters dated 12 August 2014, 13 February 2015 and 13 May 2015. No formal response has been received from Israel to these requests.

13. The Government of Israel has repeatedly sought to justify its non-cooperation by referring to its reservations regarding the mandate. Consequently, despite assurances of access made upon his appointment, and the duty of Israel, as a Member State, to extend cooperation to a special procedure mandate holder, the Special Rapporteur has effectively been denied access to the Occupied Palestinian Territory.

14. The Special Rapporteur has consistently sought to be an effective voice for the victims of violations committed under the occupation, but regrets that the policy of Israel has hampered him in fulfilling this role to the full. As noted in his report to the General Assembly presented in October 2015 (A/70/392), without access, the Special Rapporteur has had to reconsider how he can best serve the mandate (ibid., para. 7). Critically, for the current incumbent, having access to the Occupied Palestinian Territory and meaningful dialogue with both sides was the premise upon which he accepted the mandate.

15. All previous holders of this mandate since its establishment in 1993, but for the Special Rapporteur's immediate predecessor, have been permitted by Israel to access Israel and the Occupied Palestinian Territory (see A/69/301 and Corr.1, sect. III).[2] It has always been the intent of the current Special Rapporteur to fulfil this mandate by gathering information during missions to the Occupied Palestinian Territory and through face-to-face meetings with victims and witnesses, civil society representatives, United Nations representatives and Palestinian and Israeli government officials.

16. The Special Rapporteur expresses his appreciation for the broad support for his access to the Occupied Palestinian Territory by Member States.[3] He considers it of the utmost importance that the international community,

---

2   Access does not imply formal cooperation with the mandate.

3   See, e.g., statements made during the interactive dialogue following the presentation by the Special Rapporteur of his report to the Third Committee, 34th meeting, seventieth session of the General Assembly, 29 October 2015. Available from http://webtv.un.org/meetings-events/watch/third-committee-34th-meeting---70th-general-assembly/4587399067001#full-text.

UN DOCUMENTS

in particular the Human Rights Council, redouble political pressure to insist that Israel return to the level of cooperation extended when the mandate was first established and, at the very least, ceases to obstruct the mandate holder's access to the Occupied Palestinian Territory.

III   **Alleged Human Rights Violations Related to the Rise in Violence in 2015[4]**

17.   The Special Rapporteur has raised a number of concerns related to the rise in violence in the Occupied Palestinian Territory, especially of excessive use of force by Israeli security forces during clashes and in the context of attacks and alleged attacks by Palestinians. The situation escalated in October, following heightened tensions, and continued in November and December 2015.[5] The upsurge in violence[6] is a grim reminder of the unsustainable human rights situation in the Occupied Palestinian Territory and the volatile environment it engenders. On 22 October 2015, the Deputy Secretary-General in his briefing to the Security Council, while stressing that there is no justification for murder, stated that the current crisis would not have erupted "if Palestinians did not still live under a stifling and humiliating occupation that has lasted almost half a century".[7]

18.   Against the backdrop of illegal settlements in the West Bank, including East Jerusalem, the blockade of Gaza, and a general lack of accountability, including for violations and crimes by Israeli security forces and settlers, tensions rose further in September and October 2015 following restrictions imposed by Israeli authorities on Palestinians' access to the Al-Aqsa compound and what Palestinians viewed as attempts to alter the status quo at the Al-Aqsa compound.

---

4   Data available at the time of drafting primarily covered the months of October and November 2015. At the time of finalizing the present report in December 2015, the situation was ongoing.

5   Press releases, "'Extremely volatile situation across the Occupied Palestinian Territory' – UN expert expresses grave concern", 16 October 2015, and "UN rights experts express deep concern about ongoing bloodletting in the Occupied Palestinian Territory", 16 November 2015, issued together with the Special Rapporteur on extrajudicial, summary or arbitrary executions.

6   See also press release of the High Commissioner for Human Rights, "Zeid urges calm and restraint in West Bank amid deadly escalation", 8 October 2015.

7   See www.un.org/sg/dsg/statements/index.asp?nid=674.

19. On 14 September 2015, in his opening address to the thirtieth session of the Human Rights Council, the High Commissioner for Human Rights noted concerns of excessive use of force in the context of a spike in killings of Palestinians over previous months in incidents involving Israeli security forces in the West Bank. The Special Rapporteur received submissions from two Hebron-based non-governmental organizations on the case of an 18-year-old woman, Hadeel al-Hashlamoun, who was killed on 22 September 2015 by Israeli forces at a checkpoint in Hebron. There have been allegations that it constituted an extrajudicial execution, amid questions of whether the woman possessed a knife as claimed by Israeli forces.[8] Even in the context of an alleged stabbing attack, there are serious questions as to whether lethal use of force was warranted by the threat level presented by one young woman with a knife confined to the area of a checkpoint controlled by several armed Israeli soldiers.[9] She was reportedly shot multiple times and it appears there was no medical assistance attempted by the Israeli authorities.[10] The investigation by one Israeli non-governmental organization found that the allegation that she had attempted to stab soldiers could not "be reconciled with the fact that there was a metal barrier between her and the soldiers". The organization further noted that she had been shot repeatedly, when she did not pose a threat, following initial shots to her legs, and called on the Israeli military to publish its video documentation from the checkpoint's security cameras.[11]

20. October and November 2015 also saw a wave of protests and violent clashes between Palestinians and Israeli security forces. Excessive use of force by Israeli security forces against Palestinians in the context of attacks and alleged attacks on Israelis, including soldiers, and during clashes, has been widely reported. Whereas much of the initial violence centred in East Jerusalem, Hebron, where Palestinians also live in close proximity

---

8   Israel, Ministry of Foreign Affairs, "Palestinian woman attempts to stab soldier in Hebron", 24 September 2015 (communicated by the Spokesperson's Office of the Israel Defense Forces).

9   Peter Beaumont, "Dispute arises over circumstances of death of woman at Israeli checkpoint" (including a filmed witness account and photo documentation), *The Guardian*, 23 September 2015.

10   Amnesty International, "Evidence indicates West Bank killing was extrajudicial execution", 25 September 2015.

11   B'Tselem – The Israeli Information Center for Human Rights in the Occupied Territories, "B'Tselem investigation: No justification for multiple bullets that killed Hadil al-Hashlamun in Hebron", press release, 24 September 2015.

to a large settler population and with a large presence of Israeli security forces, has become a hotspot. While most fatal incidents occurred in the West Bank, including East Jerusalem, Palestinians in Gaza have also been killed in incidents involving Israeli security forces. In reported incidents on 9 and 10 October 2015, 9 Palestinians were reported killed and more than 230 injured, by Israeli security forces during protests in Gaza linked to the situation in the West Bank.[12]

21. The high number of Palestinian casualties in individual incidents and during clashes with Israeli security forces, since the violence escalated, is extremely worrying. The Office for the Coordination of Humanitarian Affairs reported that, in October and November 2015, of some 11,300 Palestinians injured, injuries were mainly caused by exposure to tear gas (60 per cent), rubber bullets (23 per cent) and live ammunition (14 per cent).[13] Of fatalities in the same period, the Office for the Coordination of Humanitarian Affairs reported that 60 Palestinians, including children, were killed in the context of attacks and alleged attacks against Israelis, and 17 Israelis were killed in such attacks. In addition, 39 Palestinians were killed in the context of clashes with Israeli security forces. Three Palestinians were killed in other types of incidents.[14]

22. On 14 October 2015, nine human rights organizations in Israel issued a joint press release against statements made by politicians and senior police officers to the effect that attackers should be killed, and noted "it seems that too often, instead of acting in a manner consistent with the nature of each incident, police officers and soldiers are quick to shoot to kill".[15] On 26 October 2015, in response to a letter from a human rights organization, the Attorney General of Israel is reported to have clarified the circumstances in which Israeli forces may use firearms: "the use of a firearm to prevent an immediate life-threatening situation is permitted

---

12 Office for the Coordination of Humanitarian Affairs, "Protection of Civilians report: 6–12 October 2015", 15 October 2015, p. 1.

13 Office for the Coordination of Humanitarian Affairs, "Casualties in the Occupied Palestinian Territory and Israel, 1 October to 30 November 2015", 14 December 2015 (figures exclude casualties within Israel except where Palestinians from the Occupied Palestinian Territory were involved in incidents). Three per cent of injuries were caused by other types of weapons.

14 Ibid.

15 Association for Civil Rights in Israel, Amnesty International – Israel branch, B'Tselem, Gisha, Public Committee Against Torture in Israel, HaMoked: Center for the Defense of the Individual, Yesh Din – Volunteers for Human Rights, Adalah: Legal Center for Arab Minority Rights in Israel, Physicians for Human Rights – Israel.

as long as there is concrete fear of such harm" and "to use a firearm after the threat to bodily integrity or human life has elapsed would constitute a deviation from the law".[16] He also, reportedly, noted that the use of fire must be proportional to the threat.

23. Among credible reports of alleged perpetrators shot dead by Israeli security forces when not posing an immediate threat to the life of Israeli soldiers or others, is the case of a 72-year-old woman killed on 6 November 2015. Israeli forces reportedly alleged that she intended to ram them with her car.[17] However, reported footage of the incident shows that soldiers continued firing after jumping out of the way of the car.[18] On 14 October 2015, a young Palestinian man from Hebron was shot dead by Israeli security forces in the context of an alleged attempted stabbing attack at the Damascus Gate entrance to the old city in East Jerusalem. A video of the incident showed the man running past police officers with what appeared to be a knife in his hand before being shot.[19] While the situation posed a level of threat, it is troubling that it appears from the footage available that there was no attempt by the Israeli security forces present to immobilize the suspect in order to apprehend him.[20] It has been claimed that a second video shows the man being shot again while lying almost motionless on the ground.[21]

24. The Special Rapporteur is deeply concerned at measures employed against the Palestinian population in the context of the escalation of violence. While Israeli authorities need to respond appropriately and proportionally to the deteriorating security situation, measures that are excessive violate international law and only add fuel to already inflamed tensions. In mid-October the Israeli Ministry of Foreign Affairs reported the approval by the Security Cabinet of a number of measures,

---

16 *Times of Israel*, "A-G: It's illegal to fire on suspects who don't pose threat", 26 October 2015.

17 *Times of Israel*, "Elderly Palestinian woman tries to run over soldiers near Hebron", 6 November 2015.

18 Amnesty International, "Israel/OPT: Investigate apparent extrajudicial execution at Hebron hospital", press release, 12 November 2015, and B'Tselem, "Unjustified use of lethal force and execution of Palestinians who stabbed or were suspected of attempted stabbings", press release, 16 December 2015.

19 From interview with a police spokesperson, with footage of the shooting (MSNBC LIVE With José Díaz-Balart, "Police: 'No doubt' man posed imminent threat" 14 October 2015).

20 B'Tselem, "Footage raises grave concern that Fadi 'Alun and Basel Sidr were shot while no longer posing danger", press release, 15 October 2015.

21 Al Jazeera, "Mapping the dead in latest Israeli-Palestinian violence" (accessed 9 December 2015).

authorizing Israeli security forces to "impose a closure on, or to surround, centers of friction and incitement in Jerusalem".[22] The measures also provided that where a punitive demolition has taken place no new construction would be permitted, that the [suspected] perpetrators' property would be confiscated and their East Jerusalem residency rights revoked.[23]

25. Punitive demolitions of the homes of perpetrators or alleged perpetrators of attacks against Israelis are in contravention of international humanitarian law and international human rights law. Israel, as the occupying Power is prohibited from destroying private property in the Occupied Palestinian Territory.[24] Such demolitions further constitute collective punishment, contrary to article 33 of the Geneva Convention relative to the Protection of Civilian Persons in Time of War, affecting not only the perpetrator or suspected perpetrator, but also the family of the targeted person and often families in adjacent homes impacted by the blast of the demolitions. Punitive demolitions violate a number of human rights, including the right to housing. According to the Office for the Coordination of Humanitarian Affairs, from mid-October to the end of November 2015, 11 homes were demolished or sealed in such punitive actions. This caused the displacement of 80 Palestinians, including 42 children. Twenty-six persons living in adjacent buildings were also temporarily displaced in connection with the demolitions.[25] On 16 November 2015, the Humanitarian Coordinator in the Occupied Palestinian Territory expressed distress at reports of punitive demolitions targeting five family homes concluding that "punitive demolitions are inherently unjust, punishing innocent people for the acts of others".[26]

26. In East Jerusalem, extensive restrictions, affecting the right to freedom of movement, in the form of roadblocks and checkpoints were imposed following approval by the Israeli Security Cabinet in mid-October 2015. At the end of November, the Office for the Coordination of Humanitarian Affairs reported that around 76,000 people in six Palestinian neigh-

---

22   Israel, Ministry of Foreign Affairs, "Security Cabinet approves anti-terror measures", 13 October 2015.

23   Ibid.

24   This prohibition (art. 53 of the Geneva Convention relative to the Protection of Civilian Persons in Time of War) applies unless an absolute necessity for military operations exists.

25   Office for the Coordination of Humanitarian Affairs, "Humanitarian Bulletin: occupied Palestinian territory – November 2015", p. 9.

26   Office for the Coordination of Humanitarian Affairs, "Humanitarian Coordinator calls for end to punitive demolitions in the occupied West Bank", Jerusalem, 16 November 2015.

bourhoods in East Jerusalem were still directly affected by additional checkpoints, roadblocks and an earth mound.[27] While such restrictions were gradually lifted in East Jerusalem, they were increasingly imposed in Hebron where several main access roads to the city were blocked by Israeli security forces and inspections and searches of Palestinians at the many checkpoints intensified. It is troubling that some international organizations providing a crucial protective presence are reported to have been denied access to the areas of Hebron city most affected and that their staff have allegedly been harassed by settlers and Israeli forces.[28] In this context, the Special Rapporteur is also seriously concerned at information received of Palestinian human rights defenders in Hebron being harassed and threatened by Israeli security forces and settlers.

27. With respect to the right to education during the period of increased tensions and clashes, the Special Rapporteur has received allegations of schoolchildren and teachers in Hebron being harassed by Israeli forces and settlers on their way to and from school in October 2015. Children attending school in the H2 area of Hebron, controlled by Israeli security forces, appear to have been particularly adversely affected. According to the organization Christian Peacemaker Teams, in the first 10 schooldays of October, more than 140 tear gas canisters were fired by Israeli forces from two military checkpoints in H2 as Palestinian children walked to and from school.[29]

28. At the time of the finalization of this report in early December 2015, the situation of heightened violence, within the context of the ongoing occupation, continued. The Special Rapporteur stresses the need to ensure respect for the human rights of Palestinians. Responding to the deteriorated security situation does not permit excessive measures or measures of collective punishment to be carried out by Israeli authorities. The Special Rapporteur reiterates that it is imperative that Israeli security forces abide by international standards on use of force, in particular the Basic Principles on the Use of Force and Firearms by Law Enforcement Officials. He renews the call on Israeli authorities to carry out independent, effective, thorough, prompt and impartial investigations into all suspected cases of extrajudicial, arbitrary and summary executions.

---

27 Office for the Coordination of Humanitarian Affairs, " Humanitarian Bulletin – November 2015", p. 6.

28 Ibid., p. 1.

29 Christian Peacemaker Teams, "Al-Khalil (Hebron): Christian Peacemaker Palestine October Newsletter", 3 November 2015.

IV Selected Universal Periodic Review Recommendations to Israel and Broad Continuing Human Rights Concerns

29. In October 2013, Israel underwent its second universal periodic review (see A/HRC/25/15). While over 200 recommendations were made, the Special Rapporteur will, as is appropriate, limit his consideration to those regarding the situation in the Occupied Palestinian Territory.

30. In March 2014, Israel submitted its responses to the recommendations in an addendum (A/HRC/25/15/Add.1) containing the Government's official responses to the recommendations, and an annex in which Israel provided its responses to recommendations that it considered beyond the scope of the universal periodic review owing to their focus on international humanitarian law.[30] In the annex, the Government of Israel questioned "the relevance of examining matters which are governed by international humanitarian law in the context of a human rights review", stating that "the applicability of human rights conventions to the West Bank and the Gaza Strip has been subject of considerable debate over the past years".[31] The Special Rapporteur refers to the determination of the International Court of Justice that international humanitarian law and human rights law apply in the Occupied Palestinian Territory.[32]

31. The Special Rapporteur notes the stated support of Israel for the following broad recommendations pertaining to its respect for international law: comply with its legal obligations under international law alongside its obligations deriving from international human rights treaties to which Israel is a party; abide by its international legal obligations, including those under the Fourth Geneva Convention; and strengthen its cooperation with international human rights mechanisms, in particular with the Human Rights Council (see A/HRC/25/15, paras. 136.46, 136.47 and 136.37, and A/HRC/25/15/Add.1, para. 13). Regrettably, however, the Government of Israel rejected many recommendations on settlements, the blockade, Palestinian prisoners and detainees and accountability. These are critical

---

30 For the purposes of this discussion the Special Rapporteur recognizes the unofficial status of responses provided by Israel in the annex, but as they represent an expression by Israel on particular areas, he will consider the support of Israel for recommendations as noted in both the addendum and in the annex.

31 The annex is available from the website of the Office of the United Nations High Commissioner for Human Rights, at www.ohchr.org/EN/HRBodies/UPR/Pages/ILSession15.aspx.

32 *Legal Consequences of the construction of a wall in the Occupied Palestinian Territory, Advisory Opinion, I.C.J. Reports 2004*, p. 136.

THE PALESTINE YEARBOOK OF INTERNATIONAL LAW, VOLUME 19 (2016)

areas to address in order to improve the situation of ongoing violations under the Israeli occupation of the West Bank, including East Jerusalem, and Gaza.

A   Settlements

32. Most of the human rights violations against Palestinians in the West Bank, including East Jerusalem, are linked to the existence and expansion of settlements. Such violations relate to home demolitions and the consequent displacement, discriminatory supply of water and provision of access to land, movement restrictions, settler violence and the discriminatory military court system which Israel applies to Palestinians. The Special Rapporteur deeply regrets that Israel rejected the following recommendations related to settlements: stop the transfer of its population to the occupied territory and put an end to all measures that encourage or perpetuate the settlements; guarantee the right to housing of the Palestinians in the occupied territories, including East Jerusalem, stopping the demolition of Palestinian houses and guaranteeing the property rights of the Palestinian population; and dismantle the separation wall and halt the expansion of illegal settlements (see A/HRC/25/15, paras. 136.173, 136.229 and 136.151, and A/HRC/25/15/Add.1, para. 53).[33]

33. The Special Rapporteur notes the partial support to the following recommendation on discrimination and access to natural resources: effectively protect the Palestinian population in the occupied West Bank, including East Jerusalem, against any form of discrimination which impairs the equitable access to basic services or natural resources, including water and land, or else the equal enjoyment of fundamental rights and freedoms, particularly the right to equal protection before the law (see A/HRC/25/15, para. 136.205).[34] However, as previously reported, Palestinians continue to face entrenched discrimination in access to land and water under the policies and practices of the Israeli occupation (see A/70/392, section III.A).

34. In view of continuing settlement activities, and the absence of a commitment by Israel to change its policy, the Special Rapporteur notes recent steps by some Member States regarding labelling of settlement produce. On 11 November 2015, in a move condemned by Israel,[35] the European

---

33   See the annex provided by Israel (footnote 31 above).

34   Ibid.

35   Israel, Ministry of Foreign Affairs "PM Netanyahu's response to EU decision regarding product labelling", 11 November 2015.

Commission adopted an interpretative notice on the indication of origin of goods from the territories occupied by Israel since June 1967, in order to ensure that European Union legislation applies to Israel within its internationally recognized, i.e. pre-1967 borders.[36] Information published by the European Union External Action Service clarifies that that marking products, such as fruit and vegetables, from Israeli settlements "made in Israel" would mislead consumers and therefore be inconsistent with existing European Union legislation.

B *Blockade*

35. In Gaza, the landscape and the people are scarred by multiple rounds of hostilities with Israel and kept in a state of de-development by the long-standing blockade, which constitutes collective punishment contrary to international humanitarian law (see A/70/392, sect. II.B). It has the effect of isolating Gaza, including from the rest of the Occupied Palestinian Territory, and affects a range of human rights, especially the right to freedom of movement and the right to an adequate standard of living. There is a dire lack of potable water and a severely limited electricity supply.[37] The United Nations Conference on Trade and Development has reported: "The over-abstraction and scarcity of drinking water have been exacerbated by crumbling sanitation infrastructure, while the blockade creates chronic shortages of electricity and fuel, which in turn aggravate contamination and the water crisis" (see TD/B/62/3, para. 46).

36. Many of the families hit hardest in terms of damage and destruction of their homes during the 2014 Israeli military operation, some 95,000 people, were still displaced as of November 2015.[38] The Office for the Coordination of Humanitarian Affairs reported that in October 2015 the reconstruction of 10 per cent of homes that had been totally destroyed in 2014 was under way (over 1,100), while 12 per cent of repairs to severely damaged homes had been completed.[39] In the same month, the

---

36 European Union External Action, Fact Sheet, Interpretive Notice, 11 November 2015. Available at http://eeas.europa.eu/delegations/israel/documents/news/20151111_indication_of_origin_fact_sheet_final_en.pdf.

37 In the context of the blockade as a primary obstacle to the right to an adequate standard of living in Gaza, the Special Rapporteur recognizes that the Palestinian political situation also impacts on the ability of civil servants to provide basic services. See e.g. Office for the Coordination of Humanitarian Affairs, "Humanitarian Bulletin – November 2015".

38 Office for the Coordination of Humanitarian Affairs, "Humanitarian Bulletin: occupied Palestinian territory – October 2015", p. 6.

39 Ibid., pp. 5–6.

United Nations Relief and Works Agency for Palestine Refugees in the Near East reported that a refugee family in Gaza was the first to complete the reconstruction of their totally destroyed home, through the Gaza Reconstruction Mechanism.[40] While progress remains limited more than a year after the 26 August 2015 ceasefire, the Special Rapporteur welcomes the assistance reaching families affected by the destruction of and damage to homes. He joins again the many calls for donors to realize their pledges made in Cairo in October 2014. The Special Rapporteur recalls, however, that the need to facilitate the entry of building materials into Gaza has been created as a result of the maintaining of the blockade by Israel. Long-term viability requires that the economy of Gaza, and people's livelihoods, be freed from the stranglehold that the blockade's restrictions on movement of goods and people presents.

37. The Special Rapporteur is dismayed that there appears to be no indication from Israel that the blockade will be lifted. The Government of Israel rejected seven recommendations expressly on lifting the blockade or closure of Gaza. In the interactive dialogue of the universal periodic review, Israel sought to justify the continuation of the blockade referring to "the volatile security situation" (see A/HRC/25/15, para. 125). The people of Gaza have suffered greatly during three escalations of hostilities with Israel between 2008 and 2014, during which time the blockade was continually imposed. Even outside of active hostilities, the people of Gaza remain victims of violations of their human rights resulting from the effects of the blockade. The Special Rapporteur recalls the joint statement, issued by 30 international aid agencies six months after the ceasefire in Gaza, warning that, "a return to hostilities is inevitable if progress is not made and the root causes of conflict are not addressed" and stressing that Israel, as the occupying Power, must comply with its obligations under international law and "must fully lift the blockade".[41]

C   *Prisoners and Detainees*

38. The Special Rapporteur has previously detailed his concerns regarding the treatment of Palestinian prisoners and detainees, including children, under the Israeli military court system (see A/HRC/28/78, sect. IV, and A/70/392, sect. IV). Figures reported by various non-governmental

---

40   "After 70 days, I held the new keys in my hands", 21 October 2015. Available from www .unrwa.org/newsroom/features/"after-70-days-i-held-new-keys-my-hands.

41   "We must not fail in Gaza", joint statement by 30 international aid agencies issued on 26 February 2015.

256 UN DOCUMENTS

organizations show a sharp rise in the number of Palestinians detained in the month of October 2015, during the escalation of violence. According to figures published by an Israeli non-governmental organization, the number of Palestinians in the custody of the Israeli security forces reached some 5,680; a rise of more than 400 persons held compared to September 2015.[42]

39. With respect to the situation of child suspects and detainees, the Special Rapporteur is astounded at the openly discriminatory approach signalled by the rejection by Israel of the following recommendation: take all steps necessary to ensure that Palestinian children in military custody receive the same level of care and have the same rights as provided by Israeli criminal law to youth offenders (see A/HRC/25/15, para. 136.114).[43] A rise in Palestinian minors held by Israel has also been recorded. Some 300 of those held by Israel at the end of October 2015 were minors, up from some 170 in September 2015.[44] In the light of the conclusion by United Nations Children's Fund (UNICEF) in February 2013 that "ill-treatment of children who come in contact with the military detention system appears to be widespread, systematic and institutionalized",[45] the rise in children in detention is alarming. Statistics collected by a professional voluntary association indicate that practices of night arrests, threats, physical and verbal abuse against children detained continue.[46]

40. In November 2015, there have been several severe legislative moves.[47] On 2 November, the Ministry of Foreign Affairs of Israel reported that the Knesset had passed a temporary law, to be reviewed in three years' time, setting a minimum sentence of three years' imprisonment for those

---

42 B'Tselem, "Statistics on Palestinians in the custody of the Israeli security forces" (accessed on 2 December 2015). This figure does not include Palestinians held in Israel Prison Service facilities for being in Israel illegally.

43 See the annex provided by Israel (footnote 31 above).

44 B'Tselem, "Statistics on Palestinian minors in the custody of the Israeli security forces" (accessed on 2 December 2015).

45 UNICEF, *Children in Israeli Military Detention: Observations and Recommendations* (Jerusalem, February 2013), executive summary.

46 Military Court Watch, "Comparative graph – Issues of concern". Statistics based on testimonies collected (accessed on 9 December 2015).

47 In addition to the previously reported amendment to the Penal Code adopted on 20 July 2015, providing for up to 20 years' imprisonment for those convicted of throwing stones or any other objects, with intent to cause harm, at moving vehicles (see A/70/392, para. 71). The Knesset, "Knesset approves harsher punishments for stone throwers", press release, 21 July 2015.

convicted of stone-throwing.[48] On 25 November 2015 the Knesset approved in a preliminary vote that children under the age of 14 can receive prison sentences, upon being convicted of terrorism, to be implemented when they turn 14.[49]

41. Israeli authorities have recommenced the practice of administrative detention of children for the first time since December 2011. The Special Rapporteur has received information in three cases concerning East Jerusalem teenagers[50] held under this practice without charge or trial. Statistics indicate another child was also under administrative detention in October 2015, although the Special Rapporteur has not received specific information on the case.[51]

42. The Government of Israel supported the following recommendation: ensure that administrative detention is carried out in accordance with international human rights standards. According to figures published by an Israeli non-governmental organization, 429 Palestinians were held under administrative detention at the end of October 2015.[52] The Special Rapporteur stresses that administrative detention is only exceptionally permissible for the shortest possible periods of time. Hundreds of Palestinians being held, now including children, often under secret evidence, and for up to six-month terms that can be renewed indefinitely, is not consistent with international human rights standards. It is fundamental that those suspected of wrongdoing be able to defend themselves and to challenge the detention. The Government of Israel should promptly charge or release all administrative detainees.

---

48 The Knesset, "Knesset approves harsher punishment for rock-throwing", 2 November 2015. It is noted that the text mentions the maximum sentence to be 15 years, although up to 20 years imprisonment was reported previously for throwing stones, with intent to cause harm, at moving vehicles (ibid.). The Ministry of Foreign Affairs website links the press release to the "Security Cabinet statement on rock-throwing" dated 24 September 2015, concerning measures against rock-throwing in Jerusalem.

49 The Knesset, "Approved in preliminary reading: Prison sentences for minors under 14 who were convicted of terrorism", 25 November 2015. The press release mentions keeping minors in "children's homes" until they can be sent to prison.

50 Defense for Children International – Palestine, "Three East Jerusalem teens held in administrative detention", 27 October 2015.

51 Military Court Watch, Newsletter, November 2015.

52 B'Tselem, "Statistics on Palestinians in the custody of the Israeli security forces" (accessed on 2 December 2015).

D   *Accountability*

43. The Special Rapporteur notes that Israel supported the following recommendation: fight impunity by thorough and impartial investigations on all the allegations of human rights violations, including when these allegations involve members of security forces or settlers (see A/HRC/25/15, para. 136.66, and A/HRC/25/15/Add.1, para. 35). However, concerns remain about a persistent and general lack of accountability for violations and crimes against Palestinians (see A/70/392, sect. V).

44. The 31 July 2015 arson attack on a family home in the West Bank village of Duma is an emblematic case illustrating the lack of accountability for the killings of Palestinians, including in incidents which are strongly suspected to have been acts of settler violence (see A/70/392, para. 47).[53] On 2 December 2015, the United Nations Special Coordinator for the Middle East Peace Process and Personal Representative of the Secretary-General to the Palestine Liberation Organization and the Palestinian Authority expressed regret at the slow progress in bringing the perpetrators in this case to justice.[54] In another high-profile case, the Special Rapporteur notes reports in Israeli media of the conviction in November 2015 of two suspects in the murder in July 2014 of 16-year-old Mohammad Khdeir. The conviction of the third and main suspect is reportedly pending a psychiatric evaluation.[55]

45. According to the Office for the Coordination of Humanitarian Affairs, in 2015, settler-related violence continued at a weekly average rate of two Palestinian casualties and three incidents of damage to Palestinian-owned property. The Office highlighted a marked increase in settler violence reported in and around Hebron in October and November 2015, with 61 attacks causing injuries to Palestinians or property damage.[56]

46. Cases of Palestinian fatalities involving Israeli security forces and failures to appropriately investigate and prosecute have also contributed to the sense of impunity for crimes committed against Palestinians. According to information released in December 2015 by an Israeli non-governmental

---

53   See also High Commissioner for Human Rights, press release, "Zeid urges calm and restraint in West Bank amid deadly escalation", 8 October 2015.

54   Statement by the United Nations Special Coordinator for the Middle East Peace Process, Nickolay Mladenov, on the Dawabsha family case, Jerusalem, 2 December 2015.

55   Nir Hasson, "Court finds two guilty in Abu Khdeir murder; conviction of main suspect suspended", *Haaretz*, 30 November 2015.

56   Office for the Coordination of Humanitarian Affairs, "Protection of civilians report: 24–30 November 2015", 4 December 2015, and "Humanitarian Bulletin – November 2015", p. 3.

organization, even when the Israeli Military Police Criminal Investigations Division has launched criminal investigations into alleged offences by Israeli soldiers against Palestinians, indictment rates are low: reportedly, over the past five years, only 3 per cent of criminal investigations resulted in indictments.[57] Concerns of lack of accountability for alleged violations during the 2014 Israeli military operation in Gaza (A/70/392, sect. V), will be further illustrated in section V B.

47.   The Special Rapporteur reiterates that settlements, the blockade, Palestinian prisoners and detainees and accountability are critical areas to address and urges Israel to take concrete steps towards addressing related ongoing violations in the Occupied Palestinian Territory.

V   Cases of Alleged Violations Raised with Israel Through Communications from Special Procedures

48.   Between June 2014 and the end November 2015, the Special Rapporteur transmitted 10 communications (joint letters of allegation or joint urgent appeals) to the Government of Israel, raising allegations of violations of international human rights law and international humanitarian law by Israeli authorities. Through communications, the Special Rapporteur seeks to intervene in individual cases but also to raise broader concerns regarding the legislation, policies and practices of the Government of Israel that give rise to human rights violations in the Occupied Palestinian Territory.

49.   In 2014, the Government of Israel responded substantively to one out of three communications sent in the second half of the year. By the end of November 2015, out of seven communications sent, the Government of Israel had responded to two.

50.   Of the 10 communications, 2 concerned the threatened forced eviction of a Palestinian family in East Jerusalem; 1 addressed the forced eviction and forcible transfer of Bedouin communities in the West Bank; 2 related to allegations of violations against Palestinian human rights defenders; 2 centred on allegations of excessive use of force by Israeli security forces; 1 concerned legislative developments affecting the human rights of Palestinians detainees and prisoners held by Israel; and 2 alleged violations of the principles of international humanitarian law in

---

57   Yesh-din, Data Sheet, "Law Enforcement on IDF Soldiers suspected of harming Palestinians: Figures for 2014", December 2015.

260 UN DOCUMENTS

Israeli strikes during the Israeli military operation in Gaza in July and August 2014.

A   *The West Bank, Including East Jerusalem*

51. The Special Rapporteur previously reported (A/70/392, paras. 61–68) on the pressure brought to bear on Palestinians in occupied East Jerusalem to leave. This is related to settlement activity and the apparent policy of the Government of Israel to establish a demographic composition in Jerusalem whereby the Jewish population outstrips the Palestinian population by a certain percentage. Combined with the declaration in Israeli law in 1980 that all of Jerusalem is the capital of Israel,[58] contrary to international law (Security Council resolutions 476 (1980) and 478 (1980)), this provides the backdrop against which the right of Palestinians to live in East Jerusalem is continually challenged.

52. On 20 November 2015, the Special Rapporteur and the Special Rapporteurs on adequate housing as a component of the right to an adequate standard of living, and on the right to non-discrimination in this context; on the independence of judges and lawyers; and on the right of everyone to the enjoyment of the highest attainable standard of physical and mental health sent a follow-up urgent appeal to the Government of Israel against a forced eviction of a Palestinian family in East Jerusalem (see A/HRC/31/79, case No. ISR 8/2015).[59] In September 2014, an eviction order was issued against the Ghaith Sub-Laban family from their home. According to information received, the main claim of the settler organization which sought to evict the family was that they had lost their protected tenancy status as a result of having abandoned the house. The case was decided against the family by a magistrate who was herself a settler. Following a failed appeal, whether the family of eight, including two children, will be able to remain in what has been their home since 1953 now depends on whether they will be granted the right to submit another appeal. Meanwhile, their social services, including health care, have reportedly been discontinued. This case is illustrative of the environment in which Palestinians in the occupied East Jerusalem live with pressure from powerful settler organizations, and the absence of proper legal pro-

---

58   Basic law: Jerusalem, Capital of Israel (1980).

59   A joint communication (case No. ISR 1/2015) with the Special Rapporteurs on adequate housing as a component of the right to an adequate standard of living and on the independence of judges and lawyers, was previously sent to the Government of Israel on this case A/70/392, para. 66.

tections for Palestinians. The Special Rapporteur regrets that no response to the original or the follow-up communication had been received as of 7 December 2015.

53. Another communication dated 14 October 2014 sent to the Government of Israel by the Special Rapporteur jointly with the Special Rapporteurs on adequate housing as a component of the right to an adequate standard of living; cultural rights; the right to food; and minority issues illustrates concerns related to moves by Israeli authorities to force Palestinians out of strategically significant locations (case previously reported, A/HRC/28/78, sect. V, and A/70/392, paras. 41–44). The communication, in which the Special Rapporteurs urged the Government of Israel to halt the plans to forcibly transfer Bedouin communities of thousands of people living in the Jordan Valley and East Jerusalem periphery, has not received a response. Demolitions occurred in some communities affected by the plans, most recently in September 2015 in the East Tayba Bedouin community.[60] Some of these communities are located in an area slated for the expansion of Israeli settlements, including in the area known as "E-1". In addition to violations of a range of human rights that the plans entail, including the right to housing, article 49 of the Fourth Geneva Convention prohibits the occupying Power from carrying out the individual or mass forcible transfers of protected persons and also prohibits Israel from transferring its civilians into occupied territory. It is feared that implementation of the plan would further isolate East Jerusalem from the rest of the West Bank and undermine the territorial contiguity of the Occupied Palestinian Territory.

54. Palestinian human rights defenders perform a critical role in documenting allegations of violations and peacefully protesting against occupation policies and practices. They are often vulnerable to acts aimed at obstructing their work, harassment, threats, reprisals and retaliatory acts, and violations of their rights including under articles 9, 19 and 21 of the International Covenant on Civil and Political Rights, which guarantee rights to liberty and security of the person, freedom of opinion and expression, and freedom of peaceful assembly. Since the beginning of the escalation in violence in 2015, the Special Rapporteur has received a higher than usual number of reports of harassment, threats and obstruction of the work of human rights defenders.

---

60   Office for the Coordination of Humanitarian Affairs, "Humanitarian Bulletin – October 2015", p. 14.

262 UN DOCUMENTS

55. In a joint communication with the Working Group on Arbitrary Detention and the Special Rapporteurs on the situation of human rights defenders; on the independence of judges and lawyers; on the promotion and protection of the right to freedom of opinion and expression; and on the rights to freedom of peaceful assembly and of association, dated 27 January 2015 (case No. ISR 11/2014), the Special Rapporteur raised a case of alleged arbitrary arrest and risk of imminent arbitrary detention of a human rights defender, and expressed concerns about the use by Israel of the military court system to try Palestinians. The facts revolved around a peaceful protest in May 2012 in front of the Israeli "Ofer" prison, in the occupied West Bank. Abdallah abu Rahma was arrested after having stood in front of bulldozers in an attempt to prevent Israeli security forces from setting up roadblocks. However, he was only charged months later, following his peaceful involvement in the Bab al-Shams protest camp against planned settlements in the West Bank in January 2013. In October 2014, he was convicted for "disturbing a soldier on duty". In its response of 10 March 2015,[61] the Israeli authorities stated that the judicial process leading to Mr. Abu Rahma's conviction complied with human rights standards, including the right to fair trial and due process guarantees. They did not address the allegation that charges against him were only brought following his participation in another peaceful process and did not indicate what measures had been taken to ensure that Palestinian human rights defenders can operate in an enabling environment and carry out their legitimate work without fear of prosecution and criminalization. In November 2015, Amnesty International reported that in rejecting Mr. Abu Rahma's appeal against his four months' suspended prison sentence and fine, the military judge allegedly stated "that the appellant's enthusiasm should be 'cooled down' in the coming years".[62]

56. In a joint communication with the Special Rapporteur on the situation of human rights defenders dated 22 October 2015, concerns were raised on measures taken against Daoud al-Ghoul, a human rights defender, who worked for a Palestinian health and development non-governmental organization in East Jerusalem (see A/HRC/31/79, case No. ISR 7/2015). In November 2014, Israeli authorities allegedly banned him from Jerusalem, with no reasons or charges initially presented. Soon after relocating to the West Bank, he was also banned from there and had to move to Haifa,

---

61 See https://spdb.ohchr.org/hrdb/29th/Israel_10.03.15_(11.2014).pdf.

62 Amnesty International, Urgent Action, "Military Court Rejects Activist's Appeal", 19 November 2015.

Israel. These sanctions imposed by Israeli military order were reportedly based on secret evidence, rendering it impossible to for him to defend himself, and were not subject to judicial review. Israeli authorities later claimed that he participated in the political party Popular Front for the Liberation of Palestine, which Israel has prohibited. Mr. Al-Ghoul was reportedly also made subject to a foreign travel ban. He was arrested in June 2015 and charged with "membership of an illegal association". The indictment against him listed activities including leading tours of Israeli settlements and participating in training courses. The Special Rapporteur regrets that no response has been received to the communication from the Government of Israel.

57. Excessive use of force by Israeli security forces is a continuing concern and is heightened during periods of increased tensions. The Special Rapporteur has previously reported (see A/HRC/28/78, para. 47) on the joint communication (case No. ISR 8/2014), with the Special Rapporteurs on the promotion and protection of the right to freedom of opinion and expression; on the rights to freedom of peaceful assembly and of association; on the situation of human rights defenders; and on extrajudicial, summary or arbitrary executions, and reflected the response of Israel of 12 November 2014.[63] The communication, dated 21 August 2014, concerned alleged excessive use of force in the case of the killings of three peaceful demonstrators in the West Bank by live ammunition fired by Israeli security forces.

58. In a joint communication with the Special Rapporteur on extrajudicial, summary or arbitrary executions dated 22 October 2015, the Special Rapporteur raised concerns in the context of the 2015 upsurge of violence, including attacks by Palestinians, regarding the many cases of injuries and killings of Palestinians involving Israeli security forces (see A/HRC/31/79, case No. ISR 6/2015). Concerns included extensive use of live ammunition and rubber-coated metal bullets against Palestinians demonstrating throughout the occupied West Bank, including East Jerusalem, and killings of Palestinian suspects of attacks on Israelis. In a joint press release of 16 November 2015, the Special Rapporteur, together with the Special Rapporteur on extrajudicial, summary or arbitrary executions called for "an end to the violence by all and strict compliance with international law" and urged "the authorities to carry out independent, thorough, prompt and impartial investigations into all suspected cases

---

63   See https://spdb.ohchr.org/hrdb/28th/Israel_12.11.14_(8.2014).pdf.

of extrajudicial, arbitrary and summary executions".[64] No response had been received as at 7 December 2015 to the communication. However, the Permanent Mission of Israel has issued a press release in response to that of the Special Rapporteurs, in which it objected, among other points, to the reference to the violence taking place within the context of long-standing Israeli occupation policies and practices.[65]

59. In a joint communication with the Special Rapporteurs on the right of everyone to the enjoyment of the highest attainable standard of physical and mental health, and on torture and other cruel, inhuman or degrading treatment or punishment dated 24 July 2015, the Special Rapporteur urged the Government of Israel to refrain from amending the Prison Act to allow the forced feeding of prisoners and detainees on hunger strike (see A/HRC/31/79, case No. ISR 3/2015). The communication made clear that such treatment would risk violating the absolute and non-derogable prohibition of torture and other ill-treatment, as codified in articles 2 and 16 of the Convention against Torture and Other Cruel, Inhuman or Degrading Treatment or Punishment. Israel responded on 14 August 2015,[66] stating that the law sought to balance the prisoner's autonomy over his/her body and right to protest with the responsibility of the State to safeguard their health care, and would only be used in cases of hunger strikes "driven by particular political purposes".

60. The amendment was resisted by the Israeli Medical Association, which noted that no prisoner or detainee in Israel had ever died during a hunger strike. It considered forced feeding equivalent to torture and concluded that it was "in conflict with accepted medical ethics in Israel and around the world".[67] As previously reported (see A/70/392, para. 70), the law was passed on 30 July 2015. However, in the high-profile case of the Palestinian hunger-striker Mohammad Allan, who was protesting against his administrative detention, it appeared that prison authorities experienced great difficulty in finding medical professionals willing to perform

---

64 Press release, "UN rights experts express deep concern about ongoing bloodletting in the Occupied Palestinian Territory", 16 November 2015.

65 "Israel expresses shock and deep regret following UN Special Rapporteurs Press Release published November 16, 2015", press release, 17 November 2015.

66 It is noted that the response received in that case omitted to acknowledge the mandate on the situation of human rights in the Palestinian territories occupied since 1967. See A/HRC/31/79.

67 Israeli Medical Association, "The Physician's Guide to treating the detainee/prisoner on a hunger strike". Policy Paper, June 2014.

the treatment envisaged by the law.[68] The Special Rapporteur applauds the principled resistance of Israeli physicians to administering the forced treatment provided for in this law.

B Gaza

61. Two communications sent by the Special Rapporteur concerned cases of alleged violations of international humanitarian law during the Israeli military operation in Gaza in July and August 2014. These communications were part of an attempt to raise with the Government of Israel the long-standing general lack of accountability for Israeli violations of international humanitarian law and international human rights law. The Special Rapporteur regrets that Israel has not responded to these communications.

62. The first of these joint communications, with the Special Rapporteur on extrajudicial, summary or arbitrary executions dated 20 August 2014 (case No. ISR 9/2014), raised four emblematic cases of alleged disproportionate or indiscriminate attacks that caused a number of Palestinian civilian fatalities, including children (previously reported, see A/HRC/28/78, para. 24). In an update of June 2015, the Israeli Military Advocate General ordered a criminal investigation into one of these cases noting that "the factual findings ... indicated the existence of grounds for reasonable suspicion that the attack was not carried out in accordance with the rules and procedures applicable" to the Israel Defense Forces.[69] This was the case of the 9 July 2014 airstrike on a beach resort in Khan Younis which killed nine young men, including four teenagers, who had been watching a football World Cup match. There was reportedly no indication that the location had been used for military purposes. As of 7 December 2015, there was no further update available.

63. The second joint communication, with the Special Rapporteur on the right of everyone to the enjoyment of the highest attainable standard of physical and mental health dated 11 June 2015, concerned alleged violations related to seven cases of attacks by the Israel Defense Forces, during the 2014 hostilities, on medical facilities and medical staff, leading to

---

68 Addameer on Mohammad Allaan, updated 16 August 2015; Amnesty International, urgent action, "Palestinian Lawyer Mohammed Allan Released", 6 November 2015.

69 All references to Israeli examinations and investigations with respect to the Israeli Military Operation in Gaza in 2014 accessed via http://www.law.idf.il/163–7353-en/Patzar.aspx, "Decisions of the IDF MAG Regarding Exceptional Incidents that Allegedly Occurred During Operation 'Protective Edge'– Updates".

destructions of health care facilities, and civilian deaths and injuries (see A/HRC/31/79, case No. ISR 2/2015). In addition, the Special Rapporteur raised allegations of wilful delay and obstruction by the Israel Defense Forces of medical evacuations. Concerns were raised of alleged failures by Israel Defense Forces to comply with principles of international humanitarian law, including special protection afforded to hospitals and medical workers, as well as violations of the right to health.[70]

64. The Special Rapporteur takes the opportunity to provide more information on one such case, which he raised during his presentation to the Human Rights Council at its twenty-eighth session and which was also mentioned in the report of the independent commission of inquiry established pursuant to Human Rights Council resolution S-21/1 (see A/HRC/29/CRP.4, para. 332). The case concerns a 7-year-old boy who was attempting to flee the area of Khuza'a in the morning of 24 July, when he was hit by shrapnel to the stomach during Israeli shelling. The boy's medical evacuation was reportedly delayed by the Israel Defense Forces, with no reason given, for more than three hours from the time he was injured, in order to achieve coordination for medical evacuation access and at checkpoints. At one point, the dying boy reportedly had to be removed from the ambulance at a checkpoint to allow the Israeli Defense Forces to inspect the ambulance with dogs. The boy passed away before reaching hospital. The Special Rapporteur is not aware of any investigation into this case.

65. The communication also included alleged violations related to attacks by Israel Defense Forces on hospitals, ambulances and medical workers. There were three cases of attacks on hospitals: Al-Aqsa, Beit Hanoun, and Al-Wafa. With respect to the Al Wafa hospital, which was attacked several times between 11 and 23 July 2014, when it was destroyed, the case was examined by the Israeli Fact Finding Assessment Mechanism. However, based on claims that it had been used for military purposes, no investigation followed. Information received by the Special Rapporteur suggested only the possibility of a launching site more than 200 metres from the hospital, but no other military activity in the area of the hospital. The independent commission of inquiry established pursuant to Human Rights Council resolution S-21/1 reported that all relevant witnesses it interviewed, including medical staff, denied that it was used for military purposes prior to its evacuation (see A/HRC/29/CRP.4, para. 477). In two

---

70 Fourth Geneva Convention, arts. 17–20, and the International Covenant on Economic, Social and Cultural Rights, art. 12.

of the three cases of attacks on ambulance and medical workers, investigations appear to have been opened by the Military Advocate General following examination by the Fact-fining Assessment Mechanism. The third case, into which there seems to have been no investigation, concerned the killing of a three-person ambulance crew when the ambulance allegedly came under attack by the Israel Defense Forces while it was on its way to attend casualties at the site of a reported drone strike. As of 7 December 2015, there were no further updates available on these cases.[71]

66. These cases illustrate a variety of effects of the policies and practices of the occupation and the related conflict on individual Palestinian lives. The Special Rapporteur reiterates the need for increased realization of the protections afforded Palestinians in the Occupied Palestinian Territory under international human rights law and international humanitarian law. Communications addressed to the Government of Israel after November 2015 are not included in the present report, but will be included in the communications report of special procedures presented at the thirty-second session of the Council.

VI   Conclusions and Recommendations

67. The Special Rapporteur recalls the well-documented violations related to the Israeli occupation policies and practices in the Occupied Palestinian Territory and sees a critical need for the international community to increase its protection of the Palestinian population.

68. He appeals to the Government of Israel, as the occupying Power, to take practical steps to implement protections under international law as it pertains to the Palestinian population living under occupation. In particular, he urges Israel to review, with a view to implementing, recommendations made to it to improve the human rights situation in the Occupied Palestinian Territory, by the Secretary-General, the High Commissioner for Human Rights and independent mandates in reports presented to the General Assembly and the Human Rights Council.

---

71   A response from Israel to the communication was received following the finalization of the present report. It will be made available in the relevant communications report of Special Procedures.

69. The Special Rapporteur reiterates recommendations previously made (see A/HRC/28/78 and A/70/392) and presents and re-emphasizes the following recommendations to the Government of Israel:

(a) Lift the blockade on Gaza, which is a primary obstacle to reconstruction, entails violations of human rights and constitutes collective punishment;

(b) Halt settlement expansion and refrain from carrying out demolitions of Palestinian property, forced evictions, and other acts causing the forced displacement of Palestinians in the West Bank, including East Jerusalem;

(c) Ensure compliance with the Basic Principles on the Use of Force and Firearms by Law Enforcement Officials and conduct full investigations into cases of excessive use of force by Israeli security forces and into allegations of settler violence;

(d) Ensure that domestic-level investigations provide accountability, including by widening the scope of investigations to include policy-level decisions guiding the Israel Defense Forces during the 2014 military operation in Gaza;

(e) End the practice of administrative detention and urgently charge or release Palestinian prisoners and detainees, especially children;

(f) Urgently redouble efforts to implement recommendations by UNICEF with respect to the detention of children, in particular, ensuring that children are detained only as a last resort;

(g) Desist from excessive measures affecting Palestinian freedom of movement and cease immediately the practice of punitive home demolitions;

(h) Cooperate with the mandate of the Special Rapporteur and any United Nations-mandated body, as required of a State Member of the United Nations, and facilitate access to the Occupied Palestinian Territory.

Human Rights Situation in the Occupied Palestinian Territory, Including East Jerusalem, Report of the Secretary-General, U.N. Doc. A/HRC/31/44

United Nations
General Assembly
A/HRC/31/44

Distr.: General

20 January 2016
Original: English

Human Rights Council
Thirty-first session
Agenda items 2 and 7
Annual report of the United Nations High Commissioner for Human Rights and reports of the Office of the High Commissioner and the Secretary-General

Human rights situation in Palestine and other occupied Arab territories
Human rights situation in the Occupied Palestinian Territory, including East Jerusalem

Report of the Secretary-General

Summary

The present report is submitted pursuant to Human Rights Council resolution 28/27 on the human rights situation in the Occupied Palestinian Territory, including East Jerusalem. It presents the human rights situation through an analysis of how the occupation and associated measures restrict freedom of movement, and examines the impact of those restrictions on Palestinians' enjoyment of their economic, social and cultural rights.

I Introduction

1. The present report, which covers the period from 1 November 2014 to 31 October 2015, assesses the implementation of Human Rights Council resolution 28/27. It is based on monitoring and other information-gathering activities carried out by the Office of the United Nations High Commissioner for Human Rights (OHCHR) and other United Nations entities in the Occupied Palestinian Territory. It also draws on information obtained from Israeli and Palestinian non-governmental organizations (NGOs) and from media sources.

2. In the present report, the human rights situation is viewed through the lens of the ongoing restrictions on the right to freedom of movement in the Occupied Palestinian Territory and their impact on the enjoyment of a wide range of other human rights. The report does not provide a comprehensive account of all human rights concerns in the Occupied Palestinian Territory. It should be read in conjunction with the reports of the Secretary-General on Israeli settlements in the Occupied Palestinian Territory, including East Jerusalem, and the occupied Syrian Golan (A/70/351) and on Israeli practices affecting the human rights of the Palestinian people in the Occupied Palestinian Territory, including East Jerusalem (A/70/421), as well as the reports of the Secretary-General (A/HRC/31/43) and the High Commissioner (A/HRC/31/40) before the Human Rights Council at its thirty-first session.

II Legal Background

3. International humanitarian law and international human rights law are applicable in the Occupied Palestinian Territory. The detailed analysis of the applicable legal framework, including the basis of the legal obligations of the duty bearers, presented in the report of the High Commissioner on the implementation of Council resolution S-9/1 (see A/HRC/12/37, paras. 5–9) and the 2014 report of the Secretary-General on Israeli practices affecting the human rights of the Palestinian people in the Occupied Palestinian Territory, including East Jerusalem (see A/69/347, paras. 3–6), remains valid.

4. Freedom of movement is guaranteed under international human rights law[1] and international humanitarian law.[2] Israel, as the occupying Power, has an obligation to facilitate the freedom of movement of persons residing in the Occupied Palestinian Territory. Palestinian duty bearers too are obliged to respect and ensure freedom of movement.

5. While certain restrictions on freedom of movement are allowed under international law, including for reasons of security,[3] they must be strictly necessary for that purpose, proportionate and non-discriminatory.[4]

6. Freedom of movement is also a prerequisite for the enjoyment of a broad range of civil, political, economic, social and cultural rights. The exercise of some rights, such as the rights to work, health and education, depends to a large extent on the ability to move freely and to choose one's residence. Thus, restrictions to freedom of movement can lead to limitations on a range of other human rights.[5]

7. Israel has positive obligations under both international humanitarian law and human rights law. Under international humanitarian law, the occupying Power retains positive obligations to ensure the welfare of the population, including the provision of medical supplies.[6] The principle of non-discrimination[7] is also relevant, especially in relation to the differential treatment of settlers and Palestinians living in the Occupied Palestinian Territory.

---

1 See the International Covenant on Civil and Political Rights, art. 12; and the Universal Declaration of Human Rights, art. 13.

2 See the Geneva Convention relative to the Protection of Civilian Persons in Time of War (Fourth Geneva Convention), art. 27; and the 1958 commentary of the International Committee of the Red Cross on that same article.

3 See the Fourth Geneva Convention, arts. 27 and 64 (2); the 1958 commentary of the International Committee of the Red Cross on that same article; and the Convention respecting the Laws and Customs of War on Land, annex, art. 43.

4 See the advisory opinion of the International Court of Justice on the legal consequences of the construction of the wall in the Occupied Palestinian Territory, paras. 135–137.

5 Ibid., paras. 133–134.

6 Fourth Geneva Convention.

7 See the International Covenant on Economic, Social and Cultural Rights, art. 2 (1); and the International Covenant on Civil and Political Rights, arts. 2 (1) and 26.

| III | Restrictions on Freedom of Movement and their Impact on Human Rights |

| A | *Introduction* |

8. During the reporting period, the human rights situation in the Occupied Palestinian Territory remained difficult, and was characterized by violations of a range of rights. Long-standing restrictions on free movement between Gaza and the West Bank and within the West Bank exacerbated the situation.

9. In the Oslo Accords it is provided that, "without derogating from Israel's security powers and responsibilities", the movement of people and vehicles in the West Bank "will be free and normal, and shall not need to be effected through checkpoints or roadblocks". Furthermore, it is recognized that the West Bank and Gaza should be maintained as a "single territorial unit ... respecting and preserving without obstacles, normal and smooth movement of people".

10. During the reporting period, movement restrictions remained in place, many of them in contradiction with previous agreements and international law. The restrictions have contributed to a fragmentation of the Occupied Palestinian Territory to a point where freedom of movement is severely impeded.

11. The current situation must be reversed. In his previous report, the Secretary-General noted that human rights violations by all duty bearers were driving the conflict in an ever-worsening cycle of violence (see A/HRC/28/45, para. 8). Movement restrictions undermine individuals' rights to health care, work, education and family life, and result in the rupture of social, economic, cultural and family ties. Cumulatively, these violations undermine the right of Palestinians to self-determination and to an adequate standard of living.

| B | *Israeli Restrictions on the Freedom of Movement of Palestinians* |
| 1 | Administrative Measures Restricting Freedom of Movement |

12. Palestinians' freedom of movement is restricted through a complex and multilayered system of administrative, bureaucratic and physical constraints that permeate almost all facets of everyday life.

13. Although the Ministry of the Interior of the State of Palestine issues identity cards for Palestinians on the basis of the Palestinian population registry, Israel retains the power to approve or reject all changes of address and permanent residency applications. In 2000, with the outbreak of the second intifada, Israel suspended updates to the register. Attempts to re-

solve the large backlog of applications between 2007 and 2009, and again in 2011,[8] had limited impact (see A/68/502, para. 9).

14. The permit regime allows Israeli authorities to limit and control Palestinians' movement in the Occupied Palestinian Territory beyond their immediate residential area. This permit regime dates back to the cancellation by Israel, during the first intifada, of the "general exit permit", which had allowed Palestinians to move freely between Gaza, the West Bank and Israel.[9] Since then, Palestinian residents of the Occupied Palestinian Territory are required to have individual permits to enter Israel and East Jerusalem. Following the outbreak of the second intifada in 2000, Israel further tightened movement restrictions, requiring Palestinians to obtain permits to cross between Gaza and the West Bank.[10] Permits are also required to enter and remain in large areas inside the West Bank, including the so-called "seam zone".[11]

15. The requirements for obtaining a permit are set out in protocols and procedures issued by the Israeli authorities, most of which have not been made public until recently. Following a series of freedom of information petitions filed by the Israeli NGO Gisha, several procedures have been posted on the website of the Coordination of Government Activities in the Territories Unit (COGAT) but a number remain unavailable to the public.[12] Moreover, of those published, only some have been translated into Arabic. As a result, both the procedures and the criteria by which applications are evaluated remain unclear to many applicants, most of whom read and understand Arabic.[13]

16. During the reporting period, COGAT eased requirements for selected groups, including by authorizing men over the age of 55 and women over the age of 50 from the West Bank to enter East Jerusalem or Israel without

---

8   See www.pmo.gov.il/English/MediaCenter/Events/Pages/eventblair040211.aspx.

9   B'Tselem and HaMoked, *One Big Prison: Freedom of Movement to and from the Gaza Strip on the Eve of the Disengagement Plan*, 2005, p. 9.

10   Ibid.

11   B'Tselem, *Ground to a Halt: Denial of Palestinians' Freedom of Movement in the West Bank* (2007), pp. 24–25. The "seam zone" is the section of Palestinian land located between the wall and the 1949 armistice line that was declared "closed" following construction of the wall.

12   Gisha, "Procedures and policies", 2015. Available from www.gisha.org/legal/procedures-and-protocols.

13   Ibid.

274 UN DOCUMENTS

a permit.[14] In June, for the first time since the second intifada broke out in 2000, the Israeli authorities reportedly allowed some 100 Palestinian doctors from the West Bank to drive their cars into East Jerusalem and Israel.[15] Movement restrictions were also eased during Ramadan when exceptions for permit requirements were extended on Fridays to men over 40 and boys under 13 and to all women and girls, although some of those steps were revoked following unrest in July.[16]

17. The monthly quota of merchants allowed to leave Gaza during the reporting period was raised from 3,000 to 5,000 and the daily number of exits increased from 400 to 800.[17] The quota of Palestinian patients allowed to exit Gaza for medical treatment in Israel was raised from 80 to 120 per day. Israeli authorities also eased restrictions on the passage of Palestinian athletes from Gaza. Thus, in March 2015, 46 runners from Gaza were granted permits to enter the West Bank to take part in the annual Palestine Marathon.[18] During Ramadan, 500 Palestinians from Gaza were given a permit to travel to participate in prayers at Al-Aqsa Mosque, in Jerusalem.[19] While those measures are welcome, they are unlikely to lead, by themselves, to a long-lasting improvement as long as the permit regime remains in place.

18. Over the years, tens of thousands of Palestinians who have sought to enter Israel, Israeli settlements and the "seam zone", or to go abroad through the Allenby crossing to Jordan, have had their permits rescinded or their applications rejected after being blacklisted by the Israel Security Agency.[20] No reasons are given for the rejection, and restrictions are usually instituted without prior warning. As a result, many Palestinians only

---

14 COGAT, "Status of permits for the entry into Israel of Palestinians, for overseas departures and the crossing points between Judea and Samaria and the Gaza Strip" (November 2015).

15 Y-Net News, "Israel increases relief measures to Palestinians in the West Bank," June 14, 2015.

16 Office for the Coordination of Humanitarian Affairs, "The monthly humanitarian bulletin", July 2015, p. 6.

17 See http://gaza.ochaopt.org/2015/02/further-easing-of-criteria-and-quotas-forisraeli-permits-to-exit-gaza/.

18 Gisha, "Forty-six runners exited this morning from Gaza", March 2015.

19 Agence France Presse, "Thousands pray at Jerusalem's Al-Aqsa for Ramadan", 19 June 2015.

20 In addition, tens of thousands of Palestinians have been blacklisted by the police, usually punitively, after having entered Israel without a valid permit. Yet others are administratively blacklisted, for example for unpaid fines. Machsom Watch, "Year-end report, January–December 2014", January 2015, pp. 16–18.

learn about the restrictions when they attempt to cross a checkpoint and are blocked.[21]

19. The Israeli NGO Machsom Watch assists blacklisted Palestinians in lodging appeals with the District Coordination Office.[22] In 59 per cent of the cases handled in 2014, the organization was able to remove individuals from the blacklist.[23] This high rate of successful challenges raises questions about the overall arbitrariness of the system.

20. Freedom of movement is a human right, yet the individual permit regime makes it a privilege to be granted or denied by Israeli authorities as an exception to the norm. While protection of national security may justify some restrictions in specific circumstances, the requirement that applicants meet narrowly defined criteria, such as visiting a sick relative or requiring hospital treatment, constitutes a fundamental breach of the International Covenant on Civil and Political Rights. The relation between rights and restrictions must not be reversed, and freedom of movement must not be made dependent on any particular purpose or reason.[24]

2   Restrictions on Freedom of Movement in the West Bank, Including East Jerusalem

21. Movement by Palestinians within the West Bank is restricted by a system of checkpoint and permit requirements, as well as by the expansion of settlements and related infrastructure. The two main areas in the West Bank that most Palestinians cannot access without a permit are the area west of the wall, known as the "seam zone", and East Jerusalem.

Movement Restrictions Linked to Settlements and Other Closed Areas

22. A number of movement restrictions are linked to the presence of Israeli settlements in Area C and East Jerusalem. There are approximately 142 settlements in the West Bank, including East Jerusalem.[25] Some restrictions on Palestinians' freedom of movement have been justified by

---

21   Ibid., p. 16.

22   The District Coordination Office is the Israeli governing body that operates in the West Bank. It was established in order to carry out practical functions within the Occupied Palestinian Territories.

23   Machsom Watch, "Year-end report, January–December 2014", January 2015, p. 17.

24   See Human Rights Committee general comment No. 27 (1999) on freedom of movement, paras. 5 and 13.

25   B'Tselem, statistics on settlements and settler population for May 2015, available from www.btselem.org/settlements/statistics.

the Israeli authorities as a means of protecting settlers and facilitating their movement throughout the West Bank. They include restrictions on Palestinians' access to private land located in the vicinity of settlements and limitations on Palestinians' use of roads used by Israeli settlers (see A/67/375 and A/HRC/31/43).

23. Particularly severe restrictions are imposed on the movement of Palestinians who live in close proximity to Israeli settlers. In the H2 area of Hebron, where approximately 6,000 Palestinians live near settlements, the vehicular and, in some cases, pedestrian movement has been restricted for the past 15 years by approximately 95 physical obstacles, including 19 permanently staffed checkpoints.[26] Consequently, access to educational and health-care institutions has been severely impeded, many Palestinian shops, as well as the city's main vegetable and wholesale markets, which are located in the closed areas, have been shut down and thousands of Palestinians have been compelled to move out of their homes.[27]

24. Since October 2015, following a series of attacks and clashes, Palestinians' movement in H2 has been further restricted. The area of Tel Rumeida was declared a closed military zone on 29 October and two of the checkpoints leading to the area have since become accessible only to Palestinian residents registered in advance with Israeli authorities.[28]

Movement Restrictions Linked to the Wall and the "Seam Zone"

25. The wall is a key obstacle to freedom of movement in the West Bank. The International Court of Justice, in its advisory opinion on the legal consequences of the construction of the wall in the Occupied Palestinian Territory, recognized as illegal those sections of the wall that depart from the Green Line. To date, however, approximately 64.2 per cent of the projected 712 km-long wall has been completed, 85 per cent of which runs through the West Bank.[29] The Secretary-General has described how the gate and permit regime, which regulates access to the "seam zone", im-

---

26 Office for the Coordination of Humanitarian Affairs, "The monthly humanitarian bulletin", November 2015, p. 4.

27 Global Protection Cluster, "Protection concerns and humanitarian impacts of settlement activity in Hebron city", April 2014.

28 Office for the Coordination of Humanitarian Affairs, "The monthly humanitarian bulletin", November 2015, p. 4.

29 Office of the United Nations Special Coordinator for the Middle East Peace Process, "Report to the Ad Hoc Liaison Committee", September 2015, para. 38.

pedes the rights of the approximately 11,000 Palestinians residing there from living normal lives and enjoying the right to work, family life and medical treatment (see A/68/502, para. 23).

26. During the reporting period, the High Court of Justice of Israel issued a decision permitting resumption of the construction of a section of the wall in the Wadi Cremisan area of Beit Jala, near Bethlehem. Preparation for construction began on 17 August 2015.[30] That section of the wall will cut the town off from 3,000 dunams of agricultural land belonging to 58 Palestinian families, which provides the community with an indispensable source of income.[31]

27. While Israeli authorities have committed to the construction of agricultural gates to facilitate farmers' access to their lands, access is expected to be limited.[32] Of the 85 agricultural gates built to facilitate Palestinians' access to agricultural land in the "seam zone", only nine are open daily.[33] As a result, many farmers have been forced to give up farming their land or have switched to lower-yielding and less-labour-intensive crops.

28. According to the military orders governing the West Bank, Israeli citizens require an Israel Defense Forces permit to enter Area A – the Palestinian urban centres under full Palestinian Authority control, covering 18 per cent of the West Bank.

Isolation of East Jerusalem from the Rest of the West Bank

29. During the reporting period, Israeli authorities continued to implement restrictions isolating East Jerusalem from the rest of the West Bank and restricting movement within East Jerusalem. Palestinians residing in East Jerusalem are required to hold Israeli-issued ID cards granting bearers the status of "permanent resident". These ID cards can be revoked if the authorities determine that Jerusalem ceases to be the bearer's "centre of life" (see A/68/502, para. 28). Hence, Palestinians in East Jerusalem who wish to travel abroad for long periods of time, whether for employment or other reasons, risk losing their residency.

---

30 Society of St. Yves, *The Last Nail in Bethlehem's Coffin: the Annexation Wall in Cremisan*, August 2015.

31 B'Tselem, "Barrier to separate Beit Jala residents from their lands, laying groundwork for annexing settlement", 12 November 2015.

32 Ibid.

33 Office for the Coordination of Humanitarian Affairs, "The monthly humanitarian bulletin", September 2015, p. 6.

278 UN DOCUMENTS

30. Palestinians from the West Bank and Gaza are required to obtain special permits to enter East Jerusalem and Israel, and can enter the city only through four established checkpoints.[34] The isolation of East Jerusalem, traditionally an important centre for Palestinian economic, cultural and social activity, has a serious impact on surrounding communities.

31. On 14 October 2015, following a series of attacks and clashes, the Israeli authorities imposed further movement restrictions on residents of neighbourhoods in East Jerusalem. As at 26 October 2015, there were 38 new obstacles, including 16 checkpoints, 20 roadblocks and one earth mound blocking the entry into and exit from the main Palestinian residential areas, curtailing the access of approximately 138,000 residents to work, school and medical treatment.[35] Some obstacles were being dismantled at the end of the reporting period.[36]

32. While the Government of Israel has a right to put in place necessary and proportionate security measures in response to specific security threats, systematically restricting the movement of thousands of Palestinians in the manner described above is prima facie disproportionate to the aim pursued.

Checkpoints

33. During the reporting period, there were 85 fixed checkpoints in the West Bank. Nine of those checkpoints were on the Green Line, while all others were located within the West Bank.[37] In addition, hundreds of "flying" checkpoints were erected each month on roads throughout the West Bank. Together with roadblocks, trenches and earth mounds, the checkpoints severely impede Palestinians' movement, including between main Palestinian cities in the West Bank.

34. Access through checkpoints is often accompanied by rigorous security checks, including vehicle inspections and bag searches, resulting in long delays. At Qalandia checkpoint – the main crossing point for West Bank Palestinians into East Jerusalem – it takes pedestrians up to 90 minutes

---

34 Office for the Coordination of Humanitarian Affairs, "The monthly humanitarian bulletin", July 2015, p. 6.

35 Office for the Coordination of Humanitarian Affairs, protection of civilians weekly report for 20–26 October 2015. Available from www.ochaopt.org/poc20october-26october-2015 .aspx.

36 Ibid., weekly update, 17–23 November 2015.

37 Ibid., *Humanitarian Atlas 2015*, p. 53.

to cross during peak times.[38] Long waiting times, uncertainties at the checkpoints and frequent clashes disrupt many aspects of Palestinians' daily life.

3   Restrictions on Movement Affecting Gaza

35.   The ongoing blockade and permit regime restricts access by Gazan residents to the West Bank and Israel. Within Gaza, movement is restricted in areas along the fence with Israel and at sea, with the Israeli security forces maintaining a buffer zone. For a detailed update on movement restrictions in Gaza, see the 2015 report of the Secretary-General on Israeli practices affecting the human rights of the Palestinian people in the Occupied Palestinian Territory, including East Jerusalem (A/70/421).

Restrictions on Movement between Gaza and the West Bank

36.   In accordance with the Oslo Accords, Israel opened a "safe passage" route in October 1999, allowing 12,000 residents of Gaza to travel to the West Bank each month. However, that route was closed in September 2000, following the outbreak of the second intifada. By March 2005, five months before the evacuation by Israel of the settlements in Gaza, travel to the West Bank from Gaza had declined by 98 per cent.[39] Movement of people was cited as "virtually impossible and expensive".[40]

37.   After Hamas took over Gaza in 2007, a strict quota system was imposed. Obtaining permits became limited to specific categories of persons, such as individuals in need of emergency medical evacuations, medical referral patients, certain businessmen and humanitarian cases (see A/70/421, paras. 23–25).

38.   During the reporting period, restrictions on movement in and out of Gaza remained in place. The easing of some measures (see para. 18 above) had a tangible effect, increasing the monthly average of exits of Palestinians to 13,800, up from a monthly average of 5,990 during 2014.[41] However, this represents only 2.8 per cent of the half a million exits recorded monthly

---

38   Ir Amim, *Displaced in Their Own City: the Impact of Israeli Policy in East Jerusalem on the Palestinian Neighbourhoods of the City Beyond the Separation Barrier*, June 2015, p. 48.

39   B'Tselem and HaMoked, *One Big Prison*.

40   Office for the Coordination of Humanitarian Affairs, "The agreement on movement and access: one year on", November 2006.

41   Office for the Coordination of Humanitarian Affairs, "Erez crossing: movement of People into and out of Gaza", 2014–2015. See gaza.ochaopt.org.

280 UN DOCUMENTS

prior to September 2000, before restrictions were tightened and when around 26,000 workers from Gaza were entering Israel on a daily basis.[42]

39. The effects of Israeli restrictions on freedom of movement have been exacerbated by the closure of Rafah crossing by the Egyptian authorities on 24 October 2014, following a suicide attack on Egyptian soldiers in the Sinai peninsula (see A/70/421, para. 29). During the reporting period, the crossing at Rafah remained closed except for on 37 partial opening days.[43] At the end of October 2015, an estimated 30,000 Palestinians registered as humanitarian cases were waiting to leave Gaza through Rafah.[44]

40. The blockade on Gaza remains a form of collective punishment and undermines civil, political economic, social and cultural rights (see A/70/421, para. 29).

Restrictions on Movement within Gaza

41. Israeli authorities have continued to impose a buffer zone within Gaza on land and at sea, in the form of access-restricted areas. Restrictions are enforced through a range of mechanisms, including the use of live fire and the destruction, damage and confiscation of property, as well as arbitrary arrest and detention (see A/70/421, paras. 30–38).

42. During the reporting period,[45] according to the Global Protection Cluster three Palestinians, including one child, were shot dead and 82, including 17 children, were injured by Israeli security forces in land-based access-restricted areas. In addition, 54 fishermen, including four children, were detained and 20 were injured, including one child.

43. The enforcement measures used by the Israeli authorities against residents living and working in access-restricted areas significantly undermine the right of Palestinian fishermen and farmers to a livelihood, and have a devastating impact on the rights to life and to physical and mental health.

---

42 Gisha, "Separating land, separating people", June 2015, p. 12; and "Rafah crossing: who holds the keys?", March 2009.

43 Office for the Coordination of Humanitarian Affairs, protection of civilians weekly report for 27 October-2 November 2015. Available from www.ochaopt.org/poc27october-2november-2015.aspx.

44 Ibid., "Gaza crossings' operations status: monthly update – October 2015".

45 This excludes the period starting 9 October 2015, when 14 demonstrators were killed and hundreds were injured.

THE PALESTINE YEARBOOK OF INTERNATIONAL LAW, VOLUME 19 (2016)   281

C   *Impact of Freedom of Movement Restrictions on Other Human Rights*

44. Restrictions on freedom of movement result in Palestinians' inability to enjoy a wide range of other human rights, particularly those related to economic, social and cultural rights.[46]

1   Right to Education

45. Access to education has been most restricted among East Jerusalem communities beyond the wall, the H2 area of Hebron, the "seam zone" and in the vicinity of closed zones and settlements in Area C. A survey of 33 communities carried out in 2015 showed that almost one in five students in the West Bank must pass a checkpoint to reach school.[47] Body and bag searches are frequent, and schoolchildren and teachers are subject to regular harassment, including verbal intimidation, by Israeli soldiers.

46. In remote parts of Area C, many schoolchildren must walk 7–10 km to reach school owing to restrictions on movement, displacement and demolitions.[48] Oftentimes, the difficulties of the commute to school are exacerbated by harassment and attacks by Israeli settlers and soldiers. During the reporting period, the United Nations Children's Fund documented 247 cases of attacks on education, including physical assault, detention and checkpoint harassment and delays, affecting 32,055 children. The majority of incidents were documented in Area C, East Jerusalem and H2, where children go to school in close proximity to Israeli settlements.

---

46   See the advisory opinion of the International Court of Justice, para. 134. Civil and political rights are also affected. During the reporting period, OHCHR continued to monitor the case of four elected members of the Palestinian Legislative Council representing East Jerusalem who have been banned from entering their constituency, in violation of political participation rights (see A/67/372, paras. 39–40).

47   Office for the Coordination of Humanitarian Affairs, *2016 Humanitarian Needs Overview: Occupied Palestinian Territory*, annex 1, p. 27. See www.ochaopt.org/documents/hno_december29_final.pdf.

48   Ibid.

Box 1

Case study: movement restrictions on school children in H2

Qurtuba School is situated in the old city of Hebron, in the H2 area. The journey to school requires students to cross a military checkpoint and walk past a settlement. Harassment, intimidation and violence from settlers, delays, bag and body searches, and abuse by soldiers are regular occurrences. During the past several years, international organizations have been providing protective presence to schools located in the area. Their presence has reduced checkpoint delays and settler violence.

On 29 October 2015, pursuant to military orders, the whole of Tel Rumeida area and Shuhada Street were declared a closed military zone, with entry into the area limited to residents recorded on soldiers' checklist. In addition, individuals or entities providing a protective presence have since been barred from accompanying children to Qurtuba School. Since then, an increase in settler harassment against students has been reported, with some settlers pointing guns and driving past children at high speed. Delays and harassment by soldiers at the checkpoint have also reportedly increased.

The situation has reinforced a sense of fear among children and teachers in an already coercive and dangerous environment. The school's headmaster noted that since the denial of a protective presence, "even teachers do not feel comfortable coming to school, due to fear of both settlers and soldiers". More than one fifth of the students did not attend school during the last days of October. According to OHCHR, the incidents have affected the well-being of students, some of whom have reportedly suffered nightmares and bedwetting.

47. The negative effects of restrictions on access to education are compounded by the limitations imposed on access to Palestinian schools by the Ministry of Education of the State of Palestine. According to the Ministry, in the "seam zone", for example, the permit regime restricts access so that the Ministry cannot effectively deliver school textbooks and furniture. In Gaza, owing to restrictions on imports, educational institutions face difficulties in acquiring teaching and learning materials, particularly for subjects like chemistry and engineering, which require items included on the "dual-use items" list.[49] These various limitations affect the availability and quality of education.

---

49   United Nations Educational, Scientific and Cultural Organization, *Rapid Assessment of Higher Education Institutions in Gaza: Data Analysis Report*, January 2015.

THE PALESTINE YEARBOOK OF INTERNATIONAL LAW, VOLUME 19 (2016)   283

48.   Movement restrictions also affect higher education. In the West Bank, Palestinian students' access to universities is impeded by checkpoints and road closures, and students can face long daily commutes if they wish to study in a university outside their immediate residential area. Al-Quds University has reported that, during the past three years, at least 38 of its students have been forced to postpone their final exams after being delayed at checkpoints. Restrictions on higher education are even more pronounced in Gaza. In 1998, approximately 1,000 Gazan students were studying in the West Bank.[50] Since the outbreak of the second intifada in 2000, sweeping bans on travel to the West Bank have been imposed on university students from Gaza, and all requests to travel for study purposes have since been rejected, even in the absence of security concerns.[51]

49.   On 16 February 2015, COGAT announced that the Government of Israel would introduce measures to ease travel restrictions, including by granting exit permits to 50 Gazan students wishing to study in the West Bank. However, the authorities retracted the decision on 18 February 2015, citing a "clerical error".[52]

50.   The impact of the ban is exacerbated by the obstacles that Gazan students face in accessing education outside the Occupied Palestinian Territory. In December 2014, Israel announced that it would allow up to 140 students from Gaza to study abroad, subject to a maximum quota of 30 per week.[53] During the reporting period, 161 students left through Erez crossing, but hundreds more remained unable to reach their academic institutions, risking losing their scholarships owing to delays and the denial of permits.

51.   The inability of students to access higher education in other parts of the Occupied Palestinian Territory or abroad affects the free choice of a university course, with a commensurate impact on future careers and livelihoods. For example, in Gaza, many important programmes, including

---

50   Gisha, "Student travel between Gaza and the West Bank 101", September 2012.

51   The Israeli army considers people aged between 16 and 35, and students in this age group in particular, as posing a general threat because of their "risk profile". Gisha, "Legal framework: higher education – rights and obligations under international and Israeli law", May 2010.

52   Gisha, "Israel will not permit students from Gaza to study in the West Bank", February 2015.

53   37 orphans stayed home", December 2014.

284 UN DOCUMENTS

medical engineering and doctoral programmes in chemistry, are not available.[54]

2 Right to Health

52. The availability, accessibility and quality of health services in the Occupied Palestinian Territory are impaired by the restricted movement of patients, doctors and other medical staff.

53. Owing to the limited capacity in hospitals run by the Ministry of Health of the State of Palestine, patients requiring specialized treatment or surgery are often referred for treatment outside of their usual area of residence. In Gaza, reliance on referrals for adequate medical care is particularly acute (see A/70/421, para. 24). There are only four oncologists to treat the 12,600 cancer patients in Gaza (cancer is the second leading cause of death in Palestine). In addition, the World Health Organization (WHO) notes that only two cardiac surgeons are available, as a result of which some 70–80 patients per month need to be treated outside Gaza.

54. Most Palestinians from the West Bank or Gaza requiring health care in East Jerusalem, Israel or abroad must apply for an Israeli-issued permit. While Israel imposes no age or quota restrictions on the process of obtaining a health permit,[55] 15–30 per cent of the applications are delayed or never approved, and the application process is reportedly slow and complicated.[56]

55. According to the General Authority for Civil Affairs of the State of Palestine, of the 173,835 applications that were received through West Bank district offices by patients and patient-companions during the first 11 months of 2015, 18 per cent were reportedly either delayed or denied.

56. WHO estimates that at least 1,500 patients travel from Gaza to the West Bank and Israel each month to receive specialized medical treatment. The approval rates dropped significantly during the last months of the reporting period, from around 80 per cent in the first eight months down to 69.85 per cent in October 2015. This represented the lowest approval rate since October 2009, with the exception of the period of escalation in 2014. As at 8 October 2015, the Ministry of Health in Gaza reported that

---

54 Ibid., "The impact of the separation between the Gaza Strip and the West Bank on higher education", May 2010.

55 COGAT, "Status of permits", p. 21.

56 Physicians for Human Rights, *Divide and Conquer: Inequality and Health*, January 2015, p. 76.

THE PALESTINE YEARBOOK OF INTERNATIONAL LAW, VOLUME 19 (2016)   285

1,180 patients had been waiting for medical treatment outside of Gaza since the beginning of 2015.

57. Over the past three years, the number of applications for patient permits by Palestinians from Gaza nearly doubled, from around 1,000 per month in early 2013 to around 2,000 between May and September 2015.[57] This increase occurred during a period in which patients' access to medical care in Egypt through the Rafah crossing became increasingly restricted.[58]

58. Patients whose applications for medical permits for urgent and specialized care are rejected or delayed have no choice but to repeat the lengthy application process, or to accept less specialized and inadequate care. This delay can place patients, particularly those in need of urgent care, at serious risk of further damage to their health or even death.

59. For those who receive a permit to cross, Israeli security forces can unpredictably deny access to patients, or can detain patients for interrogation or arrest on a charge.[59] Four patients and their companions were thus arrested by Israeli security forces at Erez during the reporting period.[60]

Box 2
Case study: movement restrictions on patients from Gaza
Medical patients in Gaza frequently experience denial or delay of care owing to the permit regime and the system of referrals.

OHCHR monitored the case of Haytham Mohamad Ghazi Shurrab, aged 22, who fell ill during the escalation of hostilities in Gaza in 2014. Following several visits to hospitals in Gaza, Mr. Shurrab was referred to a health facility in Cairo, where he was diagnosed with cancer and began treatment. Mr. Shurrab returned to Gaza in January 2015. By April, it became clear that the treatment was not working. He received a permit to attend a hospital in Tel Aviv for a scan, returning to Gaza after one day. Following the results of the scan, his treatment was adjusted but had to be stopped in June 2015 owing to swelling in his abdomen. Mr. Shurrab was referred to Al-Naja hospital in Nablus but after two weeks he received a rejection letter indicating that the type of treatment he needed was not available there.

---

57   WHO, monthly report for September 2015. Available from www.emro.who.int.
58   Ibid.
59   WHO, "Report of a field assessment of health conditions in the Occupied Palestinian Territory", April 2015.
60   WHO, monthly reports covering the period November 2014–September 2015.

Concerned about further delay in care, Mr. Shurrab's father appealed directly to the President of the State of Palestine, Mahmoud Abbas, asking that his son be referred to an Israeli hospital where the necessary treatment was available. Mr. Shurrab received a referral from the Ministry of Health in July 2015. He obtained an appointment for 5 August 2015 at a hospital in Tel Aviv and applied for a permit. On 4 August, he was informed that his exit permit was still under security review. He consequently missed his appointment and a new appointment was set for 9 September 2015. Mr. Shurrab died at the end of August 2015. His father was informed by the Civil Affairs Committee on 8 September that the permit had been granted.

60. Access to treatment is also impeded by physical restrictions on movement, including checkpoints. The checkpoints and roadblocks controlling entry to and movement within East Jerusalem since 14 October 2015 have restricted access to the six Palestinian hospitals located there, which provide a range of specialized treatment unavailable elsewhere in the West Bank and Gaza. The closures have prevented staff from getting to work and delayed and prevented patients' access to hospital treatment.[61] OHCHR monitored the case of a 65-year-old Palestinian woman with respiratory problems who died on the way to hospital on 19 October. Police had closed the road leading to the hospital, and further delays at a checkpoint hampered her access to life-saving medical care.

61. Movement restrictions compromise the quality of treatment available in health centres. Al-Quds University, in the Abu Dis district of East Jerusalem, hosts one of two medical schools in the West Bank. Clinical training for Al-Quds University students takes place primarily at Palestinian hospitals in East Jerusalem. The construction of the wall in Abu Dis separated the medical faculty from the rest of East Jerusalem. Every year, about 10 per cent of students from Al-Quds University are refused entry to East Jerusalem by the Israeli Civil Administration.[62] These restrictions limit training opportunities for medical students and staff and therefore affect the quality of medical care.

---

61   Statement of Augusta Victoria Hospital on behalf of the East Jerusalem Hospital Network, 20 October 2015.

62   Physicians for Human Rights, *Divide and Conquer*, p. 76.

3   Right to Work

62. Restrictions on movement adversely affect the right of Palestinians to work and to maintain an adequate standard of living.

63. In the West Bank, physical barriers and the permit regime particularly affect the agricultural sector, which has traditionally been the main source of employment and income for Palestinians in the West Bank. The restrictions imposed on Palestinians' access to their land in the "seam zone" and in the vicinity of settlements prevent farmers from regularly farming their lands, resulting in a drop in crop productivity and value. For example, the yield of olive trees in the zone is 40–60 per cent less than that of olive trees on the West Bank side of the wall.[63]

64. Restrictions on the movement of goods and people also affect Palestinian trade. All goods moving from the West Bank through, to and from Israel, must undergo physical inspection and commercial controls. According to the World Bank, in 2013 it took approximately 23 days to export goods from the West Bank and 38 days to import them. By way of comparison, imports and exports took on average 10 days for Israeli traders.[64] Such restrictions have a severe impact on the competitiveness of Palestinian firms, thus limiting employment in the Palestinian private sector.

65. Although still subject to severe restrictions, the situation in Gaza has improved. Since November 2014, Israel has begun allowing a limited quantity of goods to be sold to the West Bank and Israel, including agricultural produce, textiles, iron works and furniture.[65] This easing has allowed the entry of 908 truckloads during the first 10 months of 2015 compared to 228 in 2014.[66] However, the current rates remain at around 15 per cent of pre-blockade levels.[67] Moreover, restrictions on imports to Gaza of items classified as "dual-use" have weakened Palestinian productive sectors,

---

63   Office for the Coordination of Humanitarian Affairs, "The monthly humanitarian bulletin", February 2014, p. 9.

64   World Bank, *West Bank and Gaza Investment Climate Assessment: Fragmentation and Uncertainty*, 2014, pp. 32–39.

65   Gisha, "For the first time since the closure: a truckload of cucumbers left" (6 November 2014); and "Israel will allow marketing of ironworks, furniture and textile from Gaza in Israel", 21 September 2015.

66   Office for the Coordination of Humanitarian Affairs, online Gaza crossings database.

67   World Bank, *Economic Monitoring Report to the Ad Hoc Liaison Committee*, 30 September 2015.

especially in the metal,[68] engineering, agriculture, food and pharmaceutical industries.[69] In April 2015, wooden boards thicker than 5 cm and wider than 20–25 cm were added to the dual-use list, and their import to Gaza was restricted.[70] On 3 August 2015, wooden boards thicker than 1 cm were included.[71] These new restrictions on wood imports have affected Gazan furniture factories and businesses, which have been forced to cut the number of staff and working hours.[72]

Palestinian Workers in Israel and in Settlements

66. Palestinian workers from the Occupied Palestinian Territory have long sought work opportunities inside Israel. Before 1993, some 115,000 Palestinians – one third of the workforce – worked in Israel, and unemployment was at 5 per cent.[73] Restrictions on trade and the movement of people have had a long-lasting, damaging effect on the Palestinian economy, resulting in high unemployment and aid dependency. While unemployment in the reporting period saw a slight decline compared to 2014, one quarter of the Palestinian labour force remains unemployed. In Gaza, the unemployment rate was 42 per cent.[74] High unemployment rates and economic stagnation affect the standard of living. Poverty in the Occupied Palestinian Territory during 2014 reached 25 per cent, with rates in Gaza at 39 per cent.[75] This situation has increased dependency on work in Israel, despite restrictions.

67. By September 2015, 57,450 Palestinians from the West Bank held permits to work in Israel, which, according to COGAT, is the highest number

---

68 According to the Palestinian Federation of Industries in Gaza, 90 per cent of metal materials are listed as dual-use and banned from entry into Israel, affecting 1,200 factories. See also *Al-Monitor*, "Gazans scavenge for food, recyclables", 13 May 2015.

69 United Nations Conference on Trade and Development, *The 2013 World Trade Organization Agreement on Trade Facilitation: Israel's Obligations towards Palestinian Trade*, 2015, pp. 7–10.

70 Gisha, "COGAT decision to restrict entrance of wood to Gaza" (13 April 2015).

71 Israel, Ministry of Defense, instructions regarding the ban on bringing items into the Gaza Strip, 3 August 2015. See also http://gaza.ochaopt.org/2015/09/import-restrictions-impede-delivery-of-services-and-humanitarian-assistance.

72 Gisha, "Marketing of furniture from Gaza in Israel permitted –, wood to make the furniture is not", 2 November 2015.

73 See www.btselem.org/workers.

74 World Bank, *Economic Monitoring Report*, p. 4.

75 Ibid.

THE PALESTINE YEARBOOK OF INTERNATIONAL LAW, VOLUME 19 (2016)   289

since the permit system was introduced in the early 1990s.[76] A further 25,957 permits were issued for work in settlements.[77]

68. Permits to enter and work in Israel can be suddenly and arbitrarily revoked. For example, in June 2015, Israeli authorities cancelled all entry permits to Israel for Palestinians from the West Bank village of Sa'ir, apparently in an act of collective punishment after a Palestinian man from the village attacked a border police officer in East Jerusalem.[78]

69. While restricting Palestinian workers' access to work in Israel is not in and of itself a violation of international standards, such restrictions must be viewed in the overall context of the occupation and the violations of international human rights and humanitarian law accompanying it. Disproportionate Israeli restrictions on movement and trade have significantly contributed to the grave economic hardship in the West Bank and Gaza, which has interfered with access to livelihoods and work in the Occupied Palestinian Territory.

4   Right to Family Life

70. Restrictions on freedom of movement impede Palestinians' enjoyment of the right to family life and to protection of the family unit. According to a poll conducted by Gisha in 2013, almost a third of all Palestinians in Gaza had relatives in the West Bank, including East Jerusalem, or Israel.[79] Yet, under the current closure and permit regime, only those needing to visit a gravely ill, first-degree relative or to attend the wedding or the funeral of first-degree relatives may obtain approval to travel between Gaza and the West Bank. Even when narrow permit criteria are satisfied, approval remains uncertain owing to quotas and lengthy procedures.[80]

71. While it is difficult to obtain approval for family-related visits to the West Bank, permission for family reunification is nearly impossible. Relocation to the West Bank is limited to applicants satisfying one of three narrowly defined categories: minors under the age of 16 who have lost a parent in Gaza, elderly people in need of nursing care who have no first-degree

---

76   COGAT, "Status of permits", p. 21.

77   International Labour Office, *The Situation of Workers of the Occupied Arab Territories*, May 2015, para. 36.

78   Natasha Roth, "Israel responds to lone attacks with collective punishment", *+972 Magazine*, 22 June 2015.

79   Gisha, "Survey: 31 per cent of Gaza residents have relatives in Israel, East Jerusalem, West Bank" (19 December 2013).

80   Gisha, "Distant relatives", July 2015. See http://features.gisha.org/distant_relatives.

relative to care for them and chronically ill patients. Being married to someone from the West Bank or having children living there is not considered sufficient to allow relocation.[81]

72. Restrictions on movement also prevent Palestinians who are from the West Bank or Gaza and who are married to Israeli or East Jerusalem residents from realizing their right to family life. In June 2015, the Knesset extended for another year the Citizenship and Entry into Israel Law, issued as a temporary order in 2003.[82] The law prohibits Palestinians from the West Bank and Gaza from obtaining permanent or temporary resident status in East Jerusalem or Israel, even when they are married to citizens or residents of Israel.[83] In few cases, West Bank ID-holders have been granted permission to reside in Israel pursuant to renewable Israeli stay permits valid for one year at a time[84] – while family reunification with individuals from Gaza is completely prohibited pursuant to a 2008 Israeli military order.[85] Thus, the only option available for mixed families is to live in Gaza while maintaining ties to relatives in Israel – an option that Israel has facilitated since 1995 under the "split-family procedure". On 23 July 2015, following the disappearance of two Israelis who had entered Gaza without coordination or a permit, a decision was made to freeze the travel of Israelis and East Jerusalem residents to Gaza until further notice.[86] The ban creates an impossible situation for hundreds of split families living between Gaza and Israel.

73. The almost-total denial by Israel of family reunification for Palestinian or Palestinian-Israeli families and the lack of consideration for individual circumstances violate the right to family life and the prohibition of discrimination, since it makes an arbitrary distinction between mixed

---

81   B'Tselem and HaMoked, *So Near and Yet So Far: Implications of Israeli-imposed Seclusion of Gaza Strip on Palestinians' Right to Family Life*, January 2014, pp. 12–15.

82   HaMoked, "With no end in sight: for the sixteenth time, the Knesset has approved the prolongation of the Citizenship and Entry into Israel Law", 15 June 2015.

83   HaMoked, *Temporary Order?: Life in East Jerusalem under the Shadow of the Citizenship and Entry into Israel Law*, September 2014.

84   Pursuant to the 2005 amendment to the Citizenship and Entry into Israel Law, applicants must satisfy minimum age requirements: 25 years for women, 35 years for men. Entry can be prevented if the applicant or anyone in his or her family is considered a security threat (HaMoked, *Temporary Order?*, pp. 21–24).

85   HaMoked, *Temporary Order?*, p. 29.

86   Letter addressed to the Minister of Defense of Israel, Moshe Ya'alon regarding the ban on entry into Gaza by Israelis, 4 August 2015. Available from http://gisha.org/UserFiles/File/letters/letter_to_yaalon_COGAT_Israelis_11.8.15-eng.pdf.

families involving Palestinians and other foreign nationals and carries undertones of ethnic prejudice.[87]

D *Impact of Palestinian Disunity on Human Rights, Including Freedom of Movement*

74. Notwithstanding the obstacles imposed by the Israeli occupation, including movement restrictions, Palestinian duty bearers have, to the greatest extent possible, an obligation to respect, protect and fulfil the human rights of all people under their authority. This obligation has been underscored by the recent accession by the State of Palestine to seven international human rights treaties. It follows that the Government of the State of Palestine has both positive obligations to protect human rights in the Occupied Palestinian Territory and a duty to seek to mitigate the negative impact of the Israeli occupation to the extent that it can.[88]

75. In this context, the Secretary-General is particularly concerned about the negative impact of the eight-year intra-Palestinian political division between Hamas and Fatah. Palestinian disunity exacerbates the fragmentation of Palestinian territorial integrity in a way that is similar to the effect of Israeli restrictions on free movement, and thereby contributes to undermining a broad range of human rights (see A/HRC/28/45, para. 59).

76. OHCHR has received reports that the Ministry of the Interior of the State of Palestine, following instructions from the General Intelligence Service, has halted the issuance and renewal of passports of Palestinians alleged to be affiliated with Hamas.[89] During the reporting period, the Palestinian Independent Commission for Human Rights received four complaints from Palestinians from Gaza whose passport applications were reportedly denied.

77. Also of concern are reports received during the reporting period that Gazan security services have banned Gaza residents from leaving through Erez without judicial orders. According to the Independent Commission for Human Rights, on three occasions members of the Fatah Central Committee and the Fatah Revolutionary Council were denied permission

---

87 See CERD/C/ISR/CO/14–16, para. 18. See also CCPR/C/ISR/CO/3, para.15; CEDAW/C/ISR/CO/5, para. 25; and CRC/C/ISR/CO/2–4, para. 49. In 2012, in a Supreme Court ruling concluding that Israeli national security prevails over the right to family life, the then Chief Justice of Israel said: "human rights cannot be enacted at the price of national suicide". See https://www.opensocietyfoundations.org/litigation/adalah-v-israel.

88 See, for example, Human Rights Committee general comment No. 31 (2004) on the nature of the legal obligation imposed on States parties to the Covenant, para. 2.

89 See afa.ps/post/146208 (Arabic).

to travel outside of Gaza. On 28 December 2014, the Gazan authorities at the checkpoint reportedly prevented 37 children between 5 and 12 years of age, orphaned as a result of the 2014 escalation of hostilities, and five adult chaperones from exiting Gaza to visit Israel and the West Bank.[90] The authorities claimed that the children were denied travel to protect their culture and safeguard them from the normalization of ties with Israel.[91]

78. Palestinian political divisions have also had a broader negative impact on Palestinians' enjoyment of their civil and political rights. Among the acts of concern monitored by OHCHR during the reporting period are the excessive use of force, the arbitrary arrest and detention of political activists, the use of torture and other ill-treatment and restrictions on freedom of expression (A/HRC/31/40).

79. Political divisions further hinder the realization of economic, social and cultural rights. The continued non-payment of civil servants recruited by the authorities in Gaza is particularly problematic. At least 40,000 civil servants and security personnel have not received a salary, only occasional humanitarian payments, since April 2014.[92]

80. This has, in turn, negatively affected access to education, health and social welfare, among other aspects. In Gaza, the health sector recorded an absenteeism rate of approximately 50 per cent in January 2015, especially as staff could not afford transportation costs.[93] In December 2014, 750 cleaning personnel at the Ministry of Health in Gaza went on a 16-day strike because they had not been paid for six months. Consequently, cleaning services for 13 hospitals and 56 health centres were halted, and the Ministry of Health suspended some medical services, including obstetric and gynaecological services.[94]

IV Recommendations

A *Recommendations to the Government of Israel*

81. Under international human rights and humanitarian law, the Israeli authorities have the obligation to facilitate the free movement of

---

90 Gisha, "Thirty-seven students travelled abroad".

91 See http://alray.ps/ar/index.php?act=post&id=130062 (Arabic).

92 Office for the Coordination of Humanitarian Affairs, "The monthly humanitarian bulletin", January 2015, p. 1.

93 Ibid., pp. 4–5.

94 Ibid.

Palestinians within the Occupied Palestinian Territory, including East Jerusalem. Any exception must comply with international law, which means that restrictions are justified only for imperative reasons of security and only in response to a specific security threat. Israel should lift the blockade on Gaza in accordance with international human rights law and Security Council resolution 1860 (2009), and allow movement between Gaza and the West Bank. Israel should also remove physical restrictions on free movement throughout the West Bank, including East Jerusalem, and ensure that all relevant administrative rules and requirements are consistent with international human rights and humanitarian law.

82. The right to education must be respected and protected, including by facilitating free, safe and unhindered access to schools. The blanket ban on students from Gaza to access education in the West Bank must be lifted.

83. Steps should be taken immediately to remove barriers to freedom of movement that prevent medical personnel from carrying out their duties. All unnecessary or disproportionate barriers hampering Palestinians' access to medical treatment must be lifted without delay, including in Israel and East Jerusalem.

84. Steps must be taken to ease the restrictions on economic development in the Occupied Palestinian Territory, including by immediately allowing greater freedom of movement of goods and people, and lifting restrictions that prevent Palestinians from accessing land and developing their economy.

85. Israeli authorities must recognize and respect the residency rights of Palestinians, including by immediately halting the practice of revoking residence permits, ending the freeze on changes to addresses, removing any quotas on family reunification requests, and processing backlogged requests and new requests expeditiously.

B *Recommendations to the Palestinian Authorities*

86. The Palestinian authorities must implement their obligations under international human rights treaties, including with regard to freedom of movement.

87. The Palestinian authorities should take steps to encourage national political parties to resolve the political disunity that obstructs the equal implementation of the human rights obligations of the Government of the State of Palestine throughout the Occupied Palestinian Territory.

Report of the UN Secretary General on Israeli Practices Affecting the Human Rights of the Palestinian People in the Occupied Palestinian Territory, Including East Jerusalem, U.N. Doc. A/71/364

United Nations
General Assembly
A/74/364

Seventy-first session
Item 50 of the provisional agenda*
Report of the Special Committee to Investigate Israeli Practices Affecting the Human Rights of the Palestinian People and Other Arabs of the Occupied Territories

Israeli practices affecting the human rights of the Palestinian people in the Occupied Palestinian Territory, including East Jerusalem**

Report of the Secretary-General

Summary

The present report has been prepared by the Office of the United Nations High Commissioner for Human Rights pursuant to General Assembly resolution 70/90. It focuses on Israeli practices affecting the human rights of Palestinians in the Occupied Palestinian Territory, with a particular focus on the use of force by Israel, arrest and detention practices and the application of collective punishment measures across the Occupied Palestinian Territory. The report provides details on how the lack of accountability for such violations feeds the cycle of violence and compromises prospects for sustainable peace and security.

---

* A/71/150.
** The present report was submitted after the deadline to reflect the most recent developments.

THE PALESTINE YEARBOOK OF INTERNATIONAL LAW, VOLUME 19 (2016)

I   Introduction

1.   The present report covers the period from 1 June 2015 to 31 May 2016 and is primarily based on monitoring conducted by the Office of the United Nations High Commissioner for Human Rights (OHCHR) and on information collected by other United Nations entities and non-governmental organizations.

2.   The report does not provide a comprehensive account of all human rights concerns in the Occupied Palestinian Territory, nor does it address concerns arising from the actions of Palestinian authorities or Palestinian armed groups. For such an overview, the present report should be read in conjunction with other reports of the Secretary-General and the High Commissioner for Human Rights (see A/70/421, A/HRC/31/40 and Add.1, A/HRC/31/41 and A/HRC/31/44).

3.   The reporting period was marked by an upsurge in violence that started in mid-September 2015 and continued into 2016, although it declined in intensity. According to the Office for the Coordination of Humanitarian Affairs and OHCHR, in the occupied territory, a total of 232 Palestinians, including 52 children, were killed and over 5,774 seriously injured, while 32 Israelis were killed and 356 seriously injured.[1]

4.   In the occupied West Bank, the scale of deaths and injuries, in particular in the fourth quarter of 2015, made the reporting period the most deadly for Israelis and Palestinians since the end of the second intifada (2000–2005). Incarceration, including the administrative detention of children and adults, reached new records, while an increase in closures and checkpoints was reported in the occupied West Bank, including East Jerusalem. Unlawful practices, including punitive demolitions, revocations of residency and the withholding of bodies, resumed, occurring with alarming frequency.

5.   The blockade of Gaza,[2] which entered its tenth year in 2016, continued to undermine basic human rights and economic prospects, as well as the availability of essential services, exacerbating poverty and aid

---

1   Office for the Coordination of Humanitarian Affairs and OHCHR. The number of Palestinians killed does not include nine Palestinians killed by Israelis other than the Israeli security forces. The number of Palestinians injured excludes injuries sustained from tear gas inhalation. There is no record of Israeli children having been killed as a result of the upsurge in violence during the reporting period.

2   The term "blockade" has been used by the United Nations to describe Israel's imposition of prolonged closures and economic and movement restrictions in the Gaza Strip (see A/HRC/24/30, paras. 21 to 23, A/RES/69/93 and A/69/347).

dependency. Restrictions on freedom of movement and the use of force by Israel in the so-called access-restricted areas remained of particular concern.

6. The Secretary-General reiterates his view that a general sense of despair and frustration is growing under the weight of a half-century of occupation and a paralysed peace process. In the occupied West Bank, young Palestinians are resorting to violence, in particular lone-wolf attacks against Israelis, while Gaza has witnessed a rise in crime, violence and suicides, including by self-immolation. The lack of any significant movement towards a political resolution and ongoing violations of international human rights and humanitarian law are exacerbated by the lack of accountability for previous violations. That feeds the cycle of violence and compromises chances for sustainable peace and security. Tackling impunity must be the highest priority for the parties.

II   Legal Framework

7. A detailed analysis of the applicable international humanitarian and international human rights law framework and the corresponding obligations of duty bearers can be found in reports of the Human Rights Council (see A/HRC/12/37, paras. 5 to 9) and the Secretary-General (see A/69/347, paras. 3 to 6).

III   Implementation of General Assembly Resolution 70/90

A   *Use of Force by Israeli Security Forces in the Context of Law Enforcement*

8. During the reporting period, OHCHR documented several incidents of Israeli security forces using apparent excessive force in the course of law enforcement operations (see A/HRC/31/40 and A/71/355). The Secretary-General is particularly concerned by the high number of apparent unlawful killings of Palestinians, including that of a 72-year-old woman, Tharwat al-Sharawi, shot by an Israel Defense Forces soldier in Hebron on 6 November 2015, allegedly during a car-ramming incident. Concerns over extrajudicial executions also arose with the killing of a 14-year-old girl, Hadeel Wajih Awwad, who was shot repeatedly by an off-duty police officer in West Jerusalem on 23 November while she lay wounded on the ground after having attacked bystanders with scissors. In both incidents,

THE PALESTINE YEARBOOK OF INTERNATIONAL LAW, VOLUME 19 (2016)

publicly available video footage showed repeated lethal use of firearms, which continued even after any possible threat had ended.

9. Questions of extrajudicial execution also arose in the death of Abdelfattah al-Sharif and Ramzi al-Qasrawi, who were shot dead after attacking soldiers at a checkpoint in Hebron on 24 March 2016 (see A/71/355, para. 38). According to witness testimony provided to OHCHR, both men were killed after they had been wounded and "neutralized" and no longer presented an imminent threat that could justify the intentional lethal use of a firearm. The killing of Abdelfattah al-Sharif received far more attention than that of Ramzi al-Qasrawi, owing largely to a widely circulated video recording which showed an Israel Defense Forces medic fatally shooting the wounded Abdelfattah al-Sharif in the head from a few metres away.

10. Another disturbing element of the video and corroborating witness accounts was that, although seriously wounded, Abdelfattah al-Sharif did not receive medical attention, despite the presence of at least two Magen David Adom ambulances and several Israel Defense Forces medics at the site. While the medics aided the wounded Israeli soldier, who was conscious and able to walk, they disregarded the more seriously injured Palestinian. A forensic pathologist has reportedly testified that had Abdelfattah al-Sharif been given medical treatment, he could have possibly been saved.[3]

11. Throughout the reporting period, OHCHR documented and raised concerns that Palestinians wounded by Israeli security forces were not being provided medical assistance, or that such assistance was being significantly delayed, including by blocking Palestinian ambulances and first responders (see A/HRC/31/40, para. 16). Those practices are inconsistent with international standards, for example, the Basic Principles on the Use of Force and Firearms by Law Enforcement Officials, which require assistance and medical aid to be rendered at the earliest possible moment. Such practices also amount to an arbitrary deprivation of the right to life.[4]

---

3 Yonah Jeremy Bob, "Pathologist in Hebron manslaughter case says terrorist could have survived if given treatment", *Jerusalem Post*, 16 June 2016.

4 After the incident involving Abdelfattah al-Sharif, Magen David Adom clarified its policy so that staff could treat attackers after Israeli security forces had searched the attackers and declared it safe to approach. Previously, staff had to await clearance from a sapper before approaching wounded attackers. Prior to December 2015, rules of the Israeli Medical Association also contributed to failures since they permitted medical professionals to treat victims before attackers, irrespective of who was more seriously wounded.

12. Additional concerns arose over the widespread use of live ammunition by Israeli security forces, in particular against stone-throwers and in the context of clashes, protests and demonstrations. A majority of Palestinians who died in such contexts were killed by live fire, which also injured 2,129 Palestinians, despite witness accounts and video footage on several occasions indicating that there was no imminent threat to life or serious injury to Israeli security forces or other bystanders that would have warranted the use of lethal force (see A/HRC/31/40, paras. 14 and 23).

13. The use of firearms by Israeli forces appears even more rampant in access-restricted areas, in particular against protestors along the perimeter fence.[5] Most of the 20 demonstrators killed during the reporting period, and over 30 per cent of those injured, were hit by live ammunition, compared with 10 per cent of injuries caused by firearms in the occupied West Bank.[6] The use of high velocity ammunition also caused excessive and unnecessary harm, often leading to long-term disability.

14. According to the United Nations Department of Safety and Security, apart from demonstrations, there were 798 shootings into access-restricted areas by Israeli security forces on sea and land, as a result of which three Palestinians were killed and 58 others injured. Based on OHCHR monitoring and available information, none of the victims appeared to present an imminent threat to life or serious injury to Israeli security forces that would have warranted the use of firearms and, in some instances, those hit were outside the designated restricted areas. At sea, the use of force, including live fire, injured nine fishermen and led to the destruction of 18 boats.[7]

15. In a case documented by OHCHR in early 2016, the Israeli navy pursued and opened fire on two fishing boats that were reportedly within the six-nautical-mile limit in force at the time and did not present a threat. One fisherman was hit multiple times with rubber bullets and, according to medical records, sustained fractures to bones in his back, neck and face after one of the Israeli navy vessels rammed into his boat. The man is no

---

5 As recounted in previous reports, the extent where access is permissible by land remains unclear. Areas up to 300 metres from the perimeter fence are generally considered "no-go" areas, and up to 1,000 metres as "high-risk" areas. Israel continues to enforce a six-nautical-mile fishing limit along the entire coast. However, between April and June 2016, it temporarily extended the fishing area limit in the south of the Strip to nine nautical miles.

6 See www.ochaopt.org/humanitarian-overview-2015.

7 The Gaza Fishermen's Union and the Protection Cluster: Occupied Palestinian Territory.

THE PALESTINE YEARBOOK OF INTERNATIONAL LAW, VOLUME 19 (2016)

longer able to work owing to significant physical and cognitive disabilities. Moreover, Israeli security forces confiscated his boat. Three other fishermen arrested during that incident were forced to undress before their boats were boarded. They were handcuffed, blindfolded and transported to the Israeli port of Ashkelon where they were held for several hours in a container before being released. One of the fishermen was subjected to lengthy interrogation. At no point were the fishermen informed of the reasons for their arrest, nor were they allowed to communicate with their families or provided with an opportunity to contact a lawyer.

16. With respect to the use of less lethal force, the Secretary-General has concerns about the frequent and often unwarranted resort to rubber-coated metal bullets, including their use at short range, in contravention of Israeli regulations (see A/HRC/31/40, para. 26). A total of 3,786 Palestinians were wounded by rubber-coated metal bullets during the reporting period. The black sponge bullets used by the Israeli police in East Jerusalem also cause serious injury.[8] At least 15 people, including 6 children and a 67-year-old woman, were injured by such ammunition during the reporting period, and about half of them lost sight in one eye.[9] The United Nations Relief and Works Agency for Palestine Refugees in the Near East (UNRWA) raised concerns about such ammunition causing serious injuries to children in the Shu'fat refugee camp, as well as about the extensive use of tear gas by Israeli security forces in densely populated refugee camps, including in areas close to playgrounds.[10]

B   *Hostilities*

17. The 2014 ceasefire between Israel and Hamas has largely held. However low-level hostilities between Israeli security forces and Palestinian armed groups in Gaza during the reporting period resulted in 7 Palestinians being killed, of whom five were civilians, including 3 children, while at

---

8   According to the Association for Civil Rights in Israel, in July 2014, police in East Jerusalem began using black sponge-tipped bullets as a means to disperse demonstrations and riots, instead of the blue sponge-tipped bullets. The black bullets are twice as hard and heavy and their potential to cause injury is much greater.

9   Association for Civil Rights in Israel, "Injuries caused by sponge bullets in East Jerusalem", 16 March 2016. Available from www.acri.org.il/en/2016/03/16/injuries-caused-by-sponge-bullets-in-east-jerusalem/

10   UNRWA, "Children in distress: raising the alarm for 2016 and beyond", Briefing Note, April 2016. Available from http://www.unrwa.org/resources/reports/children-distress-raising-alarm-2016-and-beyond.

least 10 were wounded, including 3 children. An additional 6 Palestinians were killed and 49 wounded by explosive remnants of war. No Israeli casualties were reported.

18. During that period, Palestinian armed groups fired 112 rockets towards Israel, with 27 landing inside Israel. The launch of unguided missiles towards Israel continues to cause deep concern. Tunnel digging into Israel and Egypt, allegedly by Palestinian armed groups, was also reported. Meanwhile, Israeli forces conducted 92 incursions into Gaza and fired 80 missiles, mainly at alleged military installations of Palestinian armed groups. At least 113 shells were also reportedly fired by the Israel Defense Forces from land and sea.

19. The most significant exchange of fire took place between 4 and 7 May 2016. For the first time since the 2014 ceasefire, both the Izz el-Deen al-Qassam Brigades and Palestinian Islamic Jihad claimed responsibility for firing up to 40 mortars towards Israeli forces near the fence, reportedly in response to incursions by the Israel Defense Forces in Gaza. Israel responded with air strikes and shelling, killing one civilian and wounding five, and damaging an unspecified number of civilian structures.

20. The Secretary-General is concerned that all necessary precautions have not been taken by the Israel Defense Forces to minimize civilian casualties during its operations, as required under international humanitarian law. For example, on 12 March 2016, Israeli warplanes reportedly targeted a building in a training ground of the Izz el-Deen al-Qassam Brigades in northern Gaza in response to rocket fire the day before. Owing to the magnitude of the explosion, debris fell onto the ceiling of a nearby civilian's house, killing two children and wounding a sibling and their mother. Concerns arose over the size of the blast, especially considering that the structure targeted was 50 to 70 metres away from a civilian residential area housing approximately 500 people.

21. Similar concerns arose over an air strike conducted on 11 October 2015 that killed a child and a pregnant woman (see A/HRC/31/40, para. 54) and the shelling of an open field during the May 2016 escalation. OHCHR found that at least nine farmers were present in the field at the time and that shrapnel from shells fired nearby resulted in the death of an elderly woman.

C *Practices Raising Serious Concerns of Collective Punishment*

22. Israeli practices that may amount to collective punishment continued during the reporting period. In addition to being explicitly prohibited by

international humanitarian law,[11] collective punishment violates a range of human rights and may amount to a war crime.[12]

23. In the occupied West Bank, a commonly used form of collective punishment is the punitive demolition of homes, generally belonging to the families of attackers who killed Israelis, resulting in forced evictions and the risk of forcible transfer. According to the Office for the Coordination of Humanitarian Affairs, the practice of punitive demolitions, suspended until 2014, increased significantly during the reporting period, with 40 residential structures demolished or sealed off, displacing 237 persons, including 106 children.

24. In May 2016, the Committee against Torture observed that punitive demolitions constitute a violation of article 16 of the Convention against Torture and Other Cruel, Inhuman or Degrading Treatment or Punishment and called upon Israeli authorities to end the practice (see CAT/C/ISR/CO/5, para. 41).

25. During the reporting period, there was also an increase in the practice of Israeli authorities delaying the return of bodies of actual or alleged Palestinian attackers or suspects killed by Israeli security forces. At the time of writing, at least 12 bodies were still being held, several since October 2015. Although security considerations have been put forth at various times as the rationale for such delays, the Secretary-General is concerned that the extensive delay in returning bodies is being carried out with punitive intent against the families of the deceased. A commitment to release bodies for the purpose of burial "within a short space of time" was made by the Government of Israel to the nation's High Court of Justice in the case of *Ewisat v. The Israel Police et al.* (HCJ 2882/16) on 5 May 2016.[13] However, after a gun attack in Tel Aviv in early June 2016, the new Minister of Defence issued an order not to return bodies as a measure "to deter potential attackers and their families".[14] In addition to amounting to collective punishment, the withholding of bodies is inconsistent with Israel's obligations as an occupying Power pursuant to the

---

11 For example, see Fourth Geneva Convention (article 33), Hague regulations (article 50) and Customary International Humanitarian Law (rule 103).

12 See articles 6, 7, 9, 14 and 16 of the International Covenant on Civil and Political Rights, General Assembly resolution 2200 A (XXI), annex.

13 High Court of Justice, 2882/16.

14 "Following Tel Aviv attack, Lieberman orders holding of terrorists' bodies", *Haaretz*, 9 June 2016.

302 UN DOCUMENTS

Fourth Geneva Convention (articles 27 and 30) and violates the prohibition of torture and ill-treatment.

26. The closure of towns where actual or alleged Palestinian attackers resided is among the broadest forms of punishment employed by Israeli authorities. For example, on 3 February 2016, three residents of Qabatiya carried out an attack in East Jerusalem in which they injured a policeman prior to being killed. Immediately after, Qabatiya was raided by Israeli security forces and its seven entrances were closed off for over three days. Passage for the town's 20,000 Palestinian residents was restricted, severing family and business links. Fourteen schools were reportedly closed in that period, and approximately 700 university students from Qabatiya were barred from attending classes on 6 February. The main vegetable market in town, the largest in the northern occupied West Bank, was also forced to close as trucks and vendors were not permitted to enter or exit.

27. Israeli authorities do not give detailed reasons for their specific actions, but instead usually make generic security claims. During a media interview, however, an Israel Defense Forces colonel highlighted the importance of economic levers having a massive influence and being an extremely efficient way of sending a message. Another colonel explained the tactical use of collective punishment and intimidation measures towards "dangerous groups", comprising lists of 100 to 150 persons from various villages whom Israeli authorities considered to be potential attackers, stating that those who could be arrested, were arrested; that those for whom there was no reason to arrest were warned; and that the homes of others were mapped and then searched every night. He added that pressure was also exerted on their families and that it was made clear to them that if their children involved themselves in terror, the equipment the families used to provide for themselves, whether it was farming equipment or engineering tools, would be confiscated.[15]

28. In Gaza, the blockade and restrictions on movement continued to undermine the civil, political, economic, social and cultural rights of Palestinians. Socioeconomic indicators remain bleak, with acute crises in the public utility sectors. According to the Palestinian Central Bureau of Statistics, the unemployment rate was 41.2 per cent. According to the Office for the Coordination of Humanitarian Affairs, the rate of aid dependency was 80 per cent, and as of May 2016, an estimated 75,000 people remained displaced from the escalation of hostilities in 2014. The

15 "Israel Defense Forces colonel: Hebron soldier had 'no need to shoot'", *YnetNews*, 29 April 2016.

THE PALESTINE YEARBOOK OF INTERNATIONAL LAW, VOLUME 19 (2016)

rate of reconstruction and recovery remains well below the level needed, owing both to continued restrictions on the entry of goods and unfulfilled pledges of assistance by the international community. The impact of the blockade is further exacerbated by the almost continuous closure by the Egyptian authorities of the Rafah passenger crossing and by Jordan's increasing refusal to grant passage to Palestinians from Gaza through the Allenby crossing.

29. Following the escalation of hostilities in 2014, Israel introduced measures that considerably eased the movement of people and goods into and out of Gaza. Since the end of 2015, however, the gains started to be reversed. Worrisome measures instituted during the reporting period include the addition of crucial raw materials to the dual-use list, temporary restrictions on the entry of cement and other materials needed for reconstruction and recurring interrogations and confiscations or withdrawals of permits for traders and merchants.

30. Of particular concern was the significant drop in early 2016 of the approval rate for medical exit permits, which reached its lowest level since October 2009 (with the exception of the 2014 hostilities period).[16] There has also been a worrisome five-fold increase in the demand by the Israeli General Security Services for security interviews before medical exit applications are considered. In November 2015, the Coordinator of Government Activities in the Territories announced that only a first-degree relative would be allowed to accompany patients across the Erez checkpoint, and that security interviews would be required for all patient companions up to 55 years of age (an estimated 94 per cent of the population of Gaza).

31. Those practices raise alarm as some individuals called in for interrogations, including patients and would-be companions, have indicated to OHCHR that they had to resist pressure to collaborate with intelligence services. If substantiated, such practices can be construed as a form of coercion to extract information, which is forbidden under international law.[17]

32. The Secretary-General is particularly alarmed at the restrictions imposed by Israeli authorities on the movement and work of the staff of international and national human rights and humanitarian organizations

---

16 World Health Organization, "Health access for referral patients from the Gaza Strip", May 2016. Available from www.emro.who.int/images/stories/palestine/WHO_monthly_Gaza_access_report-May_2016_final.pdf?ua=1.

17 See Fourth Geneva Convention (article 31) and Hague regulations (article 44).

operating in Gaza. Such measures have significantly impacted the work of those organizations. According to the Office for the Coordination of Humanitarian Affairs, by April 2016, the monthly approval rate of permits for travel from Gaza of national staff of the United Nations and international NGOs dropped significantly, to 24 per cent, while averages in the previous five years ranged from 70 to 80 per cent.[18]

D   *Arrest and Detention*

33. In the context of the upsurge in attacks against Israelis, demonstrations and clashes between Palestinians and Israeli security forces, there has been an alarming surge in arrests and detentions. According to the Commission of Prisoners and Ex-Prisoners' Affairs, a total of 7,800 Palestinians from the occupied West Bank and Gaza, including 2,400 children, were arrested and detained by Israeli security forces for varying durations during the reporting period.[19] Most were held in facilities on Israeli territory, in contravention of international humanitarian law.[20]

34. The human rights organization B'Tselem issued data provided by the Israeli Prison Service showing that the overall number of Palestinians held in its facilities at any one time peaked at the end of 2015 at 6,321 inmates, the highest number since June 2010. The number of Palestinians in administrative detention steadily increased during the reporting period, peaking on 30 April 2016 at 692, including 13 children. That represents the highest number of adults and children held without charge at any given time since early 2008. In a rare move, three Jewish-Israeli men were also held in administrative detention following the suspected settler attack in Duma village on 31 July.

35. Some administrative detainees resorted to prolonged hunger strikes to draw attention to their arbitrary detention, such as journalist Mohammed Al-Qiq, whose protest lasted 94 days, until February 2016. In May, the Committee against Torture joined the Human Rights Committee in calling upon Israel to end the practice of administrative detention and to ensure that all individuals currently held in administrative detention be afforded all basic legal safeguards (see CAT/C/ISR/CO/5).

36. During the reporting period, there was also a dramatic increase in the overall number of children in detention. According to Defence for Children International, some 163 Palestinian children were in Israeli de-

---

18   See www.ochaopt.org/content/monthly-humanitarian-bulletin-may-2016.

19   See http://freedom.ps/freedom/

20   See Fourth Geneva Convention (article 76).

tention at the start of the reporting period, increasing to 414 by the end of April 2016, after peaking at 440 at the end of February. That was the highest number of detained children since January 2008. In March 2016, a bill to allow courts to sentence children under 14 years of age to imprisonment in certain limited circumstances was approved by the Ministerial Committee for Legislation.

37. According to the Higher National Commission for Prisoners and Detainees Affairs, an estimated 300 people were arrested in Gaza by Israeli security forces passing through the Erez checkpoint, at sea or while breaching the Gaza-Israel perimeter fence. At least 35 among them were reportedly children. The majority of those arrested were usually released back into Gaza within 24 to 48 hours. Fishermen are particularly vulnerable to arbitrary arrest as highlighted in paragraph 15 above. There has been a worrisome increase in the number of fishermen being detained over the years, with the number of those arrested in the first half of 2016 already outstripping the total number in 2015. Israel claims that its restrictions on maritime activities in Gaza are necessary to prevent the illicit smuggling of arms by militant groups operating there. Nevertheless, only two fishermen[21] out of 130 arrested during the reporting period were charged with a crime, although not related to smuggling,[22] with one report of an individual disguised as a fisherman arrested on a boat allegedly with contraband.[23]

E *Accountability for Human Rights and Humanitarian Law Violations Committed by Israeli Security Forces*

38. Pursuant to international law, allegations of violations and abuses of international human rights law and international humanitarian law must be promptly, thoroughly, effectively, independently, impartially and transparently investigated and perpetrators brought to justice. Victims also are to have access to a prompt, adequate and effective remedy (see General Assembly resolution 60/147). Accountability is crucial not only in order to bring perpetrators to justice but also in order to deter future violations (see A/HRC/28/45, paras. 32 and 33).

---

21 "Palestinian fishermen brought to Israeli court", *Maan News Agency*, 30 December 2015.

22 According to UNRWA, another four fishermen are in detention. Their legal status is unknown.

23 Yaakov Lappin, "Security forces arrest suspected Gazan weapons smuggler", *Jerusalem Post*, 16 May 2016.

39. The Secretary-General and the United Nations High Commissioner for Human Rights have on several occasions expressed their concern at the lack of accountability in Israel for violations of international human rights and humanitarian law.[24] Various independent committees of experts as well as international, Israeli and Palestinian human rights organizations have also expressed such concerns and extensively documented the flaws in Israel's accountability mechanisms in addressing the killing, injury, torture and ill-treatment and the destruction of Palestinian property.[25]

40. Shortcomings in the Israeli justice system identified by those organizations include physical, financial, legal and procedural barriers that restrict the ability of Palestinians, particularly those living in Gaza, to gain access to justice. Findings suggest a consistent failure by the Military Advocate General, who heads the military justice system, and the Attorney General to open investigations in cases where there is prima facie evidence, including eye-witness testimony, medical reports and audiovisual materials indicating that actions by State agents were unlawful. When investigations are opened, they frequently fail to meet human rights standards, and only a small number of alleged perpetrators, mainly at the rank-and-file level, are brought to justice, facing mainly lenient indictments and sentences.

41. The Israeli legal system does not criminalize certain international crimes, which hampers prosecution efforts. At the same time, certain cases do not trigger the duty to investigate, for example, cases in which those implicated have acted in line with military policies or open-fire regulations. The challenge here is to consider whether such policies or regulations are compliant with international law. Although the lack of an outcome in some specific cases may be justifiable, a clear pattern of impunity appears evident.

---

24 See A/68/502, paras. 29–35; A/HRC/24/30, paras. 46–48; A/69/47; A/HRC/22/35, paras. 66–82, A/HRC/28/45, paras. 26–33 and A/69/347, paras. 52–69, 81 and 84.

25 Recent examples include the report of the independent commission of inquiry established pursuant to Human Rights Council resolution S-21/1 (A/HRC/29/CRP.4); B'Tselem, *The Occupation's Fig Leaf: Israel's Military Law Enforcement System as a Whitewash Mechanism*, May 2016. Available from www.btselem.org/download/201605_occupations_fig_leaf_eng.pdf; Amnesty International, "Time to address impunity: two years after the 2014 Gaza/Israel war", 7 July 2016. Available from www.amnesty.org/en/documents/mde15/4199/2016/en/

> Accountability for Killings and Injury in Law Enforcement
> Operations

42. In 2011, the Military Advocate General adopted a policy requiring an immediate investigation into every killing of a civilian by the Israel Defense Forces. The policy, is limited, however, to the killing of individuals designated by the Military Advocate General as civilians and does not apply if it is clear that the activity in the course of which the civilian was killed was of a real combat nature.[26] The office of the Attorney General adopted a similar policy when reviewing cases where civilians were killed as a result of police action when operating alongside or under military orders in the occupied West Bank.[27] Those exceptions appear to have been interpreted very broadly over the years, and many civilian deaths have never been investigated. Furthermore, a mandatory investigation is not required in cases where civilians have survived, even when they suffer severe or life-threatening injuries due to the actions of Israeli security forces.

43. In the occupied West Bank, since the second intifada, an estimated 3.5 per cent of complaints have led to investigations that resulted in an indictment being issued.[28] Although the adoption of that policy by the Military Advocate General in 2011 led to a slight increase in the rate of investigation of fatalities compared with the previous decade, overall indictments and convictions rates did not change.

44. According to the Ministry of Justice of Israel, as of July 2016, 24 criminal investigations had been opened in connection with the death of 190 Palestinians and the injury (including by tear gas inhalation) of over 15,000 by Israeli security forces since the escalation of violence in October 2015.[29] Seventy-one cases were still under consideration for investigation by the Military Advocate General and the office of the Attorney General. In another 71 shooting incidents that resulted in death, both entities

---

26   See High Court of Justice, case No. 9594/03, and http://mfa.gov.il/MFA/AboutIsrael/ State/Law/Pages/New_investigation_policy_Palestinian_casualties_IDF_fire_Judea_ Samaria_6-Apr-2011.aspx.

27   See Turkel Commission, "Israel's Mechanisms for Examining and Investigating Complaints and Claims of Violations of the Laws of Armed Conflict According to International Law". Available from www.turkel-committee.gov.il/files/newDoc3/The%20Turkel%20 Report%20for%20 website.pdf.

28   Figures are estimates based on status of all types of claims presented by B'Tselem to the Military Advocate General and a review conducted by Yesh Din of all fatality cases investigated by the Military Police Criminal Investigations Division since 2000.

29   Letter from the Israeli Legal Counselling and Legislation Department, 15 July 2016.

UN DOCUMENTS

determined that no additional legal or disciplinary proceedings were required.

45. The only indictment pronounced so far was in the case of the above-mentioned killing of Abdelfattah al-Sharif. At the time of writing, the soldier responsible for the killing was facing trial at the Jaffa military court for manslaughter. That indictment contrasts with a decision by the court in April 2016 that upgraded the charge against an alleged Palestinian hit-and-run driver from manslaughter to murder under pressure from the victim's family, even though the driver had claimed it was an accident and had surrendered to the Palestinian police. Meanwhile, there has been no investigation in the killing of Ramzi al-Qasrawi and the cases of many other individuals allegedly killed under circumstances similar to those in the death of Abdelfattah al-Sharif.

46. In Gaza, OHCHR is not aware of any investigations related to the 23 civilians killed and over 650 injured in access-restricted areas during the reporting period, including during demonstrations. Human rights organizations have indicated that few of the incidents in which the Israel Defense Forces killed or injured Palestinians while enforcing access restrictions in Gaza's perimeter areas have ever been investigated, and no soldier has been indicted for such an offence since the end of the second intifada. One obstacle is that the 2011 policy of the Military Advocate General does not pertain to Palestinians killed or injured in Gaza, since Israel does not consider Gaza an occupied territory and thus considers all of its operations there to be of a "combat nature". Furthermore, Israeli authorities have stated to human rights organizations that investigations would not be opened because the victims had entered "prohibited areas" and/or the soldiers had acted in line with the rules of engagement.[30] However, according to the Basic Principles on Use of Force and Firearms by Law Enforcement Officials, the mere entrance into a prohibited area does not meet the threshold necessary for the use of force. Firearms may only be used when necessary to prevent risk to life or serious injury, which has not been the case in most situations within the access-restricted areas that have been documented.

47. The Secretary-General is concerned that one of the elements driving impunity is that the policies regulating the use of force may not be aligned with international human rights law and standards, in particular the Basic Principles on Use of Force and Firearms by Law Enforcement Officials.

---

30 As communicated to the Palestinian Centre for Human Rights and the Al Mezan Centre for Human Rights.

THE PALESTINE YEARBOOK OF INTERNATIONAL LAW, VOLUME 19 (2016)   309

The open-fire regulations of the Israeli police, which are applicable in East Jerusalem, were updated in September 2015 and partially declassified in July 2016 following a court petition by human rights organizations, which questioned their consistency with relevant international standards. Similar concerns arose with regard to the rules of engagement of the Israel Defense Forces for their operations in the occupied West Bank and in Gaza, which remain confidential.

48.   In April 2016, the Military Advocate General closed the investigation into an occupied West Bank brigade commander who, on 3 July 2015, had shot and killed Mohammad Qusbah, a 17-year-old who was attempting to escape after throwing a stone at the officer's vehicle, near the village of Al-Ram. The investigation reportedly found that the officer had followed proper arrest procedures, including warning calls, shots into the air and two shots aiming at the legs. According to the Military Advocate General, by firing while he was running, the officer had made "a professional mistake ... but one that was made in clearly operational circumstances" that led to the shots hitting the child in the upper body and killing him.[31] It is not known whether the officer was sanctioned.

49.   As part of OHCHR monitoring of the case, questions were raised about the factual findings of the investigation. Regardless of those questions, the arrest procedures of the Israel Defense Forces, as described by the Military Advocate General in the incident involving Mohammad Qusbah, appear to be inconsistent with international human rights law, in which it is clear that firearms may only be used against an escaping suspect if the latter poses an immediate or ongoing threat (see A/66/330, para. 88 (c)). At the time Mohammad Qusbah was shot, he did not appear to pose any such threat. Furthermore, the arrest procedures do not appear to require that use of less lethal force be considered before resorting to firearms. Following the incident, the Israel Defense Forces reportedly revised its orders to ban opening fire at fleeing suspected attackers.[32]

50.   Unfortunately, calls to review the policies of the Israeli security forces and the Government that prima facie appear to be in contravention of international law have generally gone unheeded. Some structural concerns undermine the ability of the Military Advocate General to credibly carry out such reviews, especially where the office was involved in the

---

31   Charlotte Silver, "Israel excuses killing of fleeing Palestinian teen as 'professional mistake'", *Electronic Intifada*, 12 April 2016.

32   Gili Cohern, "IDF refines orders: soldiers not to fire at fleeing Palestinian attackers", *Haaretz*, 12 August 2015.

development or implementation of those policies (see A/70/421, paras. 55 to 58). While the Attorney General and the Supreme Court both provide civilian oversight of military investigations and prosecutions, the oversight is limited and often fails to review the legality of the policies themselves or the orders issued at the highest levels.

Accountability for Violations Committed during Hostilities

51. Pursuant to international law, investigations should be opened in response to every credible allegation of a war crime.[33] However, only around 7 per cent of all claims filed with the Israeli authorities for violations committed during the last three escalations in Gaza were ever investigated, with less than 0.5 per cent resulting in convictions.[34] Often, rank-and-file soldiers are investigated for minor offences while decisions or actions by senior level commanders are not scrutinized. The longest sentence served to date for a crime perpetrated during hostilities was 15 months of imprisonment for credit card theft.[35]

52. With regard to the 2014 hostilities, only one command-level officer came under investigation after an audio recording surfaced in 2015 that indicated that he had ordered his troops to shell a protected site in reprisal for the death of one of his soldiers.[36] The Military Advocate General found fault with the officer's action but closed the case in early 2016 without issuing an indictment. Little information was given about the basis for the decision but statements from the Military Advocate General seem to indicate that the ruling relied heavily on the version of events described by the officer in question and concluded that there was no evidence suggesting that "he had not acted out of military necessity".[37]

53. Two years after the 2014 escalation, justice remains elusive. At least 354 complaints to the Military Advocate General were filed by NGOs in connection with the hostilities. The latest public update from the Military Advocate General on the status of its investigations was published in June 2015. Several organizations, including the United Nations, have

---

33   Customary international humanitarian law, rule 158.

34   Based on data from B'Tselem: the Israeli Information Centre for Human Rights in the Occupied Territories, the Palestinian Centre for Human Rights, the Al Mezan Centre for Human Rights and Adalah: the Legal Centre for Arab Minority Rights in Israel. Data cross-referenced with updates of the Military Advocate General.

35   Ibid.

36   Yonah Jeremy Bob, "Analysis: Israel on thin ice with the ICC", *Jerusalem Post*, 16 June 2016.

37   Ibid.

since been requesting updates on specific cases, but no response or details have been provided. Based on press briefings and Israel's interactive dialogue with the Committee against Torture in early 2016 (see CAT/C/SR.1419), the General Staff Mechanism for Fact-Finding Assessments[38] is said to have reviewed 225 "exceptional incidents". Of those, the Military Advocate General reportedly opened investigations into 25 cases of alleged soldier misconduct; 7 were still open as of July 2016 while the others had been closed. One indictment has been issued in a case of looting, with no convictions to date. According to recent reports, decisions in the pending investigations are not expected for several more months.[39]

54. It is not clear how many cases, if any, are being assessed by the General Staff Mechanism for Fact-Finding Assessments in relation to events in 2014, or if all the cases have been closed, including at least four involving attacks on United Nations facilities. Non-governmental organizations have appealed to the Attorney General concerning at least eight decisions by the Military Advocate General not to open investigations.

55. During the reporting period, at least one criminal complaint was filed by the Palestinian Centre for Human Rights on behalf of the family of a victim of the May 2016 escalation. The Military Advocate General has not issued any communication as to whether the General Staff Mechanism for Fact-Finding Assessments is assessing the case.

Civil Remedies

56. There is limited up-to-date and publicly available information on successful tort claims against the State of Israel for alleged wrongdoing by the Israel Defense Forces in the Occupied Palestinian Territory. According to the Government of Israel, as of March 2016, there were 196 such cases, including 85 from Gaza, pending before the courts (see CAT/C/SR.1419, para. 32). Human rights organizations have indicated, however, that less than 10 per cent of claimants have ever had any success with

---

38   The General Staff Mechanism for Fact-Finding Assessments was established by the Chief of Staff of the Israel Defense Forces to examine "exceptional incidents" that occurred during the 2014 hostilities. It was created to counter criticisms that the Military Advocate General had not collected sufficient, balanced and timely information before determining whether to open investigations. In a previous report, the Secretary-General identified some of the shortcomings of the Mechanism, which continue to exist (see A/70/421, paras. 55–58).

39   Yonah Jeremy Bob, "No decision on Hannibal Protocol incident likely for several more months", *Jerusalem Post*, 25 February 2016.

312 UN DOCUMENTS

compensation claims, and most of those have been related to cases in the occupied West Bank.[40]

57. Compensation claims in the vast majority of cases from Gaza fail owing to physical, financial, legal and procedural barriers. Those include exceptions written into Israeli law, including the 2014 declaration of Gaza as "enemy territory", that have made Israeli authorities effectively immune to civil liability for their actions in Gaza. In the context of the 2014 hostilities, civil society organizations submitted 1,148 notifications to the Ministry of Defence within the prescribed 60-day window from the time of the incident to file a compensation claim with Israeli courts. Given barriers such as a lack of permission to travel to Israel as well as the prohibitive cost of filing compensation claims, only a very small percentage of claims have actually been filed since the initial notifications were provided. As the two-year statute of limitations for Palestinians to file such claims approaches, it is unlikely that any more compensation requests will be made in relation to the 2014 hostilities.[41]

Accountability for Ill-treatment and Torture of Detainees

58. Allegations of ill-treatment and torture during arrests, transfers and interrogations of detainees have been extensively reported over the years. Accountability mechanisms differ depending on whether the official allegedly involved is a soldier, an agent of the Internal Security Agency, a police officer or a prison warden.[42]

59. The interrogation practices of the Internal Security Agency have regularly come under scrutiny since the 1970s. In 1999, Israel's High Court of Justice forbade certain types of interrogation methods, including physical pressure, that had been employed by Internal Security Agency officers. Notwithstanding, many of those practices continue to be reported. The Public Committee against Torture in Israel, an Israeli NGO, reviewed over 1,000 complaints of ill-treatment against the Internal Security Agency since the High Court of Justice ruling and found that none of them had

---

40 See Yesh Din, "Exceptions: prosecution of IDF soldiers during and after the second intifada, 2000–2007", pp. 26–30.

41 In comparison, Israelis have seven years from the time of an incident to file a compensation claim and are not required to submit a notification to authorities beforehand or pay a guarantee.

42 See http://stoptorture.org.il/wp-content/uploads/2016/04/PCATI-CAT-report.pdf.

led to the opening of a criminal investigation.[43] The Government has argued that there was "insufficient evidentiary basis" to justify the opening of criminal investigations. However, human rights organizations and OHCHR have indicated that there was credible evidence of violations that would have warranted, at the very least, the opening of investigations. Part of the challenge is that torture is not a crime in Israel and officers can refer to the so-called "necessity defence" clause, contained in section 34(11) of the Penal Law, to justify certain practices that result in death or injury to others, in contravention of international standards, as highlighted by the Committee against Torture (see CAT/C/ISR/CO/5).

60. Although a civilian torture complaint mechanism was established under the Ministry of Justice in June 2013, the mechanism has yet to issue a recommendation that a criminal investigation be launched. At the same time, organizations have claimed that the number of complaints of torture or ill-treatment against the Internal Security Agency has quadrupled since June 2013.[44] It is of great concern that the Government of Israel views the presentation of such complaints "as a method to burden and hinder the security agencies in Israel in their ongoing fight against terrorism" (see CAT/C/ISR/5, para. 11).

Addressing Challenges

61. The Government of Israel has enacted a number of measures over the years aimed at addressing some of the challenges identified above (see CAT/C/ISR/5). Those measures have been piecemeal, however, and have not resulted in significant improvements in accountability.

62. In June 2010, the Government of Israel established the Public Commission to Examine the Maritime Incident of 31 May 2010 (the Turkel Commission), which, inter alia, was entrusted with assessing the compliance of Israeli criminal investigations with international law. The report of the Commission was published in February 2013 and included 18 recommendations for addressing issues such as delays in investigations, problems with impartiality and independence, and gaps in the legal framework. Human rights groups and the United Nations welcomed the report, noting that its implementation would be a positive first step towards tackling impunity (see A/68/502, para. 29 and A/69/347, para. 60).

---

43 See http://tbinternet.ohchr.org/Treaties/CAT/Shared%20Documents/ISR/INT_CAT_CSS_ISR_23995_E.pdf.

44 The Public Committee against Torture in Israel and Physicians for Human Rights.

63. In January 2014, the Prime Minister of Israel established an interministerial team, the Ciechanover Commission, to review the implementation of the Turkel Commission recommendations. The Ciechanover Commission published its findings in September 2015, which were approved by the Security Cabinet of Israel on 3 July 2016.

64. One of the key recommendations of the Ciechanover Commission was that the Government appoint, as a matter of priority, a standing body to monitor the full and timely implementation of the Turkel Commission recommendations. It remains to be seen if that and other time-bound recommendations by the Ciechanover Commission will be implemented. It also instructed the Chief Military Prosecutor to issue a directive setting out a clear time frame for criminal complaints to be processed and investigations concluded, and demanded that the Military Advocate General and the Attorney General publish their reasoning for the opening or closing of investigations. Both measures, if implemented, could help to improve the promptness and transparency of investigations. The Ciechanover Commission also noted that, although some of the Turkel Commission recommendations had been or were in the process of being implemented, further progress would be contingent upon the allocation of additional resources to relevant bodies, including the Ministry of Justice and the Military Advocate General.

65. The High Commissioner for Human Rights has noted that the Ciechanover Commission did not issue instructions for the full implementation of the first two recommendations of the Turkel Commission, namely, incorporating international norms and standards, including with respect to war crimes, into national legislation; and holding military commanders and civilian superiors responsible for offences committed by their subordinates (see A/HRC/31/40/Add.1, para. 37). The Ciechanover Commission noted instead that the office of the Attorney General was in the process of drafting bills that would seek to anchor the crime of torture and crimes against humanity in domestic legislation. It noted, however, that little information on that process is publicly available. It is of concern is that war crimes as a category have not been included among the offences under review for incorporation into national law, and that the anchoring of responsibility of military commanders and civilian superiors in Israeli law is said to require further examination.[45]

---

45 Report of the Ciechanover Commission. Available from www.pmo.gov.il/Documents/ReportEng.pdf.

66. Concerns also remain as to whether authorities are willing to address the underlying causes of impunity. The Secretary-General and the High Commissioner for Human Rights are concerned about statements by representatives of the Government and other high officials that unambiguously condone impunity and the use of force by Israeli police and defence forces in all instances. For instance, the Jerusalem police chief stated that "anyone who stabs Jews or hurts innocents – his due is to be killed".[46] Similarly, while commenting on the ruling in the case involving Mohammad Qusbah, the then Yisrael Beytenu party leader and current Minister of Defence, Avigdor Lieberman, praised the Military Advocate General's decision to close the file and noted "that everyone should know that the blood of Israeli soldiers is not free". In reference to the case involving Abdelfattah al-Sharif, he added that the Military Advocate General should also "free from detention the soldier from Hebron".[47]

67. New challenges are arising with recent legislative measures to increase the powers of the authorities at the expense of the rights of individuals. For example, two bills have recently been presented in the Knesset that put the families of attackers and alleged attackers at risk of residency revocation, "deportation" or added restrictions on residency.[48] Similarly, recently adopted laws stiffen penalties[49] for stone-throwing, including by stripping stone throwers and their families of their national insurance benefits,[50] imposing fines and legal expenses on assailants or fines on the parents of convicted children.[51] The Counter-Terrorism Law of 2016 expands the definition of a "terrorist entity" and of "support to a terrorist entity" and contains broad and ambiguous language concerning "incitement". It also makes permanent draconian provisions that were being used as temporary measures such as those that extended detention periods for security suspects without judicial review, the extension of their detention ex parte, the use of secret evidence and the exemption of the Internal Security Agency interrogations from being recorded.

---

46   "Two stabbed in Jerusalem, teen Palestinian assailant killed", *Times of Israel*, 10 October 2015.

47   Yonah Jeremy Bob, "Case closed against IDF colonel who shot dead Palestinian rock thrower", *Jerusalem Post*, 10 April 2016.

48   The bills are expected to be discussed by the Ministerial Committee for Legislation in August 2016.

49   Penal Code, amendments 119 and 120.

50   National Insurance Law (combined version), amendment 163.

51   Youth Law, amendment 20.

68. Recent decisions by human rights organizations to cease their engagement with the Israeli justice system reflect a lack of trust in Israeli institutions to ensure accountability for violations against Palestinians. In May 2016, B'Tselem, a leading Israeli human rights organization, announced it would no longer present claims to the Military Advocate General on behalf of Palestinian victims because they had come "to the realization that there is no longer any point in pursuing justice and defending human rights by working with a system whose real function is measured by its ability to continue to successfully cover up unlawful acts and protect perpetrators".[52] Some prominent human rights organizations have started to call upon countries with universal jurisdiction and other international justice mechanisms to intervene. OHCHR has indicated also that individual rights-holders, particularly in Gaza, are disillusioned with the ability of Israeli authorities to ensure accountability for violations perpetrated against Palestinians.

69. Non-governmental organizations have played a leading role in pushing Israel's investigatory mechanisms to act on hundreds of complaints by collecting victim and witness statements on behalf of authorities, identifying evidence, facilitating transport and translation services for victims and their families and providing legal aid to plaintiffs. There is a serious risk that the already low number and quality of investigations will further decline as organizations cease their cooperation with the justice system.

IV   Conclusions

70. Serious challenges persist to ensuring accountability for violations of international human rights and humanitarian law against Palestinians. Despite efforts to strengthen the system of accountability, critical key steps, notably including those recommended by Israeli commissions, remain unimplemented, partially implemented or are not followed in practice.

71. In order for meaningful change to happen, reforms are necessary. Without them, the failure to deliver accountability will continue to create a more permissive environment for Israeli security forces to commit human rights violations. Accountability for violations committed by all parties

---

52   B'Tselem, *The Occupation's Fig Leaf: Israel's Military Law Enforcement System as a Whitewash Mechanism*, May 2016. Available from www.btselem.org/download/201605_occupations_fig_leaf_eng.pdf.

is a key factor in breaking the cycle of violence and moving towards a peaceful resolution of the conflict.

V   Recommendations

72.   The following recommendations should be read in conjunction with the numerous recommendations contained in previous reports of the Secretary-General and the High Commissioner for Human Rights.

(a)   Israel should take all measures to ensure full respect for its obligations under international humanitarian law, in particular the principles of distinction, proportionality and precaution, and ensure accountability for all violations;

(b)   Israeli authorities should take all measures necessary to prevent incidents of excessive use of force during law enforcement operations. In cases in which force is used, including in the access-restricted areas near the Gaza fence, there should be compliance with international human rights law and standards. The authorities should ensure that independent reviews are conducted promptly and that any necessary revisions to rules of engagement, open-fire regulations and arrest procedures are made in order to ensure their compliance with international law;

(c)   The use of force in the context of protests, clashes and demonstrations must be strictly consistent with international law. Regulations and practices with respect to the use of rubber-coated metal bullets and black sponge bullets should be reviewed to ensure that those weapons are only permitted to stop individuals engaged in violence, and not as a general tool to disperse a crowd. The use of firearms should only be permitted where there is an imminent threat of death or serious injury;

(d)   Israel should ensure that medical assistance is promptly provided to persons wounded by security forces, without obstruction or discrimination. To that end, Israeli security forces should issue clear instructions to the effect that the wounded must receive immediate attention, without discrimination, and that medical personnel, including Palestinian ambulance crews, are not to be obstructed in performing their duties;

(e)   Prompt, thorough, effective, independent and impartial criminal investigations should be conducted into all instances in which firearms have been used by law enforcement officials, in particular where such force has resulted in death or injury, and the outcome of the process should be made public. Those responsible for violations should be held accountable and prosecuted in fair trials, with charges and sentences commensurate with the gravity of the offences. As an initial step to reforming the investigative system, the recommendations of the Turkel Commission and Ciechanover Commission should be fully implemented;

(f) Israel should adopt legislation on international crimes, such as torture and war crimes, and establish independent mechanisms to review government and military policies and to ensure command responsibility;

(g) The blockade of Gaza should be lifted and all practices that amount to collective punishment, including restrictions on freedom of movement across the Occupied Palestinian Territory, punitive demolitions of homes, punitive residency revocations, cutting of benefits, punitive closures of towns and delays in returning bodies for burial, should be ended;

(h) Israel should end the practice of administrative detention and charge or release any detainees currently being held in administrative detention;

(i) All children should be treated with due consideration to their age, in accordance with international law, and should be detained only as a last resort;

(j) The authorities and Palestinian armed groups in Gaza should ensure respect for international humanitarian law, in particular the principles of distinction, proportionality and precaution, and should ensure accountability for all violations.

Report of the Special Rapporteur on the Situation of Human Rights in the Palestinian Territories Occupied Since 1967, U.N. Doc. A/71/554

United Nations
General Assembly
A/71/554

Distr.: General
19 October 2016
Original: English

Seventy-first session
Agenda item 68 (c)
Promotion and protection of human rights: human rights situations and reports of special rapporteurs and representatives
Situation of human rights in the Palestinian territories occupied since 1967[*]

Note by the Secretary-General
The Secretary-General has the honour to transmit to the General Assembly the report of the Special Rapporteur on the situation of human rights in the Palestinian territories occupied since 1967, Michael Lynk, submitted in accordance with Human Rights Council resolution 5/1.

Report of the Special Rapporteur on the situation of human rights in the Palestinian territories occupied since 1967

---

[*] The present report was submitted after the deadline in order to reflect the most recent developments.

> *Summary*
> The Special Rapporteur on the situation of human rights in the Palestinian territories occupied since 1967, Michael Lynk, hereby submits his first report to the General Assembly. The report is based primarily on information provided by victims, witnesses, civil society representatives, United Nations representatives and Palestinian officials in Amman, in connection with the mission of the Special Rapporteur to the region in July 2016. The report addresses a number of concerns pertaining to the situation of human rights in the West Bank, including East Jerusalem, and in Gaza.

I   Introduction

1.   The Special Rapporteur on the situation of human rights in the Palestinian territories occupied since 1967, Michael Lynk, was appointed on 24 March 2016, in accordance with Commission on Human Rights resolution 1993/2 and Human Rights Council resolution 5/1. He assumed his functions on 1 May 2016. He is the seventh person to assume the mandate.

2.   The present report is the first submitted by the Special Rapporteur. He would like to draw attention to the fact that, while he stands ready to conduct a mission to the Occupied Palestinian Territory, permission to do so has not been granted by the Israeli authorities. After assuming his position as mandate holder, the Special Rapporteur made a formal request, on 3 June 2016, to both the Israeli and Palestinian authorities for permission to visit the Occupied Palestinian Territory. As of the time of writing of the present report, no reply had been received from the Israeli authorities. The Special Rapporteur notes that the two preceding mandate holders were similarly not granted access. The Special Rapporteur met the Permanent Observer of the State of Palestine to the United Nations on 7 June 2016, during his first visit to Geneva. He also requested a meeting with the Permanent Representative of Israel, but did not receive a response. This pattern of non-cooperation with the mandate is a serious concern. A full and comprehensive understanding of the situation based on first-hand observation would be extremely beneficial to the work of a Special Rapporteur.[1]

3.   The report is based primarily on written submissions as well as consultations with civil society representatives, victims, witnesses, Palestinian

---

1   A/HRC/23/21, para. 1.

government officials, and United Nations representatives held in Amman, Jordan during the Special Rapporteur's first mission to the region in July 2016.

4. The mandate of the Special Rapporteur, as set out by the Commission on Human Rights, is to investigate Israel's violations of the principles and bases of international law, international humanitarian law and the Geneva Convention relative to the Protection of Civilian Persons in Time of War, of 12 August 1949, in the Palestinian territories occupied by Israel since 1967.[2] With this in mind, the present report focuses on the violations committed by Israel in the context of nearly 50 years of occupation. Israel, as the Occupying Power, has a responsibility to ensure the respect for and protection of the rights of Palestinians within its control.[3] The mandate of the Special Rapporteur thus focuses on the responsibilities of the Occupying Power, although he notes that human rights violations by any State party or non-state organization are deplorable and will only hinder the prospects for peace.

5. The Special Rapporteur wishes to express his appreciation for the full co-operation with his mandate extended by the Government of the State of Palestine. The Special Rapporteur also wishes to extend his thanks to all those who travelled to Amman to meet him, and to those who were unable to travel but made written or oral submissions. The Special Rapporteur acknowledges the essential work being carried by those groups in their attempts to create an environment in which human rights are respected and to ensure that violations of human rights and humanitarian law are not committed with impunity and without witnesses. The Special Rapporteur will support such work as much as possible.

6. The Special Rapporteur would like to note that several groups were unable to travel to Amman to meet him, owing to travel restrictions imposed by the Israeli authorities. This was particularly the case with individuals coming from Gaza, and all groups based in Gaza were consulted by videoconference as a result.

7. The report is structured in two parts. It first provides an overview of the situation in the Occupied Palestinian Territory, including East Jerusalem. The discussion highlights current human rights concerns while also aiming to frame the current situation in the broader context of nearly 50 years of occupation. Thus, the discussion is not limited to events within

---

2   See Commission on Human Rights resolution 1993/2.

3   Geneva Convention relative to the Protection of Civilian Persons in Time of War, 12 August 1949 (Fourth Geneva Convention), art. 47.

a specific time period, but an emphasis will be placed on issues that were highlighted as particularly critical at the time of writing, on the basis of conversations with and input from individuals and organizations during the Special Rapporteur's mission in July 2016.

8. The second part of the report examines the situation in the Occupied Palestinian Territory through the lens of the right to development, with a focus on development as a human right, and the impact of human rights violations on development in the Occupied Palestinian Territory.

II   The Current Human Rights Situation

9. A series of worrying events and trends have emerged since the upsurge in violence that began in October 2015 in the West Bank, including East Jerusalem. During the escalation of violence, more than 230 Palestinians and at least 32 Israelis were killed over the course of 2015 and 2016 in the context of demonstrations by Palestinians, as well as Palestinian attacks or alleged attacks, and the often lethal response of the Israeli security forces.[4] While the number of violent incidents has declined in recent months,[5] the continued use of administrative detention, punitive demolitions, movement restrictions and other measures continue to negatively affect the human rights of the Palestinian people on a continuous basis.

10. Violent attacks of any kind by anyone are unacceptable. The fact that the attacks and alleged attacks by Palestinians against Israelis are, not infrequently, responded to with disproportionate and deadly force only compounds the violence. Many of the attacks and alleged attacks have been committed by minors, which is particularly worrying because of the hopelessness it seems to represent. In a striking number of meetings over the course of the Special Rapporteur's mission, those working in the Occupied Palestinian Territory consistently noted a sense of desolation and desperation among children manifesting itself not only in violent outbursts but also in psychological and physical ailments such as bed-wetting, anxiety and depression. The plight of children is often a barometer for the gravity of a situation. Sadly, in the present circumstances,

---

4   Office for the Coordination of Humanitarian Affairs, Protection of civilians weekly report, 16 to 22 August 2016. Available from www.ochaopt.org/content/protection-civilians-weekly-report-16–22-august-2016.

5   Gili Cohen, "After six months of terror wave, attacks decreasing, says Israeli army", *Haaretz*, 1 April 2016. Available from www.haaretz.com/israel-news/.premium-1.712123.

children born today in the Occupied Palestinian Territory do not enjoy hope for a peaceful future.

A *Violence and Lack of Accountability*

11. The number of casualties of the escalation in violence witnessed in 2015 was the highest in the West Bank since 2005 among both Israelis and Palestinians.[6] The large majority of those killed have been Palestinians – often as a result of disproportionate use of deadly force by Israeli security forces. According to civil society representatives, of those killed in the West Bank between October 2015 and January 2016, 88 were Palestinians whom the Israeli authorities suspected were responsible for attacks or attempted attacks. Two concerns arise with respect to these cases. First, that they occurred at all – that lethal force is used so often, and frequently without justification.[7] Second, the fact that, in a majority of cases in which a member of the Israeli security forces used lethal force, no investigation was conducted or if an investigation was conducted, it was closed without any action being taken against the perpetrator.

12. In several documented cases, it is clear those killed had not posed the level of threat that, according to international standards, would merit the use of deadly force. According to the Basic Principles on the Use of Force and Firearms by Law Enforcement Officials,[8] weapons and lethal force should be used only as a last resort.[9] Human rights organizations have documented a number of cases in which it is clear that this threshold was not met.[10]

---

6   Office for the Coordination of Humanitarian Affairs, "Israel opened 24 criminal investigations into the killing and injury of Palestinians since October 2015, leading to one indictment", Monthly Humanitarian Bulletin (July 2016). Available from www.ochaopt.org/content/israel-opened-24-criminal-investigations-killing-and-injury-palestinians-october-2015.

7   See Office of the United Nations High Commissioner for Human Rights (OHCHR), "Basic principles on the use of force and firearms by law enforcement officials". Available from www.ohchr.org/EN/ProfessionalInterest/Pages/UseOfForceAndFirearms.aspx.

8   See *Eighth United Nations Congress on the Prevention of Crime and the Treatment of Offenders, Havana, 27 August-7 September 1990: report prepared by the Secretariat* (United Nations publication, Sales No. E.91.IV.2), chap. I, sect. B.

9   See OHCHR, "Basic principles on the use of force and firearms by law enforcement officials".

10   B'Tselem, "Unjustified use of lethal force and execution of Palestinians who stabbed or were suspected of attempted stabbings", 16 December 2015. Available from www.btselem.org/gunfire/20151216_cases_of_unjustified_gunfire_and_executions.

UN DOCUMENTS

13. One of the most emblematic examples, widely reported in the media, is the killing of Abd al-Fatah al-Sharif in Hebron on 24 March 2016. Al-Sharif allegedly stabbed and wounded an Israeli soldier, and was later shot and killed by an Israeli soldier while lying immobile and wounded on the ground.[11] The incident was caught on video, and the footage, which was shared on YouTube by the Israeli human rights organization B'Tselem, made international headlines. The Special Rapporteur on extrajudicial, arbitrary or summary executions noted that, "the images shown carry all the signs of a clear case of an extrajudicial execution".[12]

14. This is only one example of what appears to be an alarming trend. As noted in a statement by the spokesperson for the United Nations High Commissioner for Human Rights, "this is not the first incident to be captured on video that raises concerns of excessive use of force".[13] These few visually documented cases do not represent the true scale of the problem. Further, the recently publicized Israeli open-fire regulations, updated in December 2015, lower the threshold for use of deadly force to a level that is in contravention of international standards.[14] The Basic Principles on the Use of Force and Firearms specify that firearms should be used only in cases of "imminent threat of death or serious injury", while the new open-fire regulations allow the use of live ammunition against an individual who "appears to be throwing or is about to throw" firebombs, fireworks or stones. This change suggests that the government seeks to create an environment in which use of deadly force is questioned less and accepted more. Under such conditions, the use of excessive force is likely to occur with greater frequency.

15. Further compounding the problem is the fact that in a majority of the cases, there has been little attempt to establish accountability. Between October 2015 and June 2016, the Israeli authorities opened 24 criminal investigations into incidents in which Israeli security forces' actions led

---

11 See www.youtube.com/watch?v=S8WK2TgruMo.

12 OHCHR, "Hebron killing: 'all the signs of an extrajudicial execution' – United Nations expert expresses outrage", 30 March, 2016. Available from www.ohchr.org/EN/NewsEvents/Pages/DisplayNews.aspx?NewsID=18544&LangID=E.

13 OHCHR, "Comment by the spokesperson for the United Nations High Commissioner for Human Rights, Rupert Colville, on the killing of a Palestinian man in Hebron", 30 March 2016. Available from www.ohchr.org/EN/NewsEvents/Pages/DisplayNews.aspx?NewsID=18540&LangID=E.

14 "Israeli police reveal new open-fire regulations in response to Adalah's court petition", Adalah, 5 July 2016. Available from www.adalah.org/en/content/view/8845.

to the injury or death of Palestinians.[15] So far, only the killing of Abd al-Fatah al-Sharif in Hebron has resulted in the indictment and prosecution of a soldier. The trial is ongoing and Israel's Defense Minister, Avigdor Lieberman, reportedly said, in relation to the case, that Israel "... cannot reach a situation where a soldier must ask for a lawyer before going on a mission" and emphasized that individuals are innocent until proven guilty.[16] Such statements implicitly encourage leniency for soldiers who use deadly force against individuals, which undermines efforts to ensure accountability.

16. The problem of the lack of accountability is far from new. One striking recent illustration of this fact is the announcement by the human rights organization B'Tselem in May 2016 that it will no longer engage with Israel's military law enforcement mechanism.[17] The organization came to the conclusion, after 25 years of work, that "there is no longer any point in pursuing justice and defending human rights by working with a system whose real function is measured by its ability to continue to successfully cover up unlawful acts and protect perpetrators".[18] B'Tselem noted that, of 739 cases the organization filed with the Military Advocate General since 1989, no investigation had been launched in 182 cases, while in nearly half the cases (343), the investigation was closed with no further action. In the course of 25 years, only 25 cases led to charges being brought against implicated soldiers. In early 2015, the human rights organization Yesh Din published statistics related to indictments in 2014, noting that only 8 out of 229 investigations opened in 2014 resulted in indictments, and that in 2013 there were 199 investigations, which led to 9 indictments. Yesh Din, in interpreting the data, noted that it "reveals the deep, ongoing failure to conduct exhaustive investigations that lead to indictments. The result is near impunity from prosecution for IDF soldiers ...".[19]

---

15 Office for the Coordination of Humanitarian Affairs, "Israel opened 24 criminal investigations into the killing and injury of Palestinians since October 2015, leading to one indictment".

16 Isabel Kershner, "Israeli military investigating soldier's killing of unarmed Palestinian", *New York Times*, 29 August 2016. Available from www.nytimes.com/2016/08/30/world/ middleeast/israeli-military-investigating-soldiers-killing-of-unarmed-palestinian.html.

17 B'Tselem, *The Occupation's Fig Leaf: Israel's Military Law Enforcement System as a Whitewash Mechanism* (May 2016). Available from www.btselem.org/publications/ summaries/201605_occupations_fig_leaf.

18 Ibid.

19 Yesh Din, "December 2015 data sheet: law enforcement on IDF soldiers suspected of harming Palestinians – summary of 2014 data", 12 February 2015. Available from

326   UN DOCUMENTS

17. The lack of accountability is a systemic and deeply ingrained issue. It helps to perpetuate a cycle of continued violence, as soldiers appear to act with impunity, with the message being sent that Palestinian lives do not matter, while the Palestinian population becomes both more fearful and more desperate.

B   *Detention*

18. Coinciding with the rise in violence is a rise in arrests and in the number of Palestinians in Israeli detention, including those in administrative detention. October 2015 saw a sharp increase in the number of Palestinians in detention, which continues to hold steady at levels not seen in nearly 10 years. As of the time of writing of the present report, according to data collected by B'Tselem and the human rights organization Addameer, there are more than 6,000 detainees currently held on alleged security grounds, as well as approximately 700 administrative detainees. The numbers are staggering and are suggestive of an overarching policy that aims to intimidate and significantly restrict the freedoms of Palestinians.[20]

Administrative Detention

19. The rise in the number of administrative detainees is particularly concerning. Currently, approximately 700 Palestinians are being held on administrative detention orders.[21] This is the highest number of administrative detainees reported since 2008.[22] Detainees are often deprived of basic legal safeguards, as noted in 2016 by the Committee Against Torture in its review of the fifth periodic report of Israel, as they are held on secret evidence to which neither they nor their lawyers are granted access, and are neither charged nor tried.[23] Since administrative detention orders are indefinitely renewable, some human rights activists argue that the

---

www.yesh-din.org/en/december-2015-data-sheet-law-enforcement-on-idf-soldiers-suspected-of-harming-palestinians-summary-of-2014-data/

20 A wide-ranging set of military regulations govern the arrest and detention of Palestinians living in the occupied Palestinian territory. See Addameer Prisoner Support and Human Rights Association, "Palestinian political prisoners in Israeli prisons", June 2016. Available from www.addameer.org/sites/default/files/briefings/general_briefing_paper_-_june_2016_1.pdf.

21 Addameer, Statistics, August 2016. Available from www.addameer.org/statistics.

22 B'Tselem, Statistics on administrative detention, updated 12 September 2016. Available from www.btselem.org/administrative_detention/statistics.

23 CAT/C/ISR/CO/5, para. 22.

psychological anguish associated with this uncertainty could amount to torture.[24]

20. Israel's justification for its widespread use of administrative detention is that it is necessary for security reasons. The Israeli government has relied on article 78 of the Fourth Geneva Convention, which states that an Occupying Power "for imperative reasons of security, to take safety measures concerning protected persons, it may, at the most, subject them to assigned residence or to internment". Internment in international law is defined as "the non-criminal detention of a person based on the serious threat that his or her activity poses to the security of the detaining authority in relation to an armed conflict".[25] This means that internment can only be used in non-criminal cases, and not as a substitute for a criminal conviction nor as a form of punishment.[26] The fact that administrative detention orders are often issued against individuals whom the Israeli government initially tried to charge with a crime but failed to do so, indicates that many of these arrests are in contravention of this provision.[27] According to the commentary to the Fourth Geneva Convention, this article should be read to apply only in very limited circumstances.[28] This is among the most serious measures that an Occupying Power can use with respect to the civilian population of an occupied territory.

21. Israel's practice of holding individuals on secret evidence is in clear violation of both international humanitarian law and international human rights law and far oversteps the use of "internment" as envisioned by the Fourth Geneva Convention. The Committee Against Torture, in its review of Israel, called on the State to end the practice of administrative detention, saying concerns exist because "detainees may be deprived of basic legal safeguards as, inter alia, they can be held in detention without

---

24　Addameer, "Induced Desperation: The Psychological Torture of Administrative Detention", 26 June 2016. Available from www.addameer.org/publications/induced-desperation-psychological-torture-administrative-detention.

25　International Committee of the Red Cross, "Internment in armed conflict: basic rules and challenges", opinion paper, November 2014.

26　See Commentary (1958) to article 78 of the Fourth Geneva Convention: "The persons subjected to these measures are not, in theory, involved in the struggle. The precautions taken with regard to them cannot, therefore, be in the nature of a punishment."

27　See, for example, Amnesty International, "Israel/OPT: human rights defender administratively detained: Hasan Ghassan Ghaleb Safadi", 4 July 2016. Available from www.amnesty.org/en/documents/mde15/4376/2016/en/

28　See https://ihl-databases.icrc.org/applic/ihl/ihl.nsf/Comment.xsp?action=openDocument&documentId=D794403E436F0823C12563CD0042CF9A.

charge indefinitely on the basis of secret evidence that is not made available to the detainee or to his/her lawyer".23,[29]

22. The case of Hasan Safadi, a journalist and the media coordinator for Addameer, an organization that works to protect and promote the rights of detainees, is a clear example of those failings of the Israeli system. Safadi was arrested on 1 May 2016 and as of time of writing of the report, has been held on an administrative detention order for a period of five months. According to information provided by Addameer, Safadi was arrested and subsequently interrogated over a period of 40 days. After no evidence was found on which to hold Safadi, he was set to be released on 10 June, pursuant to the decision of the Magistrate Court. On the day of his scheduled release, the Defense Minister signed an administrative detention order, for Safadi to be detained for a period of 6 months. Addameer notes that this "exemplifies the practice of issuing an administrative detention order in the absence of adequate evidence and charges against a detainee to keep him or her in detention".[30]

Children in Detention

23. Of significant concern is the number of children currently held in detention by Israeli authorities. As of the time of writing, Addameer had documented at least 350 Palestinian minors under the age of 18 currently held in detention by the Israeli authorities.[31] At the end of 2015, the number was at 422, with at least 116 of those between the ages of 12 and 15.[32] The majority of the arrests were related to charges of stone-throwing.[33] As part of the dual legal system in existence in the Occupied Palestinian Territory, Palestinian children arrested in the West Bank are subject to

29   In article 43 of the Fourth Geneva Convention, it is noted that anyone placed in internment "shall be entitled to have such action reconsidered as soon as possible" and article 78 specifies a right of appeal. See also the International Covenant on Civil and Political Rights (art. 9 (2)), in General Assembly resolution 2200 A (XXI), annex.

30   Information published by Addameer, available from www.addameer.org/prisoner/hasan-safadi.

31   Addameer, Statistics, August 2016. Available from www.addameer.org/statistics.

32   Defense for Children International – Palestine, "No way to treat a child: Palestinian children in the Israeli military detention system", April 2016. Available from www.dci-palestine .org/palestinian_children_in_the_israeli_military_detention_system.

33   United Nations Relief and Works Agency for Palestine Refugees in the Near East (UNRWA), "Children in distress: raising the alarm for 2016 and beyond", briefing note, April 2016. Available from www.unrwa.org/sites/default/files/content/resources/children_in_distress_briefing_note.pdf.

Israeli military law (as are Palestinian adults), while Israeli settlers in the same geographic area are subject to the Israeli civil and criminal legal system. Despite numerous calls for greater attention to the protections that should be afforded children, the practice surrounding the arrest and detention of minors remains extremely problematic. Reports and documentation indicate that parents are often not informed of a child's arrest until several days after the fact. In many cases, confessions are obtained in coercive conditions and are often written in Hebrew, which most Palestinian children cannot read. Children are also often denied access to an attorney during the initial phase of arrest, and many report ill-treatment.[34] Children reported being handcuffed, hand-tied, blindfolded, beaten and subject to solitary confinement.[35]

24. These practices are not only in contravention of basic legal standards, but they fail to take into account the extremely vulnerable position of a young child. The vulnerability of children is well recognized by the international community and the special protections to which children are entitled are enshrined in a number of legal instruments, including the Convention on the Rights of the Child. A 2012 report prepared by a team of independent lawyers found Israeli claims that the Convention did not apply beyond the borders of Israel to be "factually and legally unreal".[36] The International Court of Justice, in its advisory opinion on the legal consequences of the construction of a wall in the Occupied Palestinian Territory, found that the Convention, the International Covenant on Civil and Political Rights and the International Covenant on Economic, Social and Cultural Rights do in fact apply.[37] Of the recommendations set out in the "Children in military custody" report, only 2.5 per cent had been implemented as of July 2016.[38]

---

34 Defense for Children International – Palestine, "No way to treat a child: Palestinian children in the Israeli military detention system".

35 Department of State of the United States of America, 2015 report on human rights practices in Israel and the occupied territories, available from www.state.gov/j/drl/rls/hrrpt/humanrightsreport/index.htm?dynamic_load_id=252929&year=2015#wrapper.

36 "Children in military custody", June 2012, para. 30. Available from www.childreninmilitarycustody.org.uk/

37 *Legal Consequences of the Construction of a Wall in the Occupied Palestinian Territory, Advisory Opinion of 9 July 2004, I.C.J. Reports 2004*, paras. 102–113.

38 Military Court Watch, Monitoring the treatment of children in Israeli military detention, briefing note, July 2016. Available from www.militarycourtwatch.org/files/server/MCW%20BRIEFING%20PAPER%20-%20JUL%202016.pdf.

UN DOCUMENTS

C   *Collective Punishment*

25. Israeli authorities have resorted to a number of measures, which they employ on a case-by-case basis, that often amount to collective punishment. The measures, enacted in the name of security and often in response to actions carried out by one person or a small group of people, have a significant impact on the daily lives of almost every Palestinian at some point. Road closures, checkpoints and roadblocks restrict the movement of Palestinians to and from work and school, as well for visiting family members and travelling for medical treatment. Home demolitions deprive entire families of a place to live, based on the alleged actions of one individual.

26. Collective punishment refers to the practice of punishing an entire group for the actions of a particular individual. Collective punishment is prohibited under article 33 of the Fourth Geneva Convention and the Human Rights Committee has further noted that the prohibition on collective punishment is non-derogable.[39]

     Punitive Demolitions

27. In 2014, the Israeli Government reinstituted the use of punitive home demolitions.[40] Since that time, the number of demolitions has been on the rise, with 11 demolitions displacing 85 people reported in 2015, while already, as of July 2016, there had been 16 demolitions, displacing 92 people.[41] Punitive demolitions, the purpose of which is to harm the family members of someone suspected of a crime, are in clear violation of the basic tenets of international law.[42]

28. The Human Rights Committee, in its review of the fourth periodic report of Israel, in 2014, also called on the Government to halt its policy of punitive demolitions, noting that it is incompatible with its obligations under the Covenant.[43] In addition to amounting to a prohibited form of collective punishment, punitive demolitions are a violation of the prohibition on destruction of civilian property.[44]

---

39   See General Comment No. 29 (CCPR/C/21/Rev.1/Add.11).

40   OHCHR, "Punitive demolitions destroy more than homes in occupied Palestinian territory", 28 December 2015. Available from www.ohchr.org/EN/NewsEvents/Pages/PunitivedemolitionsinOPT.aspx.

41   B'Tselem, Statistics on punitive house demolitions, updated 31 August 2016. Available from www.btselem.org/punitive_demolitions/statistics.

42   Al-Haq, "Punitive house demolitions", 31 October 2015. Available from www.alhaq.org/advocacy/topics/population-transfer-and-residency-right/983-punitive-house-demolitions.

43   See CCPR/C/ISR/CO/4.

44   Fourth Geneva Convention, article 53.

Closures, Checkpoints and Permits

29. The right to freedom of movement is adversely affected on a regular basis by road closures, checkpoints and burdensome permit regimes that affect entire towns and villages. The practices are increasingly being used in villages and areas that those suspected of attacks call home.[45] As of the end of 2015, the Office for the Coordination of Humanitarian Affairs documented a total of 543 closures in the West Bank. Hebron in particular was subject to such measures, with significantly increased restrictions imposed after a series of demonstrations and related clashes, as well as alleged attacks in the area in November 2015, which resulted in a total of 53 new obstacles deployed, in addition to the 109 already existing obstacles.[46] Israel asserts that these are security measures. However, their sweeping nature and significant impact on the entire Palestinian population of various towns and cities make them not only a violation of the right to freedom of movement,[47] but in many cases also a form of collective punishment.

30. One recent incident is particularly illustrative. On 8 June 2016, in a deplorable act, four Israelis were killed in an attack at a popular shopping area in Tel Aviv. Two Palestinian gunmen were involved and, after the attack, police noted the suspects were from Hebron.[48] In response to the attack, the Israeli Government revoked all 83,000 permits it had granted to residents of the West Bank and Gaza to travel during Ramadan, suspended 204 work permits of individuals in the alleged attackers' extended families and sealed off the suspected attackers' entire hometown.[49]

31. The blockade of Gaza is currently the longest standing measure of collective punishment of the Palestinian people.[50] The blockade, imposed in 2007, has left the vast majority of 1.8 million inhabitants of Gaza unable

---

45 See Office for the Coordination of Humanitarian Affairs, "Fragmented lives: humanitarian overview 2015", June 2016.

46 Ibid.

47 International Covenant on Civil and Political Rights, article 12, Universal Declaration of Human Rights, article 13, Fourth Geneva Convention, article 27 and commentary to article 27, and *Legal Consequences of the Construction of a Wall in the Occupied Palestinian Territory, Advisory Opinion, I.C.J. Reports 2004*, paras. 135–137.

48 Peter Beaumont, "Four dead in Tel Aviv market shooting", *The Guardian*, 8 June 2016. Available from www.theguardian.com/world/2016/jun/08/tel-aviv-market-shooting-sarona -complex.

49 OHCHR, Press briefing note on Yemen and Israel/Occupied Palestinian Territory, 10 June 2016. Available from www.ohchr.org/FR/NewsEvents/Pages/DisplayNews .aspx?NewsID=20082&LangID=E.

50 A/HRC/24/30, paras. 21–23.

to leave. The blockade has been decried as a measure of collective punishment by both the Secretary-General and the International Committee of the Red Cross.[51]

32. A recent announcement by the Defense Minister provides concerning evidence that these types of measures are likely to continue. In what has been called a "carrot and stick" approach, the Minister proposes to continue using harsh measures such as closures, the increased presence of security forces and demolitions in areas that are home to suspected attackers and, meanwhile, to build infrastructure in areas that are seen by the Israeli authorities as "seeking coexistence". Notably, this primarily implies coexistence with illegal settlements. The Minister reportedly said of the policy that "[i]ts purpose is to continue to give benefits to those who desire coexistence with us and make life difficult for those who seek to harm Jews".[52]

D   *Coercive Environment and Forcible Transfer*

33. Recent months have seen a significant increase in settlement-related activity, including more government authorization of new buildings, retroactive authorization of construction considered illegal even under Israeli domestic law, demolition of the homes of Palestinians and the continuation of discriminatory planning practices and policies that make it extremely difficult for Palestinians to build. Such policies and practices are particularly prevalent in Area C and East Jerusalem, to such an extent that the Office for the Coordination of Humanitarian Affairs has referred to the situation as a "coercive environment that undermines a Palestinian physical presence and exacerbates the risk of individual and mass forcible transfers".[53]

34. Forcible transfer is clearly prohibited by article 49 of the Fourth Geneva Convention. The same article also prohibits the transfer of the population of an Occupying Power into the occupied territory. Forcible transfer

---

51   United Nations News Centre, "In Jerusalem and Gaza, Ban urges 'courageous steps' for lasting two-State solution", 28 June 2016, available from www.un.org/apps/news/story .asp?NewsID=54341#.V8iiTJN95E4 and International Committee of the Red Cross, "Gaza closure: not another year!", news release No. 10/103, 14 June 2010, available from www.icrc .org/eng/resources/documents/update/palestine-update-140610.htm.

52   Yossi Melman, "Liberman unveils new 'carrot and stick' policy for West Bank Palestinians", *Jerusalem Post*, 17 August 2016. Available from www.jpost.com/Arab-Israeli-Conflict/ Liberman-unveils-new-carrot-and-stick-policy-for-West-Bank-Palestinians-464360.

53   Office for the Coordination of Humanitarian Affairs, "Fragmented lives: humanitarian overview 2015".

is also defined as a war crime and a crime against humanity in the Rome Statute of the International Criminal Court.[54] "Forcible" in the context of the Rome Statute has been interpreted to mean not only physical force, but may also include "threat of force or coercion, such as that caused by fear of violence, duress, detention, psychological oppression or abuse of power, against such person or persons or another person, or by taking advantage of a coercive environment".[55]

35. Bedouin communities in the West Bank are particularly vulnerable, as they are often subject to relocation plans developed by the Israeli Government. Those efforts are based on assertions, for example, that the existing structures and locations are somehow "unsustainable".[56] In order to implement relocation plans, the authorities have demolished Palestinian homes and other structures, often relying on the fact that the structures are built without Israel-issued permits. However, permits are notoriously difficult to obtain, with high application fees, frequent rejections and lengthy processes, all of which combine to form a discriminatory permit regime that makes it nearly impossible for Palestinians to "legally" build. On 8 January 2016, the United Nations Relief and Works Agency for Palestine Refugees in the Near East (UNRWA) noted, in reference to the demolition of Bedouin homes in the West Bank carried out by the Israeli authorities on 6 January, that "[d]emolishing residential structures exacerbates an already coercive environment, driving Bedouin communities off the land they have inhabited for decades".[57]

36. The Office for the Coordination of Humanitarian Affairs has further described the situation in the West Bank, including East Jerusalem, as putting many Palestinian families and communities "at risk of forcible transfer because Israeli practices have created a coercive environment that puts pressure on them to move, mainly through the unavailability

---

54 Rome Statute of the International Criminal Court, articles 8.2(a)(vii) and 7.1(d), United Nations, *Treaty Series*, vol. 2187, No. 38544.

55 International Criminal Court, *Elements of Crimes* (The Hague, 2011). Available from www.icc-cpi.int/NR/rdonlyres/336923D8-A6AD-40EC-AD7B-45BF9DE73D56/0/ElementsOfCrimesEng.pdf.

56 Office for the Coordination of Humanitarian Affairs, "At risk of forcible transfer", Monthly Humanitarian Bulletin (May 2016). Available from www.ochaopt.org/content/risk-forcible-transfer.

57 UNRWA, "UNRWA condemns demolition of the homes of Palestine refugee Bedouin families at risk of forcible transfer; decries desperate humanitarian consequences", 8 January 2016. Available from www.unrwa.org/newsroom/official-statements/unrwa-condemns-demolition-homes-palestine-refugee-bedouins-families.

of building permits, which are almost impossible to acquire".[58] In a letter signed by the ambassadors to Israel of Belgium, Germany, Ireland, Italy, Norway, Spain, Sweden and Switzerland, the ambassadors criticized Israeli forces for confiscating shelters belonging to a Bedouin community in the West Bank, saying "These confiscations as well as previous demolitions, compounded by the inability of humanitarian agencies to deliver relief items to the affected households, create a coercive environment that potentially pressures them to leave their current sites against their will".[59]

37. The destruction of homes and property is not limited to structures built by Palestinians, but now also includes, with increasing frequency, structures built and funded by international humanitarian assistance. On 16 May 2016, for example, the Israeli authorities demolished seven homes and confiscated materials for three others that had been provided by humanitarian agencies, leaving 49 Palestinian refugees without shelter, 22 of them children.[60] Since the beginning of 2016, according to civil society data, 187 of the structures destroyed or seized by the Israeli authorities had been provided through donor-funded humanitarian assistance, compared to 108 donor-funded structures destroyed in all of 2015. Destruction of much-needed infrastructure provided through humanitarian aid is in direct violation of Israel's obligations under international law. Article 59 of the Fourth Geneva Convention requires an Occupying Power to facilitate relief for a population in need "by all means at its disposal". Article 55(1) further requires the Occupying Power to ensure the provision of food and medical supplies to the civilian population.[61] If the Occupying Power is not in a position to fulfil that obligation, it has an unconditional obligation to agree to relief schemes.[62]

---

58 Office for the Coordination of Humanitarian Affairs, "At risk of forcible transfer", Monthly Humanitarian Bulletin (May 2016).

59 Peter Beaumont, "Ambassadors protest at Israel's confiscation of West Bank shelters", *The Guardian*, 18 July 2016. Available from www.theguardian.com/world/2016/jul/18/ambassadors-protest-israel-confiscation-west-bank-bedouin-shelters.

60 Office for the Coordination of Humanitarian Affairs, "Humanitarian Coordinator calls on Israeli authorities to stop destruction of humanitarian aid and respect international law", 18 May 2016. Available from www.ochaopt.org/content/humanitarian-coordinator-calls-israeli-authorities-stop-destruction-humanitarian-aid-and.

61 Felix Schwendimann, "The legal framework of humanitarian access in armed conflict", in *International Review of the Red Cross: The Future of Humanitarian Action*, vol. 93, No. 884 (Cambridge and New York, Cambridge University Press, December 2011), p. 1001.

62 Ibid., p. 1002.

III The Right to Development and the Occupied Palestinian Territory

38. Thirty years ago, the General Assembly adopted the Declaration on the Right to Development.[63] The Declaration, and its subsequent elaborations, state that every human being and all peoples have an inalienable right to economic and social development that is equitable and just, sustainable, participatory and inclusive, non-discriminatory, grounded in the rule of law and fully observant of all human rights and freedoms. The right to development has been recognized as a human right itself, which raises its status to one with universal applicability and inviolability.[64] While the Declaration is not legally binding per se, it encompasses many of the legal rights and obligations – civil, political, economic, social and cultural – that are recognized as binding on all States parties through the various human rights treaties enacted by the international community over the past 70 year[65] In turn, the Declaration has been expressly incorporated within the 2030 Agenda for Sustainable Development.[66]

39. The Declaration on the Right to Development is particularly relevant to understanding the human rights predicament in the Occupied Palestinian Territory. Among other rights, the Declaration expressly includes the following human rights that are binding in international law:

(a) The self-determination of peoples (art. 1);

(b) The elimination of foreign domination and occupation (art. 5);

(c) The prohibition against discrimination and the flagrant abuse of human rights (art. 6);

(d) The full enjoyment of all human rights and fundamental freedoms, including socioeconomic rights (arts. 6 and 8);

(e) Full sovereignty over one's natural resources (art. 1);

(f) Participatory decision-making in public affairs (arts. 2 and 8).

---

63 Resolution 41/128, annex. The right was reaffirmed in subsequent international human rights instruments, including the Vienna Declaration and Programme of Action (1993).

64 Declaration on the Right to Development, article 1, para. 1; Arjun Sengupta, "On the theory and practice of the right to development", *Human Rights Quarterly*, vol. 24, No. 4, p. 837 (Baltimore, Johns Hopkins University Press, 2002).

65 The Declaration on the Right to Development is anchored in the International Covenant on Economic, Social and Cultural Rights (United Nations, *Treaty Series*, vol. 993, No. 14531) and the International Covenant on Civil and Political Rights (United Nations, *Treaty Series*, vol. 999, No. 4668). For a table linking the rights set out in the Declaration to legally binding instruments under international law, see OHCHR, *Frequently Asked Questions on the Right to Development* fact sheet No. 37 (Geneva, 2016).

66 Resolution 70/1, para. 10.

These rights lie at the core of the binding human rights and humanitarian obligations under international law, which apply in full to the Occupied Palestinian Territory[67]. They establish not only rights for the Palestinian people, but also create obligations for Israel, the Occupying Power, to respect and protect those rights. The Palestinian people's right to self-determination is widely accepted by the international community,[68] and the International Court of Justice has stated that "Israel is bound to comply with its obligations to respect the right of the Palestinian people to self-determination and its obligations under international humanitarian law and international human rights law".[69] While the question of development is necessarily complex in the context of occupation, it is essential that human rights and humanitarian law be interpreted in a way that is consistent with the right to development, regardless of the length of occupation.

40. The Declaration on the Right to Development establishes a rights-based approach to economic growth and social progress. Human rights are to be embedded in all aspects of economic and social development as a necessary precondition to the achievement of real and sustainable progress, expanded capacities and enlarged freedoms for the entire population. Both individuals and peoples are entitled to these rights, and States parties have a responsibility to create the conditions and remove the obstacles to achieve the enjoyment of these rights. Among its core features, the right to development requires both the application of transparent and participatory procedures as well as the substantive realization of equality of opportunity for everyone in their access to basic resources and their socioeconomic rights.[70]

---

67   *Legal Consequences of the Construction of a Wall in the Occupied Palestinian Territory, Advisory Opinion, I.C.J. Reports 2004*, paras. 86–114 and para. 149. These rights are also enumerated in binding human rights treaties, including the Universal Declaration of Human Rights, the International Covenant on Civil and Political Rights and the International Covenant on Economic, Social and Cultural Rights.

68   See resolution 70/141.

69   *Legal Consequences of the Construction of a Wall in the Occupied Palestinian Territory, Advisory Opinion, I.C.J. Reports 2004*, para. 149.

70   Resolution 41/128, annex, article 8, para. 1; Paul Gready et al., "What do human rights mean in development?", in *The Palgrave Handbook of International Development*, Jean Grugel and Daniel Hammett, eds. (Palgrave Macmillan UK, 2016), p. 453.

A *Economic and Social Development in the Occupied Palestinian Territory*

41. The Palestinian economy is without parallel in the modern world. Its territorial components – the West Bank, including East Jerusalem, and Gaza – are separated physically from one other. Its largest geographic entity, the West Bank, has been divided by Israel into an archipelago of small islands of densely-populated areas disconnected from one another by the wall or by settlements, bypass roads connecting the settlements to each other and to the Israeli transportation system, roadblocks, exclusive zoning laws, restricted areas and military no-go zones. Within these areas occupied by Israel, the local political authority is likewise splintered: the Palestinian Authority has limited rule over a part of the fragmented West Bank, Gaza is governed by a separate political authority not accountable to the Palestinian Authority, and Israel has illegally annexed East Jerusalem.[71] Furthermore, Israel has imposed a comprehensive land, sea and air blockade on Gaza since 2007. Within the West Bank, Israel exercises full civil and security authority over "Area C", which makes up over 60 per cent of this part of the territory and completely surrounds and divides the archipelago of Palestinian cities and towns, a hybrid situation that one human rights group has called "occunexation".[72] The Occupied Palestinian Territory lacks any secure transit access, whether by land, sea or air, to the outside world. All of its borders, with one exception, are controlled by Israel.[73] No other society in the world faces such an array of cumulative challenges that includes belligerent occupation, territorial discontinuity, political and administrative divergence, geographic confinement and economic disconnectedness.

42. The Oslo Accords, of 1993, and the Protocol on Economic Relations between the Government of the State of Israel and the Palestine Liberation Organization (the Paris Protocol on Economic Relations, 1994) were meant to be interim arrangements and were considered by Palestine as

---

71 The Security Council has stated that Israel's annexation of East Jerusalem is contrary to international law, and that East Jerusalem is deemed to be part of the Occupied Palestinian Territory. See Security Council resolution 476 (1980) and resolution 478 (1980).

72 Association for Civil Rights in Israel, "49 years of control without rights: human rights of the Palestinians in the West Bank and East Jerusalem – what has changed?", 1 June 2016. Available from www.acri.org.il/en/wp-content/uploads/2016/06/49years2016-en.pdf.

73 The only external border point not directly controlled by Israel is the Rafah crossing between Gaza and Egypt. Rafah is used almost exclusively as a civilian crossing, and not as an economic trading junction. Egypt has kept this crossing closed for much of the past three years.

a diplomatic and economic pathway for Palestinian independence by 1999. During that transitional period, the Oslo Accords left intact the extensive Israeli settlement project and permitted Israel broad authority to act on security concerns throughout the Occupied Palestinian Territory. The Paris Protocol created an economic framework with a significant reliance on Israel for currency, customs-union style trade provisions, foreign exchange arrangements and tax collection capacity that effectively maintained Palestinian dependence on Israel. A final peace settlement between Israel and Palestine has not materialized, and those interim arrangements have now become entrenched. The consequence has been that, while the Palestinian Authority has built much of the administrative and institutional capacity for national governance, it lacks the necessary economic foundation for sovereign development.[74] Since 2000, the Palestinian economy has experienced a volatile economic growth trajectory. When growth has occurred, it has been judged to be unsustainable because (a) it has been highly dependent upon foreign aid and private consumption of imports,[75] and (b) the Israeli occupation has increasingly separated and shrunk the different regions of the Palestinian territory, creating a dysfunctional economic base deprived of the capacity for autonomous development.[76]

43. The contradictions of attempting to build a sovereign economy under a prolonged occupation, without the realization of genuine self-determination on the foreseeable horizon, have become quite apparent. A stifled and distorted Palestinian economy provides a non-viable foundation for the sustainable and equitable social development of the Occupied Palestinian Territory. Certainly, Palestine has made steady progress in several important social areas, including maternal mortality, levels of literacy and education and vaccination rates. Yet, other key indicators point

---

74   International Bank for Reconstruction and Development/World Bank, "West Bank and Gaza: towards economic sustainability of a future Palestinian State – promoting private sector-led growth" (Washington, D.C., World Bank Group, 2012).

75   The World Bank estimated that external donor aid to the Occupied Palestinian Territory declined from 32 per cent of gross domestic product (GDP) in 2008 to 6 per cent in 2015, and noted that such a donor-led growth model is unsustainable. See World Bank, "Economic monitoring report to the ad hoc liaison committee" (Washington, D.C., World Bank Group, April 2016).

76   See International Bank for Reconstruction and Development/World Bank, "West Bank and Gaza: towards economic sustainability of a future Palestinian State – promoting private sector-led growth" and UNCTAD/APP/2016/1.

to a serious situation, with social conditions and living standards stagnating or getting worse:

(a) The Palestinian economy has not advanced. In 2014, Palestinian real gross domestic product (GDP) per capita was at virtually the same level as it was in 1999, with Gaza's real GDP per capita standing at only 71 per cent of its 1999 level;[77]

(b) Unemployment is growing as a social scourge. In 2016, it stood at 27 per cent in the Occupied Palestinian Territory, compared to 12 per cent in 1999; in Gaza, the unemployment crisis is particularly acute, where it has reached 42 per cent, with 58 per cent of its youth (aged between 15 and 29) without work, among the highest rates in the world;[78]

(c) Poverty has been increasing among Palestinians since 2012, with 26 per cent of the population now deemed to be poor, and 13 per cent estimated to suffer from extreme poverty.[79] Food insecurity is endemic: an estimated 2.4 million people in the West Bank and Gaza (57 per cent of the population) are projected to require some form of humanitarian assistance in 2016;[80]

(d) The industrial, agricultural and natural resource sectors are steadily shrinking in economic significance and employment size, owing to, inter alia: Israeli restrictions on market access; low confidence among potential investors because of political uncertainty; the significant loss of arable land to the Occupying Power; lack of effective economic planning powers; limited Palestinian control over

---

77 In 2014, real GDP per capita income in the Occupied Palestinian Territory (West Bank and Gaza, not including East Jerusalem) stood at $1,737. In 1999, it stood at $1,723. In 2014, Gaza's real GDP per capita income was $971, compared to $1,372 in 1999. All figures are in constant 2004 United States dollars; current (nominal) GDP per capita figures are higher. See data published by the Palestinian Central Bureau of Statistics, available from www .pcbs.gov.ps/Portals/_Rainbow/Documents/e-napcapitacon-1994–2014.htm.

78 World Bank, "Economic monitoring report to the ad hoc liaison committee" (Washington, D.C., World Bank Group, September 2016).

79 United Nations Educational, Scientific and Cultural Organization (UNESCO), country programming document for Palestine, 2014–2017.

80 Office for the Coordination of Humanitarian Affairs, "Humanitarian dashboard: 2nd quarter 2016", 18 August 2016. Available from www.ochaopt.org/content/humanitarian-dashboard-2nd-quarter-2016. UNRWA reported in March 2016 that 70 per cent of the total refugee population in Gaza, over 930,000 people, were dependent on food assistance, dramatically up from 10 per cent in 2000. See www.unrwa.org/newsroom/emergency-reports/gaza-situation-report-137.

340 UN DOCUMENTS

important natural resources (water, land, stone quarrying, and oil and gas reserves); and the limited access to fishing resources.[81] The economy has become deindustrialized and its ability to export has been undercut by the decline of the agriculture and manufacturing sectors;[82]

(e) The Occupied Palestinian Territory continues to be a captive trading market for Israel, as it has been throughout the occupation: in recent years, about 85 per cent of Palestinian exports have gone to Israel, and it received 70 per cent of its imports from Israel. The restrictions and imbalance in the trading relationship contributed to maintaining a chronic trade deficit in the Palestinian economy of $5.2 billion in 2015, some 41 per cent of GDP;[83]

(f) Symptomatic of the Palestinian Government's precarious economic management powers are the substantial fiscal leakages that the Palestinian Government and the Palestinian economy suffer under the current revenue-sharing and collection agreements with Israel. These arrangements are estimated by the World Bank and the United Nations Conference on Trade and Development (UNCTAD) to cost the Palestinian economy at least $640 million annually (amounting to 5 per cent of GDP);[84]

(g) UNCTAD has estimated that, without the occupation, the economy of the Occupied Palestinian Territory could double its GDP, with significant reductions not only in the unemployment and poverty levels, but also in the chronic trade and budget deficits.[85]

44. Israel, the Occupying Power, effectively controls the economic and social development of the Palestinian territory, but it does so in quite different ways within each region. Measures that amount to violations of the right to development include the blockade of Gaza and the ensuing collapse of its economy, the fragmentation and cantonization of the West Bank,

---

81 See UNCTAD/APP/2016/1. The World Bank acknowledged in 2015 that "the competitiveness of the Palestinian economy has been progressively eroding since the signing of the Oslo accords, in particular its industry and agriculture". See World Bank, "Economic monitoring report to the ad hoc liaison committee" (Washington, D.C., World Bank Group, September 2015).

82 World Bank, "Economic monitoring report to the ad hoc liaison committee" (Washington, D.C., World Bank Group, September 2016).

83 See UNCTAD/APP/2016/1. All amounts are in United States dollars.

84 See World Bank, "Economic monitoring report to the ad hoc liaison committee" (Washington, D.C., World Bank Group, April 2016) and UNCTAD/APP/2016/1.

85 See UNCTAD/APP/2016/1.

including separation and neglect of East Jerusalem, exploitation and appropriation of Palestinian natural resources, the regime of formal economic dependency, unilateral control over Palestine's external borders, the encumbering of personal and business mobility, restrictions on the use of agricultural lands, limitations on Palestinian fishery, the inequitable revenue sharing and tax collection agreements, and lopsided trade arrangements. The following sections examine the particular nature of Israeli domination of these areas.

Gaza

45. Israel's continued occupation of Gaza is maintained through an extensive military, economic and social blockade of the territory, which reinforces its separation from the world and the rest of the Occupied Palestinian Territory. As a form of collective punishment imposed upon an entire population, the blockade is contrary to international law.[86] In 2007, when Israel imposed the comprehensive blockade, the economy in Gaza had already been teetering owing to Israeli closures that had begun in the early 1990s, but it has since collapsed, along with the territory's living standards. The misery of the blockade for the population of Gaza has been compounded by the three escalations of violence between Israel and Gaza, in 2008–2009, 2012 and 2014, which killed approximately 2,500 Palestinian civilians, caused tens of thousands of injuries, displaced hundreds of thousands and inflicted extensive damage to Gaza's infrastructure. All reconstruction materials that enter Gaza must be approved by Israel, which has either limited or banned the importation of such necessary items as concrete, wood and other building materials, making the efforts to rebuild slow, difficult and costly.[87] In 2016, two years after the most recent hostilities ended, only 45 per cent of Gaza's energy needs are being met, causing between 16 and 18 hours of daily power cuts; 70 per cent of Gaza's population only have piped water supplies for between

---

86 A/69/347, paras. 30–34 and A/HRC/25/40, paras. 24–30. The Special Rapporteur notes the conclusion of the Secretary-General's Panel of Inquiry on the 31 May 2010 Flotilla Incident ("Palmer Report") (September 2011) which held that the blockade is lawful, but finds that the observations of the group of United Nations independent human rights experts which criticized the conclusion of the Palmer Report to be a more persuasive reading of international law. Report available from: www.un.org/News/dh/infocus/middle_east/Gaza_Flotilla_Panel_Report.pdf.

87 Gisha – Legal Center for Freedom of Movement, "Two years later: the long road to reconstruction and recovery" (2016). Available from www.gisha.org/UserFiles/File/publications/2_years_later/Reconstruction_EN.pdf.

6 and 8 hours, every 2 to 4 days; and 65,000 displaced Gazans from the 2014 escalation of hostilities still do not have reconstructed homes. An estimated 80 per cent of the population depends upon humanitarian aid to some degree for survival. On a more positive note, many of the damaged or destroyed hospitals and schools from the most recent conflict have been repaired or rebuilt, with funding from the international community.[88]

46. Over the past decade, Gaza has undergone a process of "de-development", with Israel enforcing a policy of maintaining Gaza at a level of essential humanitarian requirements and little more.[89] A major study by the United Nations in 2012 questioned whether, under then-current conditions, Gaza would even be a sustainable place to live by 2020.[90] In 2015, the World Bank reviewed what it called "the staggering cost of violence and blockade on Gaza's economy and living standards". The World Bank, after noting the grim levels of unemployment and poverty, stated that the approximately 70 per cent of Palestinians who work in the shrunken private sector in Gaza earn an average monthly salary of $174, less than the legal minimum wage of around $400. While Israel has recently allowed a limited amount of goods produced in Gaza to be traded to the West Bank and Israel, exports from Gaza are at only 11 per cent of their level before the 2007 blockade was imposed. The World Bank found that Gaza's GDP between 2007 and 2012 would have been 51 per cent higher had it not been for the combined effects of the blockade and armed conflict. The economy is now dependent for about 90 per cent of its GDP on expenditures by the Palestinian Government, the United Nations and other external remittances and donor projects.[91]

47. With respect to agriculture, Israel has unilaterally decreed a strip of land 300 m within Gaza along the border fence as a prohibited or restricted buffer zone, thus inhibiting the use of approximately 35 per cent of Gaza's farming land. Israel has also imposed tight restrictions on the maritime zone that Gazan fishermen can utilize, with as little as 3 nautical miles

---

88   Office for the Coordination of Humanitarian Affairs, "Gaza: two years after", 26 August 2016. Available from www.ochaopt.org/sites/default/files/gaza_war_2_years_after_english.pdf.

89   Sara Roy, *The Gaza Strip: The Political Economy of De-development*, 3rd ed. (Washington, D.C., Institute for Palestine Studies, 2016).

90   UNRWA, "Gaza in 2020: a liveable place?" (Jerusalem, Office of the United Nations Special Coordinator for the Middle East Peace Process, 2012).

91   World Bank, economic monitoring reports to the ad hoc liaison committee (May 2015, September 2015 and April 2016).

available for fishing. Even within stated limits, fishermen often face arbitrary arrest, confiscation of equipment and have even been shot at.[92] The restrictions have stunted the capacity of those two sectors to generate economic growth and employment.[93]

48. The depleted economy has resulted in widespread social anguish for the Palestinians in Gaza. The World Bank reported in May 2015 that "the quality of life for the large majority of Gaza's citizens is hardly bearable".[94] Very few Gazans are able to obtain permission from Israel or Egypt to travel outside of the Strip, whether for business, family, health or educational reasons. As a consequence of the confinement and the armed conflicts, the World Bank stated in the same report that even the sky-high poverty and unemployment rates "fail to portray the degree of suffering of Gaza's citizens due to poor electricity and water/sewage availability, war-related psychological trauma, limited movement, and other adverse effects of wars and the blockade". The water aquifer, which supplies Gaza's drinking source, is vastly overdrawn and only 5 to 10 per cent of the aquifer water is still drinkable. The lack of reliable electricity not only harms the economy but also seriously degrades the quality of everyday life. Most of Gaza's sewage is dumped into the Mediterranean sea untreated, an estimated 100 million litres daily, because of unrepaired damages to the treatment plants, lack of electricity to run them to capacity and failing infrastructure, which raises the risk of infectious diseases.[95] The quality of health services continues to deteriorate, with significant shortages of essential drugs and disposables, the non-payment or underpayment of medical staff salaries and compromised health-care service delivery owing to prolonged fuel cuts. This is alarming in the face of the thousands of Gazans with major physical disabilities and the estimated 20 per cent of the population who may have acquired mental health problems in the aftermath of the recent conflicts.[96] Observing the downward slide of living conditions, one leading human rights organization has stated that

---

92 Al Mezan Center for Human Rights, "Israeli violations against Palestinian fishermen in the naval part of the access restricted area", first quarterly report, 2016, pg. 11.

93 See Gisha, "Ten years later". Available from features.gisha.org/ten-years-later/; see also Diakonia, "Within range: an analysis of the legality of the land 'buffer zone' in the Gaza Strip" (Jerusalem, Diakonia International Humanitarian Law Programme, 2011).

94 World Bank, "Economic monitoring report to the ad hoc liaison committee" (Washington, D.C., World Bank Group, May 2015).

95 Ibid.

96 See Office for the Coordination of Humanitarian Affairs, "Humanitarian dashboard: 2nd quarter 2016", 18 August 2016, available from http://www.ochaopt.org/content/humanitarian-dashboard-2nd-quarter-2016, and "Gaza two years on: the impact of the

"life in Gaza is like life in a collapsing third-world country, a reality that is not the result of a natural calamity, but purely man-made".[97]

The West Bank

49. The economy of the West Bank is not at the dire level of Gaza's, but nor is it flourishing. Between 1999 and 2014, the economy only grew by 14 per cent in real terms, in large part because of the fragmentation of the territory under the occupation and the pervasive political and economic uncertainty regarding the Occupied Palestinian Territory's future.[98] The current stage of the fragmentation can be traced to 1995, when the Oslo II Accords divided the West Bank into three areas (and illegally annexed East Jerusalem):

(a) Area A, which consists of the principal Palestinian cities and towns (except for parts of Hebron), and amounts to 18 per cent of the West Bank; it is under the civil and security governance of the Palestinian Authority, although Israel does conduct regular security intrusions with or without coordination with the Palestinian Authority;

(b) Area B, which comprises about 400 Palestinian villages and adjacent farmland, and amounts to 22 per cent of the West Bank; it is under Palestinian civil authority, but exclusive Israeli security control. The vast majority of the 2.4 million West Bank Palestinians live in Areas A and B;

(c) Area C, encompassing 60 per cent of the West Bank, is under full Israeli civil and security control. Area C contains about 225 Israeli settlements and between 370,000 and 400,000 settlers, along with about 180,000 Palestinians. Area C completely surrounds the Palestinian communities in Areas A and B.

50. In the subsequent two decades since Oslo II, the division has become ever deeper. All Palestinian travel and economic trade that requires crossing between the three Areas, to Israel or to the outside world, is subject to Israeli security arrangements. Although the Palestinian Authority has some civil jurisdiction in Areas A and B, all major military, security and economic decisions for the occupied territory rest with Israel.

2014 hostilities on the health sector", Monthly Humanitarian Bulletin (June 2016), available from www.ochaopt.org/content/gaza-two-years-impact-2014-hostilities-health-sector.

97 B'Tselem, "Reality check: almost fifty years of occupation", 5 June 2016. Available from www.btselem.org/publications/201606_reality_check.

98 In 2014, real GDP per capita income of the West Bank stood at $2,269. In 1999, it was at $1,948. Palestinian Central Bureau of Statistics, Statistical abstract of Palestine.

Meanwhile, Israel has financially and administratively devolved virtually all of the West Bank economic and social governance functions to the Palestinian Authority, funded partly by the donor community.

51. Area C is vital to the well-being of the Palestinian economy, as it is endowed with minerals and stone quarrying, productive farmland, the potential for tourism, telecommunications and new housing, and the contiguous territory required for freedom of mobility within the West Bank. The World Bank has estimated that Palestinian GDP could have grown by 35 per cent over existing levels – $3.4 billion (in 2011 United States dollars) – and Palestinian employment would similarly have increased by 35 per cent were it not for Israel's restrictions on Palestinian access to Area C.[99] Yet, rather than integrating Area C with the rest of the West Bank to prepare Palestine for sustainable independence, Israel has instead treated Area C as its own economic and political hinterland, and as the main geographic space for its illegal settlements. Despite clear prohibitions in international humanitarian law against pillage by the Occupying Power, Israel has been exploiting the natural resources in Area C for its own benefit, including quarries, Dead Sea minerals and water.[100]

52. Israel has unilaterally assigned 70 per cent of Area C for its settlements, their adjacent lands and their extensive road, military and security network; all of this is off-limits to Palestinian development. It has also created a comprehensive planning regime to facilitate the confiscation of West Bank land and the expansion of the Israeli settlements. The planning regime excludes any Palestinian participation or substantive regard for their interests. The consequences are that, in Area C, Palestinians have less than 1 per cent of the land for construction, the vast majority of building permit requests by Palestinians for housing and infrastructure are denied, Israeli military demolitions of Palestinian homes are frequent and growing, and thousands of Palestinians – many of them Bedouins – are being forcibly transferred from their homes and traditional lands.[101]

---

99   Orhan Niksic, Nur Nasser Eddin and Massimiliano Cali, *Area C and the Future of the Palestinian Economy* (Washington, D.C., International Bank for Reconstruction and Development/World Bank, 2014).

100 Fourth Geneva Convention, articles 33 (2), 47 and 53; B'Tselem, *Acting the Landlord: Israel's Policy in Area C, the West Bank* (Jerusalem, 2013).

101 See Orhan Niksic and others, *Area C and the Future of the Palestinian Economy*; Diakonia, "Planning to fail: the planning regime in Area C of the West Bank – an international law perspective" (Jerusalem, Diakonia International Humanitarian Law Resource Centre,

As one human rights organization has observed, "tens of thousands of hectares, including pastureland and farmland, have been seized from Palestinians over the years and generously allocated to settlements ... All lands allocated to settlements have been designated closed military zones which Palestinians may not enter without a permit".[102] This separate and unequal development in the West Bank, and particularly in Area C, has led to the creation of two starkly different legal, economic and political universes within one territory, with Israeli settlers enjoying a vastly superior system of laws, roads, judicial systems, personal mobility, security, economic opportunities, civil and political rights and living standards than the West Bank Palestinians among whom they live. Some informed observers have recently speculated as to whether Israel is preparing to formally annex Area C,[103] with the Government of Israel having already prepared the ostensible legal basis for such a claim.[104]

East Jerusalem

53. In recent years, East Jerusalem has become increasingly detached from its natural economic and social connections to the rest of the West Bank through Israel's construction of a ring of settlement blocs and the wall. It has also suffered as a result of long-term neglect by the Israeli Municipality of Jerusalem. After Israel's annexation of East Jerusalem and adjacent parts of the West Bank in 1967, it built 12 settlements on confiscated land in order to create a physical barrier between the city and the rest of the West Bank and to manufacture a sovereign claim over East Jerusalem. In 2014, East Jerusalem's population consisted of 315,000 Palestinians and 210,000 Israeli settlers. Human rights organizations have pointed out that Israel has sought to discourage Palestinian population

---

2013); and Office for the Coordination of Humanitarian Affairs, "Increase in West Bank demolitions during July-August", Monthly Humanitarian Bulletin (August 2016). Available from www.ochaopt.org/content/increase-west-bank-demolitions-during-july-august.

102 B'Tselem, "Reality check: almost fifty years of occupation".

103 Al-Monitor, "Is Israel annexing West Bank Area C?", 14 August 2016. Available from www.al-monitor.com/pulse/originals/2016/08/oslo-accords-area-c-annexation-economic-development-settlers.html.

104 See "Report on the Legal Status of Building in Judea and Samaria" (Jerusalem, June 2012). Available from http://israelipalestinian.procon.org/sourcefiles/The-Levy-Commission-Report-on-the-Legal-Status-of-Building-in-Judea-and-Samaria.pdf; Israel Ministry of Foreign Affairs, *Israeli Settlements and International Law*. Available from www.mfa.gov.il/mfa/foreignpolicy/peace/guide/pages/israeli%20settlements%20and%20international%20law.aspx.

growth in Jerusalem through a variety of discriminatory planning, social services and residency rights policies.[105]

54. The physical isolation of East Jerusalem has meant that its traditional role as the mercantile and trading centre for the West Bank has been significantly reduced. In 2013, a study by UNCTAD noted that the wall had created an estimated direct economic loss of over a billion dollars to Palestinian Jerusalemites since its construction, with a further estimated adverse impact of $200 million annually in lost economic opportunities. As reported by UNCTAD, "occupation has affected the economy of East Jerusalem at multiple levels, including the labour market, product market, trade and investment", resulting in the city's declining contribution to Palestinian GDP. Only 13 per cent of East Jerusalem is designated for Palestinian housing, compared to triple that area assigned for Israeli settlers.[106]

55. Socially, Palestinian East Jerusalem has been largely ignored by the Municipality and living standards are far below those in West Jerusalem and in the Israeli settlements in East Jerusalem. East Jerusalem's infrastructure has been neglected over the years and is in poor shape, with a failing road system, a lack of public parks and serious deficiencies in the public transportation system, emergency services, water, garbage collection, policing and street lighting, with some Palestinian neighbourhoods still not connected to the municipal sewage system.[107] Alarmingly, 82 per cent of Palestinian Jerusalemites in 2014 were living below the poverty line, which is three times the level of Israeli Jerusalemites, and 6 per cent higher than in 2013.[108] The construction of the wall left approximately 80,000 Palestinian Jerusalemites on its easterly side and they must now travel through checkpoints to access work and social services in the city;

---

105 See B'Tselem, "Reality check: almost fifty years of occupation"; see also Jerusalem Institute for Israeli Studies, *Statistical Yearbook* (2016), table III/4, available from www.jiis.org.il/.upload/yearbook/2016/shnaton_C0416.pdf.

106 UNCTAD, "The Palestinian economy in East Jerusalem: enduring annexation, isolation and disintegration" (Geneva, 2013).

107 See Association for Civil Rights in Israel, "East Jerusalem 2015: facts and figures", available from www.acri.org.il/en/wp-content/uploads/2015/05/EJ-Facts-and-Figures-2015.pdf; see also Jerusalem Institute for Israeli Studies, "Explosive reality and proposals for de-escalation", available from www.jiis.org/.upload/East Jerusalem summary_Sept24_2015_Final.pdf.

108 Jerusalem Institute for Israel Studies, *Statistical Yearbook* (2016), table 6.1.

while they still pay municipal taxes, many of them receive very little, if any, basic services.[109]

B   *Assessing Israel's Respect for the Right to Development in the Occupied Palestinian Territory*

56.   An Occupying Power that is administrating an occupied territory in a manner consistent with the right to development would ensure that the occupation complied fully with the range of international legal principles and obligations set out in the right to development. In particular, the Occupying Power would respect and encourage the right to self-determination. It would treat the territory as an integral whole. It would be dedicated to returning the entire territory to the sovereign power, that is to say, the people of the occupied territory, as soon as security and order permitted. It would actively assist in the creation of an effective sovereign administration to assume authority. It would make no sovereign claim on any part of the territory, nor would it transfer any of its civilian population into the occupied territory. During the occupation, it would administer the territory in good faith and in the interests of the protected population as a trustee and usufructuary, and it would respect their laws, public buildings and infrastructure, political order, economy, property regime, cultural customs and social structure. It would encourage the development of the territory's sovereign economy by allowing it to fully flourish within its potential, and it would refrain from imposing any discriminatory economic practices or unnecessary barriers. It would not plunder, enrich itself or create an economic dependency. It would recognize that the natural resources of the occupied territory belong to the sovereign power, it would act to preserve them and it would only utilize those resources that are truly necessary to effectively administer the occupation while it lasts. It would secure and promote the full enjoyment of human rights, subject only to those restrictions absolutely necessary to protect security and public life. It would not tolerate, let alone inflict, humanitarian suffering. It would prohibit discriminatory laws, practices and treatment. In addition, as much as possible, the Occupying Power would encourage participatory decision-making by the protected population, as a vital step to restoring political power to the sovereign power.

---

109   See UNCTAD, "The Palestinian economy in East Jerusalem: enduring annexation, isolation and disintegration"; see also Association for Civil Rights in Israel, "Ten years of unfulfilled promises in East Jerusalem", available from www.acri.org.il/en/2015/08/09/ej-10years/

57. Israel's occupation over the past 49 years has been seriously deficient in its respect for the legal principles and obligations embedded in the right to development. Fundamentally, Israel has obstructed the Palestinian people's right to self-determination by a range of measures. It has illegally annexed East Jerusalem. It has transferred approximately 570,000 Israeli civilians to live in State-sponsored settlements in occupied territory. It has separated Gaza's economy and people from the rest of the Occupied Palestinian Territory. It has treated much of the West Bank as its own sovereign land for economic and demographic purposes. The duration of the occupation has lasted well beyond any reasonable length for any Occupying Power acting in good faith. The diminished geographic territory available to Palestinians is directly linked to Israel's extensive and expanding settlement project, including its network of highways, adjacent lands and extensive military-security apparatus; indeed, without Israel's settlement project, there would be no rationale for the continuing occupation.

58. In turn, the entrenched occupation and its denial of self-determination has bred conditions that lead to a host of other human rights violations, such as widespread food insecurity, the denial of building permits and the destruction of housing, the confiscation of property, the ongoing imposition of collective punishment, arbitrary military raids, a punitive court and detention system and a humanitarian crisis in Gaza. One of the most serious human rights violations has been Israel's entrenchment of a colonial-like regime in the Occupied Palestinian Territory, with two separate and unequal systems as regards laws, roads, justice regimes, access to water, social services, freedom of mobility, political and civil rights, security and living standards. Taken together, Israel has reneged on its obligations to uphold, in the Occupied Palestinian Territory, the right to development and the right to the full and equal enjoyment of all human rights by the Palestinian people.

59. While the Palestinian Government has some limited planning and investment jurisdiction, its powers are subordinate to Israel's overriding ability to control or veto all major economic decisions in the Occupied Palestinian Territory. Israel's discriminatory planning regime, particularly in East Jerusalem and Area C, minimizes or excludes Palestinian participation. The economy has been functioning well below its capacity and potential and remains deeply dependent upon international donor funding. Many international agencies ascribe the Palestinian economy's weak performance primarily to the occupation and its many barriers. The social consequences of the besieged Palestinian economy are dire: very

high unemployment rates, widespread poverty, crumbling infrastructure, significant housing shortages, low standards of living and, in Gaza, widespread misery. Rather than the development of a viable economic base as a necessary path to realizing self-determination and satisfying the right to development, the occupation is instead deepening and the horizon for creating a sovereign economy is vanishing.

IV   Recommendations

60.   The Special Rapporteur recommends that the Government of Israel bring a complete end to the almost 50 years of occupation of the Palestinian territories occupied since 1967. The Special Rapporteur also recommends that the Government of Israel take the following immediate measures:

   (a)   Ensure that domestic legislation is in line with international standards as described in the Basic Principles on the Use of Force and Firearms by Law Enforcement Officials, and is rigorously applied accordingly to those standards;

   (b)   Conduct thorough, effective, independent and impartial investigations in all instances where the use of lethal or excessive force or the commission of unlawful acts are alleged against Israeli security forces, so as to ensure genuine accountability;

   (c)   Immediately end the practice of administrative detention and the use of secret evidence, and release or charge all detainees;

   (d)   Introduce effective measures to reduce the number of children in detention and ensure that any detentions are fully compliant with the protections contained in the Convention on the Rights of the Child and other applicable legal instruments;

   (e)   Immediately end the practice of collective punishment in all its forms, including punitive demolitions and unjustified restrictions on freedom of movement;

   (f)   Immediately end the practice of forcible transfer and the destruction of homes and property, including those of Palestinian Bedouin communities.

61.   With respect to the international legal obligations contained within the Declaration on the Right to Development, the Special Rapporteur recommends that the Government of Israel:

   (a)   Allow for freedom of movement of people and goods throughout the Occupied Palestinian Territory;

(b) End the blockade of Gaza and lift all restrictions on imports and exports, with due consideration to justifiable security concerns;

(c) Allow the Palestinian Authority to assume security control in Area B and civil and security control in Area C so as to end the geographic fragmentation of the Occupied Palestinian Territory;

(d) Take meaningful steps to encourage a balanced trading relationship with the Occupied Palestinian Territory, including measures that will enhance the productive capacity of Palestinian manufacturing and resource development;

(e) Immediately end the practice of utilizing the natural resources of the Occupied Palestinian Territory for its own benefit;

(f) Remove the wall and fully compensate for the economic damages that it has caused;

(g) End the punitive practice of withholding the indirect taxes collected for the benefit of the Palestinian Government;

(h) Fully implement the international legal obligations contained in the Declaration on the Right to Development.

SECTION B

United Nations Resolutions

∴

U.N. Human Rights Council Resolution 31/33 (2016) – Right of the Palestinian People to Self-determination

United Nations
A/HRC/RES/31/33
General Assembly
Distr.: General
20 April 2016

Human Rights Council
Thirty-first session
Agenda item 7

> Resolution adopted by the Human Rights Council on 24 March 2016
> 31/33. Right of the Palestinian people to self-determination
>
> *The Human Rights Council,*
> *Guided* by the purposes and principles of the Charter of the United Nations, in particular the provisions of Articles 1 and 55 thereof, which affirm the right of peoples to self-determination, and reaffirming the need for the scrupulous respect of the principle of refraining in international relations from the threat or use of force, as specified in the Declaration on Principles of International Law concerning Friendly Relations and Cooperation among States in accordance with the Charter of the United Nations, adopted by the General Assembly in its resolution 2625 (XXV) of 24 October 1970, and affirming the inadmissibility of acquisition of territory resulting from the threat or use of force,
> *Guided also* by the provisions of article 1 of the International Covenant on Economic, Social and Cultural Rights and article 1 of the International Covenant on Civil and Political Rights, which affirm that all peoples have the right to self-determination,
> *Guided further* by the International Covenants on Human Rights, the Universal Declaration of Human Rights and the Declaration on the Granting of Independence to Colonial Countries and Peoples, in particular article 1 thereof, and by the provisions of the Vienna Declaration and Programme of Action,

adopted on 25 June 1993 by the World Conference on Human Rights,[1] and in particular Part I, paragraphs 2 and 3, relating to the right of self-determination of all peoples and especially those subject to foreign occupation,

Recalling General Assembly resolutions 181 A and B (II) of 29 November 1947 and 194 (III) of 11 December 1948, and all other relevant United Nations resolutions, including those adopted by the General Assembly, the Commission on Human Rights and the Human Rights Council, that confirm and define the inalienable rights of the Palestinian people, particularly their right to self-determination,

Recalling also Security Council resolutions 242 (1967) of 22 November 1967, 338 (1973) of 22 October 1973, 1397 (2002) of 12 March 2002 and 1402 (2002) of 30 March 2002,

Taking note of General Assembly resolution 67/19 of 29 November 2012,

Reaffirming the right of the Palestinian people to self-determination in accordance with the provisions of the Charter, relevant United Nations resolutions and declarations, and the provisions of international covenants and instruments relating to the right to self-determination as an international principle and as a right of all peoples in the world, and emphasizing that this jus cogens norm of international law is a basic prerequisite for achieving a just, lasting and comprehensive peace in the Middle East,

Deploring the plight of millions of Palestine refugees and displaced persons who have been uprooted from their homes,

Affirming the applicability of the principle of permanent sovereignty over natural resources to the Palestinian situation as an integral component of the right to self-determination,

Recalling the conclusion of the International Court of Justice, in its advisory opinion of 9 July 2004, that the right to self-determination of the Palestinian people, which is a right *erga omnes*, is severely impeded by Israel, the occupying Power, through the construction of the wall in the Occupied Palestinian Territory, including East Jerusalem, which, together with the Israeli settlement enterprise and measures previously taken, results in serious violations of international humanitarian and human rights law, including forcible transfer of Palestinians and Israeli acquisition of Palestinian land,

Considering that the right to self-determination of the Palestinian people is being violated further by Israel through the existence and ongoing expansion of settlements in the Occupied Palestinian Territory, including East Jerusalem,

---

1   A/CONF.157/23.

Reaffirming that the United Nations will continue to be engaged on the question of Palestine until the question is resolved in all its aspects in accordance with international law,

1. *Reaffirms* the inalienable, permanent and unqualified right of the Palestinian people to self-determination, including their right to live in freedom, justice and dignity and the right to their independent State of Palestine;

2. *Calls upon* Israel, the occupying Power, to end its occupation of the Occupied Palestinian Territory, including East Jerusalem, and reaffirms its support for the solution of two States, Palestine and Israel, living side by side in peace and security;

3. *Expresses grave concern* at the fragmentation and the changes in the demographic composition of the Occupied Palestinian Territory, including East Jerusalem, which are resulting from Israel's continuing construction and expansion of settlements, forcible transfer of Palestinians and construction of the wall, stresses that this fragmentation, which undermines the possibility of the Palestinian people realizing their right to self-determination, is incompatible with the purposes and principles of the Charter of the United Nations, and emphasizes in this regard the need for respect for and preservation of the territorial unity, contiguity and integrity of all of the Occupied Palestinian Territory, including East Jerusalem;

4. *Confirms* that the right of the Palestinian people to permanent sovereignty over their natural wealth and resources must be used in the interest of their national development, the well-being of the Palestinian people and as part of the realization of their right to self-determination;

5. *Urges* all States to adopt measures as required to promote the realization of the right to self-determination of the Palestinian people, and to render assistance to the United Nations in carrying out the responsibilities entrusted to it by the Charter regarding the implementation of this right;

6. *Decides* to continue the consideration of this question at its thirty-fourth session.

66th meeting
24 March 2016
[Adopted without a vote.]

U.N. Human Rights Council Resolution 31/34 (2016) – Human Rights Situation in the Occupied Palestinian Territory, Including East Jerusalem

United Nations
A/HRC/RES/31/34
General Assembly
Distr.: General
20 April 2016

Human Rights Council
Thirty-first session
Agenda item 7

Resolution adopted by the Human Rights Council on 24 March 2016
31/34. Human rights situation in the Occupied Palestinian Territory, including East Jerusalem

The Human Rights Council,
Recalling the Universal Declaration of Human Rights, the International Covenant on Civil and Political Rights, the International Covenant on Economic, Social and Cultural Rights, the Convention on the Rights of the Child and the Optional Protocol thereto on the involvement of children in armed conflict, the Convention on the Elimination of All Forms of Discrimination against Women, the Convention against Torture and Other Cruel, Inhuman or Degrading Treatment or Punishment and the International Convention on the Elimination of All Forms of Racial Discrimination, and affirming that these human rights instruments, among others, are applicable to and must be respected in the Occupied Palestinian Territory, including East Jerusalem,
Recalling also relevant resolutions of the Human Rights Council,
Taking note of the recent reports of the Special Rapporteur on the situation of human rights in the Palestinian territories occupied since 1967, and of other relevant recent reports of the Human Rights Council,
Noting the recent accession by Palestine to several human rights treaties and the core humanitarian law conventions, and its accession on 2 January 2015 to the Rome Statute of the International Criminal Court,

Deploring Israel's recurrent practice of withholding Palestinian tax revenues,

Aware of the responsibility of the international community to promote human rights and ensure respect for international law,

Recalling the advisory opinion rendered on 9 July 2004 by the International Court of Justice, and recalling also General Assembly resolutions ES-10/15 of 20 July 2004 and ES-10/17 of 15 December 2006,

Noting in particular the Court's reply, including that the construction of the wall being built by Israel, the occupying Power, in the Occupied Palestinian Territory, including in and around East Jerusalem, and its associated regime are contrary to international law,

Reaffirming the principle of the inadmissibility of the acquisition of territory by force, and deeply concerned at the fragmentation of the Occupied Palestinian Territory, including East Jerusalem, through the construction of settlements, settler roads, the wall and other measures that are tantamount to de facto annexation of Palestinian land,

Emphasizing the applicability of the Geneva Convention relative to the Protection of Civilian Persons in Time of War, of 12 August 1949, to the Occupied Palestinian Territory, including East Jerusalem, and reaffirming the obligation of the States parties to the Fourth Geneva Convention under articles 146, 147 and 148 with regard to penal sanctions, grave breaches and responsibilities of the High Contracting Parties,

Reaffirming that all States have the right and the duty to take actions in conformity with international human rights law and international humanitarian law to counter deadly acts of violence against their civilian population in order to protect the lives of their citizens,

Stressing the need for full compliance with the Israeli-Palestinian agreements reached within the context of the Middle East peace process, including the Sharm el-Sheikh understandings, and the implementation of the Quartet road map to a permanent two-State solution to the Israeli-Palestinian conflict,

Also stressing the importance of accountability in preventing future conflicts and ensuring that there is no impunity for violations and abuses, thereby contributing to peace efforts and avoiding the recurrence of violations of international law, including international humanitarian law and international human rights law,

Expressing grave concern about the continuing systematic violation of the human rights of the Palestinian people by Israel, the occupying Power, including that arising from the excessive use of force and military operations causing death and injury to Palestinian civilians, including children and women, and to non-violent, peaceful demonstrators and to journalists, including through the use of live ammunition; the use of collective punishment; the closure of areas; the confiscation of land; the establishment and expansion of settlements; the construction of a wall in the Occupied Palestinian Territory in departure from the Armistice Line of 1949; the policies and practices that discriminate against and disproportionately affect the Palestinian population in the Occupied Palestinian Territory, including East Jerusalem; the discriminatory allocation of water resources between Israeli settlers, who reside illegally in the Occupied Palestinian Territory, and the Palestinian population of the said Territory; the violation of the basic right to adequate housing, which is a component of the right to an adequate standard of living; the destruction of property and infrastructure; and all other actions by it designed to change the legal status, geographical nature and demographic composition of the Occupied Palestinian Territory, including East Jerusalem,

Gravely concerned in this regard by the ongoing demolition of Palestinian homes by Israel, the occupying Power, in particular in Occupied East Jerusalem, including when carried out as an act of collective punishment in violation of international humanitarian law, and by the revocation of residence permits and the eviction of Palestinian residents of the city,

Deploring the conflict in and around the Gaza Strip in July and August 2014 and the civilian casualties caused, including the killing and injury of thousands of Palestinian civilians, including children, women and elderly persons, the widespread destruction of thousands of homes and of civilian infrastructure, including schools, hospitals, water sanitation and electricity networks, economic, industrial and agricultural properties, public institutions, religious sites and United Nations schools and facilities, the internal displacement of hundreds of thousands of civilians, and any violations of international law, including humanitarian and human rights law, in this regard,

Gravely concerned in particular about the disastrous humanitarian situation and the critical socioeconomic and security situations in the Gaza Strip, including that resulting from the prolonged continuous closures and severe economic and movement restrictions that in effect amount to a blockade, and from the continuing and vastly negative repercussions of the military operations between December 2008 and January 2009, in November 2012 and in July and August 2014, and about the firing of rockets into Israel,

Stressing that the situation in the Gaza Strip is unsustainable and that a durable ceasefire agreement must lead to a fundamental improvement in the living conditions of the Palestinian people in the Gaza Strip, including through the sustained and regular opening of crossing points, and ensure the safety and well-being of civilians on both sides,

Affirming the need to support the Palestinian national consensus Government in its assumption of full government responsibilities in both the West

Bank and the Gaza Strip, in all fields, and through its presence at Gaza crossing points,

Expressing deep concern about the short- and long-term detrimental impact of such widespread destruction and the continued impediments to the reconstruction process on the human rights situation and on the socioeconomic and humanitarian conditions of the Palestinian civilian population, and calling upon the international community to step up its efforts to provide the Gaza Strip with the assistance that it requires,

Stressing the need to end immediately the closure of the Gaza Strip and for the full implementation of the Agreement on Movement and Access and the Agreed Principles for the Rafah Crossing, both of 15 November 2005, to allow for the freedom of movement of the Palestinian civilian population within and into and out of the Gaza Strip, while taking into account Israeli concerns,

Stressing also the need for all parties, in conformity with the relevant provisions of international humanitarian law, to cooperate fully with the United Nations and other humanitarian agencies and organizations and to ensure the safe and unhindered access of humanitarian personnel, and the delivery of supplies and equipment, in order to allow such personnel to perform efficiently their task of assisting affected civilian populations, including refugees and internally displaced persons,

Expressing deep concern at the Israeli policy of closures and the imposition of severe restrictions and checkpoints, several of which have been transformed into structures akin to permanent border crossings, other physical obstacles and a permit regime, which are applied in a discriminatory manner affecting the Palestinian population only, and all of which obstruct the freedom of movement of persons and goods, including medical and humanitarian goods, throughout the Occupied Palestinian Territory, including East Jerusalem, and impair the Territory's contiguity, and deeply concerned also at the consequent violation of the human rights of the Palestinian people and the negative impact on their socioeconomic situation and the efforts aimed at rehabilitating and developing the Palestinian economy,

Convinced that the Israeli occupation has gravely impeded the efforts to achieve sustainable development and a sound economic environment in the Occupied Palestinian Territory, including East Jerusalem, and expressing grave concern at the consequent deterioration of economic and living conditions,

Deploring all policies and practices whereby Israeli settlers, who reside illegally in the Occupied Palestinian Territory, including East Jerusalem, are accorded preferential treatment over the Palestinian population in terms of access to roads, infrastructure, land, property, housing, natural resources and judicial mechanisms, resulting in widespread human rights violations of Palestinians,

Emphasizing that the destruction of property and the forced displacement of Palestinian communities in the Occupied Palestinian Territory, including East Jerusalem, constitute, in all but the most limited cases as specified under international law, violations of the prohibitions on the destruction of property and on forcible transfers, respectively, under articles 53 and 49 of the Fourth Geneva Convention,

Deeply concerned at reports of the hampering and destruction of humanitarian assistance by Israel, contributing to a coercive environment that can lead to the forcible transfer of Palestinian civilians in the Occupied Palestinian Territory,

Expressing deep concern that thousands of Palestinians, including many children and women and elected members of the Palestinian Legislative Council, continue to be detained and held in Israeli prisons or detention centres under harsh conditions, including, inter alia, unhygienic conditions, solitary confinement, lack of proper medical care, denial of family visits and denial of due process, that impair their well-being, and expressing deep concern also at the ill-treatment and harassment of any Palestinian prisoner and all reports of torture,

Expressing deep concern also at the recent hunger strikes by numerous Palestinian prisoners in protest at the harsh conditions of their imprisonment and detention by the occupying Power, while taking note of the agreement reached in May 2012 on conditions of detention in Israeli prisons and calling for its full and immediate implementation,

Recalling the United Nations Standard Minimum Rules for the Treatment of Prisoners (the Nelson Mandela Rules) and the United Nations Rules for the Treatment of Women Prisoners and Non-custodial Measures for Women Offenders (the Bangkok Rules), and calling for respect for those rules,

Expressing concern at the possible consequences of the enactment by Israel, the occupying Power, of military orders regarding the detention, imprisonment and deportation of Palestinian civilians from the Occupied Palestinian Territory, including East Jerusalem, and recalling in this regard the prohibition under international humanitarian law of the deportation of civilians from occupied territories,

Convinced of the need for an international presence to monitor the situation, to contribute to ending the violence and protecting the Palestinian civilian population and to help the parties to implement the agreements reached, and in this regard recalling the positive contribution of the Temporary International Presence in Hebron,

Recognizing the continued efforts and tangible progress made in the Palestinian security sector, noting the continued cooperation that benefits both Palestinians and Israelis, in particular by promoting security and building confidence, and expressing the hope that such progress will be extended to all major population centres,

Emphasizing the right of all people in the region to the enjoyment of human rights as enshrined in the international human rights covenants,

1. *Stresses* the need for Israel, the occupying Power, to withdraw from the Palestinian territory occupied since 1967, including East Jerusalem, so as to enable the Palestinian people to exercise its universally recognized right to self-determination;

2. *Reiterates* that all measures and actions taken by Israel, the occupying Power, in the Occupied Palestinian Territory, including East Jerusalem, in violation of the relevant provisions of the Geneva Convention relative to the Protection of Civilian Persons in Time of War, of 12 August 1949, and contrary to the relevant resolutions of the Security Council are illegal and have no validity;

3. *Demands* that Israel, the occupying Power, comply fully with the provisions of the Fourth Geneva Convention of 1949 and cease immediately all measures and actions taken in violation and in breach of the Convention;

4. *Calls for* urgent measures to ensure the safety and protection of the Palestinian civilian population in the Occupied Palestinian Territory, including East Jerusalem, in accordance with the relevant provisions of international humanitarian law and as called for by the Security Council in its resolution 904 (1994) of 18 March 1994;

5. *Demands* that Israel, the occupying Power, cease all practices and actions that violate the human rights of the Palestinian people, and that it fully respect human rights law and comply with its legal obligations in this regard, including in accordance with relevant United Nations resolutions;

6. *Reiterates* the need for respect for the territorial unity, contiguity and integrity of all of the Occupied Palestinian Territory and for guarantees of the freedom of movement of persons and goods within the Palestinian territory, including movement into and from East Jerusalem, into and from the Gaza Strip, between the West Bank and the Gaza Strip, and to and from the outside world;

7. *Also reiterates* the responsibility of Israel, the occupying Power, to respect the right to health of all persons within the Occupied Palestinian Territory and to facilitate access of medical supplies and medical practitioners to all areas under occupation, including the Gaza Strip, and

364 UN RESOLUTIONS

stresses the need for the unhindered passage of ambulances at checkpoints, especially in times of conflict;

8. *Demands* that Israel, the occupying Power, cease immediately its imposition of prolonged closures and economic and movement restrictions, including those amounting to a blockade on the Gaza Strip, which severely restricts the freedom of movement of Palestinians within, into and out of Gaza and their access to basic utilities, housing, education, work, health and an adequate standard of living via various measures, including import and export restrictions, that have a direct impact on livelihoods, economic sustainability and development throughout Gaza, and in this regard calls upon Israel to implement fully the Agreement on Movement and Access and the Agreed Principles for the Rafah Crossing in order to allow for the sustained and regular movement of persons and goods and for the acceleration of long overdue reconstruction in the Gaza Strip;

9. *Expresses grave concern* at the confiscation and damage by Israel of fishing nets in the Gaza Strip for which there is no discernible security justification;

10. *Condemns* all acts of violence, including all acts of terror, provocation, incitement and destruction, especially the excessive use of force by the Israeli occupying forces against Palestinian civilians, particularly in the Gaza Strip, where bombardment of populated areas has caused extensive loss of life and a vast number of injuries, including among thousands of children and women, massive damage and destruction to homes, economic, industrial and agricultural properties, vital infrastructure, including water, sanitation and electricity networks, religious sites and public institutions, including hospitals and schools, and United Nations facilities, and agricultural lands, and large-scale internal displacement of civilians, and the excessive use of force by the Israeli occupying forces against Palestinian civilians in the context of peaceful protests in the West Bank;

11. *Also condemns* the firing of rockets against Israeli civilian areas resulting in loss of life and injury;

12. *Calls upon* Israel to cease all violations of the right to education of Palestinians, including those stemming from restrictions on movement and incidents of harassment and attacks on school children and educational facilities by Israeli settlers and as a result of Israeli military action;

13. *Also calls upon* Israel to end all harassment, threats, intimidation and reprisals against human rights defenders and civil society actors who peacefully advocate for the rights of Palestinians in the Occupied Palestinian

Territory, including by cooperating with United Nations human rights bodies, and underscores the need to investigate all such acts, to ensure accountability and effective remedies, and to take steps to prevent any further such threats, attacks, reprisals or acts of intimidation;

14. *Expresses deep concern* at the conditions of the Palestinian prisoners and detainees, including minors, in Israeli jails and detention centres, demands that Israel, the occupying Power, fully respect and abide by its international law obligations towards all Palestinian prisoners and detainees in its custody, and also expresses its concern at the continued extensive use of administrative detention, calls for a full implementation of the agreement reached in May 2012 for a prompt and independent investigation into all cases of death custody, and also calls upon Israel to release all Palestinian prisoners detained in violation of international law;

15. *Calls for* urgent attention to the plight and the rights, in accordance with international law, of Palestinian prisoners and detainees in Israeli jails, and calls for respect for the United Nations Standard Minimum Rules for the Treatment of Prisoners (the Nelson Mandela Rules) and the United Nations Rules for the Treatment of Women Prisoners and Non-custodial Measures for Women Offenders (the Bangkok Rules);

16. *Calls upon* Israel to explicitly prohibit torture, including psychological torture and other cruel, inhuman or degrading treatment or punishment;

17. *Demands* that Israel cease its policy of transferring prisoners from the Occupied Palestinian Territory into the territory of Israel, and respect fully its obligations under article 76 of the Fourth Geneva Convention;

18. *Urges* Israel to ensure that any arrest, detention and/or trial of Palestinian children is in line with the Convention on the Rights of the Child, including by refraining from holding criminal proceedings against them in military courts that, by definition, fall short of providing the necessary guarantees to ensure respect for their rights and that infringe upon their right to non-discrimination;

19. *Deplores* Israel's resumption of the policy of punitive home demolitions and the ongoing policy of revoking the residency permits of Palestinians living in East Jerusalem through various discriminatory laws, and the demolition of residential structures and the forced eviction of Palestinian families, in violation of their basic right to adequate housing and in violation of international humanitarian law;

20. *Expresses concern* at the Citizenship and Entry into Israel Law adopted by the Knesset, which suspends the possibility, with certain rare exceptions, of family reunification between Israeli citizens and persons residing in

the Occupied Palestinian Territory, including East Jerusalem, thus adversely affecting the lives of many families;

21. *Demands* that Israel, the occupying Power, cease all of its settlement activities, the construction of the wall and any other measures aimed at altering the character, status and demographic composition of the Occupied Palestinian Territory, including in and around East Jerusalem, all of which have, inter alia, a grave and detrimental impact on the human rights of the Palestinian people and the prospects for a peaceful settlement;

22. *Also demands* that Israel, the occupying Power, comply with its legal obligations under international law, as mentioned in the advisory opinion rendered on 9 July 2004 by the International Court of Justice and as demanded by the General Assembly in its resolutions ES-10/15 of 20 July 2004 and ES-10/13 of 21 October 2003, and that it immediately cease the construction of the wall in the Occupied Palestinian Territory, including in and around East Jerusalem, dismantle forthwith the structure situated therein, repeal or render ineffective all legislative and regulatory acts relating thereto, and make reparation for all damage caused by the construction of the wall, which has had a grave impact on the human rights and the socioeconomic living conditions of the Palestinian people;

23. *Calls upon* Israel to immediately cease any demolitions or plans for demolitions that would result in the forcible transfer or forced eviction of Palestinians, particularly in the vulnerable areas of the Jordan Valley, the periphery of Jerusalem and the South Hebron Hills, to facilitate the return of those Palestinian communities already subjected to forcible transfer or eviction to their original dwellings and to ensure adequate housing and legal security of tenure;

24. *Urges* Israel to ensure that water resource allocation in the Occupied Palestinian Territory is not discriminatory and does not result in water shortages disproportionately affecting the Palestinian population of the West Bank, and to take urgent steps to facilitate the restoration of the water infrastructure of the West Bank, including in the Jordan Valley, affected by the destruction of the wells of local civilians, roof water tanks and other water and irrigation facilities under military and settler operation since 1967;

25. *Deplores* the illegal Israeli actions in occupied East Jerusalem, including home demolitions, evictions of Palestinian residents, excavations in and around religious and historic sites, and all other unilateral measures aimed at altering the character, status and demographic composition of the city and of the territory as a whole;

THE PALESTINE YEARBOOK OF INTERNATIONAL LAW, VOLUME 19 (2016)   367

26. *Expresses grave concern* at:
    (*a*)   The restrictions imposed by Israel that impede access of Christian
            and Muslim worshippers to holy sites in the Occupied Palestinian
            Territory, including East Jerusalem, and calls upon Israel to include
            guarantees for non-discrimination on grounds of religion or belief as
            well as for the preservation and peaceful access to all religious sites;
    (*b*)   The increasing tensions in occupied East Jerusalem and the wider
            region, including those stemming from attempts aimed at illegally
            changing the status quo of holy sites;
27. *Urges* Member States to continue to provide emergency assistance to the
    Palestinian people to alleviate the financial crisis and the dire socioeco-
    nomic and humanitarian situation, particularly in the Gaza Strip;
28. *Emphasizes* the need to preserve and develop the Palestinian institu-
    tions and infrastructure for the provision of vital public services to the
    Palestinian civilian population and the promotion of human rights, in-
    cluding civil, political, economic, social and cultural rights;
29. *Deplores* the persistent non-cooperation of Israel with special procedure
    mandate holders and other United Nations mechanisms, and stresses the
    need for Israel to abide by all relevant United Nations resolutions and to
    cooperate with the Human Rights Council, all special procedures and the
    Office of the United Nations High Commissioner for Human Rights;
30. *Requests* the Secretary-General to place the presence of the Office of the
    High Commissioner in the Occupied Palestinian Territory on a firmer
    basis under the regular budget, including by, inter alia, deploying the nec-
    essary personnel and expertise;
31. *Also requests* the Secretary-General to report on the implementation of
    the present resolution to the Human Rights Council, with a particular
    focus on the recurrence and persistence of human rights violations and
    the underlying policies leading to such patterns, including those involv-
    ing forcible displacement, at its thirty-fourth session;
32. *Decides* to remain seized of the matter.

66th meeting
24 March 2015

[Adopted by a recorded vote of 42 to 0, with 5 abstentions. The voting was as
follows:

In favour:
Albania, Algeria, Bangladesh, Belgium, Bolivia (Plurinational State of), Burundi, China, Congo, Côte d'Ivoire, Cuba, Ecuador, El Salvador, Ethiopia, France, Georgia, Germany, India, Indonesia, Kenya, Kyrgyzstan, Latvia, Maldives, Mexico, Mongolia, Morocco, Namibia, Netherlands, Nigeria, Panama, Philippines, Portugal, Qatar, Republic of Korea, Russian Federation, Saudi Arabia, Slovenia, South Africa, Switzerland, United Arab Emirates, United Kingdom of Great Britain and Northern Ireland, Venezuela (Bolivarian Republic of), Viet Nam

Abstaining:
Botswana, Ghana, Paraguay, the former Yugoslav Republic of Macedonia, Togo]

U.N. Human Rights Council Resolution 31/35 (2016) – Ensuring Accountability and Justice for All Violations of International Law in the Occupied Palestinian Territory, Including East Jerusalem

United Nations
A/HRC/RES/31/35
General Assembly
Distr.: General
20 April 2016

Human Rights Council
Thirty-first session
Agenda item 7

Resolution adopted by the Human Rights Council on 24 March 2016
31/35. Ensuring accountability and justice for all violations of international law in the Occupied Palestinian Territory, including East Jerusalem

The Human Rights Council,

Guided by the purposes and principles of the Charter of the United Nations,

Recalling the relevant rules and principles of international law, including international humanitarian law and human rights law, in particular the Geneva Convention relative to the Protection of Civilian Persons in Time of War, of 12 August 1949, which is applicable to the Occupied Palestinian Territory, including East Jerusalem,

Recalling also the Universal Declaration of Human Rights and the other human rights covenants, including the International Covenant on Civil and Political Rights, the International Covenant on Economic, Social and Cultural Rights and the Convention on the Rights of the Child,

Recalling further the statement of 15 July 1999 and the declarations adopted on 5 December 2001 and on 17 December 2014 by the Conference of High Contracting Parties to the Fourth Geneva Convention on measures to enforce the Convention in the Occupied Palestinian Territory, including East Jerusalem, aimed at ensuring respect for the Convention in the Occupied Palestinian Territory, including East Jerusalem,[1]

Recalling its relevant resolutions, including resolutions S-9/1 of 12 January 2009, 19/17 of 22 March 2012 and S-21/1 of 23 July 2014,

Expressing its appreciation to the independent commission of inquiry on the 2014 Gaza conflict, and all other relevant United Nations mechanisms, as well as the treaty bodies and other United Nations bodies, for their reports,

Affirming the obligation of all parties to respect international humanitarian law and international human rights law,

Emphasizing the importance of the safety and well-being of all civilians, reaffirming the obligation to ensure the protection of civilians in armed conflict, and deploring the civilian deaths that resulted from the conflict in and around the Gaza Strip in, inter alia, July and August 2014, including the killing of 1,462 Palestinian civilians, including 551 children and 299 women, and six Israeli civilians,

Gravely concerned by reports regarding serious human rights violations and grave breaches of international humanitarian law, including possible war crimes, including the findings of the United Nations Independent International Fact-Finding Mission on the Gaza Conflict, of the United Nations independent international fact-finding mission to investigate the implications of Israeli settlements on the civil, political, economic, social and cultural rights of the Palestinian people throughout the Occupied Palestinian Territory, including East Jerusalem, of the independent commission of inquiry on the 2014 Gaza conflict and of the boards of inquiry convened by the Secretary-General,

Condemning all violations of human rights and international humanitarian law, and appalled at the widespread and unprecedented levels of destruction, death and human suffering caused in the Occupied Palestinian Territory, including East Jerusalem,

Stressing the urgency of achieving without delay an end to the Israeli occupation that began in 1967,

Deploring the non-cooperation by Israel with all Human Rights Council fact-finding missions and the independent commission of inquiry on the 2014 Gaza conflict, and its refusal to grant access to and cooperate with international human rights bodies and a number of United Nations special procedures seeking to investigate alleged violations of international law in the Occupied Palestinian Territory, including East Jerusalem,

Regretting the lack of implementation of the recommendations contained in the reports of the independent commission of inquiry on the 2014 Gaza

---

1 See A/69/711-S/2015/1, annex.

conflict, the United Nations independent international fact-finding mission to investigate the implications of Israeli settlements on the civil, political, economic, social and cultural rights of the Palestinian people throughout the Occupied Palestinian Territory, including East Jerusalem, and the United Nations Fact-Finding Mission on the Gaza Conflict, which follows a pattern of lack of implementation of recommendations made by United Nations mechanisms and bodies,

Alarmed that long-standing systemic impunity for international law violations has allowed for the recurrence of grave violations without consequence, and stressing the need to ensure accountability for all violations of international humanitarian law and international human rights law in order to end impunity, ensure justice, deter further violations, protect civilians and promote peace,

Regretting the lack of progress in the conduct of domestic investigations in accordance with international law standards, and aware of the existence of numerous legal, procedural and practical obstacles in the Israeli civil and criminal legal system contributing to the denial of the right of Palestinian victims to effective judicial remedy,

Emphasizing the need for States to investigate grave breaches of the Geneva Conventions of 1949, to end impunity, to uphold their obligations to ensure respect, and to promote international accountability,

Noting the accession by Palestine on 2 January 2015 to the Rome Statute of the International Criminal Court,

1. *Welcomes* the report of the independent commission of inquiry on the 2014 Gaza conflict;[2]
2. *Calls upon* all duty bearers and United Nations bodies to pursue the implementation of the recommendations contained in the reports of the independent commission of inquiry on the 2014 Gaza conflict, the United Nations independent international fact-finding mission to investigate the implications of Israeli settlements on the civil, political, economic, social and cultural rights of the Palestinian people throughout the Occupied Palestinian Territory, including East Jerusalem, and the United Nations Fact-Finding Mission on the Gaza Conflict, in accordance with their respective mandates;
3. *Notes* the importance of the work of the independent commission of inquiry on the 2014 Gaza conflict, the United Nations independent international fact-finding mission to investigate the implications of Israeli

2 A/HRC/29/52.

settlements on the civil, political, economic, social and cultural rights of the Palestinian people throughout the Occupied Palestinian Territory, including East Jerusalem, and the United Nations Fact-Finding Mission on the Gaza Conflict and the information collected regarding grave violations in support of future accountability efforts, in particular, information on alleged perpetrators of violations of international law;

4. *Emphasizes* the need to ensure that all those responsible for violations of international humanitarian law and international human rights law are held to account through appropriate fair and independent national or international criminal justice mechanisms, and to ensure the provision of effective remedy to all victims, including full reparations, and stresses the need to pursue practical steps towards these goals;

5. *Calls upon* the parties concerned to cooperate fully with the preliminary examination of the International Criminal Court and with any subsequent investigation that may be opened;

6. *Calls upon* all States to promote compliance with international law, and all High Contracting Parties to the Fourth Geneva Convention to respect, and to ensure respect for, international humanitarian law in the Occupied Palestinian Territory, including East Jerusalem, in accordance with article 1 common to the Geneva Conventions, and to fulfil their obligations under articles 146, 147 and 148 of the said Convention with regard to penal sanctions, grave breaches and the responsibilities of the High Contracting Parties;

7. *Recommends* that the General Assembly remain apprised of the matter until it is satisfied that appropriate action with regard to implementing the recommendations made by the United Nations Fact-Finding Mission on the Gaza Conflict in its report has been or is being taken at the national or international levels to ensure justice for victims and accountability for perpetrators;

8. *Requests* the United Nations High Commissioner for Human Rights to conduct a comprehensive review detailing the status of implementation of the recommendations addressed to all parties since 2009 by the relevant Human Rights Council mechanisms, namely previous fact-finding missions, the commission of inquiry and special procedures, and by United Nations treaty bodies, the Office of the High Commissioner and the Secretary-General in his reports to the Human Rights Council, and to identify patterns of non-compliance, non-implementation and non-cooperation, to propose follow-up measures to ensure implementation, and to present a report to the Council at its thirty-fifth session;

9. *Also requests* the High Commissioner to present an oral update on the progress of the above-mentioned review to the Human Rights Council at its thirty-fourth session;

10. *Decides* to remain seized of the matter.

66th meeting
24 March 2016

[Adopted by a recorded vote of 32 to 0, with 15 abstentions. The voting was as follows:

In favour:
Algeria, Bangladesh, Belgium, Bolivia (Plurinational State of), Burundi, China, Cuba, Ecuador, El Salvador, France, Indonesia, Kenya, Kyrgyzstan, Maldives, Mexico, Mongolia, Morocco, Namibia, Nigeria, Panama, Philippines, Portugal, Qatar, Russian Federation, Saudi Arabia, Slovenia, South Africa, Switzerland, the former Yugoslav Republic of Macedonia, United Arab Emirates, Venezuela (Bolivarian Republic of), Viet Nam

Abstaining:
Albania, Botswana, Congo, Côte d'Ivoire, Ethiopia, Georgia, Germany, Ghana, India, Latvia, Netherlands, Paraguay, Republic of Korea, Togo, United Kingdom of Great Britain and Northern Ireland]

U.N. Human Rights Council Resolution 31/36 (2016) – Israeli Settlements in the Occupied Palestinian Territory, Including East Jerusalem, and in the Occupied Syrian Golan

United Nations
A/HRC/RES/31/36
General Assembly
Distr.: General
20 April 2016

Human Rights Council
Thirty-first session
Agenda item 7

Resolution adopted by the Human Rights Council on 24 March 2016
31/36. Israeli settlements in the Occupied Palestinian Territory, including East Jerusalem, and in the occupied Syrian Golan

The Human Rights Council,
Guided by the principles of the Charter of the United Nations, and affirming the inadmissibility of the acquisition of territory by force,
Reaffirming that all States have an obligation to promote and protect human rights and fundamental freedoms, as stated in the Charter and as elaborated in the Universal Declaration of Human Rights, the International Covenants on Human Rights and other applicable instruments,
Recalling relevant resolutions of the Commission on Human Rights, the Human Rights Council, the Security Council and the General Assembly reaffirming, inter alia, the illegality of the Israeli settlements in the occupied territories, including in East Jerusalem,
Recalling also Human Rights Council resolution 19/17 of 22 March 2012, in which the Council decided to establish an independent international fact-finding mission to investigate the implications of the Israeli settlements on the

THE PALESTINE YEARBOOK OF INTERNATIONAL LAW, VOLUME 19 (2016)   375

human rights of the Palestinian people throughout the Occupied Palestinian Territory, including East Jerusalem,

Reaffirming the applicability of the Geneva Convention relative to the Protection of Civilian Persons in Time of War, of 12 August 1949, to the Occupied Palestinian Territory, including East Jerusalem, and to the occupied Syrian Golan, and recalling the declarations adopted at the Conferences of High Contracting Parties to the Fourth Geneva Convention, held in Geneva on 5 December 2001 and 17 December 2014,

Noting the recent accession by Palestine to several human rights treaties and the core humanitarian law conventions, and its accession on 2 January 2015 to the Rome Statute of the International Criminal Court,

Affirming that the transfer by the occupying Power of parts of its own civilian population into the territory it occupies constitutes a breach of the Fourth Geneva Convention and relevant provisions of customary law, including those codified in Additional Protocol I to the four Geneva Conventions,

Recalling the advisory opinion rendered on 9 July 2004 by the International Court of Justice on the legal consequences of the construction of a wall in the Occupied Palestinian Territory, and recalling also General Assembly resolutions ES-10/15 of 20 July 2004 and ES-10/17 of 15 December 2006,

Noting that the International Court of Justice concluded that the Israeli settlements in the Occupied Palestinian Territory, including East Jerusalem, had been established in breach of international law,

Taking note of the recent relevant reports of the Secretary-General, the Office of the United Nations High Commissioner for Human Rights, the Special Committee to Investigate Israeli Practices Affecting the Human Rights of the Palestinian People and Other Arabs of the Occupied Territories and the treaty bodies monitoring compliance with the human rights treaties to which Israel is a party, and the recent reports of the Special Rapporteur on the situation of human rights in the Palestinian territories occupied since 1967,

Recalling the report of the independent international fact-finding mission to investigate the implications of the Israeli settlements on the civil, political, economic, social and cultural rights of the Palestinian people throughout the Occupied Palestinian Territory, including East Jerusalem,[1]

Noting that Israel has over the years been planning, implementing, supporting and encouraging the establishment and expansion of settlements in the Occupied Palestinian Territory, including East Jerusalem, through, inter alia, the granting of benefits and incentives to settlements and settlers,

---

1   A/HRC/22/63.

Recalling the Quartet road map to a permanent two-State solution to the Israeli-Palestinian conflict, and emphasizing specifically its call for a freeze on all settlement activity, including so-called natural growth, and the dismantlement of all settlement outposts erected since March 2001, and the need for Israel to uphold its obligations and commitments in this regard,

Taking note of General Assembly resolution 67/19 of 29 November 2012, by which, inter alia, Palestine was accorded the status of non-member observer State in the United Nations, and also of the follow-up report thereon of the Secretary-General,[2]

Aware that Israeli settlement activities involve, inter alia, the transfer of nationals of the occupying Power into the occupied territories, the confiscation of land, the forcible displacement of Palestinian civilians, including Bedouin families, the exploitation of natural resources, the conduct of economic activity for the benefit of the occupying Power, the disruption of the livelihood of protected persons, the de facto annexation of land and other actions against the Palestinian civilian population and the civilian population in the occupied Syrian Golan that are contrary to international law,

Affirming that the Israeli settlement activities in the Occupied Palestinian Territory, including East Jerusalem, undermine regional and international efforts aimed at the realization of the two-State solution of Israel and Palestine, living side by side in peace and security within recognized borders, on the basis of the pre-1967 borders, and stressing that the continuation of these policies seriously endangers the viability of the two-State solution, undermining the physical possibility of its realization,

Noting in this regard that the Israeli settlements fragment the West Bank, including East Jerusalem, into isolated geographical units, severely limiting the possibility of a contiguous territory and the ability to dispose freely of natural resources, both of which are required for the meaningful exercise of Palestinian self-determination,

Noting that the settlement enterprise and the impunity associated with its existence, expansion and related violence continue to be a root cause of many violations of the Palestinians' human rights, and constitute the main factors perpetuating Israel's belligerent occupation of the Palestinian Territory, including East Jerusalem, since 1967,

Condemning the continuation by Israel, the occupying Power, of settlement activities in the Occupied Palestinian Territory, including in East Jerusalem, in violation of international humanitarian law, relevant United Nations resolutions, the agreements reached between the parties and obligations under the

---

2   A/67/738.

Quartet road map, and in defiance of the calls by the international community to cease all settlement activities,

Expressing grave concern in particular at the construction and expansion by Israel of settlements in and around occupied East Jerusalem, including its so-called E-1 plan, which aims to connect its illegal settlements around and further isolate occupied East Jerusalem, the continuing demolition of Palestinian homes and eviction of Palestinian families from the city, the revocation of Palestinian residency rights in the city, and ongoing settlement activities in the Jordan Valley,

Expressing grave concern at the continuing construction by Israel of the wall inside the Occupied Palestinian Territory, including in and around East Jerusalem, in violation of international law, and expressing its concern in particular at the route of the wall in departure from the Armistice Line of 1949, which is causing humanitarian hardship and a serious decline in socioeconomic conditions for the Palestinian people, is fragmenting the territorial contiguity of the Territory and undermining its viability, and could prejudge future negotiations by creating a fait accompli on the ground that could be tantamount to de facto annexation in departure from the Armistice Line of 1949, and make the two-State solution physically impossible to implement,

Deeply concerned that the wall's route has been traced in such a way as to include the great majority of the Israeli settlements in the Occupied Palestinian Territory, including East Jerusalem,

Gravely concerned at all acts of violence, destruction, harassment, provocation and incitement by extremist Israeli settlers and groups of armed settlers in the Occupied Palestinian Territory, including East Jerusalem, against Palestinian civilians, including children, and their properties, including homes, agricultural lands and historic and religious sites, and the acts of terror carried out by several extremist Israeli settlers, which are a long-standing phenomenon aimed at, inter alia, displacing the occupied population and facilitating the expansion of settlements,

Expressing concern at ongoing impunity for acts of settler violence against Palestinian civilians and their properties, and stressing the need for Israel to investigate and to ensure accountability for all of these acts,

Aware of the detrimental impact of the Israeli settlements on Palestinian and other Arab natural resources, especially as a result of the confiscation of land and the forced diversion of water resources, including the destruction of orchards and crops and the seizure of water wells by Israeli settlers, and of the dire socioeconomic consequences in this regard, which precludes the Palestinian people from being able to exercise permanent sovereignty over their natural resources,

Noting that the agricultural sector, considered the cornerstone of Palestinian economic development, has not been able to play its strategic role because of the dispossession of land and the denial of access for farmers to agricultural areas, water resources and domestic and external markets owing to the construction, consolidation and expansion of Israeli settlements,

Recalling Human Rights Council resolution 22/29 of 22 March 2013, in follow-up to the report of the independent international fact-finding mission to investigate the implications of Israeli settlements on the civil, political, economic, social and cultural rights of the Palestinian people throughout the Occupied Palestinian Territory, including East Jerusalem,

Recalling also the Guiding Principles on Business and Human Rights, which place responsibilities on all business enterprises to respect human rights by, inter alia, refraining from contributing to human rights abuses arising from conflict, and call upon States to provide adequate assistance to business enterprises to assess and address the heightened risks of abuses in conflict-affected areas, including by ensuring that their current policies, legislation, regulations and enforcement measures are effective in addressing the risk of business involvement in gross human rights abuses,

Noting that, in situations of armed conflict, business enterprises should respect the standards of international humanitarian law, and concerned that some business enterprises have, directly and indirectly, enabled, facilitated and profited from the construction and growth of the Israeli settlements in the Occupied Palestinian Territory,

Reaffirming the fact that the High Contracting Parties to the Fourth Geneva Convention relative to the Protection of Civilian Persons in Time of War, of 12 August 1949, undertook to respect and to ensure respect for the Convention in all circumstances, and that States should not recognize an unlawful situation arising from breaches of peremptory norms of international law,

Calling upon all States not to provide Israel with any assistance to be used specifically in connection with settlements in the Occupied Palestinian Territory, including East Jerusalem, and in the occupied Syrian Golan,

Emphasizing the importance for States to act in accordance with their own national legislation on promoting compliance with international humanitarian law with regard to business activities that result in human rights abuses,

Concerned that economic activities facilitate the expansion and entrenchment of settlements, and aware that the conditions of harvesting and production for products made in settlements involve the breach of applicable legal norms, inter alia, the exploitation of the natural resources of the Occupied Palestinian Territory, including East Jerusalem, and calling upon all States to respect their legal obligations in this regard,

Aware that products wholly or partially produced in settlements have been labelled as originating from Israel,

Aware also of the role of private individuals, associations and charities in third States that are involved in providing funding to Israeli settlements and settlement-based entities, contributing to the maintenance and expansion of settlements,

Expressing its concern at the failure of Israel, the occupying Power, to co-operate fully with the relevant United Nations mechanisms, in particular the Special Rapporteur on the situation of human rights in the Palestinian territories occupied since 1967,

1. *Reaffirms* that the Israeli settlements in the Occupied Palestinian Territory, including East Jerusalem, and in the occupied Syrian Golan are illegal and an obstacle to peace and economic and social development;

2. *Calls upon* Israel to accept the de jure applicability of the Geneva Convention relative to the Protection of Civilian Persons in Time of War, of 12 August 1949, to the Occupied Palestinian Territory, including East Jerusalem, and to the occupied Syrian Golan, to abide scrupulously by the provisions of the Convention, in particular article 49 thereof, and to comply with all its obligations under international law and cease immediately all actions causing the alteration of the character, status and demographic composition of the Occupied Palestinian Territory, including East Jerusalem, and the occupied Syrian Golan;

3. *Demands* that Israel, the occupying Power, immediately cease all settlement activities in all the Occupied Palestinian Territory, including East Jerusalem, and in the occupied Syrian Golan, and calls in this regard for the full implementation of all relevant resolutions of the Security Council, including, inter alia, resolutions 446 (1979) of 22 March 1979, 452 (1979) of 20 July 1979, 465 (1980) of 1 March 1980, 476 (1980) of 30 June 1980 and 1515 (2003) of 19 November 2003;

4. *Also demands* that Israel, the occupying Power, comply fully with its legal obligations, as mentioned in the advisory opinion rendered on 9 July 2004 by the International Court of Justice;

5. *Condemns* the continuing settlement and related activities by Israel, including the expansion of settlements, the expropriation of land, the demolition of houses, the confiscation and destruction of property, the expulsion and displacement of Palestinians, including entire communities and the construction of bypass roads, which change the physical character and demographic composition of the occupied territories, including East Jerusalem and the Syrian Golan, and constitute a violation

of the Fourth Geneva Convention relative to the Protection of Civilian Persons in Time of War, of 12 August 1949, and in particular article 49 thereof;

6. *Also condemns* the construction of new housing units for Israeli settlers in the West Bank and around occupied East Jerusalem, as it seriously undermines the peace process and jeopardizes the ongoing efforts by the international community to reach a final and just peace solution compliant with international law and legitimacy, including relevant United Nations resolutions, and constitutes a threat to the two-State solution;

7. *Expresses its grave concern* at, and calls for the cessation of:

   (a) The operation by Israel of a tramway linking the settlements with West Jerusalem, which is in clear violation of international law and relevant United Nations resolutions;

   (b) The expropriation of Palestinian land, the demolition of Palestinian homes, demolition orders, forced evictions and "relocation" plans, the obstruction and destruction of humanitarian assistance and the creation of unbearable living conditions by Israel in areas identified for the expansion and construction of settlements, and other practices aimed at the forcible transfer of the Palestinian civilian population, including Bedouin communities and herders, and further settlement activities, including the denial of access to water and other basic services by Israel to Palestinians in the Occupied Palestinian Territory, including East Jerusalem, particularly in areas slated for settlement expansion, and including the appropriation of Palestinian property through, inter alia, declarations of so-called "State lands", closed "military zones", "national parks" and "archaeological" sites to facilitate and advance the expansion or construction of settlements and related infrastructure, in violation of Israel's obligations under international humanitarian law and international human rights law;

   (c) Israeli measures in the form of policies, laws and practices that have the effect of preventing Palestinians from full participation in the political, social, economic and cultural life of the Occupied Palestinian Territory, including East Jerusalem, and prevent their full development in both the West Bank and the Gaza Strip;

8. *Calls upon* Israel, the occupying Power:

   (a) To reverse the settlement policy in the occupied territories, including East Jerusalem and the Syrian Golan, and, as a first step towards the dismantlement of the settlement enterprise, to stop immediately the expansion of existing settlements, including so-called natural growth and related activities, to prevent any new installation of settlers in the occupied territories, including in East Jerusalem, and to discard its "E-1" plan;

(*b*) To put an end to all of the human rights violations linked to the presence of settlements, especially of the right to self-determination, and to fulfil its international obligations to provide effective remedy for victims;

(*c*) To take immediate measures to prohibit and eradicate all policies and practices that discriminate against and disproportionately affect the Palestinian population in the Occupied Palestinian Territory, including East Jerusalem, by, inter alia, putting an end to the system of separate roads for the exclusive use of Israeli settlers, who reside illegally in the said territory, to the complex combination of movement restrictions consisting of the wall, roadblocks and a permit regime that only affects the Palestinian population, the application of a two-tier legal system that has facilitated the establishment and consolidation of the settlements, and other violations and forms of discrimination;

(*d*) To cease the requisition and all other forms of unlawful appropriation of Palestinian land, including so-called "State land", and its allocation for the establishment and expansion of settlements, and to halt the granting of benefits and incentives to settlements and settlers;

(*e*) To put an end to all measures and policies resulting in the territorial fragmentation of the Occupied Palestinian Territory, including East Jerusalem, and which are isolating Palestinian communities into separate enclaves and changing the demographic composition of the Occupied Palestinian Territory;

(*f*) To take and implement serious measures, including confiscation of arms and enforcement of criminal sanctions, with the aim of ensuring full accountability for and preventing all acts of violence by Israeli settlers, and to take other measures to guarantee the safety and protection of Palestinian civilians and Palestinian properties in the Occupied Palestinian Territory, including East Jerusalem;

(*g*) To bring to a halt all actions, including those perpetrated by Israeli settlers, harming the environment, including the dumping of all kinds of waste materials in the Occupied Palestinian Territory, including East Jerusalem, and in the occupied Syrian Golan, which gravely threaten their natural resources, namely water and land resources, and which pose an environmental, sanitation and health threat to the civilian population;

(h) To cease the exploitation, damage, cause of loss or depletion and endangerment of the natural resources of the Occupied Palestinian Territory, including East Jerusalem, and of the occupied Syrian Golan;

9. *Welcomes* the adoption of the European Union Guidelines on the eligibility of Israeli entities and their activities in the territories occupied by Israel since June 1967 for grants, prizes and financial instruments funded by the European Union since 2014;

10. *Encourages* all States and international organizations to continue to actively pursue policies that ensure respect of their obligations under international law with regard to all illegal Israeli practices and measures in the Occupied Palestinian Territory, including East Jerusalem, particularly Israeli settlements;

11. *Reminds* all States of their legal obligations as mentioned in the advisory opinion of the International Court of Justice of 9 July 2004 on the legal consequences of the construction of a wall in the Occupied Palestinian Territory, including not to recognize the illegal situation resulting from the construction of the wall, not to render aid or assistance in maintaining the situation created by such construction, and to ensure compliance by Israel with international humanitarian law as embodied in the Geneva Convention relative to the Protection of Civilian Persons in Time of War of 12 August 1949;

12. *Urges* all States:

(a) To ensure that they are not taking actions that either recognize or assist the expansion of settlements or the construction of the wall in the Occupied Palestinian Territory, including East Jerusalem, including with regard to the issue of trading with settlements, consistent with their obligations under international law;

(b) To implement the Guiding Principles on Business and Human Rights in relation to the Occupied Palestinian Territory, including East Jerusalem, and to take appropriate measures to help to ensure that businesses domiciled in their territory and/or under their jurisdiction, including those owned or controlled by them, refrain from committing or contributing to gross human rights abuses of Palestinians, in accordance with the expected standard of conduct in the Guiding Principles and relevant international laws and standards, by taking all necessary steps;

(c) To provide guidance to individuals and businesses on the financial, reputational and legal risks, including the possibility of liability for corporate involvement in gross human rights abuses, and abuses of the rights of individuals, of becoming involved in settlement-related activities, including through financial transactions, investments, purchases, procurements, loans and the provision of services, and other economic and financial activities in or benefiting Israeli settlements, to inform businesses of these risks in the formulation of their national action plans for the implementation of the Guiding Principles on Business and Human Rights, and to ensure that their policies, legislation, regulations and enforcement measures effectively address the heightened risks of operating a business in the Occupied Palestinian Territory, including East Jerusalem;

(d) To increase monitoring of settler violence with a view to promoting accountability;

13. *Calls upon* business enterprises to take all measures necessary to comply with the Guiding Principles on Business and Human Rights and relevant international laws and standards with respect to their activities in or in relation to the Israeli settlements and the wall in the Occupied Palestinian Territory, including East Jerusalem, to avoid the adverse impact of such activities on human rights and to avoid contributing to the establishment or maintenance of Israeli settlements or the exploitation of natural resources of the Occupied Palestinian Territory;

14. *Requests* that all parties concerned, including United Nations bodies, implement and ensure the implementation of the recommendations contained in the report of the independent international fact-finding mission to investigate the implications of Israeli settlements on the civil, political, economic, social and cultural rights of the Palestinian people throughout the Occupied Palestinian Territory, including East Jerusalem,[1] and endorsed by the Human Rights Council through its resolution 22/29, in accordance with their respective mandates;

15. *Calls upon* the relevant United Nations bodies to take all necessary measures and actions within their mandates to ensure full respect for and compliance with Human Rights Council resolution 17/4 of 16 June 2011, on the Guiding Principles on Business and Human Rights and other relevant international laws and standards, and to ensure the implementation of the United Nations "Protect, Respect and Remedy" Framework, which provides a global standard for upholding human rights in relation to business activities that are connected with Israeli settlements in the Occupied Palestinian Territory, including East Jerusalem;

16. *Takes note* of the statement of the Working Group on the issue of human rights and transnational corporations and other business enterprises in follow-up to Human Rights Council resolution 22/29;

17. *Requests* the United Nations High Commissioner for Human Rights, in close consultation with the Working Group on the issue of human rights and transnational corporations and other business enterprises, in follow-up to the report of the independent international fact-finding mission to investigate the implications of the Israeli settlements on the civil, political, economic, social and cultural rights of the Palestinian people throughout the Occupied Palestinian Territory, including East Jerusalem,[1] and as a necessary step for the implementation of the recommendation contained in paragraph 117 thereof, to produce a database of all business enterprises involved in the activities detailed in paragraph 96 of the afore-mentioned report, to be updated annually, and to transmit the data therein in the form of a report to the Council at its thirty-fourth session;

18. *Requests* the Secretary-General to report on the implementation of the present resolution, with particular emphasis on the human rights and international law violations involved in the production of settlement goods and the relationship between trade in these goods and the maintenance and economic growth of settlements, at its thirty-fourth session;

19. *Decides* to remain seized of the matter.

66th meeting
24 March 2016

[Adopted by a recorded vote of 32 to 0, with 15 abstentions. The voting was as follows:

In favour:
Algeria, Bangladesh, Bolivia (Plurinational State of), Botswana, Burundi, China, Congo, Côte d'Ivoire, Cuba, Ecuador, El Salvador, Ethiopia, India, Indonesia, Kenya, Kyrgyzstan, Maldives, Mexico, Mongolia, Morocco, Namibia, Nigeria, Panama, Philippines, Qatar, Russian Federation, Saudi Arabia, South Africa, Switzerland, United Arab Emirates, Venezuela (Bolivarian Republic of), Viet Nam

Abstaining:
Albania, Belgium, France, Georgia, Germany, Ghana, Latvia, Netherlands, Paraguay, Portugal, Republic of Korea, Slovenia, the former Yugoslav Republic of Macedonia, Togo, United Kingdom of Great Britain and Northern Ireland]

U.N. Security Council Resolution 2334 (2016)

United Nations
S/RES/2334 (2016)
Security Council
Distr.: General
23 December 2016

Resolution 2334 (2016)
Adopted by the Security Council at its 7853rd meeting, on 23 December 2016

The Security Council,

Reaffirming its relevant resolutions, including resolutions 242 (1967), 338 (1973), 446 (1979), 452 (1979), 465 (1980), 476 (1980), 478 (1980), 1397 (2002), 1515 (2003), and 1850 (2008),

Guided by the purposes and principles of the Charter of the United Nations, and reaffirming, *inter alia*, the inadmissibility of the acquisition of territory by force,

Reaffirming the obligation of Israel, the occupying Power, to abide scrupulously by its legal obligations and responsibilities under the Fourth Geneva Convention relative to the Protection of Civilian Persons in Time of War, of 12 August 1949, and *recalling* the advisory opinion rendered on 9 July 2004 by the International Court of Justice,

Condemning all measures aimed at altering the demographic composition, character and status of the Palestinian Territory occupied since 1967, including East Jerusalem, including, *inter alia*, the construction and expansion of settlements, transfer of Israeli settlers, confiscation of land, demolition of homes and displacement of Palestinian civilians, in violation of international humanitarian law and relevant resolutions,

Expressing grave concern that continuing Israeli settlement activities are dangerously imperilling the viability of the two-State solution based on the 1967 lines,

Recalling the obligation under the Quartet Roadmap, endorsed by its resolution 1515 (2003), for a freeze by Israel of all settlement activity, including "natural growth", and the dismantlement of all settlement outposts erected since March 2001,

Recalling also the obligation under the Quartet roadmap for the Palestinian Authority Security Forces to maintain effective operations aimed at confronting all those engaged in terror and dismantling terrorist capabilities, including the confiscation of illegal weapons,

2/3

Condemning all acts of violence against civilians, including acts of terror, as well as all acts of provocation, incitement and destruction,

Reiterating its vision of a region where two democratic States, Israel and Palestine, live side by side in peace within secure and recognized borders,

Stressing that the status quo is not sustainable and that significant steps, consistent with the transition contemplated by prior agreements, are urgently needed in order to (i) stabilize the situation and to reverse negative trends on the ground, which are steadily eroding the two-State solution and entrenching a one-State reality, and (ii) to create the conditions for successful final status negotiations and for advancing the two-State solution through those negotiations and on the ground,

1. *Reaffirms* that the establishment by Israel of settlements in the Palestinian territory occupied since 1967, including East Jerusalem, has no legal validity and constitutes a flagrant violation under international law and a major obstacle to the achievement of the two-State solution and a just, lasting and comprehensive peace;

2. *Reiterates* its demand that Israel immediately and completely cease all settlement activities in the occupied Palestinian territory, including East Jerusalem, and that it fully respect all of its legal obligations in this regard;

3. *Underlines* that it will not recognize any changes to the 4 June 1967 lines, including with regard to Jerusalem, other than those agreed by the parties through negotiations;

4. *Stresses* that the cessation of all Israeli settlement activities is essential for salvaging the two-State solution, and calls for affirmative steps to be taken immediately to reverse the negative trends on the ground that are imperilling the two-State solution;

5. *Calls* upon all States, bearing in mind paragraph 1 of this resolution, to distinguish, in their relevant dealings, between the territory of the State of Israel and the territories occupied since 1967;

6. *Calls* for immediate steps to prevent all acts of violence against civilians, including acts of terror, as well as all acts of provocation and destruction, calls for accountability in this regard, and calls for compliance with obli-

gations under international law for the strengthening of ongoing efforts to combat terrorism, including through existing security coordination, and to clearly condemn all acts of terrorism;

7. *Calls upon* both parties to act on the basis of international law, including international humanitarian law, and their previous agreements and obligations, to observe calm and restraint, and to refrain from provocative actions, incitement and inflammatory rhetoric, with the aim, *inter alia*, of de-escalating the situation on the ground, rebuilding trust and confidence, demonstrating through policies and actions a genuine commitment to the two-State solution, and creating the conditions necessary for promoting peace;

8. *Calls upon* all parties to continue, in the interest of the promotion of peace and security, to exert collective efforts to launch credible negotiations on all final status issues in the Middle East peace process and within the time frame specified by the Quartet in its statement of 21 September 2010;

9. *Urges in this regard* the intensification and acceleration of international and regional diplomatic efforts and support aimed at achieving, without delay a comprehensive, just and lasting peace in the Middle East on the basis of the relevant United Nations resolutions, the Madrid terms of reference, including the principle of land for peace, the Arab Peace Initiative and the Quartet Roadmap and an end to the Israeli occupation that began in 1967; and *underscores* in this regard the importance of the ongoing efforts to advance the Arab Peace Initiative, the initiative of France for the convening of an international peace conference, the recent efforts of the Quartet, as well as the efforts of Egypt and the Russian Federation;

10. *Confirms* its determination to support the parties throughout the negotiations and in the implementation of an agreement;

11. *Reaffirms* its determination to examine practical ways and means to secure the full implementation of its relevant resolutions;

12. *Requests* the Secretary-General to report to the Council every three months on the implementation of the provisions of the present resolution;

13. *Decides* to remain seized of the matter.

SECTION C

European Court of Justice

∵

Opinion of Advocate General Sharpston, Case C-79/15 P, Council of the European Union v Hamas

OPINION OF ADVOCATE GENERAL SHARPSTON
delivered on 22 September 2016[1]
Case C-79/15 P
Council of the European Union
v
Hamas

(Appeal – Restrictive measures with the aim of preventing terrorism – Maintaining individuals, groups and entities on the list provided for by Article 2(3) of Regulation (EC) No 2580/2001 – Common Position 2001/931/CFSP – Article 1(4) and (6) – Procedure – Meaning of 'competent authority' – Value of information available in the public domain – Rights of the defence – Duty to state reasons)

1. The Council of the European Union has appealed against the judgment of the General Court in Case T-400/10 (2)[2] ('the judgment under appeal') annulling a series of Council decisions and Council implementing measures in so far as, with a view to combating terrorism, they included Hamas (including Hamas-Izz al-Din al-Qassem) on the list of persons, groups and entities to whom, or for whose benefit, it is prohibited to provide financial services. The General Court annulled those decisions and measures for reasons relating to, inter alia, the insufficient statement of grounds accompanying them and the grounds on which the Council had relied for maintaining Hamas (including Hamas-Izz al-Din al-Qassem) on that list.

2. The Council submits that, in the judgment under appeal, the General Court erred in law by:
   – assessing the Council's use of information in the public domain for the periodic review of the measures adopted;

---

[1] Original language: English.
[2] Judgment of 17 December 2014, *Hamas* v *Council*, T-400/10, EU:T:2014:1095.

EUROPEAN COURT OF JUSTICE

- not concluding that the decision of competent authorities of the United States of America ('USA') constituted a sufficient basis for including Hamas on the list of persons, groups and entities with respect to whom it is prohibited to provide financial services to them or for their benefit; and
- not concluding that the decision of the competent authorities of the United Kingdom constituted a sufficient basis for including Hamas on the list of persons, groups and entities with respect to whom it is prohibited to provide financial services to them or for their benefit.

Legal Background

3. The general legal background set out at points 3 to 12 of my Opinion in Case C-599/14 P *Council* v *LTTE*, delivered on the same day as my Opinion in the present appeal, is equally relevant to the present appeal. I shall not repeat it here.

4. The Council first listed 'Hamas-Izz al-Din al-Qassem (terrorist wing of Hamas)' in the respective annexes to Common Position 2001/931/CFSP[3] and to Council Decision 2001/927/EC.[4] That group remains listed. As of 12 September 2003, the group listed appears under the name 'Hamas (including Hamas-Izz al-Din al-Qassem)'. At the time of bringing its action before the General Court, that group ('"Hamas", including "Hamas-Izz al-Din al-Qassem"') was maintained on the list as a result of Council Decision 2010/386/CFSP[5] and Council Implementing Regulation (EU) No 610/2010[6] ('the Council measures of July 2010').

5. On 13 July 2010, the Council published a notice ('the July 2010 Notice') for the attention of the persons, groups and entities on the list provided

---

3 Council Common Position of 27 December 2001 on the application of specific measures to combat terrorism (OJ 2001 L 344, p. 93), as amended.

4 Decision of 27 December 2001 establishing the list provided for in Article 2(3) of Council Regulation (EC) No 2580/2001 on specific restrictive measures directed against certain persons and entities with a view to combating terrorism (OJ 2001 L 344, p. 83).

5 Decision of 12 July 2010 updating the list of persons, groups and entities subject to Articles 2, 3 and 4 of Common Position 2001/931 (OJ 2010 L 178, p. 28).

6 Implementing Regulation of 12 July 2010 implementing Article 2(3) of Regulation (EC) No 2580/2001 and repealing Implementing Regulation (EU) No 1285/2009 (OJ 2010 L 178, p. 1). The interpretation and validity of that regulation is at issue also in Case C-158/14, *A and Others*, in which I shall deliver my Opinion on 29 September 2016.

THE PALESTINE YEARBOOK OF INTERNATIONAL LAW, VOLUME 19 (2016)   393

for in Article 2(3) of Council Regulation (EC) No 2580/2001[7] ('the Article 2(3) list').[8] In the July 2010 Notice, the Council brought to the attention of the persons, groups and entities listed in Regulation No 610/2010 that it considered that the reasons for keeping them on that list remained valid and that, accordingly, it had decided to maintain them on that list. The Council further mentioned that the persons, groups and entities concerned could submit a request to obtain the Council's statement of reasons for maintaining them on the list (unless they had already received such statement). It also informed them of their right to submit at any time a request to the Council, together with any supporting documentation, that the decision to include and maintain them on the Article 2(3) list should be reconsidered.

6. Hamas was subsequently maintained on the Article 2(3) list by the following measures:

- Council Decision 2011/70/CFSP[9] and Council Implementing Regulation (EU) No 83/2011[10] ('the Council measures of January 2011'), together with a notice published on 2 February 2011[11] ('the February 2011 Notice'). The Council sent Hamas the statement of reasons for maintaining it on that list by letter of 2 February 2011, notified to Hamas on 7 February 2011 ('the letter of 2 February 2011').

- Council Decision 2011/430/CFSP[12] and Council Implementing Regulation (EU) No 687/2011[13] ('the Council measures of July 2011'), together with a notice published on 19 July 2011[14] ('the July 2011 Notice')

---

7   Regulation of 27 December 2001 on specific restrictive measures directed against certain persons and entities with a view to combating terrorism (OJ 2001 L 344, p. 70), as last amended.

8   OJ 2010 C 188, p. 13.

9   Decision of 31 January 2011 updating the list of persons, groups and entities subject to Articles 2, 3 and 4 of Common Position 2001/931/CFSP (OJ 2011 L 28, p. 57).

10   Implementing Regulation of 31 January 2011 implementing Article 2(3) of Regulation No 2580/2001 and repealing Implementing Regulation No 610/2010 (OJ 2011 L 28, p. 14).

11   Notice for the attention of the persons, groups and entities on the list provided for in Article 2(3) of Regulation No 2580/2001 (OJ 2011 C 33, p. 14).

12   Decision of 18 July 2011 updating the list of persons, groups and entities subject to Articles 2, 3 and 4 of Common Position 2001/931 (OJ 2011 L 188, p. 47).

13   Implementing Regulation of 18 July 2011 implementing Article 2(3) of Regulation No 2580/2001 and repealing Implementing Regulations No 610/2010 and No 83/2011 (OJ 2011 L 188, p. 2).

14   Notice for the attention of the persons, groups and entities on the list provided for in Article 2(3) of Regulation No 2580/2001 (OJ 2011 C 212, p. 20).

and the statement of reasons sent by the Council by letter of 19 July 2011;

- Council Decision 2011/872/CFSP[15] and Council Implementing Regulation (EU) No 1375/2011[16] ('the Council measures of December 2011'), together with a notice published on 23 December 2011[17] ('the December 2011 Notice');
- Council Decision 2012/333/CFSP[18] and Council Implementing Regulation (EU) No 542/2012[19] ('the Council measures of June 2012'), together with a notice published on 26 June 2012[20] ('the June 2012 Notice');
- Council Decision 2012/765/CFSP[21] and Council Implementing Regulation (EU) No 1169/2012[22] ('the Council measures of December 2012), together with the Notice published on 11 December 2012[23] ('the December 2012 Notice');

---

15   Decision of 22 December 2011 updating the list of persons, groups and entities subject to Articles 2, 3 and 4 of Common Position 2001/931 and repealing Decision 2011/430 (OJ 2011 L 343, p. 54).

16   Council Implementing Regulation of 22 December 2011 implementing Article 2(3) of Regulation No 2580/2001 and repealing Implementing Regulation No 687/2011 (OJ 2011 L 343, p. 10).

17   Notice for the attention of the persons, groups and entities on the list provided for in Article 2(3) of Regulation No 2580/2001 (OJ 2011 C 377, p. 17).

18   Decision of 25 June 2012 updating the list of persons, groups and entities subject to Articles 2, 3 and 4 of Common Position 2001/931 and repealing Decision 2011/872 (OJ 2012 L 165, p. 72).

19   Implementing Regulation of 25 June 2012 implementing Article 2(3) of Regulation No 2580/2001 and repealing Implementing Regulation No 1375/2011 (OJ 2012 L 165, p. 12).

20   Notice for the attention of the persons, groups and entities on the list provided for in Article 2(3) of Regulation No 2580/2001 (OJ 2012 C 186, p. 1).

21   Decision of 10 December 2012 updating the list of persons, groups and entities subject to Articles 2, 3 and 4 of Common Position 2001/931 and repealing Decision 2012/333 (OJ 2012 L 337, p. 50).

22   Council Implementing Regulation of 10 December 2012 implementing Article 2(3) of Regulation No 2580/2001 and repealing Implementing Regulation No 542/2012 (OJ 2012 L 337, p. 2).

23   Notice for the attention of the persons, groups and entities on the list provided for in Article 2(3) of Regulation No 2580/2001 (OJ 2012 C 380, p. 6).

THE PALESTINE YEARBOOK OF INTERNATIONAL LAW, VOLUME 19 (2016)   395

- Council Decision 2013/395/CFSP[24] and Council Implementing Regulation (EU) No 714/2013[25] ('the Council measures of July 2013');
- Council Decision 2014/72/CFSP[26] and Council Implementing Regulation (EU) No 125/2014[27] ('the Council measures of February 2014'); and
- Council Decision 2014/483/CFSP[28] and Council Implementing Regulation (EU) No 790/2014[29] ('the Council measures of July 2014').

7.   The General Court described the content of the statement of reasons for the Council measures of July 2011 to July 2014 as follows:

'94   The statements of reasons for the Council measures of July 2011 to July 2014 begin with a paragraph in which the Council describes the applicant as "a group involved in terrorist acts which from 1988 onwards carried out, and acknowledged responsibility for, regular attacks against Israeli targets, including kidnapping, stabbing and shooting attacks against civilians, and suicide bomb attacks on public transport and in public places". The Council states that "Hamas mounted attacks in both 'Green Line' Israel and Occupied Territories" and that "in March 2005, Hamas declared a 'tahdia' (period of calm) that resulted in a decline in their activities". The Council continues: "However, on 21 September 2005 a Hamas cell kidnapped and later killed an Israeli. In a video statement Hamasclaimed to have kidnapped the man in an attempt to negotiate the release of Palestinian prisoners held by Israel". The Council states that "Hamas militants have taken part in the firing of rockets from Gaza into

---

24   Decision of 25 July 2013 updating and amending the list of persons, groups and entities subject to Articles 2, 3 and 4 of Common Position 2001/931 and repealing Decision 2012/765 (OJ 2013 L 201, p. 57).

25   Implementing Regulation of 25 July 2013 implementing Article 2(3) of Regulation No 2580/2001 and repealing Implementing Regulation No 1169/2012 (OJ 2013 L 201, p. 10).

26   Decision of 10 February 2014 updating and amending the list of persons, groups and entities subject to Articles 2, 3 and 4 of Common Position 2001/931 and repealing Decision 2013/395 (OJ 2014 L 40, p. 56).

27   Implementing Regulation of 10 February 2014 implementing Article 2(3) of Regulation No 2580/2001 and repealing Implementing Regulation No 714/2013 (OJ 2014 L 40, p. 9).

28   Decision of 22 July 2014 updating and amending the list of persons, groups and entities subject to Articles 2, 3 and 4 of Common Position 2001/931 and repealing Decision 2014/72 (OJ 2014 L 217, p. 35).

29   Implementing Regulation of 22 July 2014 implementing Article 2(3) of Regulation No 2580/2001 and repealing Implementing Regulation No 125/2014 (OJ 2014 L 217, p. 1).

southern Israel [and that] [f]or the purpose of carrying out terrorist attacks against civilians in Israel, Hamas has in the past recruited suicide bombers by offering support to their families". The Council states that "in June 2006 Hamas[including Hamas-Izz al-Din-al-Qassem] was involved in the operation which led to the kidnap of an Israeli soldier, Gilad Shalit" (first paragraph of the statements of reasons for the Council measures of July 2011 to July 2014). Beginning with the statement of reasons for Implementing Regulation No 1375/2011 ..., the Council states that "Hamas released [the soldier] Gilad Shalit, after holding him for five years, as part of a prisoner swap deal with Israel on 11 October 2011".

95 Then, the Council draws up a list of "terrorist activities" which, according to the Council, Hamas has recently carried out, from January 2010 (second paragraph of the statements of reasons for the Council measures of July 2011 to July 2014).

96 The Council, after expressing the view that "these acts fall within the provision of Article 1(3), subpoints (a), (b), (c), (d), (f) and (g) of Common Position 2001/931, and were committed with the aims set out in Article 1(3), points (i), (ii) and (iii) thereof", and that "Hamas (including Hamas-Izz al-Din-al-Qassem) falls within Article 2(3) (ii) of Regulation No 2580/2001" (third and fourth paragraphs of the statements of reasons for the Council measures of July 2011 to July 2014), refers to decisions which the United States and United Kingdom authorities, as is apparent from the statement of reasons and from the file, adopted in 2001 against the applicant (fifth to seventh paragraphs of the statements of reasons for the Council measures of July 2011 to July 2014). In the statement of reasons for Implementing Regulation No 790/2014 ..., the Council refers for the first time to a United States decision of 18 June 2012.

97 The decisions to which the Council refers are, first, a decision of the United Kingdom Secretary of State for the Home Department of 29 March 2001 and, second, United States Government decisions adopted pursuant to section 219 of the United States Immigration and Nationality Act ("INA") and Executive Order 13224.

98 As regards those decisions, the Council mentions the fact that, in the case of the United Kingdom decision, it is reviewed regularly by an internal governmental committee and, in the case of the United States decisions, they are subject to both administrative and judicial review.

99 The Council infers from those considerations that "decisions in respect of Hamas (including Hamas-Izz al-Din-al-Qassem) have thus

been taken by competent authorities within the meaning of Article 1(4) of Common Position 2001/93" (eighth paragraph in the statements of reasons for the Council measures of July 2011 to July 2014).

100 Last, the Council "notes that the above decisions ... still remain in force, and is satisfied that the reasons for including Hamas (including Has-Izz al-Din-al-Qassem) on the list [relating to frozen funds] remain valid" (ninth paragraph of the statements of reasons for the Council measures of July 2011 to July 2014). The Council concludes that the applicant should continue to appear on that list (10th paragraph of the statements of reasons for the Council measures of July 2011 to July 2014).'

Summary of the Procedure at First Instance and the Judgment under Appeal

8. On 12 September 2010, Hamas brought an action before the General Court challenging in essence its inclusion in the Article 2(3) list. It sought the annulment of the July 2010 notice and the July 2010 Council measures in so far as they concerned Hamas and asked the General Court to order the Council to pay the costs. Hamas subsequently applied to amend the form of order sought so as to include also the Council measures of January 2011 to July 2014. The General Court therefore treated Hamas' action as asking it to annul the notice of July 2010 and the Council measures of July 2010 to July 2014 (collectively 'the contested measures'), in so far as they concerned Hamas, and to order the Council to pay the costs. The General Court found that Hamas' action retained its object with respect to the contested measures preceding the Council measures of July 2014.[30] However, it dismissed Hamas' action as being inadmissible in so far as it sought annulment of the July 2010 notice: that notice was not a challengeable act within the meaning of Article 263 TFEU.[31]

9. The Council asked the Court to dismiss the action and to order the applicant to pay the costs. The European Commission intervened in support of the Council.

10. Hamas put forward four pleas in support of its application for annulment of the Council measures of July 2010 and January 2011. Those pleas concerned, respectively, breach of its rights of defence; a manifest error of

---

30 Paragraph 60 of the judgment under appeal.
31 Paragraph 76 of the judgment under appeal.

398 EUROPEAN COURT OF JUSTICE

assessment; breach of the right to property; and breach of the obligation to state reasons.

11. Hamas put forward eight pleas in support of its application for annulment of the Council measures of July 2011 to July 2014. Those pleas included the alleged infringement of Article 1(4) of Common Position 2001/931 (first plea); the failure to take sufficient account of the development of the situation 'owing to the passage of time' (fourth plea); the principle of non-interference (fifth plea); breach of the obligation to state reasons (sixth plea); and breach of Hamas' rights of defence and of the right to effective judicial protection (seventh plea).

12. The General Court assessed the *fourth and sixth pleas, taken together*, for annulment of the Council measures of July 2011 to July 2014.

13. The General Court first set out general considerations and the case-law (concerning the review process; the duty to state reasons under Article 296 TFEU; the scope of the Council's discretion; and the legal and factual basis of a decision based on Article 1(4) of Common Position 2001/931) against the background of which it would assess the grounds on which the Council based its measures of July 2011 to July 2014.[32] After describing the content of the statement of reasons for those measures,[33] the General Court then found that, although the list of acts of violence for the period after 2004 (in particular for the period 2010 to 2011) drawn up by the Council had played a decisive role in determining the appropriateness of maintaining the freezing of Hamas' funds, none of those acts of violence had been examined in the UK and US decisions of 2001 to which the statements of reasons referred.[34] Nor indeed could those acts have been examined in those decisions because of the dates on which they took place.[35] Furthermore, whilst the statements of reasons made clear that those national decisions remained in force, they contained no reference to more recent national decisions or the reasons on which such decisions were based (with the exception of the statement of reasons for the Council measures of July 2014, which mentioned for the first time a July 2012 US decision).[36] As regards the July 2012 US decision, the General Court found that the Council had provided no evidence disclosing how the actual reasons on which that decision was based related to the list of acts of violence set out in the statement of reasons for the Council mea-

32 Paragraphs 84 to 92 of the judgment under appeal.
33 See point 7 above.
34 Paragraph 101 of the judgment under appeal.
35 Paragraph 102 of the judgment under appeal.
36 Paragraph 103 of the judgment under appeal.

sures of July 2014.[37] The General Court also rejected as inadmissible other national decisions to which reference was made at the hearing (and were not mentioned in the statement of reasons for the Council measures of July 2014 adopted after the hearing).[38]

14. As regards the Council's claim that it was sufficient to consult the press in order to establish that Hamas regularly acknowledged responsibility for terrorist acts, the General Court found that claim, together with the absence of any reference to decisions of the competent authorities postdating the imputed acts and referring to those acts, clearly showed that the Council had based its imputation of terrorist acts to Hamas (taken into account for the period after 2004) on information which it had derived from the press, not on appraisals contained in decisions of competent authorities.[39] The General Court therefore concluded that the Council had not satisfied the requirements of Common Position 2001/931 according to which the factual basis of an EU decision freezing funds is to be derived from material actually examined and accepted in decisions of national competent authorities within the meaning of that common position.[40] The General Court found the Council's reasoning to be as follows: the Council had begun with appraisals which were in reality its own, describing Hamas as 'terrorist' and imputing to it a series of acts of violence which the Council had taken from the press and the internet; it had then stated that the facts imputed to Hamas fell within the definition of terrorist acts and that Hamas was a terrorist group within the meaning of Common Position 2001/931; only *after* those assertions had the Council referred to decisions of national authorities predating the imputed facts (at least as regards the Council measures of July 2011 to February 2014).[41] According to the General Court, the Council had no longer relied on facts that were first assessed by national authorities. Rather, the Council had itself performed the role of a competent authority within the meaning of Article 1(4) of Common Position 2001/931.[42]

15. The Council had thus contravened the two-tier system established by Common Position 2001/931. Whilst the Council may, if necessary and within the context of its broad discretion, decide to maintain a person or group on the Article 2(3) list in the absence of a change in the factual

---

37   Paragraph 106 of the judgment under appeal.

38   Paragraph 107 of the judgment under appeal.

39   Paragraph 109 of the judgment under appeal.

40   Paragraphs 110 and 112 of the judgment under appeal.

41   Paragraphs 113 to 119 of the judgment under appeal.

42   Paragraph 121 of the judgment under appeal. See also paragraph 125.

situation, any new terrorist act which the Council inserts in its statement of reasons during its review must, under that system, have been the subject of examination and a decision by a competent authority.[43]

16. The General Court also rejected the argument of the Council and the Commission that the absence of any reference to decisions of competent authorities was due to the fact that Hamas could and should have contested the restrictive measures against it at the national level.[44] It found that the Council's argument corroborated its finding that the Council had relied on information obtained from the press and the internet.[45]

17. The General Court disagreed with the Council's claim that, in any event, in the context of the present action, Hamas (in its application) did not appear to contest its involvement in terrorism. According to the General Court, the Council cannot substitute before the Court the grounds for its measures of July 2011 to July 2014 by reducing those grounds to a few factual elements which (the Council alleges) Hamas has admitted before the Court. Nor can the Court itself undertake an assessment for which the Council alone is competent.[46]

18. On the basis of those considerations, the General Court concluded that, in adopting the Council measures of July 2011 to July 2014, the Council had infringed Article 1 of Common Position 2001/931 and had breached the obligation to state reasons.[47] It therefore annulled the Council measures of July 2011 to July 2014 and also the Council measures of July 2010 and January 2011. As regards the latter category of measures, the General Court found that it was not disputed that these measures likewise contained no reference to decisions of competent authorities relating to the facts imputed to the applicant. They were therefore vitiated by the same breach of the obligation to state reasons.[48]

Claims and Submissions on Appeal

19. The Council, supported by the Commission and the French Government, asks the Court to set aside the judgment under appeal, to give final judgments in the matters that are the subject of its appeal and to order Hamas

---

43 Paragraphs 126 and 127 of the judgment under appeal.
44 Paragraph 128 of the judgment under appeal.
45 Paragraphs 129 to 131 and 141 of the judgment under appeal.
46 Paragraphs 138 to 140 of the judgment under appeal.
47 Paragraph 137 of the judgment under appeal.
48 Paragraph 141 of the judgment under appeal.

to pay the costs of the Council at first instance and in this appeal. Hamas asks the Court to dismiss the appeal and to order the Council to pay the costs incurred by Hamas at first instance and at appellate level.

20. At the hearing on 3 May 2016, the same parties presented oral argument.

21. By its *first ground of appeal*, the Council submits that the General Court erred in law in its assessment of the Council's reliance on information in the public domain for the purposes of review pursuant to Article 1(6) of Common Position 2001/931.

22. *First*, the General Court was wrong to consider that the Council must regularly provide new reasons explaining why a person or group continues to be subject to restrictive measures. That principle is contrary to the Court's judgment in *Al-Aqsa* v *Council* and *Netherlands* v *Al-Aqsa*[49] and the judgments of the General Court in *People's Mojahedin Organization of Iran* v *Council*[50] and in *Al-Aqsa* v *Council*.[51] In the first case, the Council had not been required to modify the statement of reasons over a period of almost six years. It follows that the Court accepted (implicitly) the possibility of maintaining a person or group on the list during that period if there is no new information of the competent authorities supporting delisting. Like the situation of Stichting Al-Aqsa, Hamas' proscription in the UK made it extremely difficult for Hamas to commit new terrorist acts which would give rise to new decisions within the meaning of Article 1(4) of Common Position 2001/931. The same applies as regards the US decisions. Furthermore, had Hamas challenged its proscription or had there been a review *ex officio* of those decisions, that would have resulted in new decisions.

23. *Second*, the General Court erred in rejecting the Council's use of information available in the public domain. That decision is also contrary to its own previous case-law according to which a decision of a competent authority might not be sufficient to decide to maintain a person or group on the Article 2(3) list.[52] Even in the absence of any further decision of a competent authority, the Council was entitled to maintain Hamas on that list. In the present case, the publicly available information on which the Council relied was used for that purpose only (irrespective of the fact that the Council could have maintained the listing on the basis of

---

49 Judgment of 15 November 2012, *Al-Aqsa* v *Council* and *Netherlands* v *Al-Aqsa*, C-539/10 P and C-550/10 P, EU:C:2012:711 ('the judgment in *Al-Aqsa*'), paragraphs 145 and 146.

50 Judgment of 23 October 2008, *People's Mojahedin Organization of Iran* v *Council*, T-256/07, EU:T:2008:461 ('judgment of the General Court in *PMOI*'), paragraphs 109 and 112.

51 Judgment of 9 September 2010, *Al-Aqsa* v *Council*, T-348/07, EU:T:2010:373.

52 The General Court relied on its judgment in *PMOI*, paragraph 81.

existing decisions of competent authorities). That is consistent with the Court's judgment in *Al-Aqsa* v *Council* and *Netherlands* v *Al-Aqsa*.[53] Thus, a change in the factual situation may result from a change in the legal status of the initial Article 1(4) decision or new information about the activities of the listed group. In circumstances where the original Article 1(4) decision has not been annulled or withdrawn, the relevant question in the context of a review is whether there is a reason for delisting, not whether there is a reason to re-list the person or group concerned. The General Court's reasoning also leads to the absurd result that, on the one hand, the Council's decision to maintain Hamas on the Article 2(3) list would have been valid had the Council simply relied on the initial Article 2(3) list and not referred to additional information, and, on the other hand, it was publicly known that Hamas had committed new terrorist attacks (a fact which Hamas accepted in its original application before the General Court).

24. *Third*, the General Court erred in finding that the Council had made its own factual findings, based on publicly available information, for the purposes of its review. That finding too is contrary to the Court's judgment in *Al-Aqsa* v *Council* and *Netherlands* v *Al-Aqsa*. It also raises the question how the Council is to act in circumstances where it becomes aware of acts which are clearly 'terrorist' and for which a listed person or group publicly claims responsibility. In such circumstances, the two-tier system does not require procedures to be initiated at the national level.

25. *Fourth*, the General Court erred in annulling the contested measures on the basis that the Council had referred to publicly available information. That information was relevant to deciding whether to withdraw Hamas from the Article 2(3) list. In the absence of elements in support of such delisting, the Council could decide to maintain Hamas on that list.

26. Hamas' response to the first ground of appeal is as follows.

27. *First*, Hamas disagrees with the Council that the General Court required decisions within the meaning of Article 1(6) of Common Position 2001/931 to be based on new reasons or decisions of competent authorities. Rather, the General Court insisted that the grounds of the contested measures be based on facts that had been examined by competent authorities. Furthermore, the Council could not rely on previous decisions of competent authorities without examining the facts underlying those decisions. Furthermore, Hamas cannot be faulted for not having chal-

---

53   Judgment in *Al-Aqsa*, paragraph 82.

lenged the Council's factual imputations before national courts: there were no new decisions to challenge.

28. *Second,* Hamas submits that the duty to state reasons and the need for a sufficient factual basis equally apply to decisions whereby the Council maintains a person or group on the Article 2(3) list. In its review, the Council may not assume that a person or group should continue to be included in that list. In the present case, the Council had relied on its initial listing decisions (which Hamas did not challenge). However, when Hamas was first included in the Article 2(3) list, it was not yet possible to challenge those decisions before the General Court alleging that the Council had not sufficiently stated the grounds of those decisions. In fact, the Council had never communicated precise information or parts of the file showing that decisions within the meaning of Article 1(4) of Common Position 2001/931 had been taken with regard to Hamas. Nor had the Council informed Hamas of the elements justifying its inclusion in the list. That also means that the Union Courts cannot now verify whether the facts resulting in the Council's initial listing of Hamas were sufficiently credible and had been examined by a competent authority.

29. The Council also wrongly alleges that, had it not included in the statement of reasons a list of more recent facts and additional information, its decision would nevertheless still have been valid because it was based on the initial decisions of competent authorities. That presupposes that the Council would have been justified in relying solely on information taken from those decisions. Whilst the Council had relied on a series of alleged terrorist attacks committed by Hamas(both in the contested measures and in the course of the procedure before the Court), it has not shown any evidence of those facts. Nor may the Council rely on press articles for that purpose.

30. *Third,* Hamas observes that the Council appears to criticise the General Court for having reached the (logical) conclusion that the Council had made its own factual imputations. The Council is wrong to allege that there cannot be any doubt about the terrorist character of Hamas' actions. It also has no competence, when acting pursuant to Common Position 2001/931, to characterise acts in this manner. The Council's argument that it is impossible for it to ask a judicial authority to assess new facts is not relevant because the General Court did not impose such a requirement on the Council. Nor did the General Court demand that the Council ask the UK or US authorities to proscribe Hamas again. The General Court only insisted that, when the Council relies on new facts, those facts be assessed by a competent authority.

31. *Fourth,* Hamas considers that it was insufficient for the Council merely to state that the initial national decisions remained valid. It is for the Council to assess whether Hamas continued to be characterised as terrorist in a manner that is consistent with Common Position 2001/931. Whilst the Council had referred to a US decision of 18 July 2012 in the grounds for Implementing Regulation No 790/2014, the General Court correctly found that there was nothing showing that the reasoning underlying that decision attached to the acts on which the Council relied. In so far as the Council relied only on the initial decisions, the contested measures were insufficiently reasoned.

32. By its *second ground of appeal,* the Council claims that the General Court erred in not concluding that the decisions of US authorities constituted a sufficient basis for listing Hamas.

33. *First,* a decision of an administrative authority may be a decision within the meaning of Article 1(4) of Common Position 2001/931. That has been confirmed by the Court in *Al-Aqsa* v *Council* and *Netherlands* v *Al-Aqsa*[54] as well as by the General Court in *People's Mojahedin Organization of Iran* v *Council.*[55]

34. *Second,* under Common Position 2001/931, the competent national authority is to find the facts underlying the national decision. Where the decision is not taken by a judicial authority, judicial protection is guaranteed by offering the person or group concerned the possibility of challenging that decision before the national courts and tribunals. The General Court erred by requiring that the Council should know all of the factual elements on the basis of which the US Secretary of State listed Hamas. Article 1(4) of Common Position 2001/931 does not require those elements to be communicated to the Council. Nor can the Council substitute itself for the competent authority. If the General Court's position were to be upheld, it would mean that, where a person or group challenges the listing decision before the EU Courts (rather than the national courts), it would be for the EU Courts to examine the grounds underlying the listing. Furthermore, it is not realistic to require that the information underlying the decision to proscribe at a national level must constitute the factual basis of the Council's decision to apply restrictive measures. Finally, were the US authority to review the decision in a relevant manner, it would be for the Council to take that development into account.

35. *Third,* in the present case, procedures were available under US law for challenging the decision to list Hamas as a terrorist organisation.

---

54   Judgment in *Al-Aqsa,* paragraphs 70 and 71.

55   Judgment of the General Court in *PMOI,* paragraph 144.

36. *Fourth*, Hamas never contested its listing by the US authorities.

37. *Fifth*, upholding the General Court's position would mean reversing the General Court's judgment in *People's Mojahedin Organization of Iran* v *Council*,[56] including the finding that '… the Council acts reasonably and prudently when … the decision of the competent national authority on which the Community decision to freeze funds is based may be or is the subject of challenge before the courts under domestic law [and] that institution [therefore] refuses in principle to express an opinion on the validity of the arguments on substance raised by the party concerned in support of such an action, before it knows the outcome of the proceedings. If it acted otherwise, the assessment made by the Council, as a political or administrative institution, would run the risk of conflicting, on issues of fact or law, with the assessment made by the competent national court or tribunal'.[57] Upholding the General Court's position would also imply that a person or group could block its listing by deliberately not challenging the decisions of the competent authorities before the national courts and tribunals, and that an administrative authority became the final authority on the (factual) elements of the file. That approach also results in a risk of forum shopping.

38. Hamas submits that the second ground of appeal is inadmissible because the General Court made no findings on whether the US decisions were a sufficient basis for including Hamas on the Article 2(3) list. Rather, the General Court found that the Council had based its factual imputations on information found in the press and not on decisions of competent authorities. In the alternative, Hamas argues that the second plea is also inadmissible in so far as it contests factual findings made by the General Court.

39. In the further alternative, Hamas alleges that the US decisions were not taken by competent authorities within the meaning of Common Position 2001/931 and could not be a sufficient basis for including Hamas in the Article 2(3) list. In that regard, Hamas submits, the US authorities at issue only established a list of terrorist organisations to which restrictive measures should be applied. Such decisions do not satisfy the conditions of Article 1(4) of Common Position 2001/931 (except for listing decisions taken by the UN Security Council). Furthermore, as regards specifically the decisions of authorities of third States, Hamas stresses that the principle of sincere cooperation applies between the Council and the authorities of EU Member States. Hamas insists on the need to verify whether the third State pursues the same objectives as the European Union and

---

56   Judgment of the General Court in *PMOI*, paragraphs 144 to 147.

57   Judgment of the General Court in *PMOI*, paragraph 147.

offers the same guarantees as competent authorities of Member States. Hamas contests the Council's arguments regarding the level of protection of rights of defense, the duty to state reasons and the right to an effective judicial protection under US law.

40. Hamas submits that the Council is wrong to allege that the General Court erred by finding that the Council could not rely on a US decision without having access to the facts and assessments underlying that decision. It is settled case-law that it is not sufficient for the Council to rely on a decision of a competent authority. The Council must explain why it considers a group to be a terrorist group and provide the elements showing that that classification remains relevant at the time of its review.

41. By its *third ground of appeal*, the Council submits that the General Court erred in not concluding that the UK proscription order constituted a sufficient basis for listing Hamas. Even if the Council could not rely on the US decisions, the General Court was required to examine whether the 2001 UK proscription order was a sufficient and valid basis for keeping Hamas on the Article 2(3) list. Whilst the General Court accepted that the UK order remained valid, it implicitly took the position that that decision was repealed or had become outdated. The Court has already accepted that the 2001 UK proscription order was a decision of a competent authority within the meaning of Article 1(4) of Common Position 2001/931. Furthermore, the Council was justified in relying on the 2001 UK proscription order without it being necessary to have access to the facts and assessments underlying that decision.

42. Hamas submits that the third ground of appeal is inadmissible in so far as the General Court did not find that the 2001 UK proscription order was not a sufficient basis for including Hamas in the Article 2(3) list and, in the alternative, in so far as that plea contests factual findings made by the General Court. In the further alternative, Hamas argues that the 2001 UK proscription order was not taken by competent authorities within the meaning of Common Position 2001/931 and could not be a sufficient basis for including Hamas in the Article 2(3) list. It adds that, whereas the US decision concerned Hamas itself, the 2001 UK proscription order related only to Brigades Al-Qassem.

Assessment

Preliminary Remarks

43. There is considerable overlap between the issues raised in the present appeal and those in *Council* v *LTTE*, C-599/14 P. Both Opinions should be

read together. Where relevant, I shall cross-refer to my Opinion in *Council v LTTE* in assessing the Council's grounds of appeal in this case.

44. Like the appeal in that case, this appeal in essence invites the Court to (re)consider the architecture of the mechanism through which EU restrictive measures under Common Position 2001/931 and Regulation No 2580/2001 are maintained and the role of the Member States and third States in that scheme.

45. Within that scheme, a distinction can be made between: (i) the initial listing and (ii) the decision to maintain a person, entity or group on the Article 2(3) list. As regards the first type of decision, Common Position 2001/931 lays down the procedure which the Council is to apply and the materials on which it must rely. No such rules are set out for the second type of decision. It is that second type of decision that was the subject of Hamas' action before the General Court and which is at issue in the present appeal.

46. Article 1(6) of Common Position 2001/931 provides only for regular review of the names of persons and groups on the Article 2(3) list in order to ensure that there are grounds for keeping them on the list. The central issues in this appeal are how the Council may establish that such grounds exist and what the Council must communicate to the persons or groups concerned.

47. It follows from Article 1(6) of Common Position 2001/931 that, in the absence of grounds for keeping a person or group on that list, the Council must remove or 'delist' them.[58] In that regard, it is common ground that Hamas has not submitted observations and evidence to the Council which may affect the reasons for its inclusion in the Article 2(3) list and possibly result in its delisting. In the context of a different type of restrictive measure, the Court has held that, where such observations and evidence are provided and taken into account in amending the reasons for listing a person in the decision taken in the framework of the CFSP, the amendment must also appear in the regulation adopted pursuant to the TFEU.[59]

48. In its pleadings, the Council places considerable emphasis on the fact that Hamas never challenged any of the national decisions on which the Council had relied or the Council regulations through which it was initially listed and maintained on the Article 2(3) list. However, as I see it,

---

58 Judgment of 21 December 2011, *France v People's Mojahedin Organization of Iran*, C-27/09 P, EU:C:2011:853, paragraph 72.

59 Judgment of 1 March 2016, *National Iranian Oil Company v Council*, C-440/14 P, EU:C:2016:128, paragraph 55.

review of a Council regulation involves examining whether the Council complied with applicable rules of EU law, including conditions laid down in Common Position 2001/931 and fundamental rights. Nothing in those rules makes that review dependent on whether the party concerned first challenged the decision of the competent authority before the appropriate national forum.

First Ground of Appeal
Introduction

49. The Council's first ground of appeal in essence concerns whether it may rely, in the context of a review under Article 1(6) of Common Position 2001/931, on information in the public domain.

50. That ground of appeal is based on four arguments: (i) the General Court wrongly required the Council regularly to provide new reasons justifying why the party concerned should remain subject to restrictive measures; (ii) the General Court wrongly rejected the Council's use of information available in the public domain; (iii) the General Court wrongly found that the Council had made its own factual findings, based on publicly available information, for the purposes of its review within the meaning of Article 1(6) of Common Position 2001/931; and (iv) the General Court was wrong in annulling the contested measures on the basis that the Council had referred to publicly available information.

51. In my opinion, the second and third arguments are in essence the same. I shall therefore consider them together.

Must the Council regularly provide new reasons justifying why a group remains subject to restrictive measures?

52. The Council's first argument in support of its first ground of appeal in the present case corresponds with the first argument it advanced in support of its second ground of appeal in *Council* v *LTTE*.

53. What I have said in analysing that ground of appeal in my Opinion in that case applies equally here.[60] In my view, there cannot, on the one hand, be a hard and fast rule entitling the Council to maintain a person or group on the Article 2(3) list only where there are decisions of competent authorities taken or known to the Council after the initial or previous listing. On the other hand, the initial decision(s) used as a basis for the initial listing will not always be sufficient in the context of a review. Where the

---

60   See points 77 to 92 of my Opinion in Case C-599/14 P.

Council adopts an Article 1(6) decision without relying on a new decision of a competent authority, it must be satisfied that the decision of a competent authority on which it previously relied to adopt either the initial decision or a subsequent decision to keep a person or group on the Article 2(3) list is still a sufficient basis for showing that there are grounds to continue to do so.

54. Thus, when basing itself on the facts and evidence underlying the earlier decision(s) of the competent authority (even if those decisions were repealed for reasons unrelated to those facts and evidence showing involvement in terrorist acts or activities[61]), the Council must show that the facts and evidence on which the (initial or earlier) decision(s) of the competent authority was or were based continue to justify its assessment that the person or group concerned presents a risk of terrorism and that, consequently, preventive measures are justified. Because decisions of competent authorities necessarily relate to facts preceding those decisions, it follows that the longer the period between those facts and an earlier decision, on the one hand, and the Council's new decision to maintain a person or group on the Article 2(3) list, on the other hand, the greater the obligation on the Council to verify diligently whether, at the time of its review, its conclusion continues to be validly based on that decision and the facts underpinning it.[62]

55. Where that earlier decision of the competent authority has been renewed or extended, the Council must verify on what basis that was done. It follows that the Council's analysis cannot be entirely identical to that performed when adopting an earlier Article 1(6) decision based on the same decision of a competent authority. At the very least, it is necessary to take into account the time element. That must also be reflected in the statement of reasons.

56. As I read the judgment under appeal, the General Court did *not* find that the Council must regularly provide new reasons explaining why it had decided to maintain a person or group on the Article 2(3) list. Nor do I suggest that it must do so. Rather, the General Court took issue with the Council for producing a list of acts of violence, which appeared to be determinative for its decision to keep Hamas on the Article 2(3) list, without explaining in the contested measures on what grounds it considered

---

61 That was the case in the judgment in *Al-Aqsa*, paragraphs 83 to 90.

62 As regards a different type of sanction, see, by analogy, judgment of 18 July 2013, *Commission and Others* v *Kadi*, C-584/10 P, C-593/10 P and C-595/10 P, EU:C:2013:518, paragraph 156.

410   EUROPEAN COURT OF JUSTICE

those acts to have been established and examined in decisions of competent authorities. For the General Court, that could evidently not be the case of the UK and US decisions of 2001 on which the Council relied in its statement of reasons. That appears clearly from paragraphs 101 to 112 and paragraphs 119 and 127 of the judgment under appeal. Paragraph 133 of the judgment under appeal summarises the General Court's position: it had not before it, in the statement of reasons, any references to any decisions of a competent authority relating to the factual elements used by the Council against the applicant.

57.   I consider that the General Court was accordingly justified in finding that, because there was no new or other decision of a competent authority forming a satisfactory basis for maintaining that there were grounds to list Hamas, the Council was precluded from relying on a list of terrorist attacks allegedly carried out by that organisation without those facts being shown in decisions of competent authorities.

58.   I should like to add that the Council also cannot rely on the fact that, because a group's proscription renders it difficult for that group to commit new terrorist acts, new decisions of competent authorities relating to that group become less evident. The effectiveness of a group's proscription does not exonerate the Council from its obligation to ensure that a person or group is maintained on the Article 2(3) list based on decisions of competent authorities. Furthermore, a decision of a competent authority that justified initial listing can still be relevant for subsequent listings, provided that the Council finds that (and explains why) it remains a sufficient basis for finding that there is a risk justifying the application of restrictive measures.[63]

59.   I therefore reject the Council's first argument.

May the Council rely on open source materials in deciding to maintain a group on the Article 2(3) list?

60.   The Council's second and third arguments in support of its first ground of appeal mostly correspond with the second argument which it advanced in support of the second ground of appeal in *Council* v *LTTE*. In my Opinion in that case, I concluded (for the reasons given there[64]) that the Council may not, in deciding to maintain a person or group on the Article 2(3) list, rely on grounds based on facts and evidence found elsewhere

---

63   See points 77 to 92 of my Opinion in Case C-599/14 P.

64   See points 96 to 107 of my Opinion in Case C-599/14 P.

than in decisions of competent authorities. That same conclusion and reasoning apply here.

61. I therefore find no error in the General Court's interpretation of Common Position 2001/931, set out at paragraph 110 of the judgment under appeal, according to which the factual basis for a Council decision freezing funds in a terrorism matter cannot be based on material which the Council has obtained from the press or from the internet. The General Court rightly observed, at paragraph 121 of the judgment under appeal, that allowing the Council to do so would entail that institution performing the role of a competent authority within the meaning of Article 1(4) of Common Position 2001/931. However, as the General Court explained at paragraph 127 of the judgment under appeal, under the two-tier system any new terrorist act which the Council inserts in its statement of reasons must have been the subject of an examination in a decision by a competent authority.

62. I therefore reject the Council's second and third arguments.

Was the General Court justified in annulling the contested measures?

63. The Council's fourth argument in support of its first ground of appeal corresponds with the Council's third argument in support of its second ground of appeal and the second argument in support of its third ground of appeal in *Council* v *LTTE*.

64. In my Opinion in that case,[65] I rejected the logic underlying the Council's argument that, because no account can be taken of the more recent acts as documented in the press, there had been no change in the factual situation and the LTTE could therefore be maintained on the Article 2(3) list. I explained that, where there is no other or newer decision of a competent authority (regarding other facts), the Council must nonetheless review whether, based on the facts and evidence in the decision on which it previously relied, there continues to be a risk of involvement in terrorist acts and therefore a ground for listing. That also implied that the Council should have explained why the 2001 UK proscription order continued to be a sufficient basis for its decision to continue to list the LTTE and that the General Court should have addressed that argument. The General Court's findings on whether the Council had done so were the subject of the Council's third ground of appeal in that case.

65. I take the same view here.

---

65   See points 109 to 112 of my Opinion in Case C-599/14 P.

66. First, the General Court annulled the contested Council measures of July 2011 to July 2014 because it found that the Council had infringed Article 1 of Common Position 2001/931 and breached the obligation to state reasons.[66]

67. Second, it does not necessarily follow that, because the Council could not rely on facts that it found itself, the Council could nevertheless decide to maintain Hamas on the Article 2(3) list without further examination. As I have said, in circumstances where there is no other or newer decision of a competent authority (regarding other facts), the Council must nonetheless review whether, based on the facts and evidence in the decision on which it previously relied, *there continues to be a risk of involvement in terrorist acts* and therefore a ground for listing.[67] It also implies that the Council should have explained why the 2001 national decisions in the UK and in the US continued to be a sufficient basis for its decision and that the General Court should have addressed that argument. Just as in *Council* v *LTTE*, the General Court's findings on whether the Council did so are the subject of the Council's third ground of appeal.

68. I therefore reject the Council's fourth argument.

Second Ground of Appeal

69. The Council's second ground of appeal is that the General Court erred in not concluding that the decisions of US authorities constituted a sufficient basis for listing Hamas.

70. Unlike the General Court in the judgment under appeal in *Council* v *LTTE*, the General Court did not make findings here on whether a decision of a third State may constitute a decision of a competent authority within the meaning of Article 1(4) of Common Position 2001/931 and, if so, under what conditions.

71. In my opinion, the first, third and fourth arguments advanced in support of this ground of appeal must therefore be rejected as inoperative: the General Court simply did not make the findings which the Council alleges are erroneous. Indeed, the General Court made no finding on whether the decision of a US administrative authority may be a decision within the meaning of Article 1(4) of Common Position 2001/931 (first argument). That follows clearly from reading together paragraphs 99 and 101 of the judgment under appeal. Nor did it make findings on whether reliance on such a decision should be dependent on whether the listed

---

66 See paragraphs 137 and 141 of the judgment under appeal.

67 See, in particular, point 88 of my Opinion in Case C-599/14 P.

group could and in fact did challenge, under US law, the decision to list it as a terrorist organisation (the third and fourth arguments).

72. The Council also alleges that the General Court wrongly required it to know all of the factual elements on the basis of which the US Secretary of State listed Hamas (second argument). It relies, to that effect, on paragraphs 129 to 132 of the judgment under appeal. I do not read the judgment under appeal in the same manner. At paragraph 129, the General Court reiterated the need for there to be a factual basis derived from decisions of competent authorities in order to subject a person or group to restrictive measures. That is consistent with the objective of ensuring that any person or group is included in the Article 2(3) list only on a sufficiently solid factual basis.[68] At paragraph 130, the General Court found that requirement to apply irrespective of the conduct of the person or group concerned. It also focused on the need to include, in the statement of reasons, the decisions of competent national authorities that have actually examined and established the terrorist acts which the Council takes as the factual basis of its own decisions. That is consistent with the requirement that the Council must verify whether the decision of a competent authority is sufficiently precise so as (i) to identify the person or group concerned and (ii) to establish a possible nexus (as described in Article 1(2) of Common Position 2001/931) between the person or group concerned and terrorist acts as defined in Article 1(3) of that common position.[69] Paragraphs 131 and 132 concern, respectively, the General Court's earlier finding that the Council in fact relied on information which it had itself obtained and the scope of judicial review.

73. I therefore find nothing in those paragraphs to support the view that the General Court required the Council to know all of the factual elements on the basis of which a decision was adopted by a competent authority in a third State. In fact, when read together with other parts of the judgment under appeal (in particular, paragraphs 103, 106 and 110), it becomes clear that the General Court merely (and rightly) found that the Council cannot rely on a decision of a competent authority without knowing the actual reasons on which that decision was based. As the General Court stated at paragraph 114 of the judgment under appeal, the Council has to take as the factual basis of its assessment decisions adopted by competent authorities which have taken precise facts into consideration and which have acted on the basis of those facts before ascertaining that

---

68   See also my Opinion in Case C-599/14 P, point 99 and the case-law cited there.

69   See also my Opinion in Case C-599/14 P, point 80 and the case-law cited there.

414 EUROPEAN COURT OF JUSTICE

those facts are indeed 'terrorist acts' and that the group concerned is a 'group' within the meaning of Common Position 2001/931.

74. Finally, in my opinion, the Council's fifth argument cannot support its second ground of appeal according to which the General Court erred in not concluding that the decisions of US authorities constituted a sufficient basis for listing Hamas. That argument concerns the possible consequences of the General Court's logic. However, as I have already explained, the Council has misread the relevant part of the judgment under appeal.

75. In any event, the fact that a decision of the competent authority on which the Council relies has not been challenged before a national court does not relieve the Council from its obligation to verify that, as regards its reliance on that decision, the relevant conditions under Articles 1(4) and (6) of Common Position 2001/931 are satisfied and to provide an appropriate statement of reasons.

76. I therefore reject the arguments in support of the second ground of appeal.

Third Ground of Appeal

77. The Council's third ground of appeal is that the General Court erred by not concluding that the listing of Hamas could stand on the basis of the 2001 UK proscription order. That ground of appeal corresponds with the third ground of appeal in *Council* v *LTTE*.

78. The Council's first argument is that in previous cases the General Court had already accepted that same order to be a decision of a competent authority within the meaning of Article 1(4) of Common Position 2001/931. In my opinion, that argument cannot support the third ground of appeal. The General Court made no explicit findings on the status of that decision. Nor did its reasoning suggest (either expressly or implicitly) that it had taken the view that the 2001 UK proscription order was *not* a decision of a competent authority. I also do not read paragraph 105 of the judgment under appeal as meaning that the General Court found that that order had been repealed or was no longer relevant. That paragraph formed part of the General Court's discussion of the lack of decisions of competent authorities examining and establishing the acts of violence on which the Council had relied for the period after 2004.

79. The Council's second argument is that the General Court erred in law when concluding that the 2001 UK proscription order was not, or could no longer be, a valid decision within the meaning of Article 1(4) of Common Position 2001/931 and when finding that the Council should have had

available to it all the elements that resulted in the Home Secretary adopting that order. I take the same position here as in respect of the equivalent argument in *Council* v *LTTE*.[70] In my opinion, the General Court made neither finding. Having found, at paragraph 101 of the judgment under appeal, that the list of acts of violence for the period after 2004 played a decisive role in the Council's determination of whether it was appropriate to maintain Hamas on the Article 2(3) list, the General Court focused on whether the statement of reasons referred to decisions of competent authorities examining those facts. Such decisions had necessarily to post-date those facts and could therefore under no circumstances include the 2001 UK proscription order. Furthermore, I have already explained why I consider that the Council is wrong to allege that the General Court required the Council to have before it all the elements relied upon by competent authorities when proscribing Hamas.[71]

80. That said, like the third ground of appeal in *Council* v *LTTE*, it is implicit in the Council's third ground of appeal that, having found that the Council could not rely on the list of acts of violence for the period after 2004 without those acts having been examined by decisions of competent authorities, the General Court should nonetheless have found the 2001 UK proscription order (the third ground of appeal does not concern the US decision) to constitute a sufficient basis for the contested measures.

81. My position is that set out in my Opinion in *Council* v *LTTE*.[72] Thus, I take the view that, whilst the General Court accepted that the Council had cited, in the statements of reasons for the Council measures of July 2011 to July 2014, the initial national decisions (in particular, the 2001 UK proscription order), it found that the Council had stated only that they remained in force.[73] The General Court did not draw, in express terms, any conclusions from that fact. Thus, whilst the Council is wrong to allege that the General Court erred in law by finding that the 2001 UK proscription order could not, or no longer, be a valid decision of a competent authority, it is less clear whether the General Court in fact neglected to address that question (which was clearly before it, based on Hamas' pleas alleging failure to take sufficient account of the development of the

---

70 See, in particular, points 116 to 126 of my Opinion in Case C-599/14 P.

71 See point 73 above.

72 See points 117 to 123 of my Opinion in Case C-599/14 P.

73 Paragraph 103 of the judgment under appeal. See also paragraphs 100 and 119.

situation owing to the passage of time and breach of the obligation to state reasons).[74]

82. I agree with the Council that, having found that some of the reasons could not justify the decision to keep Hamas on the list and should therefore be annulled, the General Court had to go on expressly to examine the other reasons and verify whether at the very least one of those reasons was sufficient in itself to support the decision.[75] Only if those other reasons were also not sufficiently detailed and specific to form the basis for listing could the contested measures be annulled. However, the General Court here omitted to make such findings. The General Court's reasoning was in essence limited to a finding of fact, namely that the Council merely cited the earlier national decisions and stated that they remained valid. For that reason, the third plea should be upheld and the judgment of the General Court should be set aside.

83. Fortunately, the state of the proceedings in the present case enables the Court to give, in accordance with the second sentence of the first paragraph of Article 61 of the Statute of the Court of Justice, final judgment in the matter. In the context of the fourth and sixth pleas, Hamas argued that the Council merely cited a series of facts and asserted that the national decisions were still in force. It took issue with the Council for having taken insufficient account of the development of the situation owing to the passage of time. It also complained that the Council gave no indication of the facts established against it in those national decisions.

84. I have explained elsewhere in this Opinion and in my Opinion in *Council v LTTE* why I consider that the General Court rightly concluded that the Council could not, when deciding to keep Hamas on the Article 2(3) list, rely (in its statement of reasons) on a list of new acts that had not been assessed and established by decisions of competent authorities. That leaves the question of whether it was sufficient to state in the grounds for the contested measures, either that the initial decisions of the competent authorities (in particular the 2001 UK proscription order) remained valid, or (without more) that a decision of a competent authority had been taken.

85. For the reasons which I have already explained, in particular at points 77 to 91 of my Opinion in *Council v LTTE*, I consider that that was not sufficient. I therefore conclude that the contested measures must be annulled

---

74   See paragraphs 79 and 80 of the judgment under appeal.

75   Judgment of 28 November 2013, *Council v Manufacturing Support & Procurement Kala Naft*, C-348/12 P, EU:C:2013:776, paragraph 72 and the case-law cited.

THE PALESTINE YEARBOOK OF INTERNATIONAL LAW, VOLUME 19 (2016)   417

on that ground.[76] In these circumstances, it is unnecessary to examine the other pleas advanced by Hamas at first instance.

Postscript

86. Both Hamas' application at first instance and the Council's present appeal were, quintessentially, about process rather than substance. In reaching my conclusions, I deliberately refrain from expressing any view on the substantive question as to whether conduct imputed to Hamas as assessed and established by decisions of competent authorities, warrants placing and/or retaining that group and/or its affiliates on the Article 2(3) list. This Opinion should therefore be read as being concerned exclusively with upholding the rule of law, respect for due process and the rights of the defence.

Conclusion

87. In the light of all the above considerations, I conclude that the Court should:
    – uphold the appeal of the Council of the European Union;
    – set aside the judgment of the General Court in Case T-400/10;
    – annul Council Decisions 2010/386/CFSP of 12 July 2010, 2011/70/CFSP of 31 January 2011, 2011/430/CFSP of 18 July 2011 updating the list of persons, groups and entities subject to Articles 2, 3 and 4 of Common Position 2001/931/CFSP on the application of specific measures to combat terrorism, Council Decisions 2011/872/CFSP of 22 December 2011, 2012/333/CFSP of 25 June 2012, 2012/765/CFSP of 10 December 2012, 2013/395/CFSP of 25 July 2013, 2014/72/CFSP of 10 February 2014 and 2014/483/CFSP of 22 July 2014 updating and amending the list of persons, groups and entities subject to Articles 2, 3 and 4 of Common Position 2001/931/CFSP on the application of specific measures to combat terrorism and repealing, respectively, Decisions 2011/430, 2011/872, 2012/333, 2012/765, 2013/395 and 2014/72, in so far as they concern Hamas (including Hamas-Izz al-Din al-Qassem);

---

76   In so far as some of those measures concern the Common Foreign and Security Policy, the Court's jurisdiction to do so is based on Article 24(1) TEU and the second paragraph of Article 275 TFEU.

- annul Council Implementing Regulations (EU) No 610/2010 of 12 July 2010, No 83/2011 of 31 January 2011, No 687/2011 of 18 July 2011, No 1375/2011 of 22 December 2011, No 542/2012 of 25 June 2012, No 1169/2012 of 10 December 2012, No 714/2013 of 25 July 2013, No 125/2014 of 10 February 2014 and No 790/2014 of 22 July 2014 implementing Article 2(3) of Regulation (EC) No 2580/2001 on specific restrictive measures directed against certain persons and entities with a view to combating terrorism and repealing, respectively, Implementing Regulations (EU) No 1285/2009, No 610/2010, No 83/2011, No 687/2011, No 1375/2011, No 542/2012, No 1169/2012, No 714/2013 and No 125/2014 in so far as they concern Hamas (including Hamas-Izz al-Din al-Qassem);
- order, in accordance with Articles 138(3) and 184(1) of the Rules of Procedure of the Court of Justice, the Council to bear its own costs and two thirds of the costs of Hamas (including Hamas-Izz al-Din al-Qassem) incurred in this appeal;
- order, in accordance with Articles 138(3) and 184(1) of the Rules of Procedure of the Court of Justice, Hamas(including Hamas-Izz al-Din al-Qassem) to bear its remaining costs incurred in this appeal;
- order, in accordance with Articles 138(1) and 184(1) of the Rules of Procedure of the Court of Justice, the Council to pay its own costs and those of Hamas (including Hamas-Izz al-Din al-Qassem) at first instance; and,
- order, in accordance with Articles 140(1) and 184(1) of the Rules of Procedure of the Court of Justice, the French Government and the European Commission to bear their own costs.

SECTION D

International Criminal Court

∵

Report on Preliminary Examination Actions 2016 (Excerpts)

Report on Preliminary Examination Activities 2016
14 November 2016

Palestine

Procedural History

109. The situation in Palestine has been under preliminary examination since 16 January 2015.[1]
110. The Office has received more than 86 communications pursuant to article 15 in relation to crimes alleged to have been committed since 13 June 2014 in this situation.

Preliminary Jurisdictional Issues

111. On 1 January 2015, the Government of Palestine lodged a declaration under article 12(3) of the Rome Statute accepting the jurisdiction of the ICC over alleged crimes committed "in the occupied Palestinian territory, including East Jerusalem, since June 13, 2014". On 2 January 2015, the Government of Palestine acceded to the Rome Statute by depositing its instrument of accession with the UN Secretary-General. The Rome Statute entered into force for the State of Palestine on 1 April 2015.

Contextual Background
    Gaza
112. As a result of the Six-Day War in 1967, Israel acquired control over the territory of Gaza. In September 2005, Israel completed its unilateral withdrawal from Gaza, including dismantling its settlements and withdrawing its forces. Israel has maintained that following the 2005 disengagement, it is no longer an occupying power in Gaza. By contrast, it may be argued

---

1 The Prosecutor of the International Criminal Court, Fatou Bensouda, opens a preliminary examination of the situation in Palestine, 16 January 2015.

422 INTERNATIONAL CRIMINAL COURT

that Israel nonetheless remains an occupying power as a result of the scope and degree of control that Israel has retained over the territory of Gaza – a position that the Office has previously taken in the context of the preliminary examination of the situation referred by the Government of the Union of Comoros.[2]

113. Following Hamas' electoral victory in 2006 and extension of control in 2007, the territory has been the theatre of periodic hostilities between Israel and Hamas as well as other Palestinian armed groups operating in Gaza. [25]

114. Most recently, the region was affected by a new wave of hostilities, often referred to as the 2014 Gaza conflict. On 7 July 2014, Israel launched 'Operation Protective Edge', which lasted 51 days. The declared aim of the operation was to disable the military capabilities of Hamas and other groups operating in Gaza, neutralise their network of cross-border tunnels and halt their rocket and mortar attacks against Israel. The Operation consisted of three phases: after an initial phase focussed on air strikes, Israel launched a ground operation on 17 July 2014, followed by a third phase of the operation launched on 5 August characterised by alternating ceasefires and aerial strikes. The hostilities ended on 26 August 2014 with both sides agreeing to an unconditional ceasefire.

115. Since then, different national and international bodies have conducted, or are in the process of conducting, inquiries and/or investigations into incidents that occurred during the 2014 Gaza conflict, such as, for example, the United Nations Independent Commission of Inquiry on the 2014 Gaza Conflict, the UN Headquarters Board of Inquiry into certain incidents that occurred in the Gaza Strip between 8 July 2014 and 26 August 2014, the Israel Defence Forces ("IDF") Military Advocate General (along with the General Staff Mechanism for Fact Finding Assessments), and the Palestinian Independent National Committee (established by a July 2015 presidential decree in order to investigate crimes that occurred during the conflict).

West Bank and East Jerusalem

116. As a result of the Six-Day War, Israel acquired control over the West Bank and East Jerusalem. Shortly thereafter, Israel adopted laws and orders effectively extending Israeli law, jurisdiction and administration over East Jerusalem. On 30 July 1980, the Knesset, the Israeli parliament, passed a

---

2 See ICC-OTP, Situation on Registered Vessels of Comoros, Greece and Cambodia Article 53(1) Report, 6 November 2014, paras. 25–29.

'Basic Law' by which it established the city of Jerusalem 'complete and united' as the capital of Israel. The UN Security Council and International Court of Justice, among others, have regarded the annexation of East Jerusalem as a violation of the jus cogens norm prohibiting the acquisition of territory by military force.

117. Pursuant to the Oslo Accords of 1993–1995, the Palestine Liberation Organization and the State of Israel formally recognised each other, committing to the peace talks and agreeing on a progressive hand over of certain Palestinian-populated areas in the West Bank to the Palestinian National Authority (or Palestinian Authority, PA). Under the 1995 Interim Agreement, the West Bank was divided into three administrative divisions (Area A – full civil and security control by the PA; Area B – Palestinian civil control and joint Israeli-Palestinian security control; Area C – full civil and security control by Israel).

118. The peace talks between the parties grounded to a halt in 1995 and were followed over the years by a number of negotiations including the Camp [26] David Summit of 2000, the 2002/2003 Road Map for Peace, as well as intermittent peace talks and related initiatives since 2007. To date, no final peace agreement has been reached and a number of issues remain unresolved, including the determination of borders, security, water rights, control of the city of Jerusalem, Israeli settlements in the West Bank, refugees, and Palestinians' freedom of movement.

Alleged Crimes

119. The following summary of alleged crimes is without prejudice to any future determinations by the Office regarding the exercise of territorial or personal jurisdiction by the Court. It should not be taken as indicative of or implying any particular legal qualifications or factual determinations regarding the alleged conduct. Additionally, the summary below is without prejudice to the identification of any further alleged crimes which may be made by the Office in the course of its continued analysis.

Gaza Conflict

120. The conflict in Gaza between 7 July and 26 August 2014 resulted in a high number of civilian casualties, significant damage to or destruction of civilian buildings and infrastructure, and massive displacement. According to multiple sources, over 2,000 Palestinians, including allegedly over 1,000 civilians, and over 70 Israelis, including six civilians, were reportedly killed, and over 11,000 Palestinians and up to 1,600 Israelis were reportedly injured as a result of the hostilities. Figures reported by various sources

424 INTERNATIONAL CRIMINAL COURT

differ on the number of overall casualties, the proportion of civilian-to-combatant casualties, and the proportion of civilian casualties that were incidental to the targeting of military objectives.

121. It has been reported that the conflict also had a significant impact on children, in particular. For example, reportedly more than 500 children were killed, and more than 3,000 Palestinian children and around 270 Israeli children were wounded during the conflict. In addition, several instances of child recruitment by Palestinian armed groups have been reported.

122. All parties are alleged to have committed crimes during the 51-day conflict.

Acts Allegedly Committed by Members of Palestinian Armed Groups

123. *Alleged attacks against civilians*: During the 2014 conflict, Palestinian armed groups allegedly fired around 4,881 rockets and 1,753 mortar shells towards Israel, including civilian areas. The majority of these attacks were launched against areas in Israel near Gaza, but further areas, such as Tel Aviv and Dimona were also reportedly targeted. It is reported that some of the attacks resulted in civilian casualties and damage to civilian objects in Israel. [27] In addition to the injuries and displacement caused by mortar and rocket attacks by Palestinian armed groups, Israeli civilians also reportedly suffered emotional harm and psychological trauma as a result of living under the constant threat and fear of attacks. A certain number of rockets fired by Palestinian armed groups also are alleged to have fallen short and landed within Gaza, causing civilian casualties and damage to civilian objects.

124. *Alleged use of protected persons as shields*: Palestinian armed groups allegedly launched attacks directly from or nearby areas and buildings where civilians were present at the time. For example, it is alleged that attacks were launched from, or in the immediate vicinity of, residential homes and areas, hospitals, schools (including UNRWA schools), hotels, and buildings dedicated to religion. Similarly, Palestinian armed groups are also alleged to have used such buildings for other military purposes, such as for storing weapons and ammunition, tunnel entrances, and as command and control centres. It has been alleged that Palestinian armed groups engaged in such conduct in order to shield their military operations and assets from attack.

125. *Alleged ill-treatment of persons accused of being collaborators*: It is alleged that members of the Al Qassam Brigades and the Hamas' Internal Security Forces seriously ill-treated at least 20 Palestinian civilians ac-

cused of collaborating with Israel, who were later executed (some publicly) on separate occasions between 5 and 23 August 2014.

Acts Allegedly Committed by Members of the IDF

126. *Alleged attacks against residential buildings and civilians*: It is alleged that the IDF carried out numerous airstrikes on residential buildings, resulting in some cases in injuries and killings of residents and damage to, or destruction of, family homes and other residential buildings. Notable affected areas reportedly included, among others, the Shuja'iya neighbourhood, Khan Yunis, and Khuza'a. It is also alleged that during a ground operation in Khuza'a, in certain reported incidents, civilians came under fire while trying to leave the area, and others were subjected to serious ill-treatment while being detained by IDF forces. Additionally, between 1–4 August 2014, massive bombardment of the Rafah area by the IDF allegedly caused more than one hundred civilian casualties.

127. *Alleged attacks against medical facilities and personnel*: It is alleged that during the hostilities, medical facilities, ambulances, and medical personnel at times came under attack or fire from IDF forces, either reportedly as a result of being directly targeted or due to their proximity to military targets, in some cases resulting in significant damage as well as casualties to both personnel and patients. [28]

128. *Alleged attacks against UNRWA schools*: It is reported that six UNRWA schools, serving as designated emergency shelters during the conflict, were hit by projectiles, allegedly fired by the IDF, resulting in damage to the premises as well as in some cases injuries and killings of residents and other persons present at the shelters.

129. *Alleged attacks against other civilian objects and infrastructure*: During the course of the conflict, various other civilian objects and infrastructure (such as water and sanitation installations, the Gaza power plant, agricultural fields, mosques, and educational institutions) also allegedly sustained significant damage or were destroyed, reportedly due to their proximity to targeted sites or as a result of direct attacks by the IDF.

West Bank and East Jerusalem

130. *Alleged settlement activities*: The Israeli government has allegedly led and directly participated in the planning, construction, development, consolidation and/or encouragement of settlements on West Bank territory. This settlement activity is allegedly created and maintained through the implementation of a set of policies, laws, and physical measures. Such activities are alleged to include the planning and authorisation of

settlement expansions or new construction at existing settlements, including the regularisation of constructions built without the required authorisation from Israeli authorities (so-called outposts); the confiscation and appropriation of land; demolitions of Palestinian property and eviction of residents; discriminatory use of basic infrastructure and resources, such as water, soil, grazing lands, and market; imposition of other forms of access and movement restrictions upon Palestinians; and a scheme of subsidies and incentives to encourage migration to the settlements and to boost their economic development.

131. According to Israeli official data, in 2015 a total of over 62,000 dunums (or 15,300 acres) of West Bank land were declared as "state land", namely land belonging to the State of Israel, reportedly the largest total since 2005. Additionally, according to data published by the NGO Peace Now, between January and August 2016, Israeli authorities reportedly advanced plans for a total of 2,623 new units in West-Bank and East Jerusalem, including 756 retroactive approvals of unauthorised constructions. The Israeli Central Bureau of Statistics recorded 591 new construction starts and 760 constructions completed in area C of the West Bank in 2015.

132. In the same year, the Israeli government reportedly destroyed 531 Palestinian-owned structures in the West Bank, including East Jerusalem, allegedly displacing 688 people, according to figures published by the UN Office for the Coordination of Humanitarian Affairs. An additional 889 Palestinians were reportedly displaced between 1 January and 31 July 2016 due to the demolition by Israeli authorities of 684 Palestinian-owned [29] structures, including 110 in East Jerusalem. In parallel to demolitions, Israeli authorities reportedly advanced plans for the relocation of several Palestinian Bedouin or herder communities located in Area C of the West Bank, including in the Jordan Valley and in the area located immediately east of the Jerusalem municipal boundary, so-called E-1 area.

133. _Alleged ill-treatment_: Allegations concerning ill-treatment of Palestinians arrested, detained and prosecuted in the Israeli military court system have also been reported, including, for example, allegations of systematic and institutionalised ill-treatment of Palestinian children in relation to their arrest, interrogation, and detention for alleged security offences in the West Bank.

134. _Escalation of violence_: Since the beginning of October 2015, there has been an escalation of tensions and violence in Israel and Palestine, including alleged violent attacks by Palestinian assailants against Israelis and others, resulting in killings and serious injuries, as well as alleged unlawful killings and/or excessive use of force by Israeli forces against Palestinians.

In reference to the upsurge of violence in the region, allegations have also been made concerning incitement to violence against Israelis by various Palestinian political leaders and groups.

OTP Activities

135. In the past year, the Office has considered relevant submissions and other available information on issues pertaining to the exercise of territorial and personal jurisdiction by the Court in Palestine.

136. The Office meanwhile also continued to gather and review available information from a range of reliable sources on alleged crimes committed by both parties to the 2014 Gaza conflict as well as certain alleged crimes committed in the West Bank and East Jerusalem since 13 June 2014. The OTP also closely monitored relevant developments and events in the region.

137. To date, the Office has reviewed over 320 reports as well as related documentation and supporting material. This includes publicly available information and information from individuals or groups, States, and non-governmental or intergovernmental organisations. The review process has included an independent and thorough evaluation of the reliability of sources and the credibility of information received on alleged crimes. In connection with this process, during the reporting period, the Office took a number of steps to gather further information on the methodology used by various sources and to verify the seriousness of information received, including through external verification of information such as by consulting multiple reliable sources for corroboration purposes. [30]

138. Based on information collected from multiple reliable sources, the Office has produced a comprehensive database of over 3,000 reported incidents and crimes that allegedly occurred during the 2014 Gaza conflict. This database, updated as additional or new information becomes available, has enabled the Office to identify and compare the gravest incidents alleged, to conduct preliminary crime pattern analysis and to examine particular features of the conflict and of the alleged conduct of the different parties to it, such as for example, the most affected locations, timeframes and types of targets, the different *modus operandi* employed, as well as casualty figures, among others.

139. Considering the number of allegations received which also encompass a broad range of types of alleged conduct and incidents, the Office has sought to be selective in prioritising certain alleged crimes at this stage. The alleged crimes that have been the subject of analysis to date involve complicated factual and legal assessments, such as in relation to conduct

of hostilities issues, thereby necessitating careful analysis in reference to the relevant law applicable and information available.

140. During the reporting period, the Office continued to engage with State authorities and intergovernmental and non-governmental organisations in order to address a range of matters relevant to the preliminary examination as well as specifically to seek additional information to further assess the seriousness of information in its possession and other relevant issues. In this respect, the Office held numerous meetings with a variety of NGOs, including a number of Palestinian NGOs, as well as international organisations.

141. The Office also met with senior officials and representatives of the Palestinian Government on several occasions, including in November 2015 and June and September 2016. During the reporting period, the Government of Palestine also began sending monthly reports to the Office with information on alleged on-going crimes as well as other developments relevant to the preliminary examination.

142. In March 2016, the Office conducted a mission to Amman, Jordan, where it held a round of working-level meetings with representatives of the Palestinian government and Palestinian NGOs on various issues related to the ongoing preliminary examination.

143. From 5 to 10 October 2016, the Office conducted a visit to Israel and Palestine. The visit was facilitated by the Israeli and Palestinian authorities, and conducted with the logistical support of the United Nations Special [31] Coordinator for the Middle East Peace Process.[3] The purpose of the visit was to undertake outreach and education activities with a view to raising awareness about the ICC and in particular, about the work of the Office, to address any misperceptions about the ICC, and to explain the preliminary examination process. During the visit, the Office travelled to Tel Aviv, Jerusalem, and Ramallah, where meetings were held with Israeli and Palestinian officials at the working levels. Additionally, the Office engaged with the law faculty at Hebrew University and participated in an academic event at Bethlehem University and gave several interviews to the Palestinian, Israeli and international press.

144. As publically reported earlier this year, staff members of certain organisations that have gathered information of relevance to the OTP preliminary examination, such as Al-Haq and Al-Mezan Center for Human

---

3 The Government of Israel provided facilitation without prejudice to its objections to Palestine's eligibility to accede to the Rome Statute and to the Court's exercise of jurisdiction over the situation in Palestine.

Rights, have been subjected to threats and other apparent acts of intimidation and interference. The Office takes this situation very seriously and has consulted with the organisations and persons affected as well as liaised with the Dutch authorities, as the Host State to the Court, in order to ensure that appropriate steps and measures are taken to address the situation.

Conclusion and Next Steps

145. The Office is continuing to engage in a thorough factual and legal assessment of the information available, in order to establish whether there is a reasonable basis to proceed with an investigation. In this context, in accordance with its policy on preliminary examinations, the Office will assess information on potentially relevant national proceedings, as necessary and appropriate. Any alleged crimes occurring in the future in the context of the same situation could also be included in the Office's analysis.

SECTION E

Cases

∴

Sokolow v. Palestine Liberation Organization [U.S.], August 31, 2016

15-3135(L)
Sokolow v. Palestine Liberation Organization
United States Court of Appeals for the Second Circuit

August Term, 2015
Argued: April 12, 2016
Decided: August 31, 2016
Docket Nos. 15-3135-cv(L); 15-3151-cv(XAP)

Eva Waldman, Revital Bauer, individually and as natural guardian of plaintiffs Yehonathon Bauer, Binyamin Bauer, Daniel Bauer and Yehuda Bauer, Shaul Mandelkorn, Nurit Mandelkorn, Oz Joseph Guetta, minor, by his next friend and guardian Varda Guetta, Varda Guetta, individually and as natural guardian of plaintiff Oz Joseph Guetta, Norman Gritz, individually and as personal representative of the estate of David Gritz, Mark I. Sokolow, individually and as a natural guardian of plaintiff Jamie A. Sokolow, Rena M. Sokolow, individually and as a natural guardian of plaintiff Jaime A. Sokolow, Jamie A. Sokolow, minor, by her next friends and guardian Mark I. Sokolow and Rena M. Sokolow, Lauren M. Sokolow, Elana R. Sokolow, Shayna Eileen Gould, Ronald Allan Gould, Elise Janet Gould, Jessica Rine, Shmuel Waldman, Henna Novack Waldman, Morris Waldman, Alan J. Bauer, individually and as natural guardian of plaintiffs Yehonathon Bauer, Binyamin Bauer, Daniel Bauer and Yehuda Bauer, Yehonathon Bauer, minor, by his next friend and guardians Dr. Alan J. Bauer and Revital Bauer, Binyamin Bauer, minor, by his next friend and guardians Dr. Alan J. Bauer and Revital Bauer, Daniel Bauer, minor, by his next friend and guardians Dr. Alan J. Bauer and Revital Bauer, Yehuda Bauer, minor, by his next friend and guardians Dr. Alan J. Bauer and Revital Bauer, Rabbi Leonard Mandelkorn, Katherine Baker, individually and as personal representative of the estate of Benjamin Blutstein, Rebekah Blutstein, Richard Blutstein, individually and as personal representative of the estate of Benjamin Blutstein, Larry Carter, individually and as personal representative of the estate of Diane ("Dina") Carter, Shaun Coffel, Dianne Coulter Miller, Robert L. Coulter, Jr.,

434   CASES

Robert L. Coulter, Sr., individually and as personal representative of the estate of Janis Ruth Coulter, Chana Bracha Goldberg, minor, by her next friend and Guardian Karen Goldberg, Eliezer Simcha Goldberg, minor, by her next friend and guardian Karen Goldberg, Esther Zahava Goldberg, minor, by her next friend and guardian Karen Goldberg, Karen Goldberg, individually, as personal representative of the estate of Stuart Scott Goldberg/natural guardian of plaintiffs Chana Bracha Goldberg, Esther Zahava Goldberg, Yitzhak Shalom Goldberg, Shoshana Malka Goldberg, Eliezer Simcha Goldberg, Yaakov Moshe Goldberg, Tzvi Yehoshua Goldberg, Shoshana Malka Goldberg, minor, by her next friend and guardian Karen Goldberg, Tzvi Yehoshua Goldberg, minor, by her next friend and guardian Karen Goldberg, Yaakov Moshe Goldberg, minor, by her next friend and guardian Karen Goldberg, Yitzhak Shalom Goldberg, minor, by her next friend and guardian Karen Goldberg, Nevenka Gritz, sole heir of Norman Gritz, deceased,

Plaintiffs – Appellees – Cross-Appellants, – v. –
Palestine Liberation Organization, Palestinian Authority, aka Palestinian Interim Self-government Authority and or Palestinian Council and or Palestinian National Authority,

Defendants – Appellants – Cross-Appellees,
Yasser Arafat, Marwin Bin Khatib Barghouti, Ahmed Taleb Mustapha Barghouti, aka Al-Faransi, Nasser Mahmoud Ahmed Aweis, Majid Al-Masri, aka Abu Mojahed, Mahmoud Al-Titi, Mohammed Abdel Rahman Salam Masalah, aka Abu Satkhah, Faras Sadak Mohammed Ghanem, aka Hitawi, Mohammed Sami Ibrahim Abdullah, estate of Said Ramadan, deceased, Abdel Karim Ratab Yunis Aweis, Nasser Jamal Mousa Shawish, Toufik Tirawi, Hussein Al-Shaykh, Sana'a Muhammed Shehadeh, Kaira Said Ali Sadi, estate of Mohammed Hashaika, deceased, Munzar Mahmoud Khalil noor, estate of Wafa Idris, deceased, estate of Mazan Faritach, deceased, estate of Muhanad Abu Halawa, deceased, John Does, 1–99, Hassan Abdel Rahman,

Defendants. _____

2
Before: LEVAL AND DRONEY, Circuit Judges, and KOELTL, District Judge.*
    1   The defendants-appellants-cross-appellees ("defendants")
    2   appeal from a judgment of the United States District Court for

---

*   The Honorable John G. Koeltl, of the United States District Court for the Southern District of New York, sitting by designation.

3   the Southern District of New York (Daniels, *J.*) in favor of the
4   plaintiffs-appellees-cross-appellants ("plaintiffs"). A jury
5   found the defendants – the Palestine Liberation Organization and
6   the Palestinian Authority – liable under the Anti-Terrorism Act
7   ("ATA"), 18 U.S.C. § 2333(a), for various terror attacks in
8   Israel that killed or wounded United States citizens. The jury
9   awarded the plaintiffs damages of $218.5 million, an amount that
10   was trebled automatically pursuant to the ATA, 18 U.S.C.
11   § 2333(a), bringing the total award to $655.5 million. The
12   defendants appeal, arguing that the district court lacked
13   general and specific personal jurisdiction over the defendants,
14   and, in the alternative, seek a new trial because the district
15   court abused its discretion by allowing certain testimony by two
16   expert witnesses. The plaintiffs cross-appeal, asking this
17   Court to reinstate claims the district court dismissed.
18   We vacate the judgment of the district court and remand the
19   case with instructions to dismiss the action because the federal
20   courts lack personal jurisdiction over the defendants with

3

1   respect to the claims in this action. We do not reach the
2   remaining issues.
3   _____
4   KENT A. YALOWITZ, Arnold & Porter, LLP, for Plaintiffs-
5   Appellees-Cross-Appellants.
6
7   GASSAN A. BALOUL (Mitchell R. Berger, Pierre H. Bergeron, John
8   A. Burlingame, Alexandra E. Chopin, <u>on the brief</u>), Squire Patton
9   Boggs (US), LLP, <u>for Defendants-Appellants-Cross-Appellees</u>.
10
11   David A. Reiser, Zuckerman Spaeder, LLP, and Peter Raven-Hansen,
12   George Washington University Law School, <u>on the brief</u> for Amici
13   Curiae Former Federal Officials in Support of <u>Plaintiffs-</u>
14   <u>Appellees-Cross-Appellants</u>.
15
16   James P. Bonner, Stone, Bonner & Rocco, LLP, and Steven R.
17   Perles, Perles Law Firm, <u>on the brief</u> for Amici Curiae Arthur
18   Barry Sotloff, Shirley Goldie Pulwer, Lauren Sotloff, and the
19   Estate of Steven Joel Sotloff in Support of <u>Plaintiffs –</u>
20   <u>Appellees-Cross-Appellants</u>.
21

436   CASES

22 ————————

23   John G. Koeltl, District Judge:

24

25   In this case, eleven American families sued the Palestine
26   Liberation Organization ("PLO") and the Palestinian Authority
27   ("PA") (collectively, "defendants")[1] under the Anti-Terrorism Act
28   ("ATA"), 18 U.S.C. § 2333(a), for various terror attacks in
29   Israel that killed or wounded the plaintiffs-appellees-cross-
30   appellants ("plaintiffs") or their family members.[2]

4

1   The defendants repeatedly argued before the District Court
2   for the Southern District of New York that the court lacked
3   personal jurisdiction over them in light of their minimal
4   presence in, and the lack of any nexus between the facts
5   underlying the plaintiffs' claims and the United States. The
6   district court (Daniels, *J.*) concluded that it had general
7   personal jurisdiction over the defendants, even after the
8   Supreme Court narrowed the test for general jurisdiction in
9   <u>Daimler AG v. Bauman</u>, 134 S. Ct. 746 (2014). <u>See</u> <u>Sokolow v.</u>
10   <u>Palestine Liberation Org.</u>, No. 04-cv-397 (GBD), 2014 WL 6811395,
11   at *2 (S.D.N.Y. Dec. 1, 2014); <u>see also Sokolow v. Palestine</u>
12   <u>Liberation Org.</u>, No. 04-cv-397 (GBD), 2011 WL 1345086, at *7
13   (S.D.N.Y. Mar. 30, 2011).
14   After a seven-week trial, a jury found that the defendants,
15   acting through their employees, perpetrated the attacks and that
16   the defendants knowingly provided material support to
17   organizations designated by the United States State Department
18   as foreign terrorist organizations. The jury awarded the
19   plaintiffs damages of $218.5 million, an amount that was trebled
20   automatically pursuant to the ATA, 18 U.S.C. § 2333(a), bringing
21   the total award to $655.5 million.

5

1   On appeal, the defendants seek to overturn the jury's
2   verdict by arguing that the United States Constitution precludes
3   the exercise of personal jurisdiction over them. In the

---

1   While other defendants, such as Yasser Arafat, were named as defendants in the case, they
did not appear, and the Judgment was entered only against the PLO and the PA.

2   The plaintiffs are United States citizens, and the guardians, family members, and personal
representatives of the estates of United States citizens, who were killed or injured in the terrorist attacks.

4	alternative, the defendants seek a new trial, arguing that the
5	district court abused its discretion by allowing certain
6	testimony by two expert witnesses. The plaintiffs cross-appeal,
7	asking this Court to reinstate non-federal claims that the
8	district court dismissed, and reinstate the claims of two
9	plaintiffs for which the district court found insufficient
10	evidence to submit to the jury.
11	We conclude that the district court erred when it concluded
12	it had personal jurisdiction over the defendants with respect to
13	the claims at issue in this action. Therefore, we VACATE the
14	judgment of the district court and REMAND the case to the
15	district court with instructions to DISMISS the case for want of
16	personal jurisdiction. Accordingly, we do not consider the
17	defendants' other arguments on appeal or the plaintiffs' cross-
18	appeal, all of which are now moot.
19	I.
20	A.
21	The PA was established by the 1993 Oslo Accords as the
22	interim and non-sovereign government of parts of the West Bank
23	and the Gaza Strip (collectively referred to here as
24	"Palestine"). The PA is headquartered in the city of Ramallah

6

1	in the West Bank, where the Palestinian President and the PA's
2	ministers reside.
3	The PLO was founded in 1964. At all relevant times, the
4	PLO was headquartered in Ramallah, the Gaza Strip, and Amman,
5	Jordan. Because the Oslo Accords limit the PA's authority to
6	Palestine, the PLO conducts Palestine's foreign affairs.
7	During the relevant time period for this action, the PLO
8	maintained over 75 embassies, missions, and delegations around
9	the world. The PLO is registered with the United States
10	Government as a foreign agent. The PLO has two diplomatic
11	offices in the United States: a mission to the United States in
12	Washington, D.C. and a mission to the United Nations in New York
13	City. The Washington, D.C. mission had fourteen employees
14	between 2002 and 2004, including two employees of the PA,
15	although not all at the same time.[3] The Washington, D.C. and New
16	York missions engaged in diplomatic activities during the

---

3 The district court concluded that "the weight of the evidence indicates that the D.C. office simultaneously served as an office for the PLO and the PA." Sokolow, 2011 WL 1345086, at *3.

17 relevant period. The Washington, D.C. mission "had a
18 substantial commercial presence in the United States." Sokolow,
19 2011 WL 1345086, at *4. It used dozens of telephone numbers,
20 purchased office supplies, paid for certain living expenses for
21 Hassan Abdel Rahman, the chief PLO and PA representative in the

7

1 United States, and engaged in other transactions. Id. The PLO
2 also retained a consulting and lobbying firm through a multi-
3 year, multi-million-dollar contract for services from about 1999
4 to 2004. Id. The Washington, D.C. mission also promoted the
5 Palestinian cause in speeches and media appearances. Id.
6 Courts have repeatedly held that neither the PA nor the PLO
7 is a "state" under United States or international law. See
8 Klinghoffer v. S.N.C. Achille Lauro, 937 F.2d 44, 47–48 (2d Cir.
9 1991) (holding the PLO, which had no defined territory or
10 permanent population and did not have capacity to enter into
11 genuine formal relations with other nations, was not a "state"
12 for purposes of the Foreign Sovereign Immunities Act); Estates
13 of Ungar v. Palestinian Auth., 315 F. Supp. 2d 164, 178–86
14 (D.R.I. 2004) (holding that neither the PA nor the PLO is a
15 state entitled to sovereign immunity under the Foreign Sovereign
16 Immunities Act because neither entity has a defined territory
17 with a permanent population controlled by a government that has
18 the capacity to enter into foreign relations); see also Knox v.
19 Palestine Liberation Org., 306 F. Supp. 2d 424, 431 (S.D.N.Y.
20 2004) (holding that neither the PLO nor the PA was a "state" for
21 purposes of the Foreign Sovereign Immunities Act).
22 While the United States does not recognize Palestine or the
23 PA as a sovereign government, see Sokolow v. Palestine
24 Liberation Org., 583 F. Supp. 2d 451, 457–58 (S.D.N.Y. 2008)

8

1 ("Palestine, whose statehood is not recognized by the United
2 States, does not meet the definition of a 'state,' under United
3 States and international law....") (collecting cases), the
4 PA is the governing authority in Palestine and employs tens of
5 thousands of security personnel in Palestine. According to the
6 PA's Minister of Finance, the "PA funds conventional government
7 services, including developing infrastructure; public safety and
8 the judicial system; health care; public schools and education;
9 foreign affairs; economic development initiatives in

THE PALESTINE YEARBOOK OF INTERNATIONAL LAW, VOLUME 19 (2016)   439

10   agriculture, energy, public works, and public housing; the
11   payment of more than 155,000 government employee salaries and
12   related pension funds; transportation; and, communications and
13   information technology services."
14   **B.**
15   The plaintiffs sued the defendants in 2004, alleging
16   violations of the ATA for seven terror attacks committed during
17   a wave of violence known as "the al Aqsa Intifada," by
18   nonparties who the plaintiffs alleged were affiliated with the
19   defendants. The jury found the plaintiffs liable for six of the
20   attacks.[4] At trial, the plaintiffs presented evidence of the
21   following attacks.

9

1   **i. January 22, 2002: Jaffa Road Shooting**
2   On January 22, 2002, a PA police officer opened fire on a
3   pedestrian mall in Jerusalem. He shot "indiscriminately at the
4   people who were on Jaffa Street," at a nearby bus stop and
5   aboard a bus that was at the stop, and at people in the stores
6   nearby "with the aim of causing the death of as many people as
7   possible." The shooter killed two individuals and wounded
8   forty-five others before he was killed by police. The attack
9   was carried out, according to trial evidence, by six members of
10   the PA police force who planned the shooting. Two of the
11   plaintiffs were injured.
12   **ii. January 27, 2002: Jaffa Road Bombing**
13   On January 27, 2002, a PA intelligence informant named Wafa
14   Idris detonated a suicide bomb on Jaffa Road in Jerusalem,
15   killing herself and an Israeli man and seriously wounding four
16   of the plaintiffs, including two children. Evidence presented
17   at trial showed that the bombing was planned by a PA
18   intelligence officer who encouraged the assailant to conduct the
19   suicide bombing, even after the assailant had doubts about doing
20   so.
21
22

---

4   The district court found claims relating to an attack on January 8, 2001 that wounded Oz
Guetta speculative and did not allow those claims to proceed to the jury. The plaintiffs argue
that this Court should reinstate the Guetta claims. Because we conclude that there is no personal jurisdiction over the defendants for the ATA claims, it is unnecessary to reach this issue.

440 CASES

iii. March 21, 2002: King George Street Bombing

On March 21, 2002, Mohammed Hashaika, a former PA police officer, detonated a suicide bomb on King George Street in Jerusalem. Hashaika's co-conspirators chose the location because it was "full of people during the afternoon." Hashaika set-off the explosion while in a crowd "with the aim of causing the deaths of as many civilians as possible." Two plaintiffs were grievously wounded, including a seven-year-old American boy. Evidence presented at trial showed that a PA intelligence officer named Abdel Karim Aweis orchestrated the attack.

iv. June 19, 2002: French Hill Bombing

On June 19, 2002, a seventeen-year-old Palestinian man named Sa'id Awada detonated a suicide bomb at a bus stop in the French Hill neighborhood of Jerusalem. Awada was a member of a militant faction of the PLO's Fatah party called the Al Aqsa Martyr Brigades ("AAMB"), which the United States Department of State had designated as a "foreign terrorist organization" ("FTO"). The bombing killed several people and wounded dozens, including an eighteen-year-old plaintiff who was stepping off a bus when the bomb exploded.

v. July 31, 2002: Hebrew University Bombing

On July 31, 2002, military operatives of Hamas – a United States-designated FTO – detonated a bomb hidden in a black cloth bag that was packed with hardware nuts in a café at Hebrew University in Jerusalem. The explosion killed nine, including four United States citizens, whose estates bring suit here.

vi. January 29, 2004: Bus No. 19 Bombing

On January 29, 2004, in an AAMB attack, a PA police officer named Ali Al-Ja'ara detonated a suicide vest on a crowded bus, Bus No. 19 traveling from Malha Mall toward Paris Square in central Jerusalem. The suicide bombing killed eleven people, including one of the plaintiffs. The bomber's aim, according to evidence submitted at trial, was to "caus[e] the deaths of a large number of individuals."

C.

In 2004, the plaintiffs filed suit in the Southern District of New York. The defendants first moved to dismiss the claims

15 for lack of personal jurisdiction in July 2007. The district
16 court denied the motion, subject to renewal after jurisdictional
17 discovery. After the close of jurisdictional discovery, the
18 district court denied the defendants' renewed motion, holding
19 that the court had general personal jurisdiction over the
20 defendants. See Sokolow, 2011 WL 1345086, at *7.
21   The district court concluded, as an initial matter, that
22 the service of process was properly effected by serving the
23 Chief Representative of the PLO and the PA, Hassan Abdel Rahman,
24 at his home in Virginia, pursuant to Federal Rule of Civil
25 Procedure 4(h)(1)(B) (providing that a foreign association "must

12

1 be served[ ] ... in a judicial district of the United States .
2 ... by delivering a copy of the summons and of the complaint to
3 an officer, a managing or general agent....”); see also 18
4 U.S.C. § 2334(a) (providing for nationwide service of process
5 and venue under the ATA); Sokolow, 2011 WL 1345086, at *2.
6   The district court then engaged in a two-part analysis to
7 determine whether the exercise of personal jurisdiction
8 comported with the due process protections of the United States
9 Constitution. First, it determined whether the defendants had
10 sufficient minimum contacts with the forum such that the
11 maintenance of the action did not offend traditional notions of
12 fair play and substantial justice. Sokolow, 2011 WL 1345086, at
13 *2 (citing Frontera Res. Azerbaijan Corp. v. State Oil Co. of
14 Azerbaijan Republic, 582 F.3d 393, 396 (2d Cir. 2009)).
15   The district court distinguished between specific and
16 general personal jurisdiction – specific jurisdiction applies
17 where the defendants' contacts are related to the litigation and
18 general jurisdiction applies where the defendants' contacts are
19 so substantial that the defendants could be sued on all claims,
20 even those unrelated to contacts with the forum – and found that
21 the district court had general jurisdiction over the defendants.
22 Id. at *3. The court considered what it deemed the defendants'
23 "substantial commercial presence in the United States," in
24 particular "a fully and continuously functional office in

13

1 Washington, D.C.," bank accounts and commercial contracts, and
2 "a substantial promotional presence in the United States, with
3 the D.C. office having been permanently dedicated to promoting

442 CASES

4 the interests of the PLO and the PA." Id. at *4.
5 The district court concluded that activities involving the
6 defendants' New York office were exempt from jurisdictional
7 analysis under an exception for United Nations' related activity
8 articulated in Klinghoffer, 937 F.2d at 51–52 (UN participation
9 not properly considered basis for jurisdiction); see Sokolow,
10 2011 WL 1345086, at *5. The district court held that the
11 activities involving the Washington, D.C. mission were not
12 exempt from analysis and provided "a sufficient basis to
13 exercise general jurisdiction over the Defendants." Id. at *6
14 ("The PLO and the PA were continuously and systematically
15 present in the United States by virtue of their extensive public
16 relations activities.").
17 Next, the district court considered "'whether the assertion
18 of personal jurisdiction comports with "traditional notions of
19 fair play and substantial justice" – that is, whether it is
20 reasonable under the circumstances of the particular case.'"
21 Id. (quoting Metro. Life Ins. Co. v. Robertson-Ceco Corp., 84
22 F.3d 560, 568 (2d Cir. 1996)). The court found that the
23 exercise of jurisdiction did not offend "traditional notions of
24 fair play and substantial justice," pursuant to the standard

14

1 articulated by International Shoe Co. v. Washington, 326 U.S.
2 310, 316 (1945), and its progeny. See Sokolow, 2011 WL 1345086,
3 at *6–7. The district court concluded that "[t]here is a strong
4 inherent interest of the United States and Plaintiffs in
5 litigating ATA claims in the United States," and that the
6 defendants "failed to identify an alternative forum where
7 Plaintiffs' claims could be brought, and where the foreign court
8 could grant a substantially similar remedy." Id. at *7.
9 In January 2014, after the Supreme Court had significantly
10 narrowed the general personal jurisdiction test in Daimler, 134
11 S. Ct. 746, the defendants moved for reconsideration of the
12 denial of their motion to dismiss.
13 On April 11, 2014, the district court denied the
14 defendants' motions for reconsideration, ruling that Daimler did
15 not compel dismissal. The district court also denied the
16 defendants' motions to certify the jurisdictional issue for an
17 interlocutory appeal. See Sokolow, 2014 WL 6811395, at *1. The
18 defendants renewed their jurisdictional argument in their

19   motions for summary judgment, arguing that this Court's decision
20   in <u>Gucci America, Inc. v. Weixing Li</u>, 768 F.3d 122 (2d Cir.
21   2014), altered the controlling precedent in this Circuit,
22   requiring dismissal of the case. <u>See</u> <u>Sokolow</u>, 2014 WL 6811395,
23   at *1. The district court concluded that it still had general
24   personal jurisdiction over the defendants, describing the action

15

1   as presenting "'an exceptional case,'" <u>id</u>. at *2, of the kind
2   discussed in <u>Daimler</u>, 134 S. Ct. at 761 n.19, and <u>Gucci</u>, 768
3   F.3d at 135.
4   The district court held that "[u]nder both <u>Daimler</u> and
5   <u>Gucci</u>, the PA and PLO's continuous and systematic business and
6   commercial contacts within the United States are sufficient to
7   support the exercise of general jurisdiction," and that the
8   record before the court was "insufficient to conclude that
9   either defendant is 'at home' in a particular jurisdiction other
10   than the United States." <u>Sokolow</u>, 2014 WL 6811395, at *2.
11   Following the summary judgment ruling, the defendants
12   sought *mandamus* on the personal jurisdiction issue. This Court
13   denied the defendants' petition. <u>See</u> <u>In re Palestine Liberation</u>
14   <u>Org., Palestinian Authority</u>, No. 14-4449 (2d Cir. Jan. 6, 2015)
15   (summary order).
16   The case proceeded to trial in January 2015. During the
17   trial, the defendants introduced evidence about the PA's and
18   PLO's home in Palestine. The trial evidence showed that the
19   terrorist attacks occurred in the vicinity of Jerusalem. The
20   plaintiffs did not allege or submit evidence that the plaintiffs
21   were targeted in any of the six attacks at issue because of
22   their United States citizenship or that the defendants engaged
23   in conduct in the United States related to the attacks.

16

1   At the conclusion of plaintiffs' case in chief, the
2   defendants moved for judgment as a matter of law under Federal
3   Rule of Civil Procedure 50(a), arguing, among other grounds,
4   that the district court lacked personal jurisdiction over the
5   defendants. The Court denied the motion. The defendants
6   renewed that motion at the close of all the evidence and again
7   asserted that the court lacked personal jurisdiction.
8   During and immediately after trial, the District Court for
9   the District of Columbia issued three separate decisions

444 CASES

10 dismissing similar suits for lack of personal jurisdiction by
11 similar plaintiffs in cases against the PA and the PLO. <u>See</u>
12 <u>Estate of Klieman v. Palestinian Auth.</u>, 82 F. Supp. 3d 237, 245–
13 46 (D.D.C. 2015), *appeal docketed*, No. 15-7034 (D.C. Cir. Apr.
14 8, 2015); <u>Livnat v. Palestinian Auth.</u>, 82 F. Supp. 3d 19, 30
15 (D.D.C. 2015), *appeal docketed*, No. 15-7024 (D.C. Cir. Mar. 18,
16 2015); <u>Safra v. Palestinian Auth.</u>, 82 F. Supp. 3d 37, 47–48
17 (D.D.C. 2015), *appeal docketed*, No. 15-7025 (D.C. Cir. Mar. 18,
18 2015).
19   In light of these cases, on May 1, 2015, the defendants
20 renewed their motion to dismiss for lack of both general and
21 specific personal jurisdiction. The defendants also moved, in
22 the alternative, for judgment as a matter of law or for a new
23 trial pursuant to Federal Rules of Civil Procedure 50(b) and 59.
24 The district court reviewed the decisions by the District Court

17

1 for the District of Columbia, but, for the reasons articulated
2 in its 2014 decision and at oral argument, concluded that the
3 district court had general personal jurisdiction over the
4 defendants. The district court did not rule explicitly on
5 whether it had specific personal jurisdiction over the
6 defendants.
7   The jury found the defendants liable for all six attacks
8 and awarded the plaintiffs damages of $218.5 million, an amount
9 that was trebled automatically pursuant to the ATA, 18 U.S.C.
10 § 2333(a), bringing the total award to $655.5 million.
11   The parties engaged in post-trial motion practice not
12 relevant here, the defendants timely appealed, and the
13 plaintiffs cross-appealed.
14   II.
15   A.
16   "We review a district court's assertion of personal
17 jurisdiction *de novo*." <u>Dynegy Midstream Servs. v. Trammochem</u>,
18 451 F.3d 89, 94 (2d Cir. 2006).[5]

---

5 The standard of review in this case is complicated because the issue of personal jurisdiction
was raised initially on a motion to dismiss, both before and after discovery, and as a basis for
Rule 50 motions at the conclusion of the plaintiffs' case and after all the evidence was presented. This Court typically reviews factual findings in a district court's decision on personal
jurisdiction for clear error and its legal conclusions *de novo*. <u>See</u> <u>Frontera Res.</u>, 582 F.3d at

18

1   To exercise personal jurisdiction lawfully, three
2 requirements must be met. "First, the plaintiff's service of
3 process upon the defendant must have been procedurally proper.
4 Second, there must be a statutory basis for personal
5 jurisdiction that renders such service of process
6 effective.... Third, the exercise of personal jurisdiction
7 must comport with constitutional due process principles." <u>Licci</u>
8 <u>ex rel. Licci v. Lebanese Canadian Bank, SAL</u>, 673 F.3d 50, 59–60
9 (2d Cir. 2012) (footnotes and internal citations omitted),
10 *certified question accepted sub nom.* <u>Licci v. Lebanese Canadian</u>
11 <u>Bank</u>, 967 N.E.2d 697 (N.Y. 2012), *and certified question*
12 *answered sub nom.* <u>Licci v. Lebanese Canadian Bank</u>, 984 N.E.2d
13 893 (N.Y. 2012).
14   Constitutional due process assures that an individual will
15 only be subjected to the jurisdiction of a court where the
16 maintenance of a lawsuit does not offend "traditional notions of
17 fair play and substantial justice." <u>Int'l Shoe</u>, 326 U.S. at 316
18 (internal quotation marks omitted). Personal jurisdiction is "a
19 matter of individual liberty" because due process protects the
20 individual's right to be subject only to lawful power. <u>J.</u>
21 <u>McIntyre Mach., Ltd. v. Nicastro</u>, 564 U.S. 873, 884 (2011)

19

1 (plurality opinion) (quoting <u>Ins. Corp. of Ir. v. Compagnie des</u>
2 <u>Bauxites de Guinee</u>, 456 U.S. 694, 702 (1982)).
3   The ATA provides that process "may be served in any
4 district where the defendant resides, is found, or has an agent
5 ...." 18 U.S.C § 2334(a). The district court found that the
6 plaintiffs properly served the defendants because they served
7 the complaint, pursuant to Federal Rule of Civil Procedure
8 4(h)(1)(B) (providing that service on an unincorporated
9 association is proper if the complaint is served on a "general
10 agent" of the entity), on Hassan Abdel Rahman, who "based upon
11 the overwhelming competent evidence produced by Plaintiffs, was

---

395. In this case, the parties agree that this Court should review *de novo* whether the district court's exercise of personal jurisdiction was constitutional. See Pls.' Br. at 27; Defs.' Br. at 23. In any event, the issues relating to general jurisdiction are essentially legal questions that should be reviewed *de novo*. Assuming without deciding the question, we review the district court's assertion of personal jurisdiction *de novo*.

12	the Chief Representative of the PLO and the PA in the United
13	States at the time of service." <u>Sokolow</u>, 2011 WL 1345086, at *2.[6]
14	The defendants have not disputed that service was proper
15	and that there was a statutory basis pursuant to the ATA for
16	that service of process. Therefore, the only question before
17	the Court is whether the third jurisdictional requirement is
18	met – whether jurisdiction over the defendants may be exercised
19	consistent with the Constitution.
20	**B.**
21	Before we reach the analysis of constitutional due process,
22	the plaintiffs raise three threshold issues: First, whether the

20

1	defendants waived their objections to personal jurisdiction;
2	second, whether the defendants have due process rights at all;
3	and third, whether the due process clause of the Fifth Amendment
4	to the Constitution and not the Fourteenth Amendment controls
5	the personal jurisdiction analysis in this case.
6	First, the plaintiffs argue that the defendants waived
7	their argument that the district court lacked personal
8	jurisdiction over them. The plaintiffs contend that the
9	defendants could have argued that they were not subject to
10	general jurisdiction under the "at home" test before <u>Daimler</u> was
11	decided because the "at home" general jurisdiction test existed
12	after <u>Goodyear Dunlop Tire Operations, S.A. v. Brown</u>, 564 U.S.
13	915 (2011). This argument is unavailing because this Court in
14	<u>Gucci</u> looked to the test in <u>Daimler</u> as the appropriate test for
15	general jurisdiction over a corporate entity. <u>See</u> <u>Gucci</u>, 768
16	F.3d at 135–36. The defendants did not waive or forfeit their
17	objection to personal jurisdiction because they repeatedly and
18	consistently objected to personal jurisdiction and invoked
19	<u>Daimler</u> after this Court's decision in <u>Gucci</u>. Furthermore, the
20	district court explicitly noted that the "Defendants' motions
21	asserting lack of personal jurisdiction are *not* denied based on
22	a theory of waiver." <u>Sokolow</u>, 2014 WL 6811395, at *2 n.2
23	(emphasis added).

---

6 The district court found that the defendants are "unincorporated associations." See Sokolow
v. Palestine Liberation Org., 60 F. Supp. 3d 509, 523–24 (S.D.N.Y. 2014).

21

1 Second, the plaintiffs argue that the defendants have no
2 due process rights because the defendants are foreign
3 governments and share many of the attributes typically
4 associated with a sovereign government. Foreign sovereign
5 states do not have due process rights but receive the protection
6 of the Foreign Sovereign Immunities Act. See Frontera Res., 582
7 F.3d at 396–400. The plaintiffs argue that entities, like the
8 defendants, lack due process rights, because they do not view
9 themselves as part of a sovereign and are treated as a foreign
10 government in other contexts. The plaintiffs do not cite any
11 cases indicating that a non-sovereign entity with governmental
12 attributes lacks due process rights. All the cases cited by the
13 plaintiffs stand for the proposition that *sovereign* governments
14 lack due process rights, and these cases have not been extended
15 beyond the scope of entities that are separate sovereigns,
16 recognized by the United States government as sovereigns, and
17 therefore enjoy foreign sovereign immunity.
18 While sovereign states are not entitled to due process
19 protection, see id. at 399, neither the PLO nor the PA is
20 recognized by the United States as a sovereign state, and the
21 executive's determination of such a matter is conclusive. See
22 Zivotofsky v. Kerry, 135 S. Ct. 2076, 2088 (2015); see also
23 Ungar, 315 F. Supp. 2d at 177 ("The PA and PLO's argument must
24 fail because Palestine does not satisfy the four criteria for

22

1 statehood and is not a State under prevailing international
2 legal standards."); Knox, 306 F. Supp. 2d at 431 ("[T]here does
3 not exist a state of Palestine which meets the legal criteria
4 for statehood...."); accord Klinghoffer, 937 F.2d at 47 ("It
5 is quite clear that the PLO meets none of those requirements
6 [for a state]."). Because neither defendant is a state, the
7 defendants have due process rights. See O'Neill v. Asat Trust
8 Reg. (In re Terrorist Attacks on Sept. 11, 2001), 714 F.3d 659,
9 681–82 (2d Cir. 2013) ("O'Neill") (dismissing for lack of
10 personal jurisdiction claims against charities, financial
11 institutions, and other individuals who are alleged to have
12 provided support to Osama Bin Laden and al Qaeda); Livnat, 82 F.
13 Supp. 3d at 26 (due process clause applies to the PA (collecting
14 cases)).

448   CASES

15   Third, the plaintiffs and *amici curiae* Former Federal
16 Officials argue that the restrictive Fourteenth Amendment due
17 process standards cannot be imported into the Fifth Amendment
18 and that the due process clause of the Fifth Amendment to the
19 Constitution,[7] and not the Fourteenth Amendment,[8] applies to the

23

1   ATA and controls the analysis in this case. The argument is
2 particularly important in this case because the defendants rely
3 on the standard for personal jurisdiction set out in <u>Daimler</u> and
4 the <u>Daimler</u> Court explained that it was interpreting the due
5 process clause of the Fourteenth Amendment. <u>Daimler</u>, 134 S. Ct.
6 at 751.
7   The plaintiffs and amici argue that the Fourteenth
8 Amendment due process clause restricts state power but the Fifth
9 Amendment should be applied to the exercise of federal power.
10 Their argument is that the Fourteenth Amendment imposes stricter
11 limits on the personal jurisdiction that courts can exercise
12 because that Amendment, grounded in concepts of federalism, was
13 intended to referee jurisdictional conflicts among the sovereign
14 States. The Fifth Amendment, by contrast, imposes more lenient
15 restrictions because it contemplates disputes with foreign
16 nations, which, unlike States, do not follow reciprocal rules
17 and are not subject to our constitutional system. <u>See, e.g.</u>, <u>J.</u>
18 <u>McIntyre Mach.</u>, 564 U.S. at 884 (plurality opinion) ("Because
19 the United States is a distinct sovereign, a defendant may in
20 principle be subject to the jurisdiction of the courts of the
21 United States but not of any particular State. This is
22 consistent with the premises and unique genius of our
23 Constitution."). To conflate the due process requirements of
24 the Fourteenth and Fifth Amendments, the plaintiffs and *amici*

24

1   argue, would impose a unilateral constraint on United States
2 courts, even when the political branches conclude that personal
3 jurisdiction over a defendant for extraterritorial conduct is in

---

7   The Fifth Amendment states in relevant part: "... nor shall any person ... be deprived of life,
    liberty, or property, without due process of law...." U.S. CONST. amend. V.
8   The Fourteenth Amendment states in relevant part: "... nor shall any State deprive any per-
    son of life, liberty, or property, without due process of law...." U.S. CONST. amend. XIV., § 1.

4   the national interest.[9]
5   This Court's precedents clearly establish the congruence of
6   due process analysis under both the Fourteenth and Fifth
7   Amendments. This Court has explained: "[T]he due process
8   analysis [for purposes of the court's *in personam* jurisdiction]
9   is basically the same under both the Fifth and Fourteenth
10   Amendments. The principal difference is that under the Fifth
11   Amendment the court can consider the defendant's contacts
12   throughout the United States, while under the Fourteenth
13   Amendment only the contacts with the forum state may be
14   considered." Chew v. Dietrich, 143 F.3d 24, 28 n.4 (2d Cir.
15   1998).
16   Indeed, this Court has already applied Fourteenth Amendment
17   principles to Fifth Amendment civil terrorism cases. For

25

1   example, in O'Neill, 714 F.3d at 673–74, this Court applied
2   Fourteenth Amendment due process cases to terrorism claims
3   brought pursuant to the ATA in federal court. See In re
4   Terrorist Attacks on Sept. 11, 2001, 538 F.3d 71, 93 (2d Cir.
5   2008), *abrogated on other grounds by* Samantar v. Yousuf, 560
6   U.S. 305 (2010); see also Tex. Trading & Milling Corp. v. Fed.
7   Republic of Nigeria, 647 F.2d 300, 315 n.37 (2d Cir. 1981)
8   (declining to apply different due-process standards in a case
9   governed by the Fifth Amendment compared to one governed
      by the
10   Fourteenth Amendment), *overruled on other grounds by* Frontera
11   Res., 582 F.3d at 400; GSS Grp. Ltd v. Nat'l Port Auth., 680
12   F.3d 805, 816–17 (D.C. Cir. 2012) (applying Fourteenth Amendment
13   case law when considering minimum contacts under the Fifth
14   Amendment).

---

9 The plaintiffs also point to the brief filed by the United States Solicitor General in Daimler
   to support their argument that the due process standards for the Fifth and Fourteenth
   Amendments vary. However, the United States never advocated that the Fourteenth
   Amendment standard would be inapplicable to Fifth Amendment cases and, instead, urged
   the Court not to reach the issue. See Brief for the United States as Amicus Curaie Supporting
   Petitioner, DaimlerChrysler AG v. Bauman, 134 S. Ct. 746 (2014) (No. 11-965), 2013 WL
   3377321, at *3 n.1 ("This Court has consistently reserved the question whether its Fourteenth
   Amendment personal jurisdiction precedents would apply in a case governed by the Fifth
   Amendment, and it should do so here.").

450 CASES

15   *Amici* Federal Officials concede that our precedents settle
16 the issue, but they argue those cases were wrongly decided and
17 urge us not to follow them. We decline the invitation to upend
18 settled law.[10]
19   Accordingly, we conclude that the minimum contacts and
20 fairness analysis is the same under the Fifth Amendment and the

26

1 Fourteenth Amendment in civil cases and proceed to analyze the
2 jurisdictional question.

3   **III.**
4   Pursuant to the due process clauses of the Fifth and
5 Fourteenth Amendments, there are two parts to the due process
6 test for personal jurisdiction as established by International
7 Shoe, 326 U.S. 310, and its progeny: the "minimum contacts"
8 inquiry and the "reasonableness" inquiry. See Bank Brussels
9 Lambert v. Fiddler Gonzalez & Rodriguez, 305 F.3d 120, 127 (2d
10 Cir. 2002) (Sotomayor, J.). The minimum contacts inquiry
11 requires that the court determine whether a defendant has
12 sufficient minimum contacts with the forum to justify the
13 court's exercise of personal jurisdiction over the defendant.
14 See Daimler, 134 S. Ct. at 754; Calder v. Jones, 465 U.S. 783,
15 788 (1984); Int'l Shoe, 326 U.S. at 316; Metro. Life Ins., 84
16 F.3d at 567–68. The reasonableness inquiry requires the court
17 to determine whether the assertion of personal jurisdiction over
18 the defendant comports with "'traditional notions of fair play
19 and substantial justice'" under the circumstances of the
20 particular case. Daimler, 134 S. Ct. at 754 (quoting Goodyear,
21 564 U.S. at 923); Burger King Corp. v. Rudzewicz, 471 U.S. 462,
22 476–78 (1985).
23   International Shoe distinguished between two exercises of
24 personal jurisdiction: general jurisdiction and specific

27

1 jurisdiction. The district court in this case ruled only on the
2 issue of general jurisdiction. We conclude that general
3 jurisdiction is absent; the question remains whether the court

---

10   *Amici* argue for "universal" – or limitless – personal jurisdiction in terrorism cases. This Court has already rejected that suggestion. See United States v. Yousef, 327 F.3d 56, 107–08 (2d Cir. 2003) (per curiam) ("[T]errorism – unlike piracy, war crimes, and crimes against humanity – does not provide a basis for universal jurisdiction.").

4 may nonetheless assert its jurisdiction under the doctrine of
5 specific jurisdiction.
6 A court may assert general personal jurisdiction over a
7 foreign defendant to hear any and all claims against that
8 defendant only when the defendant's affiliations with the State
9 in which suit is brought "are so constant and pervasive 'as to
10 render [it] essentially at home in the forum State.'" Daimler,
11 134 S. Ct. at 751 (quoting Goodyear, 564 U.S. at 919); see also
12 Goodyear, 564 U.S. at 924. "Since International Shoe, 'specific
13 jurisdiction has become the centerpiece of modern jurisdiction
14 theory, while general jurisdiction [has played] a reduced
15 rule.'" Daimler, 134 S. Ct. at 755 (quoting Goodyear, 564 U.S.
16 at 925). Accordingly, there are "few" Supreme Court opinions
17 over the past half-century that deal with general jurisdiction.
18 Id.
19 "Specific jurisdiction, on the other hand, depends on an
20 affiliation between the forum and the underlying controversy,
21 principally, activity or an occurrence that takes place in the
22 forum State and is therefore subject to the State's regulation."
23 Goodyear, 564 U.S. at 919 (alterations, internal quotation
24 marks, and citation omitted). The exercise of specific 28
1 jurisdiction depends on in-state activity that *"gave rise to the
2 episode-in-suit."* Id. at 923 (quoting Int'l Shoe, 326 U.S. at
3 317) (emphasis in original). In certain circumstances, the
4 "commission of certain 'single or occasional acts' in a State
5 may be sufficient to render a corporation answerable in that
6 State with respect to those acts, though not with respect to
7 matters unrelated to the forum connections." Id. (quoting Int'l
8 Shoe, 326 U.S. at 318).

9 **A.**

10 The district court concluded that it had general
11 jurisdiction over the defendants; however, that conclusion
12 relies on a misreading of the Supreme Court's decision in
13 Daimler.
14 In Daimler, the plaintiffs asserted claims under the Alien
15 Tort Statute and the Torture Victim Protection Act of 1991, see
16 28 U.S.C. §§ 1350 & note, as well as other claims, arising from
17 alleged torture that was committed in Argentina by the
18 Argentinian government with the collaboration of an Argentina-
19 based subsidiary of the German corporate defendant. See

452   CASES

20 Daimler, 134 S. Ct. at 750–52. The Supreme Court rejected the
21 argument that the California federal court could exercise
22 general personal jurisdiction over the German corporation based
23 on the continuous activities in California of the German
24 corporation's indirect United States subsidiary. See id. at

29

1   751. Daimler concluded that the German corporate parent, which
2   was not incorporated in California and did not have its
3   principal place of business in California, could not be
4   considered to be "at home in California" and subject to general
5   jurisdiction there. Id. at 762.
6   Daimler analogized its "at-home test" to that of an
7   individual's domicile. "[F]or a corporation, it is an equivalent
8   place, one in which the corporation is fairly regarded as at
9   home. With respect to a corporation, the place of incorporation
10 and principal place of business are paradigm bases for general
11 jurisdiction." Id. at 760 (alterations, internal quotation
12 marks, and citations omitted).
13   As an initial matter, while Daimler involved corporations,
14 and neither the PA nor the PLO is a corporation – the PA is a
15 non-sovereign government and the PLO is a foreign agent, and
16 both are unincorporated associations, see Part I.A – Daimler's
17 reasoning was based on an analogy to general jurisdiction over
18 individuals, and there is no reason to invent a different test
19 for general personal jurisdiction depending on whether the
20 defendant is an individual, a corporation, or another entity.
21 Indeed, in Gucci this Court relied on Daimler when it found
22 there was no general personal jurisdiction over the Bank of
23 China, a non-party bank that was incorporated and headquartered
24 in China and owned by the Chinese government. The Court

30

1   described the Daimler test as applicable to "entities."
2   "General, all-purpose jurisdiction permits a court to hear 'any
3   and all claims' against an *entity*." Gucci, 768 F.3d at 134
4   (emphasis added); see id. at 134 n.13 ("The essence of general
5   personal jurisdiction is the ability to entertain 'any and all
6   claims' against an entity based solely on the entity's
7   activities in the forum, rather than on the particulars of the
8   case before the court."). Consequently, we consider the PLO and
9   the PA entities subject to the Daimler test for general

10   jurisdiction. See Klieman, 82 F. Supp. 3d at 245–46; Livnat, 82
11   F. Supp. 3d at 28; Safra, 82 F. Supp. 3d at 46.
12   Pursuant to Daimler, the question becomes, where are the PA
13   and PLO "'fairly regarded as at home'"? 134 S. Ct. at 761
14   (quoting Goodyear, 564 U.S. at 924). The overwhelming evidence
15   shows that the defendants are "at home" in Palestine, where they
16   govern. Palestine is the central seat of government for the PA
17   and PLO. The PA's authority is limited to the West Bank and
18   Gaza, and it has no independently operated offices anywhere
19   else. All PA governmental ministries, the Palestinian
20   president, the Parliament, and the Palestinian security services
21   reside in Palestine.
22   As the District Court for the District of Columbia
23   observed, "[i]t is common sense that the single ascertainable
24   place where a government such a[s] the Palestinian Authority

31

1   should be amenable to suit for all purposes is the place where
2   it governs. Here, that place is the West Bank, not the United
3   States." Livnat, 82 F. Supp. 3d at 30; see also Safra, 82 F.
4   Supp. 3d at 48. The same analysis applies equally to the PLO,
5   which during the relevant period maintained its headquarters in
6   Palestine and Amman, Jordan. See Klieman, 82 F. Supp. 3d at 245
7   ("Defendants' alleged contacts ... do not suffice to render
8   the PA and the PLO 'essentially at home' in the United States.")
9   The activities of the defendants' mission in Washington,
10   D.C. – which the district court concluded simultaneously served
11   as an office for the PLO and the PA, see Sokolow, 2011 WL
12   1345086, at *3 – were limited to maintaining an office in
13   Washington, promoting the Palestinian cause in speeches and
14   media appearances, and retaining a lobbying firm. See id. at
15   *4.
16   These contacts with the United States do not render the PA
17   and the PLO "essentially at home" in the United States. See
18   Daimler, 134 S. Ct. at 754. The commercial contacts that the
19   district court found supported general jurisdiction are like
20   those rejected as insufficient by the Supreme Court in Daimler.
21   In Daimler, the Supreme Court held as "unacceptably grasping" a
22   formulation that allowed for "the exercise of general
23   jurisdiction in every State in which a corporation 'engages in a
24   substantial, continuous, and systematic course of business.'"

32

134 S. Ct. at 761. The Supreme Court found that a court in California could not exercise general personal jurisdiction over the German parent company even though that company's indirect subsidiary was the largest supplier of luxury vehicles to the California market. Id. at 752. The Supreme Court deemed Daimler's contacts with California "slim" and concluded that they would "hardly render it at home" in California. Id. at 760.

Daimler's contacts with California were substantially greater than the defendants' contacts with the United States in this case. But still the Supreme Court rejected the proposition that Daimler should be subjected to general personal jurisdiction in California for events that occurred anywhere in the world. Such a regime would allow entities to be sued in many jurisdictions, not just the jurisdictions where the entities were centered, for worldwide events unrelated to the jurisdiction where suit was brought. The Supreme Court found such a conception of general personal jurisdiction to be incompatible with due process. The Supreme Court explained:

General jurisdiction ... calls for an appraisal of a corporation's activities in their entirety, nationwide and worldwide. A corporation that operates in many places can scarcely be deemed at home in all of them. Otherwise, "at home" would be synonymous with "doing business" tests framed before specific jurisdiction evolved in the United States. Nothing in International Shoe and its progeny suggests that "a particular quantum of local activity" should give a

33

State authority over a "far larger quantum of ... activity" having no connection to any in-state activity.

Id. at 762 n.20 (internal citations omitted). Regardless of the commercial contacts occasioned by the defendants' Washington, D.C. mission, there is no doubt that the "far larger quantum" of the defendants' activities took place in Palestine.

The district court held that the record before it was "insufficient to conclude that either defendant is 'at home' in

11 a particular jurisdiction other than the United States."
12 Sokolow, 2014 WL 6811395, at *2. That conclusion is not
13 supported by the record. The evidence demonstrates that the
14 defendants are "at home" in *Palestine*, where these entities are
15 headquartered and from where they are directed. See Daimler,
16 134 S. Ct. at 762 n.20.[11]
17 The district court also erred in placing the burden on the
18 defendants to prove that there exists "an alternative forum
19 where Plaintiffs' claims could be brought, and where the foreign
20 court could grant a substantially similar remedy." Sokolow,
21 2011 WL 1345086, at *7. Daimler imposes no such burden. In
22 fact, it is the plaintiff's burden to establish that the court
23 has personal jurisdiction over the defendants. See Koehler v.

34

1 Bank of Bermuda Ltd., 101 F.3d 863, 865 (2d Cir. 1996) ("[T]he
2 plaintiff bears the ultimate burden of establishing jurisdiction
3 over the defendant by a preponderance of evidence....");
4 Metro. Life Ins., 84 F.3d at 566–67; see also Klieman, 82 F.
5 Supp. 3d at 243; Livnat, 82 F. Supp. 3d at 30; Safra, 82 F.
6 Supp. 3d at 49.[12]
7 Finally, the district court did not dispute the defendants'
8 ties to Palestine but concluded that the court had general
9 jurisdiction pursuant to an "exception" that the Supreme Court
10 alluded to in a footnote in Daimler. In Daimler, the Supreme
11 Court did not "foreclose the possibility that in an exceptional
12 case, a corporation's operations in a forum other than its
13 formal place of incorporation or principal place of business may
14 be so substantial and of such a nature as to render the
15 corporation at home in that State." 134 S. Ct. at 761 n.19

---

11 It appears that the district court, when considering where the defendants were "at home," limited its inquiry to areas that are within a sovereign nation. We see no basis in precedent for this limitation.

12 The district court's focus on the importance of identifying an alternative forum may have been borrowed inappositely from *forum non conveniens* jurisprudence, pursuant to which a court considers (1) the degree of deference to be afforded to the plaintiff's choice of forum; (2) whether there is an adequate alternative forum for adjudicating the dispute; and (3) whether the balance of private and public interests tips in favor of adjudication in one forum or the other. See Norex Petroleum Ltd. v. Access Indus., Inc., 416 F.3d 146, 153 (2d Cir. 2005). However, that is not the test for general jurisdiction under Daimler, 134 S. Ct. at 762 n.20.

456 CASES

16 (citing <u>Perkins v. Benguet Consol. Mining Co.</u>, 342 U.S. 437,
17 447–48 (1952)).

35

1   <u>Daimler</u> analyzed the 1952 <u>Perkins</u> case, "'the textbook case
2 of general jurisdiction appropriately exercised over a foreign
3 corporation that has not consented to suit in the forum.'" <u>Id</u>.
4 at 755–56 (quoting <u>Goodyear</u>, 564 U.S. at 928). The defendant in
5 <u>Perkins</u> was a company, Benguet Consolidated Mining Company
6 ("Benguet"), which was incorporated under the laws of the
7 Philippines, where it operated gold and silver mines. During
8 World War II, the Japanese occupied the Philippines, and
9 Benguet's president relocated to Ohio, where he kept an office,
10 maintained the company's files, and oversaw the company's
11 activities. <u>Perkins</u>, 342 U.S. at 447–48. The plaintiff, a
12 nonresident of Ohio, sued Benguet in a state court in Ohio on a
13 claim that neither arose in Ohio nor related to the
14 corporation's activities in Ohio, but the Supreme Court
15 nevertheless held that the Ohio courts could constitutionally
16 exercise general personal jurisdiction over the defendant. <u>Id</u>.
17 at 438, 440. As the Supreme Court later observed: "'Ohio was
18 the corporation's principal, if temporary, place of business.'"
19 Daimler, 134 S. Ct. at 756 (quoting <u>Keeton v. Hustler Magazine</u>,
20 <u>Inc.</u>, 465 U.S. 770, 780 n.11 (1984)).
21 Such exceptional circumstances did not exist in <u>Daimler</u>,
22 id. at 761 n.19, or in <u>Gucci</u>. In <u>Gucci</u>, this Court held that,
23 while a nonparty bank had branch offices in the forum, it was
24 not an "exceptional case" in which to exercise general personal

36

1 jurisdiction where the bank was incorporated and headquartered
2 elsewhere, and its contacts were not "'so continuous and
3 systematic as to render [it] essentially at home in the forum.'"
4 768 F.3d at 135 (quoting <u>Daimler</u>, 134 S. Ct. at 761 n.19).
5   The defendants' activities in this case, as with those of
6 the defendants in <u>Daimler</u> and <u>Gucci</u>, "plainly do not approach"
7 the required level of contact to qualify as "exceptional."
8 <u>Daimler</u>, 134 S. Ct. at 761 & n.19. The PLO and PA have not
9 transported their principle "home" to the United States, even
10 temporarily, as the defendant had in <u>Perkins</u>. <u>See</u> <u>Brown v.</u>
11 <u>Lockheed Martin Corp.</u>, 814 F.3d 619, 628–30 (2d Cir. 2016).

12 Accordingly, pursuant to the Supreme Court's recent
13 decision in Daimler, the district court could not properly
14 exercise general personal jurisdiction over the defendants.

15 **B.**

16 The district court did not rule explicitly on whether it
17 had specific personal jurisdiction over the defendants, but the
18 question was sufficiently briefed and argued to allow us to
19 reach that issue.

20 "The inquiry whether a forum State may assert specific
21 jurisdiction over a nonresident defendant focuses on the
22 relationship among the defendant, the forum, and the litigation.
23 For a State to exercise jurisdiction consistent with due
24 process, the defendant's suit-related conduct must create a

37

1 substantial connection with the forum State." Walden v. Fiore,
2 134 S. Ct. 1115, 1121 (2014) (internal quotation marks and
3 citations omitted). The relationship between the defendant and
4 the forum "must arise out of contacts that the 'defendant
5 *himself*' creates with the forum." Id. at 1122 (citing Burger
6 King, 471 U.S. at 475) (emphasis in original). The "'minimum
7 contacts' analysis looks to the defendant's contacts with the
8 forum State itself, not the defendant's contacts with persons
9 who reside there." Id. And the "same principles apply when
10 intentional torts are involved." Id. at 1123.

11 The question in this case is whether the defendants' suit –
12 related conduct – their role in the six terror attacks at issue –
13 creates a substantial connection with the forum State pursuant
14 to the ATA. The relevant "suit-related conduct" by the
15 defendants was the conduct that could have subjected them to
16 liability under the ATA. On its face, the conduct in this case
17 did not involve the defendants' conduct in the United States in
18 violation of the ATA. While the plaintiff-victims were United
19 States citizens, the terrorist attacks occurred in and around
20 Jerusalem, and the defendants' activities in violation of the
21 ATA occurred outside the United States.

22 The ATA provides:

23 Any national of the United States injured in his or
24 her person, property, or business by reason of an act
25 of international terrorism, or his or her estate,

38

1   survivors, or heirs, may sue therefor in any
2   appropriate district court of the United States and
3   shall recover threefold the damages he or she sustains
4   and the cost of the suit, including attorney's fees.
5
6   18 U.S.C. § 2333(a)
7   To prevail under the ATA, a plaintiff must prove "three
8   formal elements: unlawful *action*, the requisite *mental state*,
9   and *causation*." Sokolow, 60 F. Supp. 3d at 514 (quoting Gill v.
10 Arab Bank, PLC, 893 F. Supp. 2d 542, 553 (E.D.N.Y. 2012))
11 (emphasis in original).
12   To establish an "unlawful action," the plaintiffs must show
13 that their injuries resulted from an act of "international
14 terrorism." The ATA defines "international terrorism" as
15 activities that, among other things, "involve violent acts or
16 acts dangerous to human life that are a violation of the
17 criminal laws of the United States or of any State, or that
18 would be a criminal violation if committed within the
19 jurisdiction of the United States or of any State." 18 U.S.C.
20 § 2331(1)(A). The acts must also appear to be intended "(i) to
21 intimidate or coerce a civilian population; (ii) to influence
22 the policy of a government by intimidation or coercion; or
23 (iii) to affect the conduct of a government by mass destruction,
24 assassination, or kidnapping." 18 U.S.C. § 2331(1)(B)(i)-(iii).
25   The plaintiffs asserted that the defendants were
26 responsible on a *respondeat superior* theory for a variety of

39

1   predicate acts, including murder and attempted murder, 18 U.S.C.
2   §§ 1111, 2332, use of a destructive device on a mass
3   transportation vehicle, 18 U.S.C. § 1992, detonating an
4   explosive device on a public transportation system, 18 U.S.C.
5   § 2332f, and conspiracy to commit those acts, 18 U.S.C. § 371.
6   See Sokolow, 60 F. Supp. 3d at 515. They also asserted that the
7   defendants directly violated federal and state antiterrorism
8   laws, including 18 U.S.C. § 2339B, by providing material support
9   to FTO-designated groups (the AAMB and Hamas) and by harboring
10 persons whom the defendants knew or had reasonable grounds to
11 believe committed or were about to commit an offense relating to
12 terrorism, see 18 U.S.C. § 2339 *et seq.*; see also Sokolow, 60 F.

THE PALESTINE YEARBOOK OF INTERNATIONAL LAW, VOLUME 19 (2016)   459

13   Supp. 3d at 520–21, 523.
14   The ATA further limits international terrorism to
15   activities that "occur *primarily outside* the territorial
16   jurisdiction of the United States, or transcend national
17   boundaries in terms of the means by which they are accomplished,
18   the persons they appear intended to intimidate or coerce, or the
19   locale in which their perpetrators operate or seek asylum." 18
20   U.S.C. § 2331(1)(C) (emphasis added).
21   The bombings and shootings here occurred *entirely* outside
22   the territorial jurisdiction of the United States. Thus, the
23   question becomes: What other constitutionally sufficient

40

1   connection did the commission of *these* torts by *these* defendants
2   have to *this* jurisdiction?
3   The jury found in a special verdict that the PA and the PLO
4   were liable for the attacks under several theories. In all of
5   the attacks, the jury found that the PA and the PLO were liable
6   for providing material support or resources that were used in
7   preparation for, or in carrying out, each attack.
8   In addition, the jury found that in five of the attacks –
9   the January 22, 2002 Jaffa Road Shooting, the January 27, 2002
10   Jaffa Road Bombing, the March 21, 2002 King George Street
11   Bombing, the July 31, 2002 Hebrew University Bombing, and the
12   January 29, 2004 Bus No. 19 Bombing – the PA was liable because
13   an employee of the PA, acting within the scope of the employee's
14   employment and in furtherance of the activities of the PA,
15   either carried out, or knowingly provided material support or
16   resources that were used in preparation for, or in carrying out,
17   the attack.
18   The jury also found that in one of the attacks – the July
19   31, 2002 Hebrew University Bombing – the PLO and the PA harbored
20   or concealed a person who the organizations knew, or had
21   reasonable grounds to believe, committed or was about to commit
22   the attack.
23   Finally, the jury found that in three attacks – the June
24   19, 2002 French Hill Bombing, the July 31, 2002 Hebrew

41

1   University Bombing, and the January 29, 2004 Bus No. 19 Bombing –
2   the PA and PLO knowingly provided material support to an FTO –
3   designated group (the AAMB or Hamas).

4 But these actions, as heinous as they were, were not
5 sufficiently connected to the United States to provide specific
6 personal jurisdiction in the United States. There is no basis
7 to conclude that the defendants participated in these acts in
8 the United States or that their liability for these acts
9 resulted from their actions that did occur in the United States.
10 In short, the defendants were liable for tortious
11 activities that occurred outside the United States and affected
12 United States citizens only because they were victims of
13 indiscriminate violence that occurred abroad. The residence or
14 citizenship of the plaintiffs is an insufficient basis for
15 specific jurisdiction over the defendants. A focus on the
16 relationship of the defendants, the forum, and the defendants'
17 suit-related conduct points to the conclusion that there is no
18 specific personal jurisdiction over the defendants for the torts
19 in this case. See Walden, 134 S. Ct. at 1121; see also
20 Goodyear, 564 U.S. at 923.
21 In the absence of such a relationship, the plaintiffs argue
22 on appeal that the Court has specific jurisdiction for three
23 reasons. First, the plaintiffs argue that, under the "effects
24 test," a defendant acting entirely outside the United States is

42

1 subject to jurisdiction "if the defendant expressly aimed its
2 conduct" at the United States. Licci ex rel. Licci v. Lebanese
3 Canadian Bank, SAL, 732 F.3d 161, 173 (2d Cir. 2013). The
4 plaintiffs point to the jury verdict that found that the
5 defendants provided material support to designated FTOs – the
6 AAMB and Hamas – and that the defendants' employees, acting
7 within the scope of their employment, killed and injured United
8 States citizens. They also argue that the defendants' terror
9 attacks were intended to influence United States policy to favor
10 the defendants' political goals. Second, the plaintiffs argue
11 that the defendants purposefully availed themselves of the forum
12 by establishing a continuous presence in the United States and
13 pressuring United States government policy by conducting terror
14 attacks in Israel and threatening further terrorism unless
15 Israel withdrew from Gaza and the West Bank. See Banks Brussels
16 Lambert, 305 F.3d at 128. Third, the plaintiffs argue that the
17 defendants consented to personal jurisdiction under the ATA by
18 appointing an agent to accept process.

19   Walden forecloses the plaintiffs' arguments. First, with
20   regard to the effects test, the defendant must "expressly aim[]"
21   his conduct at the United States. See Licci, 732 F. 3d at 173.
22   Pursuant to Walden, it is "insufficient to rely on a defendant's
23   'random, fortuitous, or attenuated contacts' or on the
24   'unilateral activity' of a plaintiff" with the forum to

43

1   establish specific jurisdiction. Walden, 134 S. Ct. at 1123
2   (quoting Burger King, 471 U.S. at 475). While the killings and
3   related acts of terrorism are the kind of activities that the
4   ATA proscribes, those acts were unconnected to the forum and
5   were not expressly aimed at the United States. And "[a] forum
6   State's exercise of jurisdiction over an out-of-state
7   intentional tortfeasor must be based on intentional conduct by
8   the defendant that creates the necessary contacts with the
9   forum." Id. That is not the case here.
10   The plaintiffs argue that United States citizens were
11   targets of these attacks, but their own evidence establishes the
12   random and fortuitous nature of the terror attacks. For
13   example, at trial, the plaintiffs emphasized how the "killing
14   was indeed random" and targeted "Christians and Jews, Israelis,
15   Americans, people from all over the world." J.A. 3836.
16   Evidence at trial showed that the shooters fired
17   "indiscriminately," J.A. 3944, and chose sites for their suicide
18   bomb attacks that were "full of people," J.A. 4030–31, because
19   they sought to kill "as many people as possible," J.A. 3944; see
20   also J.A. 4031.
21   The plaintiffs argue that "[i]t is a fair inference that
22   Defendants *intended to* hit American citizens by continuing a
23   terror campaign that continuously hit Americans...." Pls.'
24   Br. at 37 (emphasis in original). But the Constitution requires

44

1   much more purposefully directed contact with the forum. For
2   example, the Supreme Court has "upheld the assertion of
3   jurisdiction over defendants who have purposefully 'reach[ed]
4   out beyond' their State and into another by, for example,
5   entering a contractual relationship that 'envisioned continuing
6   and wide-reaching contacts' in the forum State," Walden, 134 S.
7   Ct. at 1122 (alteration in original) (quoting Burger King, 472
8   U.S. at 479–80), or "by circulating magazines to 'deliberately

462 CASES

9 exploi[t]' a market in the forum State." Id. (alteration in
10 original) (quoting Keeton, 465 U.S. at 781). But there was no
11 such purposeful connection to the forum in this case, and it
12 would be impermissible to speculate based on scant evidence what
13 the terrorists intended to do.
14 Furthermore, the facts of Walden also suggest that a
15 defendant's mere knowledge that a plaintiff resides in a
16 specific jurisdiction would be insufficient to subject a
17 defendant to specific jurisdiction in that jurisdiction if the
18 defendant does nothing in connection with the tort in that
19 jurisdiction. In Walden, the petitioner was a police officer in
20 Georgia who was working as a deputized Drug Enforcement
21 Administration ("DEA") agent at the Atlanta airport. He was
22 informed that the respondents, Gina Fiore and Keith Gipson, were
23 flying from San Juan, Puerto Rico through Atlanta en route to
24 their final destination in Las Vegas, Nevada. See Joint

45

1 Appendix, Walden v. Fiore, 2013 WL 2390248, *41–42 (U.S.) (Decl.
2 of Anthony Walden). Walden and his DEA team stopped the
3 respondents and searched their bags in Atlanta and examined
4 their California drivers' licenses. Id.; Walden, 134 S. Ct. at
5 1119. Walden found almost $100,000 in cash in the respondents'
6 carry-on bag and seized it, giving rise to a claim for an
7 unconstitutional search under Bivens v. Six Unknown Named
   Agents
8 of the Federal Bureau of Narcotics, 403 U.S. 388 (1971). See
9 Walden, 134 S. Ct. at 1119–20. The Supreme Court found that the
10 petitioner's contacts with Nevada were insufficient to establish
11 personal jurisdiction over the petitioner in a Nevada federal
12 court, even though Walden knew that the respondents were
13 destined for Nevada. See id. at 1119.
14 In this case, the plaintiffs point us to no evidence that
15 these indiscriminate terrorist attacks were specifically
16 targeted against United States citizens, and the mere knowledge
17 that United States citizens might be wronged in a foreign
18 country goes beyond the jurisdictional limit set forth in
19 Walden.
20 The plaintiffs cite to several cases to support their
21 argument that specific jurisdiction is warranted under an

22 "effects test." Those cases are easily distinguishable from
23 this case. Indeed, they point to the kinds of circumstances

46

1 that would give rise to specific jurisdiction under the ATA,
2 which are not present here.
3 For example, in <u>Mwani v. Bin Laden</u>, 417 F.3d 1 (D.C. Cir.
4 2005), the Court of Appeals for the District of Columbia Circuit
5 found that specific personal jurisdiction over Osama Bin Laden
6 and al Qaeda was supported by allegations that they
7 "orchestrated the bombing of the *American* embassy in Nairobi,
8 not only to kill both American and Kenyan employees inside the
9 building, but to cause pain and sow terror in the embassy's home
10 country, *the United States*," as well as allegations of "an
11 ongoing conspiracy to attack the United States, with overt acts
12 occurring *within* this country's borders." <u>Id</u>. at 13 (emphasis
13 added). The plaintiffs pointed to the 1993 World Trade Center
14 bombing, as well as the plot to bomb the United Nations, Federal
15 Plaza, and the Lincoln and Holland Tunnels in New York. <u>Id</u>.
16 Furthermore, the Court of Appeals found that bin Laden and al
17 Qaeda "'purposefully directed' [their] activities at residents"
18 of the United States, and that the case "result[ed] from
19 injuries to the plaintiffs 'that arise out of or relate to those
20 activities,'" <u>id</u>. (quoting <u>Burger King</u>, 471 U.S. at 472).
21 "[E]xercising specific jurisdiction because the victim of a
22 foreign attack happened to be an American would run afoul of the
23 Supreme Court's holding that '[d]ue process requires that a
24 defendant be haled into court in a forum State based on his own

47

1 affiliation with the State, not based on the "random,
2 fortuitous, or attenuated" contacts he makes by interacting with
3 other persons affiliated with the State.'" <u>Klieman</u>, 82 F. Supp.
4 3d at 248 (quoting <u>Walden</u>, 134 S. Ct. at 1123); see Safra, 82 F.
5 Supp. 3d at 52 (distinguishing Mwani); <u>see also</u> <u>In re Terrorist</u>
6 <u>Attacks on Sept. 11, 2001</u>, 538 F.3d at 95–96 (holding that even
7 if Saudi princes could and did foresee that Muslim charities
8 would use their donations to finance the September 11 attacks,
9 providing indirect funding to an organization that was openly
10 hostile to the United States did not constitute the type of
11 intentional conduct necessary to constitute purposeful direction

464 CASES

12 of activities at the forum); Livnat, 82 F. Supp. 3d at 33.

13 The plaintiffs also rely on O'Neill, 714 F.3d at 659, which
14 related to the September 11 attacks. In that case, this Court
15 first clarified that "specific personal jurisdiction properly
16 exists where the defendant took 'intentional, and allegedly
17 tortious, actions ... expressly aimed' at the forum." Id. at
18 674 (quoting Calder, 465 U.S. at 789). This Court also noted
19 that, "the fact that harm in the forum is foreseeable ... is
20 insufficient for the purpose of establishing specific personal
21 jurisdiction over a defendant." Id. This Court then held that
22 the plaintiffs' allegations were insufficient to establish
23 personal jurisdiction over about two dozen defendants, but that
24 jurisdictional discovery was warranted for twelve other

48

1 defendants whose "alleged support of al Qaeda [was] more
2 direct." Id. at 678; see also id. at 656–66. Those defendants
3 "allegedly controlled and managed some of [the front]
4 'charitable organizations' and, through their positions of
5 control, they allegedly sent financial and other material
6 support *directly* to al Qaeda when al Qaeda allegedly was known
7 to be *targeting the United States*." Id. (second emphasis
8 added).

9 The plaintiffs argue that this Court should likewise find
10 jurisdiction because the defendants' "direct, knowing provision
11 of material support to designated FTOs [in this case, Hamas and
12 the AAMB] is enough – standing alone – to sustain specific
13 jurisdiction because they knowingly aimed their conduct at U.S.
14 interests." Pls.' Br. at 36. But that argument misreads
15 O'Neill. In O'Neill, this Court emphasized that the mere "fact
16 that harm in the forum is foreseeable" was "insufficient for the
17 purpose of establishing specific personal jurisdiction over a
18 defendant," 714 F.3d at 674, and the Court did not end its
19 inquiry when it concluded that the defendants may have provided
20 support to terror organizations. Indeed, the Court held that
21 "factual issues persist with respect to whether this support was
22 'expressly aimed' at the United States," warranting
23 jurisdictional discovery. Id. at 678–79. The Court looked at
24 the specific aim of the group receiving support – particularly

49

1 that al Qaeda was "known to be targeting the United States" –
2 and not simply that it and other defendants were "terrorist

3   organizations." Id. at 678.[13]
4   The plaintiffs also cite Calder v. Jones, 465 U.S. at 783.
5   In that case, a California actress brought a libel suit in
6   California state court against a reporter and an editor, both of
7   whom worked for a tabloid at the tabloid's Florida headquarters.
8   Id. at 784. The plaintiff's claims were based on an article
9   written and edited by the defendants in Florida for the tabloid,
10   which had a California circulation of about 600,000. Id. at
11   784–86. The Supreme Court held that California's assertion of
12   personal jurisdiction over the defendants for a libel action was
13   proper based on the effects of the defendants' conduct in
14   California. Id. at 788. "The article was drawn from California
15   sources, and the brunt of the harm, in terms both of
16   respondent's emotional distress and the injury to her
17   professional reputation, was suffered in California," the
18   Supreme Court held. Id. at 788–89. "In sum, California is the

50

1   *focal point* both of the story and of the harm suffered." Id. at
2   789 (emphasis added); see also Walden, 134 S. Ct. at 1123
3   (describing the contacts identified in Calder as "ample" to
4   support specific jurisdiction). As the Supreme Court explained
5   in Walden, the jurisdictional inquiry in Calder focused on the
6   relationship among the defendant, the forum, and the litigation.
7   Walden, 134 S. Ct. at 1123.
8   Unlike in Calder, it cannot be said that the United States
9   is the focal point of the torts alleged in this litigation. In
10   this case, the United States is not the nucleus of the harm –
11   Israel is. See Safra, 82 F. Supp. 3d at 51.
12   Finally, the plaintiffs rely on two criminal cases, United
13   States v. Yousef, 327 F.3d 56 (2d Cir. 2003) (per curiam), and
14   United States v. Al Kassar, 660 F.3d 108 (2d Cir. 2011), for
15   their argument that the "effects test" supports jurisdiction.
16   In both cases, this Court applied the due process test for

---

13   Furthermore, the mere designation of a group as an FTO does not reflect that the organization has aimed its conduct at the United States. The Secretary of State may "designate an organization as a foreign terrorist organization" if the Secretary finds "the organization is a foreign organization," "the organization engages in terrorist activity," "or retains the capability and intent to engage in terrorist activity or terrorism," and "the terrorist activity or terrorism of the organization threatens the security of United States nationals or the national security of the United States." 8 U.S.C. § 1189(a)(1)(A)–(C).

466   CASES

17 asserting jurisdiction over extraterritorial criminal conduct,
18 which differs from the test applicable in this civil case, see
19 Al Kassar, 660 F.3d at 118; Yousef, 327 F.3d at 111–12, and does
20 not require a nexus between the specific criminal conduct and
21 harm within the United States. See also United States v.
22 Murillo, No. 15-4235, 2016 WL 3257016, at *3 (4th Cir. June 14,
23 2016)("[I]t is not arbitrary to prosecute a defendant in the
24 United States if his actions affected significant American

51

1 interests – even if the defendant did not mean to affect those
2 interests." (internal citation and quotation marks omitted)).
3 In order to apply a federal criminal statute to a defendant
4 extraterritorially consistent with due process, "'there must be
5 a sufficient nexus between the defendant and the United States,
6 so that such application would not be arbitrary or fundamentally
7 unfair.' For non-citizens acting entirely abroad, a
8 jurisdictional nexus exists when the aim of that activity is to
9 cause harm inside the United States or to U.S. citizens or
10 interests." Al Kassar, 660 F.3d 108, 118 (emphasis added)
11 (quoting Yousef, 327 F.3d at 111).
12 In a civil action, as Walden makes clear, "the defendant's
13 suit-related conduct must create a substantial connection with
14 the forum State." 134 S. Ct. at 1121.
15 Even setting aside the fact that both Yousef and Al Kassar
16 applied the more expansive due process test in criminal cases,
17 the defendants in both cases had more substantial connections
18 with the United States than the defendants have in the current
19 litigation. Yousef involved a criminal prosecution for the
20 bombing of an airplane traveling from the Philippines to Japan.
21 See 327 F.3d at 79. The Yousef defendants "conspired to attack
22 a dozen United States-flag aircraft in an effort to inflict
23 injury on this country and its people and influence American
24 foreign policy, and their attack on the Philippine Airlines

52

1 flight was a 'test-run' in furtherance of this conspiracy." Id.
2 at 112.
3 In Al Kassar, several defendants were convicted of
4 conspiring to kill United States officers, to acquire and export
5 anti-aircraft missiles, and knowingly to provide material
6 support to a terrorist organization; two were also convicted of

7	conspiring to kill United States citizens and of money
8	laundering. 660 F.3d at 115. On appeal, the defendants
9	challenged their convictions on a number of grounds, including
10	that the defendants' Fifth Amendment due process rights were
11	violated by prosecuting them for activities that occurred
12	abroad. <u>Id</u>. at 117–18. This Court rejected that argument
13	because the defendants conspired to sell arms to a group "with
14	the understanding that they would be used to kill Americans and
15	destroy U.S. property; the aim therefore was to harm U.S.
16	citizens and interests and to threaten the security of the
17	United States." <u>Id</u>. at 118.
18	In this case, the defendants undertook terror attacks
19	within Israel, and there is no evidence the attacks specifically
20	targeted United States citizens. <u>See</u> <u>Safra</u>, 82 F. Supp. 3d at
21	53–54; <u>see also</u> <u>Livnat</u>, 82 F. Supp. 3d at 34.
22	Accordingly, in the present case, specific jurisdiction is
23	not appropriate under the "effects test."

53

1	Second, <u>Walden</u> undermines the plaintiffs' arguments that
2	the defendants met the "purposeful availment" test by
3	establishing a continuous presence in the United States and
4	pressuring United States government policy. The emphasis on the
5	defendants' Washington, D.C. mission confuses the issue: <u>Walden</u>
6	requires that the "suit-related conduct" – here, the terror
7	attacks in Israel – have a "substantial connection with the
8	forum." 134 S. Ct. at 1121. The defendants' Washington mission
9	and its associated lobbying efforts do not support specific
10	personal jurisdiction on the ATA claims. The defendants cannot
11	be made to answer in this forum "with respect to matters
12	unrelated to the forum connections." <u>Goodyear</u>, 564 U.S. at 923;
13	<u>see also</u> <u>Klieman</u>, 82 F. Supp. 3d at 247 ("Courts typically
14	require that the plaintiff show some sort of causal relationship
15	between a defendant's U.S. contacts and the episode in suit.").
16	The plaintiffs argue on appeal that the defendants intended
17	their terror campaign to influence not just Israel, but also the
18	United States. They point to trial evidence – specifically
19	pamphlets published by the PA – that, the plaintiffs argue,
20	shows that the defendants were attempting to influence United
21	States policy toward the Israel-Palestinian conflict. The
22	exhibits themselves speak in broad terms of how United States

468 CASES

23 interests in the region are in danger and how the United States
24 and Europe should exert pressure on Israel to change its

54

1 practices toward the Palestinians. It is insufficient for
2 purposes of due process to rely on evidence that a political
3 organization sought to influence United States policy, without
4 some other connection among the activities underlying the
5 litigation, the defendants, and the forum. Such attenuated
6 activity is insufficient under Walden.
7   The plaintiffs cite Licci, 732 F.3d 161, to support their
8 argument that the defendants meet the purposeful availment test.
9 But the circumstances of that case are distinguishable and
10 illustrate why the defendants here do not meet that test. In
11 Licci, American, Canadian, and Israeli citizens who were injured
12 or whose family members were killed in a series of terrorist
13 rocket attacks by Hizbollah in Israel brought an action under
14 the ATA and other laws against the Lebanese Canadian Bank, SAL
15 ("LCB"), which allegedly facilitated Hizbollah's acts by using
16 correspondent banking accounts at a defendant New York bank
17 (American Express Bank Ltd.) to effectuate wire transfers
18 totaling several million dollars on Hizbollah's behalf. Id. at
19 164–66. This Court concluded that the exercise of personal
20 jurisdiction over the defendants was constitutional because of
21 the defendants' "repeated use of New York's banking system, as
22 an instrument for accomplishing the alleged wrongs for which the
23 plaintiffs seek redress." Id. at 171. These contacts
24 constituted "'purposeful[] avail[ment] ... of the privilege of

55

1 doing business in [New York],' so as to permit the subjecting of
2 LCB to specific jurisdiction within the Southern District of New
3 York...." Id. (quoting Bank Brussels Lambert, 305 F.3d at
4 127).
5   "It should hardly be unforeseeable to a bank that selects
6 and makes use of a particular forum's banking system that it
7 might be subject to the burden of a lawsuit in that forum for
8 wrongs *related to*, and *arising from, that use*." Id. at 171–72
9 (emphasis added) (footnote omitted).
10   In Licci, this Court also distinguished the "effects test"
11 theory of personal jurisdiction which is "typically invoked
12 where (*unlike here*) the conduct that forms the basis for the
13 controversy occurs entirely out-of-forum, and the only relevant

14 jurisdictional contacts with the forum are therefore in-forum
15 effects harmful to the plaintiff." Id. at 173 (emphasis added)
16 (footnote omitted). The Court held that the effects test was
17 inappropriate because "the constitutional exercise of personal
18 jurisdiction over a foreign defendant" turned on conduct that
19 "occur[ed] *within* the forum," id. (emphasis in original), namely
20 the repeated use of bank accounts in New York to support the
21 alleged wrongs for which the plaintiffs sued.
22   In this case, there is no such connection between the
23 conduct on which the alleged personal jurisdiction is based and
24 the forum. And the connections the defendants do have with the

56

1 United States – the Washington, D.C. and New York missions –
2 revolve around lobbying activities that are not proscribed by
3 the ATA and are not connected to the wrongs for which the
4 plaintiffs here seek redress.
5   At a hearing before the district court, the plaintiffs also
6 cited Bank Brussels Lambert, 305 F.3d 120, as their "best case"
7 for their purposeful availment argument. See J.A. 1128. But
8 that case, too, is distinguishable. There, a client bank sued
9 its lawyers for legal malpractice that occurred in Puerto Rico.
10 Bank Brussels Lambert, 305 F.3d at 123. This Court held that
11 the Puerto Rican law firm defendant had sufficient minimum
12 contacts with the New York forum and purposely availed itself of
13 the privilege of doing business in New York, because, although
14 the law firm did not solicit the bank as a client in New York,
15 the firm maintained an apartment in New York partially for the
16 purpose of better servicing its New York clients, the firm faxed
17 newsletters regarding Puerto Rican legal developments to persons
18 in New York, the firm had numerous New York clients, and its
19 marketing materials touted the firm's close relationship with
20 the Federal Reserve Bank of New York. Id. at 127–29. "The
21 engagement which gave rise to the dispute here is not simply one
22 of a string of fortunate coincidences for the firm. Rather, the
23 picture which emerges from the above facts is that of a law firm
24 which seeks to be known in the New York legal market, makes

57

1 efforts to promote and maintain a client base there, and profits
2 substantially therefrom." Id. at 128. This Court held that
3 there was "nothing fundamentally unfair about requiring the firm
4 to defend itself in the New York courts when a dispute arises

470 CASES

5 from its representation of a New York client – a representation
6 which developed in a market it had deliberately cultivated and
7 which, after all, the firm voluntarily undertook." Id. at 129.
8 In short, the defendants' contacts with the forum were
9 sufficiently related to the malpractice claims that were at
10 issue in the suit.
11 That is not the case here. The plaintiffs' claims did not
12 arise from the defendants' purposeful contacts with the forum.
13 And where the defendant in Bank Brussels Lambert purposefully
14 and repeatedly reached into New York to obtain New York clients –
15 and as a result of those activities, it obtained a
16 representation for which it was sued – in this case, the
17 plaintiffs' claims did not arise from any activity by the
18 defendants in this forum.
19 Thus, in this case, unlike in Licci and Bank Brussels
20 Lambert, the defendants are not subject to specific personal
21 jurisdiction based on a "purposeful availment" theory because
22 the plaintiffs' claims do not arise from the defendants'
23 activity in the forum.

58

1 Third, the plaintiffs' argue that the defendants consented
2 to personal jurisdiction under the ATA by appointing an agent to
3 accept process. It is clear that the ATA permitted service of
4 process on the representative of the PLO and PA in Washington.
5 See 18 U.S.C. § 2334(a). However, the statute does not answer
6 the constitutional question of whether due process is satisfied.
7 The plaintiffs contend that under United States v. Scophony
8 Corp. of America, 333 U.S. 795 (1948), meeting the statutory
9 requirement for service of process suffices to establish
10 personal jurisdiction. But Scophony does not stand for that
11 proposition. The defendant in Scophony "was 'transacting
12 business' of a substantial character in the New York district at
13 the times of service, so as to establish venue there," and so
14 that "such a ruling presents no conceivable element of offense
15 to 'traditional notions of fair play and substantial justice.'"
16 Id. at 818 (quoting Int'l Shoe, 326 U.S. at 316). Thus,
17 Scophony affirms the understanding, echoed by this Court in
18 Licci, 673 F.3d at 60, and O'Neill, 714 F.3d at 673–74, that due
19 process analysis – considerations of minimum contacts and
20 reasonableness – applies even when federal service-of-process

21	statutes are satisfied. Simply put, "the exercise of personal
22	jurisdiction must comport with constitutional due process
23	principles." Licci, 673 F.3d at 60; see also Brown, 814 F.3d at
24	641. As explained above, due process is not satisfied in this

59

1	case, and the courts have neither general nor specific personal
2	jurisdiction over the defendants, regardless of the service-of-
3	process statute.
4	In sum, because the terror attacks in Israel at issue here
5	were not expressly aimed at the United States and because the
6	deaths and injuries suffered by the American plaintiffs in these
7	attacks were "random [and] fortuitous" and because lobbying
8	activities regarding American policy toward Israel are
9	insufficiently "suit-related conduct" to support specific
10	jurisdiction, the Court lacks specific jurisdiction over these
11	defendants. Walden, 134 S. Ct. at 1121, 1123.
12	***
13	The terror machine gun attacks and suicide bombings that
14	triggered this suit and victimized these plaintiffs were
15	unquestionably horrific. But the federal courts cannot exercise
16	jurisdiction in a civil case beyond the limits prescribed by the
17	due process clause of the Constitution, no matter how horrendous
18	the underlying attacks or morally compelling the plaintiffs'
19	claims.
20	The district court could not constitutionally exercise
21	either general or specific personal jurisdiction over the
22	defendants in this case. Accordingly, this case must be
23	dismissed.
24	

60

1	CONCLUSION
2	We have considered all of the arguments of the parties. To
3	the extent not specifically addressed above, they are either
4	moot or without merit. For the reasons explained above, we
5	**VACATE** the judgment of the district court and **REMAND** the case to
6	the district court with instructions to **DISMISS** the case for
7	want of jurisdiction.

61

Index

2030 Agenda for Sustainable
Development 335

Abbas, Mahmoud 93–94, 244, 286
Abu Rahma, Abdallah 262
accountability
  for crimes/violations
    addressing of challenges by
      Israel 313–316
    and civil remedies 311–312
    against detainees 312–313
    during hostilities 310–311
    of Israeli officials. *see* Israeli officials
    of Israeli security forces 305–313
    lack of 258–259, 324–326
    during law enforcement 307–311
    UN resolution on 369–373
Achille Lauro (ship) 80
Ad Hoc Liaison Committee for Coordination
  of the International Assistance to
  Palestinians 64, 65
Addameer 326, 328–329
administrative detentions 257, 304, 326–328
Afghanistan 199
African Charter of Human and Peoples'
  Rights (1981) 21–22
African Union 38
Ago, Robert 154
agriculture 277, 287, 342–343
Albania 77, 89
alien residents, rights of 145–146, 150n57
Alien Tort Statute 97n1
Allan, Mohammad 264–265
Allawi, Ayad 197
Allied Powers 150–151, 227
Almog, Doron 99, 121–122, 124n103
Altstötter and Others (Justice Trial) United
  States Military Tribunal, Nuremberg,
  Germany (Dec. 4, 1947) 151
Ambiente Ufficio S.p.A. v. Argentine Republic,
  I.C.S.I.D. Case No. ARB/08/9, Decision on
  Jurisdiction and Admissibility (Feb 8,
  2013), 160–161n99
Ambrose 13
American Declaration of Independence
  (1776) 17

Amnesty International 126, 262
Andenas, Mads 217
Anglo-Egyptian Treaty of Independence
  58
Annan, Kofi 36
annexations. *see* occupations
Apartheid Convention (Convention on the
  Suppression and Punishment of the
  Crime of Apartheid) 73, 74
Application of the Convention on the
  Prevention and Punishment of the Crime
  of Genocide (Bosn. Herz. v. Serb. &
  Montenegro), Further Requests for the
  Indication of Provisional Measures
  (separate opinion of Judge Lauterpacht),
  1993 I.C.J. Rep. 407, 440, para. 10 (Sep. 13),
  203–204
Arab Charter on Human Rights (2004) 21
Arab High Committee for Palestine 54
Arab League. *see* League of Arab States
Arai-Takahashi, Yutaka 148n52, 152n65,
  168n134, 235
Argentina 128, 160–161n99
Armed Activities on the Territory of the
  Congo (Dem. Rep. Congo v. Uganda),
  Judgment, 2005 I.C.J. Rep. 168, 231
  (Dec. 19) 155–156, 159
armed conflicts
  and BITs 157–158
  definition of 157
  see also occupations
Armenia 232, 234
arrests
  in the oPt 305
  warrants for 99, 115–116, 119, 120–121,
    129n118, 132
  see also detentions
Asian Agricultural Products Ltd v. Sri Lanka,
  I.C.S.I.D. Case. No. ARB/87/3 (Final
  Award) (1991) 30 I.L.M. 173
Assad, Bashar 20n59, 35–36, 38
Australia 59, 76, 93, 185–187
Austria 64, 89, 157–158n90, 157n90
Awada, Sa'id 440
Awwad, Hadeel Wajih 296–297
Ayalon, Dani 105–106, 112–114, 122

Azarova, Valentina   223–235
Azerbaijan   232, 234

Bab al-Shams protest camp   262
Baltic States   89, 175–176n158
Ban Ki-moon   36
Barak, Ehud   115
Basic Principles on the Use of Force and
    Firearms by Law Enforcement
    Officials   251, 268, 297, 308, 323, 324, 350
Baxter, Richard, 149n53
Bedouin communities, forced relocations/
    evictions of   261, 333–334, 345, 350, 376,
    380, 426
Belgian Civil Code   167
Belgian Statute on Industrial Accidents
    (1903)   167
Belgium
    Cie des Chemins de Fer du Nord v.
        German State, Franco-German Mixed
        Tribunal (Apr. 8, 1929)   167
    and DRC   62
    Milaire v. German State, Germano-Belgian
        Mixed Arbitral Tribunal (Jan. 1,
        1923)   166, 167
    UJ cases in
        in absentia, 103
        and changes in legislation   105,
            117–118
        Sharon case, 98, 105, 117, 120
Belilos v. Switzerland, App. No. 10328/83, 1988
    Eur. Ct. H.R.   187–188
Bellal, Annyssa   27
belligerent occupation. see law of
    (belligerent) occupation; occupations
bellum justum doctrine, 13
Ben-Eliezer, Binyamin   99, 108
Benvenisti, Eyal   79n180, 86, 152–153, 235
Bicom   121
Bilateral Investment Treaties (BITs)
    binding/non-binding status of   146–150
    continuity in occupied territory
        and arbitration
            in general   160–161
            and jurisdiction of investment
                tribunals   170–172
        in armed conflicts   157–158
        and destruction of private
            property   173–174

and expropriations   173–174
and investment protection   172–175
and occupant's responsibility
    159–162
dispute resolution clauses in   160–161n99
and extraterritoriality   140–141n17
FPS standard of   172, 173
between Germany and Ukraine   142
integration of IHL   168–170
and law of occupation   168–175
between Libya and Austra   157–158n90
and occupations   141–142
between Russia and Ukraine   139–140,
    141n19, 142, 171
between UK and Argentina   160–161n99
war clause in   157–158
bilateral treaties   71
Bil'in   97n1
Bingham, Lord   198–199
Bjorge, Eirik   217
blockades, of Gaza Strip   69, 254–255,
    331–332, 341
Bodin, Jean   16
Bosnia-Herzegovina   53
Bosnian Genocide case   190
Bosnian Serb militia   180
Boyle, Francis   53
British police   114, 121–122
Broude, Tomer   217
Brownlie, Ian   192
Brunei   74
B'Tselem
    on detainees   304, 326
    and Israel's military law enforcement
        316, 324, 325
    report on settlements   131n121
building permits   333–334, 345, 349
Burke, Naomi   153n71, 158–159
Bus No. 19 Bombing (2002)   440
Bush, George H. W.   98, 117

Calvinists   14
Canada
    Bil'in case, 97n1
    one-China policy of   85
    and Palestine's statehood status   84–85
    and Resolution 67/19   66
    and UJ legislation   127
Carcano, Andrea   223–235

INDEX

Casablanca Arbitration case (1907) 147, 151–152, 162–163

Cassese, Antonio 214

Catholics 14

CCSBT (Convention for the Conservation of Southern Bluefin Tuna) 185–186

Celebisi case 190

Chad 128

Charter of the United Nations. *see* United Nations Charter

Cheney, Dick 117

Chilcot Inquiry 223, 231

child detainees 134, 256–257, 304–305, 328–329, 350

child labor 154

China
lobbying against UJ cases 115
occupation by Japan, and rights of alien residents 145–146, 150n57
recognition of 85

Cie des Chemins de Fer du Nord v. German State, Franco-German Mixed Tribunal (Apr. 8, 1929) 167

Ciechanover Commission 314

Citizenship and Entry into Israel Law 290, 365

civil law jurisdictions
and laws in force 154–155
and statehood status 79–80, 84–85, 86
of States 13–16

Clarke, Paul Kingsley 217

Class 'A' Mandate 53–54

"clean-slate" theory 87–88, 93

Coalition Provisional Authority (CPA) 154, 229–232

Cogan, Jacob 212

COGAT (Coordination of Government Activities in the Territories Unit) 273–274, 283, 288–289

colonialism 22–25, 226–228, 231

Commission of Prisoners and Ex-Prisoners' Affairs 304

Commission of the European Community v. Grand Duchy of Luxembourg and Kingdom of Belgium, 1964 E.C.R. 185

Committee against Torture 301, 304, 311, 312, 313, 326–328

Committee on the Inalienable Rights of the Palestinian People 44n5

Comm'n v. Ireland, 2006 E.C.R. I-04635 182–184

common-law jurisdictions 79–84, 86

compensation
claims 109, 312
for losses 138n10, 157–158n90, 173–174, 205

Congo. *see* Democratic Republic of Congo

Continental Shelf (Tunis. v. Libya), 1982 I.C.J. Rep. 18, 38 (Feb. 24), 205

Convention against Torture and Other Cruel, Inhuman or Degrading Treatment or Punishment 102, 113, 194, 264, 301

Convention for the Conservation of Southern Bluefin Tuna (CCSBT) 185–186

Convention on the Protection of the Marine Environment of the North-East Atlantic (OSPAR Convention) 182–183

Convention on the Rights of the Child (CRC) 140n17, 329, 350, 365

Convention on the Suppression and Punishment of the Crime of Apartheid (the Apartheid Convention) 73, 74

Cook Islands 73

Coordination of Government Activities in the Territories Unit (COGAT) 273–274, 283, 288–289

Council of the European Union 199–201

Council of the European Union v. Hamas
in general 391–392
assessment
first ground of appeal 408–412
preliminary remarks 406–408
second ground of appeal 412–414
third ground of appeal 414–417
claims and submissions on appeal 400–406
conclusion 417–418
legal background 392–397
summary of procedure at first instance 397–400

Counter-Terrorism Law 315

CPA (Coalition Provisional Authority) 154, 229–232

Craven, Matthew 214

Crawford, James 51–52, 54–55, 149n55

CRC (Convention on the Rights of the Child) 140n17, 329, 350, 365

Crimea 139–140, 175, 232, 234

crimes/violations
  in general 423
  accountability for
    addressing of challenges by Israel
      313–316
    and civil remedies 311–312
    against detainees 312–313
    during hostilities 310–311
    of Israeli officials. see Israeli officials
    of Israeli security forces 305–313
    lack of 258–259, 324–326
    during law enforcement 307–311
    UN resolution on 369–373
  committed in
    in East Jerusalem 425–427
    Gaza 43, 46, 48–49, 265–267,
      423–425
    West Bank 425–427
  and international community 9, 33–34
  and interventions 9
  role of local community in prevention
    of 28–29
  by Turkey 156n82
  victims of, right to resist of 9, 30–31, 33
  see also firearms; relocations; violence;
    war crimes
Cyprus 62
Czechoslovakia 89, 149n54

Daesh 39
Al-Daraj case 108–111, 115
De jure belli ac pacis (Grotius) 15
De Officiis Ministrorum (Ambrose) 13
debellatio doctrine 89–90, 150–151
Declaration of Principles on Interim
  Self-Government Arrangements
  (1993) 47n24, 68, 86
Declaration on Principles of International
  Law concerning Friendly Relations and
  Cooperation among States in Accordance
  with the Charter of the United Nations
  (1970) 23–24
Declaration on the Right to
  Development 335–336
decolonization 23, 24, 227
Defence for Children International 304–305
Democratic Republic of Congo (DRC) 62,
  155–156

Democratic Republic of East Timor, Fretilin,
  and Others v. The Netherlands, District
  Court of The Hague (1980) 84
demolitions 124n103, 250, 253, 301, 330,
  332–334
  see also destruction
Deserters of Casablanca arbitration
  case 147, 151–152, 162–163
desertions 147, 152, 162–163
destruction
  of property during conflicts
    in general 137, 157, 172–174
    in oPt 254–255
  see also demolitions
detentions
  in general 255–257, 304, 326
  administrative 257, 304, 326–328
  B'Tselem on 304, 326
  of children 134, 256–257, 304–305,
    328–329, 350
  Fourth Geneva Convention on 196–197
  of human rights defenders 262–263
  in international law 327
  occupants right of 196–197
  torture/ill-treatment during 264–265,
    312–313
  see also arrests
development, right to
  in general 335–336
  in East Jerusalem 346–348
  in Gaza Strip 341–344
  Israel's respect for 348–350
  in oPt 337–341
  in West Bank 344–346
Dinstein, Yoram 162n104, 235
direct/indirect consent 161
displacements. see relocations
domaine reservée 9, 34
domestic courts, and Palestine's UN
  status 79–86
domestic law
  right to rebel in 10–12, 17–18
  right to self-defense in 25–26
Dorman, Knut 166n127
Doswald-Beck, Louise 27
Draper, G.I.A.D. 145, 147
DRC (Democratic Republic of Congo) 62,
  155–156

INDEX

477

Dugard, John   53n51
duty of obedience   149n53, 168n133

East Jerusalem
  economy of   346–348
  forced relocations/evictions in   260–261
  freedom of movement in, restrictions
    on   250–251, 277–278
  ICC report on   422–423, 425–427
  isolation of   277–278, 346–347
  living standards in   347
East Timor   84, 93
ECJ (European Court of Justice). *see*
  European Court of Justice
Economic and Social Commission for
  Western Asia (ESCWA)   65
economy
  of oPt   337–348
    in general   337–340
    in East Jerusalem   346–348
    in Gaza Strip   341–344
    in West Bank   344–346
ECtHR (European Court on Human Rights).
  see European Court on Human Rights
education, access to   251, 281–283, 293, 364
effective control
  of Gaza Strip   56, 58, 63
  and Nicaragua v. United States of America
    (1986)   181
  and Palestine's statehood status   54–58,
    63–64
  as statehood criteria   53, 63–64, 89–90,
    181
effet utile principle, 164–165
EFP (Experimental Fishing Program)   185
Egypt   57–58, 280
Eichmann, Adolf   102–103
ESCWA (Economic and Social Commission
  for Western Asia)   65
espionage   147, 152, 162–163
Ethiopia   89
European Commission Law   182–185
European Community. *see* European Union
European Convention on Human Rights
  and al-Jedda case   197–199
  and extraterritoriality   156n82, 197–198
  and Kadi case   200
  on oppressed people   22

and Slivenko v. Latvia   195–196
and Turkey   188, 209
on use of force   20
European Court of Justice (ECJ)
  cases of
    Commission of the European
      Community v. Grand Duchy of
      Luxembourg and Kingdom of
      Belgium   185
    Comm'n v. Ireland, 2006 E.C.R.
      I-04635   182–184
    Council of the European Union v.
      Hamas. *see* Council of the
      European Union v. Hamas
    Flamino Costa v. E.N.E.L., 1964
      E.C.R.   185
    Kadi v. Council and Commission, 2005
      E.C.R. II-3649   200
    NV Algemene Transport-en Expeditie
      Ondememing Van Gend en Loos v.
      Nederlandse Administratie der
      Belastingen (Netherlands Inland
      Revenue Administration)
      184–185
European Court on Human Rights (ECtHR)
  cases of
    Belilos v. Switzerland, App. No.
      10328/83, 1988 Eur. Ct.
      H.R.   187–188
    Loizidou v. Turkey, App. No. 15318/89,
      1995 Eur. Ct. H.R.   156n82, 209
    Slivenko v. Latvia, App. No. 48321/99,
      Judgment, 2003 Eur. Ct. H.R.   195
    Yazar and others v. Turkey   20–21
  and ICJ   188, 209–210
European Union (EU)
  law of, and Article 103 of UN
    Charter   199–202
  and legitimacy of Qaddafi regime   35
  recognition of Bosnia-Herzegovina   53
  and UJ legislation   127
evictions. *see* relocations
Ewisat v. The Israel Police et al. (HCJ 2882/16)
  301
executions, extrajudicial   247, 296–297,
  324
Experimental Fishing Program (EFP)   185
expression, freedom of   20–21

478 INDEX

expropriations   173–174
  see also occupations
extraterritoriality
  and BITs   140–141n17
  of European Convention on Human
    Rights   156n82, 197–198
  of Human Rights Act (UK)   197–198
  of human rights treaties   155–156
  and occupant   147, 163
  through consular courts   146
  in UJ cases   131–132, 131n120

Falk, Richard   53, 107
family life, right to   289–291
FAO (Food and Agricultural
  Organization)   73
Fatah   56, 58
Fauchland, Ole Kristian   217
Ferraro, Tristan   168n135
Ferrini v. Federal Republic of
  Germany   192–193
Fifth Amendment (to US Constitution), and
  control of personal jurisdiction   433–471
firearms, use of   248–249, 263, 297, 298–299,
    309, 323–324
Flamino Costa v. E.N.E.L., 1964 E.C.R.   185
Food and Agricultural Organization
  (FAO)   73
forced feeding   264–265
Fourth Geneva Convention (1949)
  breaches of   98, 101–102, 114
  codification of law of occupation in   144
  on collective punishment   301–302, 330
  and continuity of treaties   154–155
  on destruction of private property   172
  on detention   196–197
  on internment   327
  necessity exception in   150n56, 162, 173
  persons exclude from protection
    by   170–172
  persons protected by   170–171n143, 171
  on relief for population in need   334
  on relocations   332
Fox, Gregory   213, 235
Fox, James R.   142n24
fragmentation
  definition of   179
  in international law   177–219
    in general   178–180

and Article 103 of UN
  Charter   196–204
  and EU law   199–202
  and al-Jedda case   196–199
  and *jus cogens* norms   203–204
  and Lockerbie case   203
conflicting interpretations   180–182
different approach to
  in general   210–212
  positivist   214–217
  realist   212–214
and hierarchy   191–192, 198–199,
  206–207
institutional aspect of
  in general   207–208
  jurisdictional conflicts   208–209
and *jus cogens* norms   192–194,
  203–204
and *lex posterior* principle   194–196,
  205
and *lex specialis* principle   204–206
special laws claiming exceptions
  in Belilos v. Switzerland
    case   187–188
  in Celebisi case   190
  in Lockerbie case   187
  in Martic case   189–190
  in MOX Plant case   182–185
  other examples   189–192
  in Southern Bluefin Tuna
    case   185–187
France
  Casablanca Arbitration case (1907)   147,
    151–152, 162–163
  French Declaration of the Rights of Man
    and Citizens (1789)   17–18
  recognizing Libyan NTC   37
  Waller case (1895)   147, 151–152, 162–163
Franks, Tommy   98, 117
Free Zones of Upper Savoy and District of
  Gex (Fr v. Switz), 1929 P.C.I.J. (Ser. A) no 22
  (Order of Aug. 19)   164–165
freedom of expression   20–21
freedom of movement
  restrictions on
    in oPt   272–281
      East Jerusalem   250–251, 277–278
      Gaza Strip   279–281, 331–332
      West Bank   275–277, 278–279

INDEX

French Declaration of the Rights of Man and
Citizens (1789)   17–18
French Hill Bombing (2002)   440
Fretilin Liberation Front   84
Furundžija case   193

Gabčikovo-Nagymaros Project (Hung. v.
Slovk.), Judgment, 1997 I.C.J. Rep. 7, 72
(Sept. 25)   149n54
Gaddafi, Muammar   34–35, 37
Gasser, Hans-Peter   166n127
Gaza conflict (2014)   46, 69–70, 265–267,
423–425
Gaza Freedom Flotilla attack   122–123,
129n118, 130–131n120, 131–132
Gaza Freedom Flotilla case   122–123,
130–131n120, 131–132
Gaza Strip
agriculture in   342–343
blockade of   69, 254–255, 331–332, 341
control of   56, 58, 63
de-development process in   342
economy of   341–344
education, access to   283–284
freedom of movement in, restrictions
on   279–281, 331–332
health services, access to   284–285
ICC report on   421–422, 423–425
Israel's withdrawal from   56, 68, 69
living standards in   341–342, 343
"Operation Cast Lead" against   43, 46, 48,
49n32, 69
"Operation Protective Edge" against   46,
69–70, 265–267, 423–425
power cuts   341–342
Gaza War (2008–2009)   43, 46, 48, 49n32,
69
General Staff Mechanism for Fact-Finding
Assessment   311, 422
Geneva Conventions (1949)   54, 72, 74, 227
Additional Protocols to   24, 54, 72, 74,
151
see also Fourth Geneva Convention
Gentili, Alberico   15
Georgia   232, 234
German Basic Law (1968)   18
Germany
Allied occupation of   150–151, 227
BIT between Ukraine and   142

Casablanca Arbitration (1907)   147,
151–152
Cie des Chemins de Fer du Nord v.
German State, Franco-German Mixed
Tribunal (Apr. 8, 1929)   167
Milaire v. German State, Germano-Belgian
Mixed Arbitral Tribunal (Jan. 1, 1923)
166, 167
and North Continental Shelf case   77
UJ cases in, and subsidiarity   103–104
see also Nazi Germany
Germany-Ukraine BIT   142
al-Ghoul, Daoud   262–263
Gisha Legal Center for Freedom of
Movement   273, 289
Glahn, Gerhard von   137n4, 138n10, 148n49,
160n98, 161–162
God   13–14
Goldstone report   48–49, 105, 106–107
Gowlland-Debass, Vera   55–56
Greco-Turkish war   159n96
Greece   159n96
Greenspan, Morris   152n65, 162n106,
166n126
Greenwood, Christopher   168n133
Grotius, Hugo   15, 16
Guantanamo Bay   115
Guinea-Bissau   62, 73–74

Habre, Hissene   128
Hafner, Gerhard   214
Hague Regulations (1907)
and continuity of treaties   141–143,
155–156, 158–159, 163–166
necessity exception in   150n56, 162
occupation in, codification of   144, 148
personal scope of   171
requisitions in   174
and supreme authority of occupant   151
Halkin Emek Partisi (HEP)   20–21
Hamas
control of Gaza Strip   56, 58, 63
rift between PA and   56, 69, 291–292
see also Council of the European Union v.
Hamas
Hamas-Fatah Doha Agreement (2012)   58
al-Haq   98n5, 99, 114, 124
harrassment, of human rights
defenders   261–263

Hashaika, Mohammed 440
al-Hashlamoun, Hadeel 247
health services
  access to 284–286, 297
  quality of 343
  see also medical facilities
Hebrew University Bombing (2002) 440
Hebron 68, 247, 249, 251, 276, 281–282,
  296–297, 324–325, 331
HEP (*Halkin Emek Partisi*) 20–21
High Commissioner for Human Rights 314
Higher National Commission for Prisoners
  and Detainees Affairs 305
Hoffmeister, Frank 213
Holy See (Vatican City)
  recognized as state 59
  recognizing Palestine 46
  and UN 71–72
Human Rights Act (UK) 197–199
Human Rights Committee 330
human rights defenders 261–263
human rights treaties 155–156
human rights violations. *see* crimes/
  violations
Humanitarian Coordinator in the Occupied
  Palestinian Territory 250
Hungary 149n54
hunger strikes 264, 304, 362

ICC (International Criminal Court). *see*
  International Criminal Court
ICCPR (International Covenant on Civil and
  Political Rights) 19–20, 172, 329
ICISS (International Commission on
  Intervention and State Sovereignty)
  28–29, 32
ICRC (International Committee of the Red
  Cross) 126, 128, 145, 147, 154, 161, 332
ICTR (International Criminal Tribunal for
  Rwanda) 143n25, 161
ICTY (International Criminal Tribunal for the
  former Yugoslavia). *see* International
  Criminal Tribunal for the former
  Yugoslavia
Idris, Wafa 440
ILA (International Law Association) 93
ILC (International Law Commission).
  see International Law Commission

illegitimate regimes 33–37
ill-treatment. *see* torture/ill-treatment
ILO (International Labor
  Organization) 153–154
IMF (International Monetary Fund) 63–64,
  65
immunity
  of IDF soldiers 325
  from jurisdiction 79–86
  of occupants from local law 143–144,
    163–168
  of occupation personnel from local
    law 143, 162
  from persecution 99, 119–121, 126
  special mission 120–121
impunity. *see* immunity
INA Corporation v. Iran, Iran-US C. Trib.
  Vol. 8, (1985-I) 205
independence
  as statehood criteria 51–52, 57–58, 62
  and UN membership 62
India 62
insurrection. *see* rebel, right to
Interim Agreement. *see* Israeli-Palestinian
  Interim Agreement
Interim Transitional National Council of
  Libya 37–38
International Commission on Intervention
  and State Sovereignty (ICISS) 28–29,
  32
International Committee of the Red Cross
  (ICRC) 126, 128, 145, 147, 154, 161, 332
international community 9, 27–29,
  33–34
International Court of Justice (ICJ)
  accession to 76–77
  and admission to UN 61
  cases of
    Application of the Convention on
      the Prevention and Punishment
      of the Crime of Genocide (Bosn.
      Herz. v. Serb. & Montenegro),
      Further Requests for the
      Indication of Provisional
      Measures (separate opinion
      of Judge Lauterpacht), 1993
      I.C.J. Rep. 407, 440, para. 10
      (Sep. 13), 203–204

INDEX

Armed Activities on the Territory of the Congo (Dem. Rep. Congo v. Uganda), Judgment, 2005 I.C.J. Rep. 168, 231 (Dec. 19) 155–156, 159
Bosnian Genocide case 190
Continental Shelf (Tunis. v. Libya), 1982 I.C.J. Rep. 18, 38 (Feb. 24) 205
Gabčikovo-Nagymaros Project (Hung. v. Slovk.), Judgment, 1997 I.C.J. Rep. 7, 72 (Sept. 25) 149n54
Kosovo, Advisory Opinion, 2010 I.C.J. Rep. 403 (July 22) 67–68
Libya v. U.S., Preliminary Objections, ICJ Reports (1998) 189, 199, 203
Nicaragua v. United States of America, Judgment, 1986 I.C.J. Rep. 14 (June 27) 39n153, 180–182, 190, 192, 206, 209
North Sea Continental Shelf (Fed. Rep. Ger. v. Neth./Fed. Rep. Ger. v. Den.), 1969 I.C.J. Rep. 42, para. 72 (Apr. 26) 204
North Sea Continental Shelf (Fed. Rep. of Germ. v. Den., Fed. Rep. Germ. v. Neth.), 1968 I.C.J. Rep. 77
and continuity of treaties, 155–156, 159
and ECtHR 188, 209–210
and ICTY 189–191
and Israel's construction of the wall 56
and *jus cogens* norms 192
and statehood recognition 59
Statute of 73, 76
superiority of 191–192
and UN Charter 76, 189
international courts
growth in 207–208, 212
and Palestine's UN status 76–78
see also under specific courts
International Covenant on Civil and Political Rights (ICCPR) 19–20, 172, 329
International Covenant on Economic, Social and Cultural Rights (ICESCR) 329
International Criminal Court (ICC)
accession to 77–78
jurisdiction of
for crimes committed during "Operation Cast Lead" 43, 46, 48–49
retroactive 78

and PA 49–50, 106
and Palestine 43, 77–78, 126, 130
and Palestine's status 49–50
Report on Preliminary Examination Actions (2016). *see* Report on Preliminary Examination Actions
and UJ legislation 130–131
International Criminal Tribunal for Rwanda (ICTR) 143n25, 161
International Criminal Tribunal for the former Yugoslavia (ICTY)
cases of
Prosecutor v. Anto Furundžija, Case No. IT-95-17/1, Judgment (Intl. Crim. Trib. for the Former Yugoslavia Dec. 10, 1998) 193
Prosecutor v. Milan Martić, Case No. IT-95-11-R61, T.Ch. I, (Int'l Crim. Trib. for the Former Yugoslavia Mar. 8, 1996) 189–190
Prosecutor v. Tadić, Case No.IT-94-1-A, A.Ch, Judgment (Int'l Crim. Trib. for the Former Yugoslavia July 15, 1999) 180–182, 209
Prosecutor v. Zejnil Delalić et al (Čelebići Camp), Case No. IT-96-21-A, Appeals Chamber, (Int'l Crim. Trib. for the Former Yugoslavia Feb. 20, 2001) 190
and ICJ 189–191
and indirect consent 143n25, 161
on *jus cogens* 194
review of own legality 189, 191
and UN Charter 189
international human rights law (IHRL) 9, 19, 48
international humanitarian law (IHL) 9, 33, 168–170
International Labor Conference (63rd; 1977) 153
International Labor Organization (ILO) 153–154
international law
centrality of States in 27
direct or indirect consent in 161
fragmentation in. *see* fragmentation
humanitarian obligation in 335–336
internment in 327

international law (cont.)
and *jus cogens* norms 192–194, 203–204, 206–207
and *jus dispositivum* 204
and *jus in bello* 33, 229
and *jus post bellum* 225, 233
and *lex ferenda* 232
and *lex posterior* 186, 194–196, 205
and *lex specialis* principle 144, 168, 172–173, 186, 192, 194–196, 204–206, 225
and non-State actors 9
of occupation. *see* international law of occupation
and Palestine's statehood status 53–58
and *res inter alios acta* principle 142n24
right to rebel in
codification of 18–20
neutrality towards 10–12, 18
right to self-defense in
in general 25–26
of non-State actors 25–27
specialization in 179
and struggles for self-determination
in general 22–24, 25
and external intervention 24–25
see also universal jurisdiction
International Law Association (ILA) 93
International Law Commission (ILC)
Draft Articles on the "Effects of Armed Conflict on Treaties" 156–159
and hierarchy in law 206–207
study of fragmentation 181, 210, 212
and systemic integration 169n139
international law of occupation
in general 223–226
and co-application of norms 228–229
in contemporary situations 227
deficiency of 141n18
in historical situations 226–227
minor amendments to 231
and transformative occupations 225, 226–235
see also law of (belligerent) occupation; occupant; occupations
International Monetary Fund (IMF) 63–64, 65
international territorial administration 225
international tribunals 207–208, 212
internment. *see* detentions

interventions
in general 9
historical overview 13–14
in Libya 39
paternalistic approach to 29
under R2P framework 31–32
role of international community in 27–29
and struggles for self-determination 24–25
and UN 39
UNGA on 22–23
UNSC on 9, 31–32, 39
investment laws 143n26
investment protection 172–175
investment treaties 139n2
see also Bilateral Investment Treaties
investment tribunals 170–172
investors, definition of 170
Iran-United States Treaty of Amity 205
Iraq
labor code in 154
MNF in 196–197
occupation of 223, 224, 225–226, 229–232
war crimes committed in 98, 104n27
Iraq Inquiry 223, 231
Ireland 182–184
ISIS 39
Israel
admission to UN 59–60, 63
building of wall/barrier by 56, 69, 276–277, 347
and control of Palestine 63–64
creation of 44n4
Eichmann trial 102–103
legal system of 99–100, 111, 133–134, 306
and oPt
as belligerent occupant of 63–64, 91, 98
control of economy by 340–341
labor obligation in 153–154
and "Operation Cast Lead" 43, 46, 48, 49n32, 69
and "Operation Protective Edge" 46, 69–70, 265–267, 423–425
respect for right of development 348–350

INDEX

settlements in
  in general 253–254, 332
  B'Tselem on 131n121
  growth of 69n133
  UN resolution on 374–384
  on West Bank 345–346
  status of treaties in
    concluded by PLO/PA 86–87
    Convention No. 111 of ILO
      153–154
peace process with PLO 68–70, 86
and recognition of Palestine 54
and Resolution 67/19 (2012) 44
and Resolution 181 (1947) 53–54
and UJ cases
  lobbying against 98, 105, 106–107, 111,
    114–118, 123
  opposition against
    in general 98, 104–105
    political 105–107
    responses to 105
  refusal to cooperate in 123–125
withdrawal from occupied territories 56,
  68, 69
Israel Defense Forces. see Israeli security
  forces
Israel Security Agency 273
Israeli Medical Association 268
Israeli Military Advocate General
  (MAG) 108, 110
Israeli military forces. see Israeli security
  forces
Israeli Military Police Criminal Investigations
  Division 259
Israeli navy. see Israeli security forces
Israeli officials
  UJ cases against
    in Belgium, Sharon case 98, 105, 117,
      120
    of Al-Haq 98n5, 114, 124
    in Netherlands
      Ayalon case 112–114, 122
      Riwal case 124, 128–129
    in New Zealand, Yaalon case 98, 99,
      119
    in Spain
      Al-Daraj case 109–111, 115
      Gaza Freedom Flotilla case 122–
        123, 130–131n120, 131–132

in UK
  of al-Haq 114
  Almog case 99, 121–122, 124n103
  Livni case 99, 116–117, 120–121
  Mofaz case 120
  in Western Europe 98–99
Israeli police force. see Israeli security forces
Israeli Prison Service 304
Israeli security forces
  accountability for violations 305–313
    addressing of challenges by
      Israel 313–316
    and civil remedies 311–312
    against detainees 312–313
    during hostilities 310–311
    lack of 258–259, 324–326
    during law enforcement 307–311
  crimes/violations committed by 43, 46,
    48–49, 265–267, 423–427
  hostilities between Palestinian armed
    groups and 299–300
  open-fire regulations of 309
  use of firearms by 248–249, 263, 297,
    298–299, 309, 323–324
  violence, excessive use of 246–250,
    263–264, 296–300, 315, 323–324, 350
Israeli Supreme Court 108–109, 110
Israeli-Palestinian Interim Agreement 45,
  47n24, 55, 68, 91
Italy 77
ITLOS (United Nations Law of the Sea
  Tribunal) 185–186, 191
Izz el-Din al-Qassam 300
  see also Hamas

al-Ja'ara, Ali 440
Jaffa Road Bombing (2002) 439
Jaffa Road Shooting (2002) 439
Japan 76, 145–146, 150n57, 185–187
al-Jedda, Mr. 197
al-Jedda case 196–199
Jenks, Wilfried 168n136
Jiang, Zemin 115
Jones v. Ministry of Interior of Saudi Arabia
  [2006] UKHL 26, (2007) 1 AC 270, 298
  (2006) 2 WLR 1424 [U.K.] 194
Judge Advocate General (JAG; US) 145
judicial experimentalism 191
jus ad bellum 33, 227, 229, 233

jus cogens norms   192–194, 203–204, 206–207
jus dispositivum   204
jus in bello   33, 229
jus post bellum   225, 233

Kadi & Al Barakaat v. Council of the
    European Union, 2008 3 C.M.L.R. 41
    (2008)   199–200
Kadi v. Council and Commission, 2005
    E.C.R. II-3649   200
Karmi-Ayyoub, Salma   96–135
Kennedy, David   169n140
Khan Younis   265
King George Street Bombing (2002)   440
Kleiman case   83
Klinghoffer, Leon   80
Klinghoffer v. SNC Achille Lauro, United
    States (Court of Appeals) 96 ILR 74
    80–81, 83
Koskenniemi, Martii   211–212, 214–215
Kosovo   67
Kosovo, Advisory Opinion, 2010 I.C.J. Rep. 403
    (July 22)   67–68
Kuwait   62

labor laws   153–154
LAS (League of Arab States). *see* League of
    Arab States
Latvia   195
Lauterpacht, Judge   203–204
law of (belligerent) occupation
    and BITs   168–175
    codification of   144, 148
    development of   148
    and treaty obligations   158
law of conquest   148–149
law of State succession   87–88, 93, 94, 95
lawfare   106
League of Arab States (LAS)
    and legitimacy of Assad regime   36, 38
    and legitimacy of Qaddafi regime   35, 37
    Palestine's membership of   65, 92
    and Resolution 181 (1947)   54
League of Nations   53, 58
Leathley, Christian   208
Lebanon   98, 117
legal system, of Israel   99–100, 111, 133–134,
    306

*Legality of the Threat or Use of Nuclear
    Weapons* (ICJ)   168–169n136, 172–173
legitimacy, of States   33–37
Leino, Paivi   211–212
lethal force. *see* firearms; violence
lex ferenda   232
lex posterior principle   186, 194–196, 205
lex specialis principle   144, 168, 172–173, 186,
    192, 204–206, 225
Libya
    BIT between Austria and   157–158n90
    international intervention in   30–31, 39
    legitimacy of Qaddafi regime   34–35, 37
    and Lockerbie case   189, 203
    repressing of peaceful protests in   20n59,
        21, 34
Libya v. U.S., Preliminary Objections, ICJ
    Reports (1998)   189, 199, 203
Libya-Austria BIT   157–158n90
Libyan Contact Group   37
Lieberman, Avigdor   315, 324
Liechtenstein   59, 76
life, human right to   172
living standards
    in East Jerusalem   347
    in Gaza Strip   341–342
    in West Bank   346
Livni, Tzipi   99, 116–117, 120–121
lobbying
    against UJ cases
        of China   115
        of Israel   98, 105, 106–107, 111, 114–118,
            123
        of US   98, 115, 117
local communities   28–29, 30
localized-treaty rule   146, 149
Lockerbie case   189, 199, 203
Loizidou v. Turkey, App. No. 15318/89, 1995
    Eur. Ct. H.R.   156n82, 209
losses, compensation for   138n10,
        157–158n90, 173–174, 205
Lynk, Michael
    mandate of   321
    report of   319–351
        on accountability, lack of   324–326
        on administrative detentions
            326–328
        on child detentions   328–329

on coercive environments 332
on destruction of homes 334
on freedom of movement, restrictions
on 331–332
on punitive demolitions 330
recommendations 350–351
on relocations, forced 332–334
on right to development
in general 335–336
in East Jerusalem 346–348
in Gaza Strip 341–344
Israel's respect for 348–350
in oPt 337–341
in West Bank 344–346
on violence, excessive use of 323–325
tenure of 107

Machsom Watch 275
Madagascar 147, 151–152
Magen David Adom 297
Malsko, Lauri 175n158
Martic case 189–190
Mavrommatis Palestine Concessions Case
(Greece v. UK), 1924 P.C.I.J. Ser. A No. 2
53n54, 204
Mayorga, Ofilio J. 136–176
McNeill, Mark 141n19
medical facilities 265–266
see also health services
Mégret, Frédéric 30–31, 41
Meron, Theodore 153
Milaire v. German State, Germano-Belgian
Mixed Arbitral Tribunal (Jan. 1,
1923) 166, 167
Millett, Lord 193
Ministry of Foreign Affairs of the Republic of
the Maldives 35
Mofaz, Shaul 120
Monaco 52
Mongolia 62
Montevideo Convention 51, 55, 66
Montreal Convention (1971) 203
Morgenstern, Felice 212
Morocco 147, 151–152
Moussa, Jasmine 42–95
movement, freedom of. see freedom of
movement
"moving treaty boundaries" rule 141n18, 149

MOX Plant case 182–184
multi-national forces (MNF) 196–197

NAM (Non-Aligned Movement) 65–66
National Coalition of the Syrian
Revolutionary and Opposition Forces
(NCS) 36, 37, 38, 39
national liberation movements 24
National Transitional Council (NTC) 34,
36–38
Nauru 59, 76
Nazi Germany 133
NCS (National Coalition of the Syrian
Revolutionary and Opposition
Forces) 36, 37, 38, 39
neo-colonialism 228
Netanyahu, Benjamin 104n29, 122, 131
Netanyahu case 122–123
Netherlands
and Palestine's statehood status 84
UJ cases in
Ayalon case 112–114, 122
and changes in legislation 105
and presence of suspect 112–114
Riwal case 124, 128–129
New Zealand
Southern Bluefin Tuna case 185–187
UJ cases in
and Attorneys-General decisions 119
and changes in legislation 105
Yaalon case 98, 99, 119
NIACs (non-international armed
conflicts) 9, 26
Nicaragua v. United States of America,
Judgment, 1986 I.C.J. Rep. 14 (June 27)
39n153, 180–182, 190, 192, 206, 209
Nollkaemper, Andre 217
Non-Aligned Movement (NAM) 65–66
non-international armed conflicts
(NIACs) 9, 26
non-localized treaties 149–150
non-State actors
in international law
in general 9
as parties to binding treaties 86–87,
88
right to self-defense of 25–27
and treaty succession 93

North Sea Continental Shelf (Fed. Rep. Ger. v. Neth./Fed. Rep. Ger. v. Den.), 1969 I.C.J. Rep. 42, para. 72 (Apr. 26) 204

North Sea Continental Shelf (Fed. Rep. of Germ. v. Den., Fed. Rep. Germ. v. Neth.), 1968 I.C.J. Rep. 77

Northern Cyprus 156n82, 209, 234

NTC (National Transitional Council) 34, 36–38

NV Algemene Transport-en Expeditie Ondememing Van Gend en Loos v. Nederlandse Administratie der Belastingen (Netherlands Inland Revenue Administration) 184–185

Obama, Barack 34

obedience, duty of 149n53, 168n133

occupant

  authority of 150–151, 227

  and *debellatio* doctrine 150–151

  destruction of private property by 173–174

  and extraterritoriality 147, 163

  and local law/prior treaties

    immunity from 143–144, 163–168

    as laws in force 152–161

    and necessity exception 143, 150n56, 159, 162, 167

    non-binding 145–152

    privileges of 159n96

    responsibilities of 159–163

  and relief for population in need 334

  right of detention of 196–197

  and sovereignty 57, 90–91, 148, 160n98

  and transfer of populations 332–333

  see also occupations; occupied territories

occupations

  of Azerbaijan 232, 234

  of Baltic States 89, 175n58

  and BITs 141–142

  of China 145–146, 150n57

  of Crimea 139–140, 175, 232, 234

  of Georgian territory 232, 234

  of Germany 150–151, 227

  international law of. *see* international law of occupation

  of Iraq 223, 224, 225–226, 229–232

  key principle of 148

  law of. *see* law of (belligerent) occupation

  of Northern Cyprus 156n82, 209, 234

  of Palestine. *see* Occupied Palestinian Territory

  and self-determination 225, 227, 228–232

  and sovereignty 57, 90–91, 148, 160n98

  transformative 225, 226–235

  UNSC's endorsements of 225

  see also occupant; occupied territories

Occupied Palestinian Territory (oPt)

  agriculture in 277, 287, 342–343

  economy of

    in general 337–340

    in East Jerusalem 346–348

    in Gaza Strip 341–344

    in West Bank 344–346

  human rights defenders in, harrassment of 261–263

  human rights situation in

    in general 322–323

    accountability for violations 258–259, 305–313, 324–326

    coercive environments 332, 333–334

    demolitions 124n103, 250, 253, 301, 330, 332–334

    detentions. *see* detentions

    education, access to 251, 281–283, 293, 364

    family life, right to 289–291

    forced relocations/evictions of. *see* relocations

    freedom of movement, restrictions on 272–281

      East Jerusalem 250–251, 277–278

      Gaza Strip 279–281, 331–332

      West Bank 275–277, 278–279

    health services, access to 284–286, 297

    impact of Palestinian disunity on 291–292

    poverty increase in 339

    punitive practices 250, 300–304, 330–332, 351

    recommendations of the Special Rapporteur 267–268, 350–351

    right to development

      Israel's respect for 348–350

      overview 335–348

UN resolution on 358–368
violence, excessive use of 246–250, 263–264, 296–300, 323–324, 350
work, access to
within Israel 288–289
within oPt 287–288, 339
and Israel
as belligerent occupant of 63–64, 91, 98
control of economy by 340–341
labor obligation in 153–154
and "Operation Cast Lead" 43, 46, 48, 49n32, 69
and "Operation Protective Edge" 46, 69–70, 265–267, 423–425
respect for right of development 348–350
settlements
in general 253–254, 332
B'Tselem on 131n121
growth of 69n133
UN resolution on, 374–384
on West Bank 345–346
status of treaties in
concluded by PLO/PA 86–87
Convention No. 111 of ILO 153–154
see also Palestine
occupied territories
and local law/prior treaties
as laws in force 152–161
and necessity exception 143, 150n56, 159, 162, 167
non-binding 145–152
and occupant's immunity from 143–144, 163–168
and occupant's privileges 159n96
and occupant's responsibility 159–163
and sovereignty 57, 90–91, 148, 160n98
subjugation of 150–151
O'Connell, Daniel P. 92
Office for the Coordination of Humanitarian Affairs 248, 250–251, 302, 330, 332, 333
Office of the United Nations High Commissioner for Human Rights (OHCHR)
report U.N. Doc. A/71/364 294–318

accountability for violations 305–313
addressing of challenges by Israel 313–316
and civil remedies 311–312
against detainees 312–313
during hostilities 310–311
during law enforcement 307–311
arrests 305
conclusions of 316–317
detentions 304–305
legal background 296
on punitive practices 300–304
recommendations of 317–318
on violence, excessive use of 296–300
report U.N. Doc. A/HRC/31/44, 269–293
education, access to 281–283
family life, right to 289–291
on freedom of movement, restrictions on 272–281
and East Jerusalem 277–278
and Gaza Strip 279–281
and West Bank 275–277, 278–279
health services, access to 284–286
legal background 270–271
recommendations of
to Israel 292–293
to PA 292–293
work, access to 287–289
Olmert, Ehud 109
"Operation Cast Lead" (2008–2009) 43, 46, 48, 49n32, 69
"Operation Protective Edge" (2014) 46, 69–70, 265–267, 423–425
opposition
against UJ cases
in general 133
of Israel
in general 98, 104–105
political 105–107
responses to 105
of Western States 105
see also lobbying, against UJ cases
opposition groups, support for 39
Orford, Anne 29
Organization of Islamic Conference (OIC) 66
Oslo Accords 44, 55–56, 64, 94, 337–338, 343

OSPAR Convention (Convention on the Protection of the Marine Environment of the North-East Atlantic) 182–183
Ottoman Empire 159n96
Ould Dah, Ely 124n100

Palestine
  as Class 'A' Mandate 53–54
  and Geneva Conventions and Additional Protocols 54
  and ICC 43, 77–78, 126, 130
  and ICJ 76–77
  memberships of
    Economic and Social Commission for Western Asia 65
    LAS 65, 92
    Non-Aligned Movement 65–66
    Organization of Islamic Conference 66
    UNESCO 43–44, 65, 74
  and "Operation Cast Lead" 43, 46, 48, 49n32, 69
  and "Operation Protective Edge" 46, 69–70, 265–267, 423–425
  peace process with Israel 68–70, 86
  recognition of
    by Israel 54
    by Western European States 45–46
  rift between PA and Hamas 56, 69, 291–292
  statehood status of
    in general 42–43, 44–45
    and Canada 84–85
    and effective control 54–58, 63–64
    and ICC 49–50
    and independence 57–58
    in international law 53–58
    and Netherlands 84
    and PLO 80–81
    and right to self-determination 57
    and UN status 43–44, 45–46, 65–66, 70
    in United Kingdom 80
    and US 80–84
  treaty participation of
    in general 71, 74–75
    validity in 86–94, 153–154
  and UN

application for membership of 50, 63, 65
  observer status in 43, 64–65
  see also UN non-member observer State status
Palestine Authority. see Palestinian Interim Self- Governing Authority
Palestine Liberation Organization (PLO)
  and acts of terrorism 81–82
  establishment of 47n24
  observer status in UN 54, 55, 64–65
  and Oslo Accords 55–56
  peace process with Israel 68–70, 86
  as representative of Palestinian people 44
  and statehood status, of Palestine 80–81
  status within UN 55
  validity of treaties with Israel 86–87
  see also Palestinian Interim Self-Governing Authority
Palestine Mandate 53–54, 205
Palestine National Council (PNC) 54, 64
Palestinian armed groups 299–300
Palestinian Central Bureau of Statistics 302
Palestinian Centre for Human Rights (PCHR)
  and Al-Daraj case 109–111
  and case against Ayalon 112–114
  views on UJ cases 99
Palestinian Interim Self-Governing Authority (PA)
  and acts of terrorism 81–82
  effectiveness of 56–58, 63–64
  establishment of, 47n24 55, 68
  and foreign relations 68, 91
  and ICC 49–50, 106
  and "Operation Cast Lead" 48, 49n32
  and Resolution 67/19 (2012) 44, 65
  rift between Hamas and 56, 69, 291–292
  validity of treaties with Israel 86–87
  see also Palestine Liberation Organization
Palestinian people, right to self-determination 57, 65, 69, 335–336, 355–357
Palestinian-Israeli conflict
  peace process in 68–70, 86
  two-State solution to 67, 69
Paraguayan indigenous group 128
parallelism 211

INDEX

Parent and Others v. Singapore Airlines Limited and the Civil Aeronautics Administration, Canada, Superior Court of Quebec (22 October 2003) 84

Paris Protocol on Economic Relations, 1994 (Protocol on Economic Relations between the Government of the State of Israel and the Palestine Liberation Organization) 337–338

PCHR (Palestinian Centre for Human Rights). *see* Palestinian Centre for Human Rights

PCIJ (Permanent Court of International Justice) 53n54, 164–165, 204, 205

peace process, in Palestinian-Israeli conflict 68–70, 86

peaceful assembly, right to 20–21

peaceful protest, right to 19–20

Peaceful Settlement of the Question of Palestine, Report of the Secretary General 70

Pellet, Alain 162n106

Penal Law (Israel) 313

penal laws 154–155

Permanent Court of International Justice (PCIJ) 53n54, 164–165, 204, 205

permits
building 333–334, 345, 349
residence 290, 293, 360, 365
travel 273–274, 278, 279, 283, 304, 331
medical 285, 303
work 288–289

Picciotti, Romulus A. 148n51

Pinochet, Augusto 194

Poland 89

political pressure. *see* lobbying

Portuguese Constitution (1976) 18

Potsdam Declaration 227

poverty 288, 339, 342, 343, 347

Powell, Colin 197

power cuts 341–342

Presbyterians 14

prisoner of war (POW) status 24

private property
compensation for taking 173–174
destruction of 172, 173–174

prosecution, immunity from 119–121

Prosecutor v. Anto Furundžija, Case No. IT-95-17/1, Judgment (Intl. Crim. Trib. for the Former Yugoslavia Dec. 10, 1998) 193

Prosecutor v. Milan Martić, Case No. IT-95-11-R61, T.Ch. I, (Int'l Crim. Trib. for the Former Yugoslavia Mar. 8, 1996) 189–190

Prosecutor v. Tadić, Case No. IT-94-1-A, A.Ch, Judgment (Int'l Crim. Trib. for the Former Yugoslavia July 15, 1999) 180–182, 209

Prosecutor v. Zejnil Delalić et al (Čelebići Camp), Case No. IT-96-21-A, Appeals Chamber 190

Prost, Mario 217

protected person status 170–171n143, 171

Protection of Civilian Persons in Time of War 250

Protestants 13–14

Protocol on Economic Relations between the Government of the State of Israel and the Palestine Liberation Organization (the Paris Protocol on Economic Relations, 1994) 337–338

Public Commission to Examine the Maritime Incident of 31 May 2010 313–314

Pufendorf, Samuel von 16

punitive practices, in oPt 250, 300–304, 330–332, 351

Qabatiya 302

al-Qaeda network 199

al-Qasrawi, Ramzi 297, 308

al-Qiq, Muhammed 304

Quigley, John 53, 54, 55, 56–57

Qusbah, Mohammad 309, 315

R (Al-Skeini and others) v. Secretary of State for Defence [2007] UKHL 26; [2007] 3 WLR 33, 197–198

R (In re Al-Jedda) v. Secretary of State for Defence [2007] UKHL 58; [2008] 1 A.C. 332 (appeal taken from England) 196–197

R2P doctrine (responsibility to protect doctrine). *see* responsibility to protect doctrine

Rao, Pemmaraju 216

490 INDEX

rebel, right to
  in domestic law
    in general   10–12
    codification of   17–18
  historical overview   13–16
  and human rights   19
  in international law
    codification of   18–20
    neutrality towards   10–12, 18
  neglect of   9, 10, 13
  and R2P doctrine   9
  recognition of   33, 40–41
  in regional law   20–22
rebellion. *see* rebel, right to
recognition
  of Bosnia-Herzegovina   53
  of China   85
  definition of   59
  of Holy See   59
  of National Coalition of the Syrian
    Revolutionary and Opposition Forces
    (NCS)   36, 37, 38
  of National Transitional Council
    (NTC)   34, 36–38
  of Palestine   45–46, 54
  of right to rebel   33, 40–41
  as statehood criteria   52–54, 79
  of Syrian National Council (SNC)   35–36
Redaelli, Chiara   8–41
Regina v. Bow Street Metropolitan
  Stipendiary Magistrate, Ex parte Pinochet
  Ugarte (No 3) [2000] 1 A.C. 147 (H.L. 1999)
  [U.K.]   193
regional law   20–22
relocations, forced
  in general   4
  in oPt
    in general   250, 332–333, 350, 360, 362,
      376, 380, 426
    of Bedouin communities   261,
      333–334, 345, 350, 376, 380, 426
    East Jerusalem   260–261
    West Bank   301, 333–334, 345
Report of the Special Rapporteur on the
  Situation of Human Rights in the
  Palestinian Territories Occupied Since
  1967, U.N. Doc. A/71/554. *see* Lynk, Michael

Report of the Special Rapporteur on the
  Situation of Human Rights in the
  Palestinian Territories Occupied Since
  1967, U.N. Doc. A/HRC/31/73. *see*
  Wibisono, Marakim
Report on Preliminary Examination Actions
  (2016; ICC)   421–429
  alleged crimes
    in general   423
    East Jerusalem   425–427
    Gaza   423–425
    West Bank   425–427
  conclusion   429
  contextual background
    East Jerusalem   422–423
    Gaza   421–422
    West Bank   422–423
  OTP Activities   427–429
Report on the Responsibility to Protect (of
  ICISS)   28–29, 32
requisitions in kind   174
res inter alios acta principle, 142n24
residence permits   290, 293, 360, 365
Resolution 43/177 (1988; UNGA)   54
Resolution 67/19 (2012; UNGA)
  in general   43–45
  contradiction UNSC resolutions   66–70
  legal implications for Palestine   70–94
    in general   45–47, 70–71
    and domestic courts   79–83
    institutional, with UN   71–72
    and International Courts   76–78
    and statehood status   57, 65–66, 70
    for treaty participation
      bilateral treaties   71
      multi-lateral treaties   74–75
    and validity of treaties
      in general   86–87
      and State succession   87, 88–89,
        91–94
Resolution 181 (1947; UNGA)   53–54,
  91–92
Resolution 1244 (1999; UNSC)   67
Resolution 1267 (1999; UNSC)   199
Resolution 1483 (2003; UNSC)   229–232
Resolution 1515 (2003; UNSC)   66–67
Resolution 1546 (2004; UNSC)   196–197, 199

INDEX

491

Resolution 1850 (2008; UNSC) 66–67
Resolution 2234 (2016; UNSC) 385–387
respect, definition of 165–166
responsibility to protect doctrine (R2P doctrine)
 and international intervention 31–32
 and local community 30
 and right to rebel 9
 and States 27–29
reversion, in statehood status 89–90, 91–92
Right of Passage over Indian Territory (Port. v. India), 1960 I.C.J. Rep. 6 (Apr. 12) 204
Riwal 124, 128–129
road closures 331
Road Map for Peace 45, 67, 68–69
Roberts, Adam 153n71
Rogers, A. P. V. 162n104
Rome Statute (of ICC)
 and extraterritorial jurisdiction 132
 and Goldstone report 49n32
 individual criminal responsibility in 26
 Palestine acceding to 43, 77–78, 126n105, 130
 relocations in 333
 and UJ 127
Rumsfeld, Donald 104n27
Russia
 BIT between Ukraine and 139–140, 141n19, 142, 171
 and legitimacy of Qaddafi regime 34
 occupation of Crimea 139–140, 175, 232, 234
 occupation of Georgian territory 232, 234
 and Slivenko v. Latvia 195
 see also Soviet Union
Russia-Ukraine BIT 139–140, 141n19, 142, 171
Ruys, Tom 213
Rwanda 133, 161
Rwanda Patriotic Front 30

Sabra massacre 98, 117
Safadi, Hasan 328
San Marino 59, 76
Sanctions Committee (of UNSC) 199
Sassoli, Marco 41
Saul, Ben 26
Schabas, William 107

Schwarzenberger, Georg 162n104, 163–165
Schwenk, Edmund H. 174–175n157
Scott, Karen 216
Seam Zone 276–277, 281
self-defense, right to 25–27, 56
self-determination, right to
 and interventions 24–25
 and occupation 225, 227, 228–232
 of Palestinian people 57, 65, 69, 335–336, 355–357
 and right to struggle 22–25
Sellafield plant 182–184
Senegal 128
Serbia 67
Serbia-Montenegro 180
settlements, Israeli
 in oPt
  in general 253–254, 332
  B'Tselem on 131n121
  growth of 69n133
  UN resolution on 374–384
  on West Bank 345–346
Al Shami v. Ayalon, Appeal judgment, No K08/0386 Rechtspraak.nl: BK7374, para. 15 113
al-Sharawi, Tharwat 296–297
al-Sharif, Abd al-Fatah 297, 308, 315, 324
Sharon, Ariel 98, 117, 120
Sharon case 98, 105, 117, 120
Sharpston, Advocate General 391–418
Shatila massacre 98, 117
Shaw, Malcolm 52–53, 55
Shehadeh, Saleh 108
Shongwe, Musa Njabulo 177–219
Shu'fat refugee camp 299
Shurrab, Haytham Mohamad Ghazi 285–286
Singapore 80
al-Skeini case 198–199
Slivenko v. Latvia, App. No. 48321/99, Judgment, 2003 Eur. Ct. H.R. 195
Slovakia 149n54
Smyrna 159n96
SOC (Syrian Opposition Coalition) 36, 37, 38
Societe eds Quais de Smyrna v. Greece (1929) 159n96

Sokolow v. Palestine Liberation Organization et al, 2nd U.S. Circuit Court of Appeals, (2nd Cir 2016), 31/08/2016, No. 15–3135 82, 433–471

Sokolow v. Palestine Liberation Organization et al, U.S. District Court, Southern District of New York (SDNY 2008), 9/30/2008, No. 04–00397   81–82, 83

South Africa   129n118, 132

South African police   129n118, 132

Southern Bluefin Tuna case   185–187

sovereignty
 and occupation   57, 90–91, 148, 148n51, 160n98
 of States   12, 13–16, 26

Soviet Union   89, 175–176n158
 see also Russia

Spain
 UJ cases in
  in absentia   103
  Al-Daraj case   109–111, 115
  and changes in legislation, 105, 111, 115
  Gaza Freedom Flotilla case   122–123, 130–131n120, 131–132
  and subsidiarity   103

Spanish Constitutional Court   110

Spanish police   123

Spanish Supreme Court   110

Special Committee to Investigate Israeli Practices Affecting the Human Rights of the Palestinian People and Other Arabs of the Occupied Territories, report of   294–318

Special Franco-Greek Arbitral Tribunal   159n96

special mission immunity   120–121

special rapporteurs on human rights (UN)
 in general   107
 report of Lynk, Michael   319–351
 report of Wibisono, Marakim   241–268

State Immunity Act 1978 (UK)   80

statehood
 and admission to UN   59–60, 61–63
 in civil law jurisdictions   79–80, 84–85, 86
 in common-law jurisdictions   79–84
 criteria for
  and effectiveness, illegal   89–90

effectiveness as   53, 63–64, 181
 independence as   51–52, 57–58, 62
 recognition as   52–54, 79
 and right to self-determination   57
 status of
  in general   73, 75
  Egypt   57–58
  Palestine   42–46, 49–50, 53–58, 65–66, 70
  and PLO   80–81
  reversion in   89–90, 91–92
 see also States

States
 definition of   63
 in international law, centrality of   9, 27
 legitimacy of   33–37
 and R2P doctrine   27–29
 sovereignty of   12, 13–16, 26
 succession of   87–93, 141n18, 149
 see also statehood

Statute of the International Court of Justice   73, 76

struggle, right to   22–25
 see also rebel, right to

Suarez, Francisco   14

subjugation. see debellatio doctrine

subsidiarity   103–104, 108–111

succession, of States   87–93, 141n18, 149

Suppression of Unlawful Acts against the Safety of Civil Aviation   203

Switzerland   59, 76, 187–188

Syria
 legitimacy of government of   36
 repressing of peaceful protests in   20n59, 21, 35

Syrian National Council (SNC)   35–36

Syrian Opposition Coalition (SOC)   36, 37, 38

systemic integration   169, 172

Tadić case   180–182, 209

Taiwan   84–85

Taliban regime   199

terrorism, acts of   81–82

Third United Nations Conference on the Law of the Sea   74, 205

Thomas Aquinas   13

Thrilway, Hugh   206

INDEX 493

Tibet   115
Timor Gap Treaty   93
Tinoco (Gr. Brit. v. Costa Rica), 1 R.I.A.A. 369
  (1923)   11–12
tort claims   312
Torture Victim Protection Act   97n1
torture/ill-treatment
  in general   264–265
  accountability for   312–313
  cases   104n27, 112–113, 122, 124n100,
  193–194
*The Transformation of Occupied Territory in
  International Law* (Carcano)   223–235
Transjordan   62
travel permits   273–274, 278, 279, 283, 285,
  303–304, 331
treaties
  continuity in occupied territory
    Hague Regulations on   141–143,
      155–156, 158–159, 163–166
    and ICJ   155–156, 159
    of international conventions
      153–154
    as laws in force   152–161
    and necessity exception   143, 150n56,
      159, 162, 167
    non-binding   145–152
    and occupant's immunity   143–144,
      163–168
    and occupant's privileges   159n96
    and occupant's responsibility
      159–163
  interpretation of
    in general   165
    and systemic integration   169, 172
  of Palestine
    in general   71, 74–75
    and validity   86–94, 153–154
  reservations to   188
  terms of, ordinary meaning of   165
  see also specific treaties
Treaty of Lausanne   204
Turkel Commission   313–314
Turkey
  and dissolution of HEP   20–21
  and European Convention on Human
    Rights   188, 209
  human rights violations by   156n82

occupation of Northern Cyprus   156n82,
  209, 234
UJ cases in   132
2030 Agenda for Sustainable
  Development   335

Uganda   155–156
UK-Argentina BIT   160–161n99
Ukraine
  BIT between Germany and   142
  BIT between Russia and   139–140, 141n19,
    142, 171
UN (United Nations). *see* United Nations
UN Charter. *see* United Nations Charter
U.N. Doc. A/HRC/31/44, 269–293
U.N. Doc. A/HRC/31/73, 241–268
UN non-member observer State status
  of Holy See   71–72
  of Palestine
    in general   43–44, 45–46, 65–66
    implications of   70–94
    in general   70–71
    and domestic courts   79–86
    institutional   71–72
    and International Courts   76–78
    for treaty participation   71, 72–75
    and validity of treatise   86–94
UNCLOS (United Nations Convention on the
  Law of the Sea)   182–184, 185–187
UNCTAD (United Nations Conference on
  Trade and Development)   340, 347
UNESCO (United Nations Educational,
  Scientific and Cultural
  Organization)   43–44, 65, 74
UNGA (United Nations General Assembly).
  see United Nations General Assembly
United Kingdom (UK)
  advocacy initiatives in   134
  and al-Jedda case   196–199
  and al-Skeini case   198–199
  BIT between Argentina and
    160–161n99
  and Egypt's independence   57–58
  and invasion/occupation of Iraq   223
  and Jones v. Ministry of Interior of Saudi
    Arabia   194
  and legitimacy of Assad's regime   36
  and legitimacy of Qaddafi regime   34

494   INDEX

United Kingdom (UK) (cont.)
  and Lockerbie case 203
  and MOX plant case 182–184
  and Palestine's statehood status 80
  and Pinochet case 193–194
  State Immunity Act 1978 80
  UJ cases in
    in general 99
    of al-Haq 114
    Almog case 99, 121–122, 124n103
    and Attorneys-General
      decisions 118–119
    and changes in legislation 105,
      115–117
    Livni case 99, 116–117, 120–121
    Mofaz case 120
United Nations Charter
  admission conditions in 60–61
  Article 103 of 196–204
    and EU law 199–202
    al-Jedda case 196–199
    and *jus cogens* 203–204
    and Lockerbie case 203
  and ICJ 76, 189
  and ICTY 189
  on indirect consent 143n25, 161
  on Kosovo 67
  on primacy of State obligations 196
  on right of self-defense 26, 56
  on two-State solution 67
  on use of force 39n153
United Nations Committee on Admission of
  New Members 61, 62, 63, 65
United Nations Committee on the Inalienable
  Rights of the Palestinian People 44n5
United Nations Conference on Trade and
  Development (UNCTAD) 340, 347
United Nations Convention on the Law of the
  Sea (UNCLOS) 182–184, 185–187
United Nations Department of Safety and
  Security 298
United Nations Educational, Scientific and
  Cultural Organization
  (UNESCO) 43–44,
  65, 74
United Nations Fact Finding Mission on the
  Conflict in Gaza 48–49, 105, 106–107,
  123–125

United Nations General Assembly (UNGA)
  and admission procedures 60–61
  Declaration on the Right to
    Development 335–336, 350–351
  on interventions 22–23
  Resolution 43/177 (1988) 54
  Resolution 67/19 (2012). *see* Resolution
    67/19
  Resolution 181 (1947) 53–54, 91–92
  2030 Agenda for Sustainable
    Development 335
  and UJ 126–127
United Nations High Commissioner for
  Human Rights 269–293
United Nations High Level Panel on Threats,
  Challenges and Change 32
United Nations Human Rights Council
  and crimes committed during "Operation
    Cast Lead" 48
  and Goldstone report 106
  resolutions on
    on ensuring accountability for
      violations in oPt 369–373
    human rights situation in
      oPt 358–368
    Israeli settlements in oPt 374–384
    Palestinian people's right to
      self-determination 355–357
United Nations Law of the Sea Tribunal
  (ITLOS) 185–186, 191
United Nations Relief and Works Agency for
  Palestine Refugees in the Near East
  (UNRWA) 299, 333
United Nations Security Council (UNSC)
  and admission procedures 60–61
  and endorsements of occupations 225,
    229–234
  and Goldstone report 106–107
  and ICJ 189
  and ICTY 189
  on interventions 9, 31–32, 39
  recognizing NTC 37–38
  Resolution 1244 (1999) 67
  Resolution 1267 (1999) 199
  Resolution 1483 (2003) 229–232
  Resolution 1515 (2003) 66–67
  Resolution 1546 (2004) 196–197, 199
  Resolution 1850 (2008) 66–67

INDEX

Resolution 2234 (2016)   385–387
sanction regime of   199–200
and status of Palestine   45–46
United Nations Transitional Arrangement in
East Timor (UNTAET)   93
United Nations Trusteeship system   53
United Nations (UN)
admission to
application procedures for   60–64
of Egypt   58
of Israel   59–60, 63
Palestine's application for   50, 63, 65
and statehood recognition   59–60,
61–63
and interventions   9
non-member observer State status in. *see*
UN non-member observer State status
observer status in
in general   64
of Holy See   71–72
of Palestine   43, 64–65
of PLO   54, 55, 64–65
reports of
of OHCHR
U.N. Doc. A/71/364, 294–318
U.N. Doc. A/HRC/31/44, 269–293
Special Rapporteurs on Human Rights
Lynk, Michael   319–351
Wibisono, Marakim   241–268
special rapporteurs on human rights of
Falk, Richard   53, 107
Lynk, Michael   107, 319–351
Wibisono, Marakim   107, 241–268
see also United Nations Charter
United States (US)
on admission of Israel to UN   63
Kleiman case   83
Klinghoffer case   80–81, 83
and Lockerbie case   189, 203
and Palestine's statehood status   80–84
recognition of Bosnia-Herzegovina   53
Sokolow I case   81–82, 83
Sokolow II case   82, 433–471
and UJ cases, lobbying against   98, 115,
117
and UJ legislation   127
Waller case (1895)   147, 151–152
Universal Declaration of Human Rights   19

Universal Islamic Declaration on Human
Rights (1981)   21
universal jurisdiction (UJ)
in general   97
in absentia   102–103, 132
and advocacy initiatives   133–134
application of   102–104, 126
and Attorneys-General decisions   118–119
cases against Israeli officials
in Belgium, Sharon case   98, 105, 117,
120
of al-Haq   98n5, 114, 124
in Netherlands
Ayalon case   112–114, 122
Riwal case   124, 128–129
in New Zealand, Yaalon case   98, 99,
119
and South Africa   129n118, 132
in Spain
Al-Daraj case   109–111, 115
Gaza Freedom Flotilla case
122–123, 130–131n120, 131–132
in Turkey   132
in UK
in general   99
of al-Haq   114
Almog case   99, 121–122, 124n103
Livni case   99, 116–117, 120–121
Mofaz case   120
in Western Europe   98–99
and changes in legislation   105, 111,
114–118
commitment to   126–128
definition of   101
effectiveness of   100, 125
and extraterritoriality   131–132, 131n120
future recommendations   129–134
and immunity from prosecution   119–121
and interference in judicial
processes   121–123
and Israeli non-cooperation   123–125
lobbying against
of China   115
of Israel   98, 105, 106–107, 111, 114–118,
123
of US   98, 115, 117
and low-level perpetrators   130–131
in national jurisdiction   102

universal jurisdiction (UJ) (cont.)
    opposition against
        in general   133
        of Israel
            in general   98, 104–105
            political   105–107
            responses to   105
        of Western States   105
    and perpetrators links with
        jurisdiction   132–133
    and presence of suspect   102–103, 111–114
    reasons for continuing with   125–129
    and Rome Statute   127
    and subsidiarity   103–104, 108–111
    and UNGA   126
    and victims links with
        jurisdiction   131–132
"universal succession" theory   88
UNRWA (United Nations Relief and Works
    Agency for Palestine Refugees in the Near
    East)   299, 333
UNTAET (United Nations Transitional
    Arrangement in East Timor)   93
USSR   89, 175–176n158
    see also Russia

Vattel, Emer de   15–16
VCLT (Vienna Convention on the Law of
    Treaties)   73, 86–87, 141n18, 165, 169, 172,
    194–195
VCSST (Vienna Convention on State
    Succession in Respect of Treaties)   88,
    90
victims
    of crimes/violations, right to resist of   9,
        30–31, 33
Victoria, Francisco de   13, 15
Vidmar, Jure   70
Vienna Convention on State Succession in
    Respect of Treaties (VCSST)   88, 90
Vienna Convention on the Law of Treaties
    (VCLT)   73, 86–87, 141n18, 165, 169, 172,
    194–195
"Vienna formula"   73, 74
Vietnam   62, 73–74
violations. see crimes/violations

violence, excessive use of   246–250,
    263–264, 296–300, 315, 323–324, 350
Von Glahn, Gerhard   137n4, 138n10, 148n49,
    160n98, 161–162

wall/barrier   56, 69, 276–277, 347
Waller, John   147, 151–152
Waller case (1895)   147, 151–152, 162–163
war
    justness of   13–15
    as punishment   13–14
war crimes   98, 104n27
    see also crimes/violations; firearms;
    relocations; violence
war treason, 149n53
Weiss, Jeffrey   86
West Bank
    agriculture in   287
    casualties of violence in   323
    checkpoints in   278–279
    divisions of   344
    economy of   344–346
    education, access to   281–283
    forced relocations/evictions in   301,
        333–334, 345
    freedom of movement in, restrictions
        on   275–277, 278–279
    ICC report on   422–423, 425–427
    Israeli settlements in   345–346
    Israel's withdrawal from   68
    living standards in   346
West Bank barrier   56, 69, 276–277, 347
Western States
    UJ cases in
        in general   98–99
        and Israeli lobbying   106–107
        opposition against   105
Wibisono, Marakim
    mandate of   242–243
    report of   241–268
        on accountability   258–259
        on demolitions   250
        on detention   255–257, 264–265
        on East Jerusalem   260–261
        on freedom of movement, restrictions
            to   250–251

on Gaza   265–267
on Gaza blockade   254–255
on harrassment of human rights
    defenders   261–263
on non-cooperation of
    Israel   244–246
on punitive practices   250
recommendations of   267–268
on rights to education, violations
    of   251
on settlements   253–254
on violence, excessive use of
    246–250, 263–264
on West Bank   262–264
tenure of   107
Wilde, Ralph   235
Wilmshurst, Elizabeth   234
Wolff, Christian   16
Woolsey, L. H.   145–146, 147, 150n57

work
    access to   287–289, 339
    permits   288–289
Working Group on Arbitrary Detention
    262
World Bank   63, 65, 185, 340, 342, 343
World Health Organization (WHO)   73,
    284–285
World Summit Outcome (2005)   32
Wouters, Jan   213
Wye River Agreement   68
Wye River Memorandum   44n5

Yaalon, Moshe   99, 119
Yaalon case   98, 99, 119
Yazar and others v. Turkey   20–21
Yugoslavia   133, 161, 180

Zegveld, Liesbeth   113–114